Lecture Notes in Computer Science 13708

More information about this series at https://link.springer.com/bookseries/558

Vladimir Voevodin · Sergey Sobolev ·
Mikhail Yakobovskiy · Rashit Shagaliev (Eds.)

Supercomputing

8th Russian Supercomputing Days, RuSCDays 2022
Moscow, Russia, September 26–27, 2022
Revised Selected Papers

 Springer

Editors
Vladimir Voevodin ⓘ
Research Computing Center (RCC)
Moscow State University
Moscow, Russia

Sergey Sobolev ⓘ
Research Computing Center (RCC)
Moscow State University
Moscow, Russia

Mikhail Yakobovskiy ⓘ
Keldysh Institute of Applied Mathematics
Moscow, Russia

Rashit Shagaliev
Russian Federal Nuclear Center
Sarov, Russia

ISSN 0302-9743 ISSN 1611-3349 (electronic)
Lecture Notes in Computer Science
ISBN 978-3-031-22940-4 ISBN 978-3-031-22941-1 (eBook)
https://doi.org/10.1007/978-3-031-22941-1

This Springer imprint is published by the registered company Springer Nature Switzerland AG
The registered company address is: Gewerbestrasse 11, 6330 Cham, Switzerland

Preface

The 8th Russian Supercomputing Days Conference (RuSCDays 2022) was held during September 26–27, 2022. The conference was organized by the Supercomputing Consortium of Russian Universities, the Russian Academy of Sciences, and the Moscow Center of Fundamental and Applied Mathematics. The conference organization coordinator was the Moscow State University Research Computing Center. The conference was supported by platinum sponsors (RSC, Elpitech, and ComBox Technology) and silver sponsors (Get-Rosatom and Croc).

To make the event as safe as possible, the conference was held in a hybrid way, combining offline and online sessions. Every offline session was also available online for remote attendees. There were also several online-only sessions.

RuSCDays was born in 2015 as a union of several supercomputing event series in Russia and quickly became one of the most notable Russian supercomputing international meetings. The conference caters to the interests of a wide range of representatives from science, industry, business, education, government, and academia – anyone connected to the development or the use of supercomputing technologies. The conference topics cover all aspects of supercomputing technologies: software and hardware design, solving large tasks, application of supercomputing technologies in industry, exaflops-scale computing issues, supercomputing co-design technologies, supercomputing education, and others.

All 94 papers submitted to the conference were reviewed by three referees in the first review round. During single-blind peer reviewing, the papers were evaluated according to their relevance to the conference topics, scientific contribution, presentation, approbation, and related works description. After notification of conditional acceptance, the second review round was arranged which aimed at the final polishing of papers and also at the evaluation of authors' work following revision based on the referees' comments. After the conference, the 50 best papers were carefully selected to be included in this volume.

The proceedings editors would like to thank all the conference committee members, especially the Organizing and Program Committee members, as well as the referees and reviewers for their contributions. We also thank Springer for producing these high-quality proceedings of RuSCDays 2022.

October 2022
Vladimir Voevodin
Sergey Sobolev
Rashit Shagaliev
Mikhail Yakobovskiy

Organization

Steering Committee

Victor A. Sadovnichiy (Chair)	Moscow State University, Russia
Vladimir B. Betelin (Co-chair)	Russian Academy of Sciences, Russia
Alexander V. Tikhonravov (Co-chair)	Moscow State University, Russia
Jack Dongarra (Co-chair)	University of Tennessee, USA
Alexey I. Borovkov	Peter the Great St. Petersburg Polytechnic University, Russia
Vladimir V. Voevodin	Moscow State University, Russia
Georgy S. Elizarov	NII KVANT, Russia
Vyacheslav V. Elagin	Hewlett Packard Enterprise, Russia
Elena V. Zagainova	Lobachevsky State University of Nizhni Novgorod, Russia
Alexander K. Kim	MCST, Russia
Elena V. Kudryashova	Northern (Arctic) Federal University, Russia
Nikolay S. Mester	Intel, Russia
Eugeny I. Moiseev	Moscow State University, Russia
Alexander A. Moskovskiy	RSC Group, Russia
Gennady I. Savin	Joint Supercomputer Center, Russian Academy of Sciences, Russia
Alexey S. Simonov	NICEVT, Russia
Victor A. Soyfer	Samara University, Russia
Leonid B. Sokolinskiy	South Ural State University, Russia
Igor A. Sokolov	Russian Academy of Sciences, Russia
Roman G. Strongin	Lobachevsky State University of Nizhni Novgorod, Russia
Alexey R. Khokhlov	Russian Academy of Sciences, Russia
Boris N. Chetverushkin	Keldysh Institute of Applied Mathematics, Russian Academy of Sciences, Russia

Program Committee

Vladimir V. Voevodin (Chair)	Moscow State University, Russia
Rashit M. Shagaliev (Co-chair)	Russian Federal Nuclear Center, Russia
Mikhail V. Yakobovskiy (Co-chair)	Keldysh Institute of Applied Mathematics, Russian Academy of Sciences, Russia

Thomas Sterling (Co-chair)	Indiana University, USA
Sergey I. Sobolev (Scientific Secretary)	Moscow State University, Russia
Arutyun I. Avetisyan	Institute for System Programming, Russian Academy of Sciences, Russia
David Bader	Georgia Institute of Technology, USA
Pavan Balaji	Argonne National Laboratory, USA
Alexander V. Bukhanovskiy	ITMO University, Russia
Jesus Carretero	University Carlos III of Madrid, Spain
Yury V. Vasilevskiy	Keldysh Institute of Applied Mathematics, Russian Academy of Sciences, Russia
Vasiliy E. Velikhov	National Research Center "Kurchatov Institute", Russia
Vladimir Yu. Volkonskiy	MCST, Russia
Vadim M. Volokhov	Institute of Problems of Chemical Physics, Russian Academy of Sciences, Russia
Boris M. Glinskiy	Institute of Computational Mathematics and Mathematical Geophysics, Siberian Branch of Russian Academy of Sciences, Russia
Victor M. Goloviznin	Moscow State University, Russia
Vyacheslav A. Ilyin	National Research Center "Kurchatov Institute", Russia
Vladimir P. Ilyin	Institute of Computational Mathematics and Mathematical Geophysics, Siberian Branch of Russian Academy of Sciences, Russia
Sergey I. Kabanikhin	Institute of Computational Mathematics and Mathematical Geophysics, Siberian Branch of Russian Academy of Sciences, Russia
Igor A. Kalyaev	NII MVS and South Federal University, Russia
Hiroaki Kobayashi	Tohoku University, Japan
Vladimir V. Korenkov	Joint Institute for Nuclear Research, Russia
Victor A. Kryukov	Keldysh Institute of Applied Mathematics, Russian Academy of Sciences, Russia
Julian Kunkel	University of Hamburg, Germany
Jesus Labarta	Barcelona Supercomputing Center, Spain
Alexey Lastovetsky	University College Dublin, Ireland
Mikhail P. Lobachev	Krylov State Research Centre, Russia
Yutong Lu	National University of Defense Technology, China
Thomas Ludwig	German Climate Computing Center, Germany
Iosif B. Meerov	Lobachevsky State University of Nizhni Novgorod, Russia
Marek Michalewicz	University of Warsaw, Poland

Leili Mirtaheri   Kharazmi University, Iran
Alexander V. Nemukhin   Moscow State University, Russia
Happy Sithole   Centre for High Performance Computing,
                               South Africa
Alexander V. Smirnov   Moscow State University, Russia
Hiroyuki Takizawa   Tohoku University, Japan
Michela Taufer   University of Delaware, USA
Vadim E. Turlapov   Lobachevsky State University of Nizhni
                               Novgorod, Russia
Eugeny E. Tyrtyshnikov   Institute of Numerical Mathematics, Russian
                               Academy of Sciences, Russia
Vladimir A. Fursov   Samara University, Russia
Thorsten Hoefler   Eidgenössische Technische Hochschule Zürich,
                               Switzerland
Boris M. Shabanov   Joint Supercomputer Center, Russian Academy of
                               Sciences, Russia
Lev N. Shchur   Higher School of Economics, Russia
Roman Wyrzykowski   Czestochowa University of Technology, Poland
Mitsuo Yokokawa   Kobe University, Japan

Industrial Committee

A. A. Aksenov (Co-chair)   Tesis, Russia
V. E. Velikhov (Co-chair)   National Research Center "Kurchatov Institute",
                               Russia
A. V. Murashov (Co-chair)   T-Platforms, Russia
Yu. Ya. Boldyrev   Peter the Great St. Petersburg Polytechnic
                               University, Russia
M. A. Bolshukhin   Afrikantov Experimental Design Bureau for
                               Mechanical Engineering, Russia
R. K. Gazizov   Ufa State Aviation Technical University, Russia
M. P. Lobachev   Krylov State Research Centre, Russia
V. Ya. Modorskiy   Perm National Research Polytechnic University,
                               Russia
A. P. Skibin   Gidropress, Russia
S. Stoyanov   T-Services, Russia
A. B. Shmelev   RSC Group, Russia
S. V. Strizhak   Hewlett-Packard, Russia

Educational Committee

Vl. V. Voevodin (Co-chair)   Moscow State University, Russia
L. B. Sokolinskiy (Co-chair)   South Ural State University, Russia

Yu. Ya. Boldyrev	Peter the Great St. Petersburg Polytechnic University, Russia
A. V. Bukhanovskiy	ITMO University, Russia
R. K. Gazizov	Ufa State Aviation Technical University, Russia
S. A. Ivanov	Hewlett-Packard, Russia
I. B. Meerov	Lobachevsky State University of Nizhni Novgorod, Russia
V. Ya. Modorskiy	Perm National Research Polytechnic University, Russia
S. G. Mosin	Kazan Federal University, Russia
N. N. Popova	Moscow State University, Russia
O. A. Yufryakova	Northern (Arctic) Federal University, Russia

Organizing Committee

Vl. V. Voevodin (Chair)	Moscow State University, Russia
B. M. Shabanov (Co-chair)	Joint Supercomputer Center, Russian Academy of Sciences, Russia
S. I. Sobolev (Scientific Secretary)	Moscow State University, Russia
A. A. Aksenov	Tesis, Russia
A. P. Antonova	Moscow State University, Russia
A. S. Antonov	Moscow State University, Russia
K. A. Barkalov	Lobachevsky State University of Nizhni Novgorod, Russia
M. R. Biktimirov	Russian Academy of Sciences, Russia
Vad. V. Voevodin	Moscow State University, Russia
T. A. Gamayunova	Moscow State University, Russia
O. A. Gorbachev	RSC Group, Russia
V. A. Grishagin	Lobachevsky State University of Nizhni Novgorod, Russia
S. A. Zhumatiy	Moscow State University, Russia
V. V. Korenkov	Joint Institute for Nuclear Research, Russia
I. B. Meerov	Lobachevsky State University of Nizhni Novgorod, Russia
D. A. Nikitenko	Moscow State University, Russia
I. M. Nikolskiy	Moscow State University, Russia
N. N. Popova	Moscow State University, Russia
N. M. Rudenko	Moscow State University, Russia
A. S. Semenov	NICEVT, Russia
I. Yu. Sidorov	Moscow State University, Russia
L. B. Sokolinskiy	South Ural State University, Russia
K. S. Stefanov	Moscow State University, Russia
V. M. Stepanenko	Moscow State University, Russia

Contents

HPC, BigData, AI: Architectures, Technologies, Tools

Supercomputer Simulation

A Time-Parallel Ordinary Differential Equation Solver with an Adaptive Step Size: Performance Assessment

Evgeniy Kazakov[1]($\boxtimes$), Dmitry Efremenko[2], Viacheslav Zemlyakov[1], and Jiexing Gao[1]

[1] Huawei Technologies Co., Ltd., Russian Research Institute, Moscow, Russia
`evgeniy.kazakov@huawei.com`
[2] Remote Sensing Technology Institute (IMF), German Aerospace Center (DLR), Oberpfaffenhofen, Germany

Abstract. Sequential numerical methods for integrating the ordinary differential equations can be time consuming when high accuracy is required over the large time domain. One way to accelerate computations and to get use of parallel computing is to combine computationally cheap (coarse) and expensive (fine) solvers. This approach is often referred to as the Parareal algorithm, in which a time domain is divided into subintervals. A cheap solver is used to obtain the starting points for temporal subintervals, while the fine solver which runs in parallel is used to perform accurate simulations within each subinterval. In the classical implementation of the Parareal algorithm, both coarse and fine solvers are fix step methods. However, due to inaccurate initial values at the beginnings of the subintervals, Parareal may require several iterations until the required accuracy is achieved and be slower than a serial algorithm. In this paper we analyze the performance of the Parareal algorithm based on adaptive step solvers. It is shown that such modification is more robust, requires less number of iterations and overall faster than the classical implementation. We present an error analysis and discuss possible future improvements.

Keywords: ODE solver · Parallel computing · Parareal

1 Introduction

Fast and accurate solvers for the ordinary differential equations (ODEs) are required in many fields of mathematics and natural science for describing dynamically changing phenomena. In a view of cheap multicore CPUs, it is very tempting to design parallel ODE solvers. One of the first scientists who addressed this idea was Nievergelt [1]. However, the most implementations of ODE solvers are sequential (i.e. single threaded) and hence cannot benefit from multicore CPU architectures. The reason is that the parallelization across the time direction is challenging due to a causality principle, namely, the ODE solution later in time depends on the solution earlier in time.

© The Author(s), under exclusive license to Springer Nature Switzerland AG 2022
V. Voevodin et al. (Eds.): RuSCDays 2022, LNCS 13708, pp. 3–17, 2022.
https://doi.org/10.1007/978-3-031-22941-1_1

Despite of this challenge, several approaches were proposed to accelerate the ODE solvers. The interested readers are encouraged to refer to the excellent review of Gander [2]. The straight-forward way to incorporate parallelism in an ODE solver is to parallelize some parts of it. For instance, in Ref. [3] the coefficients of the Butcher tableau in the context of the Runge-Kutta method of order 10 were computed in parallel. Nevertheless the authors did not gain a performance enhancement due to a parallel overhead, i.e. the amount of time required to coordinate parallel tasks was larger than the speedup due to the parallelism. In Refs. [4,5] the right-hand sides of an ODE system were evaluated in parallel. However, such an approach makes sense to utilize for the cases with computationally heavy right hand sizes. Otherwise, the possible gain due to parallelism is smaller than the computational overhead.

In the notable works by Lions, Maday and Turinici [6], the parallel-in-time algorithm (referred to as Parareal) was described, which exploited the idea of domain decomposition in time. Later, Parareal was adopted to the partial differential equations [7]. Essentially, Parareal is based on the use of two solvers. The first solver should be computationally cheap, but can be inaccurate (i.e. coarse). The second solver is fine, but can be computationally expensive. Keeping that in mind, the time domain is divided into N subintervals. A cheap solver is used to obtain the staring points for temporal subintervals, while the fine solver (which runs in parallel) is used to perform accurate simulations within each subinterval. If the difference between the coarse and fine solver results is larger than a threshold, the iteration (correction) procedure is applied to improve the accuracy. Although the convergence is guaranteed in $N-1$ iterations in which case no speedup is obtained, the method may converge after a small number of iterations. Although the Parareal method was applied to several applications revealing its accuracy and efficiency [8], it is not fail-safe or may require as many as $N-1$ iterations. In addition, there is an ambiguity in how actually to perform iterations. Several modifications of Parareal have been considered depending on the type of the problem [9]. However, no mathematical criteria have been formulated for the problem to be considered as suited for Parareal.

In this paper, we analyze the computational problems of the Parareal algorithm in the cases where it fails to converge in small number of iterations. These cases include the first and second order ODE systems, the Rossler system and the matrix Riccati equation. The efficiency of Parareal involving the adaptive step size is studied. The rest of the paper is organized as follows. In Sect. 2 the Parareal algorithm is summarized and the modifications of Parareal are discussed. The test cases and numerical experiments are presented in Sect. 3. The paper is concluded with a summary.

2 Theory

2.1 Classical Parareal Algorithm

In this section, we briefly outline the original Parareal algorithm.

Let us consider the following ODE within the time domain $[t_0, T]$:

$$\frac{dy(t)}{dt} = f(y(t), t), \tag{1}$$

with the following initial condition:

$$y(t_0) = y_0. \tag{2}$$

Here f is a nonlinear function with sufficiently many continuous derivatives, while $y : [t_0, T] \rightarrow \mathbb{R}$ is the time dependent solution with y_0 being the initial value of y at t_0. Defining a mesh $(t_0, t_1, ..., t_M)$ such that

$$t_{i+1} = t_i + \Delta T, \tag{3}$$

$$\Delta T = \frac{T - t_0}{M}, \tag{4}$$

we want to find a numerical solution $Y_i, i = 0, ..., M$ such that $Y_i \approx y(t_i)$.

Equation (1) can be numerically integrated by an ODE solver F, which provides y_{i+1} given y_i, namely,

$$y_{i+1} = F(y_i, t_i, t_{i+1}). \tag{5}$$

We consider J time subintervals such that the j-th subinterval is bounded by t_{kj} and $t_{k(j+1)}$, where n is the number of points per interval. In order to obtain solutions at t_{nj}, we apply an ODE solver G with a coarse step size:

$$y_{n(j+1)} = G\left(y_{nj}, t_{nj}, t_{n(j+1)}\right). \tag{6}$$

Note that solvers F and G can be the same solvers apart from using different step sizes. Once the values $y_{n(j+1)}$ are found, the solution within each sub-interval is found by applying Eq. (1) in parallel. As there is a difference between coarse and fine solvers, the following correction is performed:

$$y_{n(j+1)}^{k+1} = G\left(y_{nj}^{k+1}, t_{nj}, t_{n(j+1)}\right) + F\left(y_{nj}^{k}, t_{nj}, t_{n(j+1)}\right) - G\left(y_{nj}^{k}, t_{nj}, t_{n(j+1)}\right). \tag{7}$$

The last two terms can be regarded as a correction to a prediction $G\left(y_{nj}^{k+1}, t_{nj}, t_{n(j+1)}\right)$. However, in some cases, classical iterative formula (7) may be ineffective and it is better to use as initial points of the subintervals the endpoints provided by the fine integrator (corresponding to pink points in Fig. 1). Then the iterative formula reads as follows:

$$y_{n(j+1)}^{k+1} = F\left(y_{nj}^{k}, t_{nj}, t_{n(j+1)}\right). \tag{8}$$

Here the upper index is the iteration counter.

In both cases, the stopping condition reads as follows:

$$\left|y_{nj}^{k} - y_{nj}^{k-1}\right| < \varepsilon, nj \leq M, \tag{9}$$

where ε is the tolerance threshold. Some comments are in order:

1. at the k-th iteration, the values y_{nj}^k, $j \leq k$ and the solutions within corresponding sub-intervals are known from the fine solver F, while the rest values y_{nj}^k, $j > k$ are known approximately involving the coarse solver G;
2. the correction step (7) cannot be run in parallel;
3. although the Parareal solver is parallel in time, it converges serially in time;
4. as it follows from Eq. (9), Parareal results coincide with the fine solver F in $k = M$ iterations.

2.2 Theoretical Performance of the Parareal Algorithm

As it follows from the previous section, the accuracy of the coarse solver is crucial for the overall performance of Parareal. Technically if the solver G provides accurate solutions at the beginnings of sub-intervals, no iterations are required. It is straight-forward to estimate the maximum speedup factor (neglecting the hardware overheads). Indeed, let W_F and W_G are the wall-clocks for solvers F and G, respectively. Then the total computational time W for the Parareal algorithm can be written as follows:

$$W = MW_G + \sum_{j=1}^{k} [W_F + (M - j)W_G],$$ (10)

or rearranging,

$$W = kW_F + (k + 1)(M - k/2).$$ (11)

The theoretical speedup factor S of the Parareal algorithm over the serial solver F (with the corresponding wall-clock MW_F) is

$$S = \left[k/M + (k + 1)\left(1 - \frac{k}{2M}\right)\frac{W_G}{W_F}\right]^{-1}.$$ (12)

Thus, to achieve high performance enhancement, the ratio W_G/W_F should be small. On the other hand, as the coarse G solver becomes faster and less accurate, we might need more iterations. Taking into account a possible overhead due to managing the parallelism, convergence in $k \ll M$ is required in order to obtain a performance enhancement by Parareal over the serial solver F. From Eq. (12) it follows that in a limit $\frac{W_G}{W_F} \ll 1$ the speed factor can reach the number of processors used. However, in practice, it is impossible to achieve. For instance, in Ref. [10] twofold speedup is achieved on 8 cores, while in Ref. [11] twofold speedup is obtained on 16 cores.

2.3 Modifications of the Parareal Algorithm

In order to improve the convergence of Parareal, several approaches have been proposed. Farhat et al. [12] suggested to enhance the coarse solver by projecting it with respect to a linear space spanned by the results of previous fine integrations (Krylov subspace). This idea was adopted in Ref. [13] for linear problems.

As a matter of fact, in these methods the improvement is based on the reuse of results obtained by serial integration methods. In Ref. [11] the same idea was used but in a statistical formulation. In particular, the difference between fine and coarse solutions is predicted using a Gaussian process emulator, which allows the method to converge faster than the classical implementation. Note that in all implementations, only ODE solvers with fix step were considered, and as coarse solvers, the easiest (Euler) solver was taken to make the ratio $\frac{W_G}{W_F}$ as small as possible.

In this work we propose to use as a coarse solver an adaptive step size ODE solver (namely, ODE Runge-Kutta solver (ode45)).

The arguments in favor of this approach are as follows:

- Generally, the adaptive step size methods are more accurate than the fix step methods for nonlinear problems; therefore the faster convergence rate can be expected.
- Adaptive stepsize can deal, to some extent, with the matter of the stiffness of the problem; in this regard, the classical Parareal method may fail in some cases not because of "parallelism" but because of the stiffness of the problem.
- While using the adaptive step methods, the functions are evaluated at intermediate points. In this regard, the use of adaptive step methods implicitly use the same idea as in Refs. [11–13], namely, to estimate more accurate approximations at the staring points of subintervals by using results of previous computations.

The only possible drawback of the proposed approach is that as the functions may have to be evaluated at larger amount of points while performing the coarse integration thereby increasing the computing time of the serial part of the algorithm. However, as the obtained solutions are more accurate, the convergence is expected at lower number of iterations.

2.4   Implementation Details

The described modification of the Parareal solver has been implemented in C++ and parallelized on several CPUs by means of the MPI library. The algorithm can be summarized in the form of pseudocode 1.

Once the MPI environment is initialized and the number of processes and process ids are defined, further follows the iteration cycle. The master process only on zero ($k = 0$) iteration performs the coarse integration. Here the computations are performed by a pair of solvers with different relative tolerance values. Once the solutions agree within a given threshold, the coarse solution is sent to the slave processes. The slave processes call the fine integrator using as initial values the results of the coarse solver received from the master process. Once the fine integration is complete, the ending points of each sub-domain are collected by the master process. Next from collected Parareal solution extract new initial points for next iteration and for iterative refinement algorithm repeated K times, already without calculating coarse solution. Note that lines 23–25 are performed in parallel.

Algorithm 1. Parareal with an adaptive step solver.

	$y0$	Initial condition.
	y_0, $y1_0$, $y2_0$	Arrays for coarse integrator solution.
	$y_{parareal}^{n}$	Array for fine solution. Solver output
Input:		Upper index n - process rank.
	RelTol	Integrator relative tolerance.
	K	Number of iterations.
	i, k	Counters.

```
 1  BEGIN                                        // Main program function
 2  MPI_Init()                                        // Begin MPI section
 3  MPI_Comm_rank(proc_id)                     // Obtaining processes ranks
 4  MPI_Comm_size(num_proc)                  // Obtaining number of process
 5  for  k = 0 to K do
 6    if proc_id = 0 then                          // Master process section
 7      if  k = 0 then
 8        while |y2_0 − y1_0| > ε do
 9          y1_0 = G(y0, RelTol = a)
10          y2_0 = G(y0, RelTol = b)                              // Where a > b
11          reduce a and b
12        end
13        y_0 = y2_0
14      end
15      y_{Parareal}^{0} = F(y_0[0])           // Calculating solution in master process
16      for  i = 1 to num_proc do
17        MPI_Send(y_0[i], i)              // Sending initial points to other processes
18        MPI_Recv(y_{Parareal}^{i}, i)                    // Assembling a solution
19      end
20      y_0 = y_{Parareal}                    // Obtaining new initial points
21    end
22    else                                          // Slave processes section
23      MPI_Recv(y_0[proc_id], 0)   // Receiving 1 initial point from the Master process
24      y_{Parareal}^{proc_id} = F(y_0[proc_id])   // Calculating solution in a slave processes
25      MPI_Send(y_{Parareal}^{proc_id}, 0)    // Sending solution to the Master process
26    end
27  end
28  MPI_Finalize()                                       // End MPI section
29  END                                                     // End program
```

2.5   Illustration of the Influence of the Adaptive Step on the Convergence Rate

In this section we would like to illustrate the effects of poor accuracy of the coarse integrator. For this reason, we consider the following ODE:

$$\frac{dy}{dt} = \alpha - \beta y, y(0) = 1, \tag{13}$$

where $\alpha = 520$ and $\beta = 2$.

Figure 1 shows the solution for Eq. (13). The black points refer to the coarse solver solutions (corresponding to the initial points for subintervals). The magenta points are the end points obtained by the fine integrator. The blue curve is the solution obtained by the classical Parareal after one iteration, while the orange curve is the serial ode45 solution. Blue points show the coarse solutions at the next iteration. In Figs. 1(a) and (b) the coarse solver uses the fixed and adaptive step solvers, respectively. In the first case, after one iteration we obtain accurate results only for two subdomains. Note that even though the solution is relatively smooth and does not have an oscillatory behavior, the coarse solutions at iteration $k = 0$ and $k = 1$ are on opposite sides of the true solution. As a matter of fact, in the case of the fixed step coarse solver, Parareal requires $k = 6$ iterations to converge leaving no benefits over the serial fine integrator in terms of the computation time. Acceleration of convergence can be achieved by using the ending points of sub-domains computed by a fine solver as the initial values for the next iteration, instead of using the correction scheme according to Eq. (7).

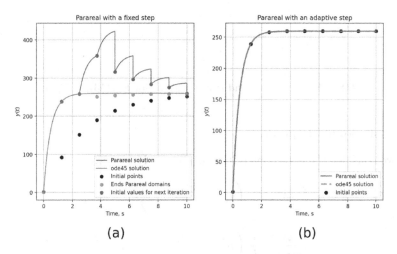

(a)   (b)

Fig. 1. Solution after one iteration for Eq. (13): (a) with the fix step coarse integrator; (b) with the adaptive step coarse integrator. The blue points refer to the coarse solver solutions, the dark blue points are the end points obtained by the fine integrator. The blue curve is the solution obtained by Parareal, while the orange curve is the serial ode45 solution. (Color figure online)

In Fig. 2 the computing time and the speedup factor are shown as functions of the number of processes for one and two iterations. For two iterations the Parareal algorithm is not faster than the serial solver. Therefore we restrict our analysis with a case of one iteration.

3 Numerical Results

The simulations are performed on a server platform with the following configuration: Intel Xeon Gold 6151 CPU 3.0 GHz with 32 CPUs, 125 GB DDR 4 RAM. As a reference solution we take those provided by the ode45 solver (the Runge-Kutta method of the 4th and 5th order) with the same step size as used in the fine integrator.

The efficiency of the proposed method is examined on the initial problems summarized below.

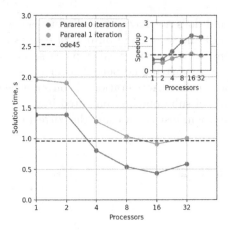

Fig. 2. Solution after one and two iterations for Eq. (13), 1e7 points.

3.1 Rotational Dynamics

Here we consider the equations of the rotational dynamics:

$$\frac{d^2 y_1}{dt^2} = \frac{1}{J_1} \left(\tau_1 - b_2 \frac{dy_1}{dt} - \tau_3 \right),$$

$$\frac{d^2 y_2}{dt^2} = \frac{1}{J_2} \left(\tau_2 - b_1 \frac{dy_2}{dt} + \tau_3 - \tau_4 \right).$$

(14)

Initial conditions are $y_1(t = 0) = 1.0$, $y_2(t = 0) = 2.0$, $\frac{dy_1}{dt} = 4.0$, and $\frac{dy_2}{dt} = 3.0$. The coefficients are chosen as follows: $J_1 = 1.0$, $J_2 = 2.0$; $b_1 = 2.0$, $b_2 = 3.0$, $\tau_1 = 3.0$, $\tau_2 = 1.0$, $\tau_3 = 3.0$, and $\tau_4 = 1.0$. The integration interval over t is $[0, 20]$ seconds, with the number of points (time steps) ranging from 1e2 points to 1e7 points. The results are summarized in Fig. 3. In particular, Fig. 3 shows an agreement between the serial and Parareal solvers within 1e−5 absolute difference, using 39 coarse solver steps. The computation time decreases with the increase of CPUs. However, starting at 16 CPUs the computation time increases with the numbers of CPUs, meaning that the overhead due to parallel computing eliminates the possible benefits of parallelization. In practice, the computation speed can be increased by a factor of 2 using 16 CPUs.

Also note that the efficiency of Parareal increases with the number of points wherein the solution is requested to be computed, as shown in Fig. 3d.

There is always an option to use an adaptive step size ODE solver on a coarse time grid and use interpolation between the nodes. In this case, the interpolation error comes into play. In the case of Parareal, integration rather than interpolation is performed in parallel. In both cases, the results obtained on a coarse time grid should be accurate enough and, in fact, they govern the overall accuracy of the method.

Parallel ODE Solver with an Adaptive Step   11

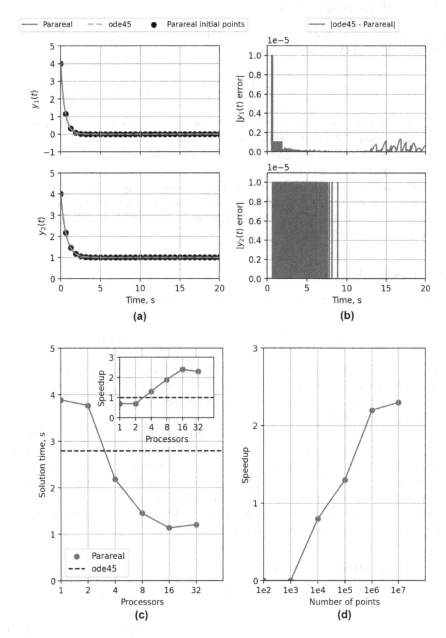

Fig. 3. Numerical results obtained solving Eq. (14). (a) Solutions for $y_1(t)$, $y_2(t)$ obtained with Parareal on 32 CPUs and serial ode45 solver; (b) Absolute errors $y_1(t)$, $y_2(t)$ of the Parareal solution; (c) Average solution time for the serial ode45 solver and Parareal as a function of CPUs for 1e7 points; (d) The speedup factor provided by Parareal as a function of points for 32 CPUs

3.2 FitzHugh-Nagumo Model

In this section we examine the efficiency of the modified Parareal algorithm using the FitzHugh-Nagumo model:

$$\frac{dy_1}{dt} = c\left(y_1 - \frac{y_1^3}{3} + y_2\right), \qquad \frac{dy_2}{dt} = -\frac{1}{c}\left(y_1 - a + by_2\right), \qquad (15)$$

where $a = 0.2$, $b = 0.2$ and $c = 3$. The integration domain is $[0, 20]$ seconds, while the number of points (time steps) ranges from 1e2 points to 1e7. This model is a good test for parallel solvers, as it describes an oscillatory behavior, and the coarse solver may fail.

The results are shown in Fig. 4. The mean absolute error is about 1e-5 using 376 coarse solver steps. The advantage of Parareal comes when the number of points is 1e6 or more. For this model, we achieved a twofold increase in performance using 16 CPUs.

3.3 Rossler System

Here we consider the Rossler model, which reads as follows:

$$\frac{dy_1}{dt} = -y_2 - y_3, \quad \frac{dy_2}{dt} = y_1 + ay_2 \quad \frac{dy_3}{dt} = b + y_3(y_1 - c), \qquad (16)$$

with $a = 0.2$, $b = 0.2$ and $c = 5.7$ within the time interval $[0, 340]$. The Rossler system belongs to stiff problems and imposes difficulties for numerical integration solvers. Figure 5 illustrates the phase trajectory of Eq. (16) obtained by the modified Parareal solver.

Even though there is a disagreement between the Parareal and reference solutions, the obtained solution is stable and the general shape of the trajectory is preserved. Nevertheless, we conclude that the Parareal solver cannot be applied for such problems. Note that the necessary condition for the Parareal to solve stiff problems in one iteration is the convergence of the coarse solver. In this regard, it is advisable to consider as a coarse solver a stiff solver with implicit integration schemes. That will be a topic of our future research.

3.4 Matrix Riccati Equation

In this section let us consider the matrix Riccati equation, which reads as follows:

$$\frac{d}{dt}\mathbf{y}(t) = \mathbf{B} + \mathbf{A}\mathbf{y}(t) + \mathbf{y}(t)\mathbf{A} + \mathbf{y}(t)\mathbf{B}\mathbf{y}(t), \qquad (17)$$

where $\mathbf{y}$ is the N-element vector to be found, while $\mathbf{A}$, $\mathbf{B}$ are the N-by-N matrices of coefficients. Such sort of equations are considered in the discrete radiative transfer theory and describe the reflection matrices of the turbid medium [14].

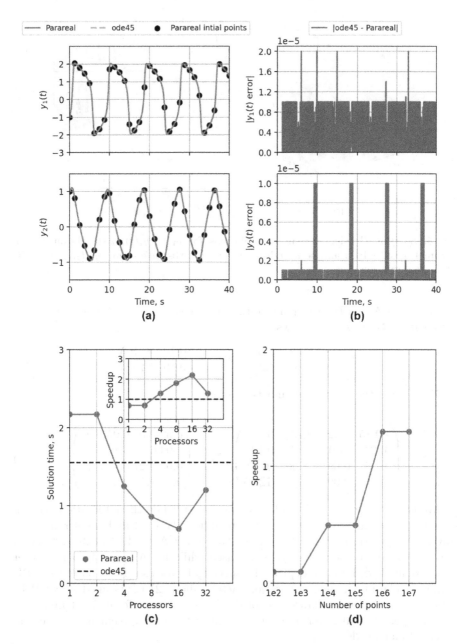

Fig. 4. The same as in Fig. 3 but for the FitzHugh-Nagumo model (Eq. (15))

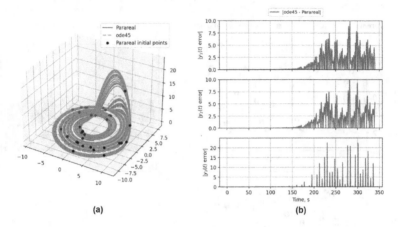

Fig. 5. Solution Rossler system. (a) Solutions for $y_1(t)$, $y_2(t)$, $y_3(t)$ obtained with Parareal on 32 CPUs and serial ode45 solver; (b) Absolute errors $y_1(t)$, $y_2(t)$, $y_3(t)$ of the Parareal solution.

The matrices $\mathbf{A}$ and $\mathbf{B}$ correspond to the case considered in Ref. [15]. For $N = 2$, the coefficients are set as follows:

$$\mathbf{A} = \begin{pmatrix} -0.62 & 0.33 \\ 1.23 & -3.21 \end{pmatrix}, \mathbf{B} = \begin{pmatrix} -0.10 & -0.19 \\ -0.69 & 1.28 \end{pmatrix}. \tag{18}$$

For $N = 4$, the matrces $\mathbf{A}$ and $\mathbf{B}$ read as

$$\mathbf{A} = \begin{pmatrix} -0.75 & 0.32 & 0.16 & 0.06 \\ 0.24 & -1.03 & 0.32 & 0.12 \\ 0.25 & 0.65 & -2.30 & -0.34 \\ 0.80 & 2.09 & 3.01 & -12.65 \end{pmatrix}, \mathbf{B} = \begin{pmatrix} 0.02 & 0.05 & 0.07 & 0.05 \\ 0.04 & 0.09 & 0.13 & 0.10 \\ 0.01 & 0.27 & 0.40 & 0.29 \\ 0.68 & 1.73 & 2.62 & 1.69 \end{pmatrix}. \tag{19}$$

We consider zero initial conditions i.e. $\mathbf{y} = 0$, while the integration domain is $[0, 1.0]$. The agreement between the modified Parareal and the serial ode45 solver is within 1.2e−7 for $N = 2$ and 3e−7 for $N = 4$ absolute difference. For $N = 2$, 16 coarse solver steps are used while for $N = 4$ 21 coarse solver steps are applied. Figure 6 depicts the speedup factor as a function of the CPU numbers. The maximum acceleration factor (about 2) is obtained at 8 CPUs. Note that the classical Parareal algorithm requires to perform $J - 1$ iterations to converge, while at fewer number of iterations, the disagreement is of several orders of magnitude.

3.5 Performance Issues

Unfortunately, one has to expect a speedup factor $S < J$ parallelizing the code on J CPUs. In the case of the Parareal algorithm, the availability and consumption of RAM, the required number of solution points (steps) and the number

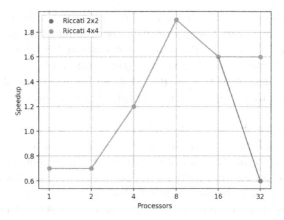

Fig. 6. Speedup of number processors for 2×2 and 4×4 matrix Riccati equation.

of available CPUs have an impact on an overall performance enhancement as compared to the serial code. As we have seen, the Parareal is faster than the serial ode45 solver when the number of points at which the solution is to be found is large (e.g. 1e6). In this case, the overhead due to the data transfer between CPUs becomes less than the computation time required for each sub-domain. However, as the number of points increases, the general consumption of RAM also increases in order to allocate memory for the arrays. In addition, the cumulative RAM consumption increases with the number of MPI processes employed since each MPI thread creates an instance of variables and arrays, as discussed in Ref. [10]. This is an issue especially for problems like matrix Riccati equations involving large matrices in the right hand side of the ODE. Therefore, if CPUs share a common RAM space, there is a limitation on maximum number of MPI processes to be taken into account. In this regrad, an implementation based on OpenMP rather than MPI might seem preferable. In Ref. [10] implementations based on MPI and OpenMP were considered. In particular, OpenMP-based implementation relied on manual control of locks for synchronisation. While OpenMP-based code appeared to be a bit more efficient, authors concluded that "its higher implementation complexity, however, might make it difficult to use in legacy codes". Also note that the overhead of parallelization increases with the number of CPUs.

Therefore, the speedup vs number of CPU curve flattens out with the increase of CPUs, as shown in Ref. [16].

4 Summary

In this paper we have analyzed the efficiency of the Parareal solver. Several problems have been selected where the classical implementation of Parareal does not provide the performance enhancement over the serial ODE solvers.

It has been shown that the accuracy of the coarse solver is the crucial factor for the Parareal algorithm, which governs its performance. Because of low accuracy of the coarse solver, the Parareal is not efficient for finding the solutions with oscillatory behavior or when the integration should be performed over the large period of time. Note that in Ref. [16], an improvement of Parareal was considered by tuning a fine solver while neglecting computational costs for the coarse solver.

There is a trade-off between the wall-clock of the coarse solver and its accuracy which automatically affects the number of iterations required. For considered problems the computational overhead due to managing the parallelism is an important factor; and in practise the Parareal algorithm should converge in one iteration in order to be more efficient than the serial solvers.

In this regard, it has been proposed to use as a coarse solver the Runge-Kutta solver with the adaptive step size. Under this setting, the Parareal algorithm surpasses a serial ODE solver. The twofold performance enhancement has been achieved using parallelism across the time without compromising the accuracy.

We showed that there is an optimal number of CPUs which provide the maximum performance (in our cases it is 16 CPUs). Note that the efficiency of a single CPU (i.e. the speedup factor divided by the number of CPU) in Parareal is small (about 0.12). These results match those presented in Ref. [16], where the CPU efficiency of about 0.15 was reported.

As a possible extension of this work, we plan to focus on stiff problems which require implicit Runge-Kutta methods. As the computational cost of implicit methods is considerably larger than that of explicit methods, the overhead due to parallelism becomes smaller in the total balance of the computational costs of the algorithm components, and so, the advantage of the Parareal approach becomes more pronounced, as discussed in Ref. [17]. Also, Parareal provides higher speedup factors for solving PDEs, where the spatial integration wall-clock is much larger than the overhead associated with parallelization, as shown in Ref. [18].

References

1. Nievergelt, J.: Parallel methods for integrating ordinary differential equations. Commun. ACM **7**(12), 731–733 (1964). https://doi.org/10.1145/355588.365137
2. Gander, M.J.: 50 years of time parallel time integration. In: Carraro, T., Geiger, M., Körkel, S., Rannacher, R. (eds.) Multiple Shooting and Time Domain Decomposition Methods. CMCS, vol. 9, pp. 69–113. Springer, Cham (2015). https://doi.org/10.1007/978-3-319-23321-5_3
3. Montejo, A.G., Michel-Manzo, O.A., Terrero-Escalante, C.A.: On parallel solution of ordinary differential equations. arXiv preprint arXiv:1601.02245 (2016)
4. Houwen, P.V.D., Sommeijer, B.: Parallel iteration of high-order Runge-Kutta methods with stepsize control. J. Comput. Appl. Math. **29**(1), 111–127 (1990). https://doi.org/10.1016/0377-0427(90)90200-j
5. Burrage, K., Suhartanto, H.: Parallel iterated methods based on multistep Runge-Kutta methods of Radau type. Adv. Comput. Math. **7**(1/2), 37–57 (1997). https://doi.org/10.1023/a:1018930415863

6. Lions, J.L., Maday, Y., Turinici, G.: Résolution d'edp par un schéma en temps "pararéel". Comptes Rendus de l'Académie des Sciences - Series I - Mathematics **332**(7), 661–668 (2001)
7. Bal, G., Maday, Y.: A parareal time discretization for non-linear PDE's with application to the pricing of an American put. In: Pavarino, L.F., Toselli, A. (eds) Recent Developments in Domain Decomposition Methods. LNCS, pp. 189–202. Springer, Heidelberg (2002). https://doi.org/10.1007/978-3-642-56118-4_12
8. Maday, Y., Turinici, G.: Parallel in time algorithms for quantum control: parareal time discretization scheme. Int. J. Quantum Chem. **93**(3), 223–228 (2003). https://doi.org/10.1002/qua.10554
9. Chen, F., Hesthaven, J.S., Zhu, X.: On the use of reduced basis methods to accelerate and stabilize the parareal method. In: Quarteroni, A., Rozza, G. (eds.) Reduced Order Methods for Modeling and Computational Reduction. MMSA, vol. 9, pp. 187–214. Springer, Cham (2014). https://doi.org/10.1007/978-3-319-02090-7_7
10. Ruprecht, D.: Implementing parareal-openmp or mpi. arXiv preprint arXiv:1509.06935 (2015)
11. Pentland, K., Tamborrino, M., Sullivan, T.J., Buchanan, J., Appel, L.C.: GParareal: a time-parallel ODE solver using Gaussian process emulation. arXiv preprint arXiv:2201.13418 (2022)
12. Farhat, C., Cortial, J., Dastillung, C., Bavestrello, H.: Time-parallel implicit integrators for the near-real-time prediction of linear structural dynamic responses. Int. J. Numer. Meth. Eng. **67**(5), 697–724 (2006). https://doi.org/10.1002/nme.1653
13. Gander, M.J., Güttel, S.: PARAEXP: a parallel integrator for linear initial-value problems. SIAM J. Sci. Comput. **35**(2), C123–C142 (2013). https://doi.org/10.1137/110856137
14. Efremenko, D.S., Molina García, V., Gimeno García, S., Doicu, A.: A review of the matrix-exponential formalism in radiative transfer. J. Quant. Spectrosc. Radiat. Transf. **196**, 17–45 (2017). https://doi.org/10.1016/j.jqsrt.2017.02.015
15. Chuprov, I., Konstantinov, D., Efremenko, D., Zemlyakov, V., Gao, J.: Solution of the radiative transfer equation for vertically inhomogeneous media by numerical integration solvers: comparative analysis. Light Eng. **30**(5) (2022)
16. Maday, Y., Mula, O.: An adaptive parareal algorithm. J. Comput. Appl. Math. **377**, 112915 (2020). https://doi.org/10.1016/j.cam.2020.112915
17. Maday, Y., Turinici, G.: The parareal in time iterative solver: a further direction to parallel implementation. In: Barth, T.J., et al. (eds.) Domain Decomposition Methods in Science and Engineering. LNCS, pp. 441–448. Springer, Heidelberg (2005), https://doi.org/10.1007/3-540-26825-1_45
18. Emmett, M., Minion, M.: Toward an efficient parallel in time method for partial differential equations. Commun. Appl. Math. Comput. Sci. **7**(1), 105–132 (2012). https://doi.org/10.2140/camcos.2012.7.105

Analysis and Elimination of Bottlenecks in Parallel Algorithm for Solving Global Optimization Problems

Konstantin Barkalov$^{(\boxtimes)}$ ⓘ, Ilya Lebedev ⓘ, and Denis Karchkov ⓘ

Lobachevsky State University of Nizhny Novgorod, Nizhny Novgorod, Russia
{konstantin.barkalov,ilya.lebedev,karchkov}@itmm.unn.ru

Abstract. The paper presents the results of investigation of efficiency of the parallelization of a global optimum search algorithm. Two stages of solving the problem were distinguished: the search of a rough approximation to the global solution and its local refining. The novelty of the parallel algorithm considered in the present paper consists in the parallelization of the whole computational process, both at the global search stage and at the one of the local refining of the solution found. The theoretical estimates of the algorithm parallelization efficiency are presented. The computational experiments were carried out. The results of the ones confirmed the theoretical conclusions.

Keywords: Multiextremal functions · Lipschitz condition · Global optimization · Local optimization · Parallel algorithms

1 Introduction

The paper is devoted to the investigation of the parallel algorithms for solving complex optimization problems arising in various fields of science and technology. Several examples of such problems are presented in the review [12].

As a rule, the objective function $\varphi(y)$ in such problems is a "black-box" function, i.e. it is defined not by a formula but as a software-implemented algorithm for computing its values at the points of the search domain D. In this case, the analytical methods for the search of the exact problem solution $y^* \in D$ are not applicable, and its numerical solving is reduced to the construction of an approximate solution $y_k^* \in D, \|y^* - y_k^*\| \leq \varepsilon$, where $\varepsilon > 0$ is a predefined accuracy. Hereafter, the process of computing the objective function at some point will be called a *search trial*.

The problem of search for the values of the parameters of complex mathematical models from the experimental data is a typical example of a global optimization problem with a "black-box" objective function. Among such problems, there are, for example, the inverse problems of chemical kinetics [1,9]. The

V. Voevodin et al. (Eds.): RuSCDays 2022, LNCS 13708, pp. 18–32, 2022.
https://doi.org/10.1007/978-3-031-22941-1_2

number of parameters in such models can be several tens that requires using the efficient parallel global optimization algorithms for solving these ones.

From the viewpoint of mathematics, the inverse problem is a global optimization one, i.e. the problem of search for the global minimizer of a function on some set. Formally, the point $y^* \in D$ is called the global minimizer for the function $\varphi(y)$ on the set D if for all $y \in D$ the inequality $\varphi(y^*) \leq \varphi(y)$ holds.

The solution of a global optimization problem always implies performing the search trials at the nodes of some grid (uniform, random, or adaptive one) in the search domain. The number of the grid nodes increases exponentially with increasing dimensionality of the problem being solved. At the same time, to find the local extremum, the function values are computed in the nodes constituting not a grid but some trajectory starting from the initial point and ending at the solution point.

Formally, the point $y' \in D$ is called the local minimizer for a function on the set D if there exists such a number $\varepsilon > 0$ that for all $y \in D$ such that $\|y - y'\| < \varepsilon$, the inequality $\varphi(y') \leq \varphi(y)$ holds. Since one needs to explore not the whole search domain D to find a local minimizer, and the descend trajectory is, generally speaking, a one-dimension object, the computational costs for the local optimization methods are essentially smaller than the ones for the global search. One can say that the local minimum search problem consists in finding the local minimizer $y^*(y^0)$ for given initial guess point $y^0 \in D$, which falls into the attraction region of y^*.

There are many cases requiring the search for the local optimum. One of such cases arises when an estimate of the global solution y_k^* is obtained with a non-satisfactory accuracy at some k^{th} iteration of the global optimization method. In this case one can find a local optimizer y_{loc}^*, which corresponds to the starting point y_k^*, with a high accuracy. The local minimum y_{loc}^* found depends, generally speaking, on y_k^*, i.e. $y_{loc}^*(y_k^*)$ will be more precise solution of the global optimization problem.

As a rule, the computational costs for the local refining of the solution is essentially smaller than the costs, which would be necessary for the multiextremal optimization procedures to achieve the same precision as the local method can ensure. However, in the case of using the parallel global optimization algorithm (at the first stage) and sequential local method (at the second stage) the work times of these ones can become comparable and the parallelization efficiency would be low.

The novelty of the parallel algorithm considered in the present paper consists in the parallelization of the whole computing process – both at the global search stage and at the stage of the local refining of the solution found. This approach can be relevant for the problems whose objective functions are ravine-type with a weak multiextremality. In such problems, the phase of searching the rough approximation of the global solution and the phase of its local refining are comparable in the computation costs. For example, in the work [5] the global search stage only was parallelized; the local refining was made with a sequential algorithm.

The main part of the paper has the following structure. In Sect. 2, the global optimization problem statement is presented and the properties of the objective function allowing developing the efficient global minimum search algorithms are described. In Sect. 3, the scheme of the parallel global optimization algorithm is presented and the theoretical estimates of its speedup are given. In Sect. 4, two local optimization methods (BFGS method and Hooke-Jeeves one) are considered, which can be applied for refining the solution found. Possible parallelization schemes for these methods are discussed. Section 5 contains the results of the computational experiments conducted using both the test problems and the applied ones.

2 Global Optimization Problem Statement

Let us consider a problem of searching the global minimum of an N-dimensional function $\varphi(y)$ in a hyperinterval D

$$\varphi(y^*) = \min\{\varphi(y) : y \in D\}, \tag{1}$$

$$D = \{y \in R^N : a_i \le y_i \le b_i, 1 \le i \le N\}. \tag{2}$$

The main assumption, which the algorithm considered are based on, is the fulfillment of Lipschitz condition for the function $\varphi(y)$, i.e.

$$|\varphi(y_1) - \varphi(y_2)| \le L\|y_1 - y_2\|, \ y_1, y_2 \in D, \ 0 < L < \infty. \tag{3}$$

Note that the Lipschitz constant L featuring the rate of variation of the function is not known *a priori*. This assumption is true for a wide class of problems and is typical of many optimization techniques (see, e.g., [2,6,10]).

The known approaches to solving the Lipschitz global optimization problems are based on a generalization of the efficient algorithms for solving the one-dimensional problems onto solving the multidimensional ones (see, for example, the methods of diagonal partitions [13] or simplicial partitions [11]). In the present work, we have also used the approach reducing the solving of a multidimensional problem to solving corresponding one-dimensional one. This approach is based on the idea of the dimensionality reduction using Peano-Hilbert curve $y(x)$ mapping the interval $[0, 1]$ of the real axis onto an N-dimensional cube

$$\{y \in R^N : -2^{-1} \le y_i \le 2^{-1}, 1 \le i \le N\} = \{y(x) : 0 \le x \le 1\}. \tag{4}$$

In theory, the Peano-Hilbert curve is a limit object. Therefore, one needs to construct an approximation to the theoretical curve for the practical application. The issues of numerical construction of such approximation (also called *evolvents*) for given dimensionality with given precision were considered in [14].

The use of the space-filling curves allows reducing the multidimensional problem (1) to a one-dimensional problem and applying the efficient one-dimensional optimization methods to solve it, i.e.

$$\varphi(y^*) = \varphi(y(x^*)) = \min\{\varphi(y(x)) : x \in [0, 1]\}. \tag{5}$$

Keeping the property of limited relative differences of the objective function is an important feature of the evolvents. If the function $\varphi(y)$ in the domain D satisfies the Lipschitz condition, the function $\varphi(y(x))$ in the interval $[0,1]$ will satisfy the Hölder condition

$$|\varphi(y(x_1)) - \varphi(y(x_2))| \leq H|x_1 - x_2|^{1/N}, \ x_1, x_2 \in [0,1], \tag{6}$$

where Hölder constant H is related to Lipschitz constant L by the relation $H = 2L\sqrt{N+3}$. Therefore, without liming the generality, one can consider the minimization of the one-dimensional function

$$f(x) = \varphi(y(x)), \ x \in [0,1], \tag{7}$$

satisfying Hölder condition.

The algorithm of solving this problem being considered implies the construction of a series of points x^k, which the values of the objective function $f(x^k) = \varphi(y(x^k))$ are computed in. We will divide the solving of the problem into two stages. At the first stage, the search of a rough approximation to the global minimum point will be performed using the global search algorithm. At the second stage, a local refining of the solution found will be conducted with a high precision. The methods applied at the first stage and at the second one are described in Sect. 3 and Sect. 4, respectively.

3 Parallel Global Search Algorithm

3.1 Computational Scheme of the Algorithm

We will consider the class of problems, in which the time of executing a single search trial doesn't depend on the trial point. In this case, one can use the synchronous parallelization scheme, which implies p trials to be carried out in parallel and synchronously within single method iteration. In this case, total number of trials executed after n parallel iterations will be $k = n \cdot p$.

The first iteration of the method is performed in a special way. The trials are performed at the boundary points $x^0 = 0$ and $x^1 = 1$ as well as at $(p-2)$ arbitrary different internal points $x^2, x^3, ..., x^{p-1}$ in the interval $[0,1]$. After executing the first iteration of the method, i.e. at $n = 1$, the number of trials will be $k = p$.

At the second iteration and at all the next ones, the following operations are performed.

Step 1. Renumber the points of the previous trials $\{x^0, ..., x^k\}$ by the lower indices in the order of increasing the coordinate values, i.e.

$$0 = x_0 < x_1 < ... < x_k = 1.$$

Step 2. Calculate the magnitudes

$$\mu = \max_{1 \leq i \leq k} \frac{|z_i - z_{i-1}|}{\Delta_i}, \ M = \begin{cases} r\mu, \mu > 0, \\ 1, \ \ \mu = 0, \end{cases} \tag{8}$$

where $z_i = f(y(x_i))$, $\Delta_i = (x_i - x_{i-1})^{1/N}$, and $r > 1$ is a predefined number (reliability parameter of the method).

Step 3. For each interval (x_{i-1}, x_i), $1 \le i \le k$, compute the *characteristic* according to the formula

$$R(i) = \Delta_i + \frac{(z_i - z_{i-1})^2}{M^2 \Delta_i} - 2\frac{z_i + z_{i-1}}{M}, 1 \le i \le k. \tag{9}$$

Step 4. Arrange the characteristics $R(i)$, $1 \le i \le k$, in the decreasing order

$$R(t_1) \ge R(t_2) \ge ... \ge R(t_{k-1}) \ge R(t_{k+1}) \tag{10}$$

and select p largest characteristics with the interval indices t_j, $1 \le j \le p$.

Step 5. Carry out new trials in parallel at the points x^{k+j}, $1 \le j \le p$, computed by the formula

$$x^{k+j} = \frac{x_{t_j} + x_{t_j-1}}{2} - sign(z_{t_j} - z_{t_j-1})\frac{1}{2r}\left[\frac{|z_{t_j} - z_{t_j-1}|}{\mu}\right]^N.$$

Put the results of the trials performed into the information database of the algorithm.

Step 6. Check the stopping criterion $\Delta_{t_j} \le \varepsilon$, where t_j are from Step 4 and $\varepsilon > 0$ is the predefined accuracy. After completing the algorithm work, take as the estimate of the solution of the problem (1)

$$f_k^* = \min_{1 \le i \le k} f(x^i), \ x_k^* = \arg \min_{1 \le i \le k} f(x^i).$$

The theoretical basis of the presented algorithm (denoted hereafter as *global search algorithm* or GSA) see in more details in [15,16]. Note briefly that the characteristics of the intervals (9) used in the algorithm can be considered as a quantitative measure how particular interval is promising from the viewpoint of finding the global minimum inside it. The inequalities (10) arrange the intervals according to their characteristics, and the trials are performed in parallel in p most promising intervals.

3.2   Theoretical Estimates of the Speedup of the Parallel Algorithm

Let us describe (according to [15]) the theoretical properties of the parallel algorithm featuring its speedup. In the problems being solved, the time of executing a single search trial essentially exceeds the time of processing its result. Therefore, the speedup in the number of trials

$$s(p) = \frac{n(1) \cdot p}{n(p)} \tag{11}$$

is the key characteristic of the efficiency of the parallel global search algorithm. Here $n(1)$ is the number of trials executed by the sequential method and $n(p)$

is the number of trials executed by the parallel method employing p parallel processes.

Obviously, the quantities of trials $n(p)$ for the algorithms with different degrees of parallelization p will differ from each other. Indeed, the sequential algorithm has the full information obtained at the previous k iterations when selecting the point x^{k+1} of the next $(k+1)^{th}$ trial. The parallel algorithm selects not one but p points x^{k+j}, $1 \leq j \leq p$, on the base of the same information. It means that the selection of the points x^{k+j} is performed without the information on the trial results at the points x^{k+i}, $1 \leq i < j$. Only the first point x^{k+1} will match to the point selected by the sequential algorithm. The points of other trials, in general, may not match the ones generated by the sequential algorithm. Therefore, we will call such trials redundant and the quantity

$$\lambda(p) = \begin{cases} (n(p) - n(1))/n(p), & n(p) > n(1) \\ 0, & n(p) \leq n(1) \end{cases}$$

we will call the redundancy of the method.

The following statements from [15] define the degree of parallelization p, which corresponds to the non-redundant (i.e. with zero redundancy) parallelization.

Let us denote the series of trials generated by the sequential algorithm and by the parallel one when solving the same problem with $\varepsilon = 0$ in the stopping conditions as $\{x^k\}$ and $\{y^m\}$, respectively.

Theorem. Let x^* be the global minimum point and x' be the local minimum one of the function $f(x)$ and let the following conditions be satisfied:

1. The inequality is fulfilled

$$f(x') - f(x^*) \leq \delta, \delta > 0. \tag{12}$$

2. The first $q(l)$ trials of the sequential method and of the parallel one match to each other, i.e.

$$\{x^1, ..., x^{q(l)}\} = \{y^1, ..., y^{q(l)}\} \tag{13}$$

where

$$\{x^1, ..., x^{q(l)}\} \subset \{x^k\}, \{y^1, ..., y^{q(l)}\} \subset \{y^m\}. \tag{14}$$

3. There exist a point $t^n \in \{y^m\}$, $n < q(l)$, such as $x' \leq y^n \leq x^*$ or $x^* \leq y^n \leq x'$.
4. For the quantity M from (8), the inequality is fulfilled

$$M > 2^{2-1/N} H, \tag{15}$$

where H is Hölder constant of the objective one-dimensional function.

Then, the parallel algorithm at $p = 2$ will be non-redundant (i.e. $s(2) = 2$, $\lambda(2) = 0$) as long as the condition is fulfilled

$$(x_{t_j} - x_{t_j-1})^{1/N} > \frac{4\delta}{M - 2^{2-1/N} H}, \tag{16}$$

where t_j is defined according to Step 4 of the algorithm.

Consequence. Let the objective function $f(x)$ have Q points of local minima $\{x'_1, ..., x'_Q\}$, which the condition (12) is fulfilled for, and let there exist the trial points y^{n_i}, $1 \leq i \leq Q$, such that

$$y^{n_i} \in \{y^1, ...y^{q(l)}\},$$
$$\alpha_i \leq y^{n_i} \leq \alpha_{i+1}, \; \alpha_i, \alpha_{i+1} \in \{x^*, x'_1, ..., x'_Q\}, 1 \leq i \leq Q.$$

Then, if the conditions of theorem are fulfilled, the parallel algorithm with the parallelization degree $Q+1$ will be non-redundant (i.e. $s(Q+1) = Q+1$, $\lambda(Q+1) = 0$) until the condition (16) is fulfilled.

The consequence from the theorem plays a special role in solving the multidimensional problems reduced to the one-dimensional ones using the evolvent $y(x)$. The evolvent $y(x)$, being an approximation to the Peano curve, has the effect of "splitting" of the global minimum point $y^* \in D$ into several (up to 2^N) preimages in the interval [0,1]. Applying the parallel algorithm to minimize the reduced one-dimensional function, one can expect a zero redundancy at the parallelization degree up to $2^N + 1$.

Now, let us consider the case when, after the stage of the search for the rough approximation to the global solution, the stage of its local refinement is performed. Assume that the fraction of the search trials necessary for the local refinement of the solution makes α of total number of trials. Then, according to Amdahl's law, the overall speedup $S(p)$, which can be obtained by parallelization into p processes, cannot exceed the quantity

$$S(p) = \left(\alpha + \frac{1 - \alpha}{p}\right)^{-1}.$$

This relation will be true if one assumes the non-redundant parallelization of the global search stage. The increase in the efficiency of the parallel algorithm will be limited by the fraction of trials at the stage of the local refinement of the solution. So far, to increase the efficiency of parallelization (especially in the case of a large number of processes employed), one needs to parallelize not only the global search but the local one as well. Two particular local methods applicable to the optimization problems with the "black-box" type functions as well as the methods of parallelization of these ones will be considered in the next section.

4   Local Optimization Methods

4.1   BFGS Method

BFGS (Broyden-Fletcher-Goldfarb-Shanno) method (see, e.g., [8]) belongs to the class of quasi-Newton methods using the values of the function $\varphi(y^k)$ and of its gradient $\nabla\varphi(y^k)$ to organize the search. In this method, the function $\varphi(y)$ is assumed to have the properties of the quadratic function that corresponds to the existence of a symmetric matrix of the second derivatives (Hessian) $\nabla^2\varphi(y)$.

The basic idea for all quasi-Newton methods consists in the construction of an approximation of the actual Hessian $\nabla^2\varphi(y^k)$ at every step of the algorithm using a special matrix B^k followed by selection of the descent direction d^k as a solution of the system

$$B^k d^k = -\nabla\varphi(y^k) \leftrightarrow d^k = -H^k \nabla\varphi(y^k),$$

where $H^k = (B^k)^{-1}$.

After obtaining the direction, a step is performed from current point y^k:

$$y^{k+1} = y^k + \alpha_k d^k,$$

where $\alpha_k > 0$ is the adjustable step length.

Assuming $B^0 = E$, the Hessian approximation is recalculated by the formula $B^{k+1} = B^k + U^k$, where U^k are the corrections represented in the form of a matrix of the rank 1. The small rank of the corrections U^k is necessary for efficient procedure of calculating the inverse matrix $H^{k+1} = (B^{k+1})^{-1} = (B^k + U^k)^{-1}$.

The main requirement to forming the corrections U^k of particular form is the condition

$$B^{k+1}(y^{k+1} - y^k) = \nabla\varphi(y^{k+1}) - \nabla\varphi(y^k),$$

that holds true for all quasi-Newton methods. For more precise determination of the matrix B^{k+1}, it is necessary to impose additional requirements on the Hessian approximation. The set of such requirements is determined by BFGS rule. Assume

$$s_k = y^{k+1} - y^k,$$

$$z^k = \nabla\varphi(y^{k+1}) - \nabla\varphi(y^k).$$

Then, the BFGS recalculation scheme takes the following form:

$$B^{k+1} = B^k - \frac{B^k s_k s_k^T B^k}{s_k^T B^k s_k} + \frac{z^k(z^k)^T}{(z^k)^T s_k},$$

$$H^{k+1} = (E - \rho_k s_k(z^k)^T)H^k(E - \rho_k z^k s_k^T) + \rho_k s_k s_k^T,$$

where $\rho_k = 1/((y^k)^T s_k)$.

For the systems with limited memory, a modification of BFGS method – the limited BFGS in the limited space (L-BFGS-B) is used. The modified method stores the history $\aleph^k = ((s_{k-i}, z^{k-i}))_i^l$ of the last l vectors s_k and z^k. From the history, the approximate form of the matrix H^k is restored.

The algorithm of the BFGS method can be represented by a sequence of the following steps.

Step 0. Initialize the starting point y^0. Set the precision $\varepsilon > 0$;

Step 1. Determine the initial approximation H^0 (either by the unit matrix E or by $\nabla^2\varphi(y^0)$);

Step 2. Determine the search direction: $d^k = -H^k \nabla\varphi(y^k)$;

Step 3. Compute $y^{k+1} = y^k + \alpha_k d^k$;

Step 4. Determine the vectors s_k and z^k;

Step 5. Compute the Hessian H^{k+1};

Step 6. Stop, if the condition $\|\nabla\varphi(y^k)\| < \varepsilon$ is fulfilled.

4.2   Hooke-Jeeves Method

Hooke-Jeeves method (see, e.g., [7]) is the first-order one, i.e. it needs only the function values for the work. In this method, the search for the minimum at every step is performed as a result of a shift along some sample direction (step by a sample), which is constructed and then corrected as a result of special trial coordinate translations called *constructing a configuration.*

Constructing a configuration from a point y is performed by a mapping of y into a point $\bar{y} = F(y)$, where F is an operator of constructing a configuration. It is constructed so that the direction $(\bar{y} - y)$ is that of the decreasing of the function φ in the nearness of y. To describe the operator F, let us introduce the following notations: e^i is the ith unit coordinate vector and h is the parameter determining the magnitude of the coordinate movement. Then, the transition from y to $\bar{y}$ (i.e. the algorithm of constricting the configuration $\bar{y} = F(y)$) is performed according to the following rules.

Step 0. Set $\bar{y} = y$.
Step 1. For y from 1 to N do:
   if $\varphi(\bar{y} + he^i) < \varphi(\bar{y})$ then
      set $\bar{y} = \bar{y} + he^i$
   else if $\varphi(\bar{y} - he^i) < \varphi(y)$ then
      set $\bar{y} = y - he^i$.

Next, the step-by-step description of the whole method is given.

Step 0. Set the starting point t^0, the parameter of the method $\varepsilon > 0$, the parameter of constructing the configuration $h \gg \varepsilon$, and the parameter α of the increasing of the step, e.g. $\alpha = 2$.

Step 1. Set $y^1 = t^0, k = 0$.
Step 2. Construct a configuration $t^{k+1} = F(y^{k+1})$.
Step 3. Determine the next step
   if $\varphi(t^{k+1}) < \varphi(t^k)$ then
      $k = k + 1$ and go to Step 4,
   else
         if $h \leq \varepsilon$ then stop the search
         else if $h > \varepsilon$ then
            if $k = 0$ then
               $h = h/2$ and go to Step 1.
            else if $k > 0$ then
               set $t^0 = t^k, k = 0$ and go to Step 1.
Step 4. Move by direction $y^{k+1} = t^k + \alpha(t^k - t^{k-1})$ and go to Step 2.

The meaning of the actions performed within the steps 2, 3, and 4 can be explained as follows. Step 4 was introduced in order to enable the method to rapidly increase the shift magnitude within a single iteration in the case when the point t^k is located far away from the solution. At that, prior to make y^{k+1} current point of the iteration, a configuration is constructed from the point y^{k+1}.

In the case of obtaining a point with $\varphi(t^{k+1}) < \varphi(t^k)$, the next step, in general, will be performed in a changed direction (relative to previous one) that allows adapting the method to variations in the function relief.

Finally, upon obtaining a value $\varphi(t^{k+1}) \geq \varphi(t^k)$ at Step 3, an attempt to run the algorithm again from the point $t^0 = t^k$ (better than the one found) is undertaken. At that, if such an attempt hasn't been undertaken yet, the parameter h is not changed, but if it has been undertaken already, h is cut in half first.

4.3   Parallelization of the Local Optimization Methods

Parallel computing of many objective function values at once is the operation, which can be performed efficiently in the optimization methods. The local optimization methods are the iteration ones, therefore, the parallelization can be organized within a single iteration only.

For example, in Hooke-Jeeves method one can parallelize the construction of configuration, i.e. parallelize the loop at the second step of the algorithm. In this loop, one may not compute the function values at the points $\bar{y} + he^i$ or $\bar{y} - he^i$ immediately but may store the coordinates of the ones in the buffer, and upon accumulating p points compute the function values at these ones in parallel. Next, the accumulated information is analyzed and the coordinates of the point $\bar{y}$ are changed. This operation is repeated until all N coordinates $\bar{y}$ are computed.

The main work of the quasi-Newton L-BFGS-B method at every iteration is spent for the computing of the function gradient. When solving the problems with the "black box" functions, the analytical calculation of the gradient is impossible. The numerical estimate of the gradient using the finite difference formulae implies multiple computing of the objective function values.

So far, in the L-BFGS-B algorithm, one can parallelize the computing of gradient at the second step of the algorithm. To do so, one needs to store all points, in which the computing of the function values for the gradient estimate are required, into an intermediate buffer, and then compute the function values at these points in parallel.

Thus, in both considered local methods the parallelization scheme will be generally the same. The vector of objective function values can be computed in parallel on a single node using shared memory (OpenMP), on a cluster with distributed memory (MPI), or on accelerator using CUDA.

5   Results of Numerical Experiments

The numerical experiments were carried out on Lobachevsky supercomputer. Each supercomputer node was a two-processor one (two Intel Sandy Bridge E5-2660 2.2 GHz, 64 Gb RAM). All methods considered in the above sections were implemented using Globalizer software [4] (development language - C++). Intel C++ 17.0.0 compiler was used to assembly the system.

The first series of experiments was carried out with the local optimization algorithms only. Rosenbrock function is a classical test function for the local search methods

$$\varphi(y) = \sum_{i=1}^{N-1} \left[(1 - y_i)^2 + 100(y_{i+1} - y_i^2)^2 \right],$$

$$D = \{ y \in R^N : -25 \le y_j \le 25, 1 \le j \le N \}.$$

Figure 1 presents the averaged numbers of iterations, which Hooke-Jeeves and BFGS methods executed for minimization of Rosenbrock function with the dimensionalities from 5 to 30. Figure 2 presents corresponding speedups in iterations. The number of parallel trials p varied from 1 to 16.

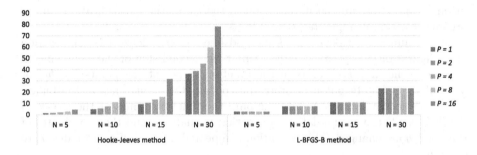

Fig. 1. Number of trials (in thousands) executed on the Rosenbrock function

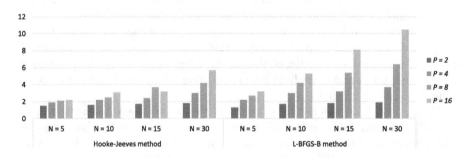

Fig. 2. Speedup on the Rosenbrock function

The results demonstrated the methods of parallelization of the local optimization algorithms described in Sect. 4 to show good results for the test function. At that, for the problems with low dimensionality (less than 30) Hooke-Jeeves method suited better. However, starting from the dimensionality of 30, L-BFGS-B method begins to execute fewer trials. Also, because of some features of parallelization, Hooke-Jeeves method executes more and more trials with increasing number of threads, whereas L-BFGS-B always performs the same number of trials. It is explained by the parallelization of the computing of gradient in L-BFGS-B so that the number of computations of the objective function is the same regardless to the number of threads while in Hooke-Jeeves method the algorithm itself is parallelized so that not all the points, at which the trials were executed earlier in the parallel algorithm match the trajectory of the sequential method.

Next, the experiments, which the global search algorithms as well as the local methods have been employed in, were carried out. In [3] GKLS (this abbreviation consists of the first letters of the authors' names) generator was described. This generator allows generating the multiextremal optimization problems with the properties known *a priori*: the number of local minima, the sizes of the attraction regions of the ones, the global minima points, the objective function value at this point, etc. The test problems generated by this generator are featured by a small time of computing the objective function values.

The global minimum y^* was considered to be found if the algorithm generates a trial point y^k near the global minimum, i.e. $\|y^k - y^*\| \leq \delta$. We use $\delta = 0.06$ for $N = 4$ and $\delta = 0.08$ for $N = 5$. When using GSA, the parameter $r = 4.5$ was selected for class Simple, and $r = 5.6$ for class Hard; the parameter of the construction of the Peano curve was fixed to be $m = 10$. The maximum allowed number of iterations was $K_{max} = 5 \cdot 10^6$.

The number of iterations for the local methods was limited to 10^4, the precision of the local methods was set to 10^{-4}. First, the problems were solved by the global search method with the parameters specified above. Then, a local method was started from the optimal point found to find the minimum more precisely.

Table 1 presents the averaged number of iterations, which GSA required to solve the problem. Figure 3 presents the numbers of trials executed by Hooke-Jeeves and L-BFGS-B local methods. Figure 4 presents the speedups achieved when solving the problem as a whole.

Table 1. Averaged number of iterations for GSA algorithm

N	Problem class	$p = 1$	$p = 2$	$p = 4$	$p = 8$	$p = 16$
4	Hard	36528	18651	9854	4808	2260
	Simple	9995	5199	2706	1333	630
5	Hard	266420	149109	90894	39873	22206
	Simple	29853	12913	7296	3618	2220

The local methods required less number of trials to refine the solution as compared to the global search method. As a result, the contributions of the local methods into total time of solving the problem were not very large. At that, L-BFGS-B method made much less computations of the objective function.

Within the last experiment an applied optimization problem was solved. This problem arose when solving the inverse problem of chemical kinetics.

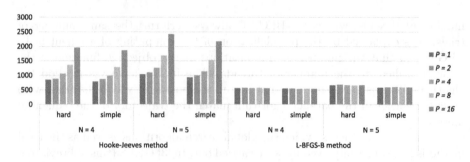

Fig. 3. Number of trials executed on the GKLS function

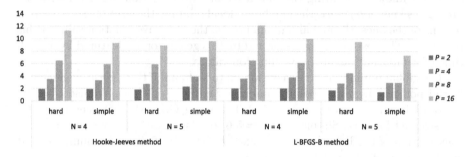

Fig. 4. Speedup on the GKLS function

The reaction investigated and respective experimental data are described in [17]. The mathematical model of the chemical kinetics problem comprises a system of differential equations, which describes the variations of the concentrations of substances in time according to the rates of the reaction stages. According to this model, one can formulate an optimization problem, which defines the objective function as a sum of absolute deviations of the calculated concentrations from the ones measured experimentally:

$$F = \sum_{i=1}^{M} \sum_{j=1}^{N} \left| x_{ij}^{calc} - x_{ij}^{exp} \right| \to \min,$$

where x_{ij}^{calc} and x_{ij}^{exp} are the calculated values of concentrations of the components and the ones measured experimentally, respectively; M is the number of measurement points, and N is the number of substances participating in the reaction. The complete problem statement is given in [17]. Here we note only that the number of the unknown parameters (i.e. the dimensionality of the optimization problem being solved) was 15, and we will consider this one as an optimization problem with a complex "black-box" objective function only.

To solve the problem stated, the synchronous parallelization scheme (using MPI) was employed. The number of processes to compute the function values was $p = 15$. Also, there was an additional managing process, which processed the accumulated search information. In the stopping criteria of the method the value $\varepsilon = 0.01$ was used and the reliability parameter of the method was set as $r = 3$. After the work of GSA, a parallel local method was started to refine the result found. The precision of the local method was set to 10^{-4} and the limitation on the number of trials was 10^4.

Table 2 presents the results of solving the optimization problem: the running time of parallel GSA without the run of a local method (column GSA), with a sequential local method (column GSA-l) and with a parallel local method run on 15 processes (column GSA-pl).

Table 2. Time of solving the applied problem, sec.

Method	GSA	GSA-l	GSA-pl
Hooke-Jeeves	158.1	299.8	177.4
L-BFGS-B	158.1	252.5	165.6

Concluding the results, one can say that the use of local methods at the final stage of search allows solving the optimization problems with higher precision. In many cases, it is enough to use sequential local methods. However, the problems with ravine-type objective function require parallelizing the whole search process including the local stage as well. In the present work, two local optimization algorithms with the parallelization variants for shared memory as well as for distributed one are described. As the experiments have shown, the methods for parallelizing the local methods (at the final stage of global search) proposed demonstrated good results in solving both the test optimization problems and the applied ones.

Acknowledgements. This study was supported by the Russian Science Foundation, project No. 21-11-00204.

References

1. Akhmadullina, L., Enikeeva, L., Gubaydullin, I.: Numerical methods for reaction kinetics parameters: identification of low-temperature propane conversion in the presence of methane. Procedia Eng. **201**, 612–616 (2017)
2. Evtushenko, Y., Posypkin, M.: A deterministic approach to global box-constrained optimization. Optim. Lett. **7**, 819–829 (2013). https://doi.org/10.1007/s11590-012-0452-1
3. Gaviano, M., Kvasov, D., Lera, D., Sergeyev, Y.: Software for generation of classes of test functions with known local and global minima for global optimization. ACM Trans. Math. Softw. **29**(4), 469–480 (2003)
4. Gergel, V., Barkalov, K., Sysoyev, A.: A novel supercomputer software system for solving time-consuming global optimization problems. Numer. Algebra Control. Optim. **8**(1), 47–62 (2018)

5. Gubaydullin, I., Enikeeva, L., Barkalov, K., Lebedev, I.: Parallel global search algorithm for optimization of the kinetic parameters of chemical reactions. Commun. Comput. Inf. Sci. **1510**, 198–211 (2021)
6. Jones, D.R.: The DIRECT global optimization algorithm. In: The Encyclopedia of Optimization, pp. 725–735. Springer, Heidelberg (2009)
7. Kelley, C.T.: Iterative Methods for Optimization. SIAM, Philadelphia (1999)
8. Nocedal, J., Wright, S.: Numerical Optimization. Springer, New York (2006). https://doi.org/10.1007/0-387-22742-3_18
9. Nurislamova, L., Gubaydullin, I., Koledina, K., Safin, R.: Kinetic model of the catalytic hydroalumination of olefins with organoaluminum compounds. React. Kinet. Mech. Catal. **117**(1), 1–14 (2016)
10. Paulavičius, R., Sergeyev, Y., Kvasov, D., Žilinskas, J.: Globally-biased DISIMPL algorithm for expensive global optimization. J. Glob. Optim. **59**(2–3), 545–567 (2014)
11. Paulavičius, R., Žilinskas, J.: Simplicial Global Optimization. Springer, New York (2014). https://doi.org/10.1007/978-1-4614-9093-7
12. Pinter, J.: Global Optimization: Scientific and Engineering Case Studies. Springer, New York (2006). https://doi.org/10.1007/0-387-30927-6
13. Sergeyev, Y.D., Kvasov, D.E.: Deterministic Global Optimization. SO, Springer, New York (2017). https://doi.org/10.1007/978-1-4939-7199-2
14. Sergeyev, Y.D., Strongin, R.G., Lera, D.: Introduction to Global Optimization Exploiting Space-Filling Curves. Springer, New York (2013). https://doi.org/10.1007/978-1-4614-8042-6
15. Strongin, R.G., Sergeyev, Y.D.: Global Optimization with Non-convex Constraints: Sequential and Parallel Algorithms. Kluwer Academic Publishers, Dordrecht (2000)
16. Strongin, R.G., Gergel, V.P., Barkalov, K.A., Sysoyev, A.V.: Generalized parallel computational schemes for time-consuming global optimization. Lobachevskii J. Math. **39**(4), 576–586 (2018). https://doi.org/10.1134/S1995080218040133
17. Uskov, S., Potemkin, D., Enikeeva, L., Snytnikov, P., Gubaydullin, I., Sobyanin, V.: Propane pre-reforming into methane-rich gas over Ni catalyst: experiment and kinetics elucidation via genetic algorithm. Energies **13**(13), 3393 (2020)

Analysis of Parallel Algorithm Efficiency for Numerical Solution of Mass Transfer Problem in Fractured-Porous Reservoir

Ravil Uzyanbaev[1,2(✉)], Yury Poveshchenko[3], Viktoriia Podryga[3,4],
Sergey Polyakov[3], Yuliya Bobreneva[2], and Irek Gubaydullin[1,2]

[1] Ufa State Petroleum Technological University, Ufa, Russia
`ravil-11@mail.ru, irekmars@mail.ru`
[2] Institute of Petrochemistry and Catalysis of Russian Academy of Sciences,
Ufa, Russia
`yu.o.bobreneva@gmail.ru`
[3] Keldysh Institute of Applied Mathematics of the Russian Academy of Sciences,
Moscow, Russia
`hecon@mail.ru, pvictoria@list.ru, polyakov@imamod.ru`
[4] Moscow Automobile and Road Construction State Technical University, Moscow,
Russia

Abstract. The work considers a parallel implementation of a mathematical model of two-phase fluid filtration in a fractured-porous reservoir during hydrodynamic studies at the well. The model is based on the mechanism of dual porosity, which complicates its numerical analysis. The model is described by a system of strongly non-linear partial differential equations. In the numerical solution, the approximations of differential operators on a Cartesian grid are used. The approximations are obtained in the framework of the finite difference method. To implement the developed implicit numerical approach, the sweep method has been chosen. The calculation of the sweep coefficients due to the strong nonlinear dependence of the coefficients of the algebraic problem leads to large computational costs. In the one-dimensional case of using detailed refining grids adaptively approximating filtration processes near the well, the use of parallel technologies is required. Therefore, to speed up the calculations, a parallel sweep algorithm adapted to this problem is used. On its basis, a number of calculations were carried out, proving the feasibility of solving the problem of modeling two-phase filtration processes in a fractured porous reservoir using parallel technologies.

Keywords: Mathematical modeling · Two-phase filtration · Fractured porous formation · Implicit finite-difference schemes · Parallel algorithms · Parallel sweep method

1 Introduction

Hydrodynamic studies of wells are one of the main and unique tools for assessing reservoir parameters today. Conducting hydrodynamic studies in fractured-

V. Voevodin et al. (Eds.): RuSCDays 2022, LNCS 13708, pp. 33–47, 2022.
https://doi.org/10.1007/978-3-031-22941-1_3

porous reservoirs is significantly complicated due to the presence of fractures and caverns [1–3]. With highly developed fracturing, two porous media are distinguished in the reservoir: the system of fractures and the pore part of the reservoir (hereinafter referred to as the matrix) which have their own porosity and permeability values [4–6]. Hydrodynamic studies make it possible to evaluate the productive and filtration characteristics of the formation. However, given that the main part of the fields in Russia is located in harsh climatic conditions, it is difficult to conduct field research on a large scale. Therefore, for the development of fractured-porous reservoirs, numerical calculations on a computer are necessary.

The mathematical foundation of hydrodynamic research is the equations of piezoconductivity [7]. Taking into account two different media and consideration of two-phase filtration, the equations describing fluid filtration in a fractured-porous reservoir become quite complex [8–11]. A large number of unknown functions and adaptively approximated filtration processes near wells lead to a large number of calculations, including due to the use of grids with a small step. The solution to the problem is the development of a parallel numerical algorithm, with the ability to run on the architecture of large supercomputer systems. This approach significantly reduces the time for solving problems and reduces the load on RAM.

The basic technology in the development of parallel application codes is the Message Passing Interface (MPI) [12]. MPI program is a set of independent processes, each of which executes the same code on a separate computer (processor, processor core, or core thread). The processes of the MPI program communicate with each other by calling the appropriate communication procedures. Each MPI process runs in its own address space, providing additional speedup and data protection. The functions of distributing MPI processes among the computing nodes of a cluster or supercomputer are usually assigned to the system for managing parallel user tasks.

In this paper, for the one-dimensional case, an effective algorithm for solving the problem of two-phase fluid filtration in a fractured-porous reservoir is proposed. The software implementation of the algorithm is based on the parallel sweep method and the MPI standard. The article analyzes the efficiency of parallelization, including the estimation of the time for calculating the coefficients of differential equations and solving a finite system of equations by the scalar sweep method. Also, the optimal number of processes for solving the considered system of difference equations depending on the grid size is determined.

2   Problem Statement

Filtration of a two-phase fluid within the dual porosity model in a fractured-porous reservoir is described by differential equations in partial derivatives in cylindrical coordinates. The mathematical model of filtration processes is based on the equations of continuum mechanics, including the law of conservation of mass and conditions of phase equilibrium [2]. As functions of fluid exchange between media, namely, a system of fractures and a matrix, the classical functions will be used, which are proposed in the works of Warren-Root [8].

$$\frac{\partial(\phi^\alpha \rho_o S_o^\alpha)}{\partial t} + \frac{1}{r}\frac{\partial}{\partial r}(r\rho_o U_o^\alpha) + q_o^\alpha = \rho_o q_j, q_o^m = -q_o^f = -\rho_o^m \sigma \lambda_o^m (P^f - P^m),$$
(1)

$$\frac{\partial(\phi^\alpha \rho_w S_w^\alpha)}{\partial t} + \frac{1}{r}\frac{\partial}{\partial r}(r\rho_w U_w^\alpha) + q_w^\alpha = \rho_w q_j, q_w^m = -q_w^f = -\rho_w^m \sigma \lambda_w^m (P^f - P^m),$$
(2)

$$\lambda_o^m = \frac{k^m k_{ro}(S_o^m)}{\mu_o}, \lambda_w^m = \frac{k^m k_{rw}(S_w^m)}{\mu_w}.$$
(3)

Here ϕ^f −porosity in the fracture system; ϕ^m −porosity in the matrix; ρ_o − density of oil (g/m^3); ρ_w − the density of water(g/m^3); S_o^f − oil saturation in the fracture system; S_w^f − water saturation in the fracture system; S_o^m − oil saturation in the matrix; S_w^m − water saturation in the matrix; U_o^α − oil flow rate, U_w^α − water flow rate, $\alpha = f, m$, where f − fracture system, m−matrix system; q_i^α − flow function between the matrix and fractures; k^α − absolute permeability (m^2); k_{rw} −relative phase permeabilities of water; k_{ro} − relative phase permeabilities of oil; μ_o − viscosity of oil (Pa·s); μ_w − viscosity of water (Pa·s); σ − coefficient of fractured rock $(1/m^2)$; P^f − pressure in the system of fractures (Pa); P^m − pressure in the matrix (Pa).

According to the generalized Darcy's law, the filtration velocities of oil and water will be equal to:

$$U_o^\alpha = -\frac{k^\alpha k_{ro}(S_o^\alpha)}{\mu_o}\frac{\partial P_o^\alpha}{\partial r}, U_w^\alpha = -\frac{k^\alpha k_{rw}(S_w^\alpha)}{\mu_w}\frac{\partial P_w^\alpha}{\partial r}.$$
(4)

We assume that the pressure for different phases in each medium will be the same: $P_o^\alpha = P_w^\alpha, \alpha = f, m$.

For the problem (1)–(4), the initial and boundary conditions are set:

$$P^m|_{t=0} = const1, P^f|_{t=0} = const1, P^f|_{r=0} = const2, \frac{\partial P^f}{\partial r}|_{r=L} = 0.$$
(5)

3 Difference Scheme for Solving the Filtering Problem

The formulated problem (1)–(5) is a quasi-linear system of equations of mathematical physics of mixed type [13]. The solution of the system causes some difficulties, due to the presence of a large number of variable parameters. Direct approximation of the initial equations by an explicit time difference scheme [14–16] leads to a limitation of the time step, which is not always acceptable in practice. To solve the above problems in the numerical solution, the algorithm of splitting by physical processes is used [17].

At the first stage, the initial system of Eqs. (1)–(2) is written in the form (6)–(7), which is equivalent to the original one. To do this, from under the sign of the time derivative in (1)–(2) we take out the saturation and get the system (6), represented by the equations of piezoconductivity [18–20].

$$\frac{S_o^f}{\rho_o^f}\frac{\partial(\phi^f\rho_o^f)}{\partial t} + \frac{S_w^f}{\rho_w^f}\frac{\partial(\phi^f\rho_w^f)}{\partial t} + \frac{\partial(r\rho_o^f U_o^f)}{\rho_o^f r\partial r} + \frac{\partial(r\rho_w^f U_w^f)}{\rho_w^f r\partial r} +$$

$$+ \sigma(P^f - P^m)(\frac{\rho_o^m}{\rho_o^f}\lambda_o^m + \frac{\rho_w^m}{\rho_w^f}\lambda_w^m) = 0,$$

$$\frac{S_o^m}{\rho_o^m}\frac{\partial(\phi^m\rho_o^f)}{\partial t} + \frac{S_w^m}{\rho_w^m}\frac{\partial(\phi^m\rho_w^m)}{\partial t} - \sigma(P^f - P^m)(\lambda_o^m + \lambda_w^m) = 0. \quad (6)$$

System (7) is written taking into account $S_o + S_w = 1$ also from (1)–(2) and describes saturation transfer:

$$\frac{\partial(\phi^f\rho_w^f S_w^f)}{\partial t} + \frac{1}{r}\frac{\partial(r\rho_w U_w^f)}{\partial r} + \frac{\sigma\rho_w k^m k_{rw}(S_w^m)}{\mu_w}(P^f - P^m) = 0,$$

$$\frac{\partial(\phi^m\rho_w^m S_w^m)}{\partial t} - \frac{\sigma\rho_w k^m k_{rw}(S_w^m)}{\mu_w}(P^f - P^m) = 0. \quad (7)$$

In Eq. (6), for convenience, we use the notation and write it in a short form:

$$\left(\frac{S_o^f}{\rho_o^f}\frac{\partial(\phi^f\rho_o^f)}{\partial t} + \frac{S_w^f}{\rho_w^f}\frac{\partial(\phi^f\rho_w^f)}{\partial t}\right) + DIG^f = 0,$$

$$DIG^f = \frac{\partial(r\rho_o^f U_o^f)}{\rho_o^f r\partial r} + \frac{\partial(r\rho_w^f U_w^f)}{\rho_w^f r\partial r} + \sigma(P^f - P^m)(\frac{\rho_o^m}{\rho_o^f}\lambda_o^m + \frac{\rho_w^m}{\rho_w^f}\lambda_w^m), \quad (8)$$

$$\left(\frac{S_o^m}{\rho_o^m}\frac{\partial(\phi^m\rho_o^m)}{\partial t} + \frac{S_w^m}{\rho_w^m}\frac{\partial(\phi^m\rho_w^m)}{\partial t}\right) + DIG^m = 0,$$

$$DIG^m = -\sigma(P^f - P^m)(\lambda_o^m + \lambda_w^m). \quad (9)$$

For the stated problem (6)–(7), the formulation in the spatially one-dimensional case is considered. To solve the problem, the finite difference method is used [21–23]. A difference grid is built in the following way:

$$W_h = \{r_i, i = 0, 1, ..I, r_0 = 0, r_I = l\}, W_\tau = \{t = \tau k, k = 0, 1, ..K\}, \quad (10)$$

where r_i are the coordinates of the nodes, τ is the grid step in time, k is the number of the time step; I and K are the numbers of nodes in space and time.

In the coordinates of the nodes r_i, the grid quantities (pressure and saturation) are determined. Ω_i is the $i + 1/2$ cell of a one-dimensional grid which corresponds to a segment $[r_i, r_{i+1}]$. $r_{i+1/2} = 1/2(r_{i+1} + r_i) \equiv r_{1/2}$, $(r_{i+1/2}^2 - r_{i-1/2}^2)/2 = ((r_{i+1/2} + r_{i-1/2})/2)\hbar$, $h_{i+1/2} = r_{i+1} - r_i$, $\hbar = 1/2(h_{i+1/2} + h_{i-1/2})$. Approximations of the quantities $r_{i+1/4} = 1/2(r_{i+1/2} + r_i) \equiv r_{1/4}$ are understood similarly.

Eqs. (6) and (7), with conditions (5) are approximated by grid analogues. Further, the resulting system of equations is linearized using the chord method.

For a system of fractures, the transformed Eq. (8) are linearized and will look like this:

$$\frac{(S_w^f)^{(\delta 1 f)\approx}}{(\rho_w^f)^{(\delta 1 f)\approx}}(\bar{\phi}^f \rho_w^f)_{P_f}'^S \delta P^f + \frac{(1 - S_w^f)^{(\delta 1 f)\approx}}{(\rho_o^f)^{(\delta 1 f)\approx}}\left(\bar{\phi}^f \rho_o^f\right)_{P_f}'^S \delta P^f + \tau \delta(DIG^{f\approx}) = -F^{fs},$$

$$\tau \delta(DIG^{f\approx}) = \frac{-\tau}{(\rho_w^f)^{(\delta 1 f)\approx}} DIN \left[\left(\frac{r \rho_w^f k^f}{\mu_w^f}\right)^s k_{rw}^{ups} GRAN \delta P^f\right]$$

$$+ \frac{\tau}{(\rho_o^f)^{(\delta 1 f)\approx}} DIN \left[\left(\frac{r \rho_o^f k^f}{\mu_o^f}\right)^s k_{ro}^{ups} GRAN \delta P^f\right]$$

$$- \frac{\tau(\rho_w^m \bar{\sigma} k_m(\lambda_w^m/k_m))^s}{(\rho_w^f)^{(\delta 1 f)\approx}}(\delta P^f - \delta P^m) - \frac{\tau(\rho_o^m \bar{\sigma} k_m(\lambda_o^m/k_m))^s}{(\rho_o^f)^{(\delta 1 f)\approx}}(\delta P^f - \delta P^m). \quad (11)$$

Here $\bar{\phi} = (r\partial r)_{1/4}\phi_{1/2} + (r\partial r)_{-1/4}\phi_{-1/2}$, F^{fs} is the difference approximation of the left-hand side of Eq. (8) (multiplied by τ), $\delta 1$ is the weight by time, a' is pressure derivative, δP is pressure increment, difference operation $DIN : (\Omega) \to (\omega)$ denotes the approximation of the divergence $dv \cdot div$ acting on functions in cells (Ω), $GRAN : (\omega) \to (\Omega)$ denotes the approximation of the gradient $grad$ in the cells (Ω) which acts on the grid functions at the nodes (ω), $k_{rw\Omega}^{up\Lambda}$ are the relative phase permeability of water in a cell Ω which is taken from the node $\omega(\Omega)$ of this cell, located upwind (up) from the implicit time layer (Λ). In grid approximations $a^{\approx}$, the values on the implicit time layer $\hat{t}$ are taken at $s + 1$ of the already calculated iteration, if they are related to pressure (P^{s+1}) and at s-th iteration if they are related to water saturation (S_w^s).

For Eq. (9), for the matrix, after linearization, we get the following:

$$\frac{(S_w^m)^{(\delta 1 m)\approx}}{(\rho_w^m)^{(\delta 1 m)\approx}}(\bar{\phi}^m \rho_w^m)_{P_m}'^S \delta P^m + \frac{(1 - S_w^m)^{(\delta 1 m)\approx}}{(\rho_o^m)^{(\delta 1 m)\approx}}\left(\bar{\phi}^m \rho_o^m\right)_{P_m}'^S \delta P^m +$$

$$+ \tau \delta(DIG^{m\approx}) = 0 - F^{ms},$$

$$\tau \delta(DIG^{m\approx}) = \frac{\tau(\rho_w^m \bar{\sigma}(\lambda_w^m))^s}{(\rho_w^m)^{(\delta 1 m)\approx}}(\delta P^f - \delta P^m) - \frac{\tau(\rho_o^m \bar{\sigma}(\lambda_o^m))^s}{(\rho_o^m)^{(\delta 1 m)\approx}}(\delta P^f - \delta P^m). \quad (12)$$

Here $\bar{\sigma}k_m = (r\partial r)_{1/4}\sigma_{1/2}k_{m,1/2} + (r\partial r)_{-1/4}\sigma_{-1/2}k_{m,-1/2}$, F^{ms} is the difference approximation of the left-hand side of Eq. (9) (multiplied by τ).

Thus, as a result of the approximation of partial differential Eq. (6) by the corresponding finite differences, we obtain a system of linear algebraic equations (SLAE):

$$- A_{pk}\delta P_{k-1}^f + C_{pk}\delta P_k^f - B_{pk}\delta P_{k+1}^f = \Phi_{pk}, \quad (13)$$

where:

$$\Phi_{pk} = -F^{fs} - \tau \left\{ \frac{(\rho_w^m \bar{\sigma} \lambda_w^m)^s}{(\rho_w^f)(\delta 1 f)^\approx} + \frac{(\rho_o^m \bar{\sigma} \lambda_o^m)^s}{(\rho_o^f)(\delta 1 f)^\approx} \right\} \Phi^{ms}, \tag{14}$$

$$A_{pk} = \frac{\tau}{\left[r(\rho_w^f)(\delta 1 f) \right]_k^\approx} \left\{ \frac{1}{h_{k-1/2}} \left(\frac{r \rho_w^f k^f}{\mu_w^f} \right)_{k-1/2}^s k_{rw(k-1/2)}^{ups} \right\} +$$

$$\frac{\tau}{\left[r(\rho_o^f)(\delta 1 f) \right]_k^\approx} \left\{ \frac{1}{h_{k-1/2}} \left(\frac{r \rho_o^f k^f}{\mu_o^f} \right)_{k-1/2}^s k_{ro(k-1/2)}^{ups} \right\}, \tag{15}$$

$$B_{pk} = \frac{\tau}{\left[r(\rho_w^f)(\delta 1 f) \right]_k^\approx} \left\{ \frac{1}{h_{k+1/2}} \left(\frac{r \rho_w^f k^f}{\mu_w^f} \right)_{k+1/2}^s k_{rw(k+1/2)}^{ups} \right\} +$$

$$\frac{\tau}{\left[r(\rho_o^f)(\delta 1 f) \right]_k^\approx} \left\{ \frac{1}{h_{k+1/2}} \left(\frac{r \rho_o^f k^f}{\mu_o^f} \right)_{k+1/2}^s k_{ro(k+1/2)}^{ups} \right\},$$

$$\tag{16}$$

$$C_{pk} = \frac{(S_w^f)(\delta 1 f)^\approx}{(\rho_w^f)(\delta 1 f)^\approx} \left(\bar{\phi}^f \rho_w^f \right)_{P_f}^{\prime S} + \frac{(1 - S_w^f)(\delta 1 f)^\approx}{(\rho_o^f)(\delta 1 f)^\approx} \left(\bar{\phi}^f \rho_o^f \right)_{P_f}^{\prime S} +$$

$$\frac{\tau}{\left[r(\rho_w^f)(\delta 1 f) \right]_k^\approx} \left\{ \frac{r_{k+1/2}}{h_{k+1/2}} \left(\frac{\rho_w^f k^f}{\mu_w^f} \right)_{k+\frac{1}{2}}^s k_{rw(k+\frac{1}{2})}^{ups} + \frac{r_{k-1/2}}{h_{k-1/2}} \left(\frac{\rho_w^f k^f}{\mu_w^f} \right)_{k-\frac{1}{2}}^s k_{rw(k-\frac{1}{2})}^{ups} \right\} +$$

$$\frac{\tau}{\left[r(\rho_o^f)(\delta 1 f) \right]_k^\approx} \left\{ \frac{r_{k+1/2}}{h_{k+1/2}} \left(\frac{\rho_o^f k^f}{\mu_o^f} \right)_{k+\frac{1}{2}}^s k_{ro(k+\frac{1}{2})}^{ups} + \frac{r_{k-1/2}}{h_{k-1/2}} \left(\frac{\rho_o^f k^f}{\mu_o^f} \right)_{k-\frac{1}{2}}^s k_{ro(k-\frac{1}{2})}^{ups} \right\} +$$

$$\left\{ \frac{\tau}{(\rho_w^f)(\delta 1 f)^\approx} (\rho_w^m \bar{\sigma} \lambda_w^m)^s (1 - \pi_m^s) \right\}_k + \left\{ \frac{\tau}{(\rho_o^f)(\delta 1 f)^\approx} (\rho_o^m \bar{\sigma} \lambda_o^m)^s (1 - \pi_m^s) \right\}_k. \tag{17}$$

Since the explicit solution scheme for this problem requires a too small time integration step, in this paper we have chosen an implicit algorithm that assumes the solution of Eqs. (13). To solve the system of Eqs. (13), the scalar sweep method was used [23,24]. The scalar sweep method has proven itself well for solving SLAEs in the spatially one-dimensional case [14].

Thus, Eq. (13) is solved by sweeping on each time layer at fixed saturations. For pressure, the accuracy is given, which is achieved using an iterative process:

$$|\delta P^m| < \varepsilon_1 |\delta P^{ms}| + \varepsilon_2, |\delta P^f| < \varepsilon_1 |\delta P^{fs}| + \varepsilon_2, \tag{18}$$

where ε_1 and ε_2 are the small quantities; the pressure increment at the iteration is represented as follows:

$$\delta P^m = \delta P^{ms+1} - P^{ms}, \delta P^f = \delta P^{fs+1} - P^{fs}. \tag{19}$$

As a result of solving (13)–(19), we obtain the pressures δP^f and δP^m, which allows us to proceed to the solution of Eq. (7).

For Eq. (7), similarly to (6), a difference scheme is constructed, then it is linearized using the chord method, and a system of equations is obtained. Based on the found pressure from (8), we find the saturation.

4 Parallel Realization

When solving the final algebraic problem in a parallel version, it was proposed to use the parallel sweep algorithm developed earlier in [25].

The corresponding program code for solving the problem is written in the C language using the MPI standard [12]. We parallelize two parts of the program:

– calculation of coefficients of Eq. (13) $A_{pk}, B_{pk}, C_{pk}, \Phi_{pk}$;
– solution of SLAE by the sweep method [14].

We introduce a uniform partition of the set of numbers of grid nodes in order to describe the parallel algorithm $\Omega = \{0, 1, ..., N\}$ into adjacent non-overlapping subsets $\Omega_m = \{i_1^m, ..., i_2^m\}$ ($m = 0, ..., p-1$ is the MPI process logical number). As a result of such a partition, the MPI process with the number m will process $(i_2^{(m)} - i_1^{(m)} + 1)$ points.

Solution for MPI process logical numbers:

$$y_i \equiv y_i^{(m)} = y_i^{(I,m)} + y_{i_1^{(m)}} y_i^{(III,m)} + y_{i_2^{(m)}} y_i^{(II,m)}, \qquad (20)$$

where $y_i^{(\alpha,m)}$ are with Roman numerals basis, and function values on the boundary $\Omega_m - y_{i_1^{(m)}}$ and $y_{i_2^{(m)}}$. From Eq. (13) we find the function $y_i^{(I,m)}$. From Eq. (13), equating the right side to zero, we find the functions $y_i^{(II,m)}$, $y_i^{(III,m)}$. $y_{i_1^{(m)}}$ and $y_{i_2^{(m)}}$ are found from the following short system:

$$-\tilde{A}_i y_{i-1} + \tilde{C}_i y_i - \tilde{B}_i y_{i+1} = \tilde{F}_i, i \in \tilde{\Omega} = \{i_2^{(0)}, i_1^{(1)}, i_2^{(1)}, ..., i_1^{(p-1)}\}, \qquad (21)$$

where the coefficients of the equation are found from the coefficients of Eq. (13) and the basis functions.

When forming the coefficients of the original algebraic problem, data exchange is organized between MPI processes within the framework of a linear topology [26,27]. The selected MPI process with number m exchanges with neighboring MPI processes with numbers (m−1) and (m+1). The code fragment that implements such exchanges is presented below:

```
if (mp_l>=0) {
    MPI_Irecv(rr_l,nn_l,MPI_DOUBLE,mp_l,MY_TAG,MPI_COMM_WORLD,R);
    R++; m++;
  }
  if (mp_r>=0) {
```

```
    MPI_Irecv(rr_r,nn_r,MPI_DOUBLE,mp_r,MY_TAG,MPI_COMM_WORLD,R);
    R++; m++;
}
if (mp_l>=0) {
    MPI_Isend(ss_l,nn_l,MPI_DOUBLE,mp_l,MY_TAG,MPI_COMM_WORLD,R);
    R++; m++;
}
if (mp_r>=0) {
    MPI_Isend(ss_r,nn_r,MPI_DOUBLE,mp_r,MY_TAG,MPI_COMM_WORLD,R);
    R++; m++;
}
```

The MPI process with number m (denoted by the variable mp in the code) uses the nonblocking functions MPI_Isend and MPI_Irecv to send the required values of the variables $\rho_o^f, \rho_w^f, k^f, \mu_o^f, \mu_w^f, P^f, S_i^f$ to its nearest neighbors (denoted mp_l and mp_r in the code). The clipboards ss_l and ss_r are used for this. The data it needs will be received from the neighbors into the rr_l and rr_r buffers. The amount of data to be sent nn_l=7.

To solve the short problem (21), all MPI processes carry out a collective exchange of coefficients. This is implemented using the code snippet below:

```
MPI_Allreduce(dd,ee,4*ncp,MPI_DOUBLE,MPI_SUM,MPI_COMM_WORLD);
for (i=0; i<ncp; i++) {
j = 4*i;
aa[i] = ee[j];
bb[i] = ee[j+1];
cc[i] = ee[j+2];
ff[i] = ee[j+3];
}
```

More details of the parallel algorithm are given in [25].

5 Calculation Results

To verify the model, the calculated data are compared with the field data [28]. To do this, we will simulate the operation of the well and its shutdown for hydrodynamic studies using the pressure build-up curve method. To do this, it is important to have initial values not only at the boundary $P^f|_{r=0} = 25$ MPa, $P^f|_{r=re} = 42.8$ MPa, but also over the entire study radius (50 m).

Figure 1 shows the field pressure (P^e), calculation pressures in the fracture (P^f) and in the matrix (P^m). Good convergence of calculated and field data is noted, the relative error does not exceed 7% that is sufficient for practical problems.

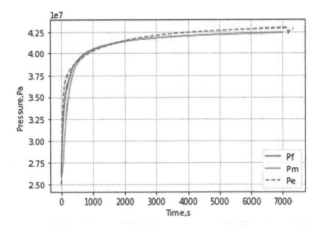

Fig. 1. Pressure build-up curves

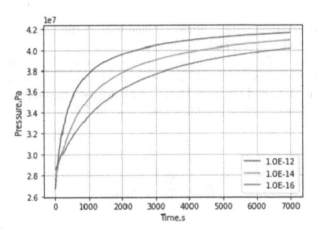

Fig. 2. Pressure build-up curves at various permeabilities

Figure 2 shows pressure build-up curves during hydrodynamic studies on a production well at various permeability values, which show that the higher the permeability, the faster the build-up velocity.

A number of calculations were also performed to analyze the efficiency of parallel computing. As mentioned earlier, two main parts of the general algorithm are parallelized in the program: calculation of the SLAE coefficients and its solution using the sweep method. Figure 3 shows the dependence of the problem solving time on the number of MPI processes. In the calculation, a study radius of 100 m and a division of the area into 1000 points of the spatial grid were chosen. The study time corresponds to 20000 s. In Fig. 3 and further, time is the total calculation time, time_c is the coefficient calculation time, time_p is the SLAE solution time by the sweep method.

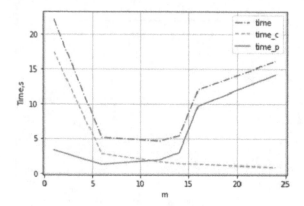

Fig. 3. Calculation time depending on the number of MPI processes on a grid with 1000 points

Figure 4 shows the calculation time depending on the number of MPI processes on a grid with 5000 points.

As we can see in Figs. 3 and 4, the time for calculating the SLAE coefficients decreases, but the time for its solution after $m = 12$ increases. This affects the overall speedup (Sm) and efficiency (Em), which are used to compare the parallel algorithm with the sequential one (see Figs. 5, 6, 7 and 8):

$$S_m = \frac{T_1}{T_m}, \tag{22}$$

$$E_m = \frac{S_m}{m} \cdot 100\%, \tag{23}$$

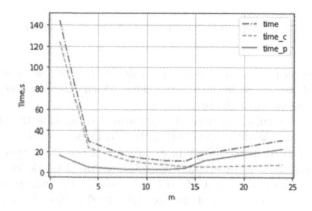

Fig. 4. Calculation time depending on the number of MPI processes on a grid with 5000 points

here T_1 is the execution time of a sequential program, T_m is the execution time of a parallel program on m MPI processes, S_m is the speedup of the parallel algorithm, E_m is the efficiency of the parallel algorithm.

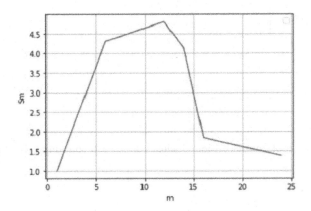

Fig. 5. Parallel speedup graph for a grid containing 1000 points

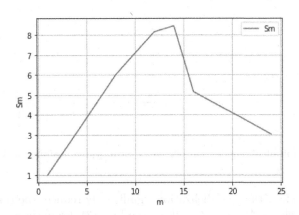

Fig. 6. Parallel speedup graph for a grid containing 5000 points

Figures 7, 8 show graphs of the parallelization efficiency when the radius is divided into 1000 and 5000 points.

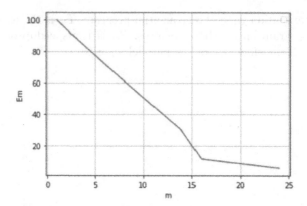

Fig. 7. Graph of parallelization efficiency for a grid containing 1000 points

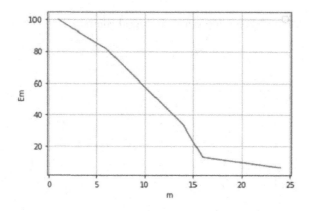

Fig. 8. Graph of parallelization efficiency for a grid containing 5000 points

Figures 3, 4 show that parallelization significantly reduces the time for calculating the coefficients $A_{pk}, B_{pk}, C_{pk}, \Phi_{pk}$ from Eq. (13). From the speedup graphs (Figs. 5,6), we note that for splitting along the radius into 1000 and 5000 points, the optimal number of MPI processes is 12 and 14, respectively. A increase in the number of MPI processes leads to a deterioration in the calculation time, which significantly reduces the efficiency (Fig. 7, 8).

The work [25] presents a detailed analysis of the possible reasons for the decrease in parallel acceleration when using more than 14 MPI processes. The acceleration is estimated from above by a finite value. Therefore, there is an optimal number of nodes m with a fixed number of grid points N for a particular computing system. The calculations were performed on the hybrid supercomputer K-100 installed in the Supercomputer Center of Collective Usage of

Keldysh Institute of Applied Mathematics of RAS [29] (see Table 1). Compiler version gcc is 4.3.4, mpicc version is 11.1, mpiexec version is OpenRTE 1.4.2.

Table 1. Description of the K-100 hardware (CPU Intel Xeon X5670 2,93 GHz)

	On node	Total
Processor cores	12	768
RAM, GB	96	6144

6   Conclusion

The work considers a mathematical model of the filtration of a two-phase fluid in a fractured-porous reservoir based on the introduction of dual porosity. To solve the problem under consideration, an original implicit finite-difference scheme on a uniform grid was proposed and implemented. The resulting system of discrete equations is linearized and solved using a parallel scalar sweep algorithm. The software implementation is based on MPI technology. The calculations performed with its help showed the following. First, good agreement between the numerical solution and field data was obtained in the calculations. Using numerical calculations, pressure build-up curves for various permeability values were constructed that is important in practical applications. Secondly, the use of the developed parallel calculation technique and the corresponding program confirmed its effectiveness and the possibility of its application in solving a multidimensional version of the problem based on numerical schemes of spatial splitting.

Acknowledgments. The work was funded by the Russian Science Foundation (project №21-71-20047). The calculations were performed on the hybrid supercomputer K-100 installed in the Supercomputer Center of Collective Usage of KIAM RAS.

References

1. Tugarova, M.A.: Reservoir Rocks: Properties, Petrographic Features, Classifications. Educational and Methodical Manual. St. Petersburg University, Saint Petersburg (2004). (in Russian)
2. Golf-Racht, T.D.: Fundamentals of Fractured Reservoir Engineering. Elsevier, Amsterdam (1982)
3. Aziz, H., Settari, E.: Mathematical Modeling of Reservoir Systems. Institute for Computer Research, Moscow-Izhevsk (2004). (in Russian)
4. Chernitskii, A.V.: Geological Modeling Of Oil Fields in Massive Type of Carbonate Fractured Reservoirs. RMNTK Nefteotdacha, Moscow (2002). (in Russian)
5. Aguilera, R.: Naturally Fractured Reservoirs. T. Pennwell Corp, Tulsa (1980)
6. Denk, S.O.: Problems of Fractured Productive Objects. Electronic Publishing, Perm (2004).(in Russian)

7. Barenblatt, G.I., Entov, V.M., Ryzhik, V.M.: The Flow of Liquids and Gases in Natural Reservoirs. Nedra, Moscow (1984). (in Russian)
8. Warren, J.E., Root, P.J.: The behavior of naturally fractured reservoirs. J. Soc. Petrol. Eng. **3**(03), 245–255 (1963). https://doi.org/10.2118/426-PA
9. Pollard, P.: Evaluation of acid treatments from pressure build-up analysis. Trans. AIME. **216**(01), 38–43 (1959). https://doi.org/10.2118/981-G
10. DeSwaan, A.O.: Analytic solutions for determining naturally fractured reservoir properties by well testing. SPE J. **16**(03), 117–122 (1976)
11. Odeh, A.S.: Unsteady-state behaviour of naturally fractured reservoirs. J. Soc. Petrol. Eng. **5**(1), 60–66 (1965). https://doi.org/10.2118/966-PA
12. Antonov, A.S.: Parallel Programming Using MPI Technology: A Textbook. MSU, Moscow (2004). (in Russian)
13. Tikhonov, A.N., Samarskii, A.A.: Equations of Mathematical Physics. Nauka, Moscow (1972). (in Russian)
14. Samarskii, A.A., Nikolaev, E.S.: Numerical Methods for Grid Equations. Nauka, Moscow (1978). (in Russian)
15. Samarskii, A.A.: Introduction to the Theory of Difference Schemes. Nauka, Moscow (1971). (in Russian)
16. Konovalov, A.N.: Introduction to Computational Methods of Linear Algebra. Siberian publishing firm, VO Nauka, Novosibirsk (1993). (in Russian)
17. Rahimly, P.I., Poveshchenko, Y.A., Rahimly, O.R., Podryga, V.O., Kazakevich, G.I., Gasilova, I.V.: The use of splitting with respect to physical processes for modeling the dissociation of gas hydrates. Math. Models Comput. Simul. **10**(1), 69–78 (2018). https://doi.org/10.1134/S2070048218010118
18. Bobreneva, Y.O., Rahimly, P.I., Poveshchenko, Y.A., Podryga, V.O., Enikeeva, L.V.: On one method of numerical modeling of piezoconductive processes of a two-phase fluid system in a fractured-porous reservoir. J. Phys: Conf. Ser. **2131**, 0220021 (2021). https://doi.org/10.1088/1742-6596/2131/2/022001
19. Bobreneva, Y.O., Rahimly, P.I., Poveshchenko, Y.A., Podryga, V.O., Enikeeva, L.V.: Numerical modeling of multiphase mass transfer processes in fractured-porous reservoirs. J. Phys: Conf. Ser. **2131**, 022002 (2021). https://doi.org/10.1088/1742-6596/2131/2/022002
20. Bobreneva, Y.O., Mazitov, A.A., Gubaydullin, I.M.: Mathematical modelling of fluid flow processes in the fracture-porous reservoir. J. Phys: Conf. Ser. **1096**, 012187 (2018). https://doi.org/10.1088/1742-6596/1096/1/012187
21. Sikovskii, D.F.: Methods of Computational Heat Transfer. Extended lecture notes, Novosibirsk (2007). (in Russian)
22. Paskonov, V.M., Polezhaev, V.I., Chudov, L.A.: Numerical Modeling of Heat and Mass Transfer Processes. Nauka, Moscow (1984). (in Russian)
23. Samarskii, A.A., Gulin, A.V.: Numerical Methods. Nauka, Moscow (1989). (in Russian)
24. Samarskii, A.A.: Introduction to Numerical Methods. Nauka, Moscow (1983). (in Russian)
25. Uzyanbaev, R.M., Bobreneva, Y.O., Poveshchenko, Y.A., Podryga, V.O., Polyakov, S.V.: Modeling of two-phase fluid flow processes in a fractured-porous type reservoir using parallel computations. In: Sokolinsky, L., Zymbler, M. (eds.) PCT 2022. Communications in Computer and Information Science, vol. 1618, pp. 276–292. Springer, Cham (2022). https://doi.org/10.1007/978-3-031-11623-0_19
26. Klochkov, M.A., Markov, K.Y., Mitrokhin, Y.S., Chirkova, L.S.: Organization of Parallel Calculations for Solving Differential Equations on the Blade Server.

Udmurt University, Educational and methodical manual, Izhevsk (2011). (in Russian)

27. Akimova, E.N.: Parallelizing the matrix sweep algorithm. Matem. Model. **6**(9), 61–67 (1994). (in Russian)
28. Cholovsky, I.P.: Handbook: Oil and Gas Geologist's Companion. Nedra, Moscow (1989). (in Russian)
29. Center for collective usage of the Keldysh institute of applied mathematics of RAS. http://ckp.kiam.ru

Black-Scholes Option Pricing on Intel CPUs and GPUs: Implementation on SYCL and Optimization Techniques

Elena Panova[1], Valentin Volokitin[1,2], Anton Gorshkov[1],
and Iosif Meyerov[1,2(✉)]

[1] oneAPI Center of Excellence, Lobachevsky University, Nizhny Novgorod 603950,
Russia
meerov@vmk.unn.ru
[2] Mathematical Center, Lobachevsky University, Nizhny Novgorod 603950, Russia

Abstract. The Black-Scholes option pricing problem is one of the
widely used financial benchmarks. We explore the possibility of developing a high-performance portable code using the SYCL (Data Parallel
C++) programming language. We start from a C++ code parallelized
with OpenMP and show optimization techniques that are beneficial on
modern Intel Xeon CPUs. Then, we port the code to SYCL and consider
important optimization aspects on CPUs and GPUs (device-friendly
memory access patterns, relevant data management, employing vector
data types). We show that the developed SYCL code is only 10% inferior to the optimized C++ code when running on CPUs while achieving
reasonable performance on Intel GPUs. We hope that our experience
of developing and optimizing the code on SYCL can be useful to other
researchers who plan to port their high-performance C++ codes to SYCL
to get all the benefits of single-source programming.

Keywords: High-performance computing · Black-Scholes formula ·
Heterogeneous computing · Parallel computing · oneAPI · DPC++ ·
SYCL · Single-source programming · Performance optimization

1 Introduction

The financial industry solves many computationally intensive problems requiring
high-performance computing. Over time some financial problems have become
traditional workload benchmarks. The Black-Scholes option pricing problem [1]
is one of the most widespread among them due to several reasons. Firstly, it
is one of the basic elements of financial market analysis and, therefore, has a
great practical interest. Secondly, ease of understanding and implementation,
combined with high computational requirements, make the Black-Scholes model
popular for learning the basics of optimization and performance testing on different architectures, including various accelerators such as GPU, Xeon Phi, and
others [2–6]. In this paper, we consider the Black-Scholes formula for a fair price

V. Voevodin et al. (Eds.): RuSCDays 2022, LNCS 13708, pp. 48–62, 2022.
https://doi.org/10.1007/978-3-031-22941-1_4

of a European call option and employ several optimization techniques to improve performance on CPUs and GPUs. Our main motivation is to understand is it possible to achieve reasonable performance on Intel CPUs and GPUs using a new oneAPI programming model.

oneAPI [7] is a new technology of single-source heterogeneous programming, introduced by Intel in 2020. Just like OpenCL [8], OpenACC [9], Kokkos [10], Alpaka [11] and many others, it is a software framework that allows implementing a single code for various hardware. With a growing diversity of architectures and their wide distribution, including among supercomputer systems, such frameworks are of increasing interest for developing high-performance applications in various problem areas. oneAPI provides a large set of tools for efficient development and performance analysis and optimization on CPUs, GPUs, FPGAs, and other devices. oneAPI includes the Data Parallel C++ (DPC++) programming language [12] based on the SYCL model [13,14]. DPC++ and SYCL are almost the same languages, so both designations will be used in the same sense in the rest of the paper.

The opportunity to write a single portable code that can be compiled and run on a variety of computing devices of various architectures and vendors is an important advantage of DPC++. This feature could allow us to develop a single portable code instead of a family of codes optimized for each computer architecture. However, whether *performance portability* is possible to achieve is still the open question.

In this paper, we address this important question by calculating the fair prices of a set of European call options. Compared to the previous paper [2] we analyze which optimization techniques to the C++ code parallelized with OpenMP improve performance on modern CPUs. We consider this implementation as a baseline for CPUs. After that, we show how to port the code to DPC++/SYCL and achieve reasonable performance not only on Intel CPUs but also on Intel GPUs. We highlight which optimization techniques are beneficial for this memory-bound application, and hope that our experience will be useful to other developers.

The paper is organized as follows. Section 2 provides the Black-Scholes formula and the corresponding algorithm. Test infrastructure and some launch parameters used in computational experiments are described in Sect. 3. The OpenMP implementation on C++ and its step-by-step optimization are presented in Sect. 4. In Sect. 5 we propose the DPC++ implementation of the Black-Scholes formula and optimize it on Intel CPUs and GPUs. Section 6 summarizes the paper.

2   Black-Scholes Option Pricing

We consider the European share call option, which is the simplest variant of an option and describes the following contract between two parties. The first party promises to sell the second one a share at a fixed strike price K at some point in time T after the contract conclusion, and the second party pays the first party an amount C for this right. After the maturity of T, the second party can decide to buy the share or not, it depends on its current price S_T: if $S_T - K - C > 0$ then it is profitable. The question is how to define the fair option price C, which is a balance of gains and losses for each party. It can be determined by the Black-Scholes formula for European call option price:

$$C = S_0 F(d_1) - K e^{-rT} F(d_2) \qquad (1)$$

$$d_1 = \ln \frac{S_0}{K} + \frac{\left(r + \frac{\sigma^2}{2}\right) T}{\sigma \sqrt{T}} \qquad (2)$$

$$d_2 = \ln \frac{S_0}{K} + \frac{\left(r - \frac{\sigma^2}{2}\right) T}{\sigma \sqrt{T}}, \qquad (3)$$

where $S_0 > 0$ is a starting price of a share, r is an interest rate (describes how many times the price of bonds in the financial market will increase), σ is volatility (a coefficient of risk assessment), K is a strike price, T is maturity, C is an option price, and $F(x)$ is a cumulative normal distribution function. We do not go into detail about key assumptions and ideas that lead to the Black-Scholes formula, this is fully described in [1,2]. In what follows, we will assume that r and σ are fixed, while S_0, K and T depend on the current state of the financial market. The main intention is to calculate the optimal option price C based on the given input parameters.

In practice, prices are calculated for a huge amount of different options for many specific market conditions. The performance of financial calculations significantly influences the decision-making speed, so reducing computational time for a large set of options is very important. Below we present the Black-Scholes formula implementation on C++ and DPC++ programming languages and optimize it step by step for CPUs and GPUs. We demonstrate that although the formula looks very simple to implement, it is a good testing ground for employing and analyzing a wide range of ideas related to performance optimization, especially when using devices of different architectures.

3   Test Infrastructure

Experiments were performed at the following infrastructures:

- A node of the Endeavour supercomputer with 2x Intel Xeon Platinum 8260L (Cascade Lake, 24 cores each, 2400 MHz), 192 GB RAM, RedHat 4.8.5, Intel C++ Compiler Classic, and Intel DPC++ Compiler from the Intel OneAPI Toolkit 2022.1 (experiments on CPUs).
- A node of the Intel DevCloud platform with Intel Iris Xe MAX (96 EU, 1650 MHz, 4 GB RAM, 68 GB/s of memory bandwidth), Intel Core i9 10920X, Ubuntu 18.04 LTS, Intel DPC++ Compiler from the Intel OneAPI Toolkit 2022.1 (experiments on GPUs).

According to peak performance and memory bandwidth, the designated GPU loses to the CPU, so we expect a worse performance on the GPU compared to the CPU. It is confirmed in practice. However, optimizations for such GPUs are of interest due to the prospect of new server GPUs being released by Intel.

The whole set of options is processed in 5 batches of 240,000,000 elements (each batch takes ∼3.8 GB). The minimum time for all batches is chosen as the resulting execution time. It is relevant for DPC++ experiments, as this way the DPC++ kernel compilation time, which increases the processing time of the first batch, is excluded from our measurements.

4 C++ Implementation and Optimization

4.1 Baseline

Even though the formulas 1–3 look quite simple, everything is not as elementary as it seems. First, we need to decide on the choice of a relevant data type and memory structure. The nature of the problem implies that it does not require high computational accuracy, so we can use single precision ('float' type) or even half precision (the last one is the subject of further research). It is worth noting that mixing 'double' and 'float' types is a typical mistake of many programmers: usage of double precision literals and inappropriate mathematical functions can significantly increase execution time. In its turn, careful handling of data types has only a positive effect on performance.

Employing a cache-friendly memory access pattern is one of the key performance optimization techniques. Applied to the Black-Scholes formula, we have two options to organize data: Array of Structures (AoS) and Structure of Arrays (SoA). In the AoS pattern case, all data related to the first option is placed into memory continued by data from the second option, and so on. In the SoA case, the data is packed in multiple arrays, and each array is responsible for storing a single parameter (initial price of a share, strike price, maturity, option price). More details about the advantages and disadvantages of each memory pattern for the option pricing problem are presented in [2]. Here we only want to point out that while SoA has given quite a significant speedup over AoS for the Black-Scholes code several years ago [2,4], now the difference has been disappeared. The AoS pattern works even a little faster than SoA on hardware described in Sect. 3. However, we need to develop code that is generally efficient across different architectures. Although the gap between SoA and AoS on the modern infrastructure does not exceed 1%, on older infrastructures SoA gives a significant increase (up to 3 times) due to the better use of vector instructions [2]. Therefore, we still use the SoA pattern.

The next issue that needs to be addressed is the choice of an appropriate mathematical library. Note that the cumulative normal distribution function ($F(x)$ in Eqs. 1–3) is of particular interest. For example, it is implemented as cdfnorm() function in the Intel Math Library of Intel C++ Compiler Classic. A more flexible and cross-platform solution is to use mathematical functions from the C++ language standard, which does not contain the normal distribution function but implements an error function and a similar complementary error function. In future computations we offer to use the next formula (Eq. 4). Note that it can work even faster than cdfnorm() in some implementations due to simpler compute approximation.

$$F(x) = 0.5 + 0.5\operatorname{erf}\frac{x}{\sigma\sqrt{T}} \tag{4}$$

Considering all of the above, the baseline implementation of the Black-Scholes formula is presented in Listing 1. Its execution time on the CPU presented in Sect. 3 was 3.062 s (Table 1).

```
const float sig = 0.2f;      // volatility (0.2 -> 20%)
const float r = 0.05f;       // interest rate (0.05 -> 5%)
// the following constants are used
// to initialize pT, pS0 and pK arrays
const float T = 3.0f;        // maturity (3 -> 3 years)
const float S0 = 100.0f;     // initial stock price
const float K = 100.0f;      // strike price

void GetOptionPrices (float *pT, float *pK, float *pS0,
   float *pC, int N) {
   for (int i = 0; i < N; i++)
   {
     float d1 = (std::log(pS0[i]/pK[i]) + (r + 0.5f*sig*sig)*
                 pT[i]) / (sig * std::sqrt(pT[i]));
     float d2 = (std::log(pS0[i]/pK[i]) + (r - 0.5f*sig*sig)*
                 pT[i]) / (sig * std::sqrt(pT[i]));
     float erf1 = 0.5f + 0.5f*std::erf(d1 / std::sqrt(2.0f));
     float erf2 = 0.5f + 0.5f*std::erf(d2 / std::sqrt(2.0f));
     pC[i] = pS0[i]*erf1 - pK[i] *
             std::exp((-1.0f)*r*pT[i])*erf2;
   }
}
```

Listing 1. Baseline C++ implementation of the Black-Scholes formula.

4.2   Loop Vectorization

Vectorization is one of the most effective optimization techniques. As to the Black-Scholes code, the absence of data dependencies between loop iterations and a suitable memory pattern are expected to provide high performance of vector calculations, which is limited by the vector register length (~8x for 256-bit registers and ~16x for 512-bit registers). Modern optimizing compilers are effective enough when it comes to vectorization; the compiler report gives detailed information on whether vector calculations are involved or not and why, as well as what speedup is expected from vectorization. As a rule, for successful vectorization, a programmer needs to specify the absence of data dependencies explicitly because it is often impossible for the compiler to prove that computations are independent even if it is true. Moreover, we have noticed that for the baseline Black-Scholes code (Sect. 4.1) and the test infrastructure we used (Sect. 3) the compiler has generated two versions of the code at once, one vectorized and one not. In this case, the decision on the possibility of using vectorized code is deferred until the program is run and much more information is available. Often the vectorized version is chosen at runtime. Thus, we just had to define a set of AVX512 instructions (**-xHost**, **-qopt-zmm-usage=high** compiler keys) instead of default SSE instructions to better utilize CPU vector units. As a result, execution time has been reduced to 1.155 s ($\sim$2.5x speedup).

4.3   Precision Reduction

We said above that the specificity of this particular financial problem allows us to involve inaccurate but fast calculations of mathematical functions. Accordingly, we used the next options of the Intel compiler:

- **fimf-precision=low** tells the compiler to use mathematical function implementations with only 11 accurate bits in mantissa instead of 24 bits available in single precision.
- **fimf-domain-exclusion=31** allows the compiler to exclude special values in mathematical functions, such as infinity, NaN, or extreme values of function arguments.

This technique has given a 2x speedup compared to the previous version (0.527 s, see Table 1). Need to mark, we got a different and less accurate result (20.927 instead of a reference 20.924 for the start parameters presented in Listing 1), but the difference does not occur until the 5th decimal digit, which is acceptable for financial models. However, the precision controls should be used with care and properly analyzed for the accuracy of the result.

4.4   Parallelism

In order to use the maximum potential of a CPU, it is expedient to distribute the computational load between its physical cores. We used the OpenMP model; in the case of the Black-Scholes code, it was enough to add **omp parallel for** pragma before the main loop and specify **-qopenmp** compiler option. The processor on which the experiments were carried out has 48 physical cores (2 CPUs with 24 cores each) and supports hyper-threading technology. The thread affinity mask is set to 'compact'. The maximal speedup of the parallel code was achieved on 48 threads, hyper-threading did not impact the performance. The best execution time was 0.053 s, that is 10 times faster (Table 1). The reason for which we do not observe better speedup is limited memory bandwidth, and we can increase performance through more efficient memory management (see Sect. 4.5 for more details).

4.5 NUMA-Friendly Memory Allocation

The heterogeneous memory structure is a characteristic of many modern CPUs. Non-Uniform Memory Access (NUMA) implies that a processor can access its memory faster than the memory of another processor on the same cluster node. We use a two-socket system, and in the worst case, we can get 50% remote (and inefficient) access because all memory is allocated on only one processor. To avoid this, it is enough to allocate memory in a NUMA-friendly manner. According to the first-touch policy [15], we should care about the appreciate initialization of a current option batch in a parallel loop before the main calculations, as shown in Listing 2. This trick gave the 2x speedup, the execution time has become final 0.022 s (Table 1).

```
#pragma omp parallel for simd
for (int i = 0; i < N; i++) {
  pT[i] = T;
  pSO[i] = SO;
  pK[i] = K;
  pC[i] = 0;
}
```

Listing 2. NUMA-friendly initialization.

Nevertheless, we have not reached the maximal speedup in parallel mode (20x instead of maximal 48x). The Roofline model [16] shown in Fig. 1 indicates that performance is limited by L3 cache bandwidth. In this case, the most common technique is to increase data locality, for example, by using cache blocking techniques, but it does not apply to the Black-Scholes code. Likely, we have reached the execution time limit.

All optimization stages of the C++ Black-Scholes code is presented in Table 1. We can see that the total speedup through all optimizations and parallelization compared to the baseline serial code is ~140x.

Table 1. Execution time of each C++ optimization stage.

Version	Time, s
Baseline	3.062
Loop vectorization	1.155
Precision reduction	0.527
Parallelism	0.053
NUMA-friendly memory allocation	*0.022*

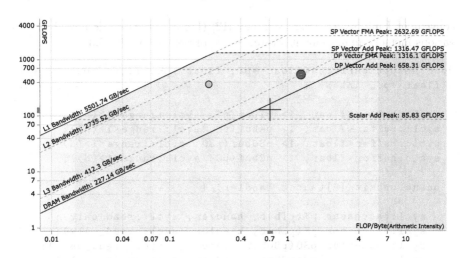

Fig. 1. The Roofline model of the optimized Black-Scholes C++ code on the CPU. The diagram is plotted by Intel Advisor from OneAPI Toolkit 2022.1. The red point denotes the main Black-Scholes computational loop. (Color figure online)

5   Porting to DPC++

5.1   Baseline and Optimizations on CPUs

The effective implementation of any algorithm on various types of accelerators implies its decomposition to a sufficiently large number of small subtasks that can be performed in parallel. In the baseline Black-Scholes formula implementation on DPC++, we choose a single option price calculation as a work item and run all of them in parallel on a device (see Listing 3). We use SYCL built-in mathematical functions.

```
handler.parallel_for(sycl::range<1>(N), [=](sycl::id<1> i) {
    float d1 = (sycl::log(pSO[i] / pK[i]) + (r + sig2*0.5f) *
                pT[i]) / (sig * std::sqrt(pT[i]));
    float d2 = (sycl::log(pSO[i] / pK[i]) + (r - sig2*0.5f) *
                pT[i]) / (sig * std::sqrt(pT[i]));
    float erf1 = 0.5f + 0.5f * sycl::erf(d1 * invsqrt2);
    float erf2 = 0.5f + 0.5f * sycl::erf(d2 * invsqrt2);
    pC[i] = pSO[i] * erf1 - pK[i] * sycl::exp((-1.0f) * r *
            pT[i]) * erf2;
});
```

Listing 3. Baseline DPC++ kernel implementation of the Black-Scholes formula and its parallel launch.

When writing high-performance code for graphics accelerators, we should consider specifics of their memory management. Discrete GPUs require a smart data transfer policy between host and device. DPC++ provides different ways to do it, explicit or implicit. In the baseline Black-Scholes code we consider a convenient Buffers&Accessors strategy [12] (Listing 4). More details about the various memory management strategies are presented in Sect. 5.3.

```
void GetOptionPrices(float *pT, float *pK, float *pSO,
  float *pC, int N) {
  // declaration of buffers
  sycl::buffer<float, 1> pTbuf(pT, sycl::range<1>(N));
  sycl::buffer<float, 1> pKbuf(pK, sycl::range<1>(N));
  sycl::buffer<float, 1> pSObuf(pSO, sycl::range<1>(N));
  sycl::buffer<float, 1> pCbuf(pC, sycl::range<1>(N));

  queue.submit([&](auto& handler) {
    // declaration of accessors
    sycl::accessor pT(pTbuf, handler, sycl::read_only);
    sycl::accessor pK(pKbuf, handler, sycl::read_only);
    sycl::accessor pSO(pSObuf, handler, sycl::read_only);
    sycl::accessor pC(pCbuf, handler, sycl::write_only);
    // here the BS computational kernel should be
  }).wait();

  // data copying from device to host
  sycl::host_accessor pCacc(pCbuf);
  // here we need to process the result
}
```

Listing 4. Buffers&Accessors data management.

As to DPC++ on CPUs, the concept of SYCL let us not think about vectorization and parallelism. However, we need to take into account non-uniform memory access to avoid problems described in Sect. 4.5, otherwise, we get a time similar to that presented in Sect. 4.4 (Table 2, Baseline). We can allocate memory in a NUMA-friendly manner by, for example, initializing parameter arrays in the separate DPC++ kernel (Listing 5).

```
handler.parallel_for(sycl::range<1>(N), [=](sycl::id<1> i) {
  pT[i] = T;
  pSO[i] = SO;
  pK[i] = K;
  pC[i] = 0;
});
```

Listing 5. Initialization in DPC++ kernel.

Nevertheless, when we just added this piece of code, the execution time was reduced to 0.035 s only instead of the expected 0.022 s observed in the case of optimized C++ code (Sect. 4.5). The issue is related to the TBB library which is used by DPC++ in this scenario. TBB threads distribute work dynamically without regard to NUMA. As a result, we have some percentage of remote memory access even after the appreciate initialization. To avoid this, the **DPCPP_CPU_PLACES** environment variable with the **numa_domains** value should be set. In this case, dynamic scheduling of work within the

TBB-based runtime occurs within each processor separately, which removes access to remote memory. After that, we got final 0.024 s, which is only 10% slower than the optimized C++ implementation (Table 2). Taking into account that DPC++ code can be run on CPUs and GPUs, we consider 10% of performance to be a reasonable price to pay for portability.

Table 2. Execution time of each DPC++ optimization stage on CPUs.

Version	Time, sec
Baseline	0.057
Initialization in a separate kernel	0.035
NUMA-friendly (DPCPP_CPU_PLACES)	*0.024*
Optimized C++ code	0.022

5.2 Experiments on GPUs

The great advantage of the DPC++ model is that a DPC++ code can be run on many devices: CPUs, GPUs, and others. However, it does not mean that the same code will work optimally on all the devices, and we still need to take into account the device specifics when developing code. But it is worth noting that the GPU-optimized code often shows high performance on CPUs as well, so it makes sense to develop and optimize for GPUs first. Some common GPU-specific optimizations are presented in Sect. 5.4, but all of them have not given any positive result for the benchmark at stake. The reason for it is the DRAM memory bandwidth limitations of the GPU (Fig. 2).

The DPC++ baseline shows 0.062 s of the kernel execution time, and this is the best result we got. It is worth saying that this is a fairly good result, corresponding to the characteristics of the device. Taking into account the characteristics of the memory bandwidth of this GPU and the fact that the benchmark is memory-bound, we expected the kernel execution time to be at least 0.056 s (3.8 GB of batch size divided by 68 GB/s of memory bandwidth).

The initialization kernel takes similar to the main kernel time – 0.061 s. However, we have noticed that the overhead of memory transfer and other operations is highly large – more than 2 s (Table 3). In the next section, we demonstrate how to reduce these additional costs.

5.3 Memory Management

As the experiments in Sect. 5.2 show, it takes a lot of time to synchronize and copy data from host to GPU and back. In this section, we attempt to reduce overhead by using different memory management strategies provided by DPC++. The code presented in Sect. 5.1 is based on the Buffers&Accessors model, whereby we create a buffer object for each parameter array and use special accessor objects to read and write buffers. Based on buffers and accessors, a decision to copy data from host to device and back is made independently of a

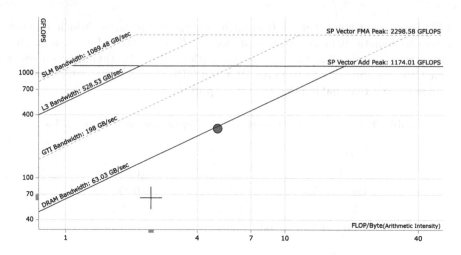

Fig. 2. The Roofline model of the Black-Scholes DPC++ code on the GPU. The diagram is plotted by Intel Advisor from OneAPI Toolkit 2022.1. The red point denotes the main computational kernel. (Color figure online)

programmer. However, we can influence this by specifying at what point in time we need the data we are interested in on a particular device by creating a buffer or accessor object in the appropriate place in a DPC++ program. For example, in Listing 5.1, the shared buffers for both the initialization and the option pricing kernels, as well as the absence of appropriate accessors between them, ensure that data is not transferred from device to host between these kernels.

It is worth paying attention that given that we process options in batches, we can allocate memory for only one batch and create the buffer objects once when the program starts. This technique had a good effect – the overhead costs were reduced by 3 times (Table 3).

An alternative approach to using buffers and accessors for data transfers relies on Unified Shared Memory (USM), which is introduced in DPC++ [12]. USM provides explicit and implicit ways to copy data from host to device and vice versa. The explicit way assumes direct APIs to move data between device and host. The implicit approach is based on shared memory support implemented in software and/or hardware, so users need just to allocate a shared memory region that will be accessible across all the devices automatically. In contrast to accessors, a user has to manage all the data dependencies manually while using USM, but at the same time, shared memory is much easier to adopt for "highly C++" codes. It is worth mentioning that the performance of USM data transfers is strongly dependent on its particular implementation and may differ for various devices. We review both implicit and explicit approaches in relation to the Black-Scholes formula and the infrastructure under consideration.

Following the implicit USM model, we create data pointers using the `malloc_shared()` function and then simply access them inside a kernel, with any necessary data movement done automatically (Listing 6). In our case, this strategy slightly reduces data transfer time, but apparently requires additional synchronizations between the host and device when calling `malloc_shared()`, which still does not matter if memory is allocated at once and common for all batches (Table 3).

```
void GetOptionPrices(float *pT, float *pK, float *pSO,
  float *pC, int N) {
  // shared memory allocation
  float *pT = sycl::malloc_shared<float>(N, queue);
  float *pSO = sycl::malloc_shared<float>(N, queue);
  float *pK = sycl::malloc_shared<float>(N, queue);
  float *pC = sycl::malloc_shared<float>(N, queue);

  // here we need to run the initialization kernel
  // and the option price calculation kernel
  // and process the result pC

  // freeing memory
  sycl::free(pT); sycl::free(pSO);
  sycl::free(pK); sycl::free(pC);
}
```

Listing 6. Implicit USM data movement.

It is worth noting that the resulting performance of implicit data movement in USM strongly depends on its internal architecture-specific implementation. Perhaps on newer hardware and software, the `malloc_shared` approach will provide more benefits. As for the current infrastructure, we suspect that some data arrays are copied from host to device and back again a few extra times. Therefore, we decided to allocate memory directly on the device and explicitly transfer only the result array `pC` to the host under the explicit USM approach. The corresponding implementation shown in Listing 7 gave the best result (0.37 s overhead, Table 3).

```
void GetOptionPrices(float *pT, float *pK, float *pSO,
  float *pC, int N) {
  // memory allocation on host to keep result
  float *pCHost = new float[N];
  // memory allocation on device
  float *pT = sycl::malloc_device<float>(N, queue);
  float *pSO = sycl::malloc_device<float>(N, queue);
  float *pK = sycl::malloc_device<float>(N, queue);
  float *pC = sycl::malloc_device<float>(N, queue);

  // here we need to run the initialization kernel
  // and the option price calculation kernel

  // data copying from device to host
  queue.memcpy(pCHost, pC, N * sizeof(float)).wait();
  // here we need to process the result pCHost
  // and free all allocated memory
}
```

Listing 7. Explicit USM data movement.

Table 3. Different DPC++ memory management models: kernel execution time and overhead time on the GPU. 'One batch' means that we allocate memory for each option batch and include its time into measurements; 'multiple batches' means that we allocate memory that is shared for all batches at once, and do not include this into measurements. The table shows the time of one batch processing.

Version	Main kernel, sec	Initialization kernel, sec	Overhead, sec	Total, sec
Buffers&Accessors, one batch	0.062	0.061	2.367	2.551
Buffers&Accessors, multiple batches			0.748	0.932
USM, implicit, one batch			2.987	3.110
USM, implicit, multiple batches			0.658	0.781
USM, explicit, one batch			1.158	1.281
USM, explicit, multiple batches			*0.369*	*0.492*

5.4   Several Common Optimization Tricks

In this subsection, we look at important optimization techniques that can provide significant performance gains on GPUs. Note that in our particular case, they did not work for various reasons. In several cases, the compiler and runtime did a great job without our help. In other cases, the nature of the task, where memory access operations are a significant part of the work compared to calculations, did not allow for achieving additional speedup. In the meantime, it seemed important to us to demonstrate these techniques for performance optimization, as they may be useful to researchers and developers in other applications.

In the baseline DPC++ implementation, we start N work items for every option. The initial one-dimensional range is divided into work-groups automatically by the DPC++ compiler and runtime. However, a programmer can vary a range, work-group or sub-group size, and here the potential for optimization lies. The trick presented in Listing 8 contributes to the solution of possible optimization problems such as underutilization of GPU cores, the overhead of maintaining a large number of threads, and suboptimal work-group size. The example demonstrates the variation in the total number of threads and the group size. It is worth paying attention that in the internal kernel loop it is necessary to walk through the iterations with a step equal to the number of threads to avoid memory bank conflicts. As to the Black-Scholes code, we checked different combinations of thread count and work-group size. Experiments on GPUs have shown that the optimal values are the maximal thread count and group size, that is, the default configuration used by the DPC++ compiler and runtime is the most beneficial.

```
handler.parallel_for(sycl::nd_range<1>(THREAD_COUNT,
  GROUP_SIZE), [=](sycl::nd_item<1> item) {
  for (int i=item.get_global_id(0); i<N; i+=THREAD_COUNT) {
    // the i-th element processing
  }});
```

Listing 8. An example of varying the number of threads and group size.

Another advantageous technique is to use vector data types [12]. In this way, we explicitly state that some elements are arranged in a row in memory. It can positively affect the speed of loading and computing on GPUs as well as on CPUs. We have tried to use **sycl::float4** data type but, in our case, it has not impacted the performance.

It should also be said that we tried using the different memory patterns in an attempt to optimize it for GPUs. The AoS pattern did not improve execution time compared to SoA, but we have noticed that it is profitable to store read-only and write-only data separately to reduce the load on the performance-limiting DRAM.

6   Conclusion

In this paper, we present a high-performance implementation of the Black-Scholes option pricing formula in the C++ and SYCL (DPC++) programming languages. We optimize it step by step and demonstrate how various optimization techniques improve performance for commonly applied Intel CPUs and GPUs. In particular, on CPUs, we employ and analyze vectorization, precision reduction, single-node parallelism, and optimal use of the NUMA architecture. For GPUs, we discuss device-friendly memory access patterns, relevant data management, and employing vector data types. Experiments showed that on CPUs, the optimized DPC++ implementation was only 10% slower than the highly optimized OpenMP implementation, while it was possible to run it also on GPUs and observe the expected performance based on the device computational capabilities. We demonstrated that the performance was limited by memory bandwidth both on CPU and GPU.

We hope that our results will be useful to other researchers who are planning to port their codes from C++ to SYCL (DPC++). In this regard, we discussed not only those optimization techniques that improved performance but also those that did not speed up our application. We believe that these techniques can work in other codes. They also can help on upcoming devices with significantly larger memory bandwidth. In general, the emergence and development of SYCL ideas within the oneAPI model looks like a promising direction in modern High Performance Computing.

Acknowledgements. The work is supported by the oneAPI Center of Excellence program and by the Ministry of Science and Higher Education of the Russian Federation, project no. 0729-2020-0055.

References

1. Black, F., Scholes, M.: The pricing of options and corporate liabilities. In: World Scientific Reference on Contingent Claims Analysis in Corporate Finance: Volume 1: Foundations of CCA and Equity Valuation, pp. 3–21. World Scientific (2019)

2. Meyerov, I., Sysoyev, A., Astafiev, N., Burylov, I.: Performance optimization of Black-Scholes pricing. In: High Performance Parallelism Pearls: Multicore and Many-core Programming Approaches, pp. 319–340. Springer, Cham (2014)
3. Grauer-Gray, S., Killian, W., Searles, R., Cavazos, J.: Accelerating financial applications on the GPU. In: Proceedings of the 6th Workshop on General Purpose Processor Using Graphics Processing Units, pp. 127–136 (2013)
4. Smelyanskiy, M., et al.: Analysis and optimization of financial analytics benchmark on modern multi-and many-core IA-based architectures. In: 2012 SC Companion: High Performance Computing, Networking Storage and Analysis, pp. 1154–1162. IEEE (2012)
5. Podlozhnyuk, V.: Black-Scholes option pricing (2007)
6. Pharr, M., Fernando, R.: GPU Gems 2: Programming Techniques for High-Performance Graphics and General-Purpose Computation (GPU Gems). Addison-Wesley Professional, Boston (2005)
7. oneAPI: A New Era of Heterogeneous Computing. https://www.intel.com/content/www/us/en/developer/tools/oneapi/overview.html
8. OpenCL: open standard for parallel programming of heterogeneous systems. https://www.khronos.org/opencl/
9. OpenACC. https://www.openacc.org/
10. Edwards, H.C., Trott, C.R.: Kokkos: enabling performance portability across manycore architectures. In: 2013 Extreme Scaling Workshop (XSW 2013), pp. 18–24. IEEE (2013)
11. Zenker, E., et al.: Alpaka-an abstraction library for parallel kernel acceleration. In: 2016 IEEE International Parallel and Distributed Processing Symposium Workshops (IPDPSW), pp. 631–640. IEEE (2016)
12. Reinders, J., Ashbaugh, B., Brodman, J., Kinsner, M., Pennycook, J., Tian, X.: Data Parallel C++: Mastering DPC++ for Programming of Heterogeneous Systems Using C++ and SYCL. Springer, Heidelberg (2021). https://doi.org/10.1007/978-1-4842-5574-2
13. Reyes, R., Lomüller, V.: SYCL: single-source C++ accelerator programming. In: Parallel Computing: On the Road to Exascale, pp. 673–682. IOS Press (2016)
14. SYCL. https://www.khronos.org/sycl/
15. Hager, G., Wellein, G.: Introduction to High Performance Computing for Scientists and Engineers. CRC Press, Boca Raton (2010)
16. Marques, D., et al.: Performance analysis with cache-aware roofline model in Intel advisor. In: 2017 International Conference on High Performance Computing & Simulation (HPCS), pp. 898–907. IEEE (2017)

CFD Simulations on Hybrid Supercomputers: Gaining Experience and Harvesting Problems

Andrey Gorobets$^{(\boxtimes)}$ (iD)

Keldysh Institute of Applied Mathematics of Russian Academy of Sciences, Moscow, Russia
gorobets@keldysh.ru

Abstract. A code for scale-resolving CFD simulations of turbulent flows on hybrid supercomputers is considered. Its heterogeneous parallelization using MPI, OpenMP and OpenCL allows engaging many GPUs and CPUs. The high performance obtained on GPUs was quite encouraging, it was an order of magnitude higher than on CPUs. Now, with more experience, we can discuss the other side of GPU computing, its dark side. It is not only about the evolution of computing devices, in which high performance computing used to lurk in the backyard of the consumer computer market and now is in the backyard of machine learning and artificial intelligence applications. It is more about problems that arise with the use GPUs, such as complicated code modifiability, fragile reliability, crucial lack of memory, and a lot of performance degradation factors. A parallel implementation is outlined, examples of applications with performance analysis on various equipment are presented. Measures to solve the problems are proposed.

Keywords: Heterogeneous computing · Supercomputer simulation · Compressible flow · Unstructured mesh · MPI+OpenMP+OpenCL · GPU architecture

1 Introduction

To begin with, computational fluid dynamics (CFD) applications are typically quite computationally demanding. Mesh methods are typically well-suited for computing on GPUs, although perhaps not everyone is still fully aware of this. Applications with memory-bound computing pattern, such as 3D CFD simulations, in which a large amount of data is being processed using floating point arithmetic, can greatly benefit from the significantly higher bandwidth of the built-in GPU memory. Because of this, GPU computing has long been widely used in CFD applications. See, for example, [1–4] among many other works.

In our previous work [5], encouraging us results were proudly reported demonstrating rather big performance advantages of GPUs. When running a scale-resolving simulation of a turbine blade, one modest rack of 9 4-GPU servers outperformed 10 thousand "Platinum" CPU cores. In the present work, having more experience accumulated, let's discuss the dark side of GPU computing: increased complexity, problems and disappointing trends.

© The Author(s), under exclusive license to Springer Nature Switzerland AG 2022
V. Voevodin et al. (Eds.): RuSCDays 2022, LNCS 13708, pp. 63–76, 2022.
https://doi.org/10.1007/978-3-031-22941-1_5

The paper is organized as follows. In the next section, mathematical models, numerical methods and a parallel simulation code are outlined. Section 3 is devoted to trends in the evolution of computing hardware. Increased complexity of development of the heterogeneous simulation code is discussed in Sect. 4. In Sect. 5, a representative example of a CFD application with CPU to GPU performance comparison is given.

2 Mathematical Basis and Parallel Framework

2.1 Mathematical Model and Numerical Method

Supercomputer modeling of turbulent flows is considered. The Navier – Stokes equations for a viscous compressible ideal gas are used as a basic mathematical model. Additionally, turbulence can be modeled using the following approaches: Reynolds-Averaged Navier – Stokes (RANS), Large Eddy Simulation (LES); non-zonal hybrid RANS-LES approaches, such as modern variants of Detached Eddy Simulation (DES) [6, 7], including alternative subgrid length scales [8] and LES models [9].

A higher-accuracy vertex-centered scheme on unstructured mixed-element meshes is used for spatial discretization. In a vertex-centered finite-volume formulation, the computational domain is split into control volumes, which are built around mesh nodes. For the discretization of convective fluxes, the edge-based reconstruction (EBR) schemes are used [10] for problems with smooth solutions, and the monotonized schemes EBR-TVD, EBR-WENO [11] for problems with discontinuities. These schemes can provide higher accuracy compared to basic 2nd order schemes, and can reach up to the 5th order of accuracy (on translationally invariant meshes).

For the discretization of viscous terms, the method of averaged element splittings [12] is used, as well as the classical mass-lumped P1-Galerkin method.

For the temporal discretization, implicit backward differentiation formula (BDF) schemes BDF1 and BDF2 with a quasi-Newton linearization of the resulting non-linear system are used. The Jacobi system of algebraic equations is solved using the preconditioned BiCGSTAB solver [13].

2.2 Parallel Software Framework

The considered simulation algorithm is implemented in the NOISEtte code. Its parallelization is based on multilevel mesh decomposition. The Message-passing interface (MPI) is used at the upper level for distributed computing on multiple cluster nodes. Then, OpenMP shared memory parallelization is used for manycore CPUs and accelerators. At this level, the mesh subdomains of MPI processes are decomposed among parallel OpenMP threads. To compute on GPUs and other kinds of accelerators, the OpenCL standard is used, which can deal with GPUs from different vendors, including NVIDIA, AMD, Intel. For co-execution on both CPUs and GPUs simultaneously, the mesh subdomains assigned to CPUs and GPUs are balanced according to the actual performance ratio.

Only the time integration algorithm itself has been ported to the GPU. All the initialization part fully remains on the CPU side: construction of incidence and adjacency topology, differential operators, interpolation constructions for the spatial scheme, etc. Resulting data arrays are copied to device buffers. Since the initialization stage is performed only once at the beginning, it does not affect the overall performance, taking about a few minutes, while the time integration process takes hours and days.

Further details on the parallel simulation technology can be found in [14] and in references therein. The heterogeneous implementation approach follows our previous works [15, 16], where the effective use of hundreds of hybrid nodes of the Lomonosov-2 supercomputer [17] was demonstrated.

In the context of the present paper, it is important to note that CPU memory can be considered infinite compared to GPU memory. Thus, all computational data remains on the CPU, and only the data necessary for the time integration process is replicated to the GPU. This allows us to switch from GPU to CPU computing at any time if needed, once the mesh functions stored on the CPU are updated from the GPU. This, in turn, allows us to leave some minor things on the CPU, such as processing of results and other small (in terms of computational cost) routines, for instance, non-trivial boundary conditions, a synthetic turbulence generator, rotor-stator interfaces, etc. Such "small things" take a very minor fraction of computing time, but may need a lot of effort to port it to the GPU efficiently.

In the previous work [5], the implementation of the parallel algorithm is described in detail and speedup plots up to 10 thousand CPU cores and dozens of GPUs are demonstrated. It was shown that a scale-resolving simulation with implicit time integration on a mesh of about 80 million nodes runs on 36 GPUs with 87% parallel efficiency and outperforms the same simulation on approximately 10 thousand CPU cores. The performance benefits of about 25% from using CPUs together with GPUs were demonstrated on the Lomonosov-2 supercomputer [17] up to several dozen nodes. In real simulations, one modern GPU NVIDIA V100 is reported to give us the equivalent of about 150–200 CPU cores. Based on such results, an overly optimistic picture regarding GPU computing may emerge. But enough of the good stuff. In the following sections, let's look for a fly in the ointment.

3   Hardware Architecture Issues

In terms of the evolution of computing hardware, high performance computing (HPC) used to lurk humbly in the backyard of the consumer computer market. Nowadays it is thrown in the backyard of machine learning and artificial intelligence applications. This artistic exaggeration is only meant to highlight some suboptimality of the currently available hardware for our applications.

3.1   CPUs

CPUs tend to widen SIMD extensions and increase the number of floating-point operations per tact, becoming more expensive and power consuming. But for us it is useless. Suppose we need to perform element-wise summation of two large vectors with multiplication on a scalar value, the so-called AXPY: $\mathbf{x} = a\mathbf{x} + \mathbf{y}$. . Suppose we have some 24-core Intel Xeon Platinum CPU, each core is operating at, say, 2 GHz and is equipped with 2 AVX-512 FMA (fused multiply-add) FP (floating point) units. This CPU can perform 24 cores times 2 (2 FMA units per core) times 8 (512-bit register fits 8 double precision floating point arguments) times 2 (multiplication and addition – two operations) times 2×10^9 (frequency) – 1.5 TFLOPS (FLOPS – floating point operations per second). The arithmetic intensity of an AXPY is 1/12 (2 operations, multiplication and addition, per 24 bytes for reading two double precision arguments, **x** and **y**, and writing one argument, **x**). This means that for one floating point operation, the CPU needs 12 bytes of memory traffic. Therefore, to do those 1.5 TFLOPS, the CPU needs at least 18 TB/s memory bandwidth. This is just a little bit, only two orders of magnitude more than what the CPU has. Well, how can this not rejoice? Perhaps, CPU vendors should stop insulting the feelings of believers in HPC and incorporate high-bandwidth embedded memory or fast external memory channels into their creatures.

3.2 GPUs

The GPUs follow the same trend as the CPUs. Computing performance grows faster than memory bandwidth, but this bandwidth is at least much higher. What's wrong then? Again, we have to pay for absolutely useless things in our applications, paying both the price of computing hardware and electricity bills. For example, modern high-end GPUs like NVIDIA V100, A100 have supposedly quite expensive tensor processors for artificial intelligence and machine learning applications. What for do we need tensor cores in our CFD applications? Then, for aur applications, high-end computing GPUs have by far too many FP units for the available memory bandwidth. We measured the execution of our simulation code on various GPU devices with orders of magnitude different number of FP units and observed no difference. For instance, we tested computing GPUs, which have the ratio of single- and double-precision FP units 1:2, and (very) cheap gaming/graphical GPUs with ratio 1:16, 1:32. The actual performance with our predominantly double precision code clearly corresponds to the memory bandwidth, but not the number of FP units, until at least 1:32 ratio (1:64 is perhaps too much). This means that in our applications, we would not even notice if the GPUs had 32 times fewer FP units. Consider a CFD simulation on a mesh of about 1 million nodes using higher-accuracy scheme EBR5 [10], implicit 2-nd order backward scheme, hybrid turbulence modelling approach [6]. The NVIDIA RTX 2070 and AMD RX 5700 GPUs have the same memory bandwidth of about 450 GB/s and single-to-double precision FP units ratio 1:32 and 1:16, respectively. Both cards perform equally and give us about 55% of the performance of the NVIDIA V100 GPU, which has twice higher bandwidth of 900 GB/s as well as an order of magnitude higher compute performance and price. The NVIDIA A5000 GPU with 768 GB/s and 1:32 ratio gives us 85% of the V100 for a several times smaller price. The actual performance ratio perfectly matches the memory bandwidth ratio, so we overpay for an order of magnitude more FP units than necessary, apart from absolutely unused tensor cores. But if these "cheap" GPUs perform so well, what's wrong with them? The amount of memory, of course. Our applications are quite memory consuming. The RTX 2070 and RX 5700 GPUs have only 8 GB of memory, the A5000 GPU has 24 GB, while, say, NVIDIA A100 has 80 GB. Thus, the ideal device for our applications should be as powerful as (very) cheap gaming GPUs in terms of FLOPS, but with the same amount of memory and bandwidth as the A100. If we could take the A100, throw out all its tensor cores and 97% of its FP units, and cheapen it accordingly, it would be a good device for our applications.

3.3   Hybrid CPU+GPU Cluster Nodes

Regarding hybrid cluster nodes (computing servers), two main things are important for us: the ratio of CPU and GPU performance and the topology of intra-node connections. As for the CPU to GPU ratio, if there are too few GPUs for the available CPU performance, we are throwing away money at the server chassis, rack space, ports in network switches, etc. If the CPU performance is not enough to handle the available GPUs (processing the results of simulation and data exchanges), then we throw money on the GPUs, which will just heat the air while waiting for the CPUs.

According to our experience, two NVIDIA V100 GPUs per one CPU with at least 16 cores and 4 DDR4 memory channels is fine. 4 GPUs per CPU can still work fine, but it requires very(-very) little computation to remain on the CPU, which is hard to achieve in practice.

In terms of memory, we used to have at least 1 to 2 GB of RAM per core when computing on CPUs. On GPUs, we have much less memory with respect to the equivalent performance. For instance, the NVIDIA V100 GPU has 32 GB of RAM and performs as about 150 cores, which means just about 200 MB per equivalent core, an order of magnitude less. But our applications, 3D CFD simulations, are rather memory consuming. Therefore, we need to use efficiently not just multiple GPUs, but multiple hybrid cluster nodes. This means that data transfer speed is important. Modern compute servers typically contain 4 to 8 GPUs (very "fat" ones even 16, which is too much for our applications due to insufficient CPU performance per GPU). Since we have to decompose the mesh between multiple GPUs and perform communications at every time step, how these GPUs are coupled is important.

Basically, there are two options (Fig. 1): A) tightly coupled GPUs that are loosely coupled to CPUs, and conversely, B) tight couplings between CPUs and GPUs rather than between GPUs. The latter is obviously preferable for our CFD applications. Since there are inter-node MPI exchanges handled by CPUs, GPUs are not communicating with each other in our algorithm. Instead, all traffic goes via CPUs, which permute interface-halo data, send and receive MPI messages, perform copy from and to GPUs. Therefore, Option B) is good, since each GPU is connected via its 16-lane PCIe link, and Option A) is totally suboptimal. In Option A), GPUs are tightly coupled by a PCIe switch with 16-lane links, but this switch is connected to the CPU with only one ×16 link. This means that all the 4 GPUs share only one link to the CPU having only 4 PCIe lanes per device. Apart from this, all devices are usually connected to only one CPU socket, which means extra delays and NUMA factors between CPUs. Note that network adapters are not shown on the diagrams, but it is also important, how they are connected.

Option A) is rather widespread, perhaps, due to machine learning applications. One might even ask what can be worse than that for CFD things? At first glance, it is difficult to imagine a worse connection topology, but such things exist and are rather common. Consider Option C) shown in Fig. 2., in which GPUs are coupled with extra very high-bandwidth bus, such as NVIDIA NVlink.

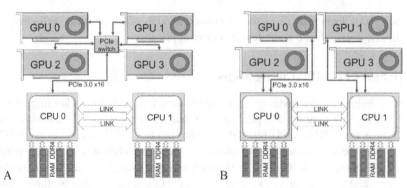

Fig. 1. Server diagram: GPUs are tightly coupled with each other (A); GPUs are tightly coupled with CPUs (B)

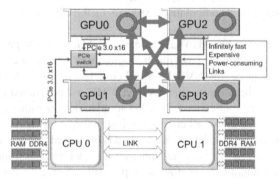

Fig. 2. Server diagram: GPUs are very tightly coupled with each other, but not with CPUs

Such a bus supposedly costs fortune and consumes a lot of energy (have you seen those massive radiators on NVlink chips?). But these links are absolutely useless for us, since CPUs and network cards are connected via PCIe links. It doesn't matter at all how infinitely fast the GPU connections are if the bottleneck is the network. Therefore, if we buy such a system, we have to pay a lot for the NVlink connection on the GPUs, NVlink chips on the server motherboard, and we have to pay the electricity it consumes, while being absolutely useless in our applications.

To conclude with, the best configuration for us is Option B), when each cluster nodes have 2 CPUs and 4 GPUs equally distributed between CPUs, each GPU is connected via its own ×16 PCIe link. Note that in this configuration, it is important to ensure that MPI processes are properly bound to CPU sockets, and GPU devices are assigned to the corresponding nearest MPI processes.

4   Small Things Grow Big

As was already mentioned above in Sect. 3, all computational data is fully present on the CPU. This allows us to switch from GPU to CPU computing at any moment.

Therefore, we can leave on the CPU those small things that take a very minor fraction of the computational time, but require a lot of effort to be ported to the GPU efficiently. Thus, for a "small thing", we just need to download from the GPU its small input dataset, quickly compute it on the CPU, and upload its small results back into the GPU. Everything seems easy, we can just leave a lot of tiny little things on the CPU and forget about it. But this approach turned out to be well suitable only for modeling the flow around a "spherical horse", preferably in a vacuum, preferably in a cubic domain. When more technologies are involved, each of them "small", e.g., non-trivial boundary conditions, immersed boundary method, rotor-stator interactions, synthetic turbulence generators, a sponge layer (dumping of turbulence), extra source terms, such small things become a lot. A lot of small things are already a "big thing".

Another complication is that the "big things" that have already been ported to the GPU have accelerated too much and become small, an order of magnitude smaller in terms of computing time. This made the "small things" that remain on the CPU, respectively, an order of magnitude bigger. Something negligible, which took 1 to 2% of computing time, now eats 10 to 20%. And if in a complex simulation there are several such formerly "small" things, then their contribution accumulates and totally kills the efficiency, eating easily 30, 40, 50% of the overall time. Yes, the calculation on the GPU may be still much faster than on the CPU, but not as fast as we would expect, for instance, 4–5 times faster instead of 7–8 times. Isn't it sad?

4.1 Processing of Small Subsets

Firstly, consider "small" things, which are small both in terms of computing time and data size, which means that its necessary data for a small subset of mesh nodes can be copied between the CPU and the GPU without significantly affecting the overall performance. When something like this remains on the CPU, we need a list of relevant mesh nodes (e.g., for a particular boundary conditions, a corresponding list of surface nodes) to update relevant mesh functions there. Such CPU-based operation is performed as follows:

- a "packing" kernel (a function running on the GPU) collects the data from mesh function arrays of the entire mesh subdomain into a continuous buffer for the given subset of nodes;
- the buffer is transferred to the CPU;
- the buffer is "unpacked" on the CPU into the corresponding mesh function arrays using OpenMP parallelization for acceleration;
- the CPU-based operation is executed;
- its output mesh functions are "packed" on the CPU side into the transfer buffer;
- the buffer for only affected mesh nodes is transferred to the GPU;
- the buffer is "unpacked" on the GPU into the entire mesh function arrays.

One might guess that the "packing" and "unpacking" stages can be eliminated with proper ordering of mesh nodes, provided that the nodes of the subset are placed continuously in the entire subdomain numeration of nodes. No, not in the case of an implicit scheme, when we have to deal with the Jacobi matrix, which is a sparse block matrix with

5×5 blocks for 5 main variables (density, velocity vector components and pressure, excluding turbulence model's variables for the sake of simplicity). If a CPU-based operation contributes to the Jacobi matrix, its affected blocks must also be transferred. For that we need to make a list of particular matrix blocks, to avoid transferring whole rows, which can take several times more traffic. And this list cannot be avoided by changing nodal numeration. The need for transferring the Jacobian blocks really spoils everything a lot.

Let's try to estimate how much laziness to port costs. Suppose we are so lazy that the boundary conditions (BC) stay on the CPU. Originally, when running everything on the CPU, the BC was taking (very roughly) about 0.5% of the overall computing time in a typical simulation on a several million nodes mesh using an implicit scheme. Then, most of the computing load was ported on the GPU, and now it goes about 7 times faster (16-core Intel Xeon Gold vs NVIDIA A5000, for instance). Then, in the worst case, the BC should grow to 3.5%, which is still quite affordable. But in fact, the BC is taking, say, 19%. Why so much? The transferring of the relevant Jacobian blocks, the biggest overhead, is responsible for 14%. Updating mesh functions in relevant nodes takes about 2%. The calculation of the BC itself accounts for less than 3%, almost negligible. Apart from matrix, at least two sets of 5 mesh functions must be updated (variables and fluxes). If we are lucky, and only the diagonal Jacobian blocks are affected, then the transfer will be rather cheap, just $\times 2.5$ compared to the mesh functions (25 coefficients in a block vs two sets of 5 variables), even $\times 1.25$, considering that the Jacobi matrix is represented in a single-precision format. Then why it takes 14% instead of some 3%? The problem is that if the BC affects off-diagonal blocks, as in the case of no-slip conditions in a rotating coordinate frame (helicopter rotors, turbomachinery, etc.), then the overhead grows to those frustrating 14%, checkmate. In complex industrial cases, when something rotates and there are a lot of walls, laziness appears to cost too much. The conclusion is that to run efficiently on GPUs, anything that can be efficiently ported should be ported, without compromise. But this can easily double the effort.

So far, only basic BCs have been ported, such as inflow, outflow, no-slip walls in a stationary domain, and still a lot of work remains for wall function BCs, no-slip BCs in the case of rotation, etc. Another representative example is the synthetic turbulence generator (STG), which costs up to 20% of the total computation time if left on the CPU. This operation affects the Jacobian, but luckily only the diagonal blocks. In a simulation on a 16-core "Gold" CPU on a mesh of 1 million nodes with the STG acting over 50 thousand nodes, it used to take less than 3% of time. When the simulation is running on the GPU (NVIDIA A5000), if the STG is left on the CPU, then it consumes 18.7%, 5.5% of which goes to CPU-GPU traffic and 13.2% to the generator itself. This is very wasteful, so the STG has been ported to GPU and now takes 4.3%.

But not all "small things" are easy to port. Some of them can hardly be ported efficiently at all, leading to unavoidable overhead. One of such things is the sliding interface, a non-stationary interface between rotating and not rotating mesh zones. On each time step, the couplings between cells at both sides of the interface must be updated. For the given angular position of the rotating subdomains, actual intersections of control volume traces on the contact surface are updated. This, in turn, requires dynamic rebuild of adjacency arrays, matrix portraits, renewing the halo update communication scheme between MPI subdomains, which must include the new couplings. This algo-rithm involves dynamic data structures, associative containers, etc., which can hardly fit into the stream processing paradigm to run on the GPU. Apart from the fact that making dynamic lists is not an easy pattern for the GPU, this operation is carried out on a relatively small dataset, hence it fits in the CPU cache. Accelerating on the GPU what fits in the CPU cache is not easy at all, because the cache bandwidth is comparable to the memory bandwidth of the GPU, but the latency is much less.

Luckily a sliding interface needs no updates of mesh functions or the Jacobian, because calculating fluxes through the sliding faces can be easily ported to the GPU. Only the partial update of the matrix portrait and adjacency arrays is required, which needs not so much traffic. In the case of a sliding interface, the main issue was to accelerate the search for intersections and rebuilding of the adjacency graph. We had to rewrite the algorithm, make implementation more complex, reconsider choice of containers, etc. Finally, after this stage was accelerated several times, the overhead fitted in some acceptable range, say, within 10%. This is another example of a labor-intensive upgrade required for GPU computing.

4.2 Processing of Results and IO

Another kind of "small things" are those things that are small only in terms of computa-tional time, but not the data size. What makes problems is the processing of simulation results. There are dozens of different variables, that can be accumulated, each computed with its own function. This set of output variables is extendable on linking time and on run time with user input using a built-in math formula parser. Then, there are inter-dependencies between those variables, which are automatically traced and dependent variables added to the hidden layer. Thus, only basic field can be easily ported, which is insufficient for complex industrial simulations. Targeted at such applications, the results processing module is too much complicated and its implementation is heavily object-oriented. But the main problem is the GPU memory, which is as precious as gold. In production simulations, dozens of mesh functions need to be accumulated, which leads to unaffordable memory consumption. This problem finally rejected the idea of porting the results processing to the GPU.

Processing of results requires downloading entire arrays of mesh functions from the GPU, which can easily eat 20–40% of the computing time of a time integration step. To eliminate this overhead, this processing is simply no longer performed at every time step. Each set of output variables has its own action interval given in the number of time steps, usually 10 to 100 steps. Calculation of integral characteristics, such as the drag and lift coefficients, is also performed with a reduced frequency. This approach reduced the overhead accordingly to a negligible level and allowed rather complicated processing of the results to remain on the CPU side. The extra labor-intensive upgrade required for GPU computing includes improvements of parallel implementation of computing and processing of output variables on the CPU in order to accelerate the performance-critical parts; implementation of dependency tracking of output variables to know what exactly mesh functions for what exactly subsets of mesh nodes need to be transferred from the GPU at each particular time step.

4.3 Modifiability, Reliability, Maintainability

Porting (and testing, and tuning, and adding buffers and exchanges) many more extra kernels is not the only effort. These kernels then need to be maintained. The function code exists in two versions, as an OpenMP-parallel function in C++ for the CPU and as an OpenCL kernel for the GPU. Consistency of these versions must be maintained, as well as the correctness and relevance of the input data and communications between the CPU and GPU. This entails additional labor costs, since for any future changes introduced into one of the versions, the other version must be updated accordingly, and consistency of the data affected by the changes must be ensured.

The code becomes much easier to break, which does not benefit the reliability that is so important in supercomputer simulations. Reliability drags new labor costs. Each new kernel must be covered by the automated quality assurance (QA) testing, which is performed for each revision of the code. And the QA procedure on a set of small tests on specific equipment is a necessary measure, but not sufficient. When running simulations on different supercomputers equipped with different hardware and compilers, errors or discrepancies between the CPU and GPU code versions that were hidden during QA testing are likely to show up. To prevent this, an automated QA procedure must be performed every time a simulation is started on a particular hardware for a particular configuration of numerical methods and models. This requires additional labor for the built-in testing infrastructure.

In our code, maintaining reliability is implemented as follows. Each function that has two implementations, for the CPU and the GPU, takes two input flags, one indicates that the CPU version must be used, the other tells to use the GPU version. In the check mode, both flags are set: both versions are executed, the output of the GPU version is copied to the CPU and compared to the output of the CPU version. Such a comparison is usually presented in the form of finding the norm of differences between two vectors of floating point values. The tolerance criterion is specified as the maximum allowable error relative to the norm of the CPU version vector (there can be some small unavoidable differences in results, e.g. due to different order of arithmetic operations in the presence of round-off errors).

When a simulation involving GPUs begins, first several time steps are performed with both flags raised. This is per-kernel testing stage when all the kernels involved in the particular numerical algorithm are tested one by one. If none of the kernels failed the test, the entire time step algorithm is checked: several time steps are performed with one or the other flag set. The mesh functions from the CPU and GPU are compared, to ensure both versions are fully equivalent at the upper level.

In the case of heterogeneous computing, both the CPU and GPU are used in computations. Second-level mesh partitioning distributes the workload between the devices of both kinds, balancing subdomains in accordance with actual performance. The MPI processes of the parallel application run in either the CPU version or the GPU version, as explained in [5]. On each hybrid node, MPI processes in CPU and GPU versions co-exist and interact. To perform correctness checks, the GPU-version processes execute the QA procedure described above. The CPU-version processes, of course, must also participate in this check, but they do not have GPU kernels. So, they just repeat the tested functions twice with the CPU flag set.

This multi-stage approach provides reliable protection against errors, but, of course, requires additional labor for its proper implementation and maintenance in the code and QA testing sets. This once again shows that GPU computing is not so easy.

5 Applications

The inconvenient complexities associated with GPU computing have been described above. To draw conclusions about whether the benefits outweigh the costs, consider a relevant example. A study of accuracy of various configurations of a scale-resolving DES turbulence modeling approach was carried out by means of simulations of an immersed subsonic turbulent jet (Fig. 3) on a set of refining meshes from 1.5 to 24 million nodes. The study involved several dozen simulations.

The use of GPUs has allowed us to perform it with unusually small computing re-sources and unusually fast. For instance, one simulation on a mesh of 9 million nodes using the NOISEtte code took about 40 h on a dual-CPU server with two 24-core Intel Xeon Platinum 8160 CPUs (time integration period is about 350 dimensionless convective time units, based on the nozzle diameter). On two NVIDIA V100 GPUs, this simulation finished in 6 h, which is about 7 times faster than on two CPUs. One GPU gave us the equivalent of about 160 CPU cores. For comparative analysis within this study, our colleagues performed the same simulations using the OpenFoam software. They finished the same simulation in 77 h on the same dual-CPU server.

Examples of comparison of DES simulation results with the experiments are shown in Fig. 4 for aerodynamics [18] and aeroacoustics [19], respectively.

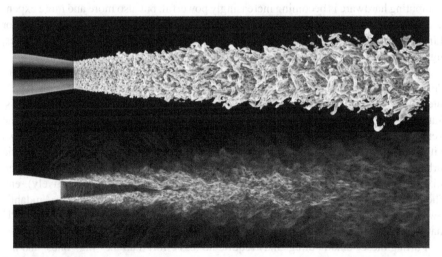

Fig. 3. Instantaneous flow fields from a turbulent jet DES on a mesh of 9 million nodes: turbulent structures (Q-criterion, top) and pressure gradient in the mid-span section (bottom)

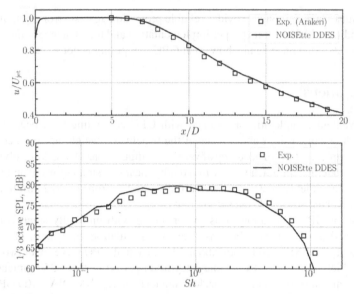

Fig. 4. Comparison of DES results on a mesh of 9 million nodes with experiments: the centerline distribution of the streamwise velocity [18] (top), the 1/3rd-octave integrated spectrum at the observer angle $\theta = 60°$ and distance of 98 nozzle diameters [19] (bottom)

6   Conclusions

Computing hardware is becoming increasingly powerful, but also more and more expensive. Floating point operations are not getting much cheaper. We tend to pay a lot for things that we don't need in our applications: excessive floating-point units, tensor cores, high-bandwidth GPU connections such as NVlink, etc.

GPU computing turned out to be more labor-consuming than expected. The entire CFD algorithm based on higher-accuracy schemes on unstructured meshes, implicit time integration, hybrid RANS-LES turbulence modelling approaches is running on GPUs. But many "small" things that used to consume a negligible fraction of computing time were planned to be left on the CPU side, such as various boundary conditions (inflows with nonstationary profiles, solid walls with wall functions, rotating surfaces), a synthetic turbulence generator, a sponge layer (turbulence dumping zone), sliding interface and mixing plane (nonstationary and stationary rotor-stator interaction, respectively), etc. These things now create too much overhead in real applications. Similar to Amdahl's law that even small serial parts limit acceleration, small parts remaining on the CPU may become dominant in the time cost.

Porting these "small" things may require no less effort than the "big" ones, and not all of them can be efficiently ported at all. Thus, unavoidable overhead remains. The need for upgrading and porting a lot of code is even more complicating in the case of scientific computing. This is routine technical work, for which it is difficult to find a place in scientific reality. Nevertheless, the benefits of using GPUs are high enough to expend all this effort.

Acknowledgments. The work has been supported by the Russian Science Foundation, project 19-11-00299. The research is carried out using the equipment of the shared research facilities of HPC computing resources at Lomonosov Moscow State University [18] and the hybrid supercomputer K60 installed in the Supercomputer Centre of Collective Usage of KIAM RAS.

References

1. Borrell, R., et al.: Heterogeneous CPU/GPU co-execution of CFD simulations on the POWER9 architecture: Application to airplane aerodynamics. Futur. Gener. Comput. Syst. **107**, 31–48 (2020). https://doi.org/10.1016/.future.2020.01.045
2. Bocharov, A., Evstigneev, N., Petrovskiy, V., Ryabkov, O., Teplyakov, I.: Implicit method for the solution of supersonic and hypersonic 3D flow problems with Lower-Upper Symmetric-Gauss-Seidel preconditioner on multiple graphics processing units. J. Comput. Phys. **406**, 109189 (2020). https://doi.org/10.1016/j.jcp.2019.109189
3. Menshov, I., Pavlukhin, P.: Highly scalable implementation of an implicit matrix-free solver for gas dynamics on GPU-accelerated clusters. J. Supercomput. **73**(2), 631–638 (2016). https://doi.org/10.1007/s11227-016-1800-1
4. Witherden, F., Vermeire, B., Vincent, P.: Heterogeneous computing on mixed unstructured grids with PyFR. Comput. Fluids **120**, 173–186 (2015). https://doi.org/10.1016/j.compfluid.2015.07.016
5. Gorobets, A., Bakhvalov, P.: Heterogeneous CPU+GPU parallelization for high-accuracy scale-resolving simulations of compressible turbulent flows on hybrid supercomputers. Comput. Phys. Commun. **271**, 108231 (2022). https://doi.org/10.1016/j.cpc.2021.108231
6. Guseva, E.K., Garbaruk, A.V., Strelets, M.K.: Assessment of delayed DES and improved delayed DES combined with a shear-layer-adapted subgrid length-scale in separated flows. Flow Turbul. Combust. **98**(2), 481–502 (2016). https://doi.org/10.1007/s10494-016-9769-7
7. Shur, M.L., Spalart, P.R., Strelets, M.K., Travin, A.K.: An enhanced version of DES with rapid transition from RANS to LES in separated flows. Flow Turbul. Combust. **95**(4), 709–737 (2015). https://doi.org/10.1007/s10494-015-9618-0
8. Trias, F.X., Gorobets, A., Silvis, M.H., Verstappen, R.W.C.P., Oliva, A.: A new subgrid characteristic length for turbulence simulations on anisotropic grids. Phys. Fluids **29**(11), 115109 (2017). https://doi.org/10.1063/1.5012546
9. Trias, F.X., Folch, D., Gorobets, A., Oliva, A.: Building proper invariants for eddy-viscosity subgrid-scale models. Phys. Fluids **27**, 065103 (2015). https://doi.org/10.1007/s10494-016-9769-7
10. Bakhvalov, P.A., Abalakin, I.V., Kozubskaya, T.K.: Edge-based reconstruction schemes for unstructured tetrahedral meshes. Int. J. Numer. Meth. Fluids **81**(6), 331–356 (2016). https://doi.org/10.1002/fld.4187
11. Bakhvalov, P., Kozubskaya, T.: EBR-WENO scheme for solving gas dynamics problems with discontinuities on unstructured meshes. Comput. Fluids **157**, 312–324 (2017). https://doi.org/10.1016/j.compfluid.2017.09.004
12. Bakhvalov, P., Surnachev, M.: Method of averaged element splittings for diffusion terms discretization in vertex-centered framework. J. Comput. Phys. **450**, 110819 (2022). https://doi.org/10.1016/j.jcp.2021.110819
13. Van der Vorst, H.A.: Bi-CGSTAB: a fast and smoothly converging variant of Bi-CG for the solution of nonsymmetric linear systems. SIAM J. Sci. Stat. Comput. **13**, 631–644 (1992)
14. Gorobets, A., Duben, P.: Technology for supercomputer simulation of turbulent flows in the good new days of exascale computing. Supercomputing Front. Innovations **8**(4), 4–10 (2021). https://doi.org/10.14529/jsfi210401

15. Gorobets, A., Soukov, S., Bogdanov, P.: Multilevel parallelization for simulating turbulent flows on most kinds of hybrid supercomputers. Comput. Fluids **173**, 171–177 (2018). https://doi.org/10.1016/j.compfluid.2018.03.011
16. Soukov, S., Gorobets, A.: Heterogeneous computing in resource-intensive CFD simulations. Dokl. Math. **98**, 472–474 (2018). https://doi.org/10.1134/S1064562418060194
17. Voevodin, V., et al.: Supercomputer lomonosov-2: large scale, deep monitoring and fine analytics for the user community. Supercomputing Front. Innovations **6**, 4–11 (2019). https://doi.org/10.14529/jsfi190201
18. Arakeri, V., Krothapalli, A., Siddavaram, V., Alkislar, M., Lourenco, L.: On the use of micro-jets to suppress turbulence in a Mach 0.9 axisymmetric jet. J. Fluid Mech. **490**, 75–98 (2003). https://doi.org/10.1017/s0022112003005202
19. Viswanathan, K.: Aeroacoustics of hot jets. J. Fluid Mech. **516**, 39–82 (2004). https://doi.org/10.1017/s0022112004000151

Development of Web Environment for Modeling the Processes of Macroscopic and Microscopic Levels for Solving Conjugate Problems of Heat and Mass Transfer

Nikita Tarasov[1], Sergey Polyakov[1], and Viktoriia Podryga[1,2(✉)]

[1] Keldysh Institute of Applied Mathematics of Russian Academy of Sciences, Moscow, Russia
{nikita_tarasov,polyakov}@imamod.ru, pvictoria@list.ru
[2] Moscow Automobile and Road Construction State Technical University, Moscow, Russia

Abstract. The work considers a way to building a system for carrying out the full cycle of computer modeling the conjugate problems of heat and mass transfer using a multiscale approach, including macroscopic and microscopic levels. The architecture of the environment was developed based on a modern view of building complex applications that led to the abandonment of the development of "thick" clients and the direction of activity towards web applications such as SaaS. The main approach in the development of the computing core remains the use of classical batch applications based on the OpenMPI/OpenMP/CUDA technology in computing on hybrid computing systems, which are controlled through an interactive web user interface.

Keywords: Web environment · Digital platform · Cloud computing · Mathematical modeling · Multiscale approach · Parallel computing

1 Introduction

With the increase in the performance of central processors, as well as the use of video cards as basic computing devices, it became possible to solve many complex scientific and engineering problems on personal computers and supercomputer systems of the collective usage. At the same time, the development of statistical and direct methods of mathematical modeling was going on, which are now linked with the technologies of neural networks and artificial intelligence. As a result, combining traditional and new approaches of mathematical and computer modeling has become a daily practice. Conventional and high-performance technology is becoming more and more available in many research organizations and in production. In this regard, the task of creating hardware and software platforms for solving a wide range of scientific and technical problems arises. The implementation of such platforms should certainly take into account the trends in the development of computer technology, including high-performance ones.

Currently, computing clusters and supercomputers are based on hybrid systems built within the framework of a distributed computing model, in which many hybrid computing nodes (containing central processors and alternative data processing devices, for example, graphics accelerators) are connected by a high-speed network [1]. Examples of such systems are the hybrid computing clusters of the Keldysh Institute of Applied Mathematics of RAS - K-100 and K-60 [2]. Such systems are ultimately able to evolve for a long time and adapt to the new ever-increasing computing needs.

In terms of system software, modern hybrid clusters and supercomputers are controlled by UNIX-like operating systems that provide multi-tasking and multi-user operation, including remote access, while observing all necessary security standards. At the same time, for the effective organization of parallel computing, various interfaces and tools for parallel and hybrid programming (MPI, OpenMP, CUDA Toolkit, etc.), as well as user task management systems are used. The main goals of such systems are the planning of supercomputations and the management of user computational tasks (from the planned allocation of resources and the launch of tasks to monitoring the state of a particular task and guaranteed saving the results of calculations carried out within its framework). An example of such a system in Russia is the control system for the passage of parallel tasks [3], developed by the Keldysh Institute of Applied Mathematics of RAS and the FSUE Research Institute «Kvant».

The use of web technologies in creating applied digital platforms for performing calculations aimed at the full cycle of supercomputer modeling the complex physical processes has a number of significant advantages over a "thick" client [4]. This approach is based on the practice of performing calculations on supercomputers, the natural access point to which is the ssh connection. This requires from developers and users of any application code not only the ability to use a command shell (based on sh, bash), but also knowledge of the features of a particular launch system. We also note the fact that it is difficult to configure computational applications before starting a specific calculation. From this point of view, a convenient user interface, equipped with interactive forms for setting initial data and control elements for applications running on remote computing systems, should significantly help.

An additional motivation for the use of web technologies is the fact that when creating a full-fledged graphical interface focused on a user computer, there is a problem with the performance of the computer, as well as the software preinstalled on it. The cloud approach eliminates these issues, since a modern browser is enough to use all the features of the web interface. In this case, the entire burden of pre- and post-processing, as well as graphical representation of data, falls on the server, which can be a supercomputer, on the basis of which the main modeling results are obtained.

In addition to the above, we note the following advantages:

- compatibility and timely updating of software on all computing resources involved in the preparation and execution of calculations now do not depend on the end user, but is the responsibility of the administrators of these resources;
- there is an effective possibility of joint work of users on one design project (multi-user mode);
- independence of the applied software environment as a whole from the state of the user's personal computer is realized, which is especially important when monitoring the completion of tasks on remote computers and timely processing of calculation data.

The final requirements for a digital platform can be defined as follows:

– support for the full cycle of mathematical modeling, including:

- setting the initial data and geometry of the computational domain;
- generation of grids and/or other modeling objects;
- preparation for parallel computing;
- carrying out a lot of numerical calculations;
- post-processing and visualization of results;
- intelligent computer analysis of the obtained results.

– secure access to computing resources, including remote access;
– possibility of efficient and controlled preparation of input data for application programs;
– possibility of expanding the set of applications and varying their parameters;
– possibility of expanding the set of computing resources;
– existence of a uniform user interface.

Today, a large number of scientific and commercial teams [5] are actively developing this topic. There are solutions such as Sim4Design [6] or Nucleonica [7]. They have a rich user interface and wide possibilities for analyzing the data obtained during the calculation, but are limited by the scope of the subject area. Another class of applications is aimed at launching and monitoring application, interacting with computers and clusters, for example, Everest [8]. Our main idea is to combine both approaches as much as possible: providing the administrator with the ability to dynamically manage the resources, the developer with a convenient platform for updating and delivering the code, and the common user with a uniform, responsive and intuitive interface for tasks preparation and management, as well as tools for analyze the calculation results.

2 Architecture

2.1 General Approach

The web environment development technology proposed below is based on the client-server approach. It allows you to select the main parts of the developed software system and place them in the server or client side, depending on the frequency of use and specific functions.

As part of the presented solution, we turn to the architecture variant shown in Fig. 1. As can be seen from the figure, the web environment consists of five main components, which are distributed over three classes of hardware. The main class is represented by the environment server (one or more) and performs the basic functions of access, storage, and comprehensive support for computing. The second class consists of basic computing facilities (supercomputers, clusters, individual workstations). The third class includes user computers (personal and/or mobile).

The proposed architecture allows to implement the following basic functions of the web environment:

- multi-user access via the HTTP/HTTPS protocol;
- interaction with remote computers via the SSH protocol;
- authorized user access to the system, separation of users by roles (access levels);
- providing clients with a uniform graphical interface for interacting with remote computers and receiving information support;
- availability of an open extensible database (DB);
- launching, managing and monitoring the progress of user tasks in a single form, regardless of the type and software of the remote computer.

An additional advantage when using the proposed approach is, as can be seen from the Fig. 1, that end users may not have direct ssh access to computing resources at all. This increases the flexibility of building remote access networks, and also makes it possible to mitigate security requirements in some cases and increase the efficiency of calculation planning.

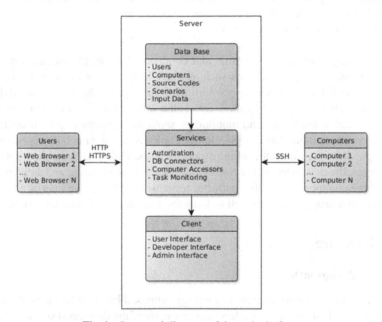

Fig. 1. Structural diagram of the web platform.

The final architecture of the web environment operates with the following set of functional entities:

1. Users are the active users of the system, divided into appropriate role levels (user, developer, administrator);
2. Applications are the applied applications and utilities managed and/or controlled by the web environment on a remote computer (for example, a grid generator, calculation code, a script for interacting with the job launch queue system, etc.);

3. Scenarios are the descriptions of a functional set of applications operating in conjunction, sequentially or in parallel, describing the relationship between input and output data. For example, a complete grid generation process may include a generator, decomposer, grinder, etc.;
4. Projects are the meta descriptions of tasks containing the parameters of one or more calculations and links to already obtained results;
5. Calculations are the specific implementation of the scenario on a user-specified computing resource, including specific calculation parameters and implying the preparation of initial data on a remote computer and the obtained results. Support from the web environment for a specific calculation consists in its launch, monitoring of its state, the possibilities of completion and continuation, including already on another computing resource.

2.2 Technology Stack

At the moment, there are a large number of ready-made libraries (frameworks) for the implementation of the server part of the digital platform, focused on various programming languages. For example, for the Python language, a library such as Django is widely used, containing all the necessary parts for implementing a server-side solution, from ORM (Object-Relational Mapping) to a web page generator. Our previous development was based on this particular framework [4]. In its research, it turned out that the interactive capabilities of server-side rendering of pages are not enough, and it is increasingly necessary to rely on the client side of the web browser using JavaScript.

As a result, it was decided to refocus on single page application (SPA) technology using a reactive approach. For this, due to the efficiency and increasing popularity and dynamism, the Vue3.js framework [9] with the Quasar component library [10] was chosen. For client-side routing (partial page refresh on the client side when the url path changes), Vue-Router [11], which is natural in this case, was used, and Vuex [12] was used as a state manager.

The transition to SPA has significantly reduced the relevance of using Django, which relies heavily on django templates. Therefore, it was decided to use Node.js [13], which is an extension of JavaScript, as the software platform for the server side of the system. Typically, the JavaScript programming language is used on the web client side and is supported in all modern browsers. However, it has significant functionality limitations, including the inability to interact directly with I/O devices and system threads. Node.js was used to build the server-side solution to extend JavaScript to a general-purpose language level.

The use of Node.js made it possible, on the one hand, to achieve uniformity of the code base between the client and server parts, and on the other hand, to use a high degree of JavaScript asynchrony on the server. This is especially useful for monitoring the progress of tasks on remote computers, the execution of long-term tasks, taking into account the subsequent scaling of the system.

The Express framework [14] was used to provide routing, as well as the use of security and authorization plugins. Interaction with the database was carried out using the ORM Sequelize library [15]. SQLite was used as a database at the development stage with the possibility of further migration to MySQL.

Since the digital platform being created is closed to the public, it was decided to organize client-server interaction based on web sockets [16]. Web sockets are an add-on for the HTTP/HTTPS protocol. Unlike the original protocol, they maintain a connection after an initial client connection request. If the connection is successfully established, the client and server can randomly exchange messages, which is a great advantage. In addition, messages sent via the web socket include only the request body, and the HTTP header is not resent, which can significantly optimize client-server communication.

To use web sockets on the server, the Express-ws library was used. Providing the HTTPS protocol was achieved through a reverse proxy of the nginx server.

3 Web Environment Prototype

Based on the described architecture and the proposed technology stack, a web platform prototype was developed, on the example of which we will consider the specific approaches used in its development. The beginning of the user's communication with the digital platform implies the access to the root url-address of the system through a web browser.

3.1 User Access

Access to the system is possible only if the user has a login-password pair specified in the standard authorization form. Otherwise, you need to get an invitation key from the system administrator and fill out the registration form.

Based on the key type, the user receives the appropriate access level:

- calculator;
- developer;
- administrator.

After a successful login, the user interface takes on the form in accordance with its role:

- the calculator has the ability to create new projects, calculations, the ability to run tasks on remote computers;
- the developer additionally gets the ability to create applications and scripts;
- the administrator, among other things, gets access to the administrator's interface - direct access to the database and the ability to register computing resources.

3.2 Applications and Scenarios

To register new applications in the system, the developer uses a special form that requires filling in an informational description of applications, specifying a unique identifier and setting a description file template in yaml format containing build instructions, run instructions, lists of input and output parameters. An example of generating the form of input parameters based on a script file is shown in Fig. 2.

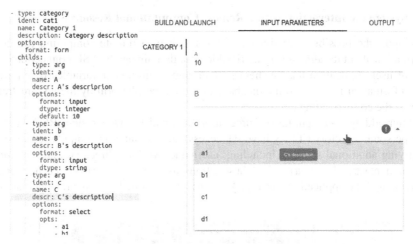

Fig. 2. Description of parameters and generated form.

Support for version control is achieved by storing their parameters in the database (passports), which require clarification of the description file (if necessary) and also store the source code to be subsequently sent to a remote computing resource. An example of the application version page is shown in Fig. 3.

To register new scripts, the developer needs to go to the script creation page. It specifies the name and the description of the script, and also sets the template of the description file in yaml format. The template contains a set of applications to use (based on a unique identifier), script input parameters, and a run order. Like applications, the final form of a script is the version generated in the database.

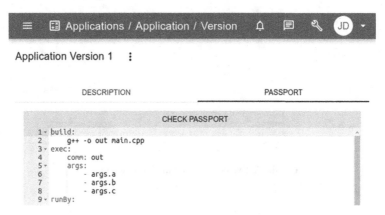

Fig. 3. Application version page.

3.3 System for Interaction with a Remote Computational Resource

To support the possibility of dynamic registration of a remote computing resource, information about its address (digital IP address or domain name), SSH connection port, type of user application management system, and environment variables is required. This information is added to the database of the digital platform by the administrator through the corresponding page.

After adding a computing resource, users can add the web system RCA keys to their personal directory (if they have ssh access) and activate the compute resource by specifying additional settings, including: username, working directory, and additional environment variables. As a result of these actions, users will be able to select and prepare the version of the application (see Fig. 4) and use the activated resource for calculations.

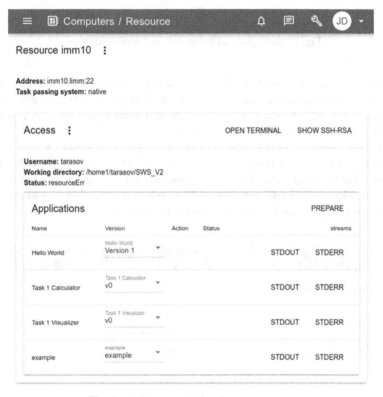

Fig. 4. Active computational resource page.

3.4 Projects and Calculations

Project creation is available for users with any type of access, for which you need to go to the project creation page, set its name, description and participants - users for whom the project will be visible.

The main functional unit for the preparation and execution of applications within the digital system is the calculation belonging to the project. When creating a calculation, it is necessary, in addition to the descriptive part, to select a scenario and its version. An example of the calculation page is shown in Fig. 5, with its help, users have the opportunity to select a calculator, set the input parameters of the calculation, launch applications and view the output data.

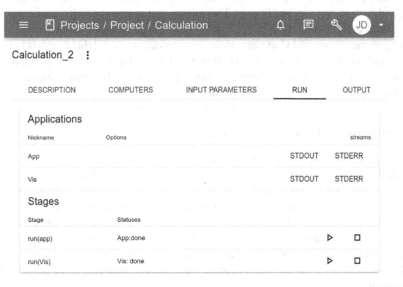

Fig. 5. An example of the interface for launching a calculation task.

The presented functional prototype of the digital platform shows the viability of the proposed approach and the selected technology stack.

4   Environment Components

4.1   Specifying the Initial Data and Geometry of the Computational Domain

The initial data can be divided into two main groups - these are the settings of the calculation codes and data files, such as grids, geometric descriptions of the calculation area and tabular data.

The settings are stored in json format, their changes are made using the generated graphical forms on the calculation page. When preparing a specific task on a remote computational resource, configuration files are generated in the format required by the application.

The main format for storing the geometric representation is brep, which is the main format of the free geometric core of Open Cascade [17]. This format allows you to use the full functionality of the library for generating and analyzing the computational domain. In the future, it is planned to prepare js-bindings of calls to Open Cascade directly on the client side to build a full-featured geometric editor based on a digital platform.

Data files are attached to the input parameters of calculations using special fields and file submission forms.

4.2 Generation of Grids and/or Other Modeling Objects

The generation of computational unstructured grids is based on the use of a freely distributed grid generator gmsh [18], which supports operation in batch mode and is equipped with an appropriate library. This allows you to use this software on a remote computing resource directly.

To generate structured Cartesian grids, an approach was used that consists in generating a uniform decomposition of a parallelepiped bordering the computational domain with its subsequent attribution using the known geometry of the computational domain with the help of Open Cascade library calls.

4.3 Preparing for Parallel Computing

The principle of geometric parallelism was used as the basis for parallelization.

For macromodels, geometric parallelism is realized by dividing the computational grid into compact domains of approximately the same size. As a partitioning algorithm, it is possible to use the inertial bisection method with unit weights at the cell centers [19], which makes it possible to achieve a good degree of balance and compactness of domains when separating regions of a simple shape. However, there are other widely used library solutions, such as the Metis, ParMetis, and Jostle packages, considered together in [20] and providing the decomposition of the computational grid of an arbitrary type and structure.

For a micromodel, a parallel algorithm is obtained in a natural way by dividing particles into subsets, the interaction forces for which are calculated in several flows. Since the number of particles in the micromodels under consideration is quite large (in aggregate, it can be tens and hundreds of millions), the chosen approach to parallelization is characterized by consistently high efficiency even with a significant increase in the number of parallel threads. This circumstance makes it possible to use graphics accelerators for the numerical calculation of particle dynamics equations. The parallel algorithm is discussed in detail in [21].

4.4 Calculation Cores

The QGD and MD codes are used as the main computing cores of the developed web environment. The first group of codes (QGD codes) includes solutions to gas dynamics problems based on a quasigasdynamic (QGD) system of equations [22, 23]. A distinctive feature of these codes is the support of parallel calculations on Cartesian and unstructured hybrid grids in two- and three-dimensional cases, as well as the possibility of using real equations of state and kinetic coefficients of the QGD system, including those obtained using molecular dynamics (MD) methods. Parallelism technologies are in line with the hybrid supercomputer platform we developed [24].

The second group of codes (MD codes) includes programs for calculating the properties of molecular systems in a wide range of thermodynamic parameters, as well as generators of microsystems for subsequent direct molecular modeling [25, 26].

In the future, it is planned to integrate QGD and MD codes within scenarios that implement a multiscale approach [27–29] to solving urgent problems of technical gas dynamics.

Although our primary goal is to integrate the internal KIAM codes discussed above in the system, it allows the use of third-party solutions. Software packages that can be used in batch mode, for example, OpenFOAM [30] or FEniCS [31], can be used within the developed digital platform by generating the corresponding application passports and scenarios.

4.5   Post-Processing and Visualization of Results

The approach used for processing calculation results and pure server-side non-interactive visualization, based on the techniques and codes developed in the framework of [32], does not differ from any other batch application (grid generators and calculation codes discussed earlier).

Another approach is also possible, based on the solution from KitWare - ParaView Web [33], which allows you to run the visualization server on a remote computer, waiting for a web connection, after which the server sends bitmap images to the client - data visualization. At the same time, the client retains interactivity, which consists in the ability to control the camera and apply data analysis methods, such as building sections, filtering elements by a scalar value, etc.

The client can be its own implementation that interacts with the visualization server using the supplied api [34]. In addition, it is possible to redirect the user to a page with a KitWare implementation, such as Visualizer [35]. The advantage of these methods lies in the high degree of development and stability of software implementation, support for VTK [36] format files, a large number of analysis tools and interaction with data out of the box.

5   Common User-Case and Results Analyzing

Consider a typical scenario of user interaction with the digital platform for solving the problem of flow modeling through complex geometry:

1. the authorized user, within an existing or new project, can create a new calculation, in the form of which the scenario should be specified;
2. after creating the calculation, the system redirects the user to the calculation page (see Fig. 5). On the «COMPUTERS» tab, the user should select the computing resources for each of the applications listed in the scenario script;
3. after the resource choosing, the user can proceed to the «INPUT PARAMETERS» tab for specifying the input data. For data files that are not connected within the scenario, two options appear - uploading the file through a special form or linking it to the results obtained from calculations carried out earlier. In case of configuration

files, the user is offered forms generated on the basis of the parameter trees specified
in the application passport;

4. after filling the input forms, user can access the task management component and
   launch the task. The status column will display the current state of the process.
   Standard program streams can be accessed by «STDOUT»/«STDERR» buttons;
5. during the calculation or after the task completion, the output data component is
   available to the user. Within this component, it is possible to interact with the output
   data of the application, including viewing text files, videos, images, and the other
   file formats known to the system. An example of interaction with data files of the
   VTK format is shown in Fig. 6.

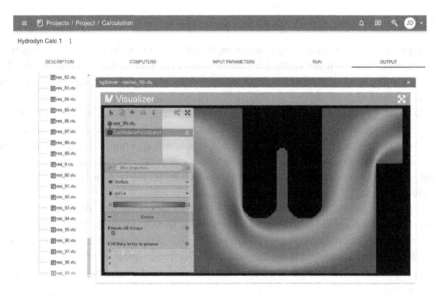

Fig. 6. Interactive 3D visualization.

The use of the ParaView package, which is widely applied in the visualization and
processing of scientific data, makes it possible to cover the needs of interaction with
the results of calculations for a wide class of problems, both grid and non-grid. Since
the application is based on the VTK library, many file formats are available for direct
reading and visualization. ParaView has a large set of data filters out of the box. This list
can be extended by the user through Python scripting. In the future, we plan to expand
support for interactive visualization for the analysis of 1D data using a component based
on Plotly library [37] that has proven itself in our previous project [4].

Moreover, the developers can add the output file handler programs to the platform
using the most suitable and familiar batch data processing tools with help of the scenario
approach to describe the interaction between applications in a single pipeline. This
technique allows users to dynamically expand the system capabilities in the way they
need.

6 Conclusion

The problem of carrying out a full cycle of computer and supercomputer modeling of conjugated problems of heat and mass transfer using a multiscale approach is considered. The specificity of such problems is to support not only the traditional chain of computational experiments in gas and hydrodynamics (initial data, geometry, grid, calculations, processing, and visualization), but also the integration of significantly heterogeneous computer models and technologies within the overall computation cycle. It is also necessary to support the work on a common project of a large number of researchers with different qualifications and specializations.

To solve the considered problem in mathematical and social terms, a cloud solution based on a multi-user digital web platform is proposed that meets the basic requirements of modern computer modeling. The common cloud space of the environment allows all project participants to work remotely or directly with all the tools of the environment, conduct joint calculations and analyze the results. In addition, application developers are provided with a powerful tool for integrating them into the environment (describing passports and creating flexible work scenarios) and linking individual components according to data using a specialized file interface. In particular, the scripting language fits well with the methodology of splitting specific calculations by physical processes and scales. From the point of view of managing calculations, an effective mechanism for the interaction of the environment with control systems for various computing resources (from a workstation to powerful computing clusters and supercomputers) has been developed.

The developed prototype of the web environment was tested in the Keldysh Institute of Applied Mathematics of RAS for the implementation of a number of projects related to solving complex problems of aerodynamics, hydrodynamics, ecology, nanoelectronics. Also, a similar solution is used for collective education of students of MEPhI, MIPT, MIET. Based on this approbation, it can be concluded that the developed architecture of the web environment and its implementation are highly operable and efficient with the support of large-scale computer experiments.

Acknowledgment. The work was funded by the Russian Science Foundation (project № 22–11-00126). Testing of the trial version of the web environment was carried out using the equipment of the Supercomputer Center of Collective Usage of KIAM RAS.

References

1. GREEN500, November 2021. https://www.top500.org/lists/green500/2021/11/
2. Center of collective usage of KIAM RAS. https://ckp.kiam.ru/?home
3. MVS-1000: Documentation. MVS-1000/K-10 user manual. https://www.kiam.ru/MVS/doc uments/k60/userguide.html
4. Puzyrkov, D.V., Podryga, V.O., Polyakov, S.V.: Cloud service for HPC management: ideas and appliance. Lobachevskii J. Math. **39**(9), 1251–1261 (2018). https://doi.org/10.1134/S19 95080218090172
5. Dubenskaya, J., Kryukov, A., Demichev, A.: Some approaches to organizing of remote access to supercomputer resources. CEUR Workshop Proc. **1482**, 712–719 (2015)

6. Sim streamlined for design: structural simulation and analysis in the cloud. https://www.sim 4design.com/index
7. Nucleonica. https://www.nucleonica.com/
8. Sukhoroslov O., Volkov S., Afanasiev A.: A web-based platform for publication and distributed execution of computing applications. In: 14th International Symposium on Parallel and Distributed Computing (ISPDC), vol. 14, pp. 175–184. IEEE (2015)
9. Vue.js – the progressive JavaScript framework | Vue.js. https://vuejs.org/
10. Quasar framework. https://quasar.dev/
11. Home | Vue router. https://router.vuejs.org/
12. What is Vuex? | Vuex. https://vuex.vuejs.org/
13. About | Node.js. https://nodejs.org/en/about/
14. Express – Node.js web application framework. https://expressjs.com/
15. Sequelize ORM. https://sequelize.org/
16. RFC 6455 - the WebSocket protocol. https://datatracker.ietf.org/doc/html/rfc6455
17. Open CASCADE technology – open cascade. https://www.opencascade.com/open-cascade-technology/
18. Gmsh: a three-dimensional finite element mesh generator with built-in pre- and post-processing facilities. https://gmsh.info/
19. Ivanov, E.G.: Automatic parallel generation of unstructured computational grids for problems of computational mechanics: dissertation for the degree of Candidate of Physical and Mathematical Sciences: 05.13.18, Novosibirsk (2007)
20. Golovchenko, E.N.: Decomposition of computational grids for solving problems of continuum mechanics on high-performance computing systems: dissertation for the degree of Candidate of Physical and Mathematical Sciences: 05.13.18, Moscow (2014)
21. Podryga, V.O., Polyakov, S.V.: Parallel implementation of a multiscale approach for calculating gas microflows. Vychislitel'nye metody i programmirovanie. 17(2), 147–165 (2016). https://doi.org/10.26089/NumMet.v17r214
22. Kudryashova, T.A., Polyakov, S.V., Sverdlin, A.A.: Calculation of gas flow parameters around a reentry vehicle. Math. Models Comput. Simul. 1(4), 445–452 (2009). https://doi.org/10.1134/S2070048209040036
23. Polyakov, S.V., Kudryashova, T.A., Sverdlin, A.A., Kononov, E.M., Kosolapov, O.A.: Parallel software package for simulation of continuum mechanics problems on modern multiprocessor systems. Math. Models Comput. Simul. 3(1), 46–57 (2011). https://doi.org/10.1134/S2070048211010091
24. Polyakov, S.V., Karamzin, Yu.N., Kosolapov, O.A., Kudryashova, T.A., Soukov, S.A.: Hybrid supercomputer platform and applications programming for the solution of continuous mechanics problems by grid methods. Izvestiya YUFU. Tekhnicheskie nauki. 6(131), 105–115 (2012)
25. Podryga, V.O., Polyakov, S.V.: Molecular dynamics simulation of thermodynamic equilibrium establishment in nickel. Math. Models Comput. Simul. 7(5), 456–466 (2015). https://doi.org/10.1134/S2070048215050105
26. Podryga, V.O., Polyakov, S.V., Puzyrkov, D.V.: Supercomputer molecular modeling of thermodynamic equilibrium in gas-metal microsystems. Vychislitel'nye metody i programmirovanie 16(1), 123–138 (2015). https://doi.org/10.26089/NumMet.v16r113
27. Podryga, V., Polyakov, S.: Parallel realization of multiscale approach for calculating the gas flows in microchannels of technical systems. In: CEUR Workshop Proceedings. vol. 1576, pp. 270–283 (2016)
28. Podryga, V.O., Karamzin, Yu.N., Kudryashova, T.A., Polyakov, S.V.: Multiscale simulation of three-dimensional unsteady gas flows in microchannels of technical systems. In: Papadrakakis, M., Papadopoulos, V., Stefanou, G., Plevris, V. (eds.) Proceedings of VII European Congress on Computational Methods in Applied Sciences and Engineering (ECCOMAS

Congress 2016), vol. 2, pp. 2331–2345. Institute of Structural Analysis and Antiseismic Research, National Technical University of Athens, Greece (2016)

29. Podryga, V.O., Polyakov, S.V.: Multiscale modeling of gas jet outflow to vacuum. KIAM Prepr. **81**, 1–52 (2016). https://doi.org/10.20948/prepr-2016-81

30. OpenFOAM: the open source CFD toolbox. https://www.openfoam.com/

31. FEniCS project. https://fenicsproject.org/

32. Puzyrkov, D.V., Podryga, V.O., Polyakov, S.V.: Parallel processing and visualization for results of molecular simulation problems. Proc. ISP RAS. **28**(2), 221–242 (2016). https://doi.org/10.15514/ISPRAS-2016-28(2)-15

33. Web | ParaView. https://www.paraview.org/web/

34. ParaViewWeb. http://kitware.github.io/paraviewweb/

35. Visualizer. https://kitware.github.io/visualizer/

36. VTK - The visualization toolkit. https://vtk.org/

37. Plotly javascript graphing library in JavaScript. https://plotly.com/javascript/

Distributed Parallel Bootstrap Adaptive Algebraic Multigrid Method

Igor Konshin[1,2,3,4] and Kirill Terekhov[1,2(✉)]

[1] Marchuk Institute of Numerical Mathematics, RAS, Moscow 119333, Russia
terekhov@inm.ras.ru
[2] Moscow Institute of Physics and Technology, Moscow 141701, Russia
[3] Dorodnicyn Computing Centre of FRC CSC, RAS, Moscow 119333, Russia
[4] Sechenov University, Moscow 119991, Russia

Abstract. We propose a fully distributed parallel adaptive generalization of the Ruge–Stuben algebraic multigrid method. In the adaptive multigrid framework, the coarse space and interpolation operator depend on the eigenvector, corresponding to the minimal eigenvalue. The bootstrap process allows to approximate the eigenvector along the setup process. Integrating the eigenvector into the Ruge–Stuben interpolation operator, we introduce the weak and strong decoupling of connections as well as parameterize the coarse space refinement process for the twice-removed interpolation. The distributed method uses single-layer matrix overlap for the coarse space refinement and the twice-removed interpolation, Luby's parallel maximal independent set method for both the initial coarse space selection as well as the coarse space refinement and a distributed Gauss–Seidel smoother. The solver is composed using S^3M framework. We demonstrate the efficiency of the method on a set of elliptic problems, on systems with rescaled matrices and finally we apply the entire method to the system, originating from the two-phase oil recovery problem.

Keywords: Sparse linear system · Numerical modeling · Adaptive multigrid method · Two-phase oil recovery problem · Parallel efficiency

1 Introduction

The multigrid idea for Poisson problems was explored early by Fedorenko and Bakhvalov in [1–4] and further developed in the works of Brandt [5] and Hackbusch [6]. It's main advantage is $O(N)$ convergence property, as well as huge potential for massive parallelization [7]. The classical multigrid method requires construction of a sequence of coarse grids with PDE discretization and intergrid interpolations, that bears a number of drawbacks. To alleviate the problem a purely algebraic multigrid method was proposed, with the most famous one by Ruge and Stüben [8,9]. It algebraically defines coarsening from matrix analysis. Since then the method gained commercial success [10]. There are numerous

V. Voevodin et al. (Eds.): RuSCDays 2022, LNCS 13708, pp. 92–111, 2022.
https://doi.org/10.1007/978-3-031-22941-1_7

open-source [11–14] (HYPRE, PETSc, Trilinos, AMGCL and others) and commercial [15–17] (SAMG, AMGX, NVAMG, Paralution and others) libraries that implement the algebraic multigrid method.

Originally, the system is required to posses weakly diagonally-dominant symmetric M-matrix properties, which simplify the theoretical analysis, see [8], whereas in practice it applies to a wider class of systems [18]. Moreover, the classical interpolation requires the system to have a vector of constants in the kernel or near the null space (i.e. $A\mathbf{1} \approx 0$), which is the property of scalar elliptic systems. To generalize the algebraic multigrid idea to systems of different nature, as well as scaled elliptic systems, an adaptive algebraic multigrid was proposed [19].

The adaptive multigrid method uses the information on near null space vector (i.e. $A\mathbf{x} \approx 0$) to properly define the interpolation operators and the coarse space [20]. Such vectors could be supplied for the system at hand or computed with the available relaxation operator, which results in a bootstrap process [21–24]. Since then the bootstrap adaptive multigrid idea was used to construct solvers for different problem types [25–27].

The algebraic multigrid method was also applied to different systems of equations [28–31]. In the systems arising from multiphase flows in oil & gas problems, an elliptic component is extracted using CPR [32,33] or DRS [34,35] techniques. Then the algebraic multigrid method is a part of multi-stage strategy, applied to rapidly solve the elliptic part of the problem. It still requires a robust first-stage preconditioner, such as an incomplete LU-factorization [36], since the remaining part of the system demonstrates elliptic component due to capillary pressure. A multigrid reduction technique was successfully applied to solve two-phase problems [37,38]. Considering rock mechanics adds an elliptic component that is also addressed with the algebraic multigrid [39,40]. However, the coupled geomechanics problem may exhibit saddle-point behavior [41,42].

Multiscale methods, similar in nature with geometric multigrid, were proposed for oil & gas problems with highly contrast coefficients [43–47]. The coarsening is performed for the pressure with the interpolation based on finite-element basis or finite-volume fluxes. These methods were applied to rapidly solve elliptic [43,48], parabolic [46], and coupled geomechanical [49,50] problems in heterogeneous media. Initially the method was applied to structured grids, but [51–53] proposed algebraic versions.

There are closely related multilevel methods [54–59], which are usually based on the incomplete LU-factorization [60–62] and approximate Schur complement serves as a coarse space. Control of the norms of inverse factors [63,64] yields optimal smoother and defining the Schur complement via the Galerkin principle (as in the algebraic multigrid) allows to reduce and control the error in the approximate Schur complement [65]. The method is applied to general types of systems [66,67], but it is much harder to extract parallelism [68–70].

In the present paper we describe our distributed parallel implementation of bootstrap adaptive multigrid method. It is implemented with the S^3M package [28], where we parallelize the main building blocks of the Ruge–Stüben method. We implement a distributed Gauss–Seidel smoother following [71] and parametrise the coarse space refinement based on the interpolation coefficient, introduce the test vector and its relaxation following [19] and supplement it with our variant of strong-weak splitting of connections. We demonstrate the parallel efficiency of the method and its ability to solve elliptic and scaled elliptic systems. Finally, we show that the adaptive method is able to solve a coupled system of equations of flow and transport, originating from the two-phase oil recovery problem that consists of parabolic and hyperbolic blocks.

The article is organised as follows. Section 2 describes the bootstrap algebraic multigrid method. In Sect. 3, the parallel implementation of the algorithms is considered. Section 4 contains the results of numerical experiments. The final section summarizes the findings.

2 Bootstrap Adaptive Algebraic Multigrid Method

Adaptive multigrid method uses available test vector $\mathbf{x}$ satisfying $A\mathbf{x} \approx \mathbf{0}$ to construct an appropriate interpolation operator. Let $A = \{a_{ij}\}, i, j \in \Omega = [1, N]$. The expression $A\mathbf{x} \approx 0$ for an i-th row is

$$a_{ii}\mathbf{x}_i \approx -\sum_{i \neq j} a_{ij}\mathbf{x}_j. \tag{1}$$

Let there exist a coarse-fine splitting $\Omega = \mathcal{C} \cup \mathcal{F}$, the i-th row connections are given by $\mathcal{N}_i = \{j | i \neq j, \, a_{ij} \neq 0\}$, and there exists some splitting to strong and weak connections $\mathcal{N}_i = \mathcal{S}_i \cup \mathcal{W}_i$. The contribution of the weak connections $\mathcal{W}_i$ is considered to be small enough, and thus they are absorbed onto the diagonal. The interpolatory connections are $\mathcal{I}_i = \mathcal{S}_i \cap \mathcal{C}$ and the remaining strong connections $\mathcal{D}_i = \mathcal{S}_i \cap \mathcal{F}$ are eliminated with the twice-removed interpolation, which requires $\forall j \in \mathcal{D}_i : \mathcal{S}_i \cap \mathcal{S}_j \cap \mathcal{C} \neq \varnothing$. To be flexible, we further split $\mathcal{D}_i = \mathcal{T}_i \cup \mathcal{E}_i$, where connections in $\mathcal{T}_i$ allow for twice-removed interpolation, whereas $\forall j \in \mathcal{E}_i : \mathcal{S}_i \cap \mathcal{S}_j \cap \mathcal{C} = \varnothing$ and connections in $\mathcal{E}_i$ are absorbed by a coefficient. The splitting into sets results in the splitting of the right-hand side in (1):

$$-\sum_{i \neq j} a_{ij}\mathbf{x}_j = -\sum_{j \in \mathcal{I}_i} a_{ij}\mathbf{x}_j - \sum_{j \in \mathcal{W}_i} a_{ij}\mathbf{x}_j - \sum_{k \in \mathcal{T}_i} a_{ik}\mathbf{x}_k - \sum_{k \in \mathcal{E}_i} a_{ik}\mathbf{x}_k.$$

Weak connections $\mathcal{W}_i$ are approximated with $\mathbf{x}_i$, whereas strong non-interpolatory connections has to be expressed using $\mathbf{x}_j, j \in \mathcal{I}_i$. The twice-removed interpolation with the account for the test vector $\mathbf{x}$ was suggested in [19], which allows to eliminate $\mathbf{x}_k, k \in \mathcal{T}_i$ by

$$a_{ik}\mathbf{x}_k = \sum_{j \in \mathcal{S}_i \cap \mathcal{S}_k \cap \mathcal{C}} \frac{a_{ik}a_{kj}\mathbf{x}_k\mathbf{x}_j}{\sum_{l \in \mathcal{S}_i \cap \mathcal{S}_k \cap \mathcal{C}} a_{kl}\mathbf{x}_l}.$$

To this end, using the introduced sets, (1) is expressed by

$$\left(a_{ii} + \sum_{j \in \mathcal{W}_i} a_{ij}\frac{\mathbf{x}_j}{\mathbf{x}_i} \right) \mathbf{x}_i \approx -\eta_i \sum_{j \in \mathcal{I}_i} \left(a_{ij} + \sum_{k \in \mathcal{T}_i} \frac{a_{ik}a_{kj}\mathbf{x}_k}{\sum_{l \in \mathcal{S}_i \cap \mathcal{S}_k \cap \mathcal{C}} a_{kl}\mathbf{x}_l} \right) \mathbf{x}_j, \tag{2}$$

where η_i is the parameter absorbing the connections from $\mathcal{E}_i$ and satisfying

$$\eta_i = 1 + \frac{\sum_{k \in \mathcal{E}_i} a_{ik} \mathbf{x}_k}{\sum_{j \in \mathcal{I}_i} a_{ij} \mathbf{x}_j + \sum_{k \in \mathcal{T}_i} a_{ik} \mathbf{x}_k} = \frac{\sum_{k \in \mathcal{S}_i} a_{ik} \mathbf{x}_k}{\sum_{k \in \mathcal{S}_i \setminus \mathcal{E}_i} a_{ik} \mathbf{x}_k}. \tag{3}$$

From (2) we obtain an interpolation formula for $\mathbf{x}_i$ in terms of $\mathbf{x}_j$ from the interpolatory set $\mathcal{I}_i$, given by

$$\mathbf{x}_i \approx \sum_{j \in \mathcal{I}_i} \omega_{ij} \mathbf{x}_j,$$

with the weights

$$\omega_{ij} = \frac{-\eta_i \mathbf{x}_i}{a_{ii} \mathbf{x}_i + \sum_{j \in \mathcal{W}_i} a_{ij} \mathbf{x}_j} \left(a_{ij} + \sum_{k \in \mathcal{T}_i} \frac{a_{ik} a_{kj} \mathbf{x}_k}{\sum_{l \in \mathcal{S}_i \cap \mathcal{S}_k \cap C} a_{kl} \mathbf{x}_l} \right). \tag{4}$$

Introducing the mapping $\forall j \in \mathcal{C} : f(j) \in \Omega_\mathcal{C}$, $\Omega_\mathcal{C} = [1, N_\mathcal{C}]$, $N_\mathcal{C} = |\mathcal{C}|$, we define the i-th row of the prolongator P as follows:

$$P_i = \begin{cases} \sum_{j \in \mathcal{I}_i} \omega_{ij} \delta_{f(j)}, & i \in \mathcal{F}, \\ \delta_{f(i)}, & i \in \mathcal{C}, \end{cases} \tag{5}$$

where $\delta_k = \mathbf{e}_k^T$ is the Kronecker delta. The system for the next level is defined by $B = P^T A P$.

In the classical method the strong points at i-th row are selected by

$$\mathcal{S}_i = \{ j | - a_{ij} \geq \theta \max_{k \in \mathcal{N}_i} (-a_{ik}) \}, \tag{6}$$

which uses an M-matrix property: off-diagonal values are negative. The recommended parameter is $\theta = 1/4$. To accommodate the test vector $\mathbf{x}$, we modify (6) as follows:

$$\mathcal{S}_i = \{ j | s_i a_{ij} \mathbf{x}_j \geq \theta \max_{k \in \mathcal{N}_i} (s_i a_{ik} \mathbf{x}_k) \}, \quad s_i = -\operatorname{sgn}(a_{ii} \mathbf{x}_i).$$

Further, the selection of weak points influences the left-hand side of (2) and hence the denominator in (4). To this end, we require the contribution of weak points to preserve the sign of the denominator:

$$a_{ii} \mathbf{x}_i \left(a_{ii} \mathbf{x}_i + \sum_{j \in \mathcal{W}_i} a_{ij} \mathbf{x}_j \right) > 0. \tag{7}$$

If (7) is violated, we turn the most influencing weak point into strong point until (7) is satisfied:

$$j = \arg \max_{k \in \mathcal{W}_i} (s_i a_{ik} \mathbf{x}_k), \quad \mathcal{S}_i = \mathcal{S}_i \cup \{ j \}, \quad \mathcal{W}_i = \mathcal{W}_i \setminus \{ j \}.$$

Ruge and Stüben [8] impose two rules on coarse-fine splitting based on the graph of strong connections $\mathcal{S}$:

- C1: $\forall i \in \mathcal{F} : \forall j \in \mathcal{S}_i \cap \mathcal{F} : \mathcal{S}_i \cap \mathcal{S}_j \cap \mathcal{C} \neq \varnothing.$
- C2: $\mathcal{C}$ is a maximal independent set of graph $\mathcal{S}$.

Exact execution of the rule C1 leads to $\mathcal{E}_i = \varnothing$ and $\eta_i = 1$ in (3) for all $i \in \mathcal{F}$. Instead of C1 we require $\forall i \in \mathcal{F} : |\eta_i - 1| \leqslant \varkappa$, where $\varkappa$ is a tunable parameter. By taking $\varkappa = 0$ we satisfy rule C1 exactly.

Taking $\mathbf{x} = \mathbf{1}$ recovers the classical algebraic multigrid method in most cases. In this work we follow [19] and apply several iterations of Gauss–Seidel smoother to the system $A\mathbf{x} = 0$, where the initial vector $\mathbf{x}$ is prescribed. After each iteration the vector $\mathbf{x}$ is normalized, the vector $\mathbf{x}$ with the minimal residual in Frobenius norm $\|A\mathbf{x}\|_F$ is taken as a solution.

After calculation of the vector $\mathbf{x}$, the prolongator P is constructed and the initial next level vector $\mathbf{y}$, satisfying $P^T A P \mathbf{y} \approx 0$, has to be calculated. A straightforward interpolation is $\mathbf{y} = (P^T P)^{-1} P^T \mathbf{x}$, where the system $P^T P \mathbf{y} = P^T \mathbf{x}$ can be solved in several iterations of conjugate gradient method using only matrix–vector multiplications. A simpler approach, suggested in [19], that we use here, is to prescribe $\forall i \in \mathcal{C} : \mathbf{y}_{f(i)} = \mathbf{x}_i$.

The setup phase is divided into steps:

- Setup the smoother for the current system;
- Improve test vector using available smoother;
- Compute graph of strong connections;
- Perform initial coarse space selection and refinement;
- Compute prolongator (Eqs. (4)–(5));
- Compute the next level system $B = P^T A P$, next level vector $\mathbf{y}$;
- Proceed to the next level: invert small system or start steps over.

The solution phase involves usual V-cycle algorithm, thus we don't present it here for brevity.

3   Parallel Implementation

3.1   Matrix Operations

We consider sparse matrices in compressed row storage (CSR) format. In parallel the rows of sparse matrix A are distributed among processors. Let $\mathcal{R}$ correspond to the local range of row indices. The column indices j, corresponding to the local rows $j \in \mathcal{R}$, are considered to be local, whereas other column indices $j \notin \mathcal{R}$ are non-local, see Fig. 1 (left). A range of values in the vector $\mathbf{x}$, corresponding to the local rows, is also considered to be local. To perform the matrix–vector multiplication operation $\mathbf{y} = A\mathbf{x}$ we have to locally reorder non-local column indices and vector values into the "tail" of the matrix and vector, respectively, see Fig. 1 (right). Let us introduce the mapping to local indices $\forall j \in \mathcal{R} : g(j) \in [1, N_R], \forall j \notin \mathcal{R} : g(j) > N_R$, $N_R = |\mathcal{R}|$. Then the matrix–vector multiplication on the local processor is expressed by

$$\mathbf{y}_{g(i)} = \sum_j a_{g(i)g(j)} \mathbf{x}_{g(j)}, \quad i \in \mathcal{R}, \quad \text{i.e. } \mathbf{y}_i = \sum_j a_{ij} \mathbf{x}_j.$$

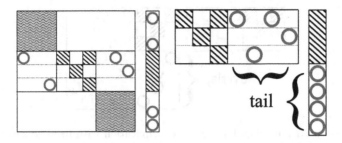

Fig. 1. Distributed sparse matrix–vector operation at the second processor (left) and its local representation with non-local connections moved to the tail (right). Boxes with wavy pattern are non-local data, boxes with lined pattern represent local non-zeroes and local data in the vector, red circles represent non-local non-zeroes and non-local data in the vector. (Color figure online)

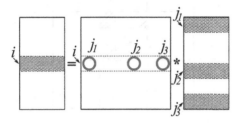

Fig. 2. Sparse matrix–matrix operation using Gustavson algorithm. Stripes with wavy pattern represent sparse rows, gray circles are non-zero entries.

We can determine the local values of the vector $\mathbf{y}$, given that the "tail" of vector $\mathbf{x}$ was synchronized. Further we present all the algorithms in the global indices but imply that the mapping is used.

The sparse matrix–matrix multiplication operation $C = AB$ is performed using Gustavson's algorithm, see Fig. 2. It is expressed by

$$\mathbf{c}_i = \sum_j a_{ij}\mathbf{b}_j,$$

where $A = \{a_{ij}\}$, and $\mathbf{c}_i$ and $\mathbf{b}_j$ are sparse rows of C and B, respectively. The algorithm can be viewed also as a matrix–vector operation, where each entry of the vector is a sparse row $\mathbf{b}_j$. To this end, the non-local sparse rows of the matrix B has to be locally accumulated at the "tail". Once this is done the sparse matrix–matrix multiplication can be performed for the local part of the matrix C.

The extension of the "tail" of sparse square matrix A for the multiplication with itself is also known as overlapping, see Fig. 3. Multiple overlapping layers are used in domain decomposition preconditioners, such as Additive Schwartz method. Here we require a single overlapping layer that allows us to use twice-removed interpolation and coarse space refinement.

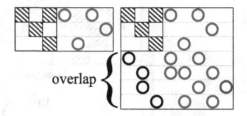

Fig. 3. Sparse matrix overlapping for the multiplication with itself. Boxes with lined pattern represent local non-zeroes and local data, black circles are non-zeroes of local range in the overlap, red and blue circles are non-local nonzeroes. Blue circle belongs to the range of the second overlapping layer. (Color figure online)

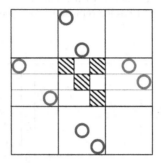

Fig. 4. Distributed sparse matrix transpose at the second processor. Boxes with lined pattern represent local non-zeroes. Red and violet circles are nonzeroes to be sent to processors one and three, respectively. Blue and green circles are nonzeroes to be received from processors one and three, respectively. (Color figure online)

Distributed sparse matrix transpose requires assembly of a range of matrix columns $\mathcal{R}_C$ at every processor, see Fig. 4. To this end, on each processor we form blocks of sparse submatrices for each other processor and communicate them. Each processor assembles received submatrices with his own block to obtain the matrix transpose. By equalizing the number of columns of the transpose prolongator at each processor we balance the number of rows in the resulting coarse space.

3.2   Coarse Space Selection

Following Ruge and Stüben [8] we split the coarse space computation into two steps: selection of a maximal independent set in graph $\mathcal{S}$ to satisfy rule C2 and coarse space refinement to satisfy modified rule C1. In [8] each new coarse space node $i \in \mathcal{U} \rightarrow i \in \mathcal{C}$ with the maximal weight $|\mathcal{S}_i^T \cap \mathcal{U}| + 2|\mathcal{S}_i^T \cap \mathcal{F}|$ is selected sequentially. Here $\mathcal{U} = \Omega \setminus (\mathcal{C} \cup \mathcal{F})$ is the set of candidates.

In this work we use the Luby's algorithm [72] for finding a maximal independent set with weights. We consider the weight $|\mathcal{S}_i \cap \mathcal{U}| + 2|\mathcal{S}_i \cap \mathcal{F}|$, which does not require graph $\mathcal{S}$ transpose. It directly motivates attributing nodes to $\mathcal{C}$ if

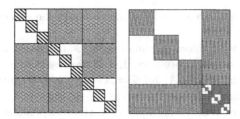

Fig. 5. Multicolor reordering (left) and doubly-bordered block-diagonal form (right). Boxes with lined pattern are diagonal entries, boxes with wavy pattern are sparse blocks.

they get more strong non-interpolatory connections and require twice-removed interpolation. It is straightforward to parallelize, if we synchronize vector **r** and sets $\mathcal{C}$, $\mathcal{F}$, and $\mathcal{U}$ after their update. Attribution of a node to a set is described by a vector with each entry bearing the set index.

Upon the initial coarse space selection, we perform its refinement. To this end, we compute the coefficient η_i using (3) for each fine node $i \in \mathcal{F}$. If the condition $|\eta_i - 1| \leqslant \varkappa$ is violated the point i is added to the candidate set $\mathcal{U}$. We search the maximal independent set in $\mathcal{U}$ with the weights $|\mathcal{E}_i|$, where $\mathcal{E}_i = \{j \in \mathcal{S}_i \cap \mathcal{F} : \mathcal{S}_i \cap \mathcal{S}_j \cap \mathcal{C} = \varnothing\}$.

For the distributed parallel algorithm, if j is a non-local column index, then j-th row of matrix A (for η_i) and strong graph $\mathcal{S}$ should be present on the local processor. To this end, a single-layer overlap of the matrix A should be locally available, whereas $\mathcal{S}_j$ can be computed locally from j-th row of A.

Upon the selection of the maximal independent set, the remaining nodes $i \in \mathcal{U}$ are checked for the condition $|\eta_i - 1| \leqslant \varkappa$. If the condition is satisfied the node is moved from $\mathcal{U}$ to $\mathcal{F}$. If there are remaining nodes in $\mathcal{U}$ we search for the maximum independent set again.

3.3   Gauss–Seidel Smoother

Let $A = L + D + U$, where D is the diagonal matrix and L, U^T are lower-triangular matrices with zero diagonal. Symmetric Gauss–Seidel iteration for the vector $\mathbf{x}^n$ to solve the system $A\mathbf{x} = \mathbf{b}$ is performed in two steps:

$$(L + D)\mathbf{x}^{n+1/2} = \mathbf{b} - U\mathbf{x}^n, \quad (U + D)\mathbf{x}^{n+1} = \mathbf{b} - L\mathbf{x}^{n+1/2},$$

where the forward and backward substitutions with triangular matrices are required.

Following [71] we utilize the doubly-bordered block-diagonal form and use multicolor ordering at the border of the matrix to extract the parallelism, see Fig. 5. In the doubly-bordered block-diagonal form the matrix is separated into a set of independent diagonal blocks and the border. The independent blocks can be eliminated simultaneously, but the border has to be solved sequentially. To this end, multicolor ordering allows to parallelise the solution at the border.

It is not required to assemble reordered matrix, only the sequence of elimination matters.

The doubly-bordered block-diagonal form is naturally available from the matrix distribution across processors. Let $\mathcal{A}$ represent the graph induced by nonzero pattern of the matrix A and $\mathcal{G} = \mathcal{A} + \mathcal{A}^T$ is its symmetrization. To this end, we prescribe the white color to node i if all indices $j \in \mathcal{G}_i$ are local, and black color otherwise. White rows appear in the independent blocks and black rows appear at the border.

The multicoloring at the border is computed by finding the maximal independent set in the graph $\mathcal{G}$ restricted to the black nodes. For the hybrid parallelism independent multicoloring can be computed in each independent block by finding the maximal independent set in the graph $\mathcal{G}$, restricted to white nodes on each processor.

We denote white set by $\mathcal{W}$ and black set by $\mathcal{B}$. Multicoloring of black set $\mathcal{B}$ results in K sets of different colors $\mathcal{B}_k, k \in [1, K]$. White nodes are attributed to $\mathcal{B}_0$.

4   Numerical Experiments

For parallel distributed tests we have used Lomonosov-2 supercomputer [73,74] with Intel Haswell-EP E5-2697v3, 2.6 GHz, 14 cores processors. MPI library for interprocessor communications was used.

In all cases we perform 6 iterations of test vector relaxation. Increasing the number of iterations may improve the convergence but also increases the setup phase cost. Tables contain: T – total solution time in seconds; Ts – total setup phase time; Tit – total time for iterations; Nit – number of iterations; Lvl – number of levels; Mem – memory consumed by the algebraic multigrid structures. Due to dependence of coarse space selection on random numbers, for reproducibility of the results we don't use multiple threads. The convergence tolerances for the bi-conjugate gradient stabilized (BiCGStab) method are $\tau_{\text{abs}} = 10^{-10}$ and $\tau_{\text{rel}} = 10^{-12}$.

4.1   Poisson Systems

First we consider a symmetric system arising from the discretization of the Poisson problem $-\nabla \cdot \nabla p = 0$ with Dirichlet boundary conditions on a 3D structured grid in a unit cube with N^3 elements. For this problem we use point Gauss–Seidel smoother. For αAMG the initial test vector is $\mathbf{x} = \mathbf{1}$.

Coarse Space Refinement. In the first test we demonstrate on a single core the effect of changing parameter $\varkappa$ for a Poisson problem with $N = 100$. The system is of size $1\,000\,000$ with $6\,940\,000$ nonzeroes. There is a trade-off in a number of iterations when using full Ruge–Stüben scheme or more aggressive coarsening. Choosing $\varkappa > 1$ potentially allows for negative parameter α_i in the interpolation weights (4) and thus it is not recommended. The results with the

Table 1. Different $\varkappa$ parameter choice in αAMG method for Poisson system.

$\varkappa$	0	0.1	0.25	0.5	0.75	1	5	10
T	36.2	28.1	23.5	19.1	16.3	15.1	11.4	**10.5**
Ts	23.2	17.8	13.7	10.3	8.9	8.2	4.7	3.8
Tit	13	10.3	9.8	8.8	7.4	6.9	6.7	6.7
Nit	**6**	**6**	7	8	8	8	12	13
Lvl	15	13	14	13	10	10	7	8
Mem	1.59 GB	1.22 GB	913 MB	674 MB	568 MB	518 MB	269 MB	**232** MB

Table 2. Applying AMG and αAMG methods to scaled systems.

	AMG					αAMG				
	A	A_s	A_w	A_m	A_r	A	A_s	A_w	A_m	A_r
T	14	14.4	14.6	14.3	20.4	15.2	16.5	15.4	15.8	15.6
Ts	5.4	5.8	5.9	5.9	5.9	8.3	8.6	8.5	9	8.6
Tit	8.5	8.6	8.7	8.5	14.6	6.9	7.9	6.8	6.9	7
Nit	10	10	10	10	**16**	8	9	8	8	8
Lvl	8	8	9	8	9	10	10	9	10	8
Mem	488 MB	493 MB	502 MB	488 MB	518 MB	518 MB	518 MB	517 MB	518 MB	520 MB

proposed method αAMG and various choice of parameters $\varkappa$ are presented in Table 1.

At $\varkappa = 10$ the coarse space refining was not required. There is no dramatic growth in the number of iterations for large $\varkappa$, but significant reduction of the setup phase time and memory. This is in contrast to the next problem, where an optimum is achieved at $\varkappa = 1$.

Rescaled Systems. We consider four variants of rescaled systems:

- Symmetric scaling $A_s \mathbf{y} = SASy = Sb$, where $\mathbf{x} = S\mathbf{y}$ [62].
- Sinkhorn scaling $A_w \mathbf{y} = D_L A D_R \mathbf{y} = D_L b = b_s$, where $\mathbf{x} = D_R \mathbf{y}$ [75].
- Maximum transversal $A_m \mathbf{y} = D_L A D_R P \mathbf{y} = D_L b$, where $\mathbf{x} = D_R P \mathbf{y}$ [76].
- Random scaling: $A_r \mathbf{y} = D_L A D_R \mathbf{y} = D_L b$, where $D_L = D_R = \text{diag}(r_i)$, where $r_i \in [0.75, 1]$ are random numbers and $\mathbf{x} = D_R \mathbf{y}$.

The comparison of the methods applied to the original system A and modified systems A_s, A_w, A_m, and A_r with the fixed unit test vector $\mathbf{x} = \mathbf{1}$ (AMG), and with test vector refinement (αAMG) are presented in Table 2. Here we use $\varkappa = 1$.

The rescaled Poisson system does not lead to dramatic convergence issues due to equilibrated row and column norms of the original matrix, except for the case with random scaling. This is in a large contrast with the next considered problem, see Table 5. Note, using the bootstrap test vector leads to a slight improvement in the number of iterations with respect to all-unit vector even for the original matrix and improves the convergence for A_r significantly.

Parallel Performance. We present the parallel performance of the method for Poisson system in Table 3, where Np is the number of cores. We use parameter $\varkappa = 1$.

Table 3. Solving Poisson system in parallel using αAMG method.

Np	1	2	4	7	14	28	56	112
T	45.19	39.14	23.63	17.72	15.57	15.17	99.60	34.41
Ts	37.98	33.06	19.81	14.59	12.30	10.98	13.40	16.58
Tit	7.21	6.08	3.82	3.13	3.27	4.18	86.19	17.83
Nit	8	9	9	9	9	9	167	10
Lvl	10	11	12	10	10	11	16	14
Mem	0.98 GB	0.93 GB	0.93 GB	0.94 GB	0.94 GB	0.95 GB	0.98 GB	1.15 GB

One can see that the number of iterations are about the same for almost all number of processors considered. One exceptional case is Np = 56, when the number of iterations is much larger, probably due to instability of BiCGStab convergence. It is interesting to note that when using 55 cores, the number of iterations decreases to 9 again.

The unsatisfactory parallel efficiency of the current implementation of the αAMG method is caused by a large number of exchanges of small size when reducing to a coarse grid. If the grid becomes too small, then the data is duplicated on all processors. The experiments performed showed that in order to increase the parallel efficiency, it is necessary to implement a gradual decrease in the number of processes used at levels with a too coarse grid.

4.2   Mimetic Finite Difference System

The mimetic finite difference method for anisotropic diffusion problem leads to more challenging systems:

$$A \begin{bmatrix} p_c \\ p_f \end{bmatrix} = \begin{bmatrix} D & B \\ B^T & C \end{bmatrix} \begin{bmatrix} p_c \\ p_f \end{bmatrix} = \begin{bmatrix} q \\ 0 \end{bmatrix}, \tag{8}$$

where D is a diagonal matrix corresponding, to the cell-centered pressure unknowns p_c; p_f and q are face-centered pressure unknowns and the right-hand side. We consider an anisotropic diffusion problem $-\nabla \cdot \mathbb{K} \nabla p = 0$ with Neumann boundary conditions on a unit cube with $11 \times 11 \times 11$ elements. Two cubes are extracted and the Dirichlet boundary conditions are prescribed to represent wells.

We consider a fine grid with $99 \times 99 \times 99$ elements. It results in a system with 3 904 281 unknowns and 44 577 664 nonzeroes.

For this problem we use point Gauss–Seidel smoother. For αAMG the initial test vector is $\mathbf{x} = \mathbf{1}$.

Coarse Space Refinement. The results with the proposed method αAMG and various choice of parameters $\varkappa$ are presented in Table 4.

For this problem the optimal balance between setup time, iteration number and iteration cost is achieved at $\varkappa = 1$. The minimal number of iterations is observed at $\varkappa = 0.1$. The memory consumption is almost double with respect to the more aggressive coarsening with $\varkappa = 10$, whence no coarse space refinement is performed.

Table 4. Different $\varkappa$ parameter choice in αAMG method for MFD system.

$\varkappa$	0	0.1	0.25	0.5	0.75	1	5	10
T	665	626.2	467.6	395.6	390.6	**352**	423.9	382
Ts	88.8	84.4	54.1	42.5	37.5	31	17.4	16.9
Tit	576.2	541.8	413.5	353.1	353.1	321.1	406.5	365.2
Nit	55	**54**	65	66	75	82	168	154
Lvl	15	15	12	12	10	10	9	9
Mem	6.2 GB	5.7 GB	3.5 GB	2.7 GB	2.3 GB	1.8 GB	838 MB	**800 MB**

Table 5. Applying AMG and αAMG methods to scaled MFD systems. [‡]Tolerance not met after 15000 iterations.

	AMG					αAMG				
	A	A_s	A_w	A_m	A_r	A	A_s	A_w	A_m	A_r
T	363	54448.5	26040.4	—	1754.9	352	383.9	**328**	596.2	492
Ts	20.6	25.5	25.2	20.5	20.5	31	33.4	33.4	34.6	31.5
Tit	342.4	54423	26065.7	—	1734.4	321.1	350.4	290.6	561.5	460.5
Nit	89	11581	5563	>15000[‡]	447	82	89	**76**	143	115
Lvl	9	17	17	11	11	10	11	10	10	10
Mem	1.8 GB	2.3 GB	2.3 GB	1.8 GB	1.8 GB	1.8 GB	1.8 GB	1.8 GB	1.8 GB	1.8 GB

Table 6. Solving MFD system in parallel using αAMG method.

Np	1	2	4	7	14	28	56	112
T	552.7	541.0	494.0	431.1	213.4	222.0	281.8	714.0
Ts	167.5	163.5	160.6	111.0	59.2	61.4	55.5	57.9
Tit	385.1	377.4	333.4	320.0	154.2	160.5	226.2	656.0
Nit	100	103	93	135	105	102	112	172
Lvl	11	12	12	12	14	12	14	15
Mem	3.77 GB	3.78 GB	3.78 GB	3.79 GB	3.80 GB	3.82 GB	3.87 GB	4.03 GB

Rescaled Systems. The comparison of algebraic multigrid method and proposed method αAMG are presented in Table 5, when applied to the original system A and modified systems A_s, A_w, A_m, and A_r.

Usage of bootstrap test vector allows to recover the convergence of the algebraic multigrid method in all the considered cases. It also slightly accelerates the convergence for the original matrix A. The scaling may also affect the performance of the Gauss–Seidel smoother. An improvement is observed with A_w.

Parallel Performance. The parallel performance of the method is explored in Table 6. The parallel efficiency of the implementation here also turns out to be insufficient, although it should be noted that the setup phase speeds up somewhat better than iterations. Of the positive features, only a slight change in the number of iterations, the number of levels, as well as the total memory costs can be noted.

4.3   Two-Phase Oil Recovery

Finally, we consider a two-phase oil recovery problem using a two-point flux approximation scheme. The mesh is generated from the SPE10 dataset [77] that is characterized by a high anisotropy ratio. The mesh is vertically distorted and the permeability tensor is rotated following the distortion resulting in a full 3×3 permeability tensor. The original dataset has $60 \times 220 \times 85$ dimensions resulting in $1\,122\,000$ cells. We prescribe the wells in the corners of the mesh, i.e. to the cells with the first index and the last index, and assign them well indices 10 and 10 and bottom hole pressures 4500 psi and 3900 psi, respectively. Initial water saturation is $S_w = 0.25$ and pressure $P = 4000$ psi. The detailed oil and water properties are omitted for brevity, see [78] for details. The problem also features rock compressibility, gravity, and capillarity.

The resulting system size is $2\,244\,000$ with $31\,120\,000$ nonzeroes.

We consider the first nonlinear iteration after 10 days of simulation and output the matrix. The comparison of the following solution methods is performed on this matrix, the system is similar to the one, we considered earlier in [28].

The system is composed of the blocks:

$$A \begin{bmatrix} p_o \\ S_w \end{bmatrix} = \begin{bmatrix} A_{pp} & A_{ps} \\ A_{sp} & A_{ss} \end{bmatrix} \begin{bmatrix} p_o \\ S_w \end{bmatrix} = \begin{bmatrix} q_o \\ q_w \end{bmatrix},$$

where p_o is oil pressure, S_w is water saturation, q_o and q_w are right-hand sides for oil and water, respectively. The blocks of the system have the following properties [37]: A is nonsymmetric and indefinite; A_{pp} is a parabolic problem for oil pressure; A_{ps} is the first-order hyperbolic problem for oil saturation; A_{sp} is a parabolic problem for water pressure; A_{ss} is a parabolic problem for water saturation with capillary effects; for small time step size A_{pp}, A_{ps}, and A_{ss} are diagonally dominant. A_{pp} is not purely elliptic due to rock compressibility, furthermore gravity and mobility add convective component into A_{pp} and A_{ps}.

After left scaling by S the system is transferred to

$$S = \begin{bmatrix} I & -D_{ps}D_{ss}^{-1} \\ 0 & I \end{bmatrix}, \quad \begin{bmatrix} B_{pp} & Z_{ps} \\ A_{sp} & A_{ss} \end{bmatrix} \begin{bmatrix} p_o \\ S_w \end{bmatrix} = \begin{bmatrix} q_o - D_{ps}D_{ss}^{-1}q_w \\ q_w \end{bmatrix},$$

where $B_{pp} \equiv A_{pp} - D_{ps}D_{ss}^{-1}A_{ps}$ with

- "true-IMPES": $D_{ps} = \mathrm{colsum}(A_{ps})$, $D_{ss} = \mathrm{colsum}(A_{ss})$,
- "quasi-IMPES": $D_{ps} = \mathrm{diag}(A_{ps})$, $D_{ss} = \mathrm{diag}(A_{ss})$,

and $Z_{ps} \equiv A_{ps} - D_{ps}D_{ss}^{-1}A_{ss} \approx 0$ is assumed, resulting in decoupled system. We also consider S obtained by a more sophisticated dynamic row scaling, "DRS", with the recommended parameters, see [34, 35] for more details.

In this problem, the initial guess for the test vector is $\mathbf{x} = \begin{bmatrix} \mathbf{1}^T & \mathbf{1}^T \cdot 10^{-9} \end{bmatrix}^T$, where $\mathbf{1}$ corresponds to oil pressures and $\mathbf{1} \cdot 10^{-9}$ to water saturations. We first explore applicability of various smoothers in sequential setting. Then we demonstrate distributed solution of the scaled problem with point Gauss–Seidel method.

Solution Strategies. We first consider sequential problem solution with αAMG, where we use two types of smoothers: Gauss–Seidel (GS) and block Gauss-Seidel

Table 7. Solution of the original two-phase oil recovery system. †Tolerance diverged above 10^{10}. ‡Tolerance not met after 15000 iterations. ◇Factorization step requires 6.4 GB. °Factorization step requires 5.6 GB. ♡Factorization step requires 3.7 GB.

	TS-ILUC2	TS-BGS	GS	αAMG-GS	BGS	αAMG-BGS	ILUC2	αAMG-ILUC2
A								
T	334	738	—	—	4274	1344.1	508.3	—
Ts	128.5	8	0.4	15.3	1.6	26.6	122.8	1012
Tit	205.5	730	—	—	4272.5	1317.5	385.4	—
Nit	80	233	2108†	>15000‡	3094	193	430	866†
Lvl	9	9	—	11	—	12	—	15
Mem	3.1 GB◇	793 MB	9 MB	931 MB	9 MB	1.1 GB	2.0 GB◇	6.1 GB◇
A_{QUASI}								
T	**202.6**	967.4	—	494	11747.4	1155.8	428	284.7
Ts	94	7.8	0.2	15.6	1.7	26.8	88.8	193.3
Tit	108.5	959.6	—	478.4	11745.7	1129	340.1	91.37
Nit	44	295	>15000‡	207	7628	161	423	**27**
Lvl	10	10	—	12	—	11	—	11
Mem	2.3 GB°	774 MB	9 MB	945 MB	84 MB	1.2 GB	1.2 GB°	4.4 GB°
A_{TRUE}								
T	903.3	520.6	1688.9	510.7	6132.7	812.5	1229.6	3401.2
Ts	64.1	7.8	0.3	15.3	1.6	26.6	57	160.6
Tit	839.2	512.8	1688.6	495.4	6131.1	786	1172.6	3240.5
Nit	343	164	3374	212	4346	117	1623	977
Lvl	11	11	—	11	—	11	—	11
Mem	2.0 GB♡	793 MB	9 MB	933 MB	97 MB	1.1 GB	834 MB♡	3.8 GB♡
A_{DRS}								
T	543.3	522.3	1997.4	583.5	4085.8	798.4	1129.7	2134.9
Ts	70	7.9	0.3	53.5	1.4	26.7	63.2	168.8
Tit	473.3	514.4	1997.1	529.99	4084.3	771.7	1066.6	1966
Nit	192	163	3984	221	2898	115	1462	594
Lvl	10	10	—	10	—	11	—	12
Mem	2.0 GB♡	793 MB	9 MB	1.1 GB	97 MB	1.1 GB	834 MB♡	3.9 GB♡

(BGS), inverse-based second-order incomplete Crout-LU factorization with maximum transversal preordering and scaling (ILUC2). In BGS blocks are identified automatically as in [79]. In ILUC2 the dropping tolerances are $\tau_1 = 5 \cdot 10^{-2}$ and $\tau_2 = \tau_1^2 = 2.5 \cdot 10^{-3}$ and additionally 12 iterations are preformed to improve I-dominance [76]. The CPR-scaled system was shown to be easier to solve [28]. To this end, we consider either original system A and pre-scaled systems A_{QUASI}, A_{TRUE} and A_{DRS} scaled using "quasi-IMPES", "true-IMPES" CPR methods and "DRS" method, respectively. For comparison we consider two stage (TS) strategy that applies adaptive algebraic multigrid to pressure block and either ILUC2 or BGS as a preconditioner for the entire system. At the lowest level of algebraic multigrid we use direct LU factorization with full pivoting. The results for the problem with 1 million cells are presented in Table 7.

It follows that the point Gauss–Seidel smoother is a poor choice for the system in question. Therefore, it fails to reduce the norm of the test vector during iterations, and does not produce appropriate approximation to the test vector for αAMG. On the other hand, it is able to address the scaled systems and performs the best on A_{TRUE}. Block Gauss–Seidel method is applicable to the original system, albeit it performs less efficient with the rescaled system, it turns out a better smoother within algebraic multigrid method. Its distributed implementation is out of scope of the present work. In terms of the number of iterations the best is adaptive multigrid with incomplete factorization as a smoother applied to A_{QUASI}, which required only 27 iterations to converge. In terms of time the fastest is two stage strategy, applied to A_{QUASI}, with incomplete factorization as a first stage preconditioner. The complexity of the incomplete factorization does not scale linearly and the memory requirement is substantial. Neither maximal transversal nor incomplete factorization methods are trivial to parallelise. On the other hand, block Gauss–Seidel is either able to serve as a first stage preconditioner in two stage strategy. It appears even more efficient than the incomplete factorization for A_{DRS}. In all cases there are less iterations when block Gauss–Seidel is a smoother for adaptive algebraic multigrid rather then within the two stage strategy. To this end, we further consider point Gauss–Seidel method with the CPR-scaled system for the distributed tests. It follows that the multigrid method is applicable without CPR-scaling, given that a capable smoother is provided.

Parallel Implementation. Parallel implementation of the αAMG method for two-phase flow problems is not fundamentally difficult; the main stages have already been described above. At present, we continue to work on an efficient parallel code and plan to present the results of a parallel solution of this problem elsewhere.

5   Conclusions

In this work we implemented a distributed parallel bootstrap adaptive algebraic multigrid method. We introduce our strong-weak decomposition of connections with account of test vector, which influences the coarse space selection and parameterise the coarse space refinement process based on the coefficient in the interpolation. We demonstrate the method efficiency, as well as its ability to solve rescaled elliptic systems and complex coupled system of two-phase oil recovery in a monolithic way.

In the further work, we shall consider block variant of the method. This includes automatic block detection, parallel block Gauss–Seidel smoother, multiple orthogonal test vectors and extension of the strong-weak decoupling of connections to blocks. The block version of adaptive algebraic multigrid method may prove to be an appropriate way to solve coupled systems with the monolithic algebraic multigrid method. Another direction is to explore unsymmetric restriction operator and more complex coupled systems, originating from three-phase black-oil, incompressible elasticity, poroelasticity, incompressible fluid flow.

Acknowledgements. This work has been supported by Russian Science Foundation grant 21-71-20024. The research is carried out using the equipment of the shared research facilities of HPC computing resources at Lomonosov Moscow State University.

References

1. Fedorenko, R.P.: A relaxation method for solving elliptic difference equations. Zh. Vychisl. Mat. Mat. Fiz. **1**(5), 922–927 (1961). Comput. Math. Math. Phys. **1**(4), 1092–1096 (1962)
2. Fedorenko, R.P.: The speed of convergence of one iterative process. USSR Comput. Math. Math. Phys. **4**(3), 227–235 (1964)
3. Bakhvalov, N.S.: On the convergence of a relaxation method with natural constraints on the elliptic operator. USSR Comput. Math. Math. Phys. **6**(5), 101–135 (1996)
4. Fedorenko, R.P.: Iterative methods for elliptic difference equations. Russ. Math. Surv. **28**, 129–195 (1973)
5. Brandt, A., McCormick, S., Ruge, J.: Algebraic multigrid (AMG) for automatic algorithm design and problem solution. Report, Comp. Studies, Colorado State University, Ft. Collins (1982)
6. Hackbusch, W.: Multi-grid Methods and Applications, vol. 4. Springer, Heidelberg (2013/1985). https://doi.org/10.1007/978-3-662-02427-0
7. Hülsemann, F., Kowarschik, M., Mohr, M., Rüde, U.: Parallel geometric multigrid. In: Bruaset, A.M., Tveito, A. (eds.) Numerical Solution of Partial Differential Equations on Parallel Computers. LNCSE, vol. 51, pp. 165–208. Springer, Heidelberg (2006). https://doi.org/10.1007/3-540-31619-1_5
8. Ruge, J.W., Stüben, K.: Algebraic multigrid. In: Multigrid Methods, pp. 73–130. SIAM (1987)
9. Stüben, K.: A review of algebraic multigrid. In: Numerical Analysis: Historical Developments in the 20th Century, pp. 331–359 (2001)
10. Stüben, K., Ruge, J.W., Clees, T., Gries, S.: Algebraic multigrid: from academia to industry. In: Griebel, M., Schüller, A., Schweitzer, M.A. (eds.) Scientific Computing and Algorithms in Industrial Simulations, pp. 83–119. Springer, Cham (2017). https://doi.org/10.1007/978-3-319-62458-7_5
11. HYPRE: Scalable Linear Solvers and Multigrid Methods. https://computing.llnl.gov/projects/hypre
12. PETSc - Portable, Extensible Toolkit for Scientific Computation. https://www.mcs.anl.gov/petsc
13. Trilinos - platform for the solution of large-scale, complex multi-physics engineering and scientific problems. http://trilinos.org/
14. AMGCL - a header-only C++ library for solving with AMG method. https://amgcl.readthedocs.io/en/latest/index.html
15. SAMG (Algebraic Multigrid Methods for Systems) - Efficiently solving large linear systems of equations. https://www.scai.fraunhofer.de/en/business-research-areas/fast-solvers/products/samg.html
16. Naumov, M., Arsaev, M., Castonguay, P., Cohen, J., Demouth, J., et al.: AmgX: a library for GPU accelerated algebraic multigrid and preconditioned iterative methods. SIAM J. Sci. Comput. **37**(5), S602–S626 (2015)
17. PARALUTION - Library for Iterative Sparse Methods. https://www.paralution.com/
18. Manteuffel, T.A., Münzenmaier, S., Ruge, J., Southworth, B.: Nonsymmetric reduction-based algebraic multigrid. SIAM J. Sci. Comput. **41**(5), S242–S268 (2019)
19. Brezina, M., Falgout, R., MacLachlan, S., Manteuffel, T., McCormick, S., Ruge, J.: Adaptive algebraic multigrid. SIAM J. Sci. Comput. **27**(4), 1261–1286 (2006)

20. Brannick, J., Frommer, A., Kahl, K., MacLachlan, S., Zikatanov, L.: Adaptive reduction-based multigrid for nearly singular and highly disordered physical systems. Electron. Trans. Numer. Anal. **37**, 276–295 (2010)
21. Brezina, M., Ketelsen, Ch., Manteuffel, T., McCormick, S., Park, M., Ruge, J.: Relaxation-corrected bootstrap algebraic multigrid (rBAMG). Numer. Linear Algebra Appl. **19**(2), 178–193 (2012)
22. Franceschini, A., Magri, V., Paludetto, A., Mazzucco, G., Spiezia, N., Janna, C.: A robust adaptive algebraic multigrid linear solver for structural mechanics. Comput. Meth. Appl. Mech. Eng. **352**, 389–416 (2019)
23. Brandt, A., Brannick, J., Kahl, K., Livshits, I.: Bootstrap AMG. SIAM J. Sci. Comput. **33**(2), 612–632 (2011)
24. Brandt, A., Brannick, J., Kahl, K., Livshits, I.: Bootstrap algebraic multigrid: status report, open problems, and outlook. Numer. Math.: Theory Methods Appl. **8**(1), 112–135 (2015)
25. D'Ambra, P., Vassilevski, P.S.: Compatible matching adaptive AMG (α−AMG) preconditioners for Laplacian matrices on general graphs. Technical report, LLNL-TR-676601 (2015)
26. D'ambra, P., Filippone, S., Vassilevski, P.S.: BootCMatch: a software package for bootstrap AMG based on graph weighted matching. ACM Trans. Math. Softw. **44**(4), 1–25 (2018)
27. D'Ambra, P., Cutillo, L., Vassilevski, P.S.: Bootstrap AMG for spectral clustering. Comput. Math. Methods **1**(2), e1020 (2019)
28. Konshin, I., Terekhov, K.: Sparse system solution methods for complex problems. In: Malyshkin, V. (ed.) PaCT 2021. LNCS, vol. 12942, pp. 53–73. Springer, Cham (2021). https://doi.org/10.1007/978-3-030-86359-3_5
29. Shu, S., Liu, M., Xu, X., Yue, X., Li, S.: Algebraic multigrid block triangular preconditioning for multidimensional three-temperature radiation diffusion equations. Adv. Appl. Math. Mech. **13**(5), 0210–1226 (2021)
30. Gries, S.: System-AMG approaches for industrial fully and adaptive implicit oil reservoir simulations. Dissertation. Universität zu Köln (2015)
31. Gries, S.: On the convergence of System-AMG in reservoir simulation. SPE J. **23**(2), 589–597 (2018)
32. Cusini, M., Lukyanov, A., Natvig, J.R., Hajibeygi, H.: A constrained pressure residual multiscale (CPR-MS) compositional solver. In: Proceedings of ECMOR XIV-14th European Conference on the Mathematics of Oil Recovery, Catania, Sicily, Italy (2014)
33. Lacroix, S., Vassilevski, Y.V., Wheeler, M.F.: Decoupling preconditioners in the implicit parallel accurate reservoir simulator (IPARS). Numer. Lin. Alg. Appl. **8**(8), 537–549 (2001)
34. Gries, S.: System-AMG approaches for industrial fully and adaptive implicit oil reservoir simulations. Ph.D. thesis. Der Universität zu Köln, Köln (2016)
35. Kayum, S., Cancellierei, M., Rogowski, M., Al-Zawawi, A.: Application of algebraic multigrid in fully implicit massive reservoir simulations. In: Proceedings of SPE Europec Featured at 81st EAGE Conference and Exhibition. SPE-195472-MS (2019)
36. Gries, S.: Algebraic wavefront parallelization for ILU(0) smoothing in reservoir simulation. ECMOR XVII **1**, 1–17 (2020)
37. Bui, Q.M., Elman, H.C., Moulton, J.D.: Algebraic multigrid preconditioners for multiphase flow in porous media. SIAM J. Sci. Comput. **39**(5), 5662–5680 (2017)

38. Bui, Q.M., Wang, L., Osei-Kuffuor, D.: Algebraic multigrid preconditioners for two-phase flow in porous media with phase transitions. Adv. Water Resour. **114**, 19–28 (2018)
39. Gries, S., Metsch, B., Terekhov, K.M., Tomin, P.: System-AMG for fully coupled reservoir simulation with geomechanics. In: SPE Reservoir Simulation Conference (2019)
40. Bui, Q.M., Osei-Kuffuor, D., Castelletto, N., White, J.A.: A scalable multigrid reduction framework for multiphase poromechanics of heterogeneous media. SIAM J. Sci. Comput. **42**(2), 8379–8396 (2020)
41. Terekhov, K.M.: Cell-centered finite-volume method for heterogeneous anisotropic poromechanics problem. J. Comput. Appl. Math. **365**, 112357 (2020)
42. Terekhov, K.M., Vassilevski, Yu.V.: Finite volume method for coupled subsurface flow problems, II: poroelasticity. J. Comput. Phys. **462**, 111225 (2022)
43. Jenny, P., Lee, S.H., Tchelepi, H.A.: Multi-scale finite-volume method for elliptic problems in subsurface flow simulation. J. Comput. Phys. **187**(1), 47–67 (2003)
44. Efendiev, Y., Hou, T.Y., Ginting, V.: Multiscale finite element methods for nonlinear problems and their applications. Commun. Math. Sci. **2**(4), 553–589 (2004)
45. Pergament, A.Kh., Semiletov, V.A., Zaslavsky, M.Yu.: Multiscale averaging algorithms for flow modeling in heterogeneous reservoir. In: ECMOR X-10th European Conference on the Mathematics of Oil Recovery, p. 23 (2006)
46. Hajibeygi, H., Jenny, P.: Multiscale finite-volume method for parabolic problems arising from compressible multiphase flow in porous media. J. Comput. Phys. **228**(14), 5129–5147 (2009)
47. Tomin, P., Lunati, I.: Hybrid multiscale finite volume method for two-phase flow in porous media. J. Comput. Phys. **250**, 293–307 (2013)
48. Hajibeygi, H., Jenny, P.: Adaptive iterative multiscale finite volume method. J. Comput. Phys. **230**(3), 628–643 (2011)
49. Sokolova, I.V., Hajibeygi, H.: Multiscale finite volume method for finite-volume-based poromechanics simulations. ECMOR XVI **1**, 1–13 (2018)
50. Castelletto, N., Klevtsov, S., Hajibeygi, H., Tchelepi, H.A.: Multiscale two-stage solver for Biot's poroelasticity equations in subsurface media. Comput. Geosci. **23**(2), 207–224 (2019)
51. Wang, Y., Hajibeygi, H., Tchelepi, H.A.: Algebraic multiscale solver for flow in heterogeneous porous media. J. Comput. Phys. **259**, 284–303 (2014)
52. Cusini, M., van Kruijsdijk, C., Hajibeygi, H.: Algebraic dynamic multilevel (ADM) method for fully implicit simulations of multiphase flow in porous media. J. Comput. Phys. **314**, 60–79 (2016)
53. Bosma, S., Hajibeygi, H., Tene, M., Tchelepi, H.A.: Multiscale finite volume method for discrete fracture modeling on unstructured grids (MS-DFM). J. Comput. Phys. **351**, 145–164 (2017)
54. Saad, Y., Suchomel, B.: ARMS: an algebraic recursive multilevel solver for general sparse linear systems. Numer. Lin. Algebra Appl. **9**(5), 359–378 (2002)
55. Li, Z., Saad, Y., Sosonkina, M.: pARMS: a parallel version of the algebraic recursive multilevel solver. Numer. Lin. Algebra Appl. **5–6**, 485–509 (2003)
56. Bollhöfer, M., Schenk, O., Verbosio, F.: A high performance level-block approximate LU factorization preconditioner algorithm. Appl. Numer. Math. **162**, 265–282 (2021)
57. Kaporin, I.E.: Multilevel ILU preconditionings for general unsymmetric matrices. In: Numerical Geometry, Grid Generation, and Highperformance Computing (2008)

58. Kuznetsov, Y.A.: Algebraic multigrid domain decomposition methods. Russ. J. Numer. Anal. Math. Model. **4**(5), 351–379 (1989)
59. Terekhov, K.: Parallel multilevel linear solver within INMOST platform. In: Voevodin, V., Sobolev, S. (eds.) RuSCDays 2020. CCIS, vol. 1331, pp. 297–309. Springer, Cham (2020). https://doi.org/10.1007/978-3-030-64616-5_26
60. Li, N., Saad, Y., Chow, E.: Crout versions of ILU for general sparse matrices. SIAM J. Sci. Comput. **25**(2), 716–728 (2003)
61. Kaporin, I.E.: High quality preconditioning of a general symmetric positive definite matrix based on its $U^T U + U^T R + R^T U$-decomposition. Numer. Lin. Algebra Appl. **5**(6), 483–509 (1998)
62. Kaporin, I.E.: Scaling, reordering, and diagonal pivoting in ILU preconditionings. Russ. J. Numer. Anal. Math. Model. **22**(4), 341–375 (2007)
63. Bollhöfer, M.: A robust ILU with pivoting based on monitoring the growth of the inverse factors. Lin. Algebra Appl. **338**(1–3), 201–218 (2001)
64. Bollhöfer, M.: A robust and efficient ILU that incorporates the growth of the inverse triangular factors. SIAM J. Sci. Comput. **25**(1), 86–103 (2003)
65. Bollhöfer, M., Saad, Y.: Multilevel preconditioners constructed from inverse-based ILUs. SIAM J. Sci. Comput. **27**(5), 1627–1650 (2006)
66. Bollhöfer, M., Grote, M.J., Schenk, O.: Algebraic multilevel preconditioner for the Helmholtz equation in heterogeneous media. SIAM J. Sci. Comput. **31**(5), 3781–3805 (2009)
67. Chen, Q., Ghai, A., Jiao, X.: HILUCSI: simple, robust, and fast multilevel ILU for large-scale saddle-point problems from PDEs. Numer. Lin. Algebra Appl. **28**(6), e2400 (2021)
68. Aliaga, J.I., Bollhöfer, M., Martín, A.F., Quintana-Ortí, E.S.: Parallelization of multilevel ILU preconditioners on distributed-memory multiprocessors. In: Jónasson, K. (ed.) PARA 2010. LNCS, vol. 7133, pp. 162–172. Springer, Heidelberg (2012). https://doi.org/10.1007/978-3-642-28151-8_16
69. Kaporin, I.E., Konshin, I.N.: Parallel solution of large sparse SPD linear systems based on overlapping domain decomposition. In: Malyshkin, V. (ed.) PaCT 1999. LNCS, vol. 1662, pp. 436–446. Springer, Heidelberg (1999). https://doi.org/10.1007/3-540-48387-X_45
70. Terekhov, K.: Greedy dissection method for shared parallelism in incomplete factorization within INMOST platform. In: Voevodin, V., Sobolev, S. (eds.) RuSCDays 2021. CCIS, vol. 1510, pp. 87–101. Springer, Cham (2021). https://doi.org/10.1007/978-3-030-92864-3_7
71. Koester, D.P., Ranka, S., Fox, G.C.: A parallel Gauss-Seidel algorithm for sparse power system matrices. In: Supercomputing 1994: Proceedings of the 1994 ACM/IEEE Conference on Supercomputing, pp. 184–193 (1994)
72. Luby, M.: A simple parallel algorithm for the maximal independent set problem. SIAM J. Comput. **15**(4), 1036–1053 (1986)
73. Voevodin, Vl.V., Antonov, A.S., Nikitenko, D.A., Shvets, P.A., Sobolev, S.I., et al.: Supercomputer Lomonosov-2: large scale, deep monitoring and fine analytics for the user community. Supercomput. Front. Innov. **6**(2), 4–11 (2019)
74. Sadovnichy, V., Tikhonravov, A., Voevodin, Vl., Opanasenko, V.: Lomonosov: supercomputing at Moscow state university. In: Contemporary High Performance Computing, pp. 283–307. Chapman and Hall/CRC (2017)
75. Sinkhorn, R.: Diagonal equivalence to matrices with prescribed row and column sums, II. Proc. Am. Math. Soc. **45**, 195–198 (1974)
76. Olschowka, M., Arnold, N.: A new pivoting strategy for Gaussian elimination. Lin. Algebra Appl. **240**, 131–151 (1996)

77. SPE10 distorted grid generator. https://github.com/kirill-terekhov/spe10grdecl
78. Nikitin, K., Terekhov, K., Vassilevski, Y.: A monotone nonlinear finite volume
    method for diffusion equations and multiphase flows. Comput. Geosci. **18**(3–4),
    311–324 (2014)
79. Bollhöfer, M., Schenk, O., Verbosio, F.: High performance block incomplete LU
    factorization. arXiv preprint arXiv:1908.10169 (2019)

GPU-Based Algorithm for Numerical Simulation of CO_2 Sorption

Tatyana Khachkova, Vadim Lisitsa$^{(\boxtimes)}$ (iD), Vladimir Derevschikov,
and Yaroslav Bazaikin

Institute of Mathematics SB RAS, Koptyug ave. 4, Novosibirsk 630090, Russia
lisitsavv@ipgg.sbras.ru

Abstract. In this article, we propose an original algorithm for numerical
simulation of the conjugated reactive transport. The algorithm is essentially oriented toward the use of GPUs. We simulate the CO_2 chemosorption by soda-lime sorbent, assuming a multi-scale process. Macropore
space supports both advective and diffusive transport of the reactive
species, whereas impermeable microporous sorbent granules admit diffusion as the only transport mechanism. We simulated CO_2 pass-through
an evenly distributed granules illustrating agreement with lab measurements. We also studied the CO_2 break-through rates in dependence of
sorbent granules compaction in the reactor.

Keywords: Reactive transport · Chemosorption · Finite differences ·
GPU

1 Introduction

Chemical sorption of CO_2 from gas mixtures is an actual problem in chemical
engineering with a wide range of applications, including inhalation anesthesia
and respiratory care in medicine, underwater diving gear, marine rescue equipment, fire safety devices, and others. One of the most commonly used CO_2
sorbent is the solid soda-lime, which reacts as follows: $Ca(OH)_2 + CO_2 \rightarrow$
$CaCO_3 \downarrow +H_2O$. The efficiency of the sorption is affected by several factors,
such as the shape and size of the sorbent granules, the porosity of the material and inter-granular porosity or granules compaction in the reactive chamber,
specific surface of the packed granules, gas flow rate, CO_2 concentration, temperature, humidity, presence of other pollutants, etc. [1]. Optimization of these
parameters requires numerous time-consuming laboratory experiments.

On the contrary, computational fluid dynamics (CFD) in combination with
multi-scale conjugated reactive transport (advection-diffusion-reaction equation
(ADR)) allows for performing numerical experiments with varying input parameters in a routine manner. Nowadays, there are several commercial and free
software allowing for CFD and ADR simulation, such as Comsol, FreeFEM, and
others. However, they are mainly based on finite element solvers, which require a

V. Voevodin et al. (Eds.): RuSCDays 2022, LNCS 13708, pp. 112–126, 2022.
https://doi.org/10.1007/978-3-031-22941-1_8

detailed description of the model geometry to generate a grid. Thus, it is getting troublesome to perform simulations for randomly generated granule packing, complex granules shapes, etc. Moreover, finite element implementation of the conjugate reactive transport requires explicit flow and transport coupling at the interfaces of each granule assuming a free flow in the interparticle space and filtration flow inside the particles. Instead, we focused on the finite difference solvers to simulate both reactive transport and fluid flow. To follow the complex interface geometry it's applied the level-set method [2,3] in combination with the immersed boundary conditions [4], which allows easy change in the geometry of the model, including the particle packing, size, and shape.

Note, that due to the computational intensity of the direct CFD-based simulations of the chemical reactors, the problem is typically split into two almost independent steps. First, the averaged reaction rates are estimated by solving the diffusion-reaction equation for a single sorbent particle. Second, CFD-based simulation is implemented under the assumption of Darcy flow inside the reactor [5]. In opposite to this workflow, we present the algorithm implemented using CUDA technology, which allows directly simulating CO_2 chemisorption in a typical inhalation anesthesia machine using a single GPU. To demonstrate how the approach should be used, we provide the study of the CO_2 break-through time in dependence on the packing of the particles.

2   Statement of the Problem

We define the model (reactor) as a cylindrical domain $D_0 = \{0 \le x_1 \le X, x_3^2 + x_3^2 \le R^2\}$, where X is the reactor length and R is the reactor radius. Inside the domain D_0 we consider two non-overlapping multiply-connected subdomains D_g and D_p, so that $D_0 = D_g \cup D_p$. Domain D_g represents the space occupied by the granules where the media is assumed as microporous. Domain D_p represents the macropores or inter-granular pores where the free fluid flow is considered. In this research, we assume, that micropores do not keep up the fluid flow; i.e., the permeability of the microporous space is set to zero. Thus, the only mechanism of reactive transport in the microporous space is diffusion. On the contrary, macro-pores support the fluid flow and free molecular diffusion in the fluid.

In our research, we assume the fluid's physical characteristics are unaffected by the concentration of active species, the process is isotermal and the geometry of the model is fixed. Thus, we may consider the steady-state fluid flow, satisfying Stokes formulas:

$$\begin{aligned}
\nabla p - \mu \Delta \vec{u} &= 0, \ \vec{x} \in D_p, \\
\nabla \cdot \vec{u} &= 0, \quad \vec{x} \in D_p, \\
\vec{u} &= 0, \quad \vec{x} \in D_g,
\end{aligned} \tag{1}$$

where u is the velocity of fluid, p is the pressure, μ is fluid viscosity. We do not consider Darcy flow in the microporous space, which allows us to avoid using Stokes-Brinkmann equation [19]. Thus, the problem of the fluid flow simulation can be reformulated as follows: seek for velocity and pressure field inside domain D_g satisfying the boundary-value problem:

$$
\begin{aligned}
\nabla p - \mu \Delta \vec{u} &= 0, & \vec{x} &\in D_p, \\
\nabla \cdot \vec{u} &= 0, & \vec{x} &\in D_p, \\
\int_{x_2, x_3} v_1(0, x_2, x_3) dx_2 dx_3 &= Q_{in}, & x_1 &= 0, \\
p(X, x_2, x_3) &= p^{out}, & x_1 &= X, \\
\vec{u} &= 0, & \vec{x} &\in \partial D_p / (x_1 = x_1^{in} \cup x_1 = x_1^{out}),
\end{aligned} \tag{2}
$$

where ∂D_p is the macroporous space's boundary.

To simulate reactive transfer we use the advection-diffusion-reaction (ADR) equation which is valid in either micro- and macroporous space:

$$
\frac{\partial}{\partial t} (\phi C_j) + \nabla \cdot (\vec{u} C_j) - \nabla \cdot (D \nabla C_j) = g_j. \tag{3}
$$

In these notations, ϕ is the micro-porosity, C_j is the species's molar concentration, D is the coefficient of effective diffusion, and g_j is the exterior term caused by the chemical process. We assume a free flow in the macroporous space; thus, we state $\phi = 1$, the free-flow rate $\vec{u} \neq 0$, and the molecular diffusion coefficient for species in the fluid $D = D_0$. In the micro-porous space, porosity is less than one and will be specified below, the flow rate is zero, and the diffusion coefficient is $D = \phi D_0 / F$, where the formation factor F characterize the geometry of the microporous space [6]. Typical values of form factor are $F \in [1; 10]$.

Consider the chemical interaction between the soda-lime sorbent and CO_2:

$$
Ca(OH)_2 + CO_2 \rightarrow CaCO_3 \downarrow + H_2O. \tag{4}
$$

Among the presented species CO_2 and H_2O are mobile species, which satisfy the ADR equation, whereas $Ca(OH)_2$ and $CaCO_3$ are solids and assumed to be immobile and the reaction is the only mechanism of concentration evolution. The considered reaction is the first-order reaction, thus its kinetics can be represented as:

$$
g_j = \pm k C_{CO_2} C_{Ca(OH)_2},
$$

where plus sign corresponds to products of the reaction and minus sign corresponds to the reactants. The reaction rate k is assumed constant in this research due to assumption of isothermal reaction. Taking everything into account one may state the entire system of ADR equations for the considered process:

$$
\begin{aligned}
\frac{\partial}{\partial t} (\phi C_{CO_2}) + \nabla \cdot (\vec{u} C_{CO_2}) - \nabla \cdot (D_{CO_2} \nabla C_{CO_2}) &= -k\phi C_{CO_2} C_{Ca(OH)_2}, \\
\frac{\partial}{\partial t} (\phi C_{H_2O}) + \nabla \cdot (\vec{u} C_{H_2O}) - \nabla \cdot (D_{H_2O} \nabla C_{H_2O}) &= k\phi C_{CO_2} C_{Ca(OH)_2}, \\
\frac{\partial}{\partial t} \left(C_{Ca(OH)_2} \right) &= -k\phi C_{CO_2} C_{Ca(OH)_2}, \\
\frac{\partial}{\partial t} \left(C_{CaCO_3} \right) &= k\phi C_{CO_2} C_{Ca(OH)_2}.
\end{aligned} \tag{5}
$$

We also need to state the initial and boundary conditions to close the equations. The initial conditions are

$$
\begin{array}{ll}
C_{CO_2}(0, \vec{x}) = 0, & \vec{x} \in D_p \cup D_g, \\
C_{H_2O}(0, \vec{x}) = 0, & \vec{x} \in D_p \cup D_g, \\
C_{Ca(OH)_2}(0, \vec{x}) = 0, & \vec{x} \in D_p, \\
C_{Ca(OH)_2}(0, \vec{x}) = C_{Ca(OH)_2}^0, & \vec{x} \in D_g, \\
C_{CaCO_3}(0, \vec{x}) = 0, & \vec{x} \in D_p, \\
C_{CaCO_3}(0, \vec{x}) = C_{CaCO_3}^0, & \vec{x} \in D_g,
\end{array}
\tag{6}
$$

which means that no CO_2 or water initially existing in the system, while the solid species present in their initial concentrations in the sorbent granules.

The boundary conditions should be imposed for the mobile species only:

$$
\begin{array}{ll}
C_{CO_2} = C_{CO_2}^{in}, & x_1 = 0, \\
\frac{\partial C_{CO_2}}{\partial \vec{n}} = 0, & \vec{x} \in x_1 = X \cup S_{ext}, \\
C_{H_2O} = C_{H_2O}^{in} = 0, & x_1 = 0, \\
\frac{\partial C_{H_2O}}{\partial \vec{n}} = 0, & \vec{x} \in x_1 = X \cup S_{ext},
\end{array}
\tag{7}
$$

where S_{ext} corresponds to the sides of the reactor; i.e., $S_{ext} = x_2^2 + x_3^2 - R^2$.

Formally, we provided the system of ADR equations for the entire system, however, we assumed that the coefficients of the equations do not depend on the solution. Thus, the presence of H_2O does not affect considered reactive transport, and the H_2O transport equation can be excluded from the considerations.

3   Numerical Methods

As we mentioned before, we use finite difference scheme to simulate both the fluid flow and the reactive transport. However, the geometry of the model may be complex enough, so a straightforward projection of the model to a regular cuboid mesh may cause a high error. To overcome this effect we suggest use the level-set approach in combination with the immersed boundary conditions.

3.1   Level-Set

Level-set approach is used for the implicit representation of complex surface [3] using a regular grid. Moreover, it allows simulating the evolution of the surface including topology changes. Application of the level-set to fluid-solid interaction is presented in [7], to multi-phase fluid flow is provided in [8], and to chemical fluid-solid interaction is presented in [9,10]. In our research, we need to introduce two level-sets. One defines the entire reactor; i.e., the domain D. This level-set is denoted as φ^e and it satisfies the relations

$$
\varphi^e(\vec{x}) : \begin{cases} \varphi^e(\vec{x}) > 0, \vec{x} \in D, \\ \varphi^e(\vec{x}) < 0, \vec{x} \notin D, \end{cases}
$$

Typically, the signed distance to interface is used to determine the level-set. Note, that we assume the reactor is a tube with radius R; thus, level-set $\varphi^e(\vec{x})$ can be constructed analytically:

$$\varphi^e(\vec{x}) = sign(x_2^2 + x_3^2 - R^2)\sqrt{|x_2^2 + x_3^2 - R^2|}.$$

This level-set will be needed to properly simulate the reactive transport, stating the boundary conditions (7).

The second level-set is applied to model fluid movement in a macroporous area, thus we require

$$\varphi^p(\vec{x}) : \begin{cases} \varphi^p(\vec{x}) > 0, \vec{x} \in D_p, \\ \varphi^p(\vec{x}) < 0, \vec{x} \notin D_p. \end{cases}$$

The construction of this level-set is more complex and will be described below.

Note, that we consider stationary domains D_g and D and we need to construct both level-set only at the preliminary steps. Moreover, in the particular implementation of the algorithm, we use this level-set as the input parameters.

3.2   Stokes Equation

We use standard staggered grid scheme to approximate Stokes equation (1) in the domain D_p. The grid has integer and half-integer grid points, so that $(x_1)_i = ih_1$ and $(x_1)_{i+1/2} = (i + 1/2)h_1$, where h_1 is the grid step in x_1 direction. By reversing the function of the spatial indices, grid points may be produced along the other two spatial directions. After that one may introduce the grid cell $C_{i,j,k} = [(x_1)_{i-1/2}, (x_1)_{i+1/2}] \times [(x_2)_{j-1/2}, (x_2)_{j+1/2}] \times [(x_3)_{k-1/2}, (x_3)_{k+1/2}]$. The components of the velocity vector are set at the centers of cell sides, whereas the pressure is specified in the centers of the cells; for example $(u_1)_{i+1/2,j,k} = u_1((i + 1/2)h_1, jh_2, kh_3)$. Also, level-sets are defined in the grid cell centers.

Approximation of Stokes equation on a staggered grid is

$$\begin{aligned}
\mu L[u_1]_{i+1/2,j,k} - D_1^c[p]_{i+1/2,j,k} &= 0, & if \ \varphi_{i+1/2,j,k}^p &> 0, \\
\mu L[u_2]_{i,j+1/2,k} - D_2^c[p]_{i,j+1/2,} &= 0, & if \ \varphi_{i,j+1/2,k}^p &> 0, \\
\mu L[u_3]_{i,j,k+1/2} - D_3^c[p]_{i,j,k+1/2} &= 0, & if \ \varphi_{i,j,k+1/2}^p &> 0, \\
D_1^c[u_1]_{i,j,k} + D_2^c[u_2]_{i,j,k} + D_3^c[u_3]_{i,j,k} &= 0, & if \ \varphi_{i,j,k}^p &> 0.
\end{aligned} \tag{8}$$

Here the Laplace operator's approximation is

$$L[f]_{I,J,K} = D_1^2[f]_{I,J,K} + D_2^2[f]_{I,J,K} + D_2^2[f]_{I,J,K}, \tag{9}$$

where

$$D_1^2[f]_{I,J,K} = \frac{f_{I+1,J,K} - 2f_{I,J,K} + f_{I,J,K}}{h_1^2} = \left.\frac{\partial^2 f}{\partial x_1^2}\right|_{I,J,K} + O(h_1^2), \tag{10}$$

and the approximation of the divergence operator's j-th component

$$D_1^c[f]_{I,J,K} = \frac{f_{I+1,J,K} - f_{I,J-1/2,K}}{h_1} = \left.\frac{\partial f}{\partial x_1}\right|_{I,J,K} + O(h_1^2). \tag{11}$$

In this case, the indices I, J and K may all be integers or half-integers, but i, j and k are the only integers. The permutations of the function of spatial indices can be used to get the operators for approximation of derivatives with regard to the other spatial direction.

We solve Eq. (1) in the macroporous space D_p and need to apply the immersed boundary condition approach at the interface $\varphi^g = 0$. At this interface, we must resolve the equation $\vec{u} = 0$, and due to the use of the projection method in order to solve the Stokes equation we need to apply the condition $\frac{\partial p}{\partial \tilde{n}} = 0$. The idea of the immersed boundary condition is the extrapolation of the solution to such points outside of D which are used by the finite difference scheme when computing the solution inside D. To do so, one needs to compute the distance between the point and the interface as well as its normal direction. Both these values can be calculated using the level-set; indeed by the construction φ^g is the distance with sign to the interface, and the normal direction is just $\vec{n} = \nabla \varphi^d$. Details of the immersed boundary condition implementation can be found in [9, 11–13].

To solve the Stokes equation, we use the projection technique [14] to get the steady-state solution for time-dependent Navier-Stokes equation. According to this technique, the Poisson equation for pressure must be solved, which may be done effectively by employing Krylov-type methods with the proper preconditioner [6], that are founded on the pseudo-spectral approximation [15].

3.3   The Solution of the Equations of Advection-Diffusion-Reaction

The equations of advection-diffusion-reaction are solved using the first-order splitting scheme, which can be represented as the AD-R scheme. It means that at each time instant we solve advection-diffusion first and then correct it by resolving the reactive part. To approximate the AD equation we apply the explicit in time WENO scheme of third-order approximating the advective part [10, 16] and standard second-order approximation of the diffusive part. Note, that the balance-technique [6, 17] is used to deal with discontinuous diffusion coefficient at the interface between macro- and microporous spaces:

$$\frac{\partial}{\partial x_1}\left(D\frac{\partial}{\partial x_1}\right) \approx \frac{1}{h_1}\left[\tilde{D}_{i+1/2,j,k}\frac{C^n_{i+1,j,k}-C^n_{i,j,k}}{h_1} - \tilde{D}_{i-1/2,j,k}\frac{C^n_{i,j,k}-C^n_{i-1,j,k}}{h_1}\right],$$

where

$$D_{i+1/2,j,k} = 2\left(D^{-1}_{i+1,j,k} + D^{-1}_{i,j,k}\right)^{-1}.$$

This operator was developed using the conservative scheme theory [17]. If the coefficients are constant, it is second-order accurate; however, if the coefficients are discontinuous, it may degrade to the first order.

Correction of the solution due to the reactive part is performed using an implicit scheme. Take the system of ordinary differential equations representing the reactions:

$$\frac{\partial}{\partial t}\left(\phi C_{CO_2}\right) = -k\phi C_{CO_2} C_{Ca(OH)_2},$$
$$\frac{\partial}{\partial t}\left(C_{Ca(OH)_2}\right) = -k\phi C_{CO_2} C_{Ca(OH)_2},$$
$$\frac{\partial}{\partial t}\left(\phi C_{H_2O}\right) = k\phi C_{CO_2} C_{Ca(OH)_2}, \tag{12}$$
$$\frac{\partial}{\partial t}\left(C_{CaCO_3}\right) = k\phi C_{CO_2} C_{Ca(OH)_2},$$

it is approximated by the scheme:

$$\frac{C_{CO_2}^{n+1} - \tilde{C}_{CO_2}^{n+1}}{dt} = -k C_{CO_2}^{n+1} \tilde{C}_{Ca(OH)_2}^{n+1},$$
$$\frac{C_{Ca(OH)_2}^{n+1} - \tilde{C}_{Ca(OH)_2}^{n+1}}{dt} = -k\varphi \tilde{C}_{CO_2}^{n+1} C_{Ca(OH)_2}^{n+1},$$
$$\frac{C_{H_2O}^{n+1} - \tilde{C}_{H_2O}^{n+1}}{dt} = k C_{CO_2}^{n+1} C_{Ca(OH)_2}^{n+1},$$
$$\frac{C_{CaCO_3}^{n+1} - \tilde{C}_{CaCO_3}^{n+1}}{dt} = k\varphi C_{CO_2}^{n+1} C_{Ca(OH)_2}^{n+1}.$$

First-order accuracy and unconditional stability characterize this scheme.

4   Algorithm Implementation

The algorithm is essentially oriented on the use of GPUs with minimal data transfer from host to device and vice versa. Only the preliminary steps are executed by the CPU. It includes the input data processing, memory allocation for the level-sets, and field variables. As presented above we use explicit finite-difference schemes to perform numerical simulations. Thus the algorithm uses stencil computations which are naturally parallelized with technology CUDA. The only the algorithm's part which requires solving a system of linear algebraic equations is the Poisson equation resolved for pressure when the Navier-Stokes equation is treated. However, it is solved with BiCGStab, where matrix-vector multiplication is needed, which is also based on stencil computations and can be efficiently implemented using CUDA technology. A detailed description of the GPU-based solver of 3D Poisson equations is provided in [6]. Note, that in this research we assume the fluid flow is steady, thus the Stokes equation is solved only once. Moreover, as presented in the next section, we are interested in the chemical model parameters optimization which requires several simulations for fixed geometry. Thus, we add the option of reading the fluid flow as input data if the model geometry does not change.

The output parameters of the algorithm are spatial distributions of the species concentrations at few time instants and time-dependent CO_2 concentration at the outflow. The spatial distributions of the concentrations are transferred from device to host at a small number (up to 20 snapshots per simulation) of time instants during the algorithm execution. The concentration of CO_2 at the outlet is estimated and accumulated on GPU at each time step and it is uploaded to the host memory at the end of algorithm execution.

5 Numerical Experiments

5.1 Parameters Calibration

The initial batch of numerical tests were done to calibrate the model parameters. In particular, two coefficients in ADR equations (5) are not available from technical sorbents descriptions or lab experiments. They are the effective diffusion coefficient in microporous media and the reaction rate. We assumed that the effective diffusion coefficient can be represented as $D = D_0/F$, where D_0 refers to the diffusion coefficient of species in fluid, and F is a form factor of microporous media. Typically, the form factor varies from two to ten, with higher values corresponding to a more complex pore space structure. The reaction rate for the considered chemical reaction may take a wide range of values from 10^{-4} to 10^1 mol/s. So, we focus on the analysis of the effect of these two parameters on the change in the immovable species concentrations inside the particles.

We considered the Soda-lime Loflosorb (Intersurgical Ltd., UK) sorbent, that is a commercially accessible CO_2 sorbent. Loflosorb consists of $Ca(OH)_2$ (60 wt%), water (15 wt%), and indicator (ethyl violet, less than 0.1 wt%). The pellets of Loflosorb sorbent are round particles with a 3 mm diameter [18]. Table 1 contains the results of laboratory measurement of the initial porosity (expressed in m^3/kg), mass density of the granules and mass fraction of $Ca(OH)_2$ and $CaCO_3$.

Table 1. The results of laboratory measurement for Soda-lime Loflosorb.

Property	Notation	Loflosorb
Density (kg/m^3)	ρ	1080
Chem. porosity (m^3/kg)	v_p	$4.6 \cdot 10^{-4}$
Mass fraction of $Ca(OH)_2$	$\mu_{Ca(OH)_2}$	0.76
Mass fraction of $CaCO_3$	μ_{CaCO_3}	0.05

Carbon dioxide chemisorption was investigated in a lab. We placed the sorbent particles in a single layer along the reactor grid. The distance between the granules was much higher than their diameters to ensure free flow access to all particles. With a constant flow rate of 100 L/h, the gas-air mixture with a fixed amount of CO_2 (1 vol. % or 5 vol. %) was introduced into the reactor. Each sample was exposed to the gas-air combination for a predetermined amount of time before being taken out of the reactor and placed into the sealed container.

Thermo Scientific's ARL Perform'X X-Ray Fluorescence Spectrometer was used to analyze the elements in the sorbent samples both before and after chemisorption. Using the STA 449 Jupiter instrument (Netzsch, Germany), the synchronous thermal analysis approach (thermogravimetry (TG) combined with differential thermal analysis (DTA)) was used to examine the chemical composition of the sorbent samples. Ca(OH)2 and CaCO3's weight contents were

Table 2. $CaCO_3$ and $Ca(OH)_2$ mass fractions measured at various time instants

	$t = 0$	$t = 15$	$t = 30$	$t = 60$
Concentration of CO_2 is 5%				
μ_{CaCO_3}	0.05	0.5	0.72	0.78
$\mu_{Ca(OH)_2}$	0.76	0.32	0.19	0.13
Concentration of CO_2 is 1%				
μ_{CaCO_3}	0.0522	0.2318	0.3818	0.475
$\mu_{Ca(OH)_2}$	0.6948	0.4604	0.3535	0.2672

determined using the effects of mass loss at temperatures of 450 and 750 °C, respectively. Table 2 provides the results of laboratory measurements.

To reproduce the lab experiments we considered a reactor model with the length of 15 mm and diameter of 15 mm. We placed a single granule (3 mm diameter) in the center. We used a 0.3 mm discretization which ensures 10 grid points per diameter of granules and leads to the problem size of 50^3 voxels. Thus, a single GPU may be used for the simulation. The flow rate was reduced to $1.73 \cdot 10^{-6}$ m^3/s to scale the fluid velocity to the laboratory setup. We used the following model parameters: fluid dynamic viscosity $\mu = 2.8 \cdot 10^{-4}$, that corresponds to air under typical circumstances. The air's CO_2 diffusion coefficient is $D_0 = 1.5 \cdot 10^{-5}$ m^2/s. These parameters correspond to the Reynolds number of about $10^{-3} - 10^{-2}$, Peclet number of about 10^2, and Schmidt number of about 10. The Microporosity of the particles is 0.49. It supposes to drop down to 0.45 during the chemisorption, but we neglect this effect. To construct the effective diffusion in the microporous space we use the formula $D = \phi D_0/F$. Here F denotes the form factor. We varied the form factor within the set $F \in \{1, 2, \ldots, 10\}$. Also the reaction rate is unknown and we consider several values $k \in \{10^{-4}, 10^{-3}, 10^{-2}, 10^{-1}\}$ m^3/(mol · s). We used the Polytechnic Tornado supercomputer of Saint-Petersburg Polytechnic University equipped with NVIDIA K40 GPUs.

To match the lab experiments we deal with two volumetric fractions of CO_2 in the air at the inlet. They are 5% (corresponds to 2.2321 mol/m^2) and 1% (0.4464 mol/m^3). Figures 1, 2, 3 and 4 represent the plots of weight fraction of $Ca(OH)_2$ and $CaCO_3$ in the granules as functions of time. Each figure corresponds to a fixed reaction rate but contains a result for all values of the form factor. One may note, that for the high reaction rates the concentrations reach their equilibrium concentrations much faster, than in the experiment. On the contrary, the low reaction rate does not let the reaction develop, and mass fractions remain almost unchanged, especially for low CO_2 concentrations. However, if the reaction rate is about 10^{-2} (Fig. 3) the simulated data is close to the lab measurements. Also, a decrease in the form factor causes an increase in the diffusion coefficient, thus, it improves the reactant delivery and increases the sorption.

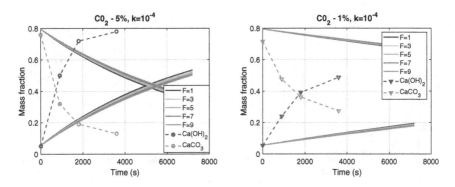

Fig. 1. The mass fraction for $Ca(OH)_2$ and $CaCO_3$ in particle as function of time for different values of the formation factor and a constant reaction rate of $k = 10^{-4}$. The right plot corresponds to a CO_2 volume concentration of 1% and the left plot a CO_2 volume concentration of 5%.

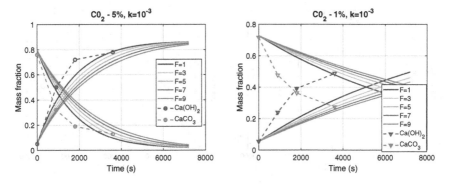

Fig. 2. The mass fraction for $Ca(OH)_2$ and $CaCO_3$ in particle as function of time for different values of the formation factor and a constant reaction rate of $k = 10^{-3}$. The right plot corresponds to a CO_2 volume concentration of 1% and the left plot a CO_2 volume concentration of 5%.

The experiments show that the values of $k = 10^{-4}$ and $k = 10^{-3}$ are so small to correspond the experimental results. Particularly, at $k = 10^{-4}$ concentrations fluctuate practically linearly over time up to $7200\,\mathrm{s}$ ($2\,\mathrm{h}$).

5.2 CO_2 Break-Through Time

The second series of the numerical experiments were done to study CO_2 break-though time depending on the initial concentration at the inlet and particle packing density. We considered a simplified reactor model with dimensions of $30\,\mathrm{mm}$ in length and $30\,\mathrm{mm}$ in diameter. We generated the spherical particles $3\,\mathrm{mm}$ in diameter being uniformly distributed inside the reactor and varied the number of the particles. Same as before, we used the grid with steps of $0.3\,\mathrm{mm}$ to discretize the domain which led to the problem size of 100^3 voxels. Thus, a

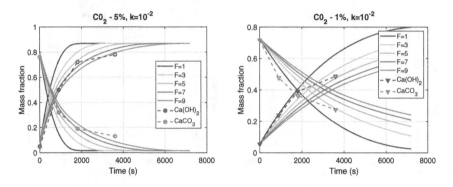

Fig. 3. The mass fraction for $Ca(OH)_2$ and $CaCO_3$ in particle as function of time for different values of the formation factor and a constant reaction rate of $k = 10^{-2}$. The right plot corresponds to a CO_2 volume concentration of 1% and the left plot a CO_2 volume concentration of 5%.

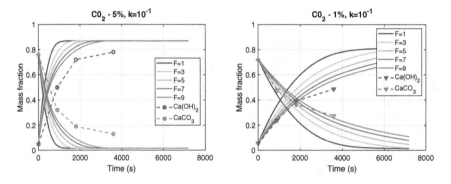

Fig. 4. The mass fraction for $Ca(OH)_2$ and $CaCO_3$ in particle as function of time for different values of the formation factor and a constant reaction rate of $k = 10^{-1}$. The right plot corresponds to a CO_2 volume concentration of 1% and the left plot a CO_2 volume concentration of 5%.

single GPU may be used for the simulation. We admit that such a model is not consistent with the physical assumption, that the particles are rigid bodies and can not overlap, but it still can be used to derive the main relations between the particles compaction and the break-through time. We generated models with 50, 100, 200, 400, 800, and 1600 particles inside the reactor. Note, that in the last case the particles must overlap to ensure macroporosity. We assumed the flow rate at the inlet equals $7.5 \cdot 10^{-5}$ m^3/s. We considered three CO_2 concentrations at the inlet 1, 5, 7 volume %. Simulations were performed up to 1200 s. For each number of particles, we generated five realizations, thus the total number of simulations was 90 (six statistical models, five realizations per model, and three concentrations at the inlet).

We recorded the CO_2 concentration at the outlet as function of time, as presented in Figs. 5, 6 and 7. In general, an almost instant break-through is observed

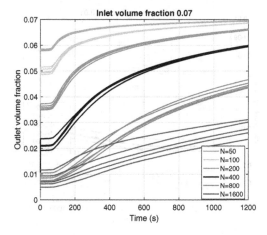

Fig. 5. CO_2 volume fraction in the gas mixture at the outlet in dependence on time. Line colors correspond to the different number of particles packed in the reactor. Inlet volume fraction is 7%. (Color figure online)

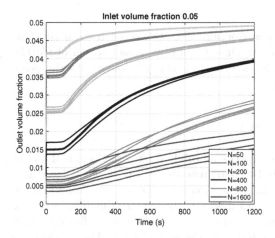

Fig. 6. CO_2 volume fraction in the gas mixture at the outlet in dependence on time. Line colors correspond to the different number of particles packed in the reactor. Inlet volume fraction is 7%. (Color figure online)

in all considered cases due to high fluid flow in the macroporous space. However, high particle concentrations lead to a high specific surface of the macroporous space, thus improving CO_2 sorption that reduces the initial break-through CO_2 concentration. After that concentration at the outlet stabilizes for some time, which is due to the easy reactant access to $Ca(OH)_2$ near the granule surface. Later on, the concentration increases because the delivery of the reactant to $Ca(OH)_2$ is mainly governed by the diffusion in the microporous space which limits the reaction. In the scenario of the minimal amount of particles in the

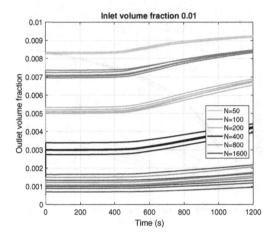

Fig. 7. CO_2 volume fraction in the gas mixture at the outlet in dependence on time. Line colors correspond to the different number of particles packed in the reactor. Inlet volume fraction is 7%. (Color figure online)

reactor, the volume fraction of CO_2 almost reaches the input concentration, which corresponds to almost complete consumption of $Ca(OH)_2$ from the sorbent particles. The described effects get slower with the decrease of the initial CO_2 at the inlet.

6   Conclusions

In this article, we propose an original numerical method and algorithm to simulate the conjugate two-scale reactive transport. This algorithm is oriented on the modeling of gas chemosorption with the use of microporous sorbents impermeable for the supporting fluid but allowing for the diffusion of the reactive species. Thus, we solve Stokes equations and advection-diffusion equations for the reactive transport simulation at the macroscale; which is the inter-pore space, but we deal with the diffusion-reaction equation in the microporous space inside the sorbent particles. Only stencil calculations are used in the algorithm, which is founded on explicit finite differences, and they are implemented on GPUs. To illustrate the applicability of the algorithm we performed two series of numerical experiments. First, we optimize the model parameters (effective diffusion and rate of reaction in the micro-porous space) to correspond the lab results of concentration changes rate. Second, we numerically studied the CO_2 breakthrough curves for different particles packing inside the reactor, defining three main stages of the break-through: initial break-through, the kinetics-limiting stage when the reactant has easy access to the active component of the sorbent, and diffusion-limiting stage when access to $Ca(OH)_2$ is restricted by diffusion in the microporous space.

Acknowledgements. The study was carried out with funding provided by RSCF grant number 21-71-20003. The Saint-Petersburg Polytechnic University's supercomputer resources were used for numerical simulations.

References

1. Derevschikov, V.S., Kazakova, E.D., Yatsenko, D.A., Veselovskaya, J.V.: Multiscale study of carbon dioxide chemisorption in the plug flow adsorber of the anesthesia machine. Sep. Sci. Technol. **56**(3), 485–497 (2021)
2. Osher, S., Fedkiw, R.P.: Level set methods: an overview and some recent results. J. Comput. Phys. **169**(2), 463–502 (2001)
3. Gibou, F., Fedkiw, R., Osher, S.: A review of level-set methods and some recent applications. J. Comput. Phys. **353**, 82–109 (2018)
4. Mittal, R., Iaccarino, G.: Immersed boundary methods. Annu. Rev. Fluid Mech. **37**(1), 239–261 (2005)
5. Niegodajew, P., Asendrych, D.: Amine based CO_2 capture – CFD simulation of absorber performance. Appl. Math. Model. **40**(23), 10222–10237 (2016)
6. Khachkova, T., Lisitsa, V., Reshetova, G., Tcheverda, V.: GPU-based algorithm for evaluating the electrical resistivity of digital rocks. Comput. Math. Appl. **82**, 200–211 (2021)
7. Coco, A.: A multigrid ghost-point level-set method for incompressible Navier-Stokes equations on moving domains with curved boundaries. J. Comput. Phys. **418**, 109623 (2020)
8. Grave, M., Camata, J.J., Coutinho, A.L.G.A.: A new convected level-set method for gas bubble dynamics. Comput. Fluids **209**, 104667 (2020)
9. Lisitsa, V., Bazaikin, Y., Khachkova, T.: Computational topology-based characterization of pore space changes due to chemical dissolution of rocks. Appl. Math. Model. **88**, 21–37 (2020). https://doi.org/10.1016/j.apm.2020.06.037
10. Prokhorov, D., Lisitsa, V., Khachkova, T., Bazaikin, Y., Yang, Y.: Topology-based characterization of chemically-induced pore space changes using reduction of 3D digital images. J. Comput. Sci. **58**, 101550 (2022)
11. Johansen, H., Colella, P.: A cartesian grid embedded boundary method for Poisson's equation on irregular domains. J. Comput. Phys. **147**(1), 60–85 (1998)
12. Li, X., Huang, H., Meakin, P.: Level set simulation of coupled advection-diffusion and pore structure evolution due to mineral precipitation in porous media. Water Resour. Res. **44**(12), W12407 (2008)
13. Luo, K., Zhuang, Z., Fan, J., Haugen, N.E.L.: A ghost-cell immersed boundary method for simulations of heat transfer in compressible flows under different boundary conditions. Int. J. Heat Mass Transf. **92**, 708–717 (2016)
14. Brown, D.L., Cortez, R., Minion, M.L.: Accurate projection methods for the incompressible Navier-Stokes equations. J. Comput. Phys. **168**(2), 464–499 (2001)
15. Pleshkevich, A., Vishnevskiy, D., Lisitsa, V.: Sixth-order accurate pseudo-spectral method for solving one-way wave equation. Appl. Math. Comput. **359**, 34–51 (2019)
16. Liu, X.D., Osher, S., Chan, T.: Weighted essentially non-oscillatory schemes. J. Comput. Phys. **115**(1), 200–212 (1994)
17. Samarskii, A.A.: The Theory of Difference Schemes, Pure and Applied Mathematics, vol. 240. CRC Press, Boca Raton (2001)

18. Derevshchikov, V.S., Kazakova, E.D.: Comparative analysis of the chemical composition and sorption, textural, and strength properties of commercial medical CO_2 sorbents. Catal. Ind. **12**(1), 1–6 (2020)
19. Hwang, W.R., Advani, S.G.: Numerical simulations of Stokes-Brinkman equations for permeability prediction of dual scale fibrous porous media. Phys. Fluids **22**(11), 113101 (2010)

Heterogeneous Computing Systems in Problems of Modeling Filaments Formation and Pre-stellar Objects

Boris Rybakin[1]([✉]) and Valery Goryachev[2]

[1] Moscow State University, Moscow, Russia
`boris.rybakin@math.msu.ru`
[2] Tver State Technical University, Tver, Russia

Abstract. Modeling of astrophysical processes requires the use of modern means of supporting labor-intensive calculations with more efficient parallelization of operations. In this paper, we apply our proposed methods for constructing parallel algorithms for heterogeneous parallelization on the CPU and GPU. To numerically solve the Poisson and Euler equations, the adaptive mesh refinement (AMR) method was used for five levels of nesting. A comparison is made of the acceleration of the numerical solution of the Poisson equation on the CPU and GPU on grids from 128^3 to 4096^3. Of great importance in such a transfer is the combination of computation time on different processors, that is, code profiling. Serial numerical modeling was carried out for the case of a direct collision of clouds in a head-on scenario without rotation or collision of clouds rotating and moving in opposite directions. Collisions of molecular clouds with mutual matter penetrations are accompanied by periodic perturbations of the matter density in impact core and inside newly formed remnants, fragmented clumps and filaments. To increase the accuracy of calculations of the main variables in the areas of flow movement with high gradients, grid refinement by the AMR patch method is used. In modeling, it was found that in residual clumps with more condensed matter the gas density can reach values that are at the initial level of the matter of prestellar formations. In the zones of these formations, the emergence of new stars is more likely. It was revealed how the coherent structures of new formation, unbalanced during a collision and caused by the Kelvin-Helmholtz effects, together with other instabilities can change in their shape due to rotation, can affect the transformation of the remains.

Keywords: Parallel computing · Heterogeneous computing systems · Instability

1 Introduction

Solving multidimensional problems of astrophysics and gas dynamics, taking into account additional forces acting on objects, such as gravity, magnetic fields, cooling or heating effects, requires very large computing resources. With the increase in new additions that need to be taken into account in the created and debugged mathematical model, it becomes necessary to rebuild and adapt the developed program codes to

© The Author(s), under exclusive license to Springer Nature Switzerland AG 2022
V. Voevodin et al. (Eds.): RuSCDays 2022, LNCS 13708, pp. 127–139, 2022.
https://doi.org/10.1007/978-3-031-22941-1_9

new requirements. Such a need also arises when transferring modified software, with an increase in the possibilities of using processors and video cards of a new generation, modernized for parallel computing, and new ones that did not exist before. An example is the emergence of the ability to perform calculations on GPU tensor cores (NVIDIA), or the emergence of two different types of cores in the latest Intel processors. When modifying existing, well-functioning programs, it is necessary to preserve and, if possible, improve their adaptation to modern computing systems and parallel software.

This paper presents examples of constructing parallel algorithms for heterogeneous systems designed to solve problems in astrophysics. For this, the author's program was modified and an algorithm was proposed for parallelizing the problem of gas space collapse on the CPU and GPU, taking into account gravitational forces.

The use of the program for the parallel solution of the Poisson equation in a three-dimensional setting on the used high-resolution grids requires a very large amount of processor time for calculations. In the modified program, the CPU is used to calculate gas-dynamic processes. In systems with shared memory, OpenMP technology is used, which implements the parallelization of multiple threads running in a common address space. This allows you to exchange data without complex and time-consuming transmission of interprocessor messages [1].

The use of OpenMP technology makes it possible to almost completely load the processors of one node of the computer system [2]. Coarrays [3] technology is used for interconnection. If there are graphics processors (GPU) in the computer system, it is possible to organize parallel solution of other tasks using this hardware parallel by computing on CPU. In this paper, the OpenACC technology is used to solve the Poisson equation. This technology is essentially a set of compiler directives for specifying parts of the code that should be accelerated by the GPU. To date, the OpenACC 3.2 standard has been implemented [4]. This technology largely complies with the OpenMP standards and allows you to create high-level programs on the CPU and GPU without significant rebuilding of existing code. Both OpenMP and OpenACC allow parallel programming based on a small number of directives. OpenACC uses directives that tell the compiler how to parallelize loops and also allows you to control the flow of data between two types of memory located on the CPU and GPU. The creation of threads, their activation and completion on these two technologies require significantly less overhead for the operating system. In addition, the parallel loop in OpenACC allows the computer to generate code for a large number of cores that are in CPUs.

In recent years, there has been a sharp increase in computational codes for solving the equations of gravitational hydrodynamics. Most computational codes use particle-in-cell (PIC) algorithm, N-body simulation, mesh-less smoothed particle hydrodynamics (SPH), mesh-based and finite-volumes methods. A detailed review of the software used in this area of modeling gigantic in space and time scale processes in the Universe is given in [5, 6]. Many of existing astrophysical codes use the MPI technology to parallelize algorithms for solving partial differential equations. Can be given as example RAMSES software [7], it can be cited as example of computational code for solving large-scale problems of astrophysics. It is a mesh-based solver with adaptive refinement of grids using patch-based AMR and MPI/OpenMP hybrid parallelism model. The computer structuring and parallelism in solving are convenient for implementing grid modeling using Euler description of hypersonic flows with large matter flux gradient changes, great energy transfer and radiation characteristics including simulation of some gravitationally bounded gas objects such stars.

The combination of the use of AMR and SPH codes with a high parallelism of calculations is a characteristic feature of the known models to simulate the formation of prestellar zones in high compressed gravitationally bounded clumps and filament areas originating during collisions of molecular clouds [8–11]. Among the computational models, it can be noted as one of pioneering, highly detailed and substantiated studies carried out by Habe A. and K. Ohta on gravitational instability caused by a cloud-cloud collision (CCC) [8]. To date, more and more detailed 3D gravitational-turbulent models are appearing that take into account the effects of the interaction of matter of oncoming hypersonic gas streams with the mutual penetration of gravitationally bounded spatial formation into each other. Sharp form transformations during collision are accompanied by significant vortex generation at the boundaries of interpenetrating deformable clouds. In many studies, this is taken into account with the involvement of a description of various physical instabilities: Rayleigh–Taylor (RT), Richtmyer–Meshkov (RM), Kelvin-Helmholtz (KH), non-linear thin shell (NTS) instability, and others effects, which initiate shape forming on front of corrugated MCs core during CCC [12–15].

Interacting molecular clouds formations in various galaxies, as a rule, are rotating objects. The number of computational experiments performed on cloud-cloud collision modeling taking into account the rotation of clouds is not too large compared to the studied situations of frontal collision without rotation [16, 17].

Our study takes into account the latest results noted in the cited studies, taking into account the preferences in understanding the processes of formation of prestellar formations as a result of the pure dynamic interaction of matter streams in the ISM, as the main one in understanding of such processes.

2 Implementation of Parallelized Numerical Code

During of interplay between hypersonic streams of matter in the Universe, compact regions of highly compressed molecular gas arise, in which the density exceeds the density of the interstellar medium by many orders of magnitude. In the emerging gravitationally bound regions formed during the collision, under certain conditions, future stars can be born.

An original program for solving the Poisson equation was created to simulate the gravitational effect on emerging objects (clumps). The calculations in the program were carried out using parallelization on the CPU and GPU. The Euler equations are solved at CPU using OpenMP. In parallel with this, the Poisson equations can be solved on GPU and the gravitational potential can be found. The promising OpenACC technology mentioned above [4] was used to simultaneously solve various types of equations (hyperbolic and elliptic) at the GPU and CPU. Directives of OpenACC enable to easily develop portable applications that maximize the performance and power efficiency benefits of the hybrid CPU/GPU architectures computers. They allow complete access to the massive parallel power of a GPU and making GPU programming straightforward and portable across parallel and multi-core processors.

In the codes to solve the Poisson and Euler equations, the AMR (Advanced Mesh Refinement) method is used, which whish could be very successive to increase the accuracy of calculations without a significant increase in computational costs.

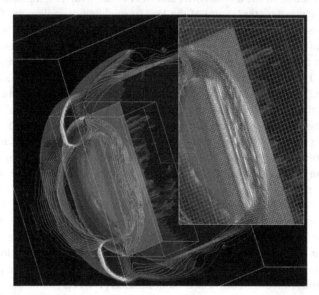

Fig. 1. Two levels of AMR patches generated near compressed core layer in one of modelling case of head-on collision.

The fragment of two levels of AMR patches in dynamical behavior used in one of cloud-cloud collision scenario is shown in Fig. 1.

In the case of calculating the gravitational potential in bounded volume, five levels of the refinement grid were used to more accurately simulate the evolution of matter near the center of the simulated spherical region. In solution performed reducing the size of the cells and increase the accuracy by 25 times and helped to accelerate sharply time effectiveness of calculations. To balance the load, operations with emerging refinement patches of higher spatial resolution were transferred to the GPU, where they were effectively redistributed to free SM (Streaming Multiprocessor).

The numerical calculation of the gravitational potential based on five AMR levels refinement grids was confirmed by comparison with the analytical solution obtained in [18].

In test performed we simulated the gravitational collapse of a gas volume, repeating the initial data on the distribution of the matter density of a centrally condensed sphere of radius R in the form of the following function:

$$\rho(r) = \begin{cases} \frac{\rho_c}{1+(r/r_c)^2} & if \quad r \leq R \\ 0 & if \quad r > R \end{cases}. \tag{1}$$

The solution of the Poisson equation with density distribution (1) has an analytical solution for $\Phi(r)$ and for the gravitational potential:

$$\Phi(r) = \begin{cases} 4\pi G\rho_c r_c^2 \left[\frac{arctan(r/r_c)}{r/r_c} + \frac{1}{2}ln\left(\frac{1+(r/r_c)^2}{1+(R/r_c)^2}\right) - 1 \right] & if \ \ r \leq R \\ -4\pi G\rho_c \frac{r_c^3}{r}[R/r_c - arctan(R/r_c)] & if \ \ r > R \end{cases}, \quad (2)$$

$$\nabla\Phi(r) = \frac{GM(r)}{r^2} = \begin{cases} 4\pi G\rho_c \frac{r_c^3}{r^2}[r/r^c - arctan(r/r_c)] & if \ \ r \leq R \\ -4\pi G\rho_c \frac{r_c^3}{r^2}[R/r_c - arctan(R/r_c)] & if \ \ r > R \end{cases}. \quad (3)$$

An example of the numerical solution of one of the options, which was compared with the analytical solution, is illustrated in Fig. 2. The solution was carried out on the computational grid $128 \times 128 \times 128$ using five levels of mesh refinement with a twofold increase in the number of nodes at each step of the transition.

Calculations for finding the gravitational potential for this test problem were carried out as follows. On the original coarse grid, iterations were carried out until the convergence criterion for the coarse grid was met. Then the transition to the second-level grid was completed using procedure *CoarseToFine*. Then the procedure with doubling the number of partitions of grid nodes was repeated until the results were obtained on grids of the fifth level. 12502 iterations were performed on the coarsest grid, 8131 iterations on the second level grid, 2311 iterations on the third level, 1874 iterations on the fourth level, and 1665 iterations on the fifth level. After the calculations, the transition to the first level grid was carried out, taking into account all the calculations. At the 5th level, the residual accuracy $\varepsilon = 9.994178 \cdot 10^{-7}$ was achieved, which exceeds the specified one. Thus, it was shown that the numerical solution practically coincides with the analytical solution, described by formulas 2 and 3.

To build an efficient parallelization algorithm at the CPU and GPU, it is necessary to optimize the processes of data exchange between the processors and to manage the allocation of time for the calculation of the Euler equations and gravitational potential change, at each time step. To select an efficient solution, test calculations were carried out with control over the acceleration of calculation obtained by parallelization using OpenACC, in comparison with OpenMP procedures. Some results of data treatment acceleration obtained on the NVIDIA GeForce GTX 980 Ti GPU, compared with those obtained on two Intel Xeon E5 2620 processor using 12 cores (total 12 cores, 24 threads, 64 Gb RAM) are shown in Fig. 3. The main calculations were carried out on a 4-node heterogeneous server of the High Performance Computing Department, Moscow State University. The most powerful node has two Intel Xeon E5 2630 processors with 40 threads, 256 Gb RAM and NVIDIA GeForce which has 24 Gb DDR5, 3840 CUDA cores. The Intel Cluster Edition 2018 compiler was used to implement the code. PGI Fortran was used for GPU computing.

It can be noted that calculations using relatively small grids show the advantage of choosing an Intel processor. On large grids, choosing a GPU gives better acceleration results. The fastest increase in the acceleration of calculations falls on calculations with grids in the size range 512×512–1024×1024. In the analyzed cases, we are not interested in absolute results of velocity calculation change, but in comparing CPU and GPU performance in order to obtain information about load balancing between them.

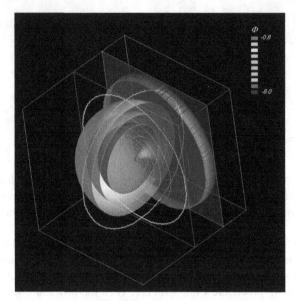

Fig. 2. Surface of gravitation potential and some isodense in calculation of $\nabla\Phi(r)$ using fifth-level mesh refinement.

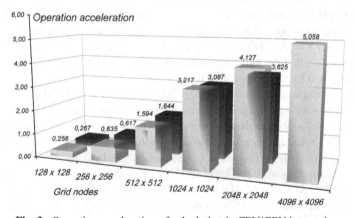

Fig. 3. Operation acceleration of calculation in CPU/GPU interaction.

Analyzed problem of optimization was done taking into account that the calculation of the gravitational potential takes more time than the calculation of the equations of gas dynamics, so for a good load balancing on the processors, you need to have information about the time of work on them.

Next problem using AMR patches method is numerical simulation of a head-on collision of two molecular clouds moving with and without rotation. The main attention was paid to the dynamics of this process, highlighting the features of the mutual penetration of the MCs substance with an analysis of the influence of instabilities and rotation effects on the corrugated core of the shock zone with its destruction and fragmentation.

Simulation is performed with an emphasis on taking into account, first of all, the force impact and turbulent perturbations during a collision, to analyze mainly this dynamical effect.

The problems being solved consider supersonic compressible hydrodynamics using the nonsteady set of conservation equations using laws of mass, momentum, and energy transfer:

$$\frac{\partial U}{\partial t} + \frac{\partial F_i}{\partial x_i} = 0,$$

(4)

$U = (\rho, \rho u_i, E)^T$ - vector of conservative variables; $E = \rho\left(\frac{1}{2}u^i u_j + \frac{P}{(\gamma-1)\rho}\right)$ - is a full energy; $F(U)_i = \left(\rho u_i, \rho u_i u_j + P\delta_{ij}u^j, u_i E + P\delta_{ij}u^j\right)^T$ - are fluxes of main variables. The total energy E and gas pressure P are related through the ideal gas closure.

In presented modeling new MCs formation starts in large-scale supersonic compressions in impact zone between MCs. According head-on collision scenarios oppositely moving clouds MC_1 and MC_2 of different masses, sizes, and density distribution collide with each other at oncoming velocity of 5.32 km s^{-1}, spinning with angular velocity $\Omega = 2.6 \times 10^{-15}$ s^{-1} in the case with clouds rotation. The calculations are carried out using suppose about diameters of initially spherical clouds MC_1 - 13.44 pc and MC_2 - 13.76 pc. The cloud masses for this scenario were taken equal to 694 $M_\odot$ and 675 $M_\odot$, which corresponds to giant molecular clouds (GMC) characteristics. Density contrast - the ratio $\chi = \rho_{cl}/\rho_{ism}$ denoted by the values between of the MCs center and value in ISM, was taken equal to 500 in clouds cores at the initial moment of collision. The ambient gas density in ISM was taken as $\rho_{ism} = 1 \times 10^{-25}$ g·cm^{-3}. The present study considers the collision and mutual penetration with supersonic speeds of molecular clouds in computing spatial volume 40 × 40 × 40 pc.

General equations were solved on high refinement grids in the range 256^3–1024^3 nodes, using the schemes of TVD type and implementing Row's adaptive solver. The numerical realization was done using in-house code developed for high-performance computer systems. The program has been created using Coarray Fortran and patch AMR refinement of grids in zones with large gradients of main variables. When implementing the author's computational code, the problems of substantial improvement of the adopted computer architecture were taken into account. Given the capabilities, which modern processors and GPUs provide, changes have been made to the program to improve performance and time realization of solution. Programmatic changes made it possible to smooth out the problem of the influence of the memory cache size in computational threads. Cache sizes for each thread, as well as the overhead of data transfer in the implementation of calculations, began to matter less than data localization. It's advisable in the implementation of multigrid algorithms, which are widely used in solving problems of gravitational gas dynamics.

Calculation is carried out for Xeon E2630 and Xeon E5 2650 Ivy Bridge processors used. The parallelization efficiency was observed using the Intel VTune Amplifier XE program. To realize parallel computations, new noted technologies for CPU were tested. Some routines used in tested numerical code were performed using GPU and CUDA implementation.

Advanced postprocessing video system HDVIS with parallelization options to analyze a very large output of numerical results is used to treatment results after simulation.

3   Results of Modeling for Two Case of Cloud-Cloud Collision

Taking into account the rotation of molecular clouds in simulation of nebular interplay in ISM made possible to reveal additional effects of clouds fragmentation in in two CCC scenario of head-on impact and penetration of ongoing molecular gas streams with shock wave interplay.

The performed calculations are illustrated below in figures in order to compare the changes in the structure of flows for these two scenarios and highlighting the main moments of the restructuring of new formations in different cases.

The clouds transformation in CCC process and the appearance of a corrugated structure with blobs in core of impact during collision is continue at all stages of the development of the collision process. Spatial evolution of pre- and post-impact gas formation for different stages of collision is illustrated in Figs. 4, 5, 6, 7.

It can be seen how the distribution of compressed clumps changing when passing through before and past of resulting passage of cloud MC_1 through MC_2. This is shown for two comparable in time CCC episodes: for the case of an impact without rotation (a) and for the case of mutual penetration of clouds with rotation (b). As addition to numerical study of no rotated MCs collision, conducted early, new calculation show that MCs rotation leads to significant redistribution of the final mass of the arising clumps and filaments in compressed lenticular disk - in core of collision.

The animation frames in Fig. 4 shows how the local redistribution of oncoming gas flows occurs in the region of the collision core. The RGB images color coding of velocity field distribution on the isodense shows the local change of value U_x component. It can be seen how the local swirl of interpenetrating gas jets affects the structure of the formed filaments in bow like layer of impact area. In the case of a frontal impact, lumpy blobs are formed. They are grouping in concentric ring structures. Upon impact of swirling clouds, filaments of overcompressed gas are formed with elongation in the direction of rotation with periodical clumps inclusions.

It can be seen how the size of the clouds novo formation increases, the diametrical dimensions of the possible prestellar areas increase approximately by one and a half times in the compared options of two scenarios. It can be noted that in the case a) of a clouds collision without rotation, MC_1 enters the area of MC_2. When moving according to the scenario b) - with counter moving of rotated clouds, the opposite picture is observed - cloud MC_1 creeps on cloud MC_2. This is a rather indicative effect of a sharp change in the structure of CCC by different scenario.

The radial propagation of compacted lumpy gas formations is well observed in the early evolutionary times in the calculations according to the first scenario (a). The radius of the rings with patches of cloud remnants monotonically increases until the time of complete passage of one cloud through another.

In the case of mutual counter penetration of oncoming and rotating clouds, wave redistribution and displacement of clumps with increased density along spiral trajectories

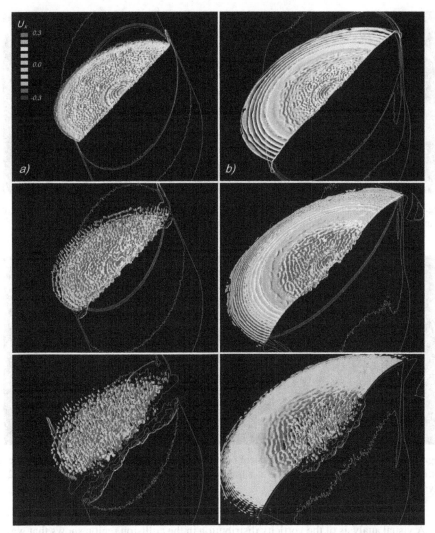

Fig. 4. Isodense ($\chi = 5000$) with map distribution of axial velocity component and contours of flow velocity in meridional plane of the calculation domain for MCs collision without rotation (a) and for the case of rotated clouds (b) in the CCC evolution from t = 1.0 to 2.0 Myr.

is observed. Illustration of such moving is shown in Fig. 5. Density ripples with oscillation of local compression spots inside conditional lenticular core are triggered from local instabilities between forming clumps.

The tangential and streamlines shown in Fig. 5 are most intensively deformed in the areas around the gas clumps and spot tufts with the highest values of matter density. When organizing flows according to scenario b) a spiral structure of the local redistribution of flows near these formations with an increased gas density is revealed.

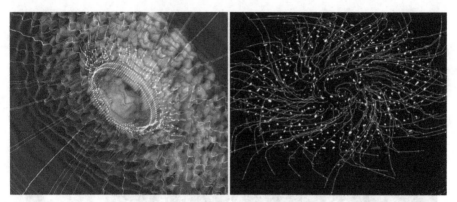

Fig. 5. Streamlines and tangential pathlines over fragmented clumps conditionally bounded in diapason $100 < \chi < 70000$ during mutual penetration of rotated nebulae at time t = 1.5 Myr.

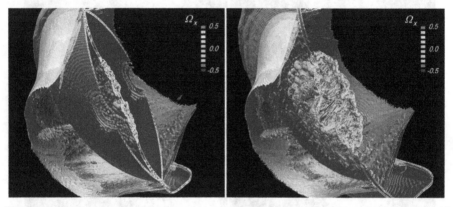

Fig. 6. Contours of rotation Ω_x component on magnitude iso-surface $|\Omega| = 0.5$ in vortex field for case of clouds mutual penetration at a transitional interval of evolution from t = 1.5 to 2.0 Myr.

A visual analysis of the vorticity distribution in the collision region shows that wave density changes are provoked by the Kelvin-Helmholtz instability and periodic changes in the direction of gas jets penetration through stagnation surface, there velocity try to rich zero value when flows collide and corresponding density distribution near this surface, that change rapidly. The instability accelerates the generation of vortices inside the cloud formation, which is reflected in the corrugated forms of the core layers with over density gas blob-like inclusions (Fig. 6). In a head-on collision a), the main compressed gas blobs accumulate above the stagnation surface of oncoming gas flows in repeating ring-like structures, more or less uniformly in radius. In case b) - with the mutual penetration of rotating clouds, the influence of centrifugal forces leads to a more complex redistribution of the masses of the formed clumps, their stretching and the formation of filamentous structures with an oscillatory change in density inside them. A slow movement of matter along spiral trajectories through annular gas zones alternating in density is observed.

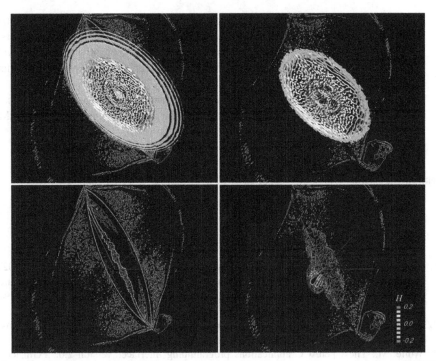

Fig. 7. Helicity contours in meridional section of CCC domain and contrast density $\chi = 20000$ distribution of fragmented clumps at a transitional time interval of collision evolution from t = 1.5 to 2.0 Myr

A distinct influence of gas stream instabilities on the nucleation and deformation of clumps and filaments is observed clear at visual analyze of fluid structures transformation. This is shown in Fig. 7. To illustrate the process of decay of vortices, a display of the distribution pattern of the characteristic of helisity $H = U \cdot (\nabla \times U)$ is used here. The close distribution of helicity contours in high-gradient regions correlates with the zone where the local flow vorticity increases and the negative value of velocity divergence - $divU$ increases. This situation is an indicator of the possible location of protostellar gas clumps and filaments, where self-gravity is possible and trigger to star generation can start. The calculations revealed that the possibility of the formation of zones with a higher density in the collision of rotating MCs can be greater than in similar places of the origin of cloud remnants under instability in a collision without rotation. The density of originated clumps can vary on a level of 10^{-19} g·cm^{-3}, which corresponds to the generally accepted values for the prestellar conglomeration [5, 19, 20].

4   Conclusion

1. The OpenACC technology using heterogeneous computing systems was tested at the problems of formation of gravitationally bound regions, which arise when modeling cloud-cloud collisions.

2. Simulation of rotated colliding molecular clouds made it possible to clarify the details of the origin of turbulization and shape morphing of structures inside MCs remnants, in clumps and filaments. The consequences of the influence of the instability of KH and NTSI on the change in the shape and distribution of remnant clumps and filaments were analyzed.
3. The simulation of the GMC collision revealed the conditions for reaching the critical density in fragmented clumps corresponding to the prestellar consolidation of ISM matter.

Acknowledgements. This work supported by RFBR Grant 19–29-09070 mk.

References

1. Voevodin, V.V., Voevodin, Vl.V.: Parallelnye vychisleniya. SPb: BCV-Petersburg, 608 s (2002)
2. Rybakin, B., Goryachev, V.: Modeling of density stratification and filamentous structure formation in molecular clouds after shock wave collision. Comput. Fluids **173**, 189–194 (2018)
3. Rybakin, B., Goryachev, V.: Applying Coarray Fortran to simulate rotating nebulae collisions. Comput. Fluids (in print)
4. Wolfe, M.: The OpenACC applications programming interface. Version 2.0., PGInsider, Technical News from PGI (2013)
5. Dobbs, C.L., et al.: Formation of molecular clouds and global conditions for star formation. In: Beuther, H., Klessen, R., Dullemont, C., Henning, Th. (eds.) Protostars and Planets VI, pp. 3–26. University of Arizona Press (2014)
6. Skinner, M.A., Dolence, J.C., Burrows, A., Radice, D., Vartanyan, D.: FORNAX: a flexible code for multiphysics astrophysical simulations. Astrophys. J. Suppl. Ser. **241**(7), 27 (2019)
7. RAMSES. https://www.ics.uzh.ch/~teyssier/ramses/RAMSES.html
8. Habe, A., Ohta, K.: Gravitational instability induced by a cloud-cloud collision: the case of head-on collision between clouds with different sizes and densities. Publ. Astron. Soc. Japan **44**, 203–226 (1992)
9. Vazquez-Semadeni, E., Gomez, G., Jappsen, A.K., Ballesteros-Paredes, J., Gonzalez, R.F., Klessen, R.: Molecular cloud evolution. II. From cloud formation to the early stages of star formation in decaying conditions. Astrophys. J. **657**, 870–883 (2007)
10. Special Issue: Star formation triggering by cloud-cloud collision, Publication of the Astronomical Society of Japan – PASJ, 70 (SP2) (2018)
11. Parkin, E.R., Pittard, J.M.: Numerical heat conduction in hydrodynamical models of colliding hypersonic flows. Mon. Not. R. Astron. Soc. **406**, 2373–2385 (2010)
12. Vishniac, E.T.: Nonlinear instabilities in shock-bounded slabs. Astrophys. J. **428**, 186–208 (1994)
13. Folini, D., Walder, R.: Supersonic turbulence in shock-bound interaction zones I. Symmetric settings. Astron. Astrophys. **459**, 1–19 (2006)
14. McLeod, A.D., Whitworth, A.P.: Simulations of the non-linear thin shell instability. Mon. Not. R. Astron. Soc. **431**, 710–721 (2013)
15. Calderón, D., Cuadra, J., Schartmann, M., Burkert, A., Prieto, J., Russell, C.: Three-dimensional simulations of clump formation in stellar wind collision. Mon. Not. R. Astron. Soc. **493**, 447–467 (2020)

16. Li, G.-X., Wyrowski, F., Menten, K.: Revealing a spiral-shaped molecular cloud in our galaxy: cloud fragmentation under rotation and gravity. Astron. Astrophys. **598**(A96), 1–15 (2017)
17. Arreaga-García, G., Klapp, J.: Accretion centers induced in a molecular cloud core after a penetrating collision. In: Klapp, J., Ruíz Chavarría, G., Medina Ovando, A., López Villa, A., Di G. Sigalotti, L. (eds.) Selected Topics of Computational and Experimental Fluid Mechanics. ESE, pp. 505–513. Springer, Cham (2015). https://doi.org/10.1007/978-3-319-11487-3_41
18. Stone, J.M., Norman, M.L.: ZEUS-2D: a radiation magnetnohydrodynamics code for astrophysical flows in two space dimensions I. The hydrodynamic algorithms and tests. Astrophys. J. Suppl. Ser. **80**, 753–790 (1992)
19. Nakamura, F., McKee, C.F., Klein, R.I., Fisher, R.T.: On the hydrodynamic interaction of shock waves with interstellar clouds II. The effect of smooth cloud boundaries on cloud destruction and cloud turbulence. Astrophys. J. **164**, 477–505 (2006)
20. Pittard, J.M., Falle, S.A.E.G., Hartquist, T.W., Dyson, J.E.: The turbulent destruction of clouds. Mon. Not. R. Astron. Soc. **394**, 1351–1378 (2009)

High-Performance Computing in Solving the Electron Correlation Problem

Artem Danshin$^{(\boxtimes)}$ (iD) and Alexey Kovalishin

NRC Kurchatov Institute, Moscow 123182, Russia
danshin_aa@nrcki.ru, kovalishin_aa@nrcki.ru

Abstract. In this work we analyze the solution of the Schrödinger equation for light atoms obtained by the quantum Monte Carlo method using a supercomputer. The general properties of electron correlations are determined, which are further used to improve deterministic methods of solving the Schrödinger equation.

Keywords: Schrödinger equation · Quantum Monte Carlo · Electron correlation · Hartree-Fock method

1 Introduction

The main problem of deterministic methods used to solve the Schrödinger equation is the incorrect allowance for interelectronic correlations [1–3]. In this case, to refine them, a solution obtained by the stochastic method, the quantum Monte Carlo method (QMC), can be used. Different versions of QMC simulations give an exact solution for boson systems in the sense that the error is determined only by statistics. But in the case of fermion systems with an antisymmetric wave function, successful application of QMC requires knowledge of the nodal surfaces due to the sign problem [4,5]. An additional approximation associated with the use of Slater determinants introduces an uncontrollable error, and is also very inconvenient for the implementation of Monte Carlo methods.

In [6] we proposed a new approach—Kurchatov Quantum Monte Carlo (KQMC)—that differs from the traditional diffusion Monte Carlo methods [5] by using the stationary Green's function of the Helmholtz equation. The implementation of the KQMC algorithm on a supercomputer makes it possible to bypass the problems associated with the use of normalization algorithms and to obtain an actually exact solution from a chemical point of view for a number of light atoms.

This paper presents the main aspects related to the parallel implementation of the KQMC method. The calculation results obtained with a supercomputer are analyzed and an assumption is made about the form of the correlation function. Further, the correlation function is used to refine the classical Hartree-Fock method (HF) in terms of the error associated with taking into account correlations of electrons with oppositely directed spins.

V. Voevodin et al. (Eds.): RuSCDays 2022, LNCS 13708, pp. 140–151, 2022.
https://doi.org/10.1007/978-3-031-22941-1_10

2   Parallel Implementation of KQMC

The wave function describing a multifermion system has the well-known antisymmetry property, which is expressed in the Pauli principle. If the QMC methods allowed integrating the entire domain of definition of the wave function, then the solution would converge to the exact solution of the Schrödinger equation. However, this is not the case for the reason that Monte Carlo methods cannot work with sign-changing functions (the sign problem) [4,5].

Due to the properties of antisymmetry, the wave function of N fermions of the same spin divides the entire space into $N!$ subdomains, in each of which the wave function is of constant sign. In [6] we proposed a method for constructing such a subdomain for the KQMC algorithm, which made it possible to bypass the sign problem at least for some simple fermionic systems. However, the use of normalization algorithms to prevent an unlimited growth of the eigenfunction norm leads to the appearance of an additional error associated with electronic fluctuations in shells located far from the nucleus. Figure 1 shows the magnitude of these fluctuations.

In KQMC, the integral Schrödinger equation of the form (1) is solved:

$$\lambda \Psi(\mathbf{r}) = \int_V G(\mathbf{r}' \to \mathbf{r}) k_0(\mathbf{r}') \Psi(\mathbf{r}') \, dV', \tag{1}$$

where

$\lambda = \sqrt{\frac{E_0}{E}}$—eigenvalue to be determined, $E_0 = -\frac{me^4}{32\pi^2 \hbar^2 \varepsilon_0^2}$;

Ψ—wave function of the system, defined in $\mathbf{R}^{3N}$, N—number of electrons;

$G(r) = r^{1-\frac{3N}{2}} K_{\frac{3N}{2}-1}(r)$;

$k_0 = \left(\sum_{i=1}^{N} \frac{2Z}{|\tilde{\mathbf{r}}_0 - \tilde{\mathbf{r}}_i|} - \sum_{i=1}^{N-1} \sum_{j>i}^{N} \frac{2}{|\tilde{\mathbf{r}}_i - \tilde{\mathbf{r}}_j|} \right)$, $\tilde{\mathbf{r}}_i = \frac{\mathbf{r}_i}{a_0} \sqrt{\frac{E}{E_0}}$, $a_0 = \frac{4\pi\varepsilon_0 \hbar^2}{me^2}$, $\mathbf{r}_0 \in$
$\mathbf{R}^3$—nuclear radius vector, $\mathbf{r}_i \in \mathbf{R}^3$—radius vector of the i-th electron.

In operator form, Eq. (1) is written as:

$$\lambda \Psi = \mathbf{KG}\Psi, \tag{2}$$

where $\mathbf{G}$—non-local translation operator, $\mathbf{K}$—local production operator.

To find the maximum modulo eigenvalue and corresponding eigenfunction of the ground state of the calculated system, the following iterative process is realized [7]:

$$\Psi^{(n+1)} = \mathbf{A}\Psi^{(n)}, \tag{3}$$

where n—iteration number, $\mathbf{A} = \mathbf{KG}$.

The eigenvalue corresponding to the ground eigenstate is defined as:

$$\left| \lambda_0^{(n+1)} \right| = \frac{\|\Psi^{(n+1)}\|}{\|\Psi^{(n)}\|} \xrightarrow[n \to \infty]{} |\lambda_0|, \tag{4}$$

where $\|\Psi\|$ is any norm of Ψ. The sequence $\Psi^{(n)}$ converges to an eigenfunction Ψ_0 corresponding to λ_0.

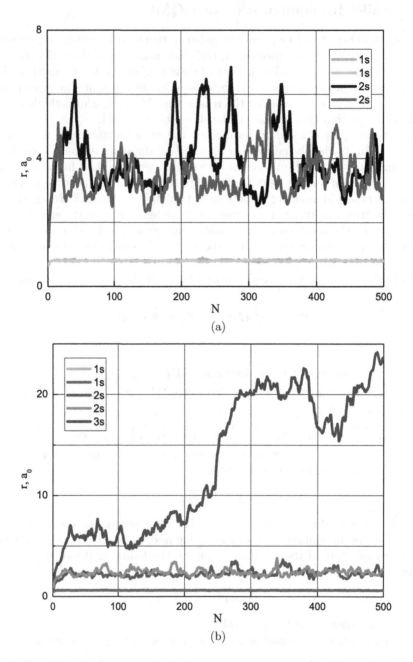

Fig. 1. Dependence of an average distance over generations (in Bohr radii) of each electron on a series number (20 generations in a series) in Be atom (a) and in B (3s ^2S) atom (b), obtained by KQMC calculation using normalization algorithm.

The distribution $\Psi(\mathbf{r})$ is represented by a set of discrete sampling points (random walkers) with weights [8]:

$$\Psi(\mathbf{r}) \xrightarrow{discrete} \sum_k \omega_k \delta(\mathbf{r} - \mathbf{r}_k). \tag{5}$$

At each iteration (3), the operator $\mathbf{A}$ acts on each such point. Since the operator $\mathbf{A}$ is stochastic itself, its action on $\sum_k \omega_k \delta(\mathbf{r} - \mathbf{r}_k)$ is understood as the generation of a set of points $\sum_k \widetilde{\omega}_k \delta(\mathbf{r} - \widetilde{\mathbf{r}}_k)$. A set of points with weights (delta functions with weights) corresponding to one iteration (3) is called a generation.

To estimate the eigenvalue, use not the $\lambda^{(n)}$ number for a particular n, but the averaging:

$$\Lambda_{M,N} = \frac{\lambda^{(M+1)} + \lambda^{(M+2)} + \ldots + \lambda^{(N)}}{N - M}. \tag{6}$$

Similarly, the functionals of an eigenfunction are estimated by averaging.

Monte Carlo calculations are inherently parallel in nature. At their most basic they involve calculation of a large set of independent random numbers and then averaging of the set of results obtained by each of these random numbers. The central idea in doing QMC on massively parallel processors is the master-slave paradigm when one processor controlls the whole simulation. In KQMC, each core, generating its own sequence of pseudorandom numbers [9], independently runs a simulation and accumulates its own set of eigenvalues; the eigenvalues from different cores are gathered, averaged, and written by the master core at the end of the run. Due to this, the KQMC parallel algorithm achieves linear scaling on machines with any number of nodes.

The calculations were carried out on the second-generation HPC2 cluster of Complex for Simulation and Data Processing for Mega-science Facilities at NRC "Kurchatov Institute". One compute node has two Intel Xeon E5450 processors (3.00 GHz, 4 cores), 16 GB of RAM. Interprocessor communications involving sending packets of data between processors are carried out using the MPI standard.

To solve the problem of electronic fluctuations, we abandoned the use of normalization algorithms and introduced a corridor according to the number of particles in a packet—an approach that does not affect the accuracy of the solution obtained [10]. At the same time, it was obtained that when calculating using the corridor on insufficient statistics, a residual fluctuation remains (Fig. 2(a)). To completely solve the problem of electronic fluctuations, at least for the first three periods of the periodic table, a sample of the order of 10^{12} points is needed (Fig. 2(b)). Sampling about 10^9–10^{10} points (the average number of points in the corridor is several hundred thousand, the number of generations is several tens of thousands) for elements of the first two periods of periodic table on one core of Intel Xeon E5450 3.00 GHz processor takes up to 10–20 h. Calculation on the same statistics per core, but using 512 cores, allows increasing the total number of sampled points to about 10^{12}, while the calculation time in fact remains the same as on one core due to the linear scaling of KQMC.

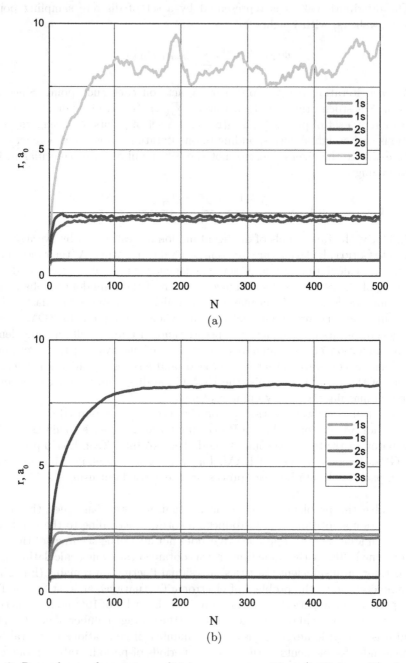

Fig. 2. Dependence of an average distance over generations (in Bohr radii) of each electron on a series number (20 generations in a series) in B ($3s\,^2S$) atom, calculated using a corridor by a number of particles in a packet per 1 (a) and 512 (b) cores.

3   Analysis of the Results

The HF method is one of the main tools in the theory of electronic structure in chemistry, materials science and other related fields. In this, the wave function of the system is represented as a product of determinants built on one-electron orbital functions with the same spin projection [1,11]. The problem of the method is that the subspace of solutions chosen in this way does not make it possible to take into account the correlation in the motion of electrons with oppositely directed spins [1]. Therefore, in order to somehow take into account this correlation, in practice, the wave function is usually represented as a linear combination of determinants (configuration interaction), or perturbation theory is used [12]. However, the computational complexity grows with the use of more and more determinants in the configuration interaction, or a larger order of perturbation theory, and the calculation becomes more laborious, which severely limits the scope of these methods. Therefore, the urgent task is to develop fundamentally new methods to account for electron-electron correlation.

The exact functional E of the system can be represented as:

$$E = E_{HF} + \delta E_c^{\uparrow\uparrow} + \delta E_c^{\downarrow\downarrow} + \delta E_c^{\uparrow\downarrow}, \tag{7}$$

where E_{HF} is the HF functional; $\delta E_c^{\uparrow\uparrow}$, $\delta E_c^{\downarrow\downarrow}$ and $\delta E_c^{\uparrow\downarrow}$ are correlation corrections for electron pairs with the corresponding spin projection. Correlation corrections $\delta E_c^{\uparrow\uparrow}$ and $\delta E_c^{\downarrow\downarrow}$ for pairs of electrons with the same spin projection are second-order corrections, since in the first order the correlation in the motion of these pairs is taken into account by means of the exchange interactions in E_{HF}. The most significant correction will be $\delta E_c^{\uparrow\downarrow}$, the form of which is determined by the term with the two-particle density $\rho(\mathbf{r}_1^{\uparrow}, \mathbf{r}_2^{\downarrow})$ in the expression for E:

$$
\begin{aligned}
E = &-N_1 \int_{\mathbf{R}^{3N}} \Psi(\mathbf{r})\Delta_{\uparrow}\Psi(\mathbf{r})d\mathbf{r} - N_2 \int_{\mathbf{R}^{3N}} \Psi(\mathbf{r})\Delta_{\downarrow}\Psi(\mathbf{r})d\mathbf{r} - N_1 \int_{\mathbf{R}^3} 2Z\frac{\rho(\mathbf{r}^{\uparrow})}{|\mathbf{r}^{\uparrow}|}d\mathbf{r}^{\uparrow} \\
&- N_2 \int_{\mathbf{R}^3} 2Z\frac{\rho(\mathbf{r}^{\downarrow})}{|\mathbf{r}^{\downarrow}|}d\mathbf{r}^{\downarrow} + N_1(N_1-1) \int_{\mathbf{R}^3}\int_{\mathbf{R}^3} \frac{\rho(\mathbf{r}_1^{\uparrow},\mathbf{r}_2^{\uparrow})}{|\mathbf{r}_1^{\uparrow}-\mathbf{r}_2^{\uparrow}|}d\mathbf{r}_1^{\uparrow}d\mathbf{r}_2^{\uparrow} \\
&+ N_2(N_2-1) \int_{\mathbf{R}^3}\int_{\mathbf{R}^3} \frac{\rho(\mathbf{r}_1^{\downarrow},\mathbf{r}_2^{\downarrow})}{|\mathbf{r}_1^{\downarrow}-\mathbf{r}_2^{\downarrow}|}d\mathbf{r}_1^{\downarrow}d\mathbf{r}_2^{\downarrow} + N_1N_2 \int_{\mathbf{R}^3}\int_{\mathbf{R}^3} \frac{\rho(\mathbf{r}_1^{\uparrow},\mathbf{r}_2^{\downarrow})}{|\mathbf{r}_1^{\uparrow}-\mathbf{r}_2^{\downarrow}|}d\mathbf{r}_1^{\uparrow}d\mathbf{r}_2^{\downarrow}.
\end{aligned}
\tag{8}
$$

To register the functional $\rho(\mathbf{r}_1^{\uparrow}, \mathbf{r}_2^{\downarrow}) \equiv \rho(r_1, r_2, \mu_{12})$ in KQMC, we used a spatial grid. Based on the conditions, the grid was chosen so that the change in the solution inside the grid would be significantly less than we are interested in from a practical point of view. Over these areas, the solution obtained by KQMC was integrated with an average statistical error of order $\frac{1}{\sqrt{N}}$, where N is the number sampling points.

Next, we represent the exact density function in the form:

$$\rho(r_1, r_2, \mu_{12}) = \frac{\rho(r_1, r_2, \mu_{12})}{\overline{\rho}(r_1, r_2)} \overline{\rho}(r_1, r_2) = \xi(r_1, r_2, \mu_{12}) \overline{\rho}(r_1, r_2),$$

$$\overline{\rho}(r_1, r_2) = \int_{-1}^{1} \rho(r_1, r_2, \mu_{12}) d\mu. \tag{9}$$

Theoretically, the function ξ can be expanded into a series using Legendre polynomials in μ_{12}. For He atom, the simplest system with two electrons having different values of the spin projection, it was found that the dependence of the function ξ on μ_{12} is close to linear (Fig. 3(a)), so the first two terms of the expansion are sufficient:

$$\xi(r_1, r_2, \mu_{12}) \cong 1 - a(r_1, r_2)\mu_{12}. \tag{10}$$

A similar result for ξ was obtained for pairs of electrons with opposite values of the spin projection in Li atom (for example, for a pair of $1s2s$-electrons in Fig. 3(b)).

The following boundary conditions for the coefficient a are obvious:

$$a(r_1, r_2) = a(r_2, r_1),$$
$$a(0, r_2) = a(r_1, 0),$$
$$a(r_1, r_2) \xrightarrow[|r_1 - r_2| \to \infty]{} 0. \tag{11}$$

The form of the dependence of the function $a(r_1, r_2)$ on r_1 at different values of r_2, obtained by the KQMC for He atom, is shown in Fig. 4. The function $a(r_1, r_2)$ has a minimum at $r_1 = r_2$. The function $max(a(r_1, r_2)) = a(r, r)$ is well approximated by a power law:

$$a(r, r) = e^{-\frac{p}{r^q}}, \tag{12}$$

where p and q are some numbers (Fig. 5). The same type of dependence of the function $a(r_1, r_2)$ on r_1 at different values of r_2 with a minimum at $r_1 = r_2$ was obtained for pairs of electrons with different values of the spin projection in Li atom. The only difference is in the values of p and q for $max(a(r_1, r_2))$ in the expression (12).

The form of the function $a(r_1, r_2)$ for He and Li atoms defined from the KQMC calculation turned out to be the same:

$$a(r_1, r_2) = -\exp\left\{-\frac{p}{r_2^q}\right\}\left(-2\left(\frac{r_1}{r_2}\right)^3 + 3\left(\frac{r_1}{r_2}\right)^2\right), \quad r_1 \leq r_2. \tag{13}$$

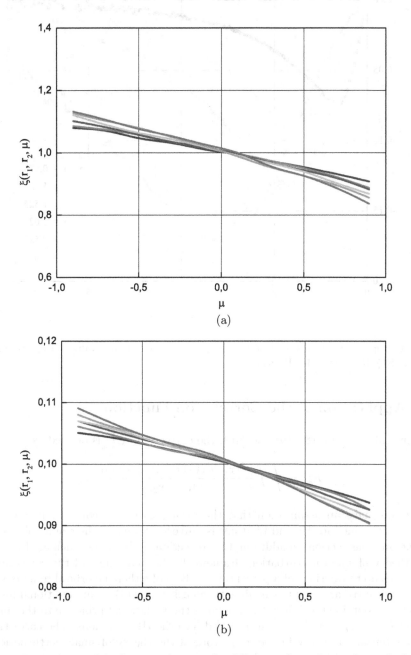

Fig. 3. Dependence of the function ξ on μ_{12} for different values of r_1 and r_2, calculated by the KQMC method for He atom (a) and for a pair of $1s2s$-electrons with opposite values of the spin projection in Li atom (b).

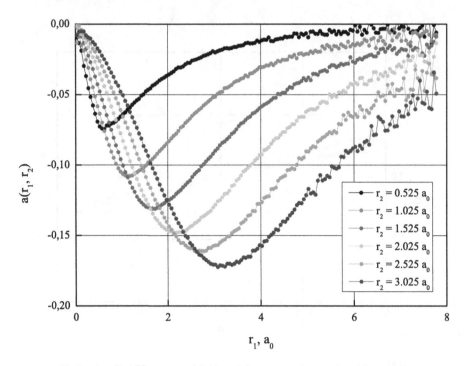

Fig. 4. Dependence of the function $a(r_1, r_2)$ on r_1 for different values of r_2 obtained by the KQMC method for He atom.

4 Application of the Correlation Function

Taking into account (8), (9) and (10), the correction $\delta E_c^{\uparrow\downarrow}$ is defined as follows:

$$\delta E_c^{\uparrow\downarrow} = \int \int \frac{\rho^{\uparrow}(\mathbf{r}_1)\rho^{\downarrow}(\mathbf{r}_2)a(\mathbf{r}_1,\mathbf{r}_2)\mu d\mathbf{r}_1 d\mathbf{r}_2}{|\mathbf{r}_1 - \mathbf{r}_2|}. \tag{14}$$

Next, we make an assumption that the form (13) of the correlation function $a(r_1, r_2)$ obtained for He and Li atoms is universal based on the results obtained in the previous section. In addition, the corrections (14) can be calculated within the theory of small perturbations framework: the magnitude of the corrections coincides up to fractions of a percent, regardless of either the orbital functions of the classical HF are used to calculate the densities in (14), or an additional term, which was obtained as a result of applying the variational principle to the functional $E = E_{HF} + \delta E_c^{\uparrow\downarrow}$, was introduced into the HF equations. The correction to the ionization energy in the framework of the theory of small perturbations can be calculated by the formula:

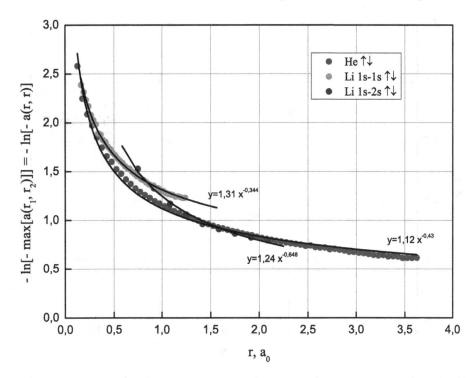

Fig. 5. Approximation of the function $max[a(r_1, r_2)] = a(r, r)$ obtained by the KQMC method for He and Li atoms.

$$\delta I_i = \iint \frac{\varphi_i^{\uparrow^2}(\mathbf{r}_1)\rho^\downarrow(\mathbf{r}_2)a(\mathbf{r}_1, \mathbf{r}_2)\mu d\mathbf{r}_1 d\mathbf{r}_2}{|\mathbf{r}_1 - \mathbf{r}_2|}, \qquad (15)$$

where $\varphi_i^\uparrow$ is the orbital function of the i-th valence electron with spin projection $+\frac{1}{2}$.

Figure 6 demonstrates that the rather simple corrections introduced in this way, which take into account the correlation, made it possible to refine the HF to an almost chemical accuracy practically without increasing computational costs at least for the first two periods of the periodic table. The exceptions are elements with completely filled shells with valence s-electrons: He and Be. We identified the source of this error as an exceptional feature associated with the spatial dependence of HF wave function on $\bar{p}(r_1, r_2)$, which can be refined by introducing additional corrections.

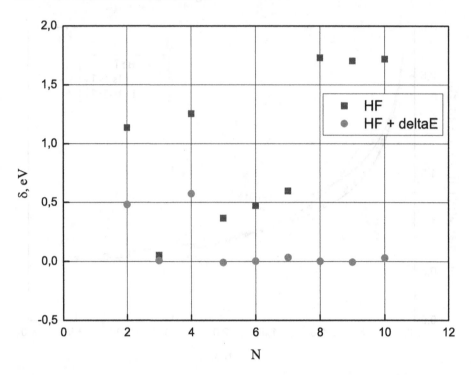

Fig. 6. Value of the error in the energy of the valence electron for the calculation by the HF method without and with corrections of the form (15) depending on the element number N.

5   Conclusions

In this work, the results of calculations of light atoms on a supercomputer using a program that implements the parallel KQMC algorithm were investigated to determine the general properties of electron correlations. The form of the correlation function was obtained from the analysis of the two-particle electron density of He and Li atoms, using which the correlation corrections to the HF ionization energies for the elements of the first two periods of the periodic table were calculated. These corrections made it possible to refine the HF method to an almost chemical accuracy with exception of elements with completely filled shells with valence s-electrons. In the future, it is planned to introduce corrections of this type for all elements of the periodic table.

Acknowledgements. This work was supported by National Research Center "Kurchatov Institute" (order No 2770 of 28.10.2021) and has been carried out using computing resources of the federal collective usage center Complex for Simulation and Data Processing for Mega-science Facilities at NRC "Kurchatov Institute", http://ckp.nrcki.ru/.

References

1. Pople, J.A.: Nobel lecture: quantum chemical models. Rev. Mod. Phys. **71**, 1267 (1999)
2. Kohn, W.: Nobel lecture: electronic structure of matter - wave functions and density functionals. Rev. Mod. Phys. **71**, 1253 (1999)
3. Tew, D.P., Klopper, W., Helgaker, T.: Electron correlation: the many-body problem at the heart of chemistry. J. Comput. Chem. **28**, 1307–1320 (2007)
4. Ceperley, D.M.: Fermion nodes. J. Stat. Phys. **63**, 1237–1267 (1991)
5. Foulkes, W.M.C.: Quantum Monte Carlo simulations of solids. Rev. Mod. Phys. **10**, 33–83 (2001)
6. Danshin, A.A., Gurevich, M.I., Ilyin, V.A., Kovalishin, A.A., Velikhov, V.E.: The extension of the Monte Carlo method for neutron transfer problems calculating to the problems of quantum mechanics. Lobachevskii J. Math. **39**(4), 513–523 (2018). https://doi.org/10.1134/S1995080218040066
7. Lebedev, V.I.: Functional Analysis and Computational Mathematics. Fizmatlit (2005)
8. Sobol, I.M.: Numerical Monte Carlo Methods. Nauka (1973)
9. Marsaglia, G., Zaman, A., Tsang, W.W.: Toward a universal random number generator. Stat. Probab. Lett. **9**, 35–39 (1990)
10. Zolotykhin, V.P., Maiorov, L.V.: Evaluation of the Criticality Parameters of Reactors by the Monte Carlo Method. Energoatomizdat (1984)
11. Fock, V.: Näherungsmethode zur Lösung des quantenmechanischen Mehrkörperproblems. Z. Phys. **61**, 126–148 (1930)
12. Cramer, C.J.: Essentials of Computational Chemistry. Wiley, Hoboken (2002)

Implementation of Discrete Element Method to the Simulation of Solid Materials Fracturing

Veronica Chepelenkova and Vadim Lisitsa[✉][ID]

Institute of Mathematics SB RAS, Koptyug ave. 4, Novosibirsk 630090, Russia
lisitsavv@ipgg.sbras.ru

Abstract. We present an algorithm that implements the discrete element method for numerical simulation of large deformations including those leading to the destruction of solid materials. In the discrete element method, a continuous medium is represented by a set of model particles with given interaction laws. Under the action of external forces and forces of interaction of particles, they can change their position in space according to the equations of motion for a discrete set of particles, which allows effectively taking into account large deformations. The peculiarity of the Discrete Element Method is the absence of theoretically substantiated relationships between the model parameters at the level of interaction of individual particles and the macroscopic mechanical parameters of the medium. The paper presents a systematic numerical study of the influence of model parameters on the effective Young's modulus and breaking point of the simulated elastic body.

Keywords: Discrete element method · Uniaxial loading · Fracturing

1 Introduction

Granular porous materials are widely used in chemical engineering [4,6], which includes CO_2 sorption [4,5], spherical alumina-supported catalysts of catalytic reforming [13], and fuel consumption [15]. The efficiency of the chemosorption or catalytic capacity of such materials is mainly governed by the geometry and topology of the pore space. However, the higher the porosity of the porous material the lower the mechanical properties. In the meanwhile mechanical strength of the material may be an important property of catalyst support or a sorbent to allow their use in technological conditions; such as high pressure, rapid pressure and temperature change, etc. Thus, the design of granular porous materials should not only include the optimization of the pore space geometry, but also the estimation of the Young modulus and critical stress (strain) that can be applied to the material before crushing.

Nowadays, material design is mainly performed using numerical simulations. In particular, the sintering [3] manufacturing process is simulated with a further numerical estimation of porosity, specific surface of pore space, hydraulic permeability, etc. Numerical experiments include the direct simulation of sorption and combustion processes in designed models. However, there is a lack of numerical investigation of the mechanical properties, even though numerical methods for such simulations are well developed. One of the most widely used approaches to simulate mechanical loading of complex structures is the finite element method [7]. It allows to consider finite deformations and even fracturing. However, its implementation requires accurate mesh generation which may be a time and resources consuming procedure, especially if randomly packed granular porous materials are considered. On the contrary, the discrete element method (DEM) is widely used to simulate dynamics of granular media [11,14]. Moreover, this approach is extended to simulate the uniaxial and triaxial loading of rock samples [2,12] and geological faults forming [8–10]. This approach can be applied to granular porous materials because the granules can be naturally represented by the elements. Moreover, the main mechanical properties of the granules are known, which include bulk modulus, shear modulus, etc. Thus, we need to develop an appropriate DEM model of the interaction of the pair-wise particles to match the macroscopic mechanical properties of the material.

In this paper, we present an original DEM bonded-particles model, that accounts for the initial particle packing due to the sintering. It means that we initiate both normal and tangential bonds which ensure additional resistance to deformations and the breakage of the bond is considered as fracture formation. To calibrate the model, we performed a series of simulations varying input parameters and estimating their effect on the Young modulus and compressive strength of the entire sample.

The remainder of the paper has the following structure. We present the discrete element bonded-particles model, input and output parameters in Sect. 2. Description of the algorithm and its implementation are provided in Sect. 3. We present numerical experiments in Sect. 4.

2   Discrete Element Method

2.1   Forces

The force acting on particle i from particle j can be decomposed into normal and tangential components as $\vec{f}_{ij} = f^n_{ij}\vec{n}_{ij} + f^t_{ij}\vec{t}_{ij}$, where $\vec{n}_{ij} = (\vec{x}_i - \vec{x}_j) \,/\, \|\vec{x}_i - \vec{x}_j\|$ and $\vec{t}_{ij} \perp \vec{n}_{ij}$ denote normal and tangential unit vectors, respectively. For ease of notation subscripts ij are hereafter omitted, if possible (Fig. 1).

Normal force component for two bonded particles is calculated as

$$f^n = \begin{cases} k^n_r\delta, & \delta \geq 0, \\ k^n_a\delta, & -d_{crit} < \delta < 0, \\ 0, & \delta \leq -d_{crit}, \end{cases}$$

with k^n_r and k^n_a being normal stiffnesses of repulsive and attractive springs respectively, $\delta = R_i + R_j - \|\vec{x}_i - \vec{x}_j\|$ is the particles overlap and d_{crit} is the bond length.

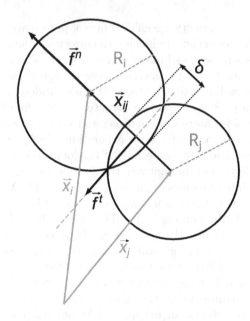

Fig. 1. Decomposition to normal and tangential components of the force acting on particle i from particle j.

If the distance between particles exceeds the value of d_{crit}, the bond breaks, and from this moment only repulsive force can arise

$$f^n = \begin{cases} k_r^n \delta, & \delta \geq 0, \\ 0, & \delta < 0. \end{cases}$$

The tangential force represents sliding friction and therefore can act only on contacting particles, i.e. with $\delta > 0$.

Let $\vec{\xi}^{(n)}$ denote a vector of particles displacement in a contact plane, which is computed iteratively. At the moment the contact is established, its value is set to zero. After calculating a force value on each step, the shear-displacement vector has to be updated as

$$\vec{\xi}^{(n+1)} = \begin{cases} \vec{\xi}^{(n)} + \tau \vec{v}^t, & f_0^t < \mu_s f^n, \\ -\dfrac{\mu_d f^n}{k^t} \dfrac{\vec{f}_0^t}{\|\vec{f}_0^t\|}, & f_0^t \geq \mu_s f^n, \end{cases}$$

where $\vec{v}_t$ is the relative tangential velocity of particles.

Note that the contact plane on the n-th step might have rotated since the previous one. Hence the vector $\vec{\xi}^{(n)}$ should also be rotated accordingly.

At each time instant t^n, the vector of test force $\vec{f}_0^t = -k^t \vec{\xi}^{(n)}$ is computed. Therefore the tangential force component $\vec{f}^t$ acting on bonded particles is given by

$$\vec{f}^t = \begin{cases} \vec{f}_0^t, & \|\vec{\xi}\| < d_{crit}, \\ \mu_d f^n \dfrac{\vec{f}_0^t}{\|\vec{f}_0^t\|}, & \|\vec{\xi}\| \geq d_{crit}. \end{cases}$$

The second case, when reached, breaks the bond, and particles then interact with force

$$\vec{f}^t = \begin{cases} \vec{f}_0^t, & f_0^t < \mu_s f^n, \\ \mu_d f^n \dfrac{\vec{f}_0^t}{\|\vec{f}_0^t\|}, & f_0^t \geq \mu_s f^n, \end{cases}$$

corresponding to the Coulomb friction law.

2.2   Time Integration

Particles move in space according to the classical Newtonian mechanics. The equation of motion for i-th particle is given by

$$m_i \frac{d^2 \vec{x}_i}{dt^2} = m_i \vec{g} + \sum_{j \in J_i} \vec{f}_{ij}\left(t, \vec{x}_i, \vec{x}_j, \vec{v}_i, \vec{x}_j\right) + \vec{f}_d^i, \tag{1}$$

where m_i is the mass of the considered particle, $\vec{f}_{ij}$ are the forces acting on i-th particle from the neighboring particles, J_i is a set of indices of the i-th particle neighbours, $\vec{f}_d^i$ is the dissipative forces which are introduced to ensure the system to rest down at high times.

We follow [9] using the velocity Verlet algorithm to approximate Eq. (1):

$$\begin{aligned} \frac{\vec{v}_i^{n+1/2} - \vec{v}_i^n}{\tau/2} &= \frac{1}{m_i}\vec{F}_i\left(t^n, \vec{x}_i^n, \vec{x}_j^n, \vec{v}_i^n, \vec{v}_j^n\right), \\ \frac{\vec{x}_i^{n+1} - \vec{x}_i^n}{\tau} &= \vec{v}_i^{n+1/2}, \\ \frac{\vec{v}_i^{n+1} - \vec{v}_i^{n+1/2}}{\tau/2} &= \frac{1}{m_i}\vec{F}_i\left(t^{n+1}, \vec{x}_i^{n+1}, \vec{x}_j^{n+1}, \vec{v}_i^{n+1/2}, \vec{v}_j^{n+1/2}\right), \\ j &\in J(i). \end{aligned} \tag{2}$$

This is the second-order scheme if forces do not explicitly depend on velocities, but it is only the first-order accurate otherwise.

Stability condition for the Verlet scheme can be formulated as follows [9]:

$$\tau \leq 0.2 \frac{D_{min}}{V_p} = 0.2 D_{min} \sqrt{\frac{\rho}{E}}, \tag{3}$$

where D_{min} is the minimum diameter of particles, and $V_p = \sqrt{\frac{E}{\rho}}$ is the speed of p-waves in the material with density ρ and Young's modulus E.

2.3   Boundary Conditions

During all the simulation time particles are located inside a rectangular area to prevent any of them from falling. All the boundaries forming this area are supposed to be rigid. Hence we implement each wall as a set of particles, consecutively placed along the lines $x = $ const and $y = $ const. These particles should be regarded as the ones being able to interact with particles of the material itself, but there is no need to update their new positions and velocities as in (2) if they do not move.

However on a stage of uniaxial loading we move the upper boundary with the specified speed $\dot{\varepsilon} = $ const, so in that case we should also take into account this motion and update their new positions as follows: $\vec{x}^{n+1,top} = \vec{x}^{n,top} + \tau\dot{\varepsilon} \cdot \vec{n}^y$, where $\vec{n}^y = [0, -1]^\top$ is the direction of motion.

2.4   Output Parameters

While running the algorithm, one can compute the average stress in a sample and; thus, get a stress-strain curve. Using this curve, one can obtain the Young modulus E as a slope of a linear part, and the compressive strength σ_{max} as peak stress.

To compute the average stress in the sample we use the method described in [12].

For any given tensor s_{ij}

$$s_{ij} = \delta_{ik}s_{kj} = \frac{\partial x_i}{\partial x_k}s_{kj} = \frac{\partial(x_i s_{kj})}{\partial x_k} - x_i\frac{\partial s_{kj}}{\partial x_k} = \mathrm{div}(x_i s_{kj}) - x_i\frac{\partial s_{kj}}{\partial x_k}.$$

Taking into account the expression above, one may compute the average stress in a particle of volume V^p as

$$\langle\sigma_{ij}^p\rangle = \frac{1}{V^p}\iiint\limits_{V^p}\sigma_{ij}^p dV = \frac{1}{V^p}\iiint\limits_{V^p}\left(\mathrm{div}(x_i\sigma_{kj}^p) - x_i\frac{\partial\sigma_{kj}^p}{\partial x_k}\right)dV.$$

Using the divergence theorem and assuming the particles are in the state of equilibrium, which leads to $\frac{\partial\sigma_{kj}^p}{\partial x_k} = 0$, the following equation is obtained:

$$\langle\sigma_{ij}^p\rangle = \frac{1}{V^p}\iint\limits_{\partial V^p}x_i\sigma_{kj}^p n_k dS = \frac{1}{V^p}\iint\limits_{\partial V^p}x_i\sigma_j^p dS = \frac{1}{V^p}\iint\limits_{\partial V^p}x_i dF_j^p,$$

where σ_j^p denotes a traction vector, n_k – an outer unit normal to the particle surface.

In DEM the forces between interacting particles arise only at contact points. Hence the integral can be replaced with a sum over a set of the particle neighbours or over a number of direct contacts

$$\langle\sigma_{ij}^p\rangle = \frac{1}{V^p}\sum_{q\in J_p}x_i^{c,q}F_j^{pq},$$

with $x_i^{c,q} = x_i^p - n_i^{pq}\left(R^p + \frac{\delta^{pq}}{2}\right)$ being a contact point of the particle p and particle q.

In order to symmetrize the stress tensor the force value is replaced by

$$x_i^{c,q} F_j^{pq} \rightarrow \frac{1}{2}(x_i^{c,q} F_j^{pq} + x_j^{c,q} F_i^{pq}).$$

Finally, the overall stress in the given volume V containing N particles can be computed as

$$\langle \sigma_{ij} \rangle = -\frac{1}{2 \sum_N V^p} \sum_N \sum_{J_p} (x_i^{c,q} F_j^{pq} + x_j^{c,q} F_i^{pq}).$$

Average stress is computed at each time instant. Note, that we use the constant strain rate boundary conditions. Thus, time-dependent stress can be mapped to the stress-strain relation. To obtain a slope of the linear part on a stress-strain curve, we shrink the line segment $[0, \sigma_{max}]$ by one quarter from each endpoint, and define the set $S = \{(\varepsilon, \sigma) \mid \frac{\sigma_{max}}{4} < \sigma(\varepsilon) < \frac{3\sigma_{max}}{4}\}$, after that we compute the linear stress-strain relation minimizing the least-square residual between the straight line and the original curve. The slope of this line gives us the value of the Young modulus inasmuch as by definition

$$E = \frac{\sigma}{\varepsilon}.$$

3   Implementation of the Algorithm

There are two main steps in the algorithm: computation of the forces for the fixed particle positions and updating the positions. For a given array of particles both steps are free from data dependencies; thus they can be efficiently parallelized under the shared memory and implemented using CUDA technology. However, there is a hidden step in the algorithm, which includes the search for the neighboring particles to be used in forces computation.

Particle-based methods, including DEM, require computing of the pairwise particles' interactions. But the calculation of all-to-all interactions would require $O(N^2)$ operations, where N is the total number of particles. Thus, it is typically assumed, that for each particle i there exists a domain of influence J_i defining the number of particles $N_i = \dim\{J_i\} << N$ able to interact with a given one. In this case, the computational complexity of the algorithm becomes $O(N < N_i >)$, where $< N_i >$ is the mean value of the neighbor amount per particle. However, if the dynamical system is considered, one needs to reconstruct the list of neighbors at each time instant. Thus, we need to be able to construct and then reconstruct the adjacency matrix.

The construction of the adjacency matrix can not be parallelized and it is implemented as a sequential CPU-based code. Following [10] we use the lattice method. According to the definition of the forces of interaction, the particles affect each other only if they intersect or are linked by a bond, which means that

$$\|\vec{x}_i - \vec{x}_j\| \leq R_i + R_j + d_{crit},$$

where R_i and R_j are the particles radii and d_{crit} is the critical distance or bond length. Thus, the domain of dependence of each particle does not exceed $2R_{max} + d_{crit}$, where R_{max} is the maximal radius. Moreover, the particle displacement at a single time step is considered to be much smaller than its radius, which follows from the stability condition of the Verlet scheme.

Using the assumptions above one can build a regular rectangular grid with cell size $h_1 = h_2 = h = 2R_{max} + d_{crit}$ and define the grid cells $C_{kl} = \{(x_1, x_2) \in \mathbb{R}^2 \mid kh \leq x_1 \leq (k+1)h, \ lh \leq x_2 \leq (l+1)h\}$. We state that the i-th element belongs to the cell C_{kl} ($E_i \in C_{kl}$) if its center belongs to the cell; i.e., $\vec{x}^i \in C_{kl}$. Due to the choice of the grid cell size if i-th particle belongs to cell C_{kl}, then all its neighbours may only belong to directly adjacent cells $C_{k'l'}$, where $k' \in \{k+1, k, k-1\}$ and $l' \in \{l+1, l, l-1\}$. Thus, at the preliminary step of the algorithm, the adjacency matrix can be constructed in the following form. For each particle we find the grid cell to which it belongs: $k = \text{round}(x_1^i/h)$ and $l = \text{round}(x_2^i/h)$. Then we update the list of particles belonging to each cell C_{kl}. Finally, for each particle, we get the cell number, and for each cell, we get the number of particles belonging to this cell and their numbers. Note, that this part of the algorithm has data dependencies; i.e., if parallelized with respect to particles, different threads may try to update the list of particles in the same cell. Thus, this stage is implemented as a CPU-based code.

Reconstruction of the adjacency matrix can be parallelized if split into two steps. We assume that the matrix is known at the time instant n and then we apply the time stepping to recompute the particles' positions. After that for each particle independently we may update the cell number, using the formula above. However, we do not update the list of particles belonging to cells to prevent data dependency, which is done one the second step. Due to the choice of the grid cells, a particle may either stay in the same cell or move to one of the adjacent cells after one time step. Thus, to update the list of the particles within a fixed C_{kl} we need only to take into account adjacent cells $C_{k'l'}$ and check out what particles within these cells (including the cell C_{kl}) belong to C_{kl} at the new instant. This step is parallelized with respect to grid cells. Similar ideas, but with different principles of lattice construction, are used in molecular dynamics and lattice Boltzmann methods [1].

The pseudo-code of the entire algorithm is provided below in Algorithm 1.

4   Numerical Experiments

In this section, we present the result of numerical experiments on samples containing 4000 particles each, simulating a uniaxial compression test. The test results in getting a stress-strain curve allowing us to estimate the Young modulus and compressive strength of the given sample. Numerical experiments in this

Algorithm 1. DEM algorithm used for simulation of uniaxial sample loading

if packing **then**
  Set the computational area
  Generate paticles
  Set the grid
if removing lateral walls **then**
  Set bonded neighbours
  Adjust the upper wall to the highest of particles
while non-zero energy (if packing) $\|$ $\varepsilon < \varepsilon^*$ (if loading) **do**
  For each particle p update C_{kl}
  For each C_{kl} update its contents
  Update neighbours of each particle p
  $\vec{x}_p^n \leftarrow \vec{x}_p^{n+1}$
  $\vec{v}_p^n \leftarrow \vec{v}_p^{n+1/2}$
  For each particle p update C_{kl}
  For each C_{kl} update its contents
  Update neighbours of each particle p
  $\vec{v}_p^{n+1/2} \leftarrow \vec{v}_p^{n+1}$
  if loading **then**
    $\langle \sigma_{ij} \rangle \leftarrow -\frac{1}{2\sum_N V^p} \sum_N \sum_{J_p} (x_i^{c,q} F_j^{pq} + x_j^{c,q} F_i^{pq})$

study are conducted using NVIDIA Tesla K40 as a graphics accelerator. Average time needed for one experiment is estimated at approximately 4 h.

Note, that the peculiarity of the discrete element method is the lack of direct relations between the input model parameters, or microscopic parameters and the macroscopic properties of the sample or output parameters. Hence, the calibration of the model is always needed prior to real-life simulation. Among the input parameters we need to distinguish the minimal and maximal sizes of particles R_{min} and R_{max}, repulsive and attractive stiffness k_r^n and k_a^n, tangential stiffness k^t, critical distance d_{crit} and static and dynamic friction coefficients μ_s and μ^d. Following [12] we suggest that the particle size does not affect the macroproperties examined in this paper. Additionally, we assume that repulsive and attractive stiffness coincide; i.e., $k_r^n = k_a^n = k^n$, and set its value to $k^n = 128 \cdot 10^9$ N/m. The same is considered for friction coefficients: $\mu_s = \mu_d = \mu$. Thus, we reduce the number of parameters to only three of them: d_{crit}, k^t, and μ. These three parameters has been varied to study their effect on the resulting estimations of the mechanical properties of the material. We consider $d_{crit} \in \{0.01R_{max}, 0.03R_{max}, 0.05R_{max}, 0.07R_{max}\}$, $k^t \in \{0.1k^n, 0.3k^n, 0.5k^n, 0.7k^n, k^n\}$, $\mu \in \{0, 0.1, 0.3, 0.5\}$. Particles radii were generated as uniformly distributed random numbers on the interval of $[10, 15]$ m. For every set of parameters we generate five samples within a region 1260×2520 m each. The overall view of a packed sample is given in Fig. 2a.

After the packing stage is finished, vertical boundaries are removed, and particles are allowed to reach the new state of equilibrium. At this point the sample is considered unloaded; i.e., we assume strains to be equal to zero. After that, the upper boundary starts to move down with a constant speed of $0.01R_{min}$ per time step which corresponds to a constant strain rate. At each time step, one can compute the stress tensor, current strain value, and positions of all bonds being broken on this step. A sample at different time instants is shown in Fig. 2. Broken bonds distribution in the sample representing the microfracturing is given in Fig. 3.

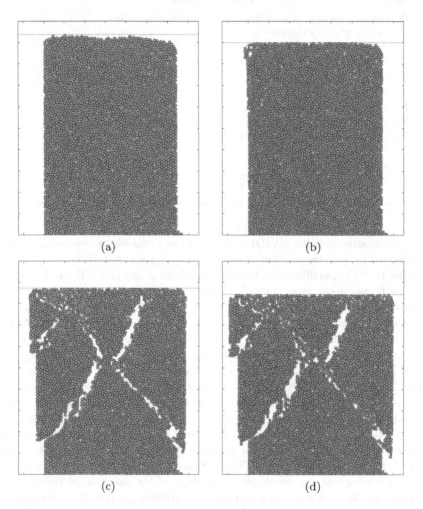

(a)

(b)

(c)

(d)

Fig. 2. A sample with $k^t = k^n$, $d_{crit} = 0.05R_{max}$, $\mu = 0.1$ on different stages of loading: (a) $\varepsilon = 0$, (b) $\varepsilon = 0.04$, (c) $\varepsilon = 0.07$, (d) $\varepsilon = 0.1$

The main output of the algorithm simulating the uniaxial loading is the stress-strain relation, which is computed for all 400 experiments. We examined the dependence of the stress-strain response on every varied parameter

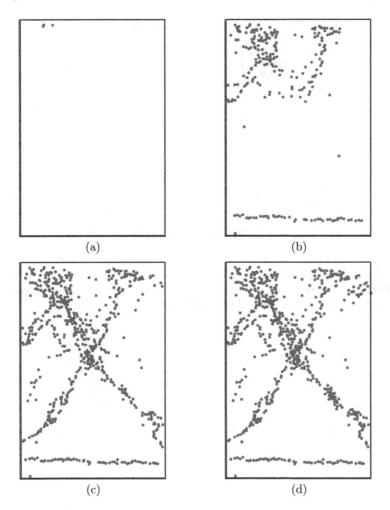

Fig. 3. Distribution of broken bonds in the sample with $k^t = k^n$, $d_{crit} = 0.05R_{max}$, $\mu = 0.1$ on different stages of loading: (a) $\varepsilon = 0.01$, (b) $\varepsilon = 0.04$, (c) $\varepsilon = 0.07$, (d) $\varepsilon = 0.1$.

with two others being fixed. We took the central point in the parameter space $(d_{crit}, k^t, \mu) = (0.03R_{max}, 0.3k^n, 0.1)$. Stress-strain curves for various critical distances with fixed tangential stiffness and dynamic friction coefficient are given in Fig. 4. Same plots for the fixed critical distance and dynamic friction coefficient but various tangential stiffness are presented in Fig. 5. The last figure in

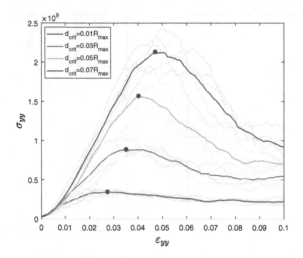

Fig. 4. Stress-strain curves for fixed $k^t = k^n$ and $\mu = 0.1$ and for different values of d_{crit}. Thin lines represent single statistical realizations, thick lines correspond to the mean curve over the realizations. Markers represent the critical stress.

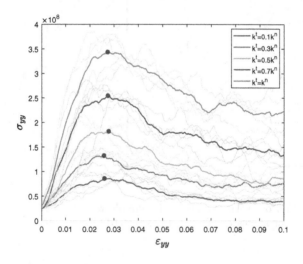

Fig. 5. Stress-strain relations for fixed $d_{crit} = 0.01R_{max}$ and $\mu = 0.1$ and for different values of k^t. Thin lines represent single statistical realizations, thick lines correspond to mean curve over the realizations. Markers represent the critical stress.

the series (Fig. 6) represents the stress-strain curves for fixed critical distance and tangential stiffness with various dynamic friction coefficients. In all cases, we observe the increase of a slope of a linear part on stress-strain curves; i.e., the increase of the Young modulus with the increase of a parameter value. Compressive strength also tends to increase with the growth of any parameter.

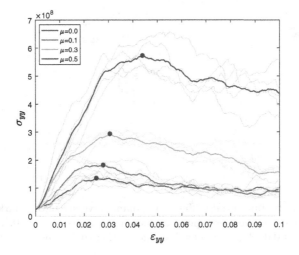

Fig. 6. Stress-strain relations for fixed $d_{crit} = 0.01R_{max}$ and $k^t = 0.5k^n$ and for different values of μ. Thin lines represent single statistical realizations, thick lines correspond to mean curve over the realizations. Markers represent the critical stress.

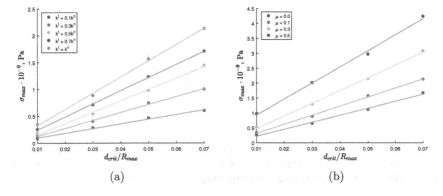

Fig. 7. Effect of the bond length on compressive strength. Markers represent the experimental data, lines correspond to linear regressions. (a) $\mu = 0.1$, various tangential stiffness; (b) $k^t = k^n$, various dynamic friction coefficients.

To construct a quantitative relation between input and output parameters we consider critical stresses to be functions of the tangential stiffness, dynamic friction coefficient, and bond length. It is shown (see Figs. 7, 8 and 9) that compressive strength linearly depends on the bond length and the tangential stiffness, whereas dependence on the friction coefficient is matched by a quadratic function. With these estimations, we may now construct the models with pre-

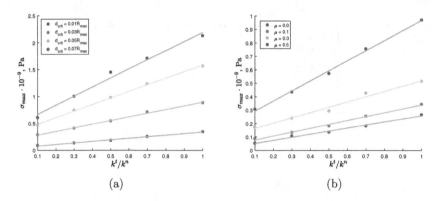

Fig. 8. Effect of the tangential stiffness on compressive strength. Markers represent the experimental data, lines correspond to linear regressions. (a) $\mu = 0.1$, various bond length; (b) $d_{crit} = 0.01R_{max}$, various dynamic friction coefficients.

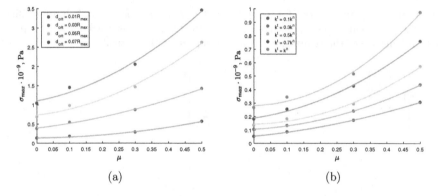

Fig. 9. Effect of the friction coefficient on compressive strength. Markers represent the experimental data, lines correspond to polynomial regressions. (a) $k^t = 0.5k^n$, various bond length; (b) $d_{crit} = 0.01R_{max}$, various tangential stiffness.

scribed limiting stresses to perform predictive modeling by the discrete element method. However, as it follows from Fig. 10 estimations of the Young modulus are less stable and may require more statistical realizations to construct suitable regressions describing their dependence on input parameters. Nevertheless, the qualitative analysis illustrates the increase of the Young modulus with the increase of the input parameters.

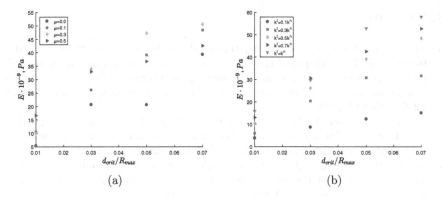

Fig. 10. Effect of the bond length on the Young modulus. Markers represent the experimental data. (a) $k^t = 0.5k^n$, various friction coefficients; (b) $\mu = 0.1$, various tangential stiffness.

5   Conclusions

We presented an original algorithm to simulate the uniaxial loading of granular porous materials to estimate their Young modulus and limiting stress value. The algorithm is based on the Discrete Element Method (DEM) with the use of bonded elements model which allows attraction of the particles as well as repulsion. However, the bonds are allowed to break which simulates fracturing. The algorithm was implemented using CUDA technology so that only the pre- and postprocessing is performed using CPU, whereas all main stages of the numerical simulation (forces computation and integration of the equations of motion) are performed on GPUs.

The peculiarity of the DEM is that there are no theoretically derived relations between the model parameters used at the particles level and the macroscopic elastic modulus of the sample. To reconstruct these relations we performed a series of numerical experiments changing three microscopic parameters and considering their effect on the Young modulus and the limiting stress of the sample. We showed that the limiting stress linearly depends on the limiting bonds' length and tangential stiffness, but it is proportional to the squared dynamic friction coefficient. The Young modulus illustrates an almost monotonic increase with the increase of the considered microscopic parameters. However, a small number of numerical experiments (only five statistical realizations per a fixed set of parameters) did not let us construct statistically confident functional relations.

Acknowledgement. The research was supported by the RSCF grant no. 21-71-20003. Numerical simulations were performed using the supercomputer facilities of Saint-Petersburg State Technical University.

References

1. Alpak, F.O., Gray, F., Saxena, N., Dietderich, J., Hofmann, R., Berg, S.: A distributed parallel multiple-relaxation-time lattice Boltzmann method on general-purpose graphics processing units for the rapid and scalable computation of absolute permeability from high-resolution 3D micro-CT images. Comput. Geosci. **22**(3), 815–832 (2018)
2. Bobet, A., Fakhimi, A., Johnson, S., Morris, J., Tonon, F., Yeung, M.R.: Numerical models in discontinuous media: review of advances for rock mechanics applications. J. Geotech. Geoenviron. Eng. **135**(11), 1547–1561 (2009)
3. Bordia, R.K., Kang, S.J.L., Olevsky, E.A.: Current understanding and future research directions at the onset of the next century of sintering science and technology. J. Am. Ceram. Soc. **100**(6), 2314–2352 (2017)
4. Derevschikov, V.S., Kazakova, E.D., Yatsenko, D.A., Veselovskaya, J.V.: Multiscale study of carbon dioxide chemisorption in the plug flow adsorber of the anesthesia machine. Sep. Sci. Technol. **56**(3), 485–497 (2021)
5. Derevshchikov, V.S., Kazakova, E.D.: Comparative analysis of the chemical composition and sorption, textural, and strength properties of commercial medical CO_2 sorbents. Catal. Ind. **12**(1), 1–6 (2020)
6. Fedorov, A.V., Gulyaeva, Y.K.: Strength statistics for porous alumina. Powder Technol. **343**, 783–791 (2019)
7. Guiton, M.L.E., Sassi, W., Leroy, Y.M., Gauthier, B.D.M.: Mechanical constraints on the chronology of fracture activation in folded Devonian sandstone of the western Moroccan Anti-Atlas. J. Struct. Geol. **25**(8), 1317–1330 (2003)
8. Hardy, S., Finch, E.: Discrete-element modelling of detachment folding. Basin Res. **17**(4), 507–520 (2005)
9. Hardy, S., McClayc, K., Munozb, J.A.: Deformation and fault activity in space and time in high-resolution numerical models of doubly vergent thrust wedges. Mar. Pet. Geol. **26**, 232–248 (2009)
10. Lisitsa, V., Kolyukhin, D., Tcheverda, V., Volianskaia, V., Priimenko, V.: GPU-based discrete element modeling of geological faults. In: Voevodin, V., Sobolev, S. (eds.) RuSCDays 2019. CCIS, vol. 1129, pp. 225–236. Springer, Cham (2019). https://doi.org/10.1007/978-3-030-36592-9_19
11. Meng, J., Huang, J., Sheng, D., Sloan, S.W.: Granular contact dynamics with elastic bond model. Acta Geotech. **12**(3), 479–493 (2017)
12. Potyondy, D.O., Cundall, P.A.: A bonded-particle model for rock. Int. J. Rock Mech. Min. Sci. **41**(8), 1329–1364 (2004)
13. Rahimpour, M.R., Jafari, M., Iranshahi, D.: Progress in catalytic naphtha reforming process: a review. Appl. Energy **109**, 79–93 (2013)
14. Theocharis, A., Roux, J.N., Langlois, V.: Elasticity of model weakly cemented granular materials: a numerical study. Int. J. Solids Struct. **193–194**, 13–27 (2020)
15. Yazykov, N.A., Dubinin, Y.V., Simonov, A.D., Reshetnikov, S.I., Yakovlev, V.A.: Features of sulfur oils catalytic combustion in fluidized bed. Chem. Eng. J. **283**, 649–655 (2016)

Information Entropy Initialized Concrete Autoencoder for Optimal Sensor Placement and Reconstruction of Geophysical Fields

Nikita Turko[1]([envelope]), Alexander Lobashev[2], Konstantin Ushakov[1,3], Maxim Kaurkin[3], and Rashit Ibrayev[3,4]

[1] Moscow Institute of Physics and Technology, Dolgoprudny, Russia
`turko@phystech.edu`
[2] Skolkovo Institute of Science and Technology, Skolkovo, Russia
[3] Shirshov Institute of Oceanology, Russian Academy of Sciences, Moscow, Russia
[4] Marchuk Institute of Numerical Mathematics, Russian Academy of Sciences, Moscow, Russia

Abstract. We propose a new approach to the optimal placement of sensors for the problem of reconstructing geophysical fields from sparse measurements. Our method consists of two stages. In the first stage, we estimate the variability of the physical field as a function of spatial coordinates by approximating its information entropy through the Conditional PixelCNN network. To calculate the entropy, a new ordering of a two-dimensional data array (spiral ordering) is proposed, which makes it possible to obtain the entropy of a physical field simultaneously for several spatial scales. In the second stage, the entropy of the physical field is used to initialize the distribution of optimal sensor locations. This distribution is further optimized with the Concrete Autoencoder architecture with the straight-through gradient estimator and adversarial loss to simultaneously minimize the number of sensors and maximize reconstruction accuracy. Our method scales linearly with data size, unlike commonly used Principal Component Analysis. We demonstrate our method on the two examples: (a) temperature and (b) salinity fields around the Barents Sea and the Svalbard group of islands. For these examples, we compute the reconstruction error of our method and a few baselines. We test our approach against two baselines (1) PCA with QR factorization and (2) climatology. We find out that the obtained optimal sensor locations have clear physical interpretation and correspond to the boundaries between sea currents.

Keywords: Concrete Autoencoder · Optimal sensor placement · Information entropy · Ocean state reconstruction

1 Introduction

The motivation to study optimal sensor placement problems is two-fold: firstly, we want to find locations where to place new sensors or observational sta-tions, secondly, we want to optimize data assimilation methods such as ensemble Kalman filters that use the singular value decomposition (SVD) and slow-down ocean model simulation. In real-time ocean forecast systems, a typical number of observations for data assimilation is about 300 observations for temperature and salinity fields and about 5000 observations for altimetry and sea ice concentration [1]. With the growing number of observations coming from satellites, it is important to find a balance between the amount of assimilated data and the speed of the data assimilation algorithm. One of the ways to find the optimal amount of data is to solve the problem of estimation of informativity of the measurements.

In this work, we will focus on solving the following problem: suppose we have a data set of historical measurements of some physical field. We want to reconstruct these fields using only a small fraction of the observations while maintaining good reconstruction quality. If we want to select k sensors from n grid nodes, where k lies in the interval $[k_{min}, k_{max}]$, then our search space grows as $\sum_{k=k_{min}}^{k_{max}} C_n^k$, which for large n makes it impossible to use direct combinatorial search by measuring the reconstruction error for each possible placement of sensors. Since the exact solution of the optimal sensor placement problem is associated with laborious combinatorial search, one has to use approximate algorithms.

Classical approximate optimization methods for sensor selection assume that the measurement vector at sparse sensor locations is related to the full observation vector via a linear transformation. The Fisher Information Matrix is used to measure the error between the true and reconstructed fields. The Fisher information matrix can be computed as the inverse covariance matrix of the reconstruction errors. Classical methods can be divided into three main groups depending on the loss function used [2]. The first set of methods maximizes the determinant of the Fisher information matrix or, equivalently, minimizes the determinant of the errors covariance matrix [3–5]. The second set of methods is based on minimizing the trace of the Fisher information matrix [6–8]. In particular, if diagonal error covariance is assumed, the loss function becomes the well-known mean square error (MSE) between the observed and reconstructed fields. The third group of classical methods minimizes the minimum eigenvalue of the Fisher information matrix or, in other words, minimizes the spectral norm of the error covariance matrix [6,7].

In high-dimensional cases even calculating the error covariance matrix is intractable, for example, if we consider global ocean circulation models with a resolution of $1/4°$ or $1/10°$, the covariance matrix has size up to $10^6 \times 10^6$. After the introduction of the Gumbel-softmax trick [9] and the concrete distribution [10] which allowed to use traditional gradient methods to learn parameters of discrete probability distributions several deep learning approaches were proposed for optimal sensor placement including concrete autoencodes [11,12], deep probabilistic subsampling [13] and feature selection network [14]. These deep learning methods are more memory-efficient and don't require costly computation of the covariance matrix. However, during optimization with help of the Gumbel-softmax trick the long period of exploration of the space of optimal sensor locations is needed. Despite its memory-efficiency, deep learning-based methods may experience slow convergence in case of high-dimensional data. To solve the problem of slow convergence we introduce a prior distribution on the optimal sensor locations by using information entropy.

2   Information Entropy Approximation

2.1   Information Entropy

To apply optimization algorithms consistently in the high-dimensional space of sensor locations, we need to introduce an informative prior distribution. For example, it is advisable to place sensors at points where the physical field has high variability. If we have a non-negative scalar field $V(x, y)$ reflecting the historical variability of the physical field, then the prior distribution becomes

$$\mathbb{P}(x, y) = \frac{e^{\frac{1}{\tau} V(x,y)}}{\int e^{\frac{1}{\tau} V(x,y)} dx dy} \tag{1}$$

where τ is a temperature parameter that controls the concentration of sensors near the maximum of the variability field $V(x, y)$.

The variability of the physical field as a function of spatial coordinates can be estimated as the standard deviation of the values of the physical field, taken along the temporal dimension. This estimate using the historical standard deviation is a special case of information entropy, assuming that at each spatial location we have an independent Gaussian random variable with density

$$\mathbb{P}(\xi|x, y) = \frac{1}{\sqrt{2\pi}\sigma(x, y)} e^{-\frac{1}{2}(\frac{\xi - \mu(x,y)}{\sigma(x,y)})^2} \tag{2}$$

The entropy of a normally distributed random variable is the logarithm of its standard deviation up to a constant

$$H(x, y) = -\int \mathbb{P}(\xi|x, y) \log \mathbb{P}(\xi|x, y) d\xi = \frac{1}{2} + \log(\sqrt{2\pi}\sigma(x, y))$$
$$= \log(\sigma(x, y)) + \text{const.} \tag{3}$$

Information entropy as a quantitative measure of variability can be generalized to the case of spatially correlated non-Gaussian random variables. One way to implement such an approximation is to use neural networks to approximate the joint probability density of patches taken from a data set of historical values of physical fields.

Examples of patches are provided in Fig. 1. We are interested in approximating the conditional density of physical field values in a patch given its center location $P(\xi|x, y)$. The entropy of a physical field could be obtained from the density by the Monte-Carlo approximation

$$H(x, y) = -\int \mathbb{P}(\xi|x, y) \log \mathbb{P}(\xi|x, y) d\xi = -\frac{1}{N} \sum_{i=1}^{N} \log \mathbb{P}(\xi_i|x, y), \ \xi_i \sim \mathbb{P}(\xi_i|x, y). \tag{4}$$

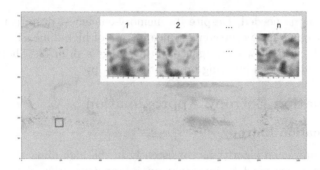

Fig. 1. Example of patches extracted from sea the surface temperature anomaly field. Indices $1, 2, \ldots, n$ correspond to patches taken in the same spatial location at different time moments.

2.2   Density Estimation Using Conditional PixelCNN

Suppose our set of physical fields is encoded as a set of $L \times L$ images or patches s_i cropped from the domain of interest $\mathcal{D}$, each of which is labeled with spatial coordinates of the patch center $\mathbf{r} = \{r_1, \ldots, r_K\} \in \mathcal{D}$

$$\mathcal{S}^{(\mathbf{r}_i \in \mathcal{D})} = \{s_1^{\mathbf{r}_1}, \ldots, s_N^{\mathbf{r}_N}\}. \tag{5}$$

We want to approximate probability density of physical fields $\mathbb{P}(s^{\mathbf{r}}|\mathbf{r})$ conditioned on a vector $\mathbf{r}$ of spatial coordinates. The image could be represented as the vector of dimension $L \times L$ and the probability density can be expanded as the product of probabilities of individual pixels conditioned on all previous pixels

$$\mathbb{P}(s^{\mathbf{r}}|\mathbf{r}) = \prod_{i=1}^{L \times L} \mathbb{P}([s^{\mathbf{r}}]_i | [s^{\mathbf{r}}]_1, \ldots, [s^{\mathbf{r}}]_{i-1}, \mathbf{r}), \tag{6}$$

where $[s^{\mathbf{r}}]_i$ stands for the i-th pixel of the image $s^{\mathbf{r}}$ with respect to the chosen ordering.

In Conditional PixelCNN approach [15] all conditional distributions are modeled by a single convolutional network. Auto-regressive structure is achieved by applying masked convolutions. Convolution kernels at every layer are multiplied by a tensor masking all pixels with larger order than the current one.

In (6) we need to specify the particular ordering of pixels in an image. Examples of possible orderings are shown in Fig. 2. We introduce the so-called spiral ordering (e). Spiral ordering allows one to train a Conditional PixelCNN once at the largest patch size $L \times L$ and then obtain information entropy on several spatial scales $L' \times L'$, $L' < L$ by taking product only of the first $L' \times L'$ conditional distributions in (6).

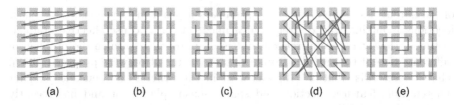

Fig. 2. (a) Raster ordering; (b) S-curve ordering; (c) Arbitrary continuous ordering; (d) Arbitrary discontinuous ordering. It is favorable to use continuous orderings like (b) and (c) since they don't suffer from the blind spot problem as it does the raster ordering (a) used in the original PixelCNN architecture [16]. We propose to use spiral ordering (e) since it allows one to compute information entropy at several scales simultaneously.

The network is trained on the dataset $\mathcal{S}^{(\mathbf{r}_i \in \mathcal{D})}$ maximizing probability of observed physical fields or equivalently by minimizing negative log-likelihood

$$L(\theta) = -\sum_{i=1}^{N} \log \mathbb{P}_\theta(s_i^{\mathbf{r}_i}|\mathbf{r}_i), \tag{7}$$

where θ is the vector of parameters of Conditional PixelCNN.

Given a trained network we compute the entropy of a physical field as a function of spatial coordinates by averaging negative log-likelihoods over ensemble of physical fields generated at fixed values of spatial coordinates

$$H(\mathbf{r}) = -\mathbb{E}_s \log \mathbb{P}_\theta(s|\mathbf{r}) = -\frac{1}{\#\{\mathbf{r}^i : |\mathbf{r}^i - \mathbf{r}| < \varepsilon\}} \sum_{|\mathbf{r}^i - \mathbf{r}| < \varepsilon} \log \mathbb{P}_\theta(s_i^{\mathbf{r}_i}|\mathbf{r}), \tag{8}$$

where $\#s$ is the number of elements in a set s.

Computed information entropy field can be used to propose optimal sensor locations by sampling from the distribution

$$\mathbb{P}(\mathbf{r}) = \frac{e^{\frac{1}{\tau}H(\mathbf{r})}}{\int_\mathcal{D} e^{\frac{1}{\tau}H(\mathbf{r})} d\mathbf{r}} \tag{9}$$

where we set hyperparameter $\tau = 0.2$ for the entropy field measured in nats per computational grid cell.

3 Optimization of Sensors Locations and Reconstruction of Fields

3.1 Concrete Autoencoder

The initial sensor locations sampled from the prior distribution (9) need to be further optimized since we also want to find an operator that takes as input sparse measurements and reconstructs the full field from the as small number of measurements as possible. The optimization problem in the space of sensor locations is intrinsically discrete which makes it hard to use effective gradient methods. However, several relaxation-based approaches to solve the problem of differentiation of the samples from a discrete distribution were proposed [9,10]. The Concrete distribution [10] was used in the concrete autoencoder [12] for differentiable feature selection and sparse sensor placement and has recently been applied in CFD-based sensor placement problems [11].

One of the drawbacks of the concrete autoencoder is that we need to apriori specify the desired number of sensors. To automatically define the necessary number of sensors we propose to optimize parameters of the binary mask using a straight-through gradient estimator, i.e. in the backward pass we replace the ill-defined gradients of the step function with the gradients of the identity function.

Our binary mask is parametrized by the scalar field of parameters w, and the binary mask representing sensor locations is obtained via a step function

$$\text{mask}(w) = \text{step}(w) \tag{10}$$

Straight-through gradient estimator allows us to use a single matrix w of parameters for a different number of sensors. However, the Gumbel-Softmax reparametrization is more efficient at initial exploration the space of sensor locations. We argue that good initialization of optimal sensor location with straight-through gradient estimator allows one to achieve similar performance with better- scaling properties with growing computational grid size and the number of sensors.

Our architecture consists of a trainable binary mask and a reconstructing image-to-image neural network with U-Net architecture with bilinear upsampling. Another version of the reconstructing image-to-image network is a convolutional autoencoder with a discrete binary latent vector.

When training the Concrete Autoencoder G neural network, we find the optimal parameters by minimizing the loss function

$$\mathcal{L}_G = \mathbb{E}_{S_{\text{full}}} \| G(S_{\text{full}} \cdot \text{mask}, w) - S_{\text{full}} \|_{L_2} + \lambda \cdot \mathbb{E} |\text{mask}| \tag{11}$$

where the function G takes as input the physical field S_{full} in the entire simulation area, multiplies it component by the binary mask mask and tries to restore the original field. The binary mask must remain as sparse as possible, λ is a factor that determines the sparseness of the binary mask. The average value of the average $\mathbb{E} |\text{mask}|$ is proportional to the number of sensors.

3.2 Concrete Autoencoder with Adversarial Loss

Once we have a set of pairs from the exact and sparsely measured physical fields (which we obtain using initialization of the binary input mask using information entropy prior), we can solve the inverse problem of recovering the exact physical field from the sparsely measured one by solving the image-to-image translation problem. To do this, we introduce two neural networks following the Pix-2-Pix framework [17].

The generator takes a sparsely measured physical field as input and tries to restore the exact one. A network with UNet architecture with bilinear upsampling [18] and with trainable binary input mask is used as a generator $G : \hat{S} \to S$. The discriminator in the space of physical fields tries to distinguish the real exact physical fields from those generated by the generator, $D : S \times \hat{S} \to [\mathbb{O}, \mathbb{I}]$, where $[\mathbb{O}, \mathbb{I}]$ is the set of matrices of size $k \times k$ with entries in the interval $[0, 1]$. The specific value of k depends on the size of the input matrix M. Discriminator D has PatchGAN architecture used in [17].

The loss function of the generator has three main terms

$$\mathcal{L}_G = \lambda_1 \mathcal{L}_{\text{LSGAN}} + \lambda_2 \mathcal{L}_{\text{pixel-wise}} + \lambda_3 \mathcal{L}_{\text{sensors}} \tag{12}$$

where we use $\lambda_1 = 10^{-4}$, $\lambda_2 = 1$ and λ_3 dynamically changes during training from 0 to 1. This is done to initially achieve good reconstruction quality and only after to minimize the number of sensors without significant increase of the reconstruction error.

The loss function $\mathcal{L}_{\text{LSGAN}}$ requires that the generator produces physical fields that are indistinguishable by the discriminator from the real fields

$$\mathcal{L}_{\text{LSGAN}} = \text{MSE}(D(G(\hat{M})), \mathbb{I}) \equiv ||D(G(\hat{M})) - \mathbb{I}||_{L_2}$$

In addition to the requirement for the realism of the generated physical fields, we require an element-by-element correspondence of the restored physical fields with the ground true ones. The L_2-norm is used to measure pixel-wise error

$$\mathcal{L}_{\text{pixel-wise}} = ||G(\hat{M}) - M)||_{L_2}$$

The control of sensors number is achieved by adding average value of the binary mask to the loss function

$$\mathcal{L}_{\text{sensors}} = \mathbb{E}||\text{mask}||_{L_1}$$

For the discriminator, we require that it distinguish the physical fields produced by the generator from the real ones.

$$\mathcal{L}_D = \frac{1}{2} \left[\text{MSE}(D(G(\hat{M})), \mathbb{O}) + \text{MSE}(D(M), \mathbb{I}) \right]$$

4 Numerical Experiments

The dataset contains daily temperature and salinity fields taken from the INMIO COMPASS global ocean circulation model for $3\,\text{m}$ and $45\,\text{m}$ depth near the Svalbard group of islands from 2 Jan 2004 to 31 Dec 2020. The full ocean model dataset was obtained using supercomputer resources of JSCC RAS and INM RAS. Calculation of 17 model years took about $340\,\text{h}$, using 176 cores for the ocean, 60 cores for ice, and 3 cores for coupler, atmospheric forcing and rivers runoff, so in total 239 cores. The number of processors was chosen so that the time for calculating the integration steps for the ice and ocean models was approximately equal. This choice leads to more efficient use of computing resources when scaling the model to larger grids. A detailed study of this issue is presented in [19]. The dataset is divided into the train and test sets by taking the first 80% of the historical values for training and the other 20% is taken for testing. We train the concrete autoencoder, PCA-QR, and compute daily climate based on the training set. After training, we compute the reconstruction error on the test set and compare all three methods using bias and root mean square error (RMSE) metrics.

All neural networks were trained using the compute nodes with 4 Nvidia Tesla V100 GPUs of the Zhores HPC [20]. The information entropy field was computed by averaging across the ensemble of Conditional PixelCNN networks. For every physical field out of four considered, an ensemble of 30 Conditional PixelCNN networks was trained using 10 V100 GPUs. The training of a single PixelCNN takes 1 h on a single V100 for patch size 16×16. The training of a single Concrete Autoencoder takes 6 h on a single V100 for a computational grid 104×284.

4.1   Dataset Description

INMIO COMPASS Ocean General Circulation Model. The system of equations of three-dimensional ocean dynamics and thermodynamics in the Boussinesq and hydrostatic approximations is solved by the finite volume method [21] on the type B grid [22–24]. The ocean model INMIO COMPASS [25] and the sea ice model CICE [26] operate on the same global tripolar grid with a nominal resolution of $0.25°$. The vertical axis of the ocean model uses z-coordinates on 49 levels with a spacing from 6 m in the upper layer to 250 m at the depth. The barotropic dynamics is described with the help of a two-dimensional system of shallow water equations by the scheme [27]. Horizontal turbulent mixing of heat and salt is parameterized with a background (time-independent) diffusion coefficient equal to the nominal value at the equator and scaled towards the poles proportionally to the square root of the grid cell area. To ensure numerical stability in the equations of momentum transfer, the biharmonic filter is applied with a background coefficient scaled proportionally to the cell area to the power $3/2$ and with the local addition by Smagorinsky scheme in formulation [28] for maintaining sharp fronts. Vertical mixing is parameterized by the Munk-Anderson scheme [29] with convective adjustment performed in case of unstable vertical density profile. On the ocean-atmosphere interface, the nonlinear kinematic free surface condition is imposed with heat, water and momentum fluxes calculated by the CORE bulk formulae [30]. Except for vertical turbulent mixing, all the processes were described using time-explicit numerical methods which allow simple and effective parallel scaling. The time steps of the main cycle for solving model equations are equal for the ocean and the ice. The ocean model, within the restrictions of its resolution, implements the eddy-permitting mode by not using the laplacian viscosity in the momentum equations.

The Sea Ice Model CICE v. 5.1. The simulation regime includes processing of five thickness categories of ice and one of snow, the upwind transport scheme, and the description of melting ponds. The ice dynamics is parameterized with the elastic - viscous - plastic rheology model which requires the subcycle with small time steps for explicit resolving of elastic waves. In the calculation of ice thermodynamics, the zero layer approximation is applied.

ERA5 Atmospheric Forcing. The ERA-5 reanalysis [31] for the period 2004–2020 was used as the external forcing needed to determine the water and momentum fluxes on the ocean-atmosphere and ice-atmosphere interfaces. Wind speed at 10 m above sea level, temperature and dew point temperature at 2 m were transmitted to the ice-ocean system every 3 h. In addition, the accumulated fluxes of incident solar and long-wave radiation, precipitation (snow and rain) are read with the same period.

4.2   Baselines

Climate. The simplest baseline in ocean modeling, reconstruction, and forecasting is climate interpolated in time to the correct date. We calculated our climate values on the train set for each day in a year, according to the formula

$$S^{climate}(i,j,d) = \frac{1}{N^{years}} \sum_{y=1}^{N^{years}} S(i,j,y,d), \tag{13}$$

where $S(i,j,y,d)$ - the value of physical field with coordinates (i,j) at day number $d = \{1,2,\ldots,365\}$ in year y from train set, N^{years} - number of years with day d in train set.

PCA-QR. Principal component analysis (in the geophysics literature also known as Proper Orthogonal Decomposition or the method of Empirical Orthogonal Functions) with pivoted QR decomposition is a common baseline for sparse sensor placement [4,5,32]. This method approximately minimizes the determinant of the covariance matrix of reconstruction errors to find optimal sensor locations. The main assumption of PCA is that the joint density of the data and the low-dimensional latent variables has the form

$$\mathbb{P}(x,z|\theta) = \mathbb{P}(x|z,\theta)\mathbb{P}(z) = \mathcal{N}(x|\mu + Wz, \sigma^2 I) \cdot \mathcal{N}(z|0,I), \tag{14}$$

where $\theta = \{\mu, W, \sigma\}$ represents tunable parameters. These parameters could be found from maximization of the marginal likelihood of the observed dataset

$$\mathbb{P}(x|\theta) = \int \mathbb{P}(x,z|\theta)dz \to \max_{\theta} \tag{15}$$

which in the limit of $\sigma \to 0$ is equivalent to computation of the eigenvalues of the covariance matrix of the data. By applying the QR decomposition with column pivoting to the matrix of eigenvalues W^T we will obtain matrices P, Q, R such that

$$W^T P = QR, \tag{16}$$

where Q is an orthogonal matrix, R is an upper triangular matrix and P is a permutation matrix. The permutation matrix P contains optimal sensor positions and plays the role of an operator which extracts a measurement vector M at optimal sensor locations $M = PX$. Then the full field could be reconstructed from the sparse measurements M as

$$X^{rec} = WM(W^T P)^{-1} \qquad (17)$$

4.3 Evaluation Metrics

Evaluation metrics used in this study were based on GODAE OceanView Class 4 forecast verification framework [33]. *Bias* demonstrates correspondence between mean forecast and mean observation. For the analysis the *Bias* was calculated in every spatial location (i, j) with averaging along the time using Eq. (18) and for each time moment in the test set with averaging across the spatial coordinates using Eq. (19)

$$Bias(i,j) = \frac{1}{\#\{\tau \in TestSet\}} \sum_{\tau \in TestSet} (S^{recon}(i,j,\tau) - S^{ref}(i,j,\tau)), \qquad (18)$$

where $S^{recon}(i,j,\tau)$ - reconstructed values of a physical field at a point with coordinates (i, j) and at time moment τ, $S^{ref}(i,j,\tau)$ - original values of a physical field in the same point.

$$Bias(\tau) = \frac{1}{N^i} \frac{1}{N^j} \sum_{i=1}^{N^i} \sum_{j=1}^{N^j} (S^{recon}(i,j,\tau) - S^{ref}(i,j,\tau)), \qquad (19)$$

where $N^i \cdot N^j$ - total number of computational cells for a physical field.

The second metric used is the Root Mean Square Error ($RMSE$). It was calculated in every grid point (i, j) with averaging along the time dimension using Eq. (20) and for each time moment in test set with averaging along the spatial dimensions using Eq. (21)

$$RMSE(i,j) = \sqrt{\frac{1}{\#\{\tau \in TestSet\}} \sum_{\tau \in TestSet} (S^{recon}(i,j,\tau) - S^{ref}(i,j,\tau))^2}$$
$$(20)$$

$$RMSE(\tau) = \sqrt{\frac{1}{N^i} \frac{1}{N^j} \sum_{i=1}^{N^i} \sum_{j=1}^{N^j} (S^{recon}(i,j,\tau) - S^{ref}(i,j,\tau))^2} \qquad (21)$$

The scalar metric presented in the Table 1 was calculated by taking the median along the time dimension in the $RMSE(\tau)$ time series.

4.4   Results

Information Entropy. Figure 3 shows the information entropy of the temperature field on the under-surface sea layer, calculated from the test dataset. The color indicates the value of information entropy in nats per computational grid cell. The value characterizes the average level of "uncertainty" inherent to the variable's possible outcomes. A small value means that we had more a priori information about the temperature at this point than in a point with higher information entropy. The black contour highlights the areas of various sizes from $1 \times 1°$ to $4 \times 4°$ along which smoothing is performed. Smoothing allows one to remove anomaly and noise, but the smoothing scale should be chosen carefully because the land boundaries and hydro-physical features of the region should be preserved. We chose the size $2 \times 2°$, because it allows one to meet the specified requirements.

Figure 4 shows the information entropy fields calculated from the test set for temperature and salinity fields at under-surface and depth layers. The result obtained is consistent with the hydrophysics of the region under consideration. Temperature fields show low uncertainty northwest of Svalbard. Because most of the time the surface of the ocean is covered with ice with constant close to the ice formation temperature. And south of Svalbard and in the Barents Sea, high information entropy values are observed. These are areas of mixing of relatively warm North Atlantic waters and cold waters from the Arctic Ocean. For salinity, the situation is significantly different in the northwestern part of the region, since although the area of ice cover varies to a lesser extent, the growth and melting occur constantly, which in turn changes the salinity each time, and as a result, there is a high degree of uncertainty. High values of information entropy on the 3m depth along the border with land and estuaries in the southeastern part of the region are observed. This also corresponds to physical considerations: river freshwater reduces salinity, and in shallow water, the movement of water masses has a high degree of variability due to the influence of wind.

Reconstruction Accuracy. The accuracy metrics calculated by the formulas (18) and (20) are shown in the Fig. 5. The median MED value was calculated from the time series of $Bias$ and $RMSE$ using the formulas (19) and (21). Corresponding historical time series are shown in the Fig. 6. And the total reconstruction accuracy for all methods is shown at Table 1.

The dipole error structure for climate Fig. 5 errors fields (a) and (b) shows the presence of the interannual variability in the dataset, this is also confirmed by the absence of such a structure for calculating the error on the training set. There is significant noise in field reconstruction errors using PCA-QR, which is caused by the use of high-order modes that learn to resolve mesoscale eddies on the training set and, due to the presence of interannual variability, make a significant contribution to the increase in reconstruction errors. In the Concrete Autoencoder (e) error picture, artifacts are visible along the parallels, which can be removed by replacing MSE with LSGAN loss function. It should be noted that there is an excessive number of sensors along the coast for the PCA-QR and Concrete Autoencoder methods. This can be explained by the fact

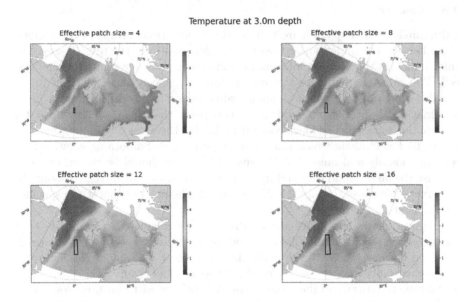

Fig. 3. Smoothed ensemble average information entropy of temperature field at 3 m depth calculated by application of PixellCNN to test data set. The black outline shows the size of the smoothing region with different side size: (a) $1 \times 1°$ (b) $2 \times 2°$ (c) $3 \times 3°$ (d) $4 \times 4°$ (Color figure online)

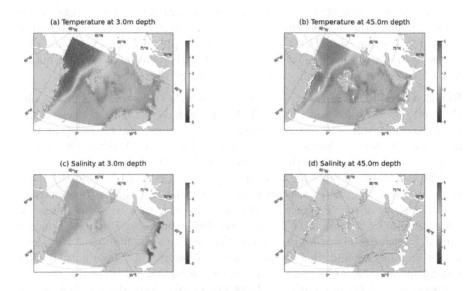

Fig. 4. Smoothed ensemble mean information entropy of geophysical fields: temperature at (a) 3 m and (b) 45 m depth; salinity at (c) 3 m and (d) 45 m depth.

that, through atmospheric forcing, the ocean feels the influence of the earth, whose temperature has a higher annual variability due to lower heat capacity. Thus, Concrete Autoencoder with LSGAN better reconstructs the instantaneous physical field using fewer sensors.

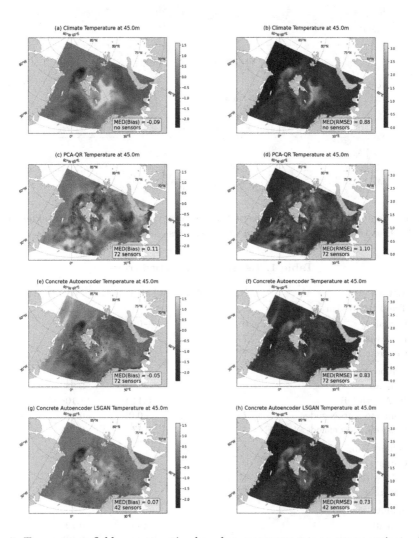

Fig. 5. Temperature field reconstruction based on measurements accuracy against original model data. Bias/RMSE temperature reconstruction at depth 45 m by methods: (a)/(b) Climate, (c)/(d) PCA-QR, (e)/(f) Concrete Autoencoder, (g)/(h) Concrete Autoencoder with LSGAN. At the left corner of each plot shown the time median field value and number of measurements.

Finally, the Fig. 6 shows the graphs of *Bias* and *RMSE* versus time, calculated using the formulas (19) and (21) on the test sample. From the shape of the

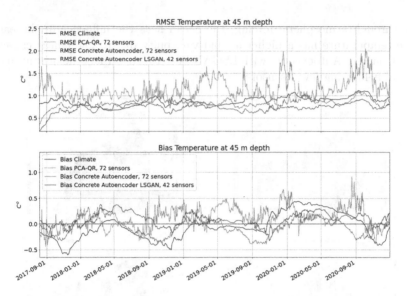

Fig. 6. Temperature field reconstruction accuracy against original model data. RMSE/Bias time series based on data from the test dataset.

Table 1. Test set reconstruction errors

Method	Number of sensors	MED (Bias)	MED (RMSE)
Temperature 3 m			
Climate	0	−0.19	0.98
PCA with QR	77	0.13	1.03
Concrete Autoencoder	77	−0.07	**0.73**
Temperature 45 m			
Climate	0	−0.09	0.88
PCA with QR	72	0.11	1.10
Concrete Autoencoder	72	−0.05	0.83
Concrete Autoencoder LSGAN	42	0.07	**0.73**
Salinity 3 m			
Climate	0	0.58	0.84
PCA with QR	57	−0.03	0.66
Concrete Autoencoder	57	0.05	**0.53**
Salinity 45 m			
Climate	0	0.59	0.72
PCA with QR	61	0.02	**0.30**
Concrete Autoencoder	61	0.26	0.41

Bias climate error curve, one can quantify the scale of interannual variability. It can also be seen from the graphs that the PCA-QR method shows the worst result in terms of field reconstruction accuracy due to over-fitting to the training set. Concrete Autoencoder with LSGAN loss demonstrates the best restoration accuracy, and the *Bias* graph shows a clear correlation with the climate error up to the spring of 2019. In general, the influence of seasonal variability is expressed in a cyclical change in *Bias* for all methods, which can be partially eliminated if the physical field anomaly relative to the climate is initially used for training and testing.

Concrete Autoencoder with LSGAN loss demonstrates the best restoration accuracy, and the *Bias* graph shows a clear correlation with the climate error up to the spring of 2019. In general, the influence of seasonal variability is expressed in a cyclical change in *Bias* for all methods, which can be partially eliminated if the physical field anomaly relative to the climate is initially used for training and testing.

5 Conclusion

We proposed a method for optimal sensor placement and reconstruction of geophysical fields. The method consists of two stages. At the first stage, we estimate the variability of the physical field as a function of spatial coordinates by approximating the information entropy of patches of field values through the Conditional PixelCNN. We proposed a modification to the Conditional PixelCNN architecture by introducing spiral ordering. This new ordering allows one to compute entropy at several scales using the network trained with a relatively large patch size. In our experiments, we observe that the patch size of 8 corresponding to the square $2 \times 2°$ produces the information entropy field that captures spatial characteristics of the sea currents near the Svalbard group of islands in the most consistent way.

In the second stage, the information entropy field is used to initialize the binary mask of the Concrete Autoencoder, and corresponding sensor locations are further optimized to maximize the reconstruction accuracy of the physical fields and minimize the total number of sensors. The reconstruction accuracy was measured by two losses. Firstly, we try to mean square error as a loss. Secondly, we use adversarial LSGAN loss.

As a result, we observe that the proposed method outperforms baselines and that the addition of LSGAN loss improves reconstruction accuracy. PCA-QR overfits on the training data more severely than the Concrete Autoencoder both with MSE and LSGAN loss. We observe that LSGAN loss gives the lowest reconstruction RMSE and Bias out of the considered methods while maintaining a spatially well-distributed set of sensors and avoiding clustering of sensors in some particular areas of the considered region.

Such an approach could reconstruct the synoptic variability from a limited number of measurements, and at the same time allows one to explore the inter-annual variability.

Acknowledgements. This research was funded by the state assignment of IO RAS, theme FMWE-2021-0003 (analysis of the temperature and salinity fields near the Svalbard group of islands, final experiments and assessment of reconstruction accuracy for the considered optimal sensor placement methods), and by the BASIS Foundation, Grant No. 19-1-1-48-1 (development of the information entropy approximation scheme and initial experiments with the concrete autoencoder by A. L.). The authors acknowledge the use of Zhores HPC [20] for obtaining the results presented in this paper. The ocean model dataset was obtained using supercomputer resources of JSCC RAS and INM RAS.

References

1. Kaurkin, M.N., Ibrayev, R.A.: Multivariate EnOI-based data assimilation in the high resolution ocean model. J. Phys.: Conf. Ser. **1128**(1), 012144 (2018). IOP Publishing
2. Nakai, K., et al.: Effect of objective function on data-driven greedy sparse sensor optimization. IEEE Access **9**, 46731–46743 (2021)
3. Saito, Y., et al.: Determinant-based fast greedy sensor selection algorithm. IEEE Access **9**, 68535–68551 (2021)
4. Wolf, P., Moura, S., Krstic, M.: On optimizing sensor placement for spatio-temporal temperature estimation in large battery packs. In: Proceedings of the IEEE Conference on Decision Control (CDC), pp. 973–978 (2012). https://doi.org/10.1109/CDC.2012.6426191
5. Kumar, P., Sayed, Y.M.E., Semaan, R.: Optimized sensor placement using stochastic estimation for a flow over a 2D airfoil with Coanda blowing. In: Proceedings of the 7th AIAA Flow Control Conference, Atlanta, GA, USA (2014)
6. Krause, A., Singh, A., Guestrin, C.: Near-optimal sensor placements in Gaussian processes: theory, efficient algorithms and empirical studies. J. Mach. Learn. Res. **9**(2), 235–284 (2008)
7. Nguyen, L.V., Guoqiang, H., Spanos, C.J.: Efficient sensor deployments for spatio-temporal environmental monitoring. IEEE Trans. Syst. Man. Cybern.: Syst. **50**(12), 5306–5316 (2018)
8. Nagata, T., et al.: Data-driven sparse sensor selection based on A-optimal design of experiment with ADMM. IEEE Sens. J. **21**(13), 15248–15257 (2021)
9. Jang, E., Gu, S., Poole, B.: Categorical reparameterization with Gumbel-Softmax. arXiv preprint arXiv:1611.01144 (2016)
10. Maddison, C.J., Mnih, A., Teh, Y.W.: The concrete distribution: a continuous relaxation of discrete random variables. arXiv preprint arXiv:1611.00712 (2016)
11. Wang, Z.-K., et al.: Optimization and assessment of blade tip timing probe layout with concrete autoencoder and reconstruction error. Appl. Soft Comput. **119**, 108590 (2022)
12. Balın, M.F., Abid, A., Zou, J.: Concrete autoencoders: differentiable feature selection and reconstruction. In: International Conference on Machine Learning. PMLR (2019)
13. Huijben, I.A.M., Veeling, B.S., van Sloun, R.J.G.: Deep probabilistic subsampling for task-adaptive compressed sensing. In: International Conference on Learning Representations (2019)
14. Singh, D., et al.: FsNet: feature selection network on high-dimensional biological data. arXiv preprint arXiv:2001.08322 (2020)
15. Van den Oord, A., et al.: Conditional image generation with PixelCNN decoders. In: Advances in Neural Information Processing Systems, vol. 29 (2016)
16. Van Oord, A., Kalchbrenner, N., Kavukcuoglu, K.: Pixel recurrent neural networks. In: International Conference on Machine Learning. PMLR (2016)

17. Isola, P., et al.: Image-to-image translation with conditional adversarial networks. In: Proceedings of the IEEE Conference on Computer Vision and Pattern Recognition (2017)
18. Ronneberger, O., Fischer, P., Brox, T.: U-Net: convolutional networks for biomedical image segmentation. In: Navab, N., Hornegger, J., Wells, W.M., Frangi, A.F. (eds.) MICCAI 2015. LNCS, vol. 9351, pp. 234–241. Springer, Cham (2015). https://doi.org/10.1007/978-3-319-24574-4_28
19. Kalnitskii, L., Kaurkin, M., Ushakov, K., Ibrayev, R.: Supercomputer implementation of a high resolution coupled ice-ocean model for forecasting the state of the Arctic Ocean. In: Voevodin, V., Sobolev, S. (eds.) RuSCDays 2020. CCIS, vol. 1331, pp. 332–340. Springer, Cham (2020). https://doi.org/10.1007/978-3-030-64616-5_29
20. Zacharov, I., et al.: "Zhores" - petaflops supercomputer for data-driven modeling, machine learning and artificial intelligence installed in Skolkovo Institute of Science and Technology. Open Eng. **9**(1), 512–520 (2019). https://doi.org/10.1515/eng-2019-0059
21. Bryan, K.: A numerical method for the study of the circulation of the world ocean. J. Comput. Phys. **135**(2), 154–169 (1997). https://doi.org/10.1016/0021-9991(69)90004-7
22. Lebedev, V.I.: Difference analogues of orthogonal decompositions, basic differential operators and some boundary problems of mathematical physics. I. USSR Comput. Math. Math. Phys. **4**(3), 69–92 (1964). https://doi.org/10.1016/0041-5553(64)90240-X
23. Lebedev, V.I.: Difference analogues of orthogonal decompositions, basic differential operators and some boundary problems of mathematical physics. II. USSR Comput. Math. Math. Phys. **4**(4), 36–50 (1964). https://doi.org/10.1016/0041-5553(64)90003-5
24. Mesinger, F., Arakawa, A.: Numerical Methods Used in Atmospheric Models. GARP Publ. Series # 17, vol. I, p. 64 pp. WMO/ISCU Joint Org. Committee, Geneva (1976)
25. Ushakov, K.V., Ibrayev, R.A.: Assessment of mean world ocean meridional heat transport characteristics by a high-resolution model. Russ. J. Earth. Sci. **18**, ES1004 (2018). https://doi.org/10.2205/2018ES000616
26. Hunke, E.C., Lipscomb, W.H., Turner, A.K., Jeffery, N., Elliott, S.: CICE: the Los Alamos Sea Ice Model documentation and software user's manual, version 5.1. Technical report LA-CC-06-012. Los Alamos National Laboratory, Los Alamos, NM (2015). http://www.ccpo.odu.edu/klinck/Reprints/PDF/cicedoc2015.pdf
27. Killworth, P.D., et al.: The development of a free-surface Bryan-Cox-Semtner ocean model. J. Phys. Oceanogr. **21**(9), 1333–1348 (1991)
28. Griffies, S.M., Hallberg, R.W.: Biharmonic friction with a Smagorinsky-like viscosity for use in large-scale eddy-permitting ocean models. Mon. Weather Rev. **128**, 2935–2946 (2000). https://doi.org/10.1175/1520-0493(2000)1282935:BFWASL2.0.CO;2
29. Munk, W.H., Anderson, E.R.: Note on the theory of the thermocline. J. Mar. Res. **7**, 276–295 (1948)
30. Griffies, S.M., et al.: Coordinated ocean-ice reference experiments (COREs). Ocean Model. **26**(1–2), 1–46 (2009). https://doi.org/10.1016/j.ocemod.2008.08.007
31. Hersbach, H., Bell, B., Berrisford, P., et al.: The ERA5 global reanalysis. Q. J. R. Meteorol. Soc. **146**(730), 1999–2049 (2020)

32. Manohar, K., et al.: Data-driven sparse sensor placement for reconstruction: demonstrating the benefits of exploiting known patterns. IEEE Control Syst. Mag. **38**(3), 63–86 (2018)
33. Ryan, A.G., et al.: GODAE OceanView Class 4 forecast verification framework: global ocean inter-comparison. J. Oper. Oceanogr. **8**(sup1), s98–s111 (2015). https://doi.org/10.1080/1755876X.2015.1022330

Microwave Radiometric Mapping of Broken Cumulus Cloud Fields from Space: Numerical Simulations

Yaroslav Kopcov[1], Yaroslaw Ilyushin[1,2(✉)], Boris Kutuza[2],
and Dobroslav Egorov[2]

[1] Physical Faculty, Moscow State University, Moscow, Russia
koptcov.iv17@physics.msu.ru, ilyushin@phys.msu.ru
[2] Kotel'nikov Institute of Radio Engineering and Electronics,
Russian Academy of Sciences, Moscow, Russia
kutuza@cplire.ru

Abstract. Monitoring the atmosphere characteristics is an important task in remote sensing of the environment. In this paper, the question is raised about taking into account the influence of clouds on the characteristics of thermal radiation. The aim is to analyze the applicability of models for cloud correction during microwave radio sounding of thermal radiation. The result of the work is to determine the parameters that best correspond to the cloud fields of the Earth's atmosphere.

For the applicability of the calculated values to account for the structure of clouds in the atmosphere, it is necessary to generate model cloud fields comparable in size to real cloud fields in the Earth's troposphere. This results in significant computational costs required for their modeling and analysis.

Numerical modeling of the statistical properties of thermal radio emission of separated cloudiness field models implies the need to perform calculations with an ensemble of simulated random fields of a sufficiently large size, and the use of projections with good resolution, therefore, the optimal use for computing high-performance computers.

As a result, the developed algorithms and computer models of cloud fields significantly form a practical basis for further studies of radiation processes in the cloud atmosphere. Two-dimensional (2D) distributions of the brightness temperature of the outgoing thermal radiation of the separated cloudiness fields were calculated. For simplified statistical models of separated cloudiness fields, numerical estimates of the radio brightness temperatures of microwave radiation of the cloud layer are obtained depending on the model statistical parameters.

Keywords: Plank model · Cumulus clouds · Microwave radiometric sensing

1 Introduction

Monitoring of atmospheric characteristics is an important task in remote sensing of the environment. In this paper, the question is raised about taking into

V. Voevodin et al. (Eds.): RuSCDays 2022, LNCS 13708, pp. 185–198, 2022.
https://doi.org/10.1007/978-3-031-22941-1_13

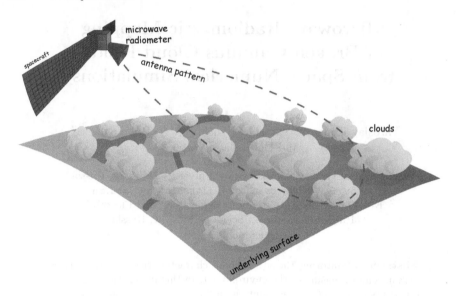

Fig. 1. General sketch of the experimental radiometry of cloud fields.

account the influence of clouds on the characteristics of thermal radiation. Atmospheric sounding by the method of receiving atmospheric thermal radiation is the development of ground-based studies of atmospheric thermal radiation. One of the methods of such research is microwave radiometric sounding from artificial Earth satellites. Passive microwave radiometry [1–5] has long been used as a remote sensing approach in geophysics [7,8], meteorology [9] and astronomy [6,10,11]. Observations of the thermal radiation of the atmosphere-ocean surface system [13–15] allow us to obtain information about the state of cloud fields in the atmosphere and quantify many meteorological parameters, for example, the mass of water vapor [18], water reserve [17] and the effective temperature of clouds [16]. The disadvantage of a significant part of most previous studies is the use of a homogeneous plane-layered model of the cloud layer, ignoring its heterogeneous structure [20].

Clouds in the troposphere are involved in the scattering and reflection of sunlight and thermal radiation of the atmosphere. For this reason, cloud cover makes a significant contribution to the radiation and energy balance of the atmosphere, which plays a key role in climatic processes on the planet. To understand this role, it is necessary to study the radiation properties of cloud cover. Cloud fields are characterized by a random structure, so their properties are random and can be studied by statistical methods. One of the possible approaches is a direct numerical evaluation of the properties of the cloud fields of interest based on their specific implementations, followed by averaging. This approach is also used in this study.

The aim of this work is to numerically simulate the statistical properties of the thermal radio emission of Plank fields of broken clouds in the microwave range and to study systematic errors of meteorological parameters of the atmosphere associated with the random nature of real broken cloud fields. For this purpose, direct numerical modeling of cloud fields is carried out in the work and the characteristics determining the radio brightness temperatures of broken clouds at various frequencies of the microwave wavelength range are calculated. The calculated characteristics are directly compared with the results obtained in the works of other authors in the study of real fields of broken clouds.

2 Size Distributions and Geometry of Broken Cloud Fields

In the article [12] it is shown that when calculating the characteristics of radiation fields in the microwave range, the assumption of the cylindrical shape of clouds is acceptable.

2.1 The Plank Model

Plank [22] proposed the following distribution:

$$n\left(D\right) = Ke^{-\alpha D}, \quad 0 \le D \le D_m \tag{1}$$

where D is the diameter of the cloud, D_m is the maximum possible diameter of the cloud in the field, K is a normalization constant, α is a constant parameter depending on local conditions [22].

The cumulative distribution of the number of clouds by size is, respectively, equal to:

$$N\left(D\right) = \frac{1 - e^{-\alpha D}}{1 - e^{-\alpha D_m}} \tag{2}$$

Average diameter of clouds:

$$\langle D \rangle = D_m \left(\frac{1}{\alpha D_m} - \frac{1}{e^{\alpha D_m} - 1} \right) \tag{3}$$

2.2 Alternative Model

Distribution proposed in [19] based on aircraft measurements over Ukraine:

$$n\left(D\right) = KD \cdot \left(1 - \frac{D}{D_m}\right)^{p_0}, \quad 0 \le D \le D_m \tag{4}$$

where D is the diameter of the cloud, D_m is the maximum possible diameter of the cloud in the field, K is a normalization constant, p_0 is a constant parameter depending on local conditions [19].

The cumulative distribution of the number of clouds by size is, respectively, writes as follows:

$$N\left(D\right) = 1 - \left(\left(1 + p_0\right)\frac{D}{D_m} + 1\right)\left(1 - \frac{D}{D_m}\right)^{p_0+1} \tag{5}$$

Average diameter of clouds, respectively, is

$$\langle D \rangle = \frac{2D_m}{3 + p_0} \tag{6}$$

2.3   The Cloud Height Distribution

Following the work of [22], the power of the cloud and its diameter can be linked unambiguously by the ratio:

$$H = \eta D \left(\frac{D}{D_m}\right)^{\beta} \tag{7}$$

where η and β are the adjustable model parameters.

Since the height of the cloud is unambiguously related to its diameter by the formula (7), the cloud height in the cloud field is also a random variable with the corresponding statistical distribution. Since in a given model the height of a cloud is uniquely related to its diameter, the probability density of the height distribution is

$$p\left(H\right) = \frac{1}{N\left(D_m\right)} n\left(D\right)\frac{dD\left(H\right)}{dH} \tag{8}$$

where $N\left(D_m\right)$ is the total number of clouds in the field. So a certain density of the distribution of random heights of clouds (8) obviously satisfies the condition of normalization by one

$$\int_0^{D_m} p\left(H\right) dH = 1 \tag{9}$$

In frequency, for the Plank model of broken clouds (1) probability density of the cloud height distribution $p\left(H\right)$ is equal to

$$P\left(H\right) = \frac{\left(D_m/\left(\alpha\eta H\right)\right)^{\beta/\left(\beta+1\right)}}{\left(1 - e^{-\alpha D_m}\right)\left(\beta + 1\right)} \exp\left(-\left(D_m/\alpha\eta\right)^{\beta/\left(\beta+1\right)} H^{1/\left(\beta+1\right)}\right) \tag{10}$$

For the non-Plank model (4) the density function of the height probability distribution is

$$P\left(H\right) = \frac{\left(p_0 + 1\right)\left(p_0 + 2\right)\eta^{2\beta/\left(\beta+1\right)}}{H^{\left(1-\beta\right)/\left(\beta+1\right)} D_m^{2/\left(1+\beta\right)}\left(\beta + 1\right)}\left(1 - \left(\frac{H}{\eta^{\beta}D_m}\right)^{1/\left(\beta+1\right)}\right)^{p_0} \tag{11}$$

It is obvious that the essential parameters of both cloud abundance distributions by diameter (1) and (4) and the corresponding cloud height distributions (10) and (11), the dependence on which is not reduced to a simple linear scaling of the values and arguments of the distribution functions, are in and, respectively, α and p_0. Otherwise, these distributions can be reduced to dimensionless normalized parameters D/D_m and $H/\eta D_m$. In practice, this means that in further research, the values of the parameters η and D_m can be assumed to be equal to one without limitation of generality. Then, in particular, for $\beta = 0, \eta = 1, D_m = 1$ for the non-Plank cloud model (11) we get

$$p(H) = (1 - H)^{p_0} H (p_0 + 1) (p_0 + 2) \tag{12}$$

This height distribution has a well-defined maximum at $H = (1 + p_0)^{-1}$. For $\beta = 1/2, \eta = 1, D_m = 1$, respectively, the distribution (11) takes the form

$$p(H) = \frac{2}{3} \left(1 - H^{2/3}\right)^{p_0} \cdot \sqrt[3]{H} (p_0 + 1) (p_0 + 2) \tag{13}$$

with a maximum at

$$H = \frac{1}{\sqrt{8p_0^3 + 12p_0^2 + 6p_0 + 1}} \tag{14}$$

For $\beta = -1/2, \eta = 1, D_m = 1$, respectively, the distribution (11) takes the form

$$p(H) = 2H^3 \left(1 - H^2\right)^{p_0} (p_0 + 1) (p_0 + 2) \tag{15}$$

with a maximum at

$$H = \frac{\sqrt{3}}{\sqrt{2p_0 + 3}} \tag{16}$$

Probability density distributions (12), (13) and (15) for different values of the parameter p_0 are shown in Figs. 2, 3 and 4, respectively. Thus, these random models of broken clouds can be identified with one of the types of cumulus clouds Cumulus [30] by matching the height of the clouds (according to the maximum probability of distribution or average values) by selecting appropriate combinations of model parameters.

We developed a simple numerical procedure which generates the set of randomly distributed diameters of clouds and then places it randomly over the given rectangular area. The calculation was carried out in the C++ programming language using Intel C++ compiler. The distribution of clouds by size was controlled by the Kolmogorov statistical agreement criterion. The sample random cloud field generated with that procedure is shown in the Fig. 5. Cloud sizes are distributed according the Plank distribution (1) with $D_m = 4\,\mathrm{km}$ and $\alpha = 1., \beta = 0.5, \eta = 1.0$. Size of the whole cloud field area is $100 \times 100\,\mathrm{km}$, relative sky coverage parameter $S = 0.5$.

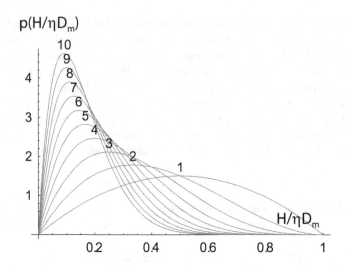

Fig. 2. Probability density functions of the cloud heights distribution (12) for different values of the distribution parameter p_0 (indicated by numbers with corresponding curves).

3   Radiative Properties of the Clouds and the Atmosphere

The total absorption coefficient $\gamma_\lambda(h)$ in a cloudy atmosphere consists of molecular absorption in oxygen and water vapor, as well as absorption in small cloud droplets. Absorption in molecular oxygen depends on temperature and pressure, information about it can be found, for example, in [7,7,23]. The absorption coefficient in water vapor, in addition, has a close to linear dependence on absolute humidity [21,23,24].

The size distribution of droplets of layered clouds and cumulus clouds of good weather is given in [25]. The average droplet sizes of these clouds are 3.9–7.5 microns, and the maximum contribution to the water content is made by droplets with a radius of 10–20 microns [19]. Radar studies by E. Gossard [26] show the presence of droplets with a radius of 70 microns or more in powerful cumulus clouds, and the largest contribution to water content is made by droplets with a size of about 50 microns.

Taking the scattering of microwave radiation on spherical water particles in a cloud by Rayleigh, it is not difficult to obtain the formula [2] for the volume absorption coefficient of the liquid droplet phase in the cloud [20]

$$k = \frac{3w}{\rho} kIm\left(\frac{m^2 - 1}{m^2 + 2}\right) \tag{17}$$

where w is the water content of the cloud, kg/m^3, ρ is the density of water, kg/m^3, $k = \omega/c$ is the wave number of radiation, m is the refractive index of water.

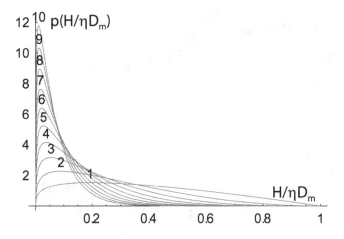

Fig. 3. Probability density functions of the cloud heights distribution (13) for different values of the distribution parameter p_0 (indicated by numbers with corresponding curves).

The coefficients of absorption of radiation by water vapor and the values of total integral oxygen absorption in a vertical column of atmospheric air for different wavelengths can be calculated using the well-known formulas [23]. The complex permittivity of liquid water is determined by the Debye formula (see, for example, [2])

$$\varepsilon = \varepsilon_0 + \frac{\varepsilon_s - \varepsilon_0}{1 + i\frac{\Delta\lambda}{\lambda}} \tag{18}$$

where

$$\Delta\lambda = 2\pi\tau_p \frac{\varepsilon_s + 2}{\varepsilon_0 + 2} \tag{19}$$

ε_s - static permittivity of water (at frequencies $\nu \ll 1/\tau_p$), $\varepsilon_0 = 4,9$ - optical permittivity of water (at frequencies $\nu \gg 1/\tau_p$), relaxation time [3]

$$\tau_p = exp\left[9,8\left(\frac{273}{T + 273} - 0,955\right)\right] \cdot 10^{-12}s \tag{20}$$

The static permittivity of water is described by the approximate formula [3]

$$\varepsilon_s(T) = 88,045 - 0,4147 \cdot T + 6,295 \cdot 10^{-4} \cdot T^2 + 1,075 \cdot 10^{-5} \cdot T^3 \tag{21}$$

Values of temperature, water reserve and cloud power for Cu cong and Cu med are given in [2,30]. The altitude profile of the water content of each cloud was calculated using the formula [27,30]

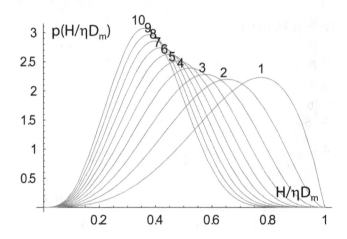

Fig. 4. Probability density functions of the cloud heights distribution (15) for different values of the distribution parameter p_0 (indicated by numbers with corresponding curves).

$$w\left(\xi\right) = w\left(\xi_0\right) \frac{\xi^{\mu_0}\left(1-\xi\right)^{\psi_0}}{\xi_0^{\mu_0}\left(1-\xi_0\right)^{\psi_0}} = \frac{W}{H}\frac{\Gamma\left(2+\mu_0+\psi_0\right)}{\Gamma\left(1+\mu_0\right)\Gamma\left(1+\psi_0\right)}\xi^{\mu_0}\left(1-\xi\right)^{\psi_0} \quad (22)$$

where $\xi = h/H$ is the reduced height inside the cloud, H is the power of the cloud, km, W is the water reserve of the cloud, kg/m^2, $w\left(\xi_0\right)$ is the water content of the cloud, kg/m^3, w is the maximum water content clouds, ξ_0 – the reduced height of the maximum water content of the cloud, μ_0, ψ_0 - dimensionless parameters of the model. According to [30], the parameter values are $\mu_0 = 3.27, \psi_0 = 0.67, \xi_0 = 0.83$. The dependence of the water reserve of Cumulus-type clouds (kg/m^2) on the cloud power (km) according to the tabular data given in [30] was approximated by the formula

$$W = 0,132574 \cdot H^{2,30215} \quad (23)$$

4   Microwave Thermal Radiation Simulation

In the microwave range, the influence of scattering processes in a cloudy atmosphere can be neglected. If the quantum energy at the radiation frequency is small compared to the temperature $\hbar\omega \ll kT$, the Planck function is almost proportional to the temperature, which is known as the so-called Rayleigh-Jeans approximation [4,5]. Thus the observed intensity can be expressed directly in the radio brightness temperature T_b units (degrees). Under these conditions, and also under the assumption of local thermodynamic equilibrium, the radio brightness temperature of a plane-layered atmosphere when observed from the Earth's surface can be represented as [28,29]

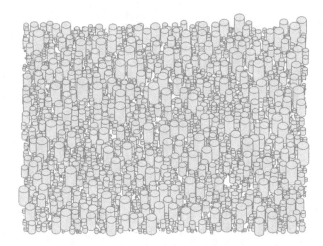

Fig. 5. Sample of the random cloud field model generated with the algorithm developed here. Cloud sizes are distributed according the Plank distribution (1) with $D_m = 4\,\text{km}$ and $\alpha = 1.$, $\beta = 0.5$, $\eta = 1.0$. Size of the whole cloud field area is $100 \times 100\,\text{km}$, relative sky coverage parameter $S = 0.5$.

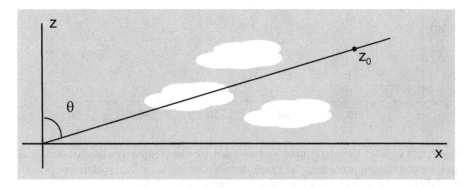

Fig. 6. Sounding ray direction.

$$T_b\left(\lambda, \theta\right) = \int_0^\infty T\left(z\right) \gamma_\lambda\left(z\right) exp\left(-\int_0^z \gamma_\lambda\left(z'\right) sec\theta dz'\right) sec\theta dz \qquad (24)$$

where $T(z)$ is the temperature of the atmosphere at an altitude of z, $\gamma_\lambda\left(z\right)$ is the total absorption coefficient, θ is the zenith angle of the viewing direction (see the Fig. 6), λ is the wavelength. Similar integral equation can be written down also for the case of the space-borne observations

$$T_b\left(\lambda, \theta\right) = T_{b0}\, exp\left(-\int_0^{z_0} \gamma_\lambda\left(z'\right) sec\theta dz'\right) + \qquad (25)$$

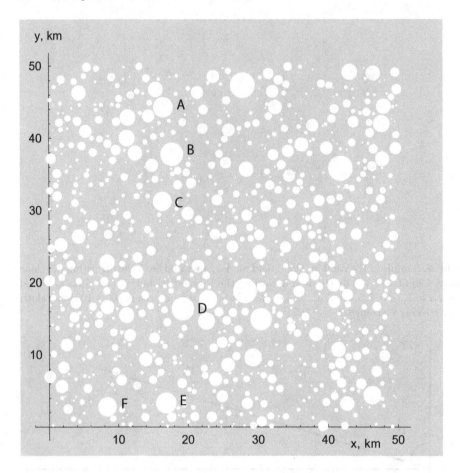

Fig. 7. 2D view of the cloud field portion used for the sample T_b simulation. Cloud sizes are distributed according the Plank distribution (1) with $D_m = 4\,\mathrm{km}$ and $\alpha = 1.$, $\beta = 0.5$, $\eta = 1.0$. Size of the whole cloud field area is $50 \times 50\,\mathrm{km}$.

$$\int_0^{z_0} T(z)\,\gamma_\lambda(z)\,exp\!\left(-\int_z^{z_0}\gamma_\lambda(z')\,sec\theta dz'\right)sec\theta dz\,,$$

where T_{b0} is the radio brightness temperature of the underlying surface.

The expressions (24) and (25) can be immediately integrated numerically, which readily yields the radio brightness temperature T_b. Repeating these calculations for a set of observation points and directions, one gets map of the radio brightness temperatures over the desired sea or land area.

5   Parallelization Efficiency Analysis

Since the integrand does not exhibit any singularities or irregularities, an integration procedure is rather simple. It can be easily parallelized dividing the integration domain or parametrically, using different threads for different sounding ray

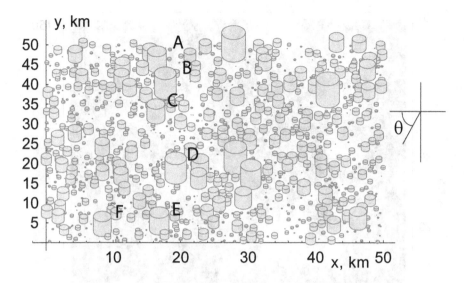

Fig. 8. 3D view of the cloud field portion used for the sample T_b simulation. Cloud sizes are distributed according the Plank distribution (1) with $D_m = 4$ km and $\alpha = 1.$, $\beta = 0.5$, $\eta = 1.0$. Size of the whole cloud field area is 50×50 km.

trajectories. However, for realistic practical purposes these routine calculations should be performed for rather large areas covered by the clouds. In addition, to investigate statistical characteristics of the radio brightness distributions they should be repeated many times. This implies the ultimate need in using high-performance parallel computer systems. The algorithm itself can be implemented using only the basic parallel programming techniques, e.g. the OpenMP or MPI standards.

Since all the integrals (24) and (25) can be evaluated independently from each other, parallelization of these calculations is rather effective both on MPP and SMP architectures. Namely, the computing work can be distributed among any reasonable number of processing cores. Because the threads do not interact with each other, the acceleration is roughly proportional to the number of the cores used. For relatively small cloud fields, SMP architectures are rather effective in practice.

For example, we performed these calculations for the sample portion of the broken cloud field shown in the Figs. 7 and 8 over the sea surface ($T_{b0} = 100\,K$). The node with 8 computing cores (two 4-core CPUs) was used with the code using OpenMP standard. The result is shown in the Fig. 9. For simpler identification of characteristic features of the cloud field and corresponding features of the radio brightness map, we labeled some of them with the capital letters (A–F). Warm clouds can be clearly seen over the relatively cold sea surface. To account for the instrumental distortions, the calculated T_b map was convolved with the simple model Point Spreading Function (PSF). The PSF was chosen

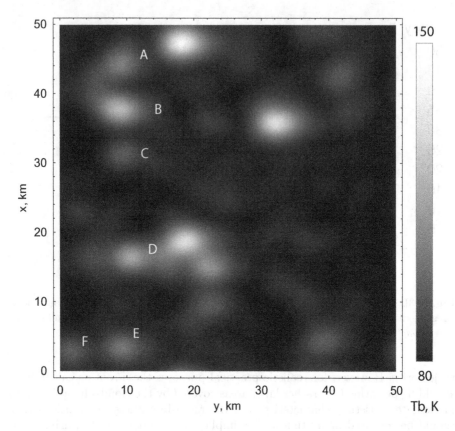

Fig. 9. Sample 2D mapping of the simulated distribution of the radio brightness temperature T_b (25) observed from space. Random cloud field is shown in the Figs. 7 and 8 over the sea surface ($T_{b0} = 100\,K$). Viewing zenith angle $\theta = 70°$, radiometer frequency 70 GHz.

Gaussian with 2 km half width. This PSF is rather idealistic, however it is used here to show the distortion visually just for the illustrative purposes.

6   Conclusions and Remarks

In the course of the study, algorithms for generating cloud fields were developed based on well-known stochastic models of broken cumulus clouds proposed for real cloud distributions obtained empirically. For the obtained implementations of random cloud fields, numerical estimates of shading curves are made, i.e., the probability of sky overlap in a given direction, depending on the total cloud cover score. The estimates obtained are compared with published observational data on the probabilities of sky overlap.

As a result of the study, the compliance of the models of the broken cloud cover with the known observational data was verified. In addition, the developed algorithms and computer models of cloud fields form a significant practical basis for further studies of radiation processes in the cloud atmosphere.

The research is carried out using the equipment of the shared research facilities of HPC computing resources at Lomonosov Moscow State University [31]. The authors thank both reviewers for valuable comments.

References

1. Nicoll, G.R.: The measurement of thermal and similar radiations at millimetre wavelengths. Proc. IEEE B Radio Electron. Eng. **104**(17), 519–527 (1957)
2. Akvilonova, A.B., Kutuza, B.G.: Thermal radiation of clouds. J. Com. Tech. Elect. **23**(9), 1792–1806 (1978)
3. Ulaby, F.T., Moore, R.K., Fung, A.K.: Microwave Remote Sensing, Active and Passive, vol. 1. Addison-Wesley, Reading, MA (1981)
4. Drusch, M., Crewell, S.: Principles of radiative transfer. In: Anderson, M.G. (ed.) Encyclopedia of Hydrological Sciences. Wiley (2006)
5. Janssen, M.A. (ed.): Wiley series in remote sensing and image processing, Vol. 6, Atmospheric Remote Sensing by Microwave Radiometry, 1st edn. Wiley (1993)
6. Schloerb, P.F., Keihm, S., Von Allmen, P., et al.: Astron. Astrophys. **583** (2015)
7. Zhevakin, S.A., Naumov, A.P.: Radio Eng. Electron. **19**, 6 (1965)
8. Zhevakin, S.A., Naumov, A.P.: Izv. Univ. Radiophys. **10**, 9–10 (1967)
9. Staelin, D.H., et al.: Microwave spectrometer on the Nimbus 5 satellite meteorological and geophysical data. Science **182**(4119), 1339–1341 (1973)
10. Ilyushin, Y.A., Hartogh, P.: Submillimeter wave instrument radiometry of the Jovian icy moons-numerical simulation of the microwave thermal radiative transfer and Bayesian retrieval of the physical properties. Astron. Astrophys. **644**, A24 (2020)
11. Hagfors, T., Dahlstrom, I., Gold, T., Hamran, S.-E., Hansen, R.: Icarus **130** (1997)
12. Kutuza, B.G., Smirnov, M.T.: The influence of clouds on the averaged thermal radiation of the Atmosphere-Ocean surface system. Earth Studies from Space (No. 3) (1980)
13. Egorov, D.P., Ilyushin, Y.A., Koptsov, Y.V., Kutuza, B.G.: Simulation of microwave spatial field of atmospheric brightness temperature under discontinuous cumulus cloudiness. J. Phys: Conf. Ser. **1991**(1), 012015 (2021)
14. Egorov, D.P., Ilyushin, Y.A., Kutuza, B.G.: Microwave radiometric sensing of cumulus cloudiness from space. Radiophys. Quantum Electron. **64**, 564–572 (2022). https://doi.org/10.1007/s11141-022-10159-2
15. lyushin, Y.A., Kutuza, B.G., Sprenger, A.A., Merzlikin, V.G.: Intensity and polarization of thermal radiation of three-dimensional rain cells in the microwave band. AIP Conf. Proc. **1810**(1), 040003 (2017)
16. Ilyushin, Y., Kutuza, B.: Microwave radiometry of atmospheric precipitation: radiative transfer simulations with parallel supercomputers. In: Voevodin, V., Sobolev, S. (eds.) RuSCDays 2018. CCIS, vol. 965, pp. 254–265. Springer, Cham (2019). https://doi.org/10.1007/978-3-030-05807-4_22
17. Ilyushin, Y.A., Kutuza, B.G.: Microwave band radiative transfer in the rain medium: implications for radar sounding and radiometry. In: 2017 Progress in Electromagnetics Research Symposium-Spring (PIERS), pp. 1430–1437. IEEE (2017)

18. Ilyushin, Y.A., Kutuza, B.G.: New possibilities of the use of synthetic aperture millimeter-wave radiometric interferometer for precipitation remote sensing from space. In: 2013 International Kharkov Symposium on Physics and Engineering of Microwaves, Millimeter and Submillimeter Waves, pp. 300–302. IEEE (2013)
19. Mazin, I.P., Shmeter, S.M. (eds.): Cumulus clouds and associated deformation of meteorological element fields. In: Proceedings of the CAO. Hydrometeoizdat, Moscow Issue 134 (1977)
20. Ilyushin, Y.A., Kutuza, B.G.: Influence of a spatial structure of precipitates on polarization characteristics of the outgoing microwave radiation of the atmosphere. Izv. Atmos. Ocean. Phys. **52**(1), 74–81 (2016). https://doi.org/10.1134/S0001433816010047
21. Barrett, A.H., Chung, V.K.: J. Geophys. Res. **67** (1962)
22. Plank, V.G.: The size distribution of cumulus clouds in representative Florida populations. J. Appl. Meteorol. Climatol. **8**(1), 46–67 (1969)
23. Rec. ITU-R P.676-3 1 recommendation ITU-R P.676-3 attenuation by atmospheric gases (Question ITU-R 201/3) (1990-1992-1995-1997)
24. Zhevakin, S.A., Naumov, A.P.: Izv. Univ. Radiophys. **6**, 4 (1963)
25. Hrgian, A.H.: Atmospheric Physics. Hydrometeoizdat (1969)
26. Gossard, E.E.: The use of radar for studies of clouds. Proc. Wave Prop. Lab, NOAA/ERL (1978)
27. Voit, F.Y., Mazin, I.P.: Water content of cumulus clouds. Izv. Akad. Nauk SSSR, Fiz. Atmos. Okeana **8**(11), 1166–1176 (1972)
28. Kislyakov, A.G., Stankevich, K.S.: Investigation of tropospheric absorption of radio waves by radio astronomy methods. Izv. VUZov, Radiophys. **10**(9–10) (1967)
29. Kondratyev, K.Y.: Radiant heat transfer in the atmosphere. Hydrometeoizdat (1956)
30. Kutuza, B.G., Danilychev, M.V., Yakovlev, O.I.: Satellite monitoring of the earth: microwave radiometry of the atmosphere and surface (2017)
31. Sadovnichy, V., Tikhonravov, A., Voevodin, V., Opanasenko, V.: "Lomonosov": supercomputing at Moscow state university. In: Contemporary High Performance Computing: From Petascale Toward Exascale. Chapman & Hall/CRC Computational Science, Boca Raton (2013)

Parallel Computations by the Grid-Characteristic Method on Chimera Computational Grids in 3D Problems of Railway Non-destructive Testing

Alena Favorskaya$^{(\boxtimes)}$ ⓘ, Nikolay Khokhlov ⓘ, Vitaly Sagan ⓘ,
and Dmitry Podlesnykh ⓘ

Moscow Institute of Physics and Technology, 9 Institutsky Lane, Dolgoprudny,
Moscow 141701, Russian Federation
{favorskaya,sagan.vs}@phystech.edu, {khokhlov.ni,
podlesnykh.da}@mipt.ru

Abstract. Our work is devoted to the numerical solution of direct problems of non-destructive testing of rails in a full-wave three-dimensional formulation. The complexity of this class of problems is due to the high frequencies of the waves, which imposes a limitation on the step size of the computational grid, including along the rail, as well as the complex geometry of the object under study. Therefore, it is advisable to use supercomputer calculations and the grid-characteristic method on Chimera computational grids. The Chimera grid allows to both accurately define the shape of the rail and to use structured computational grids as background grids. Interpolation is used between the background grids and the Chimera grid. However, although the sequential implementation of this numerical method provides significant savings not only in the cost of RAM, but also in the time for performing calculations, the issue arises of choosing an efficient parallel implementation. The complexity of this issue is due to the fact that calculations are performed at different speeds in the Chimera grid and in structured regular grids, since the number of computational operations differs significantly. Also, when creating a set of background grids to reduce the total number of points, there is a need for additional interpolation between these grids, which means data transfer in the case of using high-performance computational systems with distributed memory. This paper contains a number of preliminary studies of the scalability of a three-dimensional problem of rail ultrasonic non-destructive testing using various configurations of computational background grids.

Keywords: Parallel computing · Grid-characteristic method · Chimera computational grids · Overlapping grids · Non-destructive testing · Full-wave simulation · Railway · Parallel mesh partitioning

1 Introduction

The numerical solution of the direct problem of ultrasonic non-destructive testing of railway can be reduced to the solution of the initial-boundary value problem for the

V. Voevodin et al. (Eds.): RuSCDays 2022, LNCS 13708, pp. 199–213, 2022.
https://doi.org/10.1007/978-3-031-22941-1_14

elastic wave equation. Computational methods for solving this problem can be divided into finite-difference [1], finite-element [2] methods, and not related to these two classes [3]. Among finite-difference methods, the method of staggered grids has been the most popular in recent years [4, 5]. Among the finite element methods, the discontinuous Galerkin method [6, 7] and the method of spectral elements [8, 9] are of the most interest. The finite-difference methods also include the grid-characteristic method [10, 11], which we use in this work.

Chimera or overlapping grids [12–15] have been proposed for solving hydrodynamic problems. In recent years, their application has expanded to the solution of other equations of mathematical physics. In particular, earlier we proposed a grid-characteristic method on Chimera computational grids for solving the initial-boundary value problem for the elastic wave equation [11, 16].

The essence of the grid-characteristic method using Chimera grids is in generation curved structured grids, overlapped on background regular (with constant coordinate steps) structured grids and mutual interpolation between them. With the help of Chimera computational grids, it is possible to describe boundaries and contact boundaries of complex shape [16] or not co-directed with the coordinate axes [11].

Basically, studies of algorithms for distribution of computational grids among processes and parallel mesh partitioning are carried out, firstly, for one computational grid, and secondly, for the case of tetrahedral and hexahedral grids [17–19], apparently, because the case of regular structured grids seems trivial to scientists.

However, the studies carried out in this paper show that the complexity is the distribution of grids among processes in the case of a large number of structured computational grids of different sizes. Therefore, the direct construction of a system of computational grids, in which ultrasonic wave phenomena in a rail are calculated, by minimizing the total number of nodes may not give the expected increase in the speed of calculations. And the problems of both the optimal choice of a set of background grids and the algorithm for their distribution among processes require study and solution. In this paper, we study the dependence of scalability on the configuration of background computational grids and the used algorithm of their distribution among processes. We mean as the scalability the change in acceleration on the number of parallel processors and, generally, the ability to proportionally increase in performance with an increase in hardware resources.

The paper is organized as follows. We introduce the mathematical model of ultrasonic wave propagation in Sect. 2. The used computational algorithm is discussed in Sect. 3. Some features of the used numerical method are presented in Sect. 4. Computational curved grid generation and the choice of background regular grids are discussed in Sect. 5. We describe the tested algorithms of the distribution of computational grids among processes in Sect. 6. The results of scalability testing are presented in Sect. 7. Section 8 concludes the paper.

2 Mathematical Model

To simulate the ultrasonic waves phenomena in a rail, we solve the following boundary value problem for the elastic wave equation with zero initial conditions:

$$\frac{\partial \sigma(t, \mathbf{r})}{\partial t} = \rho\left(c_P^2 - 2c_S^2\right)(\nabla \cdot \mathbf{v}(t, \mathbf{r}))\mathbf{I} + \rho c_S^2\left(\nabla \otimes \mathbf{v}(t, \mathbf{r}) + (\nabla \otimes \mathbf{v}(t, \mathbf{r}))^T\right) \quad (1)$$

$$\rho\frac{\partial \mathbf{v}(t, \mathbf{r})}{\partial t} = (\nabla \cdot \sigma(t, \mathbf{r}))^T + \mathbf{f}(t, \mathbf{r}), \ \mathbf{r} \in \Omega, \ t \in [0, T] \quad (2)$$

$$\mathbf{f}(t, \mathbf{r}) = \begin{cases} \{0, \ f_0 \sin(2\pi\eta t) \sin \ \alpha, \ f_0 \sin(2\pi\eta t) \cos \ \alpha\}^T, \ t \in \left[0, \dfrac{N_{IMP}}{\eta}\right], \ \mathbf{r} \in \Theta \\[2ex] 0, \ t \notin \left[0, \dfrac{N_{IMP}}{\eta}\right], \ \mathbf{r} \notin \Theta \end{cases}$$

$$(3)$$

$$\mathbf{m}(\tilde{r}) \cdot \sigma(t, \tilde{r}) = 0, \ \mathbf{m}(\tilde{r}) \perp \partial\Omega, \ |\mathbf{m}(\tilde{r})| = 1, \ \tilde{r} \in \partial\Omega, \ t \in [0, T] \quad (4)$$

In Eqs. 1–5, we used the following notations. $\mathbf{v}(t, \mathbf{r})$, $\sigma(t, \mathbf{r})$ are unknown functions, i.e. velocity and symmetric Cauchy stress tensor of 2nd rank; ρ is the density of the rail and is of 7,800 kg/m^3, c_P and c_S mean the speeds of P- (pressure) and S- (shear) elastic waves, 6,250.1282 m/s and 3,188.521 m/s, respectively; $\mathbf{f}$ is the volume density of external forces, η is the frequency of ultrasonic waves in Hz, 625.01282 kHz, N_{IMP} is the number of periods in the wavelet, 0.5, α is the given angle; Ω is the integration domain, the rail volume, $\partial\Omega$ means it's out boundary except the perpendicular to OZ axis; Θ is a circle inside Ω, near the rail surface and the location of the piezoelectric element. This type of elastic wave source was chosen because the non-destructive testing of rails uses directed sources of ultrasonic waves that generate a wavelet of P-waves propagating at an angle α to the surface. In further studies, we plan to improve the method of modeling the impact of a piezoelectric element on a rail and take it into account as a boundary condition in the form of a plane P-wave locally incident on the rail surface at the place of contact with the piezoelectric element. At the moment, the software implements to set at the boundary the density of external forces, which changes only depending on time, which generates either a superposition of P- and S-waves propagating perpendicular to the surface. Also, the developed software implements the impact of wheelsets on the rail [20, 21], but it is not considered in this paper.

3 Computational Algorithm

Firstly, consider the computational algorithm in its sequential version. In general, for each time step, the following stages can be distinguished.

0. Initial conditions. They are performed once before the first time step. Whereas the steps below are performed for each time step. Moreover, the stages of the algorithm, except for *.1 and *.5, are performed in a cycle over all computational grids, and only then should the transition to the next stage take place.

1.1   Preconditions between grids on planes perpendicular to OX.
1.2   Fillers on planes perpendicular to OX.
1.3   Calculation of the solution at internal points along the X direction.
1.4   Correctors for planes perpendicular to OX.
1.5. Contact conditions between grids on planes perpendicular to OX.
2.1   Preconditions between grids on planes perpendicular to OY.
2.2   Fillers on planes perpendicular to OY.
2.3   Calculation of the solution at internal points along the Y direction.
2.4   Correctors for planes perpendicular to OY.
2.5. Contact conditions between grids on planes perpendicular to OY.
3.1   Preconditions between grids on planes perpendicular to OZ.
3.2   Fillers on planes perpendicular to OZ.
3.3   Calculation of the solution at internal points along the Z direction.
3.4   Correctors for planes perpendicular to OZ.
3.5. Contact conditions between grids on planes perpendicular to OZ.

Interpolation between grids can be implemented as *.1st or *.5th stages.

Thus, let's present the algorithm used in the considered direct problem of ultrasonic rail non-destructive testing. At each time step, the following stages are performed.

1. Interpolation from all background computational grids to points $[1, 2] \times [1, N_L^G] \times [1, N_Z]$ of the Chimera computational grid.

2. Non-reflective fillers for Chimera grid on the inner plane perpendicular to the X-axis. In the cycle of $[N_S^G + 1, N_S^G + 2] \times [1, N_L^G] \times [1, N_Z]$, the filling occurs corresponding to the non-reflective boundary conditions.

3. Calculation of the solution at internal points of all computational grids along the X direction, i.e. calculation of the solution at the $\sum\limits_{g=1}^{G} [1, N_X^g] \times [1, N_Y^g] \times [1, N_Z]$ points.

4. Corrector of zero external force in the Chimera computational grid, correction of values on the external boundary in points $\{N_S^G\} \times [1, N_L^G] \times [1, N_Z]$.

5. Copying data in points from the beginning to the end of the Chimera computational grid, and vice versa. That is, copying the data to the following points:

$$\left[3, N_S^G\right] \times [1, 2] \times [1, N_Z] \rightarrow \left[3, N_S^G\right] \times \left[N_L^G, N_L^G + 1\right] \times [1, N_Z] \quad (5)$$

$$\left[3, N_S^G\right] \times \left[N_L^G - 2, N_L^G - 1\right] \times [1, N_Z] \rightarrow \left[3, N_S^G\right] \times [-1, 0] \times [1, N_Z] \quad (6)$$

Interpolation perpendicular to OY between background computational grids into the upper and lower cells:

$$\left[1, N_X^g\right] \times \left[N_Y^g, N_Y^g + 1\right] \times [1, N_Z], \ \left[1, N_X^{g+1}\right] \times [-1, 0] \times [1, N_Z], \ g \in [1, G - 2] \quad (7)$$

Interpolation from all background computational grids to points $[1, 2] \times [1, N_L^G] \times [1, N_Z]$ of the Chimera computational grid.

       Interpolation from the points $[3, N_S^G] \times [1, N_L^G] \times [1, N_Z]$ of the Chimera computational grid to all points of the background computational grids lying inside the corresponding cells of the Chimera computational grid.

6. Calculation of the solution at internal points of all computational grids along the Y direction, i.e. calculation of the solution at the $\sum_{g=1}^{G} [1, N_X^g] \times [1, N_Y^g] \times [1, N_Z]$ points.

7. For all grids, non-reflective fillers on planes perpendicular to the Z direction, filling values at the following points $\sum_{g=1}^{G} [1, N_X^g] \times [1, N_Y^g] \times \{-1, 0, N_Z + 1, N_Z + 2\}$.

8. Calculation of the solution at internal points of all computational grids along the Z direction, i.e. calculation of the solution at the $\sum_{g=1}^{G} [1, N_X^g] \times [1, N_Y^g] \times [1, N_Z]$ points.

9. For the points of the upper background grid $G - 1$ and the Chimera grid, a correction is made in accordance with the specified right side. The solution value is modified at the points $[1, N_X^{G-1}] \times [1, N_Y^{G-1}] \times [1, N_Z]$ and $[1, N_S^G] \times [1, N_L^G] \times [1, N_Z]$. Since the right side imitates a source, that acts localized in a short period of time and in local space, this part of the algorithm, of course, needs to be optimized, since all the algorithms for distributing grids among processes considered below will work with less efficiency, since they will not take into account double run of 2 grids from G.

10. Interpolation from the points $[3, N_S^G] \times [1, N_L^G] \times [1, N_Z]$ of the Chimera computational grid to all points of the background computational grids lying inside the corresponding cells of the Chimera computational grid.

Here G is the number of computational grids, the index $g = G$ corresponds to the Chimera computational grid, N_S^G (short) is the size across the Chimera grid, corresponding to the nominal direction OX, N_L^G (long) is the dimension along the Chimera grid, corresponding to the nominal direction OY, N_Z means the number of points along the OZ direction, the same for all computational grids, $N_X^g \times N_Y^g \times N_Z$ are the sizes of the background computational grids, $g \in [1, G - 1]$. Note that for each computational grid, the data will be stored in an extended grid $(N_X^g + 4) \times (N_Y^g + 4) \times (N_Z + 4)$ with ghost nodes [11], however, calculations will be made only in the following ranges of variation of node indices $[1, N_X^g] \times [1, N_Y^g] \times [1, N_Z]$.

Note that 1th and 10th stages conditionally correspond to one stage. However, we moved the interpolation from the Chimera grid to the background grids to the last 10th stage of the considered time step, since the calculation data is saved to the HDD or SSD after 10th stage, if necessary. Thus, in order to the incorrect solution in the background grids not to be saved, we shifted the interpolation from the Chimera grid to the background grids to 10th stage from 1th one. Since we use zero initial conditions, this is permissible and does not affect the result of the calculations. Also note that the interpolation from the Chimera grid to the background grid and vice versa is repeated both before calculating the solution at internal points along the X direction and before calculating the solution at internal points along the Y direction. This is necessary due to the curvature of the considered Chimera grid with respect to the both axes OX and OY.

When using a parallel implementation, each computational grid can be partition into several grids, which is specified by a set of numbers L_X, L_Y, L_Z of partitions along each direction. Next, the grid is partitioned into approximately equal parallelepipeds in the number of $L_X \cdot L_Y \cdot L_Z$. Each of the additional grids is given to one of the processes. Calculations can be performed at points of several additional grids from one or different initial grids at one process. In connection with the use of the Rusanov difference scheme on a five-point template, it is necessary to send two lines of points closest to the boundary to neighboring additional grids [11, 22]. Also, at the preprocessing stage, the interpolation algorithm is analyzed and it is determined, which data should be sent from this process and which data should be received. Interpolation at one point in the 3D case may require sending data from 1 (hitting a node), 2 (hit on an edge), 4 (hit on a face), or 8 (hit inside a cell) nodes of another computational grid. Accordingly, if at the preprocessing stage it turned out that one or several of these nodes are assigned to other processes, the corresponding data sending is protocoled. Synchronization is required after each element of the above sequential algorithm.

The implementation of the software allows to test various algorithms for the distribution of grids among processes, since there are significant options of setting process numbers, which will calculate the solution in a specific computational grid, and of a specific partition of this grid along each of the axes.

4   Numerical Method

The used grid-characteristic computational method on structured curved and regular computational grids for solving initial-boundary value problems for the elastic wave equation is described in detail in [10, 11, 22]. To compare the number of calculations, we present here the formulae for the transition to the Riemann invariants and back to the unknown functions in the case of the X direction in the background grid

$$\omega_{1,2}^X = v_X \mp \frac{1}{\rho c_P}\sigma_{XX}, \quad \omega_{3,4}^X = v_Y \mp \frac{1}{\rho c_S}\sigma_{XY}, \quad \omega_{5,6}^X = v_Z \mp \frac{1}{\rho c_S}\sigma_{XZ} \quad (8)$$

$$\omega_7^X = \sigma_{YZ}, \quad \omega_8^X = \sigma_{YY} - \sigma_{ZZ}, \quad \omega_9^X = \sigma_{YY} + \sigma_{ZZ} - 2k\sigma_{XX} \quad (9)$$

$$\mathbf{v} = \frac{1}{2}\left\{\omega_1^X + \omega_2^X, \omega_3^X + \omega_4^X, \omega_5^X + \omega_6^X\right\}^T \quad (10)$$

$$\sigma_{XX} = \rho c_P\left(\omega_2^X - \omega_1^X\right)/2, \quad \sigma_{XY} = \rho c_S\left(\omega_4^X - \omega_3^X\right)/2, \quad \sigma_{XZ} = \rho c_S\left(\omega_6^X - \omega_5^X\right)/2 \quad (11)$$

$$\sigma_{YZ} = \omega_7^X, \quad \sigma_{YY,ZZ} = \left(k\rho_P\left(\omega_2^X - \omega_1^X\right) + \omega_9^X \pm \omega_8^X\right)/2 \quad (12)$$

and in the Chimera computational grid:

$$\omega_{1,2} = \mathbf{n} \cdot \mathbf{v} \mp \frac{1}{lc_P\rho}(\mathbf{N}_{00} : \sigma), \quad \omega_{3,4} = \mathbf{n}_1 \cdot \mathbf{v} \mp \frac{1}{lc_S\rho}(\mathbf{N}_{01} : \sigma), \quad \omega_7 = 2\mathbf{N}_{12} : \sigma \quad (13)$$

$$\omega_{5,6} = \mathbf{n}_2 \cdot \mathbf{v} \mp \frac{1}{lc_S\rho}(\mathbf{N}_{02} : \sigma), \quad \omega_8 = (\mathbf{N}_{11} - \mathbf{N}_{22}) : \sigma, \quad \omega_9 = (\mathbf{N}_{11} + \mathbf{N}_{22} - 2k\mathbf{N}_{00}) : \sigma$$

$$(14)$$

$$\mathbf{v} = \frac{\omega_1 + \omega_2}{2}\mathbf{n} + \frac{\omega_3 + \omega_4}{2}\mathbf{n}_1 + \frac{\omega_5 + \omega_6}{2}\mathbf{n}_2 \tag{15}$$

$$\sigma = l\rho((c_P - c_3)\mathbf{N}_{00} + c_3\mathbf{I})(\omega_2 - \omega_1)/2 + lc_S\rho(\omega_4 - \omega_3)\mathbf{N}_{01} + lc_S\rho(\omega_6 - \omega_5)\mathbf{N}_{02}$$

$$+2\omega_7\mathbf{N}_{12} + \omega_8/2(\mathbf{N}_{11} - \mathbf{N}_{22}) + \omega_9/2(\mathbf{I} - \mathbf{N}_{00}) \tag{16}$$

Here, ω_i^X are the Riemann invariants, $k = 1 - 2c_S^2/c_P^2$; l depends on the Jacobian of the transformation of the considered cell of the Chimera grid into a unit cube and is different at each point of the Chimera grid, vectors $\mathbf{n}$, $\mathbf{n}_1$, $\mathbf{n}_2$ and symmetric tensors of 2nd rank $\mathbf{N}_{ij}$, $i,j \in \{0, 1, 2\}$, are also different for each point of the Chimera grid.

5   Computational Meshes

As mentioned in the previous Sects., for the calculation we will need one or more structured regular background grids and one Chimera curved structured grid (Fig. 1).

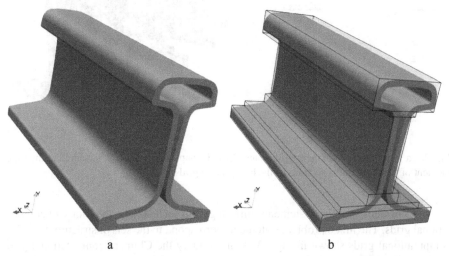

a   b

Fig. 1. Computational grids: **a** Chimera computational grid; **b** Chimera computational grid and structured regular (with constant coordinate steps) background grids for a set of grids No. 1.

To generate the Chimera grid, we used an analytical algorithm, setting the geometry of the outer surface of the rail in the OXY plane as a set of arcs of circles and segments in accordance with the engineering drawing of the considered rail model. The inner boundary was also calculated analytically as a set of arcs of circles and segments. Next, we naturally parametrized both curves and split them with automatic thickening in areas with a significant radius of curvature (the developed software allows to set the minimal angle of rotation of the edges of two neighboring cells and the minimal increase in the length of the edge of two neighboring cells). Further, based on these sets of points, using the analytical algorithm described in [23], Sect. 5, a curved structured grid is generated. The parts of the used Chimera grid are shown in Fig. 2a.

One of the snapshots of the ultrasonic wave field in the rail is shown in Fig. 2b for an example. However, we note that in real problems of ultrasonic non-destructive testing, it may not be necessary to study the wave field in sections and volume, but only on the detector, therefore, in further testing of scalability, we did not take into account the time spent on saving volumetric data and slices. But we can note that due to the large amount of data, it is expedient to use ghost slicing grids shown in Fig. 2b, in which the calculation is not carried out, and in which copying is carried out from real grids.

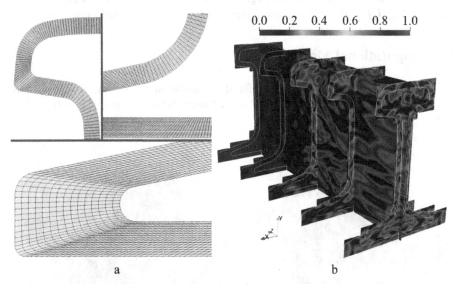

Fig. 2. **a** Fragments of Chimera grid, plane OXY; **b** snapshot of velocity wavefield at the time moment of 0.566 μs in the sections of the background grids.

We consider 8 problem statements, differing from each other in the choice of computational grids. The first 6 problem statements correspond to the sets of structured regular computational grids shown in Figs. 3, 4 and 5. Only the Chimera computational grid participates in the seventh formulation (the Chimera grid is the same for all formulations, see Figs. 1, 2). In the eighth formulation, the calculation is carried out only in one structured regular computational grid from the set of grids No. 4. The seventh and eighth formulations have no physical meaning. They were tested to show how different algorithms for distributing grids among processes work in the case of one Chimera grid and one regular structured grid.

In all calculations, the step along the Z axis was taken equal to 2 mm. Unless otherwise stated, a rail length along the Z axis of 30 cm was considered, that is, 151 points in the Z

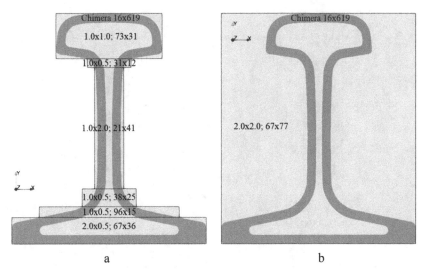

Fig. 3. Sets of computational grids, plane OXY, cell dimensions in this plane are indicated in mm, followed by the number of points in the X and Y directions: **a** No. 1, the total number of points for a rail length of 30 cm is 3,533,690; **b** No. 2, the total number of points for a rail length of 30 cm is 2,274,513.

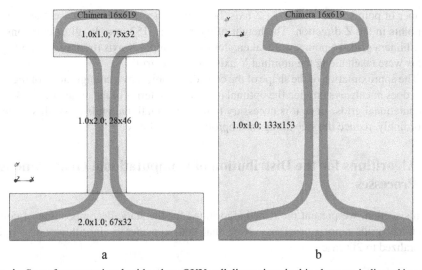

Fig. 4. Sets of computational grids, plane OXY, cell dimensions in this plane are indicated in mm, followed by the number of points in the X and Y directions: **a** No. 3, the total number of points for a rail length of 30 cm is 2,366,472; **b** No. 4, total number of points for a rail length of 30 cm is 4,568,203.

direction. Also, for the grid distribution algorithm with minimization of cross-sectional areas, a version of the calculations with a rail length of 7 cm was considered to show how this algorithm behaves in the case when for half of the computational grids the maximum

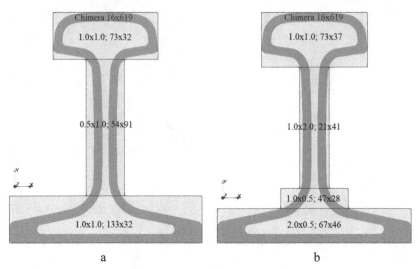

Fig. 5. Sets of computational grids, plane OXY, cell dimensions in this plane are indicated in mm, followed by the number of points in the X and Y directions: **a** No. 5, the total number of points for a rail length of 30 cm is 3,232,910; **b** No. 6, the total number of points for a rail length of 30 cm is 2,697,464.

number of points is not along the Z axis, but along other axes. In this case, there were 36 points in the Z direction. The height of the rail was 152 mm. In all calculations in the Chimera grid, 16 points were taken along the nominal X axis (transverse), and 619 points were taken along the nominal Y axis (along the grid).

The approximation of the shape of the considered object by a configuration of regular grids does not always provide the optimal result even in terms of the number of nodes of computational grids, since it is necessary to use computational grids of small size and, accordingly, reduce the step along the appropriate coordinate.

6   Algorithms for the Distribution of Computational Grids Among Processes

In this section, we present the tested algorithms for the static decomposition of computational grids among processes. Note that both considered algorithms are simply generalized to 2D case.

6.1   Greedy Method for a Large Number of Processes

In a case of a large number of processes, it seems appropriate to use the following greedy algorithm:

1. The total number of nodes N of all grids is calculated, at that Chimera grids being taken into account with a coefficient $a > 1$, since they are curved and, as discussed above, require a large amount of calculations to find solution at a node. This

coefficient a is calculated empirically. For example, in geophysical problems where Chimera grids are built around fractures in the geological media, the coefficient $a \approx 7$.

2. $P \cdot N_X \cdot N_Y \cdot N_Z / N$ processes are allocated for each regular grid with sizes of $N_X \times N_Y \times N_Z$, where P is the total number of processes.
3. $a \cdot P \cdot N_X \cdot N_Y \cdot N_Z / N$ processes are allocated for each Chimera grid with sizes of $N_X \times N_Y \times N_Z$.
4. Next, the grids are divided into subdomains using the simple geometric decomposition method, i.e. MPI_Dims_Create with default options.

6.2 Minimal Cross Section Algorithm for Parallel Mesh Partitioning

When using a simple geometric decomposition and the MPI_Dims_Create function with default options, the distribution of the grid among the processes occurs as follows. If possible, 3 divisors of the number of processes are considered, closest to each other in value. According to the maximum of them, the grid is divided along OX, then along OY, then along OZ. That is, for example, for the number of processes 24, we obtain a partition along OX by 4, along OY by 3 and along OZ by 2.

This variant of grid partitioning among processes is bad for real problems with a large number of grids, since they are often elongated along an arbitrary axis. The use of the minimal cross section algorithm (the minimal total area of sections) seems to be more effective, which was shown by further testing. This algorithm is as follows.

1. Based on the known tables of divisors of natural numbers, all possible partitions of the number of processes into 3 divisors are considered, without repetitions.
2. And for each partition, the sum of the sections is calculated using the formula:

$$S = (L_X - 1) \cdot N_Y \cdot N_Z + (L_Y - 1) \cdot N_X \cdot N_Z + (L_Z - 1) \cdot N_X \cdot N_Y \qquad (17)$$

Here, $N_X \times N_Y \times N_Z$ are sizes of the considered structured computational grid, L_X, L_Y, L_Z means the numbers of partitions of this grid along appropriate axes.
3. Such a variant of grid partitioning is chosen, which provides the minimal value of cross section S.

In the case when the number of processes varies in large ranges and there are natural numbers with a large amount of divisors, one can choose not all divisors for these natural numbers, but only some. Note that the selected set of divisors must include limiting cases of 1 and the natural number itself, since they correspond to the absence of grid splitting along some axes, which can be an optimal solution for highly elongated computational grids, for which not too many processes are allocated.

7 Scalability Testing

In this section, we present the results of the scalability testing in Figs. 6, 7 and 8 for various problem statements and algorithms for the distribution of grids among processes.

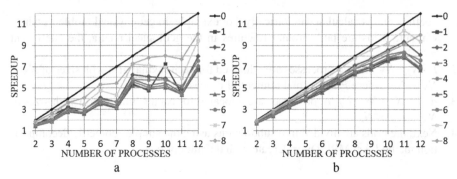

Fig. 6. Scalability graphs for all problem statements, 0 means the ideal, other numbers mean the numbers of problem statements: **a** simple geometric decomposition of each computational grid using MPI_Dims_Create; **b** splitting all grids along the Z axis by the number of processes.

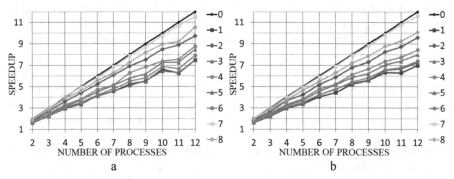

Fig. 7. Scalability graphs for all problem statements using the minimal cross section algorithm, 0 means the ideal, other numbers mean the numbers of problem statements: **a** rail length of 30 cm as in other calculations; **b** rail length of 7 cm.

The problem of the minimal cross section algorithm is that in its current version it does not take into account the data transfer between different grids, which is already necessary in the numerical method. This explains the fact that on a middle number of processes, the algorithm with splitting each grid along the Z axis works better.

Note that in the problem considered in the paper, the coefficient a from the greedy algorithm was taken equal to 1.5, which is due both to the features of the used structured curved grid and to the absence of contact boundaries inside it.

It is also interesting to compare the time costs for solving the same problem with a different choice of computational grids and algorithms for their distribution among processes. We present these results in Figs. 9, 10.

In Figs. 9, 10, one can see how, due to a higher increase in speedup, the use of a smaller number of nodes due to an increase in the number of background grids ceases to justify itself.

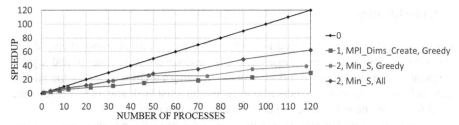

Fig. 8. Scalability graph with the greedy algorithm (Greedy) or allocating all processes to each grid (All), using a simple geometric decomposition (MPI_Dims_Create), or minimal cross section algorithm (Min_S), 1st and 2nd problem statements with sets of grids No. 1 and 2, respectively. 0 means the ideal. Calculations were performed on the cluster of the National Research Center "Kurchatov Institute".

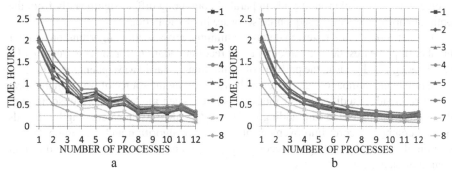

Fig. 9. Time costs (in hours) for all problem statements 1–8: **a** simple geometric decomposition of each computational grid using MPI_Dims_Create; **b** splitting all grids along the Z axis by the number of processes.

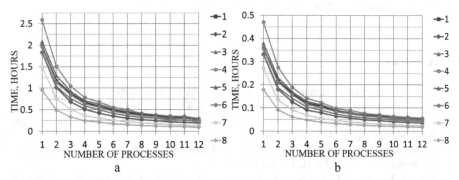

Fig. 10. Time costs (in hours) for all problem statements 1–8 using the minimal cross section algorithm: **a** rail length of 30 cm as in other calculations; **b** rail length of 7 cm.

8 Conclusions

A software package was developed for carrying out parallel calculations of elastic and acoustic wave phenomena on a large number of separate structured curved and regular computational grids. Various algorithms for constructing a set of separate computational grids and various algorithms for distributing computational grids among processes were tested for one problem of modeling ultrasonic waves in a rail.

The performed studies have shown the promise of using the minimal cross sections algorithm in comparison with a simple geometric decomposition (MPI_Dims_Create) for solving applied problems using a large number of separate structured computational grids, i.e. curved and regular. The developed curved grid generator also proved itself well, allowing to reduce the difference in the calculation in the node of the curved grid and the calculation in the node of the regular grid. It was also found that the optimal choice of a set of background grids in parallel computing differs significantly from the optimal choice when using sequential software implementation.

Further research are to test in detail the minimal cross section algorithm on a larger number of processes; determination of exact recommendations for the construction of a set of background grids in the problem of simulation of elastic wave phenomena in rails; reduction in the number of calculations when specifying the source of waves in the form of the right side; modification of the wave source when modeling the ultrasonic non-destructive testing of the rail; adding the use of OpenMP when calculating by threads on one computing core; improvement of the greedy algorithm and the minimal cross section algorithm by adding an account of the amount of data sent between different computational grids.

Acknowledgments. This work has been performed with the financial support of the Russian Science Foundation (project No. 20-71-10028). This work has been carried out using computing resources of the federal collective usage center Complex for Simulation and Data Processing for Mega-science Facilities at NRC "Kurchatov Institute", http://ckp.nrcki.ru/.

References

1. Cao, J., Chen, J.B.: A parameter-modified method for implementing surface topography in elastic-wave finite-difference modeling. Geophysics **83**(6), T313–T332 (2018)
2. Li, S., Wu, Y.: Energy-preserving mixed finite element methods for the elastic wave equation. Appl. Math. Comput. **422** (2022). Art. no. 126963
3. Li, B., Stovas, A.: Decoupling approximation of P-and S-wave phase velocities in orthorhombic media. Geophysics **87**(2), T169–T182 (2022)
4. Gordon, R., Turkel, E., Gordon, D.: A compact three-dimensional fourth-order scheme for elasticity using the first-order formulation. Int. J. Numer. Meth. Eng. **122**(21), 6341–6360 (2021)
5. Lu, Z., Ma, Y., Wang, S., Zhang, H., Guo, J., Wan, Y.: Numerical simulation of seismic wave triggered by low-frequency sound source with 3D staggered-grid difference method in shallow water. Arab. J. Geosci. **14**(6), 1–8 (2021). https://doi.org/10.1007/s12517-021-06854-5

6. Duru, K., Rannabauer, L., Gabriel, A.A., Igel, H.: A new discontinuous Galerkin method for elastic waves with physically motivated numerical fluxes. J. Sci. Comput. **88**(3), 1–32 (2021)
7. Huang, J., Hu, T., Li, Y., Song, J., Liang, S.: Numerical dispersion and dissipation of the triangle-based discontinuous Galerkin method for acoustic and elastic velocity-stress equations. Comput. Geosci. **159** (2022). Art. no. 104979
8. Sepehry, N., Ehsani, M., Asadi, S., Shamshirsaz, M., Nejad, F.B.: Fourier spectral element for simulation of vibro-acoustic modulation caused by contact nonlinearity in the beam. Thin-Walled Struct. **174** (2022). Art. no. 109112
9. Trinh, P.T., Brossier, R., Métivier, L., Tavard, L., Virieux, J.: Efficient time-domain 3D elastic and viscoelastic full-waveform inversion using a spectral-element method on flexible Cartesian-based mesh. Geophysics **84**(1), R61–R83 (2019)
10. Favorskaya, A.V., Zhdanov, M.S., Khokhlov, N.I., Petrov, I.B.: Modelling the wave phenomena in acoustic and elastic media with sharp variations of physical properties using the grid-characteristic method. Geophys. Prospect. **66**(8), 1485–1502 (2018)
11. Khokhlov, N., Favorskaya, A., Stetsyuk, V., Mitskovets, I.: Grid-characteristic method using Chimera meshes for simulation of elastic waves scattering on geological fractured zones. J. Comput. Phys. **446** (2021). Art. no. 110637
12. Steger, J.L.: A Chimera grid scheme: advances in grid generation. Am. Soc. Mech. Eng. Fluids Eng. Div. **5**, 55–70 (1983)
13. Chesshire, G., Henshaw, W.D.: Composite overlapping meshes for the solution of partial differential equations. J. Comput. Phys. **90**(1), 1–64 (1990)
14. Henshaw, W.D., Schwendeman, D.W.: Parallel computation of three-dimensional flows using overlapping grids with adaptive mesh refinement. J. Comput. Phys. **227**(16), 7469–7502 (2008)
15. Chang, X.H., Ma, R., Wang, N.H., Zhao, Z., Zhang, L.P.: A parallel implicit hole-cutting method based on background mesh for unstructured Chimera grid. Comput. Fluids **198** (2020). Art. no. 104403
16. Favorskaya, A., Khokhlov, N.: Accounting for curved boundaries in rocks by using curvilinear and Chimera grids. Proc. Comput. Sci. **192**, 3787–3794 (2021)
17. Walshaw, C., Cross, M.: Parallel optimisation algorithms for multilevel mesh partitioning. Parallel Comput. **26**(12), 1635–1660 (2000)
18. Borrell, R., et al.: Parallel mesh partitioning based on space filling curves. Comput. Fluids **173**, 264–272 (2018)
19. Horne, W.J., Mahesh, K.: A massively-parallel, unstructured overset method for mesh connectivity. J. Comput. Phys. **376**, 585–596 (2019)
20. Favorskaya, A., Khokhlov, N.: Modeling the impact of wheelsets with flat spots on a railway track. Proc. Comput. Sci. **126**, 1100–1109 (2018)
21. Kozhemyachenko, A.A., Petrov, I.B., Favorskaya, A.V., Khokhlov, N.I.: Boundary conditions for modeling the impact of wheels on railway track. Comput. Math. Math. Phys. **60**(9), 1539–1554 (2020)
22. Favorskaya, A.V., Khokhlov, N.I., Petrov, I.B.: Grid-characteristic method on joint structured regular and curved grids for modeling coupled elastic and acoustic wave phenomena in objects of complex shape. Lobachevskii J. Math. **41**(4), 512–525 (2020)
23. Favorskaya, A.V.: Simulation of the human head ultrasound study by grid-characteristic method on analytically generated curved meshes. Smart Innov. Syst. Technol. **214**, 249–263 (2021)

Parallel Computing in Solving the Problem of Interval Multicriteria Optimization in Chemical Kinetics

Sergey Koledin[1] , Kamila Koledina[2(✉)] , and Irek Gubaydullin[2]

[1] Ufa State Petroleum Technological University, Ufa, Russia
[2] Institute of Petrochemistry and Catalysis of RAS, Ufa, Russia
koledinakamila@mail.ru

Abstract. Interval multi-criteria optimization (MCO) of the conditions based on the kinetic model is relevant for both laboratory and industrial processes. In the work for the laboratory catalytic reaction of the synthesis of benzylbutyl ether, the problem of interval MCO of the conditions of conducting based on a kinetic model is solved. The problem was solved in the form of Pareto approximation using the evolutionary algorithm of multiobjective optimization NSGA-II and parallel computing. The solution of the MCO interval problem was obtained by varying the temperature from 160 °C to 175 °C, with a temperature spread of no more than 5 °C. An increase in temperature leads to an increase in the yield of the target product, but the concentration of the by-product also increases. A parallel scheme has been developed for solving the interval problem of the MCO and an assessment of the efficiency of the execution of the parallel program has been carried out.

Keywords: Parallel computing · Interval multicriteria optimization · Chemical kinetics · Benzylbutyl ether

1 Introduction

The basis for optimizing the conditions of complex chemical processes is their kinetic model. The kinetic model reflects the regularities of the reaction, the effect of the conditions on the reaction rate, on the yield of target and by-products and reaction time. In a complex chemical process, including the process of oil production [1], oil refining, it is difficult to single out one optimization criterion. Often several criteria are set, which may be contradictory and have different dimensions. Such a task is defined as multi-criteria optimization. Due to the fact that in practice it is difficult to maintain the calculated exact optimal mode of the process, it is necessary to select the optimal interval of conditions [2]. Which requires solving the problem of interval multi-criteria optimization, including the development of an interval kinetic model [3, 4]. The range of variation of the conditions can be quite wide when searching for the optimal solution, and the dimension of the mathematical model can reach several dozen differential equations in the number

© The Author(s), under exclusive license to Springer Nature Switzerland AG 2022
V. Voevodin et al. (Eds.): RuSCDays 2022, LNCS 13708, pp. 214–224, 2022.
https://doi.org/10.1007/978-3-031-22941-1_15

of reaction components, so it is relevant to develop a parallel calculation scheme when solving the problem of interval multicriteria optimization in chemical kinetics.

The object of the study is the catalytic reaction of the synthesis of benzylalkyl esters, namely benzylbutyl ether. The catalytic reaction of the synthesis of benzylalkyl esters occurs by intermolecular dehydration of benzyl and n-butyl alcohols with the formation of three esters: target benzylbutyl and side dibenzyl, dibutyl [5, 6]. The development of a detailed kinetic model will solve the problem of multi-criteria optimization of the reaction conditions in order to maximize the target yield and minimize the output of by-products.

2 Mathematical Model

The mathematical model of the kinetics of complex chemical reactions in the form of a system of ordinary nonlinear differential equations (SONDE) has the form [7]:

$$\frac{dy_i}{dt} = \varphi_i(y_i, k_j), \quad i = 1, ..., I, \quad j = 1, ..., J, \tag{1}$$

$$k_j = k_j^0 \exp(-\frac{E_j}{RT}) \tag{2}$$

$y_i(0) = y_i^0, \quad t \in [0, t^*],$

where y_i – concentration of chemical reaction substances, mol/l; t^* - reaction time, min; φ_i - functions of the right parts according to the rate of reaction steps; I - number of chemical reaction substances; J - number of chemical reaction stages; k_j - stage rate constants; k_j^0 - pre-exponential factors; E_j - activation energy of stages, kcal/mol; R - universal gas constant, 2 cal/(mol*K); T - temperature, K.

When calculating a task with interval values of the process temperature $T \in (\underline{T}, \overline{T})$, the rate constants of the stages will have interval values according to (2) $k_j \in (\underline{k_j}, \overline{k_j})$. To solve the system of differential Eqs. (1), a two-sided method for solving the interval problem will be used [8, 9]. For each component y_i it is possible to introduce a dependence on the boundaries of kinetic parameters: y_i isotone by parameter k_j, if $\frac{\partial \varphi_i}{\partial k_j} > 0$ and antiton by k_j, if $\frac{\partial \varphi_i}{\partial k_j} < 0$, otherwise φ_i does not depend on k_j.

Then, accordingly, it is possible to define two systems of differential equations of the form (1) for the lower bound of the concentration change $\underline{y_i}$ – dib_low and for the upper bound $\overline{y_i}$- dib_up.

3 Interval Mathematical Model of the Catalytic Reaction for the Synthesis of Benzylalkyl Ethers

Benzyl butyl ether is widely used as a flavoring agent in various industries. Is a large-capacity, industrial product [6]. The preparation of esters in the reaction of dehydration of benzyl alcohol is best carried out in the presence of catalysts containing copper, in particular $CuBr_2$ [10].

Table 1 shows the stages of chemical transformations and the values of the kinetic parameters of the stages, calculated in the works [11].

Table 1. Stages of chemical transformations and values of the kinetic parameters in the catalytic synthesis of benzyl butyl ethers

N	Stages of chemical transformations	E_j	lnk_j^0
1	$PhCH_2OH(Y_1) + CuBr_2(Y_2) \rightarrow [PhCH_2]^+[CuBr_2(OH)]^-(Y_3)$	5.40	7.00
2	$[PhCH_2]^+[CuBr_2(OH)]^-(Y_3) + BuOH(Y_4) \rightarrow [PhCH_2OBu]H^+$ $[CuBr_2(OH)]^-(Y_5)$	12.2	15.4
3	$[PhCH_2OBu]H^+ [CuBr_2(OH)]^-(Y_5) \rightarrow PhCH_2OBu(Y_6) + H_2O(Y_7) +$ $CuBr_2(Y_2)$	10.3	9.50
4	$[PhCH_2]^+[CuBr_2(OH)]^-(Y_3) + PhCH_2OH(Y_1) \rightarrow [PhCH_2OHCH_2Ph]^+$ $[CuBr_2(OH)]^-(Y_8)$	14.0	17.6
5	$[PhCH_2OHCH_2Ph]^+ [CuBr_2(OH)]^-(Y_8) \rightarrow PhCH_2OCH_2Ph (Y_9) +$ $H_2O(Y_7) + CuBr_2(Y_2)$	21.7	24.1
6	$BuOH(Y_4) + CuBr_2(Y_2) \rightarrow [Bu]^+[CuBr_2(OH)]^- (Y_{10})$	15.0	10.7
7	$[Bu]^+[CuBr_2(OH)]^- (Y_{10}) + BuOH(Y_4) \rightarrow [BuOHBu]^+[CuBr_2(OH)]^-$ (Y_{11})	18.5	20.4
8	$[BuOHBu]^+[CuBr_2(OH)]^- (Y_{11}) \rightarrow BuOBu(Y_{12}) + H_2O(Y_7) +$ $CuBr_2(Y_2)$	35.1	34.1
9	$[Bu]^+[CuBr_2(OH)]^- (Y_{10}) + PhCH_2OH(Y_1) \rightarrow [PhCH_2OBu]H^+$ $[CuBr_2(OH)]^-(Y_5)$	11.9	12.4

The mathematical model using the two-sided method for solving the interval problem will have the form of two SONDE for calculating the lower and upper limits of the concentrations of the components (3).

The direct interval kinetic problem was solved using the two-sided method in combination with the multi-step Gear method of variable order [12]. The scheme of chemical transformations of the reaction and the corresponding ranges of values of kinetic parameters are given in Table 1.

$$
\begin{cases}
\dfrac{dy_1}{dt} = -\overline{k}_1 y_1 y_2 - \overline{k}_4 y_3 y_1 - \overline{k}_9 y_1 y_{10}; \\[4pt]
\dfrac{dy_2}{dt} = -\overline{k}_1 y_1 y_2 + k_3 y_5 + k_5 y_8 + k_8 y_{11}; \\[4pt]
\dfrac{dy_3}{dt} = k_1 y_1 y_2 + \overline{k}_2 y_3 y_4 - \overline{k}_4 y_3 y_1; \\[4pt]
\dfrac{dy_4}{dt} = -\overline{k}_2 y_3 y_4 + \overline{k}_6 y_2 y_4 - \overline{k}_7 y_{10} y_4; \\[4pt]
\dfrac{dy_5}{dt} = k_2 y_3 y_4 - \overline{k}_3 y_5 + k_9 y_{10} y_1; \\[4pt]
\dfrac{dy_6}{dt} = k_3 y_5; \\[4pt]
\dfrac{dy_7}{dt} = k_3 y_5 + k_5 y_8 + k_8 y_{11}; \\[4pt]
\dfrac{dy_8}{dt} = k_4 y_3 y_1 - \overline{k}_5 y_8; \\[4pt]
\dfrac{dy_9}{dt} = k_5 y_8; \\[4pt]
\dfrac{dy_{10}}{dt} = k_6 y_2 y_4 - \overline{k}_7 y_{10} y_4 - \overline{k}_9 y_1 y_{10}; \\[4pt]
\dfrac{dy_{11}}{dt} = k_7 y_{10} y_4 - \overline{k}_8 y_{11}; \\[4pt]
\dfrac{dy_{12}}{dt} = k_8 y_{11};
\end{cases}
\qquad
\begin{cases}
\dfrac{d\overline{y}_1}{dt} = -k_1 \overline{y}_1 \overline{y}_2 - k_4 \overline{y}_3 \overline{y}_1 - k_9 \overline{y}_1 \overline{y}_{10}; \\[4pt]
\dfrac{d\overline{y}_2}{dt} = -k_1 \overline{y}_1 \overline{y}_2 + \overline{k}_3 \overline{y}_5 + \overline{k}_5 \overline{y}_8 + \overline{k}_8 \overline{y}_{11}; \\[4pt]
\dfrac{d\overline{y}_3}{dt} = \overline{k}_1 \overline{y}_1 \overline{y}_2 + k_2 \overline{y}_3 \overline{y}_4 - k_4 \overline{y}_3 \overline{y}_1; \\[4pt]
\dfrac{d\overline{y}_4}{dt} = -k_2 \overline{y}_3 \overline{y}_4 + k_6 \overline{y}_2 \overline{y}_4 - k_7 \overline{y}_{10} \overline{y}_4; \\[4pt]
\dfrac{d\overline{y}_5}{dt} = \overline{k}_2 \overline{y}_3 \overline{y}_4 - k_3 \overline{y}_5 + k_9 \overline{y}_{10} \overline{y}_1; \\[4pt]
\dfrac{d\overline{y}_6}{dt} = \overline{k}_3 \overline{y}_5; \\[4pt]
\dfrac{d\overline{y}_7}{dt} = \overline{k}_3 \overline{y}_5 + \overline{k}_5 \overline{y}_8 + \overline{k}_8 \overline{y}_{11}; \\[4pt]
\dfrac{d\overline{y}_8}{dt} = \overline{k}_4 \overline{y}_3 \overline{y}_1 - k_5 \overline{y}_8; \\[4pt]
\dfrac{d\overline{y}_9}{dt} = \overline{k}_5 \overline{y}_8; \\[4pt]
\dfrac{d\overline{y}_{10}}{dt} = \overline{k}_6 \overline{y}_2 \overline{y}_4 - k_7 \overline{y}_{10} \overline{y}_4 - k_9 \overline{y}_{10} \overline{y}_1; \\[4pt]
\dfrac{d\overline{y}_{11}}{dt} = \overline{k}_7 \overline{y}_{10} \overline{y}_4 - k_8 \overline{y}_{11}; \\[4pt]
\dfrac{d\overline{y}_{12}}{dt} = \overline{k}_8 \overline{y}_{11};
\end{cases}
$$

$$
y_i(0) = \overline{y}_i(0) = y_i^0, \quad t \in [0, t*],
$$

(3)

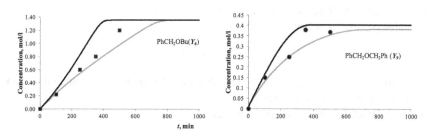

Fig. 1. Correspondence graphs between experimental data (dots) and intervals of calculated values (lines) of changes in the concentration of observed substrates in the temperature range [160 °C, 175 °C] in the reaction of the synthesis of benzyl butyl ethers (average values of the experimental concentrations of the components are given)

Figure 1 shows the correspondence of the experimental data with the intervals of calculated values of the measured substrates of the catalytic reaction of the synthesis of benzyl butyl ethers. The observed substrates are the target reaction product benzylbutyl ether $PhCH_2OBu(Y_6)$ and reaction by-product dibenzyl ether $PhCH_2OCH_2Ph$ (Y_9). The graphs show the values of concentrations in the temperature range [160 °C, 175 °C]. Experimental data on component concentrations are included in the calculated interval (Fig. 1). Thus, the interval values of the parameters obtained for the given temperature intervals describe the experimental data within the error. This gives grounds to conclude that this mechanism is reliable for the catalytic reaction of the synthesis of benzyl butyl ethers when using interval values of variable parameters.

The subsequent introduction of the process into production requires determining the optimal reaction conditions in order to obtain the highest yield of the target benzyl butyl ether PhCH2OBu(Y6) and the smallest by-product of dibenzyl ether PhCH2OCH2Ph (Y9). Based on the values of the kinetic parameters, it is possible to formulate a multicriteria interval optimization problem [13–15].

4 Statement of the Multi-criteria Interval Optimization Problem

Statement and solution of the optimization problem requires the definition of optimality criteria. It is also necessary to define variable parameters and restrictions on them. The process in the optimization problem is a chemical reaction. In chemical technology, such parameters can be: reaction temperature, pressure, initial concentrations of reagents, type of catalyst, reaction time. Restrictions on variable parameters are determined by the nature of the process and technical capabilities.

The mathematical model of problems of chemical kinetics has the form of a system of nonlinear differential equations for changing the concentration of reaction substances. The change occurs in time with known values of kinetic parameters: pre-exponential factors and activation energies of the rates of stages (1).

To determine the optimal conditions for the reaction, it is necessary to solve the problem of multicriteria optimization according to the set optimality criteria, using the described model.

The mathematical formulation of the MCO problem of the conditions of the chemical process according to the kinetic model has the form [14]:

Variable parameter vector

$$X = (x_1, \ x_2, \ x_3, \ x_4, \ x_5, \ \ldots), \tag{4}$$

x_1 – reaction temperature; x_2 – initial concentrations of reagents; x_3 – reaction time; x_4 – type of catalyst; x_5 – catalyst supply, etc.

Direct restrictions on variable parameters

$$X \in [X^{\min}, X^{\max}] : x_1 \in [x_1^-, x_1^+]; \ x_2 \in [x_2^-, x_2^+]; \ x_3 \in [x_3^-, x_3^+]; \ x_4 \in [x_4^-, x_4^+]; \ x_5 \in [x_5^-, x_5^+]; \ldots$$

Vector function of optimality criteria

$$F(X) = (f_1(X), \ f_2(X), \ f_3(X), \ \ldots) \tag{5}$$

Then the maximization (minimization similarly, with a "–" sign) of the optimality criteria in the area DX can be written as [15]

$$\max_{X \in D_X} F(X) = F(X^*) = F^* \tag{6}$$

Then the MCO task of the conditions for conducting a catalytic reaction is to determine the values of the variable parameters (4), in order to achieve the extrema of the optimality criteria (5) according to (6).

5 Multi-criteria Interval Optimization Problem for the Catalytic Reaction of Benzylbutyl Ether Synthesis

In the reaction of the synthesis of benzyl butyl ether in the presence of a metal complex catalyst, products are formed $PhCH_2OBu$ (Y_6), $PhCH_2OCH_2Ph$ (Y_9), $BuOBu$ (Y_{12}). Then the task of the MCO of the reaction conditions for the synthesis of benzylbutyl ether has the form:

- Variable parameter vector $X = (x_1, x_2)$, where x_1 – reaction temperature, T; x_2 – temperature change radius.
- Vector function of optimality criteria $F(X) = (f_1(X), f_2(X))$: $f_1(X) = y_{PhCH_2OBu(Y_6)}(t^*, T, N) \to$ max; $f_2(X) = y_{PhCH_2OCH_2Ph(Y_9)}(t^*, T, N) \to$ min.

To solve multicriteria interval optimization, it is necessary to calculate the values of optimality criteria that depend on interval parameters. An interval can be uniquely defined by its midpoint and width.

Then for $F(X)$, $l = 1, 2$:

$$mid\, f_l = \frac{\underline{f_l} + \overline{f_l}}{2} - \text{interval midpoint,} \tag{7}$$

$$wid\, f_l = \overline{f_l} - \underline{f_l} - \text{interval width.} \tag{8}$$

The task of the MCO is to maximize the optimality criteria in the area D_X by (6).

6 Parallel Scheme for Implementing the Computational Process

Work on the development of efficient evolutionary algorithms for solving the problem of multicriteria optimization has been actively carried out in recent decades [16]. The advantages are obtained by methods that take into account the principles of Paretto-dominance based on genetic algorithms. Increasing the performance of computing resources allows for high-performance computing in a reasonable time.

The basis of parallelization of multiobjective optimization algorithms is the decomposition and structuring of the population (a set of possible solutions). That is, the division of the original population into several subsets (subpopulations). Decomposition can be implemented in various ways. Partitioning methods define parallelization models. The most popular parallelization models are: the island parallelization model [17], the global client/server model [18], and the cellular model [19]. The most common model of parallelization of the computational process is the island model of parallelization (Fig. 2).

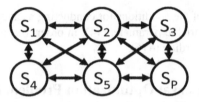

Fig. 2. Island parallelization model for solving the multi-criteria optimization problem

$$S = \bigcup_{i=1}^{|P|} S_i, \tag{9}$$

where S – multipopulation, S_i – subpopulations (islands), $|P|$ - number of processors.

From a multipopulation of values of variable parameters (desired conditions for carrying out a catalytic reaction), subpopulations are created according to the number of available processors. According to Fig. 2 individuals settle on several isolated islands. These subpopulations will develop independently, with subsequent synchronization of results.

This scientific study proposes a modification of the island parallelization model according to the distribution of intervals of variation of kinetic parameters.

If P – the number of available processors, then the intervals of parameter variation can be divided into processors and calculated in parallel (similarly (9)):

$$\left[x_i^{min}, x_i^{max}\right] = \left[x_i^{min,0}, x_i^{max,1}\right) \cup \left[x_i^{min,1}, x_i^{max,2}\right) \cup \cdots \cup \left[x_i^{min,P-1}, x_i^{max,P}\right), \; i = 1, 2, \ldots I, \tag{10}$$

Figure 3 shows the parallelization scheme of the computational process for solving the problem of interval multicriteria optimization in chemical kinetics. The input data are: kinetic model of the process in the form of a system of differential Eqs. (1), values of kinetic parameters - pre-exponential factors and activation energy of stages, a list of variable parameters and optimality criteria. An interval is set for the vector of variable parameters $[X^{min}, X^{max}]$. And the corresponding subintervals are distributed among the available processors by (10). For the value (selected using the NSGA-II Pareto approximation algorithm [20]), lower and upper values of component concentrations are calculated from this subinterval using two systems of differential equations for the lower bound *dib_low* and for the upper bound *dib_up*. The values of the optimality criteria (7), (8) are calculated from the concentrations of the components. After checking the nondominability condition of the solution, the optimal value of the vector is determined $X^{opt,p}$ and $F^{opt,p}$ on each subinterval. At the last stage, the total values are calculated X^{opt} and F^{opt} over the entire range of variation.

7 Research Results

For the catalytic reaction of the synthesis of benzylbutyl ether, the effect of the temperature change intervals of the process on the values of the optimality criteria will be

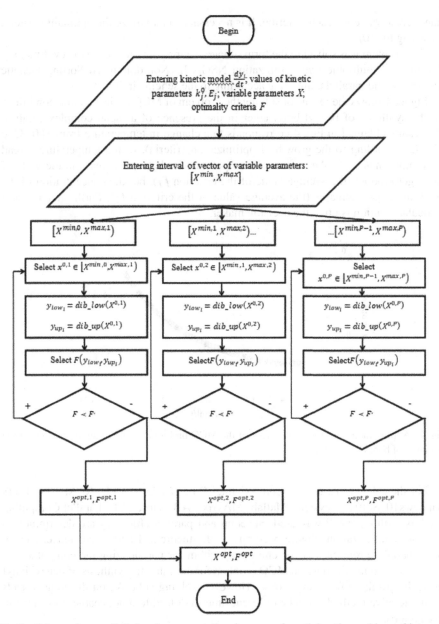

Fig. 3. Scheme for parallelizing the computational process for solving the problem of interval multicriteria optimization in chemical kinetics

calculated. The variable parameters are $x_1 \in [160, 175]$; $x_2 \in [1, 5]$. Optimization criteria $F(X) = (f_1(X), f_2(X))$. The values of the optimality criteria are subject to restrictions on changing the width of the interval depending on the temperature spread no more than a given value for each criterion. It is necessary to maximize the optimality criteria according to (10).

The problem was solved in the form of Pareto approximation using the evolutionary algorithm of multiobjective optimization NSGA-II (Non-dominated Sorting Genetic Algorithm) and parallel computing according to the scheme in Fig. 3.

Figure 4 shows the results of solving the problem of MCO of the reaction conditions for the synthesis of benzyl butyl ether in the presence of a metal complex catalyst. The results obtained in Fig. 4 corresponds to a change in temperature from 160 °C to 175 °C (according to the growth of optimization criteria), with a temperature spread of no more than 5 °C. An increase in temperature leads to an increase in the yield of the target product (the average value of the criterion f_1), but the concentration of the by-product also increases (the average value of the criterion f_2). Further choice of a particular solution is up to the decision maker.

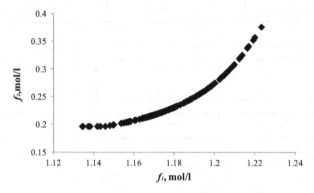

Fig. 4. Approximation of the Pareto front of the MCO problem for the catalytic reaction of the synthesis of benzyl butyl ether

For the calculation, use a 4-core PC Intel Core i7-8550U CPU, RAM 16 GB, OS Windows10, Software system: Matlab (MATrix LABoratore). The Parallel Computing Toolbox with OpenMP was used. Speedup and parallel efficiency are determined to evaluate parallelization. Figure 5 compares the theoretical and calculated efficiency of the parallel program. For the chosen algorithm for parallelizing the computational process for solving the interval MCO problem for the catalytic synthesis of benzyl butyl ether, the parallel efficiency is 68%. However, solving subtasks on different threads by the iterative method can take different times and lead to a noticeable imbalance in calculations.

Perhaps the use of a larger number of cores will make it possible to conduct a computational experiment more efficiently. What will be implemented in further research.

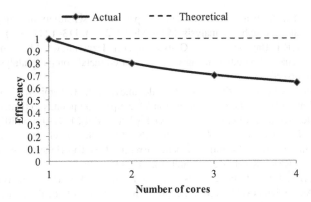

Fig. 5. Efficiency of the parallel program for solving the interval MCO-task of catalytic synthesis of benzylbutyl ether

8 Conclusion

Interval multi-criteria optimization of the conditions based on the kinetic model is relevant for both laboratory and industrial processes. In the work for the laboratory catalytic reaction of the synthesis of benzylbutyl ether, the problem of interval MCO of the conditions of conducting based on a kinetic model is solved. The solution of the MCO interval problem was obtained by varying the temperature from 160 °C to 175 °C, with a temperature spread of no more than 5 °C. An increase in temperature leads to an increase in the yield of the target product, but the concentration of the by-product also increases. A parallel scheme has been developed for solving the interval problem of the MCO and an assessment of the efficiency of the execution of the parallel program has been carried out. The efficiency of the developed parallelization algorithm was 68%. The developed parallel algorithm for solving the interval problem of the MCO will be used to analyze other catalytic industrial and laboratory processes.

Acknowledgement. This research was performed due to the Russian Science Foundation grant (project No. 21-71-20047).

References

1. Bobreneva, Yu.O., Ragimli, P.I., Poveshchenko, Yu.A., Podryga, V.O., Enikeeva, L.V.: On one method of numerical modeling of piezoconductive processes of a two-phase fluid system in a fractured-porous reservoir. J. Phys.: Conf. Ser. 022001 (2021). In: Intelligent Information Technology and Mathematical Modeling 2021 (IITMM 2021), Gelendzhik
2. Koledina, K., Gubaydullin, I., Koledin, S.: Parameter analysis of stability of the Pareto front for optimal conditions of catalytic processes. Lobachevskii J. Math. **42**(12), 2834–2840 (2021). https://doi.org/10.1134/S1995080221120192
3. Bukhtoyarov, S.E., Emelichev, V.A.: Parametrization of the optimality principle (from Pareto to Slater) and stability of multicriteria trajectory problems. J. Appl. Ind. Math **10**(2), 3–18 (2003)

4. Mikhailov, V.B., Rumyantsev, V.V.: Theory of parametric sensitivity of natural frequencies and its application to stability analysis. Math. Model. **24**(9), 113–124 (2012)
5. Khusnutdinov, R.I., Bayguzina, A.R., Gallyamova, L.I., Dzhemilev, U.M.: A novel method for synthesis of benzyl alkyl ethers using vanadium-based metal complex catalysts. Pet. Chem. **52**(4), 261–266 (2012)
6. Khusnutdinov, R.I., Bayguzina, A.R., Gimaletdinova, L.I., Dzhemilev, U.M.: Intermolecular dehydration of alcohols by the action of copper compounds activated with carbon tetrabromide. Synthesis of ethers. Russ. J. Org. Chem. **48**(9), 1191–1196 (2012)
7. Koledina, K.F., Gubaydullin, I.M., Koledin, S.N., Zagidullin, Sh.G.: Multicriteria optimization of gasoline catalytic reforming temperature regime based on a kinetic model with grouped hydrocarbons. React. Kinet. Mech. Catal. **135**, 135–153 (2022)
8. Dobronets, B.S.: Interval Mathematics. Tutorial. Krasnoyarsk State University (2004). 216 p.
9. Morozov, A., Reviznikov, D.L.: Modification of methods for solving the Cauchy problem for systems of ordinary differential equations with interval parameters. Trudy MAI **89**, 15 (2016)
10. Tsai, C.-Y., Sung, R., Zhuang, B.-R., Sung, K.: TICl$_4$-activated selective nucleophilic substitutions of tert-butyl alcohol and benzyl alcohols with π-donating substituents. Tetrahedron **66**(34), 6869 (2010)
11. Koledina, K.F., Gubaidullin, I.M., Koledin, S.N., Baiguzina, A.R., Gallyamova, L.I., Khusnutdinov, R.I.: Kinetics and mechanism of the synthesis of Benzylbutyl ether in the presence of copper-containing catalyst. Russ. J. Phys. Chem. A **93**(11), 2146–2151 (2019)
12. Gear, C.V. Numerical Initial Value Problems in Ordinary Differential Equations. Prentice-Hall, Englewood Cliffs (1971). 252 p.
13. Lotov, A.V., Ryabikov, A.I.: Launch pad method in multi-extremal problems of multi-criteria optimization. J. Comput. Math. Math. Phys. **59**(12), 2111–2128 (2019)
14. Koledina, K.F., Koledin, S.N., Karpenko, A.P., Gubaydullin, I.M., Vovdenko, M.K.: Multi-objective optimization of chemical reaction conditions based on a kinetic model. J. Math. Chem. **57**(2), 484–493 (2019)
15. Koledina, K.F., Koledin, S.N., Nurislamova, L.F., Gubaydullin, I.M.: Internal parallelism of multi-objective optimization and optimal control based on a compact kinetic model for the catalytic reaction of dimethyl carbonate with alcohols. In: Sokolinsky, L., Zymbler, M. (eds.) PCT 2019. CCIS, vol. 1063, pp. 242–255. Springer, Cham (2019). https://doi.org/10.1007/978-3-030-28163-2_17
16. Awrejcewicz, J., Lind, Yu.B., Gubaidullin, I.M., Koledina, K.F.: Modern technologies of high-performance computing for modeling of detailed olefins hydroalumination reaction mechanism. Dynamical systems. In: Nonlinear Dynamics and Control, Lodz, Poland (2011). 6 p.
17. Baynazarova, N.M., Koledina, K.F., Pichugina, D.A.: Parallelization of calculation the kinetic model of selective hydrogenation of acetylene on a gold clusters. In: CEUR Workshop Proceedings, vol. 1576, pp. 425–431 (2016)
18. Karpenko, A.P. Modern search engine optimization algorithms. Algorithms Inspired by Nature. Publishing House of MSTU im. N.E. Bauman, Moscow (2014). 446 p.
19. Skolicki, Z.: Linkage in island models. In: Chen, Y.P., Lim, M.H. (eds.) Linkage in Evolutionary Computation. SCI, vol. 157, pp. 41–60. Springer, Heidelberg (2008). https://doi.org/10.1007/978-3-540-85068-7_3
20. Deb, K., Mohan, M., Mishra, S.: Towards a quick computation of well-spread Pareto-optimal solutions. In: Fonseca, C.M., Fleming, P.J., Zitzler, E., Thiele, L., Deb, K. (eds.) EMO 2003. LNCS, vol. 2632, pp. 22–236. Springer, Heidelberg (2003). https://doi.org/10.1007/3-540-36970-8_16

Parallel Efficiency for Poroelasticity

Denis Anuprienko[(✉)]

Nuclear Safety Institute RAS, Moscow 115191, Russian Federation
`anuprienko@ibrae.ac.ru`

Abstract. Poroelasticity is an example of coupled processes which are crucial for many applications including safety assessment of radioactive waste repositories. Numerical solution of poroelasticity problems discretized with finite volume – virtual element scheme leads to systems of algebraic equations, which may be solved simultaneously or iteratively. In this work, parallel scalability of the monolithic strategy and of the fixed-strain splitting strategy is examined, which depends mostly on linear solver performance. It was expected that splitting strategy would show better scalability due to better performance of a black-box linear solver on systems with simpler structure. However, this is not always the case.

Keywords: Poroelasticity · Multiphysics · Splitting · Linear solvers · Parallel efficiency

1 Poroelasticity Problem

Modeling of coupled physical processes is important in many engineering applications, such as safety assessment of radioactive waste repositories. It is acknowledged that complex thermo-hydro-mechanical-chemical (THMC) processes should be taken into account in such modeling [1]. Software package GeRa (Geomigration of Radionuclides) [2,3] which is developed by INM RAS and Nuclear Safety Institute RAS already has some coupled modeling capabilities [4,5] and is now moving toward hydromechanical processes. Poroelasticity is the simplest example of such processes.

Numerical solution of coupled problems is a computationally expensive task. Arising discrete systems require efficient solution strategies, and parallel computations are a necessity. In this work, two solution strategies are tested in their scalability when a black-box linear solver is used.

1.1 Mathematical Formulation

This work is restricted to the simplest case of elastic media filled with water only. Following theory introduced by Biot [6], the following equations are considered:

$$s_{stor}\frac{\partial h}{\partial t} + \nabla \cdot \mathbf{q} + \alpha\nabla \cdot \frac{\partial \mathbf{u}}{\partial t} = Q, \tag{1}$$

V. Voevodin et al. (Eds.): RuSCDays 2022, LNCS 13708, pp. 225–236, 2022.
https://doi.org/10.1007/978-3-031-22941-1_16

$$\nabla \cdot (\sigma - \alpha P\mathbf{I}) = \mathbf{f}. \tag{2}$$

Equation (1) represents water mass conservation taking into account porous medium deformation. Equation (2) represents mechanical equilibrium in porous medium in presence of water pressure and external forces. Here h is water head, s_{stor} is the specific storage coefficient, Q is specific sink and source term, σ is the stress tensor, $\mathbf{f}$ is the external force vector, water pressure P is related to water head h as $P = \rho g (h - z)$; α is the Biot coefficient, which is equal to 1 in this work.

The following constitutive relationships complete the equations: Darcy law

$$\mathbf{q} = -\mathbf{K}\nabla h \tag{3}$$

and generalized Hooke's law:

$$\sigma = \mathbf{C}\varepsilon = \mathbf{C}\frac{\nabla \mathbf{u} + (\nabla \mathbf{u})^T}{2}. \tag{4}$$

Here $\mathbf{q}$ is the water flux, $\mathbf{K}$ is the hydraulic conductivity tensor, a $3{\times}3$ s.p.d. matrix, $\mathbf{C}$ is the stiffness tensor, ε is the strain tensor and $\mathbf{u}$ is the displacement vector.

Water head h and solid displacement $\mathbf{u}$ are the primary variables.

The system is closed with initial and boundary conditions. The following boundary conditions are available:

- specified head h or normal flux $\mathbf{q} \cdot \mathbf{n}$ for flow;
- specified displacement $\mathbf{u}$, traction $\sigma \cdot \mathbf{n}$ or roller boundary condition with zero normal displacement for mechanics.

1.2   Discretization

Subsurface flow modeling is a well-established technology in GeRa and uses the finite volume method (FVM). Choice of the discretization method for elasticity was guided by following criteria: (a) applicability on general grids, (b) ability to work with arbitrary tensor $\mathbf{C}$, (c) sufficient history of application in multiphysics. Criterion (a) makes use of traditional finite element method (FEM) problematic, since meshes for subsurface domains can contain cells which are general polyhedra. While FVM for geomechanics exists [7,8] and is applied in poroelastic case [10] and more complex ones [9], it is still somewhat new and not so widely used option. Recent developments include FVM scheme achieving improved robustness by avoiding decoupling into subproblems and introducing stable approximation of vector fluxes [11].

For discretization of elasticity equations in GeRa the virtual element method (VEM) [12] was ultimately chosen. VEM, applied to elasticity equation [13], can handle cells which are non-convex and degenerate, its simplest version uses only nodal unknowns and is similar to FEM with piece-wise linear functions. An important feature of VEM is existence of FVM-VEM scheme for poroelasticity with proved properties [14]. A drawback of this scheme is the use of simplest FVM option, the linear two-point flux approximation (TPFA) which is inconsistent in general case. In this work, TPFA is replaced with a multi-point flux approximation, MPFA-O scheme [15]. This scheme gives reasonable solutions on a wider class of grids, capturing media anisotropy, but is not monotone which is important for more complex physical processes.

Discretization in time uses first-order backward Euler scheme, which results in a system of linear equations at each time step.

2   Solution Strategies for Discrete Systems

The system of discrete equations has the form

$$\begin{bmatrix} A_F & A_{FM} \\ A_{MF} & A_M \end{bmatrix} \cdot \begin{bmatrix} h \\ \mathbf{u} \end{bmatrix} = \begin{bmatrix} b_F \\ b_M \end{bmatrix}, \tag{5}$$

where subscripts F and M denote parts related to flow and mechanics subproblems, respectively. Here h and $\mathbf{u}$ denote vectors of discrete unknowns on a given time step. The system matrix has block form with square block A_F representing FVM discretization of equation (1), square block A_M representing VEM discretization of equation (2) and off-diagonal blocks A_{FM} and A_{MF} representing coupling terms discretized with VEM (example of matrix A is depicted at Fig. 1). Right-hand side terms b_F and b_M contain contributions from boundary conditions, source and force terms and previous time step values.

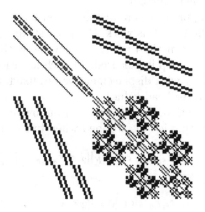

Fig. 1. Matrix pattern for a $4 \times 4 \times 4$ cubic grid

In multiphysics applications, different approaches to solution of coupled problems exist.

2.1 Monolithic Strategy

An intuitive approach is the monolithic strategy, in which system (5) is solved as is and water head and displacement values are obtained simultaneously. This approach results in one linear system solution per time step and is unconditionally stable [16]. However, both flow and mechanics modules should be implemented in a single simulator. Moreover, complex structure of the system matrix requires robust linear solvers with some efforts being centered around specialized physics-based preconditioners [17] and other sophisticated approaches. In case of more relevant physics like unsaturated or multiphase flow, the discrete system becomes nonlinear, and monolithic approach may lead to convergence problems of nonlinear solver, e.g. Newton method.

2.2 Fixed-Strain Splitting Strategy

This solution method belongs to the class of iterative splitting schemes. Such strategies split flow and mechanics subproblems and solve each separately, iterating between then two until convergence. Notice that this splitting is not mere decomposition of matrix A into blocks to solve the linear systems. The splitting involves two different solution procedures for both subproblems. With splitting strategy it possible to use tailored solvers and even separate dedicated simulators for each subproblem. One can also expect satisfactory performance from black-box linear solvers since subproblem matrices A_F and A_M have simpler structure compared to the full matrix A. In case of nonlinear flow equations, nonlinearity stays in the flow subsystem, while mechanics part remains linear and still needs to compute preconditioner only once.

Different splitting approaches are distinguished by constraints and by which subproblem is solved first. In this work, the fixed-strain approach is examined. It is the simplest splitting method where the flow subproblem is solved first. At each time step a splitting loop is executed. At each iteration of the loop the flow subproblem is solved first with displacement values fixed, then the mechanics is solved with obtained water head values.

At each splitting iteration, residuals r_F, r_M of flow and mechanics equations are evaluated. The splitting loop is stopped when two conditions are satisfied:

$$||r_F||_2 < \varepsilon_{spl,abs} \text{ or } ||r_F||_2 < \varepsilon_{spl,rel} \cdot ||r_F^0||_2$$

and

$$||r_M||_2 < \varepsilon_{spl,abs} \text{ or } ||r_M||_2 < \varepsilon_{spl,rel} \cdot ||r_M^0||_2,$$

where r_*^0 is the residual at first splitting iteration.

Fixed-strain splitting is only conditionally stable [16] and is presented here only as an example of a splitting solution strategy.

3   Numerical Experiments

3.1   Implementation Details

GeRa is based on INMOST [18,19], a platform for parallel computing. INMOST provides tools for mesh handling, assembly of systems via automatic differentiation as well as variety of linear solvers. Multiphysics tools of INMOST are able to switch submodels on and off in the global coupled model, which allows for easy implementation of different splitting strategies with minimal code modification.

The idea of this work is to use a black-box solver with minimal parameter tuning and compare performance of full and splitting strategies in this case. INMOST internal solver `Inner_MPTILUC` is used. It is a robust solver which has been successfully used in GeRa, including parallel computations in nonlinear problems with highly heterogeneous and anisotropic domains [20]. The solver is based on Bi-CGSTAB with preconditioner performing second order Crout-ILU with inverse-based condition estimation and maximum product transversal reordering [19]. Convergence of the solver is governed by relative and absolute tolerances which are set to 10^{-9} and 10^{-12}, respectively. Other parameters are set to default values except drop tolerance.

3.2   Problem A: Faulted Reservoir

Problem A is a model problem similar to one presented in [21]. It describes coupled water flow and elastic deformation in a faulted reservoir. The domain is cube 900 m × 900 m × 900 m composed of three layers. One 100 m thick layer located in the center is storage aquifer, other two layers are low-permeable sedimentary fill. An almost vertical fault crosses all three layers (see Fig. 2). The fault is modeled as another porous medium with increased hydraulic conductivity. All three media are isotropic, their hydraulic conductivity is characterized by a single value K, while stiffness tensor is completely defined by Young's modulus E and Poisson ratio ν. Media parameters are listed in Table 1.

At the top boundary, a constant water head value $h = 305.81$ m is set. At the left side of storage aquifer, a constant water head value $h = 10193.7$ is set. All other boundaries have zero normal flux conditions. The top boundary is free (zero traction BC), all other boundaries are sliding planes with fixed zero normal displacement. Initial water head is set constant at $h = 305.81$ m.

Simulation time covers $4 \cdot 10^9$ s ($\approx$127 years) with 4 time steps for both monolithic and fixed-strain strategies. For the linear solver, drop tolerance of 0.1 was set.

A series of tests was conducted on triangular prismatic mesh of 672300 cells and 356356 nodes, which makes total number of unknowns 1741368. Computations were carried out on INM RAS cluster [22] on up to 100 computational cores.

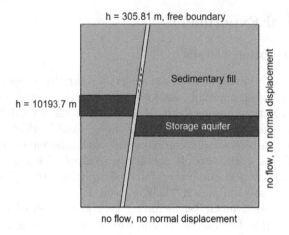

Fig. 2. Problem A setup. XZ cross-section

Table 1. Media parameters for the problem A

Media	K, m/s	s_{stor}, 1/m	E, MPa	ν
Storage aquifer	$1.5 \cdot 10^{-10}$	$8.20116 \cdot 10^{-7}$	14400	0.2
Sedimentary fill	$2 \cdot 10^{-13}$	$8.46603 \cdot 10^{-7}$	29400	0.12
Fault	$1.5 \cdot 10^{-9}$	$1.92276 \cdot 10^{-6}$	14400	0.2

Computed water head and displacement and stress tensor magnitudes are depicted in Fig. 3. Water head builds up in high-permeable aquifer and fault, resulting in stress changes which uplift surface of the domain.

Measured computation times for monolithic and fixed-strain splitting methods are presented in Tables 2 and 3. Total speed-up is presented at Fig. 4, while speed-ups for different computational stages for both strategies are presented in Fig. 5. Profiling results are presented in Fig. 6. Results show that fixed-strain strategy takes more time than monolithic one due to relatively large numbers (13 to 14) of splitting iterations at time steps. The fixed-strain strategy, however, scales better due to better scaling of iterations time, which is the most time-consuming part. Sublinear scaling of assembly procedure is explained by non-ideal partitioning by INMOST internal partitioner Inner_RCM, which is based on reverse Cuthill–McKee algorithm.

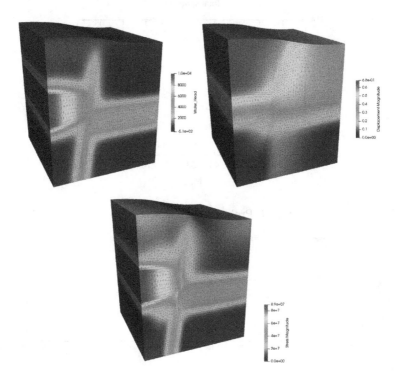

Fig. 3. Problem A: water head, displacement and stress tensor in the domain, mesh distorted by displacement magnified 300 times

Table 2. Problem A: results of cluster computations, monolithic strategy

N_{proc}	T_{total}, s	T_{assmbl}, s	$T_{precond}$, s	T_{iter}, s	#lin.it
8	2103	184	130	1761	1673
16	1592	148	101	1318	1637
40	457	40.3	16	379	2298
80	295	23.2	8.7	250	2522
100	235	17.9	5.8	206	2639

Table 3. Problem A: results of cluster computations, fixed-strain splitting strategy

N_{proc}	T_{total}, s	T_{assmbl}, s	$T_{precond}$, s	T_{iter}, s	#lin.it
8	7684	2479	219.5	4961	15162
16	4390	1483	71.5	2817	18121
40	1733	601.2	21.1	1091	19575
80	896	305.6	8.6	558.8	21099
100	749	251.7	6.4	480.8	21395

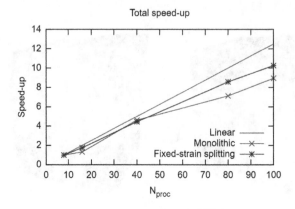

Fig. 4. Problem A: total speed-up

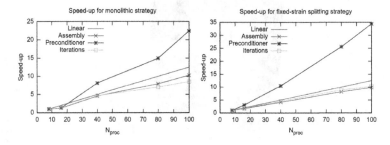

Fig. 5. Problem A: detailed speed-up

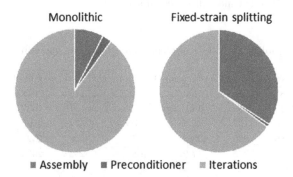

Fig. 6. Problem A: time distributions for different computational stages

3.3   Problem B: Real-Life Domain with Synthetic Elastic Parameters

In this problem, a part of a real site is considered. The part is a quadrilateral cut in XY-plane from a domain with 9 geological layers and 11 different media. The media are anisotropic with their hydraulic conductivity being a diagonal tensor

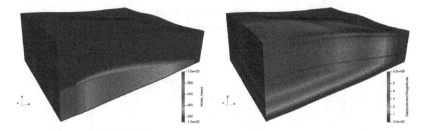

Fig. 7. Problem B: water head and displacement in the domain, mesh distorted by displacement magnified 30 times

Table 4. Problem B: results of cluster computations, monolithic strategy

N_{proc}	T_{total}, s	T_{assmbl}, s	$T_{precond}$, s	T_{iter}, s	#lin.it
40	1490	52.0	688	731.5	470
120	490.5	19.5	58.0	406.7	680
200	247.5	11.5	51.1	180.5	742
280	157.8	9.4	16.2	129.5	779
360	141.0	7.0	24.6	107.1	902
440	100.6	6.1	10.1	82.4	821
520	84.7	5.2	6.3	71.6	840
600	81.9	4.7	5.7	69.9	993

Table 5. Problem B: results of cluster computations, fixed-strain splitting strategy

N_{proc}	T_{total}, s	T_{assmbl}, s	$T_{precond}$, s	T_{iter}, s	#lin.it
40	1101	81.3	475.3	537.4	728
120	340.3	31.0	28.9	278.1	1079
200	177.4	16.8	32.0	125.0	1101
280	114.9	14.8	8.6	90.5	1175
360	100.7	10.5	15.2	73.2	1290
440	85.8	8.9	5.5	69.5	1408
520	69.5	7.7	3.5	57.1	1399
600	64.0	7.1	3.3	52.4	1503

with values ranging from $1.2 \cdot 10^{-12}$ to $2 \cdot 10^{-5}$ m/s. Specific storage coefficient varies from 10^{-6} to 10^{-5} m^{-1}. Elastic parameters are not known and are set constant for all media: $E = 10000$ MPa, $\nu = 0.2$. One corner of the model has prescribed water head value $h = 1000$ m at 8th layer, which imitates injection in that layer. On the opposite side of the domain, constant water head value of $h = 100$ m is set. Other boundaries are impermeable. Bottom boundary is fixed ($\mathbf{u} = 0$), top boundary is free ($\sigma \cdot \mathbf{n} = 0$), side boundaries have roller boundary conditions (zero normal displacement $\mathbf{u} \cdot \mathbf{n} = 0$). Simulation starts with constant initial water head value $h = 100$ m and covers $2 \cdot 10^8$ s ($\approx$6.3 years).

Triangular prismatic mesh of 2205400 cells and 1142714 (total number of unknowns is 5461942) was constructed in the domain. Computations were per-

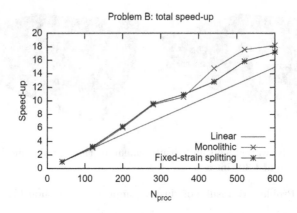

Fig. 8. Problem B: total speed-up

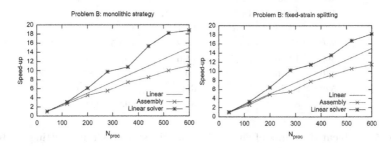

Fig. 9. Problem B: speed-up for assembly and linear solver

formed on INM cluster using 40–600 cores. In order to obtain better balanced partitioning of the mesh, the ParMETIS [23] partitioner was used, interface to which is provided by INMOST. Calculated water head and displacement distributions are depicted in Fig. 7. Time measurements and linear iterations count are presented in Tables 4 and 5. Total speed-up is presented in Fig. 8 and shows superlinear scaling with monolithic strategy reaching slightly larger speed-up. In order to better understand this scaling behavior of the two strategies, speed-up for both assembly and linear solver are presented in Fig. 9 and profiling results are presented in Fig. 10. It can be seen that superlinear scaling is caused by linear solver, namely, scaling of the preconditioner. At the same time, assembly scales sublinearly, which is explained again by non-ideal partitioning of the mesh. Since profiling shows that assembly takes large percentage of time in the fixed-strain splitting, this strategy reaches lower overall speed-up.

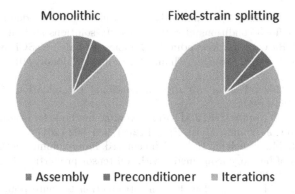

Fig. 10. Problem B: time distributions for different computational stages

4   Conclusion

Two solution strategies for finite volume – virtual element discretizations of coupled poroelastic problems were tested in their parallel performance. Implemented using INMOST numerical platform, the model used a robust general-purpose linear solver. Calculations for two problems on meshes with millions of unknowns and up to 600 computational cores gave mixed results. Fixed-strain splitting strategy was expected to scale better due to performance of the linear solver, as separate systems for flow and mechanics have simpler structure. This, however, was not always observed. This is explained by the following reasons. First, performance of the linear solver is mostly determined by preconditioner, which exhibits superlinear scalability depending on the problem. Second, non-ideal performance of mesh partitioner results in sublinear scalability of systems assembly process, which affects splitting strategy more as assembly takes larger fraction of time in this case. Overall, there was no clear answer as to which strategy scales better. Partly this may imply that the linear solver used can successfully handle fully coupled multiphysical systems. However, with additional partitioner tuning to better balance mesh between processes, scalability of assembly may approach linear rate, resulting in better overall scalability of splitting strategy.

References

1. Birkholzer, J.T., Tsang, C.F., Bond, A.E., Hudson, J.A., Jing, L., Stephansson, O.: 25 years of DECOVALEX-scientific advances and lessons learned from an international research collaboration in coupled subsurface processes. Int. J. Rock Mech. Min. Sci. **122**, 103995 (2019)
2. Kapyrin, I.V., Ivanov, V.A., Kopytov, G.V., Utkin, S.S.: Integral code GeRa for radioactive waste disposal safety validation. Gornyi Zh (10), 44–50 (2015)
3. GeRa website. gera.ibrae.ac.ru
4. Grigor'ev, F.V., Kapyrin, I.V., Vassilevskii, Y.V.: Modeling of thermal convection in porous media with volumetric heat source using the GeRa code. Chebyshevskii Sbornik **18**(3), 235–254 (2017)

5. Kapyrin, I., Konshin, I., Kramarenko, V., Grigoriev, F.: Modeling groundwater flow in unconfined conditions of variable density solutions in dual-porosity media using the GeRa code. In: Voevodin, V., Sobolev, S. (eds.) RuSCDays 2018. CCIS, vol. 965, pp. 266–278. Springer, Cham (2019). https://doi.org/10.1007/978-3-030-05807-4_23

6. Biot, M.A.: General theory of three-dimensional consolidation. J. Appl. Phys. **12**(2), 155–164 (1941)

7. Keilegavlen, E., Nordbotten, J.M.: Finite volume methods for elasticity with weak symmetry. Int. J. Numer. Meth. Eng. **112**(8), 939–962 (2017)

8. Terekhov, K.M., Tchelepi, H.A.: Cell-centered finite-volume method for elastic deformation of heterogeneous media with full-tensor properties. J. Comput. Appl. Math. **364**, 112331 (2020)

9. Nordbotten, J.M., Keilegavlen, E.: An introduction to multi-point flux (MPFA) and stress (MPSA) finite volume methods for thermo-poroelasticity. In: Di Pietro, D.A., Formaggia, L., Masson, R. (eds.) Polyhedral Methods in Geosciences. SSSS, vol. 27, pp. 119–158. Springer, Cham (2021). https://doi.org/10.1007/978-3-030-69363-3_4

10. Terekhov, K.M.: Cell-centered finite-volume method for heterogeneous anisotropic poromechanics problem. J. Comput. Appl. Math. **365**, 112357 (2020)

11. Terekhov, K.M., Vassilevski, Y.V.: Finite volume method for coupled subsurface flow problems, II: Poroelasticity. J. Comput. Phys. **462**, 111225 (2022)

12. Beirão da Veiga, L., Brezzi, F., Marini, L.D., Russo, A.: The hitchhiker's guide to the virtual element method. Math. Models Methods Appl. Sci. **24**(08), 1541–1573 (2014)

13. Gain, A.L., Talischi, C., Paulino, G.H.: On the virtual element method for three-dimensional linear elasticity problems on arbitrary polyhedral meshes. Comput. Methods Appl. Mech. Eng. **282**, 132–160 (2014)

14. Coulet, J., Faille, I., Girault, V., Guy, N., Nataf, F.: A fully coupled scheme using virtual element method and finite volume for poroelasticity. Comput. Geosci. **24**(2), 381–403 (2020)

15. Aavatsmark, I., Barkve, T., Bøe, O., Mannseth, T.: Discretization on unstructured grids for inhomogeneous, anisotropic media. Part I: derivation of the methods. SIAM J. Sci. Comput. **19**(5), 1700–1716 (1998)

16. Kim, J., Tchelepi, H.A., Juanes, R.: Stability and convergence of sequential methods for coupled flow and geomechanics: fixed-stress and fixed-strain splits. Comput. Methods Appl. Mech. Eng. **200**, 1591–1606 (2011)

17. Frigo, M., Castelletto, N., Ferronato, M.: Enhanced relaxed physical factorization preconditioner for coupled poromechanics. Comput. Math. Appl. **106**, 27–39 (2022)

18. INMOST website. inmost.org

19. Vassilevski, Y., Terekhov, K., Nikitin, K., Kapyrin, I.: Parallel Finite Volume Computation on General Meshes. Springer, New York (2020). https://doi.org/10.1007/978-3-030-47232-0

20. Anuprienko, D., Kapyrin, I.: Nonlinearity continuation method for steady-state groundwater flow modeling in variably saturated conditions. J. Comput. Appl. Math. **393**, 113502 (2021)

21. Kolditz, O., Shao, H., Wang, W., Bauer, S.: Thermo-Hydro-Mechanical Chemical Processes in Fractured Porous Media: Modelling and Benchmarking, vol. 25. Springer, Berlin (2016)

22. INM RAS cluster. cluster2.inm.ras.ru

23. Karypis, G., Schloegel, K., Kumar, V.: Parmetis: Parallel graph partitioning and sparse matrix ordering library (1997)

Parallel Implementation of Fast 3D Travel Time Tomography for Depth-Velocity Model Building in Seismic Exploration Problems

Dmitry Neklyudov$^{(\boxtimes)}$, Kirill Gadylshin, and Maxim Protasov

Institute of Petroleum Geology and Geophysics, Novosibirsk 630090, Russia
{neklyudovda,gadylshinkg,protasovmi}@ipgg.sbras.ru

Abstract. We present a parallel algorithm for 3D seismic tomography that reconstructs the depth velocity model. The aim is to provide the parallelization of the developed method for processing 3D seismic data in the production mode. Time migration results are the input data for tomography. The tomography algorithm contains three blocks: data preparation for tomography from results of time processing, tomography matrix construction via ray tracing and tomography matrix inversion. Each block uses MPI technology. The paper provides numerical experiments performed using real data got from the field in Eastern Siberia.

Keywords: Seismic tomography · Time migration · Macro-velocity model · MPI technology

1 Introduction

Currently, tomographic algorithms for velocity model building use the kinematic characteristics of the recorded wave fields (travel times seismic waves). A detailed review of the existing methods for constructing depth-velocity models in seismic exploration can be found in review monographs [1–3]. We note the principal features of reflection travel time tomography algorithms. Picking the travel times of the reflected waves is a nontrivial task. First, because the amount of seismic data recorded during seismic exploration process is very large and often reaches tens (and hundreds) of terabytes. Second, the identification of reflected waves is a very challenging and time-consuming procedure because the reflected waves are masked by a strong background noise. Together, these factors almost completely exclude the possibility of "manual" picking of the travel times of reflected waves.

It is necessary to involve new methods of seismic data processing to extract as complete and reliable information about the structure as the possible. One of such methods that has attracted the increased attention of specialists in recent years is the Full Waveform Inversion (FWI) [4–6]. Modern implementations of FWI attempt to recover a sufficiently broad spatial spectrum of the model, combining the construction of a macro velocity model and a migration image in one procedure. Examples of wide azimuth data illustrate the possibility of recovering all spatial spectrums of the medium [7]. But, there

V. Voevodin et al. (Eds.): RuSCDays 2022, LNCS 13708, pp. 237–249, 2022.
https://doi.org/10.1007/978-3-031-22941-1_17

is the need for huge computing resources, such that FWI calculations take several months on a supercomputer [8]. Therefore, developing new fast methods of the macro-velocity model recovery is of high importance.

Migration velocity analysis (MVA, [9] provides an effective alternative solution). Now, it is the practical method for recovery depth-velocity models from seismic data. We summarize the main idea of MVA in a simplified way. Starting from the initial model, we use pre-stack depth migration (PSDM). As a result, we get common image gathers (CIGs). Each trace of CIG corresponds to a depth image at a fixed area point at a specific azimuth and offset. If "correct" velocity model is used during PSDM, then the migrated reflections in the CIG will be flat (i.e. it will image reflections at the same depth). If the velocity model is not adequate, the migrated reflections in the CIG will be non-flat, i.e. it will have so called "residual move-out". Curvatures of in each event in a CIG provide the travel time residuals of the target waves. The travel time tomography procedure uses the residuals as input data for inversion and, as a result, provides a velocity model update, minimizing the travel time residuals and reducing the curvature (or "non-flatness") of events in the CIGs. The major weakness of MVA is the necessity to repeat expensive PSDM at each step of the velocity model refinement process. When processing 3D seismic data, this can be very time-consuming.

Previously, we developed a simple and relatively cheap 3D tomography algorithm [10] in order to reduce the number of expensive MVA iterations for depth-velocity model building. To do this, we use the data obtained during seismic time processing. Despite the essential improvement of computational speed, there is a practical need to use the parallel technologies to process large volumes of 3D seismic data in production mode. Therefore, here we propose the parallel scheme and its implementation of the tomographic algorithm. Also, we describe its main general aspects briefly. We test the efficiency of the parallel tomography implementation on a rather big number of data sets and with the help of TraceAnalizer program. Data sets include synthetic and real data from different regions, particularly from Eastern Siberia.

2   Reflection Tomography Using Time Migrated Images

2.1   General Tomography Scheme

Geophysicists use time processing results i.e. time images for interpretation of reflection horizons. Another important time processing results are normal move-out velocities and velocities of time migration [11]. Using time processing results, we developed an efficient travel time tomography algorithm [10]. Here we describe it briefly.

Primarily, we formulate what is the input data for the proposed algorithm: a) initial depth velocity model; b) reflection horizons picked in the PSTM image, T_{IM}^{j} (X_{IM}, Y_{IM}), $j = 1, ..N$ (N is several horizons).

Next, we describe the algorithm for constructing a depth-velocity model in six stages.

1. First, for each point on the picked "time-migrated" surface $T_{IM}^{j}(X_{IM}, Y_{IM})$, ,, we trace an "image" ray (Fig. 1a) within the initial depth model [12]. As a result, we determine the position of the corresponding point (X, Y, Z) in depth.

2. Second, the surface $Z_j(X, Y)$ normal is determined numerically.
3. Third, a relation between the time-migrated horizon $T^j_{IM}(X_{IM}, Y_{IM})$ and corresponding zero-offset travel times $T^j_0(X_{CMP}, Y_{CMP})$ is numerically constructed via normal ray tracing.
4. Then, we built a cone of reflected rays from each reflecting area with a known normal (Fig. 1b). The rays come to the points on the acquisition surface, to the source (X_S, Y_S), and receiver (X_R, Y_R). Therefore, we define reflected ray by the midpoint coordinates (X_{CMP}, Y_{CMP}), absolute offset $h = \sqrt{(X_R - X_S)^2 + (Y_R - Y_S)^2}$, and azimuth α. Thus, we compute travel time $T_{CALC} = T_{CALC}(X_{CMP}, Y_{CMP}, h, \alpha)$ and corresponding elements of tomography matrix along each reflected ray.
5. Next, we determine "observed" reflection travel times in each point on the acquisition surface. We provide "observed" reflection travel time using hyperbolic approximation [13, 14]:

$$T_{OBS}(X_{CMP}, Y_{CMP}, h, \alpha) = \sqrt{T_0^2(X_{CMP}, Y_{CMP}) + \frac{h^2}{V_{NMO}^2(X_{CMP}, Y_{CMP}, T_0, \alpha)}}$$

$$(1)$$

Thus, we get travel times residuals of reflected waves:

$$dT(X_{CMP}, Y_{CMP}, h, \alpha) = T_{OBS}(X_{CMP}, Y_{CMP}, h, \alpha) - T_{CALC}(X_{CMP}, Y_{CMP}, h, \alpha)$$

$$(2)$$

6. Finally, we provide a solution of the inverse kinematic problem in the tomographic formulation, i.e. determination of the model update according to the reflected wave travel time residuals.

   After we solve the linearized problem, we get an update to the initial velocity model. Then we repeat the solution of the linear problem in the updated velocity model. Thus, we get a rather fast iterative model refinement without the usage of the expensive depth migration.

2.2 Inversion Tomographic Kernel

At the described above stages 4 and 5 we construct a tomographic system of linear algebraic equations (SLAE). This system provides a linear relationship between the travel time residuals dT and the model update v:

$$dT = M \, \Delta v. \tag{3}$$

Here M is a tomographic matrix, where its elements represent derivatives of reflection travel times with respect to parameters of the model defined on a 3D regular grid. Thus, we come to a classical "grid" tomography problem [3]. Here instead of the Eqs. (3), we solve a pre-conditioned SLAE:

$$LMSR\Delta v' = LdT, \tag{4}$$

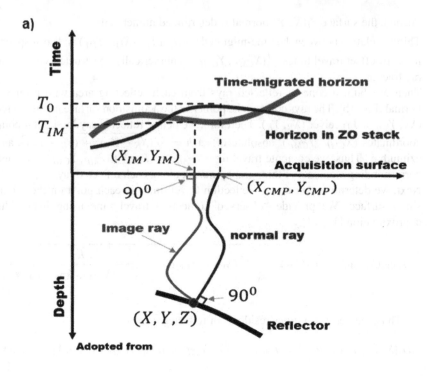

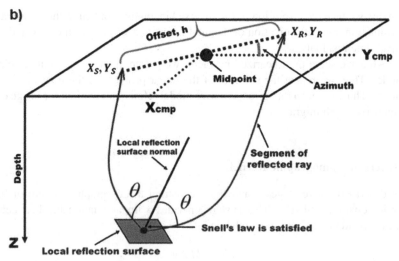

Fig. 1. a) Image ray and normal ray. b) Calculation of up-going reflected ray emitted from a local reflection surface in depth.

where L, R are a diagonal weighting matrix of rows and columns correspondingly, S is a smoother matrix with respect to spatial coordinates. We solve the pre-conditioned SLAE (4) via the iterative reweighted least-squares (IRLS) method [15] with the norm $l_{1.5}$. In this case, the cost functional has the following representation:

$$F = \|LMSR\Delta v' - LdT\|_{1.5}^{1.5} + \lambda^2 \|\Delta v'\|_2^2 = \|A\vec{x} - \vec{b}\|_{1.5}^{1.5} + \lambda^2 \|\vec{x}\|_2^2, \qquad (5)$$

where $A = LMSR$, $\vec{x} = \Delta v'$, $\vec{b} = LdT$.

Following [9], we implement the classical multi-scale approach. It is efficient in MVA applications [9], and we use it in all examples below.

We solve SLAE's (4) via IRLS method based on usage the LSQR algorithm [16]. We utilize IRLS instead of LSQR because it allows getting more stable solutions, which allows handling noisy input data.

3 Parallel Implementation of Tomography

For the described above general tomography scheme, we propose parallel implementation, which comprises three different blocks (Fig. 2). The first one contains time-to-depth conversion using image rays, determination of surfaces in depth, and tracing normal rays from depth to acquisition. It corresponds to the first, second and third step in the described above scheme. We call this block as data preparation for tomographic inversion because

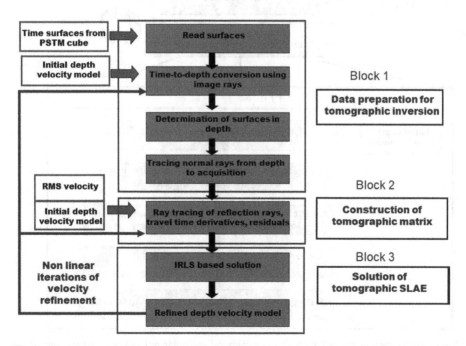

Fig. 2. Block scheme of the tomography algorithm (data in red rectangular, functions – blue background).

it provides mapping that connects necessary data (for tomographic matrix and SLAE construction and inversion) in depth and on the acquisition. Second block calculates reflected rays, the corresponding travel times and travel time derivatives, which construct the elements of tomography matrix. Also here we compute the observed travel times using normal move-out approximation, and we calculate the travel time residuals using data mapping computed at first block. Travel time residuals provide the right-hand side of the tomographic SLAE. Thus, the second block corresponds to the fourth and fifth steps of the described above tomographic scheme. The third block corresponds to the sixths step of the scheme, and it solves the tomographic SLAE using IRLS method. Finally, the last step provides a velocity update, which we use as an initial model to repeat the described scheme providing non-linear tomographic iterations. After such decomposition into blocks, we propose effective parallelization of each of them using MPI technology.

3.1   Parallelization Schemes for Data Preparation and Matrix Construction

In the first and the second blocks, the main computational cost is ray tracing. Therefore, the algorithm has to be oriented toward parallelization of exactly these parts. The parallelization scheme for data preparation starts from reading time surfaces on the master

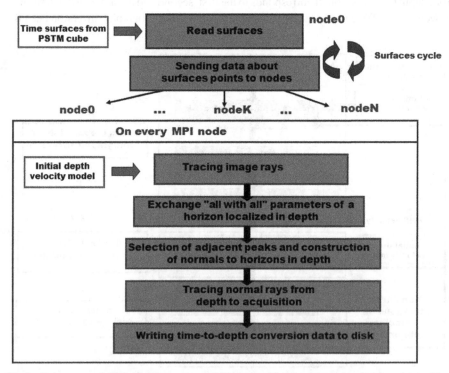

Fig.3. Data preparation block for tomographic inversion (data in red rectangular, functions – blue background) (Color figure online).

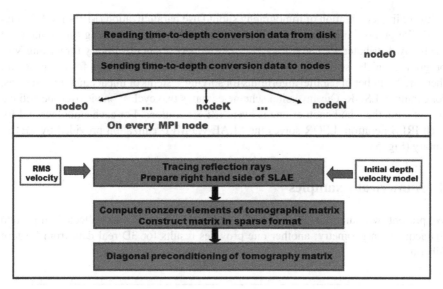

Fig. 4. Block scheme for construction of the tomographic matrix (data in red rectangular, functions – blue background).

node. Then, this node divides surface points and sends the corresponding portion of them to each MPI node. Every MPI node load initial velocity model and has its own copy of the model. Such operations with the model provide the possibility of making ray tracing independently on each node. However, the exchange of information about ray parameters between nodes is necessary between the nodes after tracing of image rays. After that, we do the selection of surface peaks and tracing normal rays also independently on each node. Finally, we get time-to-depth conversion data, and we write them to the disk (Fig. 3).

In the second block, parallelization starts from reading time-to-depth conversion data into master node. Then each peak from the data connects with the number of events that corresponds to the same number of rays. We divide these events and send a portion of them to each MPI node. Again, every node loads its own copy of the depth velocity model and additionally normal move-out velocity in this case (Fig. 4). Each node independently performs ray tracing, and each node provides a set of rows of tomographic matrix. In this construction, each event corresponds to one row of the tomographic matrix. We finish tomographic matrix construction by its diagonal pre-conditioning (Fig. 4). Thus, at the end of the second block, we have SLAE that is ready for inversion.

3.2 Matrix Inversion Parallelization

Let us note the key features of systems of linear equations (SLAE) that arise in seismic tomography problems: very large matrices dimension (more than $10^6 \times 10^8$ elements); matrices have a relatively small number of nonzero elements; ill-condition problems, i.e. solving SLAE, require the use of regularizing procedures. For real applications, such matrices may reach hundreds of gigabytes (even considering their sparseness). The software implementation of tomography should use parallelization (MPI - implementation). We propose implementation of the tomography algorithm using functionality of the freely distributed PETSc library [17]. Developers orient this library for writing MPI programs, which use linear algebra. It provides the major advantage for our problem: there are a number of parallel algorithms for solving systems of linear equations, such as, for example, LSQR. Our inversion scheme contains two cycles: one is over the defined row of smoothers and another one is overs IRLS iterations. For each smoother and for each IRLS iteration, LSQR solves the SLAE via MPI realization provided by PETSc library (Fig. 5).

4   Numerical Examples

We present two numerical examples: the first one is for real data collected on pseudo 3D acquisition geometry; another one provides results for 3D real data from Eastern Siberia.

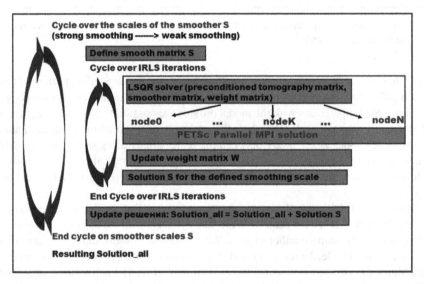

Fig. 5. Block scheme for tomographic matrix inversion (data in red rectangular, functions – blue background).

4.1   Pseudo 3D Real Data

We provide promising numerical results for the real data got on complex pseudo 3D geometry. As one can observe the geometry is very sparse (Fig. 6). Therefore, any kind of the processing is very challenging in this case. However, the proposed approach is stable regarding geometry type because the input data is rather stable time processing results. The input data contains 5 interfaces peaked on the PSTM cube and the initial velocity model which has the sizes 18.5 km, 7.5 km, 8 km that correspond to x, y and depth directions (Fig. 7a). We do different inversion strategies using variations of inversion parameters. Refinement of the velocity model when the reconstruction area is limited in depth from 1500 to 7500 m. Refinement of the velocity model occurs when using two runs of the whole inversion scheme presented on Fig. 2. For the first run, we use ten nonlinear iterations, and we use just one smoother with the rather big width: $w_x = w_y = 8km$, $w_z = 4km$. For the second run, we use ten nonlinear iterations also, but we use the lower smoother width: $w_x = w_y = 4km$, $w_z = 1km$. Finally, we get the quite satisfactory model update (Fig. 7b). The improvement of the quality one can observe on the depth migration results obtained in the initial model and the reconstructed one (Fig. 8). The CIGs are flatted in the updated part of the model, while in the initial model they are rather curved.

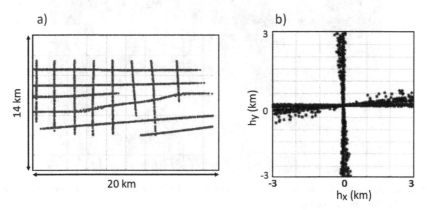

Fig. 6. Geometry of pseudo-3D acquisition system: a) common midpoint coordinates; b) offset coordinates.

4.2   3D Real Data from Eastern Siberia

Next experiments we do on the 3D real data from Eastern Siberia. Here, the acquisition geometry has essential topography. The input data contains 4 interfaces peaked on the PSTM cube and the initial velocity model which has the rather big sizes 40 km, 21 km, and 4 km that correspond to x, y and depth directions (Fig. 9a). In this experiment, we get edge effects in the x direction. Therefore, we use «strong» regularization parameters and smoothers with the huge width: $w_x = 10km$, $w_y = w_z = 2km$. These allow us to get the reasonable model update (Fig. 9b). Again, the improvement of the model quality one can observe on the depth migration results obtained in the initial model and the recovered one (Fig. 8). Here, the initial model is already quite satisfactory, therefore the CIGs are quite flattened. However, the in many areas CIGs are flatted in the updated part of the model, while in the initial model they are curved. Therefore, we conclude model update is necessary still, and we get satisfactory model update. Here, the size of the investigated area is 820 km^2. Here, the size of data needed for depth migration achieves several

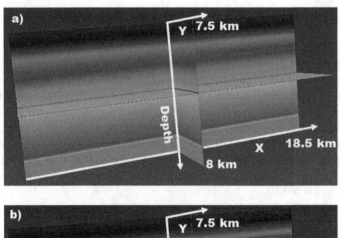

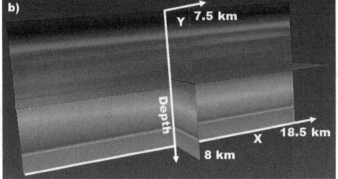

Fig. 7. a) The initial velocity model. b) The recovered velocity model using the proposed approach for pseudo-3D data geometry.

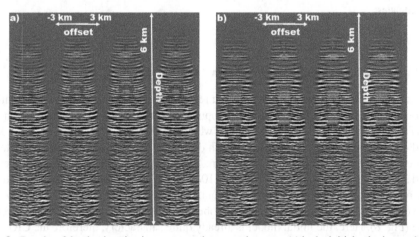

Fig. 8. Results of depth migration i.e. common-image gathers got: (a) in the initial velocity model; (b) in the velocity model obtained using the proposed approach for 3D data from Eastern Siberia.

terabytes. Therefore, application of standard common image point tomography becomes time-consuming. To get a satisfactory model via such algorithms, service companies spend months, even using high performance computing technologies. In the described experiment, we use 38 MPI nodes, and the total computational time for running the proposed tomography is about 2 h 46 min (Fig. 11a). The computation time for the first and second block (data preparation and matrix construction) is 2 h 13 min (about 1 h for each block), however, computational time for the inversion is about 33 min (Fig. 11a). We use TraceAnalyzer program to analyze the efficiency of the presented tomographic MPI realization. The efficiency of the whole tomographic code reaches over 93%, and each parallelized block via MPI also shows similar high efficiency (Fig. 11). Also, we have got linear speedup of the computations with respect to the number of MPI nodes, where the coefficient is between 0.8 and 1.0. We reach such a good efficiency because of two factors: 1) we provide independent parallelization of the computationally expensive part that is ray tracing inside first and second block; 2) we use efficiently realized PETSc library (Fig. 10).

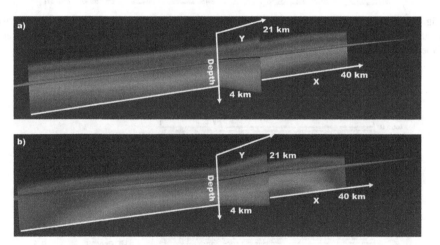

Fig. 9. a) The initial velocity model. b) The recovered velocity model using the proposed approach for 3D data from Eastern Siberia.

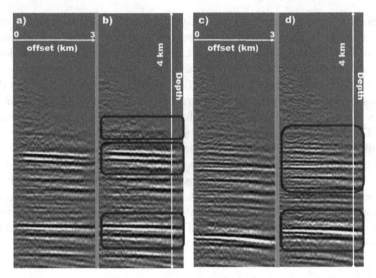

Fig. 10. Results of depth migration i.e. common-image gathers got: (a, c) in the initial velocity model; (b, d) in the velocity model obtained using the proposed approach for 3D data from Eastern Siberia.

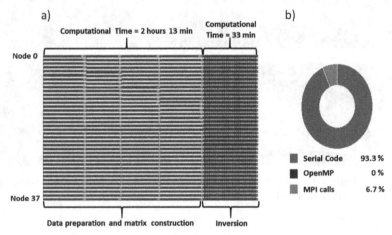

Fig. 11. Efficiency analysis for 3D tomography implementation using the TraceAnalyzer program: a) distribution of computational costs by stages (blue – computations only, red – idle time); b) MPI efficiency table.

5 Conclusions

The parallel implementation of tomography algorithm is presented. The advantages of the proposed approach include: the input data for the algorithm are time processing results, which can be borrowed from existing processing software systems; algorithm does not require expensive dynamic or two-point ray tracing; and it does not need very expensive depth migration. We associate major limitation with normal move-out approximation of the real travel times of the reflected waves.

The parallelization of the algorithm uses MPI technology for each of its block: data preparation for tomography, tomography matrix construction, solution of tomographic SLAE. The numerical experiments performed on real data confirm the efficiency of the proposed parallel algorithm. It provides computationally cheap solution while the velocity model quality improves essentially. Finally, the parallel implementation provides the possibility for processing large volumes of 3D seismic data in production mode.

Acknowledgments. The work is supported by RSF grant 21–71-20002. The numerical results were obtained using the computational resources of Peter the Great Saint-Petersburg Polytechnic University Supercomputing Center (scc.spbstu.ru).

References

1. Claerbout, J.F.: Imaging the Earth's Interior. Publ, Blackwell Sci (1985)
2. Goldin S.V.: Seismic Traveltime Inversion: Investigations in Geophysics. SEG (1986)
3. Nolet, G.: A Breviary of Seismic Tomography: Imaging the Interior of the Earth and Sun. Cambridge (2008)
4. Tarantola, A.: Inversion of seismic reflection data in the acoustic approximation. Geophysics **49**(8), 1259–1266 (1984)
5. Tarantola, A.: Inverse problem theory: Methods for data fitting and model parameter estimation. Elsevier Science Publ. Co., Inc. (1987)
6. Virieux, J., Operto, S.: An overview of full-waveform inversion in exploration geophysics. Geophysics **78**, WCC1–WCC26 (2009)
7. Pratt, R.G.: Seismic waveform inversion in the frequency domain, part 1: theory and verification in a physical scale model. Geophysics **64**(3), 888–901 (1999)
8. Warner, M., et al.: Anisotropic 3D full-waveform inversion. Geophysics **78**, R59–R80 (2013)
9. Stork, C.: Reflection tomography in the postmigrated domain. Geophysics **57**, 680–692 (1992)
10. Neklyudov, D., Gadylshin, K., Protasov, M., Klimes, L.: Fast three-dimensional depth-velocity model building based on reflection traveltime tomography and pre-stack time migrated images. In: Gervasi, O., et al. (eds.) ICCSA 2021. LNCS, vol. 12950, pp. 282–295. Springer, Cham (2021). https://doi.org/10.1007/978-3-030-86960-1_20
11. Yilmaz O.: Seismic Data Analysis: Processing, Inversion, and Interpretation of Seismic Data. SEG (2001)
12. Hubral P., Krey T.: Interval velocities from seismic reflection time measurements. SEG (1980)
13. Dix, C.H.: Seismic velocities from surface measurements. Geophysics **20**, 68–86 (1955)
14. Bishop, T.N., et al.: Tomographic determination of velocity and depth in laterally varying media. Geophysics **50**, 903–923 (1985)
15. Scales, J.A., Gersztenkorn, A.: Robust methods in inverse theory. Inverse Prob. **4**, 1071–1091 (1988)
16. Paige, C.C., Saunders, M.A.: Algorithm 583. LSQR: sparse linear equations and least squares problems. ACM Trans. Mathematical Software **8**(2), 195–209 (1982)
17. Balay, S., et al.: PETSc user's manual, Tech. Rep. ANL-95/11 - Revision 3.13, Argonne National Laboratory (2020). https://www.mcs.anl.gov/petsc

Parallel Implementation of Multioperators-Based Scheme of the 16-th Order for Three-Dimensional Calculation of the Jet Flows

Mihael Lipavskii[1(✉)] and Igor Konshin[1,2]

[1] Dorodnicyn Computing Centre, FRC CSC RAS, Moscow 119333, Russia
m.lipavskiy@yandex.ru, igor.konshin@gmail.com
[2] Sechenov University, Moscow 119991, Russia

Abstract. Numerical simulation of the outflow of a round subsonic jet into a flooded space is considered. The non-stationary three-dimensional Euler equations are approximated by means of the multioperators-based 16-th order scheme. The results of flow calculations are given. The main attention is paid to the study of the parallel implementation efficiency. The optimization of the running computations pipeline is investigated, theoretical estimates of parallel efficiency are presented. Numerical experiments were performed using from 1 to 1024 computational cores.

Keywords: Multioperators-based scheme · Euler equation · Jet flow · Parallel efficiency

1 Introduction

The multioperator principle for constructing difference schemes was proposed by A. I. Tolstykh in [1]. The main idea of the method is to represent the approximating difference operator as a linear superposition of compact basis operators depending on the parameter. The weights of the basic operators included in the multioperator are determined from the condition of approximation of the total multioperator. This approach makes it possible to construct difference schemes of arbitrarily high order of accuracy. In [2] a multi-operator scheme with the inversion of two-point compact basis operators has been proposed. This paper uses a variant of the multi-operator scheme described in [3]. The most complete description of the multi-operator technique and its application to computational fluid dynamics problems can be found in [4].

A multioperator difference scheme is used to solve the problem of the flow of a circular jet into a flooded space. Depending on the parameters of the problem, such as shear layer thickness, Mach number, temperature and density ratios of the jet and the surrounding space, different vortex structures may arise [5,6].

2 Problem Formulation

The unsteady problem of the flow of a circular subsonic jet into a flooded space is solved. Molecular viscosity is not taken into account, Euler equations are used.

V. Voevodin et al. (Eds.): RuSCDays 2022, LNCS 13708, pp. 250–261, 2022.
https://doi.org/10.1007/978-3-031-22941-1_18

The Cartesian coordinate system x, y, z is given. The computational domain is a rectangular parallelepiped in which the jet is directed along the x-axis, i.e. along the line $y = 0$, $z = 0$. The velocity components along the axes of the Cartesian coordinate system x, y, z are denoted by u, v, w, respectively. The following notations for gas-dynamic quantities are used: ρ is density, e is specific internal energy, p is pressure.

The following quantities are taken as units: R is a jet radius, ρ_0 and u_0 are density and velocity in the center of unperturbed jet, respectively. In this case, the unit of specific energy is u_0^2, and that of pressure is $\rho_0 u_0^2$.

At the initial moment of time, an unperturbed axisymmetric jet and a flooded space are given. These fields do not depend on the longitudinal coordinate x. The longitudinal velocity component was calculated either by the formula

$$u = \frac{1}{2} + \frac{1}{2} \tanh\left[\frac{1}{4\theta}\left(\frac{1}{r} - r\right)\right],$$

where θ is the conditional thickness of the transition layer between the jet core and the surrounding space, r is the distance from the jet axis, or as a table of values. Both transverse velocity components are taken equal to zero $v = 0$, $w = 0$. The parameter $s = \rho_0/\rho_\infty$ is the ratio of density in the center of the jet to the density in the surrounding space. The pressure is assumed constant throughout the entire computational domain. The density and specific internal energy are calculated from the Crocco–Buzemann relations. The Mach number is defined as the ratio of the local speed of sound to the speed in the center of the unperturbed jet:

$$M = \frac{c_c}{u_c}.$$

In this formulation of the problem, the solution is defined by three dimensionless parameters:

$$s, \theta, M.$$

3   Numerical Method

To approximate the spatial derivatives included in the Euler equations, we use multioperators with inverse two-point grid operators [3]. Using the model equation $u_t + f(u)_x = 0$ as an example, the approximation of the spatial derivative is as follows:

$$\frac{\partial u}{\partial t} + K(c_1, c_2, \ldots, c_I)f(u) + CD(d_1, d_2, \ldots, d_J)u = 0.$$

Here K and D are multioperators providing approximation and dissipation, respectively, $C > 0$ is a constant reflecting the intensity of the scheme dissipation.

By changing the parameter sets $c_1, c_2, \ldots, c_I$ and $d_1, d_2, \ldots, d_J$ we can control the spectral and dissipative properties of the difference scheme, respectively. In the present work, operators with $I = J = 8$ were used. At these values, the scheme provides the 16-th order of approximation of the derivative and dissipation of the 15-th order of smallness. The distribution of the parameters of the multioperators is assumed to be uniform $c_i = c_{min} + (i-1)(c_{max} - c_{min})/(I - 1), i = 1, \ldots, I$, $d_i = d_{min} + (i-1)(d_{max} - d_{min})/(J-1), i = 1, \ldots, J$. In this case, multioperators can be considered as depending only on two parameters $K = K(c_{min}, c_{max})$, $D = D(d_{min}, d_{max})$.

The classical Runge–Kutta method of 4-th order of accuracy is used for time integration. At all boundaries of the computational domain characteristic boundary conditions are set.

For each of the spatial directions, the nodes of the grid are densified in the areas of the supposed rapid change of the solution. To ensure computational stability, some additional reduction of the step along the longitudinal coordinate x near the input boundary is required. The node densification and sparsification is done for each spatial coordinate independently of the other coordinates. This somewhat simplifies the system of equations to be solved. All grids are constructed as elements of families of quasi-uniform grids [7]. The computational domain is a rectangular parallelepiped $0 \leqslant x \leqslant 300$, $-300 \leqslant y \leqslant 300$, $-300 \leqslant z \leqslant 300$. The work area, that is, the part of the computational area in which you can calculate an adequate solution, is much smaller: $0 \leqslant x \leqslant 30$, $-3.8 \leqslant y \leqslant 3.8$, $-3.8 \leqslant z \leqslant 3.8$. In the rest of the area, the grid step is chosen rather rapidly increasing, which ensures that the influence of the boundaries of the computational area is reduced. In the working area, the step size for all coordinates is limited to 0.08, and the ratio of neighboring steps does not exceed 1.04.

4   Parallel Implementation and Efficiency Estimation

A parallel implementation of a similar algorithm was partially described in [8]. In the present study, we consider it in more detail and obtain a new parallel efficiency estimates for this algorithm.

When implementing the described algorithm in parallel, it is necessary to take into account that operators are two-point instead of three-point, so instead of sweep solution along one line, the so-called "running" computations should be used. In this case, calculations can be started on both sides of the line at the same time. This increases parallel efficiency by halving the start time of the pipeline. The organization of the running computations pipeline is shown in Fig. 1. At the kth step of pipeline, a series of running computations are performed on each process simultaneously to both sides of the calculation line. Running computations can be combined into groups, e.g. by m runs, using a single "package" for inter-process communications. This reduces significantly the impact of message initialization time. In Fig. 1 by letters from "a" to "f" we denote 6 different packages of running computations, which are performed on 3 processes ($p = 0, 1, 2$) in 8 steps, $k = 0, \ldots, 7$.

Now we can proceed to the estimation of the algorithm total solution time to find the optimal value of the parameter m, which affects the parallel efficiency of the computation. The methodology proposed in [9,10] can be used as a speedup estimation technique.

```
                [:p=0:] [:p=1:] [:p=2:]
        k       ------------------------------>X
        0       [>>a>>> ------- ------]
        0       [------ ------- <<<a<<]
        1       [>>b>>> >>>a>>> ------]
        1       [------ <<<a<<< <<<b<<]
        2       [>>c>>> >>>b>>> >>>a>>]
        2       [<<a<<< <<<b<<< <<<c<<]
        3       [>>d>>> >>>c>>> >>>b>>]
        3       [<<b<<< <<<c<<< <<<d<<]
        4       [>>e>>> >>>d>>> >>>c>>]
        4       [<<c<<< <<<d<<< <<<e<<]
        5       [>>f>>> >>>e>>> >>>d>>]
        5       [<<d<<< <<<e<<< <<<f<<]
        6       [------ >>>f>>> >>>e>>]
        6       [<<e<<< <<<f<<< ------]
        7       [------ ------- >>>f>>]
        7       [<<f<<< ------- ------]
```

Fig. 1. Pipeline structure for parallel "running" computations on each step $k = 0, .., 7$ for $P = 3$ processes.

Let computations are carried out in the 3D domain with $N_x \times N_y \times N_z$ nodes using $P = p_x \times p_y \times p_z$ processes, while simultaneously transmitting in one package the results of running computations along m lines. The length of one communication package in one direction will be equal to

$$L_{1c} = mN_o,$$

where N_o is a number of operators. In addition, let us denote by N_a a number of arithmetic operations per node when processing one operator in one direction, then the total number of arithmetic operations at one stage of the running computations pipeline for one process is the following:

$$L_{1a} = 2n_x N_o N_a m.$$

The time spent to arithmetic operations and data transfers at each stage of the running computations pipeline can be estimated using the formulas

$$T_{1a} = \tau_a L_{1a}, \quad T_{1c} = \tau_0 + \tau_c L_{1c},$$

respectively. Here τ_a is the average time per one arithmetic operation, τ_c is the average transfer time of one number for sufficiently large messages, τ_0 is the initialization time of communication. Usually, we have $\tau_a \ll \tau_c \ll \tau_0$.

We will further assume that the traditional blocking data exchanges are performed, which means

$$T_1 = T_{1c} + T_{1a} = \tau_0 + (\tau_c N_o + 2\tau_a n_x N_o N_a)m.$$

Let us note that for non-blocking exchanges, the reasonable estimates of the parallel efficiency cannot be obtained, since in this case, the dependence of T_1 on m will be linear, and the optimal size of the transfer package in this case will be equal to $m = 1$. By the way, the same optimal value $m = 1$ is obtained if τ_0 is neglected.

The total number of lines along one direction per one process is equal to $n_y n_z$. Then the total number of pipeline stages along one direction can be estimated as $N_s = p_x - 1 + n_y n_z / m$. Finally, we can write out the total computation time along the x direction:

$$T = N_s T_1 = \left(p_x - 1 + \frac{N_y N_z}{p_y p_z m} \right) \left(\tau_0 + \left(\tau_c + 2\tau_a N_a \frac{N_x}{p_x} \right) N_o m \right). \qquad (1)$$

Note that for fixed domain sizes ($N_x \times N_y \times N_z$) and scheme parameters, this value depends both on the partition of the domain by processes ($p_x \times p_y \times p_z$) and on the transfer package size m.

For the case of a cubic domain with $N = N_x = N_y = N_z$ and $p = p_x = p_y = p_z$, or just approximately putting $N = \sqrt[3]{N_x \cdot N_y \cdot N_z}$ and $p = \sqrt[3]{P}$, we can write

$$T = \left(p - 1 + \frac{N^2}{p^2 m} \right) \left(\tau_0 + \left(\tau_c + 2\tau_a N_a \frac{N}{p} \right) N_o m \right). \qquad (2)$$

If one is interested in the optimal transfer package size m, then it suffices to write $T'(m) = 0$ and solve the resulting quadratic equation. Up to principal terms, it gives

$$m = \sqrt{\frac{\tau_0 \frac{N^2}{p^2}}{(p-1)\left(\tau_c + 2\tau_a N_a \frac{N}{p}\right) N_o}}. \qquad (3)$$

If we substitute in the resulting Eq. (3) the characteristic dimensions of the domain $200 \times 200 \times 200$ partitioned into $4 \times 4 \times 4$ processes, with $N_a = 10$, $N_o = 8$, $\tau_c = 30\tau_a$, and $\tau_0 = 30\tau_c$, then we obtain $m \approx 5$. This result is consistent with the results of calculations for the considered problem given in Table 1, in which, in addition to the calculation time T for one time step, the average transfer length L_{sr} in double words and the total number of transfer stages N_{sr} are presented. It can be seen that the actual calculation time does not change very much in the range $3 < m < 60$. This fact indicates the flatness of the minimum of the solution time function, which means that in the above range it is possible to change the selected value of m without significant loss of parallel efficiency. This may be necessary, for example, when the total number of calculation lines is divisible by m without a remainder so that the sizes of all packages are the same. This is important for balancing calculations on different processes. In our experiments, we set $m = 20$ and, taking into account the number of nodes in the domain in different directions, we chose the lowermost value for m.

Let us now turn to estimation of the parallel efficiency of the algorithm. Using formula (2) one can write out the full theoretical speedup estimate

Table 1. Calculation time of one time step depending on the transfer package size m.

m	T	L_{sr}	N_{sr}
1	3.110	85	18905
3	2.655	254	6425
10	2.445	836	2057
15	2.453	1244	1433
18	2.451	1487	1225
20	2.407	1648	1121
30	2.409	2442	809
36	2.416	2911	705
60	2.474	4747	497
90	2.541	6980	393

$$S = \frac{T(1)}{T(P)}, \tag{4}$$

where for more accurate estimate one may set

$$T(1) = 2\tau_a N_a N_o N^3.$$

Following the technique described in [9, 10], one can also write out a simplified asymptotic speedup estimate using the main characteristic of the parallelism resource inherent to the considered algorithm

$$L = \frac{L_c}{L_a} \approx \frac{L_{1c}}{L_{1a}} = \frac{p}{2\,NN_a}.$$

In view of the reduction in value N_o, which characterizes the number of support operators, one can, in particular, conclude that the parallelism resource of this algorithm will be approximately the same for high-order and low-order schemes of approximation. Here, for simplicity of estimate, $\tau_0 = 0$ is assumed, which means that the time of initialization of the running computations pipeline is neglected. Thus, for one value involved in the transfer, on average, there are about $1/L = 2N_a N/p$ double addition/multiplication operations (for example, for $N = 200$, $p = 10$ and $N_a = 10$ this parameter is equal to 400, which allows us to hope for high parallel efficiency). In this case, the speedup can be estimated as

$$S = \frac{T(1)}{T(P)} = \frac{T_a}{T_c + T_a} = \frac{P}{1 + \tau L} \approx \frac{P}{1 + \dfrac{\tau \sqrt[3]{P}}{2\,NN_a}},$$

where $\tau = \tau_c/\tau_a$ is the ratio of data transfer rate and arithmetic operation rate. The value of τ expresses the "parallelism" characteristic of the computer itself and can be easily measured on a case-by-case basis. Usually τ is in the range $10 < \tau < 50$. For the above speedup estimate, it can be noted that for not very efficient algorithms with $\tau L = 1$, a twofold drop in parallel efficiency will occur. As follows from the above estimates for a specific set of problem parameters, the algorithm we consider has a strong margin of parallel efficiency.

For a detailed practical study of parallel efficiency on the $541 \times 145 \times 145$ grid, calculations were performed using from 1 to 1024 MPI processes. The results of numerical experiments are presented in Table 2. Here, P is the number of MPI processes, "Config." is the MPI processes configuration, T is the solution time for a single time step, T_{mpi} is the total time of all MPI exchanges at one time step, S_{run} is the runtime speedup estimate considering T_{mpi}, $S_{1/2}$ is the speedup relative to the solution time for $P/2$ processes, S_{theor} is the theoretical speedup estimate calculated by formula (4), and finally, S is the actual speedup relative to the solution time for one process.

It is most convenient to analyze the calculation time T directly on a special graph (see Fig. 2), where the dependence of T on the number of processes P is presented in a logarithmic scale. It can be seen that the deviations from the straight line are minimal, which indicates the stability of both the calculations themselves and the time measurement technique used. In this case, the slope of the straight line is quite close to $45°$, i.e. to calculations with the ideal parallelism $S = P$.

The value of S_{run} was calculated on the basis of the total solution time $T(P)$ for a particular program run in parallel mode, providing an additional measurement of the total execution time T_{mpi} of all MPI functions. Then the program execution time on one process can be represented as $T(1) = (T(P) - T_{\mathrm{mpi}})P$, in such a way the speedup can be estimated directly during a parallel run of the MPI program as

$$S_{\mathrm{run}} = \frac{T(1)}{T(P)} = \frac{(T(P) - T_{\mathrm{mpi}})P}{T(P)} = \left(1 - \frac{T_{\mathrm{mpi}}}{T(P)}\right)P.$$

Such a speedup estimate can be justified, for example, when running the program on one process is impossible, for example, due to the extremely long problem solution time or some memory limitations. It is interesting to note that estimate S_{theor}, calculated using the original formula (4), and also shown in Fig. 3, almost coincides with the value of S_{run} for $p = 1, ..., 256$. The results presented in Table 2 and Fig. 3 show that the use of the S_{run} estimate in such cases can be considered quite reasonable.

The value of $S_{1/2}$ expresses the speedup of a particular run with a doubling of the number of processes. In the ideal case we have $S_{1/2} = 2$. Some jumps in the behavior of this value (see Table 2 and Fig. 4) may occur due to a change in the configuration of MPI processes and a corresponding change in the size of the local subdomain along one of the directions, implementation features communications for such a configuration of the processes network, as well as just fluctuations in the parallel solution time of a particular program run (see, for example, [11]).

The estimate S_{theor}, also shown in Fig. 4, was calculated using a more accurate original formula (4). To obtain an estimate, we have used the following values:

Table 2. Results of calculations per time step depending on the number of processes $P = 1, ..., 1024$.

P	Config.	T	T_{mpi}	S_{run}	$S_{1/2}$	S_{theor}	S
1	1×1×1	85.649	—	1.0	—	1.00	1.00
2	2×1×1	43.423	0.471	2.0	1.97	1.97	1.97
4	2×1×2	22.187	0.250	4.0	1.96	3.94	3.86
8	2×2×2	12.378	0.078	7.9	1.79	7.86	6.92
16	4×2×2	6.666	0.211	15.5	1.85	15.62	12.84
32	4×2×4	3.660	0.084	31.3	1.82	30.94	23.39
64	4×4×4	1.838	0.062	62.3	1.99	60.87	46.58
128	8×4×4	0.956	0.046	121.8	1.92	118.27	89.59
256	8×4×8	0.492	0.047	231.2	1.94	224.56	173.83
512	8×8×8	0.298	0.101	338.9	1.65	408.93	287.02
1024	16×8×8	0.157	0.057	651.5	1.89	694.59	543.59

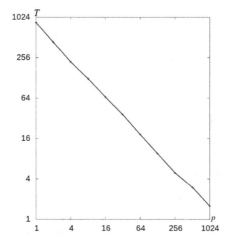

Fig. 2. The problem solution time depending on the number of processes.

$$N = \sqrt[3]{N_x N_y N_z} = \sqrt[3]{541 \cdot 145 \cdot 145}, \quad p = \sqrt[3]{P},$$
$$N_a = 10, \quad N_o = 8, \quad m = 20, \quad \tau_c = 30\tau_a, \quad \tau_0 = 30\tau_c.$$

The closeness to the case of ideal parallelism $S_{1/2} = 2$ as well as to the theoretical estimate S_{theor} reflects the high parallel efficiency of the method under consideration, as well as the validity of using this specification in evaluating the efficiency of calculations.

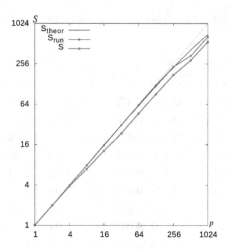

Fig. 3. Actual relative speedup S, run-time estimated speedup S_{run}, and theoretical estimate S_{theor}.

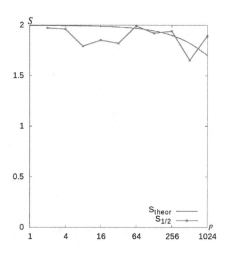

Fig. 4. Speedup $S_{1/2}$ for P processes relative to the solution time for $P/2$ processes, as well as theoretical estimate S_{theor} for the same value.

In conclusion to this section, it is worth noting that all the studies performed have shown a high parallel efficiency of the considered difference scheme implementation.

5 Numerical Results

The computations were performed using supercomputer MVS-10Q of Joint Supercomputer Center of the Russian Academy of Sciences [12].

Fig. 5. Isosurface of the vorticity vector modulus, $|\boldsymbol{\Omega}| = 3.85$.

At the initial moment of time, the longitudinal velocity is set in the form of a table of values. The transition zone between the jet and the flooded space has only three nodes of the computational grid. The Mach number M = 0.47 is set, temperature and pressure are constant in the entire computational domain.

The shear layer, which is a transition zone between the jet and the flooded space, begins to deform due to instability with subsequent formation of toroidal vortex structures. Toroidal vortices are drifted down the stream and in their turn are deformed with formation of smaller structures. At some values of the parameters, quasi-periodic vortex formation with subsequent movement down the flow and collapse occurs; at some other values, the formed vortices merge in pairs while moving; at some other values, non-periodic flow with chaotic vortex formation and collapse occurs. At the initial parameters selected for the calculations, the third of the described scenarios is realized, in which irregular vortex formation takes place. The axial symmetry of each vortex begins to break slightly as the vortices are drifted down the flow.

Figure 5 shows the isosurface of the vorticity module $|\boldsymbol{\Omega}| = 3.85$ at time $t = 1637$. Three toroidal vortices can be clearly seen. Breach of axial symmetry is noticeable already on the vortex closest to the inflow. The distortion of the jet shape near the entrance boundary is caused by too small a number of nodes of the computational grid falling on the shear layer.

Figure 6 is a space-time diagram. Here the overpressure in the line $y = 1.2$, $z = 0$ as a function of coordinate x and time t is given. In this image, elongated regions of reduced pressure generally correspond to moving vortices. Thus, we can get an idea of the regularity of vortex formation, merging, collapse, and displacement. In our case, the emergence of vortices occurred irregularly. Such events as merging of two vortices into one are also observed. The difference scheme used allows us to numerically obtain fine details of the solution. In the solution, vortices with a diameter of only three steps of the computational grid are clearly visible.

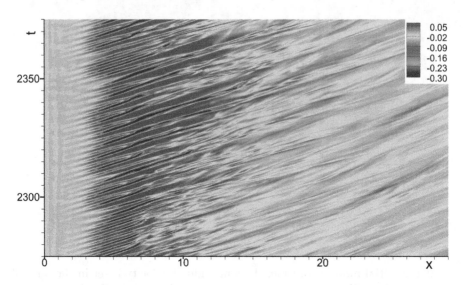

Fig. 6. Excess pressure at $y = 1.2$, $z = 0$, as a function of coordinate x and time t.

6   Conclusion

In the present paper we consider a parallel implementation of a multi-operator scheme with two-point operator reversal. Its high parallel efficiency was demonstrated on the example of a high-precision 16-order scheme. This scheme was used for direct numerical simulation of the flow of a circular subsonic jet into a flooded space based on the Euler equations. As a result, the process of occurrence of vortex structures of various intensities has been studied and described in detail.

In further studies, it is supposed to take into account molecular viscosity in the algorithm under consideration and add a turbulence model, which will make it possible to compare the calculation results with the data of a physical experiment.

A detailed description of the computation paralleling scheme is given. Theoretical estimations of the optimal data packet size for the running computations pipeline are obtained. The dependence of the counting time on the packet size was also investigated practically, which confirmed the theoretical investigations. A theoretical estimation of the counting acceleration was obtained, which was also confirmed by numerical experiments.

Numerical experiments have shown the possibility of using the considered schemes for modeling the emergence and development of vortex structures on a coarse grid. The conducted investigations confirmed the high parallelism resource inherent in the multi-operator method itself when using two-point operators. High parallel efficiency of the considered algorithm implementation was also shown by numerical examples.

Acknowledgements. The computations were performed using facilities of the Joint SuperComputer Center of the Russian Academy of Sciences.

The authors are grateful to anonymous reviewers for valuable comments, which improved the quality of the paper presentation and avoided many items that could cause ambiguous interpretation.

References

1. Tolstykh, A.I.: Multioperator high-order compact upwind methods for CFD parallel calculations. In: Emerson, D., Fox, P., Satofuka, N. (eds.) Parallel Computational Fluid Dynamics: Recent Developments and Advances Using Parallel Computing, pp. 383–390. Elsevier, Amsterdam (1998)
2. Tolstykh, A.I.: A family of compact approximations and related multioperator approximations of a given order. Dokl. Math. **72**(1), 519–524 (2005)
3. Tolstykh, A.I.: 16th and 32nd multioperators based schemes for smooth and discontinuous solutions. Commun. Comput. Phys. **22**(2), 572–598 (2017). https://doi.org/10.4208/cicp.141015.240217a
4. Tolstykh, A.I.: High Accuracy Compact and Multioperators Approximations for Partial Differential Equations. Nauka, Moscow (2015).(in Russian)
5. Monkewitz, P., Bechert, D., Barsikow, B., Lehmann, B.: Self-excited oscillations and mixing in a heated round jet. J. Fluid Mech. **213**, 611–639 (1990). https://doi.org/10.1017/S0022112090002476
6. Lesshafft, L., Huerre, P.: Frequency selection in globally unstable round jets. Phys. Fluids **19**, 054108 (2007). https://doi.org/10.1063/1.2732247
7. Kalitkin, N.N., Alshin, A.B., Alshina, E.A., Rogov, B.V.: Computations on Quasiuniform Grids. Fizmatlit, Moscow (2005).(in Russian)
8. Tolstykh, A.I., Shirobokov, D.A.: Using 16-th order multioperators-based scheme for supercomputer simulation of the initial stage of laminar-turbulent transitions. In: Voevodin, V., Sobolev, S. (eds.) RuSCDays 2021. CCIS, vol. 1510, pp. 270–282. Springer, Cham (2021). https://doi.org/10.1007/978-3-030-92864-3_21
9. Konshin, I.: Parallel computational models to estimate an actual speedup of analyzed algorithm. In: Voevodin, V., Sobolev, S. (eds.) RuSCDays 2016. CCIS, vol. 687, pp. 304–317. Springer, Cham (2016). https://doi.org/10.1007/978-3-319-55669-7_24
10. Konshin, I.: Efficiency estimation for the mathematical physics algorithms for distributed memory computers. In: Voevodin, V., Sobolev, S. (eds.) RuSCDays 2018. CCIS, vol. 965, pp. 63–75. Springer, Cham (2019). https://doi.org/10.1007/978-3-030-05807-4_6
11. Konshin, I.: Efficiency of basic linear algebra operations on parallel computers. In: Voevodin, V., Sobolev, S. (eds.) RuSCDays 2019. CCIS, vol. 1129, pp. 26–38. Springer, Cham (2019). https://doi.org/10.1007/978-3-030-36592-9_3
12. Joint SuperComputer Center of the Russian Academy of Sciences. https://www.jscc.ru. Accessed 15 April 2021

Parallel Implementation of the Seismic Sources Recovery in Randomly Heterogeneous Media

Galina Reshetova$^{(\boxtimes)}$ (ID) and Vitaly Koynov

The Institute of Computational Mathematics and Mathematical,
Geophysics SB RAS, Novosibirsk, Russia
kgv@nmsf.sscc.ru

Abstract. A parallel algorithm to solve the problem of seismic source location inside a randomly heterogeneous medium is considered. To recover the source position, we propose using information about recorded seismograms on the free surface and the knowledge about the statistical properties of a random medium. This approach requires a solution to a large number of dynamic elasticity problems to simulate seismic wavefields for different statistically equivalent velocity models. This is the most time-consuming part of the solution algorithm. To speed up the calculations, we use a two-level strategy for the parallelization with the help of creating subgroups with the domain decomposition technique inside each group.

Keywords: Wave propagation · Random media · Computational seismic · Numerical solution · Time reversal mirror · Parallel domain decomposition

1 Introduction

The numerical solution of most problems arising in exploration geophysics require the development of efficient methods of numerical calculations using modern powerful computers. Applications of the finite element methods [1,2], pseudospectral methods [3,4], spectral element methods [5] and the finite difference methods [6–9] allow modeling the propagation of seismic waves with a high accuracy in heterogeneous media based on the equations of dynamic elasticity theory for elastic/anisotropic/viscoelastic media [6,10–12]. However, the calculations with a high accuracy are associated with high computational costs and a large amount of computational resources. In addition, one of the features of the problems solution in exploration seismology and global tomography of the Earth is the necessity to solve minimization problems by simultaneously or sequentially considering and analyzing solutions for at least several thousand wave propagation models. Therefore, methods for increasing the efficiency of solving such problems directly affect not only the efficiency, but also the very possibility of solving them.

During the last decade, several directions in improving the efficiency of solving seismic problems methods were developed. One of them is related with the development of faster modelling methods for parallel computing synthetic seismograms in a three-dimensional heterogeneous model of the Earth. Among these approaches, one can single out the approach using the two-dimensional modeling to calculate the three-dimensional seismograms [13] or an approach based on limiting the calculations of wave propagation within a subregion [14].

The paper considers the problem of restoring the location of a seismic source inside a randomly inhomogeneous medium. This problem is of great interest and arises, for example, in seismological applications when determining the location of an earthquake source. The solution technique is based on the simulation of seismic wavefields applied to heterogeneous geological media with a random structure. To recover a seismic source we propose to use the Time Reversal Mirror (TRM) technique [15–17].

To speed up calculations, a two-level parallelization strategy is used, which naturally follows from the features of the algorithm for solving the problem. The scheme of the numerical solution of the problem is described below, as well as the method of parallelization technique.

2 Statement of the Problem

The propagation of elastic waves within linear, isotropic, heterogeneous two-dimensional elastic media is described by sets of first order partial differential equations known as a system of the dynamic elasticity theory written down in the velocity-stress formulation [18]. These equations are written down below.

Stress-strain relations:

$$
\frac{\partial \tau_{xx}}{\partial t} = (\lambda + 2\mu)\frac{\partial v_x}{\partial x} + \lambda\frac{\partial v_y}{\partial y} + F_{xx}
$$
$$
\frac{\partial \tau_{yy}}{\partial t} = (\lambda + 2\mu)\frac{\partial v_y}{\partial y} + \lambda\frac{\partial v_x}{\partial x} + F_{yy} \tag{1}
$$
$$
\frac{\partial \tau_{xy}}{\partial t} = \mu\left(\frac{\partial v_x}{\partial y} + \frac{\partial v_y}{\partial z}\right)
$$

Equations of momentum conservation:

$$
\rho\frac{\partial v_x}{\partial t} = \frac{\partial \tau_{xx}}{\partial x} + \frac{\partial \tau_{xy}}{\partial y}
$$
$$
\rho\frac{\partial v_y}{\partial t} = \frac{\partial \tau_{xy}}{\partial x} + \frac{\partial \tau_{yy}}{\partial y} \tag{2}
$$

Initial conditions:

$$
\boldsymbol{v}|_{t=0} = 0, \qquad \boldsymbol{\tau}|_{t=0} = 0 \tag{3}
$$

Boundary conditions on the free-surface:

$$
\tau_{yy} = 0, \qquad \tau_{xy} = 0. \tag{4}
$$

In these equations, the elastic waves are described in terms of $\boldsymbol{v} = (v_x, v_y)$ displacement velocity components and $\boldsymbol{\tau} = (\tau_{xx}, \tau_{yy}, \tau_{xy})$ stress tensor components. The medium is characterized by the Lame elasticity modules λ, μ and the density ρ. The Lame parameters are expressed in terms of the velocities of the compression V_p and the shear V_s waves as follows:

$$\lambda = \rho \left(V_p^2 - 2V_s^2\right), \qquad \mu = \rho V_s^2. \tag{5}$$

The functions F_{xx}, F_{yy} in the right-hand side of equations (1) determine the body-force components acting as a seismic moment tensor of the elastic motion. In particular, the volumetric type source is defined by the components

$$F_{xx} = F_{yy} = f(t) \cdot \delta(x - x_0, y - y_0), \tag{6}$$

where $f(t)$ is the signal time wavelet in the source and δ is the Dirac delta function centered at the source point (x_0, y_0). In our simulations we use the Ricker impulse

$$f(t) = (1 - 2\pi^2 \, f_0^2(t - t_0)^2)exp(-\pi^2 \, f_0^2(t - t_0)^2), \tag{7}$$

where f_0 is the dominant frequency in the source, and t_0 is the time delay of the impulse.

To avoid artificial reflections from computational domain boundaries we apply the absorbing boundary conditions in the form of Berenge's formulation of the Perfectly Matched Layer (PML method) with splitting [19].

3   Source Recovery Algorithm

The problem to recover the seismic source location inside a randomly heterogeneous medium using only recorded seismograms on the free surface and the knowledge about the statistical properties of a random medium is of great interest in practical geophysical and seismological applications. It has been shown, for example, that typical seismograms resulting from earthquakes are not described in terms of simplified piece-wise homogeneous models [20], but could be the result of interactions between elastic waves and underlying randomly heterogeneities in the medium [21].

The solution technique of the problem under study is based on the simulation of seismic wavefields applied to multi-scale heterogeneous geological media with random models of the soil. The elastic properties of a randomly heterogeneous medium are characterized of elastic moduli and density with strong variations in space. In many cases a random medium can be described in terms of a random function with specific statistical properties such, for example, as a standard deviation and a correlation length. This fact gives the possibility to produce a set of statistically equivalent velocity models (realizations) of a random medium. The term "equivalence" means that the parameters of the standard deviation, the correlation length and the mathematical expectation are the same with the initial random model.

To recover a seismic source in a randomly heterogeneous medium, we propose to use the Time Reversal Mirror (TRM) technique [15–17]. This approach is based on the property of time invariance of the wave equation in a non-dissipating case and the source-receiver reciprocity. This means that if we record by a receiver array on the free surface, the wavefield radiated by a seismic source with the use of the backwards traces of a seismogram as a set of sources (at the same locations as receivers) to generate the waves traveling backward to the same medium, then the resulting wavefield must theoretically refocus synchronously at the original source position. The key point here is that the wavefild travels backwards in the *same medium*. In the case of a random medium we do not know its exact fine structure, but only its statistical properties. In this case we offer to use statistically equivalent velocity models to recover the source position in random media.

The proposed algorithm consists of three steps and is schematically presented in Fig. 1. A brief description of each step is given below.

- **Step one**. Let us fix a randomly heterogeneous medium (call it the initial model). Suppose that we have a seismogram on the free surface from the source inside this model in case of real seismic data. At the stage of the algorithm verification, we use the synthetic data obtained by the numerical simulation;
- **Step two**. At this stage, we "forget" about the initial model and only keep the seismogram and knowledge about the statistical properties of the initial model. Using this information, we calculate a set of statistically equivalent velocity models. For each generated model we apply the TRM technique and calculate the wavefield traveling backward. For the numerical simulation we use a staggered-grid finite difference technique [7,8]. As a result, we have a set of snapshots of the wavefield components for each realization at the time corresponding to the source refocusing;
- **Step three**. At this stage, it is necessary to recover the source location in the initial model using the simulation results from Step two. To image and clarify the position of the source, we use and analyze various recovery methods, such as the simple summation, finding the center of mass, calculation of the semblance, and the summation of the snapshots components in conjunction with the search for the global maximum.

4   Numerical Simulations

To verify the algorithm, we have chosen an initial model as a randomly heterogeneous model of the medium with the following statistical parameters: the average velocities $V_p = 3000$ m/s, $V_s = V_p/\sqrt{3}$, the density $\rho = 2000$ kg/m^3, the correlation length 30 m and standard deviation 10%. To build this model, we use the method based on the spectral representation of random media, which allows one to mathematically generate a series of statistically equivalent media fields [22]. The distribution of the velocity V_p for this model is presented in Fig. 2.

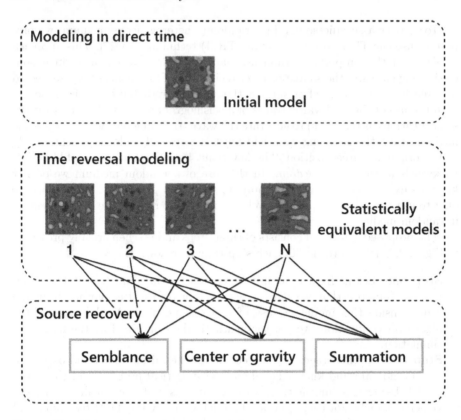

Fig. 1. The schematic steps description of the proposed seismic source recovery algorithm in a random medium using the TRM applied to a set of statistically equivalent velocity models.

Let us consider a 2000×2000 m square computational domain with a uniform finite difference grid step of 4 m. Suppose that the wavefield was excited by a source of the volumetric type at the center of the computational domain. The generated wavefield was recorded by receivers located on the free surface every 24 m. The simulation time was 1.5 s with a sampling interval of 0.7 ms.

Now we will sequentially perform the Steps described in the previous section to solve the problem.

Step One. To construct a numerical solution of system (1)-(4) for the initial model and obtaining a synthetic seismogram, we use a highly efficient and concise staggered-grid finite difference technique with second order of accuracy in space and time [7,8]. The PML method was used to remove non-physical reflections from the boundaries of the computational domain [19]. The snapshots of the wavefield excited from the source are presented in Fig. 3.

Step Two. For each statistically equivalent velocity model we solve the inverse problem that is to continue the wavefield in reverse time by the TRM

Randomly inhomogeneous medium

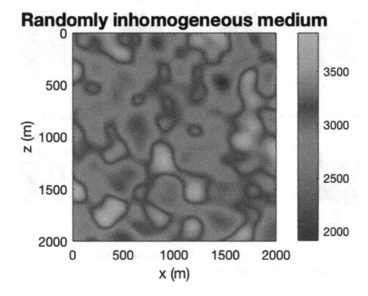

Fig. 2. The velocity distribution V_p of a randomly heterogeneous model with the following statistical parameters: the average velocity $V_p = 3000\ m/s$, $V_s = V_p/\sqrt{3}$, $\rho = 2000\ kg/m^3$, the correlation length $30\ m$ and the standard deviation 10%.

technique. As we have already mentioned, the receivers on the free surface now act as sources. The snapshots of the solution of the inverse problem for the initial model are presented in Fig. 4.

Step Three. To recover the seismic source location in the initial model, several approaches have been proposed and investigated to enhance the spatial resolution. These approaches are listed below.

1. The calculation of the elastic energy density was used to eliminate the local extrema of the wavefields [23]. In order to enhance the coherent component of the total wavefield calculated in reverse time, the idea of calculating the "accumulated" elastic energy was used. To do this, at each moment of time t^k for all points of the finite difference grid, the square of the total energy density E for all previous computational time steps t^m was calculated:

$$E_{\text{sum}}(x_i, z_j, t^k) = \sum_{t^m \le t^k} E(x_i, z_j, t^m) \tag{8}$$

where the elastic energy density at the time t^m is expressed by the formula

$$E(x_i, z_j, t^m) = \tau_{\text{xx}}(x_i, z_j, t^m)\varepsilon_{\text{xx}}(x_i, z_j, t^m)+$$
$$+\tau_{\text{zz}}(x_i, z_j, t^m)\varepsilon_{\text{zz}}(x_i, z_j, t^m)+2\tau_{\text{xz}}(x_i, z_j, t^m)\varepsilon_{\text{xz}}(x_i, z_j, t^m) \tag{9}$$

In this formula, τ and ε are the stress and the strain components, respectively.

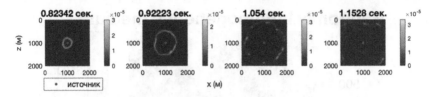

Fig. 3. The wavefield snapshots for the stress component simulated for the initial model.

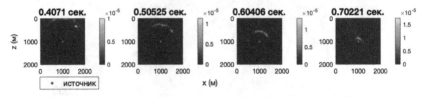

Fig. 4. The wavefield snapshots for the stress component simulated in reverse time by the TRM technique for the initial model.

2. Peak-to-Average Power Ratio (PAPR) was used to enhance the spatial focus of seismic event detection:

$$PAPR(x,z) = \frac{E_{\max}^2(x,z)}{E_{\text{total}}^2/T_{\text{global}}}, \qquad E_{\text{total}}^2(x,z) = \sum_{t=0}^{T_{\text{end}}} E^2(x,z,t). \qquad (10)$$

3. To search for the location of a seismic source position we have used a simple summation of the different wavefield components of the TRM inversion for all statistically equivalent models.

4. Another approach that has been explored is to calculate the semblance. The semblance is defined as the quadrature of the correlation coefficient with a constant:

$$S = (\sum_{i=0}^{n} E_i)^2 / n (\sum_{i=0}^{n} E_i^2), \qquad (11)$$

where n is the number of equivalent models used in the calculation process. If for a fixed point the value of the sum is less than a certain percentage of its maximum value, then it is assumed to be equal to zero. Specify that the semblance elements here are the elastic energy density obtained for each realization.

5. And the two last approaches we have tested were to find the global maximum of the wavefield and to find the center of the mass (a geometric point, which is determined by the distribution of the mass in the body).

The calculation results of Step 3 are shown in Fig. 5. This figure shows the wavefield images of the source recovery obtained by the TRM method for initial model and three different realizations. As we can see, almost all the approaches give a good source position recovery for the initial model. This is not true for each realization. That is why we apply different summation techniques over statistically equivalent models to compare them and choose a better result. The results of comparison are presented in Fig. 6.

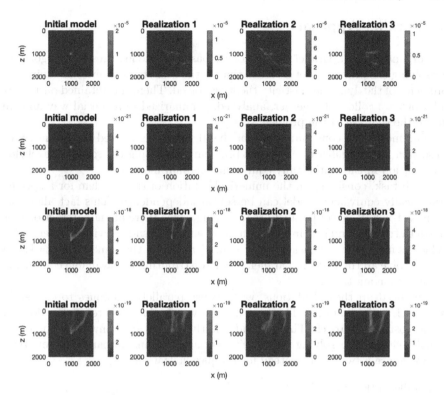

Fig. 5. Wavefield images of the source recovery obtained by the TRM method for the initial model and three different realizations: 1 line - stress components, 2 line - elastic energy, 3 line - time summed elastic energy, 4 line - Peak-to-Average Power Ratio (PAPR).

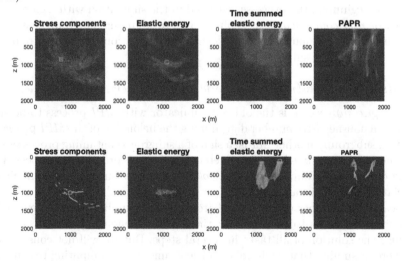

Fig. 6. Seismic source recovery results. The first line is the summation over realizations for different components, the second line is the semblance applied to the same components as above.

5   Parallel Approach

The organization of parallel calculations is based on the features of an algorithm for solving the problem. Let us recall that at the first stage, a series of equivalent problems of the dynamic elasticity theory is solved. Then, the obtained particular solutions are collected together, analyzed, summarized in a special way and we define the solution of the problem.

The most time-consuming part of the algorithm is related to the necessity to solve a large number of numerical problems describing the seismic wavefields propagation in the statistically equivalent medium models.

Each task, consisting in the numerical solution of the problem for a specific statistically equivalent model can be solved independently. This fact allows us to make the best use of parallel programming, since there are no interactions for the data transfer and synchronization between the threads servicing other tasks. Which is more, the dimension of the numerical grid is the same for all tasks, so we can solve all the tasks in parallel, evenly distributing the available computing resources among them.

To speed up the calculations, we also use parallel techniques to efficiently solve each individual task. The most natural way to do this is to use the domain decomposition approach. This method is fairly general and convenient computational technique for solving partial differential equations on parallel computers.

So we use a two-level strategy for the parallelization:

- parallelization by tasks;
- parallelization to solve an individual task.

Figure 7 shows a general scheme of the *MPI* processes interaction within the designed parallel algorithm. Let us schematically describe it.

In the beginning, the processes engaged in the simulation with a global communicator *mpi_comm_world* are split to non-overlapping subgroups associated with their local communicator and local communication domain. Grouping is done using the *MPI* subroutine

$$MPI\_Comm\_split(mpi\_comm\_world, color, key, new\_comm\_color, ierr)$$

where *mpi_comm_world* is the old communicator with *MPI* process to be split; *colour* is a non-negative number determining the belonging of the *MPI* process to a certain subgroup, in other words, a sign of a subgroup containing processes only with the color value; *key* is the parameter that controls ordering the process rank in the created subgroup; *new_comm_color* is the new subgroup communicator associated with color value.

Ideally, the number of created subgroups (color number) should be equal to the number of tasks to be solved. If there are not enough processes, one can organize the solution of all tasks in several steps. But we will not consider this case here, assuming that we have a sufficient amount of computing resources.

The next step of our algorithm is to create a local topology in each subgroup that is convenient for applying the domain decomposition approach to solve the dynamic elasticity TRM problem (task) in parallel. This is a very important step in the parallel implementation, because, in fact, the total solution time is equal to the calculation time of one task at Step two. Indeed, if we distribute the solution of a set of tasks into groups of processes (each group calculates one task), then this step of parallelization gives a linear acceleration of the algorithm. Further, the solution of each task in each group is carried out at the same time, since these tasks are of the same type. Therefore, the total time is just the time to solve one task. Processing and imaging at the third stage takes a negligible time and does not affect the efficiency of the parallel algorithm.

To speed up the solution of the task, we have chosen the domain decomposition method in the two directions (vertical and horizontal) to split the computational region by processes (Fig. 8). The computational domain is divided into several subdomains with overlap at one point using the *MPI_Cart_create* subroutine. This function assigns each subdomain to an individual process according to the Cartesian topology presented in Fig. 8. Each process usually handles one subdomain in the partition and calculates the partial solution using the boundary values obtained from the neighbour processes. To solve the problem by the finite difference scheme on staggered grids, it is necessary to perform the data exchange at each computational time step. This raises the problem of optimizing the data exchange between processes to minimize time losses caused by slow data exchange operations. Instead of using the *MPI_send* and *MPI_recv* point-to-point routines for data exchange, we took advantage of the new opportunities of the Coarray Fortran approach [24]. In our previous research [25], we have compared in detail various data exchanges between processes including the Coarray Fortran technique and have revealed the advantages of the delayed non-blocking *MPI_Isend, MPI_Irecv* and the Coarray Fortran routines for the data exchange in domain decomposition technique when the problem size (the number of elements) increases. The comparison of the computational time and acceleration coefficient by applying different communication approaches among processes can be found in [25].

Testing and analysis of the parallel algorithm were carried out on the computers of the Siberian Branch of the Russian Academy of Sciences of Siberian Supercomputer Center NKS-1P, at the Broadwell nodes [26].

To analyse the performance of our algorithm, we have ran a series of tests for medium model described in Sect. 4. Figure (9) shows the "Event Timeline" trace section (0.025 s) from Intel® Trace Analyzer and Collector for 20 processes on 1 node. Processes are divided into 5 groups of 4 processes. Each group uses the 2 × 2 domain decomposition to solve a separate TRM problem. We can observe the same distribution of the computational load on the MPI processes within each group and the lack of interaction between the groups.

Figure (10) shows the strong and weak scaling behavior when we increase the number of groups, keeping the number of processes in each group constant. The solid line shows the ideal speedup and efficiency, while the dotted line shows the

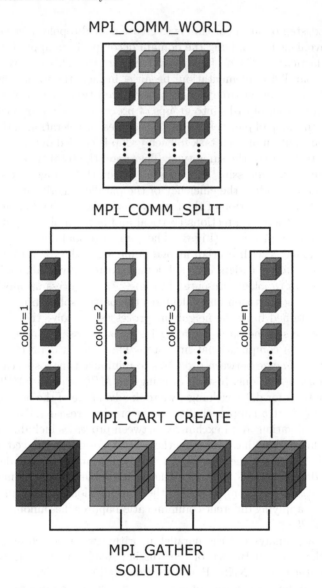

Fig. 7. The two-level strategy for the parallelization algorithm.

measured speedup and efficiency. This figure shows the good performance of the parallel program. This is not surprising, since the structure of the algorithm is ideal for very efficient parallelization, which is confirmed by numerical tests.

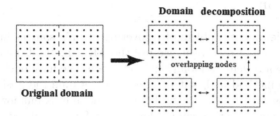

Fig. 8. An example of the Cartesian two-dimensional domain decomposition scheme between among four processes. Red dots indicate one layer of overlapping elements participating in inter-processes boundary conditions. (Color figure online)

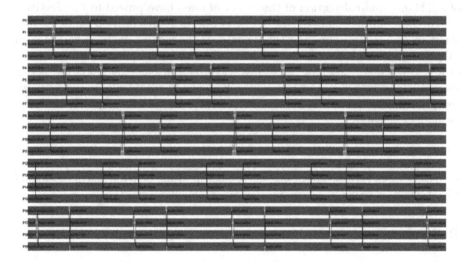

Fig. 9. The "Event Timeline" trace section (0.025 s) from Intel® Trace Analyzer and Collector for 20 processes on 1 node. Red - the MPI functions, blue - program operations, black lines show the MPI communications.

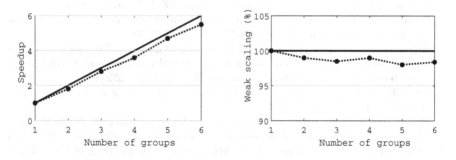

Fig. 10. Strong scaling speedup and weak scaling efficiency. Solid line - ideal speedup and efficiency, dotted line - measured speedup and efficiency.

6   Conclusion

The paper considers the problem of recovering seismic sources inside randomly heterogeneous media. To solve it, we use the TRM method applied to a series of statistically equivalent randomly heterogeneous media models. Unlike other approaches, the method makes it possible to determine the position of sources under conditions when the exact model of the medium is unknown.

In the course of numerical simulation, it was found that the method of calculating the elastic energy is the most effective way to filter local extrema. To search for sources using the summed elastic wave energy and the PAPR method, additional techniques must be applied. To restore the position of the source from a series of realizations for the stress and energy components, the methods of semblance and calculation of the center of mass have proved to be effective.

To speed up calculations, we use a two-level parallelization strategy, creating subgroups and applying the domain decomposition method within each subgroup. Although the method under study is quite laborious, since it is necessary to calculate tasks for many statistical realizations (the more, the better the result), nevertheless, this technique allows one to effectively use the available computing resources and achieve a linear acceleration of the algorithm relative to model realizations.

Acknowledgements. This work was financially supported by the Russian Science Foundation, grant No. 22-21-00759, https://rscf.ru/en/project/22-21-00759/.

The research is carried out using the equipment of the shared research facilities of HPC computing resources at the Siberian Supercomputer Center [26].

References

1. Yoshimura, Ch., Bielak, J., et al.: Domain reduction method for three-dimensional earthquake modeling in localized regions, Part II: verification and applications. Bull. seism. Soc. Am. **93**, 825–840 (2003)
2. Moczo, P., Kristek, J., et al.: 3-D finitedifference, finite-element, discontinuous-Galerkin and spectral-element schemes analysed for their accuracy with respect to P-wave to S-wave speed ratio. Geophys. J. Int. **187**, 1645–1667 (2011)
3. Fornberg, B.: The pseudospectral method: accurate representation of interfaces in elastic wave calculations. Geophysics **53**(5), 625–637 (1988)
4. Takenaka, H., Wang, Y., Furumura, T.: An efficient approach of the pseudospectral method for modelling of geometrically symmetric seismic wavefield. Earth Planets Space **51**(2), 73–79 (1999). https://doi.org/10.1186/BF03352212
5. Chaljub, E., Komatitsch, D., et al.: Spectral element analysis in seismology. Geophysics **50**(4), 705–708 (2007)
6. Moczo, P., Kristek, J., et al.: 3D fourth-order staggered-grid finite-difference schemes: stability and grid dispersion. Bull. seism. Soc. Am. **90**(3), 587–603 (2000)
7. Virieux, J.: P-SV wave propagation in heterogeneous media: Velocity-stress finite-difference method. Geophysics **51**(1), 889–901 (1986)
8. Levander, A.R.: Fourth-order finite-difference P-W seismograms. Geophysics **53**(11), 1425–1436 (1988)

9. Tessmer, E.: Seismic finite-difference modeling with spatially varying time steps. Geophysics **65**(4), 1290–1293 (2000)

10. Moczo, P., Kristek, J., Vavrycuk, V., Archuleta, R.J., Halada, L.: 3D heterogeneous staggered-grid finite-difference modeling of seismic motion with volume harmonic and arithmetic averaging of elastic moduli and densities. Bull. seism. Soc. Am. **92**(8), 3042–3066 (2002)

11. Dumbser, M., Kaser, M., De La Puente, J.: Arbitrary high-order finite volume schemes for seismic wave propagation on unstructured meshes in 2D and 3D. Geophys. J. Int. **171**(2), 665–694 (2007)

12. Peter, D., et al.: Forward and adjoint simulations of seismic wave propagation on fully unstructured hexahedral meshes. Geophys. J. Int. **186**(2), 721–739 (2011)

13. Nissen-Meyer, T., Fournier, A., Dahlen, F.A.: A two-dimensional spectral-element method for computing spherical-earth seismograms: I. Moment-tensor source. Geophys. J. Int. **168**(3), 1067–1092 (2007)

14. Robertsson, J.O.A., Chapman, C.H.: An efficient method for calculating finite-difference seismograms after model alterations. Geophysics **65**(3), 907–918 (2000)

15. Fink, M.: Time reversal in acoustics. Contemp. Phys. **37**(2), 95–109 (1996)

16. Fink, M.: Time reversed acoustics. Phys. Today **50**(3), 34–40 (1997)

17. Fink, M., Montaldo, G., Tanter, M.: Time reversal acoustics in biomedical engineering. Annu. Rev. Biomed. Eng. **5**, 465–497 (2003)

18. Graves, R.W.: Simulating seismic wave propagation in 3D elastic media using staggered-grid finite differences. Bull. Seismol. Soc. Am. **86**(4), 1091–1106 (1996). https://doi.org/10.1785/BSSA0860041091

19. Collino, F., Tsogka, C.: Application of the PML absorbing layer model to the linear elastodynamic problem in anisotropic heterogeneous media. Geophysics **66**(1), 294–307 (2001)

20. Sato, H., Fehler, M., Maeda, T.: Seismic Wave Propagation and Scattering in the Heterogeneous Earth, 2nd edn. Springer, Heidelberg (2012)

21. Aki, K., Chouet, B.: Origin of coda waves: source, attenuation, and scattering effects. J. Geophys. Res. **80**(23), 3322–3342 (1975)

22. Sabelfeld, K., Kurbanmuradov, O.: Two-particle stochastic eulerian-lagrangian models of turbulent dispersion. Environ. Sci. Phys. (1998)

23. Reshetova, G.V., Anchugov, A.V.: Digital core: time reversal modeling of acoustic emission events. Russ. Geol. Geophys. **62**(4), 486–494 (2021). https://doi.org/10.2113/RGG20194152

24. TS18508: Additional Parallel Features in Fortran [Electronic resource], ISO/IEC JTC1/SC22/WG5 N 2074 (2015)

25. Reshetova, G., Cheverda, V., Koinov, V.: Comparative efficiency analysis of mpi blocking and non-blocking communications with coarray fortran. In: Voevodin, V., Sobolev, S. (eds.) RuSCDays 2021. CCIS, vol. 1510, pp. 322–336. Springer, Cham (2021). https://doi.org/10.1007/978-3-030-92864-3_25

26. Novosibirsk Supercomputer Center of SB RAS. https://www.sscc.icmmg.nsc.ru

Performance Analysis of GPU-Based Code for Complex Plasma Simulation

Daniil Kolotinskii[1,2(✉)] and Alexei Timofeev[2,1,3]

[1] Moscow Institute of Physics and Technology, Dolgoprudnyi, Moscow 141701, Russia
kolotinskiy.da@phystech.edu, timofeev@jiht.ru
[2] Joint Institute for High Temperatures, Russian Academy of Sciences,
Moscow 125412, Russia
[3] HSE University,
Moscow 101000, Russia

Abstract. According to the TOP-500 supercomputer ranking [27], since 2017, the share of supercomputers which have NVIDIA V100 and A100 graphics accelerators has been continuously growing, reaching 80% by November 2021 from the total number of supercomputers with accelerators and co-processors. This paper presents the results of an assessment of energy and economic efficiency, as well as the performance study of using V100 and A100 graphics accelerators in the framework of complex plasma physics. In addition, the use of several accelerators for one calculation is considered. In order to quantify the effectiveness of the considered devices, we use the following metrics: calculation time, resource efficiency, economical efficiency, power efficiency.

Keywords: Parallel computing · HPC · GPU · Complex plasma physics

1 Introduction

Numerical modeling of complex plasmas [1–11] is an important area of computational physics and has extensive practical applications. The problem of numerical simulation of complex plasmas arises in applications related to extreme ultraviolet lithography [12], thin film deposition [13], production of materials for the space industry [14], and dusty plasma physics [15–17]. One of the most recently developed approaches for modeling complex plasmas is the method of asymmetric molecular dynamics proposed in [18]. The method of asymmetric molecular dynamics is implemented in such packages as Mad [18], DRIAD [19]. One of the advantages of this approach is the possibility of porting calculations from central processors to graphic accelerators, which makes it possible to significantly speed up the solution of actual problems of complex plasma physics.

The use of graphic processors are showed to be more efficient than the use of distributed systems based on central processors, not only within the framework of complex plasma tasks. In addition, graphics accelerators are successfully used to

V. Voevodin et al. (Eds.): RuSCDays 2022, LNCS 13708, pp. 276–289, 2022.
https://doi.org/10.1007/978-3-031-22941-1_20

accelerate calculations by the method of molecular dynamics [20–24], quantum calculations [25] and modeling of continuous media [26]. An important factor influencing the choice of computing resources for calculations in a particular problem of computational physics is their availability. Therefore, speaking of graphics accelerators, it is useful to look at the trend in the development of supercomputers and see what types of graphics accelerators have been used in the world top supercomputers in recent years. According to the TOP-500 supercomputer ranking [27], since 2017, share of supercomputers which have NVIDIA V100 and A100 graphics accelerators has been continuously growing, reaching 80% by November 2021 from the total number of supercomputers with accelerators and co-processors, see Fig. 1. In connection with such an increase in the use of this type of graphics accelerators, the question arises of how effective their application is in computational physics problems, in particular, the problem of complex plasma modeling.

In this paper, we present a study of the efficiency of using NVIDIA V100 and NVIDIA A100 graphics accelerators on a test problem arising in complex plasmas physics: simulation of a collisionless plasma flow around a condensed matter macroparticle. The paper presents the results of an assessment of energy and economic efficiency, as well as the performance study of using V100 and A100 graphics accelerators in the framework of the test problem. The results obtained for the V100 and A100 are then compared with the results obtained on the NVIDIA A30 GPU and the Intel Xeon Gold 6152 CPU. In the second section, the test problem for performance analysis is formulated. In the third section, we presents the efficiency and performance results analysis. The conclusion and summary are given in the fourth section.

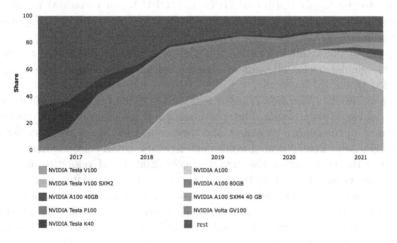

Fig. 1. Development of share of various types of accelerators in the top 500 super-computers [27] over time.

2   Methods

As a test problem for studying the efficiency and performance of the V100 and A100 graphics accelerators, we use the classical problem of complex plasma physics: simulation of a collisionless plasma flow around a solitary macroparticle. For modeling, the method of asymmetric molecular dynamics is used. The exhaustive description of the test task and the asymmetric molecular dynamics method can be find in [18], here we discuss it briefly. Within the framework of the asymmetric molecular dynamics, the motion of discrete particles interacting with each other and with a macroparticle is considered. The trajectories of these discrete particles are used to calculate the time evolution of the spatial distribution of plasma parameters. The Velocity Verlet scheme [28] is used to calculate the trajectories of the discrete particles. The bottleneck of the simulation is the calculation of pair forces between all discrete particles. The pair force between two discrete particle is expressed via the following formula:

$$F_{ij} = \frac{q_i q_j}{4\pi\varepsilon_0} \frac{1 + |r_i - r_j|/r_{D_e}}{|r_i - r_j|^3} \exp\left(-\frac{|r_i - r_j|}{r_{D_e}}\right)(r_j - r_i), \qquad (1)$$

where i, j are the discrete particles' indexes, q_i, q_j are the discrete particles' charges, r_i, r_j are the radius-vectors of discrete particles, ε_0 is the vacuum permittivity.

The complexity of the algorithm for calculating all such pair interactions scales as $O(N^2)$, where N is the number of discrete particles. In typical complex plasma simulations, the number of used discrete particles starts from 2^{15} value [18], which means that interparticle force (1) must be calculated for more than 1 billion pairs every simulation time step. We have developed a Python interface to the highly optimized GPU- and CPU-based OpenMM library [20] to accelerate such resource-intensive simulations. The written interface performs only auxiliary calculations, while the main computational load falls on the internal OpenMM algorithms. That means the most resource-intensive routine of force (1) calculation for all pairs are conducted and parallelized by the highly-optimized OpenMM backend.

Now we describe the data transfer logic in the case of using a graphics accelerator to solve a test problem. The coordinates and velocities of discrete particles are created on the central processor and then copied to the graphics accelerator. Trajectories are calculated on graphics accelerators. Upon completion of the calculation of the trajectories, the arrays of coordinates and velocities of discrete particles are copied back from the GPU to the central one. After that, they are processed and the spatial distribution of plasma parameters is calculated. The illustration of the data transfer and processing is presented in the Fig. 2 Copying arrays from the CPU to the GPU and vice versa, as well as subsequent processing, take much less time than the calculation of trajectories. Therefore, in the further analysis of efficiency and performance, the discrete particles trajectories calculation time is used.

The described data transfer between several GPUs for parallelizing force calculation is illustrated in the Fig. 3.

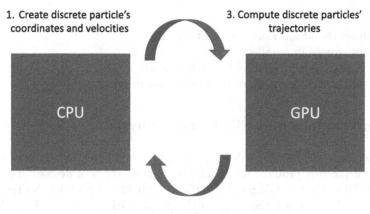

Fig. 2. Illustration of the discrete particles data transfer between GPU and CPU.

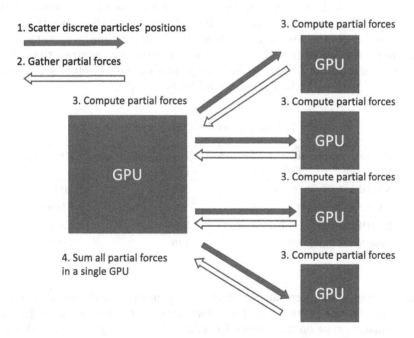

Fig. 3. Illustration of the data transfer between multiple GPUs for parallelizing force calculation.

In addition, the test problem is run on several graphics accelerators located within the same node with shared memory. In this case, at each numerical integration step, the computational load is distributed among the graphics accelerators as follows:

- Broadcast the atom positions to all GPUs;
- Compute forces in parallel;
- Send the forces from each GPU back to a single GPU;
- That single GPU sums all of them and does integration;

3 Performance and Efficiency Analysis

In this section, we present results of performance and efficiency study of various devices for the test problem described above. Four types of devices are considered: NVIDIA A100 80 GB SXM, NVIDIA V100 32 GB NVLink, NVIDIA A30 (Ampere), 22-core Intel Xeon Gold 6152 2.1–3.7 GHz processor. For NVIDIA A100, we also present the dependence of test problem acceleration on the number of used graphics accelerators. Characteristics of the listed devices are presented in the Table 1. All calculations are performed with the single precision.

Four test problem sizes are utilized for analysis: 2^{15}, 2^{16}, 2^{17}, 2^{18}. The size of the problem is determined by the number of discrete particles used in the calculation. Since the time for copying data from the graphics accelerator to the central processor and vice versa, as well as the time for calculating the spatial distribution of plasma parameters, is much less than the time for calculating the trajectories of discrete particles, it is assumed during the analysis that all the measured computational time is spent on calculating the trajectories. Estimated time is measured using the Python time library.

Table 1. Characteristics of the tested devices.

Device	Peak performance (TFLOPS)	Energy consumption (Watt)	Price ($)
NVIDIA A30	10.32	165	5000
NVIDIA A100	19.5	400	31000
NVIDIA V100	15.7	300	13000
Intel Xeon Gold	10	140	3600

In the Fig. 4, the dependence of the test problem calculation time on the amount of discrete particles is shown for all the devices under consideration. The calculation time on the 22-core Intel Xeon Gold 6152 processor is about an order of magnitude longer than the calculation time on any of the used graphics accelerators. The calculation time on NVIDIA Tesla A100 is about twice time faster than on NVIDIA A30, and about 20% faster than on NVIDIA V100. The

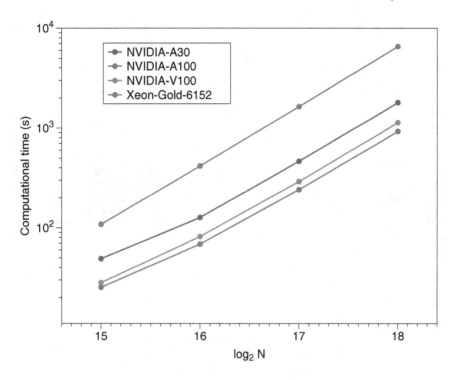

Fig. 4. Dependence of the calculation time on number of discrete particles for different devices. Measured time is depicted with points, lines serve as an eye-guide.

horizontal axis of the graph shows the base 2 logarithm of the number of used discrete particles. The vertical axis, which has a logarithmic scale, shows the calculation time in seconds. For all devices, the time grows quadratically from the number of discrete particles, which is explained by the fact that the most of the calculation time is spent on computation of all pairwise interactions in the simulated system.

In the Fig. 5, the dependence of the resource efficiency on the number of discrete particles is presented for all the devices we study. Resource efficiency is calculated as the ratio of the relative number of operations per second to

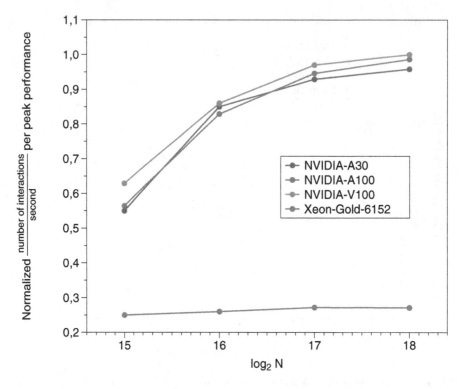

Fig. 5. Resource efficiency for different devices. Calculated efficiency is depicted with points, lines serve as an eye-guide.

the values of device peak performance and then normalized on the value of calculation with best efficiency. The relative number of operations per second is calculated as the square of the number of discrete particles divided by the total calculation time. As far as the main computational time is spent on calculating pair interactions according to the formula 1, the relative number of operations is proportional with good accuracy to the total number of float operations. The peak performance values are taken from the websites of device manufacturers, see Table 1. All three graphics accelerators give very close dependencies of resource efficiency on the number of discrete particles, which significantly exceed the data for the central processor. The NVIDIA V100 graphics accelerator demonstrates the highest resource efficiency of the three video cards. A30 is better than A100 for small task sizes, and A100 is better for large ones.

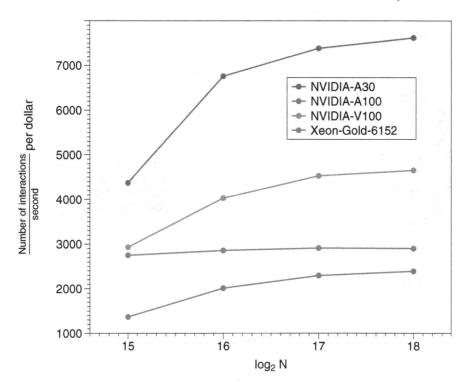

Fig. 6. Economical efficiency of using different devices. Calculated efficiency is depicted with points, lines serve as an eye-guide.

In the Fig. 6, the results of a study of the economic efficiency of using the devices under consideration are shown. The economic efficiency metric is the relative number of operations per second per one US dollar. That metric is calculated as the square of the number of discrete particles divided by the total computation time and the cost of the device used. A30 video card shows the best economical efficiency for the given test problem, almost reaching 8000 relative operations per second per dollar for a number of discrete particles of 2^{18}. Number of operations per dollar reached with V100 is approximately a half of the number of operations per dollar reached with A30. With the number of simulated discrete particles equal to 2^{15}, the CPU shows close results with the V100, however, for larger values of the number of discrete particles, the economic efficiency of using the CPU becomes worse in comparison with the V100. The smallest number of operations per dollar is demonstrated by A100, which, according to this metric, is even lower than for CPU.

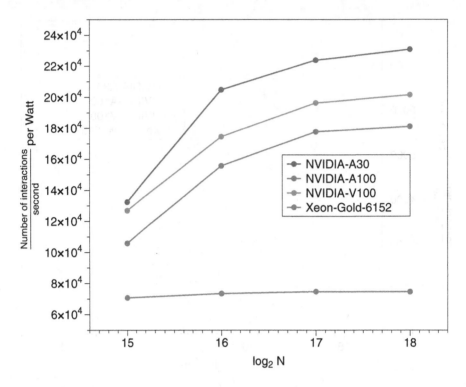

Fig. 7. Power efficiency of using different devices. Calculated efficiency is depicted with points, lines serve as an eye-guide.

Finally, in Fig. 7, a study of the power efficiency of the usage of the considered types of devices for solving a test problem is presented. The ratio of the number of operations per second to the power, consumed by the device, is used as a power efficiency metric. The power consumption of the device is estimated from the reference TDP values specified on the developer's website. The lowest energy efficiency is obtained for the central processor. The highest efficiency is achieved with the A30, followed by the V100, then the A100.

To study the acceleration of the test problem calculation with an increase in the number of used graphics accelerators, we measure the simulation time for a different number of graphics accelerators for two values of the number of discrete particles. In the Fig. 8, the dependence of the acceleration on the number of used graphics accelerators is shown. The acceleration is defined as the ratio of the calculation time on a given number of graphics accelerators to the calculation time on a single graphics accelerator. The speedup for $N = 2^{15}$ peaks when using six GPUs and reaches the maximum value 2.5. The acceleration for $N = 2^{17}$ does not reach the local maximum for the considered number of graphic accelerators. The largest value of acceleration for the number of discrete particles 2^{17} is 5.5.

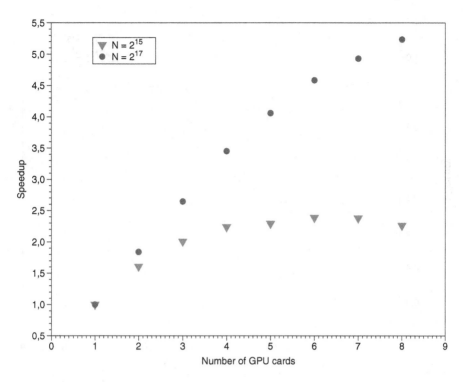

Fig. 8. The dependence of speedup on the number of used GPU cards. Green triangles and red circles denote simulations with 2^{15} and 2^{17} ions correspondingly. (Color figure online)

In the Fig. 9, dependency of efficiency on the number of used graphic accelerators is shown. Efficiency of usage of graphic processors is higher for the number of discrete particles $N = 2^{17}$.

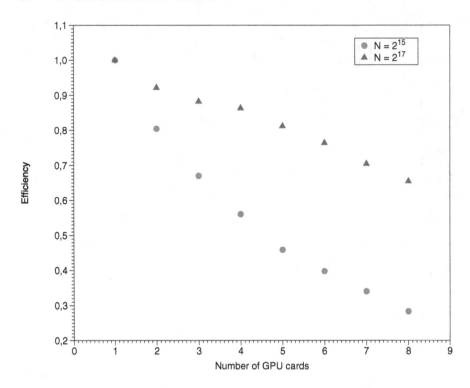

Fig. 9. The dependence of efficiency on the number of used GPU cards. Green triangles and red circles denote simulations with 2^{15} and 2^{17} ions correspondingly. (Color figure online)

4   Conclusion

In this work, we have studied the efficiency of using NVIDIA A100 and NVIDIA V100 graphics accelerators for solving problems which arise in applications of complex plasma physics. For comparison, we also studied the efficiency of using the A30 graphics accelerator and the Intel Xeon Gold 6152 CPU. As a benchmarking task, we used a test problem, which is common in complex plasma physics: modeling a plasma flow around a condensed matter macroparticle. To quantify the effectiveness of the selected devices, we used the following metrics: calculation time, the ratio of the number of operations per second to the theoretical values of device performance (resource efficiency), the number of operations per second per one US dollar (economical efficiency), the number of operations per second per consumed Watt (power efficiency).

We have shown that the use of accelerators like NVIDIA A100 and NVIDIA V100 makes it possible to speed up the calculation of the test problem by an order of magnitude compared to the 22-core processor, Intel Xeon Gold 6152, and approximately twice the speed of calculation in comparison with the NVIDIA A30 graphics accelerator. This suggests that NVIDIA A100 and NVIDIA V100 accelerators can be used to significantly accelerate complex plasma tasks. Furthermore, the analysis of the acceleration of the calculation time of the test problem showed that the use of several GPUs within one calculation can further significantly reduce the calculation time. At the same time, the acceleration asymptotics is quite close to the ideal case, giving a 5.5 times acceleration with usage of 8 graphics cards.

In addition, the NVIDIA A100 and NVIDIA V100 accelerators use resources efficiently, outperforming the central processor Intel Xeon Gold 6152 by about one order of magnitude according to the used metric. However, economically, the use of NVIDIA A100 and NVIDIA V100 graphics accelerators for solving such tasks may not be fully justified. The best economic efficiency is achieved when using the A30 graphics accelerator, the V100 performed slightly worse, and the use of the A100 is even less economically effective than the use of the Intel Xeon Gold 6152 central processor. From the point of view of power efficiency to the solution of the test problem, all graphic cards showed themselves better in comparison to the Intel Xeon Gold 6152 central processor and are approximately equal to each other.

Thus, in this work, we have shown that the use of NVIDIA A100 and NVIDIA V100 graphics accelerators, which are now utilized in the most part of the world's leading supercomputers with accelerators of co-processors, both Green500 and TOP500 [27], can be effectively used to solve complex plasma problems. When comparing V100 and A100 in terms of economic and energy efficiency, V100 should be preferred.

Acknowledgments. The study was carried out with a grant from the Russian Science Foundation (project no. 20-71-10127). This research was supported in part through computational resources of HPC facilities at HSE University and at JIHT RAS. The calculations were also performed on the hybrid supercomputer K60 (K100) installed in the Supercomputer Centre of Collective Usage of KIAM RAS.

References

1. Fortov, V.E., Ivlev, A.V., Khrapak, S.A., Khrapak, A.G., Morfill, G.E.: Complex (dusty) plasmas: current status, open issues, perspectives. Phys. Rep. **421**(1–2), 1–103 (2005). https://doi.org/10.1016/j.physrep.2005.08.007
2. Schweigert, V.A., Schweigert, I.V., Melzer, A., Homann, A., Piel, A.: Alignment and instability of dust crystals in plasmas. Phys. Rev. E **54**(4), 4155 (1996)
3. Vladimirov, S.V., Maiorov, S.A., Ishihara, O.: Molecular dynamics simulation of plasma flow around two stationary dust grains. Phys. Plasmas **10**(10), 3867–3873 (2003)
4. Sukhinin, G.I., et al.: Plasma anisotropy around a dust particle placed in an external electric field. Phys. Rev. E **95**(6), 063207 (2017)
5. Kompaneets, R., Morfill, G.E., Ivlev, A.V.: Wakes in complex plasmas: a self-consistent kinetic theory. Phys. Rev. E **93**(6), 063201 (2016)
6. Lisin, E.A., et al.: Experimental study of the nonreciprocal effective interactions between microparticles in an anisotropic plasma. Sci. Rep. **10**(1), 1–12 (2020)

7. Khrapak, S.A., Ivlev, A.V., Morfill, G.E., Thomas, H.M.: Ion drag force in complex plasmas. Phys. Rev. E **66**(4), 046414 (2002)
8. Ignatov, A.M.: Collective ion drag force. Plasma Phys. Rep. **45**(9), 850–854 (2019). https://doi.org/10.1134/S1063780X19090046
9. Klumov, B.A.: On the effect of confinement on the structure of a complex (dusty) plasma. JETP Lett. **110**(11), 715–721 (2019). https://doi.org/10.1134/S0021364019230097
10. Salnikov, M., Fedoseev, A., Sukhinin, G.: Plasma parameters around a chain-like structure of dust particles in an external electric field. Molecules **26**(13), 3846 (2021)
11. Yakovlev, E.V., Ovcharov, P.V., Dukhopelnikov, D.V., Yurchenko, S.O.: Experimental approach for obtaining a complex (dusty) plasma fluid. In: Journal of Physics: Conference Series, vol. 1348(1), p. 012094. IOP Publishing (2019)
12. Nguyen, T.T.N., Sasaki, M., Tsutsumi, T., et al.: Formation of spherical Sn particles by reducing $SnO2$ film in floating wire-assisted $H2/Ar$ plasma at atmospheric pressure. Sci. Rep. **10**, 17770 (2020). https://doi.org/10.1038/s41598-020-74663-z
13. Martinu, L., Poitras, D.: Plasma deposition of optical films and coatings: a review. J. Vacuum Sci. Technol. A Vacuum Surf. Films **18**(6), 2619–2645 (2000). https://doi.org/10.1116/1.1314395
14. Shoyama, M., Yoshioka, H., Matsusaka, S.: Charging and levitation of particles using UV irradiation and electric field. IEEE Trans. Indus. Appl. **58**, 776–782 (2021). https://doi.org/10.1109/TIA.2021.3123930
15. Nikolaev, V.S., Timofeev, A.V.: Nonhomogeneity of phase state in a dusty plasma monolayer with nonreciprocal particle interactions. Phys. Plasmas **28**(3), 033704 (2021). https://doi.org/10.1063/5.0031081
16. Hariprasad, M.G., et al.: Self-sustained non-equilibrium co-existence of fluid and solid states in a strongly coupled complex plasma system. Sci. Rep. **12**(1), 1–12 (2022)
17. Kolotinskii, D.A., Nikolaev, V.S., Timofeev, A.V.: Effect of structural inhomogeneity and nonreciprocal effects in the interaction of macroparticles on the dynamic properties of a dusty plasma monolayer. JETP Lett. **113**, 510–517 (2021). https://doi.org/10.1134/S0021364021080063
18. Piel, A.: Molecular dynamics simulation of ion flows around microparticles. Phys. Plasmas **24**(3), 033712 (2017). https://doi.org/10.1063/1.4978791
19. Matthews, L.S., et al.: Dust charging in dynamic ion wakes. Phys. Plasmas **27**(2), 023703 (2020). https://doi.org/10.1063/1.5124246
20. Eastman, P., et al.: OpenMM 7: rapid development of high performance algorithms for molecular dynamics. PLoS Comput. Biol. **13**(7), e1005659 (2017). https://doi.org/10.1371/journal.pcbi.1005659
21. Kondratyuk, N., Nikolskiy, V., Pavlov, D., Stegailov, V.: GPU-accelerated molecular dynamics: state-of-art software performance and porting from Nvidia CUDA to AMD HIP. Int. J. High Perform. Comput. Appl. **35**(4), 312–324 (2021). https://doi.org/10.1177/10943420211008288
22. Kostenetskiy, P.S., Chulkevich, R.A., Kozyrev, V.I.: HPC resources of the higher school of economics. In: Journal of Physics: Conference Series, vol. 1740(1), P. 012050 (2021). https://doi.org/10.1088/1742-6596/1740/1/012050
23. Stegailov, V., et al.: Early performance evaluation of the hybrid cluster with torus interconnect aimed at molecular-dynamics simulations. In: Wyrzykowski, R., Dongarra, J., Deelman, E., Karczewski, K. (eds.) PPAM 2017. LNCS, vol. 10777, pp. 327–336. Springer, Cham (2018). https://doi.org/10.1007/978-3-319-78024-5_29

24. Stegailov, V., et al.: Angara interconnect makes GPU-based Desmos supercomputer an efficient tool for molecular dynamics calculations. Int. J. High Perform. Comput. Appl. **33**(3), 507–521 (2019). https://doi.org/10.1177/1094342019826667
25. Wiśniewska, J., Sawerwain, M.: GPU: accelerated computation routines for quantum trajectories method. In: Kindratenko, V. (ed.) Numerical Computations with GPUs, pp. 299–318. Springer, Cham (2014). https://doi.org/10.1007/978-3-319-06548-9_14
26. Habich, J., Zeiser, T., Hager, G., Wellein, G.: Performance analysis and optimization strategies for a D3Q19 lattice Boltzmann kernel on NVIDIA GPUs using CUDA. Adv. Eng. Softw. **42**(5), 266–272 (2011). https://doi.org/10.1016/j.advengsoft.2010.10.007
27. Dongarra J., Luszczek P.: TOP500. In: Padua D. (eds.) Encyclopedia of Parallel Computing. Springer, Boston (2011). https://doi.org/10.1007/978-0-387-09766-4_157
28. Scott, R.: Computer simulation of liquids (1991)

PIConGPU on Desmos Supercomputer: GPU Acceleration, Scalability and Storage Bottleneck

Leonid Pugachev[1,2], Iskander Umarov[1,2], Vyacheslav Popov[1],
Nikolay Andreev[1,2], Vladimir Stegailov[1,2,3], and Alexei Timofeev[1,2,3(✉)]

[1] Joint Institute for High Temperatures of RAS, Moscow, Russia
pugachev@ihed.ras.ru, andreev@ras.ru, timofeev@jiht.ru
[2] Moscow Institute of Physics and Technology, Dolgoprudny, Russia
[3] HSE University, Moscow, Russia

Abstract. Particle-in-Cell models are among the most demanding computational problems that require appropriate supercomputing hardware. In this paper we consider the solution of generic PIC problems on the Desmos supercomputer equipped with novel AMD MI50 GPUs and Angara interconnect. The open-source PIConGPU code is used. The acceleration limits and bottlenecks for this type of calculations are considered.

Keywords: PIC · GPU computing · Benchmarking · Scalability · Storage · PIConGPU

1 Introduction

The particle-in-cell (PIC) algorithm [1,2] is one of the most widely used algorithms in computational plasma physics. In the PIC method, individual particles or fluid elements in a Lagrangian frame of reference are tracked in continuous phase space, and density and flux are computed at Euler grid points.

The range of application of the PIC method is very wide and includes the following areas: calculation of the dynamics of charged particles in self-consistent electromagnetic fields, laser-plasma interactions, electron acceleration and heating of ions in the ionosphere under the influence of auroras, magnetohydrodynamics, magnetic reconnection, as well as ion-temperature-gradient and other microinstabilities in tokamaks, vacuum discharges, dusty plasmas and even some problems of solid state mechanics and liquids [3,4].

The application of the method for a wide range of scientific problems contributed to its implementation on a computer. At the same time a paradigm shift in high-performance computing was occurred: a sharp increase in the number of cores and an increased emphasis on massive parallelism. Current and future supercomputer architectures are hybrid systems using both distributed and shared memory. These features of memory make it harder to manage workloads, schedule resources, and create an efficient computational code. It is quite

V. Voevodin et al. (Eds.): RuSCDays 2022, LNCS 13708, pp. 290–302, 2022.
https://doi.org/10.1007/978-3-031-22941-1_21

understandable that the development of software lags behind the development of computer technology. Particle-in-cell codes produced by the plasma science community also have difficulty meeting these challenges. A significant part of these problems can be solved in close cooperation between physicists and specialists in high-performance computing. Physicists and programmers are trying to make code more efficient in terms of both computing resources and energy. There are several popular and fairly high-performance codes for particle-in-cell simulation and tools for their acceleration, such as Alpaka [5], EPOCH [6], LSP [7], oneAPI [8,9], OSIRIS [10], SMILEI [11], iPIC3D [12], VPIC [13], Warp [14], which can be used on high-performance central processing units (CPU). With the advent of graphics processing units (GPUs) good enough for high-performance computing, large-scale plasma simulations on GPU computing clusters have become possible. The PIConGPU [15] and PICADOR [16] simulation codes were among the first scalable implementations of the PIC algorithm in plasma physics on GPU. The work of the former software package on graphics accelerators from NVIDIA [17] was extensively studied. In recent years, there has been a trend towards a market transition to AMD graphics accelerators.

In this paper, we consider the efficiency of code operation on the Desmos supercomputer [18,19] with 32 nodes with graphics accelerators from AMD and a high-speed Angara interconnect [20]. The scalability of PIConGPU is considered using a relatively small test problem SPEC and a larger Laser wakefield acceleration (LWFA) problem. Very good scalability for this test shown in this study can serve as a guidance for developing new GPU-based supercomputers with Angara interconnect. The revealed limitations caused by the storage subsystem is another critical aspect that needs to be carefully addressed in new supercomputers oriented on calculations with PIConGPU.

2   PIConGPU

PIConGPU simulation code [15,21] uses Particle-in-Cell (PIC) algorithm at its core. In this algorithm average particle motion is represented by the dynamics of macroparticles with charges q and masses m. Fields $\vec{E}, \vec{B}$ and current $\vec{J}$ are described by a mesh – grid decomposition of simulated plasma volume. In the most basic form, a simulation of relativistic plasma dynamics using the PIC algorithm can be represented as the following four consecutive steps that are computed at each time step for all particles in each cell on the mesh (Fig. 1):

1. Starting with a given distribution of the electric field $\vec{E}$ and magnetic field $\vec{B}$, those fields are interpolated from the grid cells onto the particle position $\vec{r}$, and the Lorentz force $\vec{F}_{Lorentz}$ is calculated.
2. The Lorentz force is used to integrate the equation of motion $m\ddot{\vec{r}} = \vec{F}_{Lorentz}$, changing the velocity $\vec{v}$ and the position $\vec{r}$ for all macroparticles. This step is usually called the particle pusher.

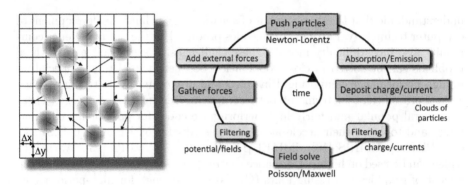

Fig. 1. Schematic illustration of grid decomposition in particle-in-cell (PIC) method (left). The PIC method follows the evolution of a collection of charged macroparticles (blue and red for positive and negative charged particles respectively) that evolve self-consistently with their electromagnetic fields. Schematic illustration of time step cycle (right). Yellow color boxes represent four main stages of time step, while the blue ones represent additional operations, which can account for additional physics. (Figures from [22] (Color figure online))

3. The new positions and momenta of the macroparticles are used to calculate the value of current $\vec{J}$ at the grid cells.
4. Using the principle of superposition of fields, the change in field strength for both $\vec{B}$ and $\vec{E}$ is calculated from the local current and neighbor cells following Maxwell's equations.

The Lorentz force is given by

$$\vec{F}_{Lorentz} = q(\vec{E} + \frac{\vec{v}}{c} \times \vec{B})$$

and the Maxwell equations are given by

$$\nabla \cdot \vec{E} = 4\pi\rho,$$
$$\nabla \cdot \vec{B} = 0,$$
$$\partial\vec{B}/\partial t = -c(\nabla \times \vec{E}),$$
$$\partial\vec{E}/\partial t = c(\nabla \times \vec{B}) - 4\pi\vec{J}.$$

For relativistic plasma simulation usually only the last two equations are used during time steps, while the first two can be used at the field initialization stage at the beginning of the simulation.

As was mentioned earlier, for the particle push stage and for the field evolution stage the local integration of the equations requires information on the local fields and currents only from the nearest neighbor cells or next to the nearest neighbor cells. Since all operations are local on a mesh this enables natural distribution of computation onto different computing units (CPU or GPU) with domain decomposition into several subdomains, each of them is local to the corresponding computing unit, with good scalability. In this case additional data transfer between subdomains during each step is required: transfer of field information in boundary cells (Fig. 2) and transfer of particles that are crossing boundary. While time associated with data transfer overhead is negligible compared with computation time, it is possible to achieve almost linear scalability of computation speed.

PIConGPU uses Alpaka library that provides performance portability across different types of accelerators through the abstraction of the underlying levels of parallelism. The first variant of the HIP backend of Alpaka was released in version 0.4.0 (January 2020) that opened possibility to run PIConGPU on AMD GPUs.

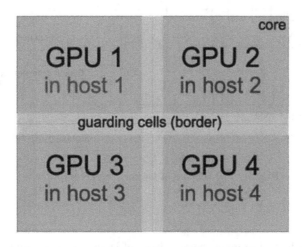

Fig. 2. Simulation domain is decomposed into subdomains. Each GPU device manages its own subdomain. Each subdomain is composed of (blue) a core and (gray) a border. The border consists of guarding cells that are mirrored on all neighbor GPUs. (Figure from [21] (Color figure online))

3 Hardware

The hybrid supercomputer Desmos in JIHT RAS was the first supercomputer based on the Angara network with the in-depth analysis of performance for various applications [18–20]. The MPI communication over the Angara network was reviewed for the systems with torus topology, Desmos including [24,25]. In September 2018, Desmos (equipped with AMD FirePro S9150 GPUs) was ranked as No.45 in the Top50 list of supercomputers of Russian Federation (the

open-source HPL-GPU benchmark based on OpenCL [26] was used for running
LINPACK). The upgraded Desmos with AMD MI50 GPUs is No. 46 in the
current Top50 list (March 2022).

The main details of the current configuration of Desmos supercomputer used
in this work are given in Table 1 and illustrated in Fig. 3.

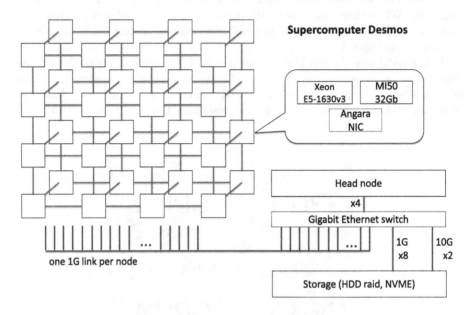

Fig. 3. The scheme of Desmos supercomputer.

Table 1. The main characteristics of Desmos supercomputer.

Compute nodes	Host[1-32]
Chassis	Supermicro 1018GR-T
Processor/Memory	Xeon E5-1650v3 6c/32 GB
GPU/ROCm	AMD MI50 32 GB/version 5.0
Interconnect	Angara 4D-Torus
OS	SUSE Linux Enterprise Server 15 SP1
Kernel version	4.12.14-195-default
MPI	MPICH 3.3 for Angara

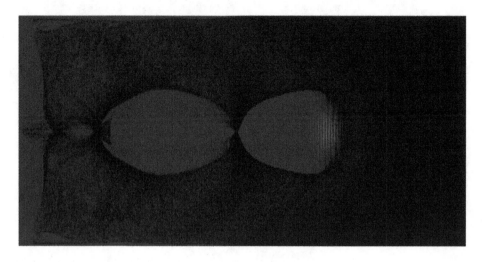

Fig. 4. The illustration of the laser wake field acceleration model.

4   Models

SPEC and LWFA tasks provided in the PIConGPU repository were used as benchmarks.

SPEC task. Electron and positron species are presented in the simulation. Both particle species have a drift velocity along the z axis with gamma factor equal 5. Electrons move in the positive direction and positrons move in the opposite direction. The electron specie has 1, 2 and 4 particles per cell in x, y and z directions, correspondingly. In contrast, the positron specie has 4, 1 and 2 particles per cell along x, y and z. Totally, both species have 8 particles per cell. Density of each specie equals 10^{25} m^{-3} and has a homogeneous profile. Time step is 30 as. Cell size is 18 nm along all directions. The computation grid has 256 cells in each direction. The simulation lasts for 150 time steps. Such a task allows for a large number of particle exchanges between computational subdomains while particles of different species move toward each other and mix. Calculations are done with single precision.

LWFA task. Pre-ionized plasma is considered. An electron specie is presented in the simulation. Electrons field is compensated by fixed neutralizing background field at the initial moment since the movement of ions is irrelevant on time scales considered in the task. The density equals 10^{25} m^{-3}. Gaussian laser pulse enters the simulation domain, propagates along the y axis and generates a wakefield in the blowout regime. The dimensionless laser amplitude equals 8. The laser wavelength is 0.8 μm and the duration is 5 ps. Time step is 0.139 ps. Cell sizes are 0.1772 μm along x and z directions and 0.0443 μm along the y direction. The grid sizes are 320, 3072 and 320 along corresponding axes. Such a grid allows for a simulation of close to realistic laser-plasma settings. The sim-

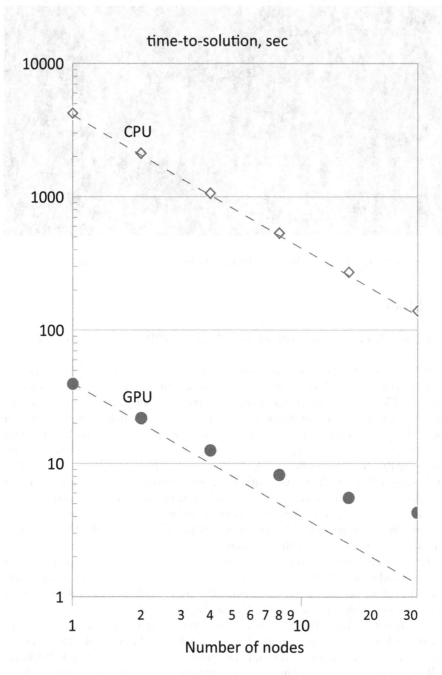

Fig. 5. Strong scaling of PIConGPU for the SPEC model ($256 \times 256 \times 256$ grid, 150 steps): diamonds show the results of CPU runs, circles show the results of GPU runs.

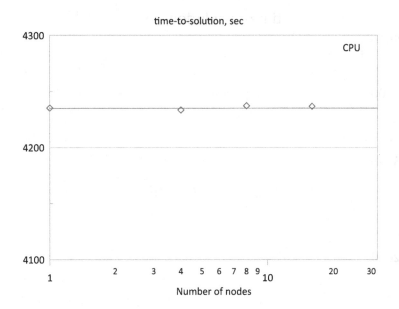

Fig. 6. Weak scaling of CPU runs of PIConGPU for the SPEC model ($256 \times 256 \times 256$ grid for 1 node, 150 steps).

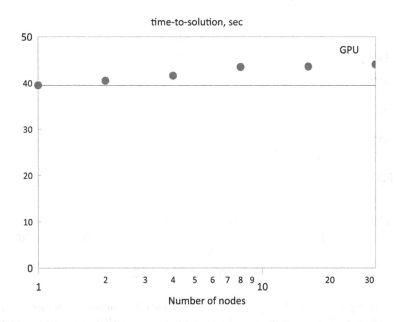

Fig. 7. Weak scaling of GPU runs of PIConGPU for the SPEC model ($256 \times 256 \times 256$ grid for 1 node, 150 steps).

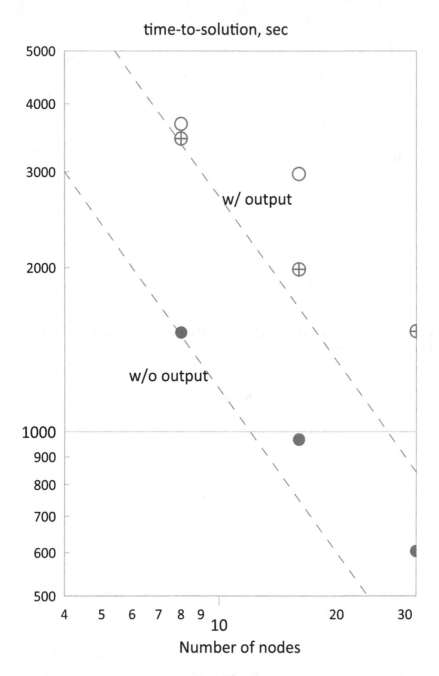

Fig. 8. Strong scaling of PIConGPU for the laser wake field acceleration model (320 × 3072 × 320 grid, 2 particles per cell, 10000 steps, output each 250 steps): filled circles show the results of GPU runs without data output. The effect of storage is shown by open circles (for HDD storage) and crossed circles (for NVME storage).

ulation lasts for 10000 steps. Particle and field data are dumped each 250 steps. Calculations are done with single precision.

5 Discussion

Figure 5 shows strong scaling of a relatively small benchmark SPEC problem. CPU runs have been performed with OpenMP backend of PIConGPU (with 6 threads per CPU). GPU runs have been performed with the HIP backend with 1 MPI rank per node (per GPU). Angara interconnect provides nearly ideal scaling for CPU time-to-solution. Non-ideal GPU time-to-solution should be therefore attributed to lower saturation of GPU compute units at higher numbers of nodes. Some other factors can also affect scalability.

The code has been optimized for the use of NVIDIA GPUs for a long time. The ability to run simulations on AMD GPUs is a recent addition. Therefore, the deviation from the optimum scaling may be due to the use of AMD GPUs, and additional steps may need to be taken to optimize the code for this architecture. Our work is one of the first to demonstrate the results of PIConGPU scaling on AMD GPUs.

The number of exchanges also affects scaling. The authors of the code in [1] found that during the transition from the initial ordered state to a completely disordered state, the time step increases from 17 s to 30.7 s during simulation. From the description of the models in this work, one can assume that in the SPEC problem the average number of exchanges will be greater than in the LWFA problem, since in the SPEC problem the entire volume of particles moves initially, and in the LWFA the particles start moving when a laser pulse reaches them. This may be the reason for the better strong scaling for the LWFA task compared to the SPEC observed in Figs. 5 and 8. SPEC runs 8.2 s on 8 nodes and 5.5 s on 16 nodes, and LWFA - 1520 s on 8 and 967 s on 16.

Figures 6 and 7 show the results of weak scaling benchmarks based on the SPEC problem for OpenMP and HIP backends. The weak scaling of the GPU-accelerated runs shows no signs of performance degradation up to 32 nodes.

LWFA model ($320 \times 3072 \times 320$ grid, 2 particles per cell) is a larger and a more real-life model (see Fig. 4). Figure 8 illustrate the strong scaling for this model (10000 steps).

Using this LWFA model we have considered the delays for storing the calculation data during the runs. Data output is performed each 250 steps (this generates about 1 TB of data). The OpenPMD schema is used for parallel data storage. Initially, the Desmos storage server has been used with 8 Gig/E links. At this time Angara interconnect can not be used for data output that is why storage operation proceeds via gigabit ethernet. Open circles on Fig. 8 show that this type of storage mechanism can not give reasonable performance.

The next benchmarks have been made with the PCIe NVME disk installed in the storage server, two 10G links have been used to connect the gigabit switch with the storage server. This type of data output scales better with the number of nodes (see the crossed circles in Fig. 8).

6 Related Work

Simulations of future particle accelerators have been considered [27] as an important scientific and technological challenge that requires massively parallel supercomputing. Portability of PIConGPU to OpenPower architecture has been described [28]. Data reduction techniques and scalability of data output for the upcoming HPC systems have been analyzed [29]. New frameworks for performance portable implementation of PIC algorithms (KOKKOS and RAJA) have been considered [30]. Metrics and design of an instruction roofline model for AMD GPUs are the topics of a recent paper by Leinhauser et al. [31].

7 Conclusion

The HIP backend of the PIConGPU code allows us to perform calculations on the new AMD GPUs. The GPU acceleration reduces time-to-solution for PIC calculations considerably. The Angara interconnect provides very good strong and weak scaling for PIConGPU calculations. Running PIConGPU on 32 nodes of the Desmos supercomputer with CPUs only does not show any signs of performance degradation, larger supercomputers are required to study the interconnect-determined scalability limits. Data storage is an important bottleneck for PIConGPU calculations. Some hardware steps to decrease data storage penalty have been implemented for the Desmos supercomputer.

Additional steps may need to be taken to further optimize the code for better scaling on AMD GPUS. The number of exchanges affects scaling and additional experimentation is required to evaluate performance for other tasks and for a larger number of nodes.

Our results can be useful for all specialists who use PIC simulations in their work. We demonstrated that different important types of problems can be studied with the use of the appropriate code and relatively small cluster Desmos equipped with GPU accelerators. In light of this, specialists from other areas may consider developing GPU-enabled codes and applying them to their tasks.

Acknowledgments. The study was carried out with a grant from the Russian Science Foundation (project no. 20-71-10127).

References

1. Harlow, F.H., Evans, M., Richtmyer, R.D.: A machine calculation method for hydrodynamic problems. Los Alamos Scientific Laboratory of the University of California (1955)
2. Dawson, J.M.: Particle simulation of plasmas. Rev. Mod. Phys. **55**(2), 403 (1983)
3. Liu, G.R., Liu, M.B.: Smoothed Particle Hydrodynamics: A Meshfree Particle Method. World Scientific, Singapore (2003)
4. Harlow, F.H.: The particle-in-cell computing method for fluid dynamics. Methods Comput. Phys. **3**, 319–343 (1964)

5. Matthes, A., Widera, R., Zenker, E., Worpitz, B., Huebl, A., Bussmann, M.: Tuning and optimization for a variety of many-core architectures without changing a single line of implementation code using the Apaka library. In: Kunkel, J.M., Yokota, R., Taufer, M., Shalf, J. (eds.) ISC High Performance 2017. LNCS, vol. 10524, pp. 496–514. Springer, Cham (2017). https://doi.org/10.1007/978-3-319-67630-2_36
6. Arber, T., Bennett, K., Brady, C., Lawrence-Douglas, A., Ramsay, M., Sircombe, N., Gillies, P., Evans, R., Schmitz, H., Bell, A., et al.: Contemporary particle-in-cell approach to laser-plasma modelling. Plasma Phys. Control. Fusion **57**(11), 113001 (2015)
7. Welch, D.R., Rose, D., Oliver, B., Clark, R.: Simulation techniques for heavy ion fusion chamber transport. Nucl. Instrum. Methods Phys. Res., Sect. A **464**(1–3), 134–139 (2001)
8. Reinders, J., Ashbaugh, B., Brodman, J., Kinsner, M., Pennycook, J., Tian, X.: Data Parallel C++. Apress, Berkeley, CA (2021). https://doi.org/10.1007/978-1-4842-5574-2
9. Volokitin, V., Bashinov, A., Efimenko, E., Gonoskov, A., Meyerov, I.: High performance implementation of Boris particle pusher on DPC++. A first look at oneAPI. In: Malyshkin, V. (ed.) PaCT 2021. LNCS, vol. 12942, pp. 288–300. Springer, Cham (2021). https://doi.org/10.1007/978-3-030-86359-3_22
10. Fonseca, R.A., et al.: OSIRIS: a three-dimensional, fully relativistic particle in cell code for modeling plasma based accelerators. In: Sloot, P.M.A., Hoekstra, A.G., Tan, C.J.K., Dongarra, J.J. (eds.) ICCS 2002. LNCS, vol. 2331, pp. 342–351. Springer, Heidelberg (2002). https://doi.org/10.1007/3-540-47789-6_36
11. Derouillat, J., et al.: Smilei: a collaborative, open-source, multi-purpose particle-in-cell code for plasma simulation. Comput. Phys. Commun. **222**, 351–373 (2018)
12. Markidis, S., Lapenta, G., et al.: Multi-scale simulations of plasma with iPIC3D. Math. Comput. Simul. **80**(7), 1509–1519 (2010)
13. Bowers, K.J., Albright, B., Yin, L., Bergen, B., Kwan, T.: Ultrahigh performance three-dimensional electromagnetic relativistic kinetic plasma simulation. Phys. Plasmas **15**(5), 055703 (2008)
14. Friedman, A., Grote, D.P., Haber, I.: Three-dimensional particle simulation of heavy-ion fusion beams. Phys. Fluids B **4**(7), 2203–2210 (1992)
15. Bussmann, M., et al.: Radiative signatures of the relativistic Kelvin-Helmholtz instability. In: Proceedings of the International Conference on High Performance Computing, Networking, Storage and Analysis. pp. 5:1–5:12. SC 2013, ACM, NY (2013). https://doi.acm.org/10.1145/2503210.2504564
16. Bastrakov, S., et al.: Particle-in-cell plasma simulation on heterogeneous cluster systems. J. Comput. Sci. **3**(6), 474–479 (2012)
17. Leinhauser, M., Young, J., Bastrakov, S., Widera, R., Chatterjee, R., Chandrasekaran, S.: Performance analysis of PIConGPU: particle-in-cell on GPUs using NVIDIA's NSight systems and NSight compute. Tech. rep., Oak Ridge National Lab (ORNL), Oak Ridge, TN, USA (2021)
18. Stegailov, V., et al.: Early performance evaluation of the hybrid cluster with torus interconnect aimed at molecular-dynamics simulations. In: Wyrzykowski, R., Dongarra, J., Deelman, E., Karczewski, K. (eds.) PPAM 2017. LNCS, vol. 10777, pp. 327–336. Springer, Cham (2018). https://doi.org/10.1007/978-3-319-78024-5_29
19. Kondratyuk, N., Smirnov, G., Dlinnova, E., Biryukov, S., Stegailov, V.: Hybrid supercomputer Desmos with Torus Angara interconnect: efficiency analysis and optimization. In: Sokolinsky, L., Zymbler, M. (eds.) PCT 2018. CCIS, vol. 910, pp. 77–91. Springer, Cham (2018). https://doi.org/10.1007/978-3-319-99673-8_6

20. Stegailov, V., et al.: Angara interconnect makes GPU-based Desmos supercomputer an efficient tool for molecular dynamics calculations. Int. J. High Perform. Comput. Appl. **33**(3), 507–521 (2019)
21. Burau, H., et al.: PIConGPU: a fully relativistic particle-in-cell code for a GPU cluster. IEEE Trans. Plasma Sci. **38**(10), 2831–2839 (2010)
22. Vay, J.L., Lehe, R.: Simulations for plasma and laser acceleration. Rev. Accelerator Sci. Technol. **09**, 165–186 (2016). https://doi.org/10.1142/S1793626816300085
23. Kondratyuk, N., Smirnov, G., Stegailov, V.: Hybrid codes for atomistic simulations on the Desmos supercomputer: GPU-acceleration, scalability and parallel I/O. In: Voevodin, V., Sobolev, S. (eds.) RuSCDays 2018. CCIS, vol. 965, pp. 218–229. Springer, Cham (2019). https://doi.org/10.1007/978-3-030-05807-4_19
24. Khalilov, M.R., Timofeev, A.V.: Optimization of MPI-process mapping for clusters with Angara interconnect. Lobachevskii J. Math. **39**(9), 1188–1198 (2018). https://doi.org/10.1134/S1995080218090111
25. Kondratyuk, N., et al.: Performance and scalability of materials science and machine learning codes on the state-of-art hybrid supercomputer architecture. In: Voevodin, V., Sobolev, S. (eds.) RuSCDays 2019. CCIS, vol. 1129, pp. 597–609. Springer, Cham (2019). https://doi.org/10.1007/978-3-030-36592-9_49
26. Rohr, D., Neskovic, G., Lindenstruth, V.: The L-CSC cluster: optimizing power efficiency to become the greenest supercomputer in the world in the Green500 list of November 2014. Supercomput. Front. Innov. Int. J. **2**(3), 41–48 (2015)
27. Sagan, D., et al.: Simulations of future particle accelerators: issues and mitigations. J. Instrum. **16**(10), T10002 (2021)
28. Zenker, E., et al.: Performance-portable many-core plasma simulations: porting PIConGPU to OpenPower and beyond. In: Taufer, M., Mohr, B., Kunkel, J.M. (eds.) ISC High Performance 2016. LNCS, vol. 9945, pp. 293–301. Springer, Cham (2016). https://doi.org/10.1007/978-3-319-46079-6_21
29. Huebl, A., et al.: On the scalability of data reduction techniques in current and upcoming HPC systems from an application perspective. In: Kunkel, J.M., Yokota, R., Taufer, M., Shalf, J. (eds.) ISC High Performance 2017. LNCS, vol. 10524, pp. 15–29. Springer, Cham (2017). https://doi.org/10.1007/978-3-319-67630-2_2
30. Artigues, V., Kormann, K., Rampp, M., Reuter, K.: Evaluation of performance portability frameworks for the implementation of a particle-in-cell code. Concurr. Comput. Pract. Exp. **32**(11), e5640 (2020)
31. Leinhauser, M., Widera, R., Bastrakov, S., Debus, A., Bussmann, M., Chandrasekaran, S.: Metrics and design of an instruction roofline model for AMD GPUs. ACM Trans. Parallel Comput. **9**(1), 1–14 (2022)

Quasi-one-Dimensional Polarized Superfluids: A DMRG Study

Anastasia Potapova, Ian Pile[ID], and Evgeni Burovski[✉][ID]

HSE University, 101000 Moscow, Russia
evgeny.burovskiy@gmail.com

Abstract. We study the dimensional crossover of polarized superfluids. Employing large-scale numerical simulations the attractive Hubbard on multi-leg ladders with up to five legs, we construct ground-state phase diagrams which feature polarized (Fulde-Ferrell-Larkin-Ovchinnikov like) and unpolarized (Bardeen-Cooper-Schrieffer like) phases and trace the crossover from strictly one-dimensional behavior to higher dimensions. We pay special attention to the quasi-one-dimensional regime, where mean-field approximate approaches lead to artifacts due to uncontrollable nature of approximations.

Keywords: Hubbard model · FFLO · DMRG · Superconductivity

1 Introduction

Recent developments of experimental techniques for confining and cooling ultra-cold gases in optical lattices allow the experimental creation of strongly correlated quantum systems described by model Hamiltonian. Unlike traditional implementations in solids, experimental implementations of model systems in optical lattices provide unprecedented control over system parameters: lattice geometry, interparticle interactions, tunneling amplitudes, and degree of polarization. The last decade saw an active study of variants of Fermi- and Bose-Hubbard models. Among the experimental achievements are the observation of an antiferromagnetic state in the two-dimensional Hubbard model [1,2], the implementation of the extended Bose-Hubbard model [3], the observation of polaron behavior in a heterogeneous mixture of bosonic atoms [4], the controlled study of the transition between the quasi-one-dimensional and three-dimensional behavior of a polarized superconductor [5], and the direct observation of magnetically mediated hole pairing in Fermi-Hubbard ladders [6].

Of particular interest for possible implementations of quantum technologies is the study of low-dimensional strongly correlated systems, since spatial confinement tends to amplify quantum mechanical effects. Experimental technologies open up the possibility of studying polarized superfluid systems, a one-dimensional analog of the celebrated Fulde-Ferrel-Larkin-Ovchinnikov (FFLO) quantum phase [7,8], which proves elusive in solid-state systems, as well as the

V. Voevodin et al. (Eds.): RuSCDays 2022, LNCS 13708, pp. 303–312, 2022.
https://doi.org/10.1007/978-3-031-22941-1_22

transition between strictly one-dimensional (1D) and three-dimensional (3D) behavior [4,9,10].

The physics of formation of the FFLO phase is widely discussed both in the context ultracold gases (see, e.g., [11,12] and references therein), and in the context of unconventional superconductors (see, e.g., [13] and references therein). From a theoretical point of view, it has been established that, in a strictly one-dimensional (1D) geometry, the FFLO-like phase is stable in a wide range of parameters [14,15].[1] In a two-dimensional geometry, the FFLO physics was studied numerically via Monte Carlo simulations [16,17]. In three dimensions, the FFLO phase proves elusive both in solid-state systems [13] and cold atom experiments [9]—the samples phase separate into an unpolarized gas and a single-component gas of excess fermions.

This way, a detailed investigation of a dimensional crossover from a strictly one-dimensional behavior (algebraic ordering) to higher dimensions (formation of a long-range order) is called for. Semi-analytic studies of dimensional crossover of the FFLO phase are based on the mean-field approximation and suffer from artifacts due to uncontrollable approximations [19,20]. Previous numerical studies were limited to two-leg Hubbard ladders [18] and three-leg ladders [32]—which do not allow to trace the dimensional crossover.

In this paper, we perform large-scale numerical simulations of the attractive Hubbard model on multi-leg ladders using the density-matrix renormalization group (DMRG) simulations [21,22]. We perform simulations of ladders with up to five legs and varying boundary conditions in the perpendicular direction. We construct the grand canonical ground state phase diagram of the model, and trace the crossover from a strictly 1D limit to higher dimensions—concentrating on the quasi-1D regime which is most difficult for approximate mean-field studies [20].

We note that our approach of simulating multi-leg ladders is conceptually similar to previous studies of the superconductor-insulator transition in anisotropic quasi-one-dimensional bosonic systems [26] and variants of the repulsive Hubbard model [27–29].

2   Model and Methods

We consider an attractive Hubbard model of spin-1/2 fermions, with the Hamiltonian

$$\hat{H} = -t \sum_{\langle i,j \rangle, \sigma} \left(\hat{c}^{\dagger}_{i,\sigma} \hat{c}_{j,\sigma} + h.c. \right) + U \sum_{i} \hat{n}_{i,\uparrow} \hat{n}_{i,\downarrow}. \tag{1}$$

Here the indices i enumerate sites of a $W \times L$ ladder lattice and $\langle i,j \rangle$ are nearest neighbors on the lattice. $\hat{c}_{i,\sigma}$ annihilates a fermion with spin $\sigma = \uparrow, \downarrow$ on a site i, $\hat{c}^{\dagger}_{i,\sigma}$ is its Hermitian conjugate and the local number operator $\hat{n}_{i,\sigma} = \hat{c}^{\dagger}_{i,\sigma} \hat{c}_{i,\sigma}$. The Hubbard onsite coupling $U < 0$ since we consider an attractive model, and the

---

[1] Strictly speaking, the 1D FFLO analog has only algebraic long-range order, where the correlations decay as a power law *and* are spatially modulated.

hopping amplitude t can be set to unity without loss of generality since the only dimensionless parameter in the model is U/t. For ladder lattices typically $L \gg W$ and we use the open boundary conditions in the ladder direction. The boundary conditions in the perpendicular direction can be varied, and we consider both open and periodic boundary conditions.

Let $E(N_\uparrow, N_\downarrow)$ is the ground state energy of Eq. (1) with $N_\uparrow$ spin-up particles and $N_\downarrow$ spin-down particles on $W \times L$ sites. We define the total particle number $N = N_\uparrow + N_\downarrow$ and the total polarization $P = N_\uparrow - N_\downarrow$. We then define the conjugate variables, the effective magnetic field, h, and the chemical potential, μ, via

$$\mu = \left(\frac{\partial E}{\partial N}\right)_P, \qquad h = \left(\frac{\partial E}{\partial P}\right)_N. \tag{2}$$

A system in a weak external potential, $V(r)$, which we take to be spin-independent, can be treated in the local density approximation, $\mu \to \mu - V(r)$. In experiments with ultracold gases, atomic clouds are subject to a weak trapping potential, so that the structure of the local density profile can be directly read off a phase diagram of the uniform model ($V(x) = 0$) (1) on the h-μ plane.

Depending on values of μ and h, the following ground states are of interest (for simplicity, we restrict ourselves to $h > 0$ and $\mu < U/2$):

Equal Densities (ED) Here $N_\uparrow = N_\downarrow > 0$. This phase is expected to be equivalent to a BCS superconductor. This phase can be expected for small values of the effective magnetic field h.

Fully Polarized (FP) Here $N_\uparrow > 0$ and $N_\downarrow = 0$. This is a single-component non-interacting gas. This phase can be expected for large values of h.

Partially Polarized (PP) Here $N_\uparrow > N_\downarrow > 0$. This phase is expected to exhibit the FFLO correlation properties.

Vacuum (V) This is a trivial state with $N_\uparrow = N_\downarrow = 0$ which is realized e.g. at $h = 0$ and μ smaller then $E(1,1)$, the energy of a single pair.

For a lattice model, additional states appear when either a single-spin or both spin bands are full, $N_\sigma/LW = 1$.

The main objective of our work is to determine the region of stability of the PP phase for various ladder widths W and boundary conditions in the perpendicular direction. The lengths of the ladder, L, is taken to be large enough to be close to the thermodynamic limit $L \gg 1$.

To this end, we compute the ground state energies of the Hubbard model (1) in the canonical ensemble, $E(N_\uparrow, N_\downarrow)$, using DMRG simulations [21,22]. The phase boundaries on the h-μ plane are constructed by comparing the energies of the states.

V-ED phase boundary corresponds to creation of a single pair from the empty band by increasing the chemical potential, i.e., $\mu = E(1,1)/2$.

V-FP boundary corresponds to creation of a single spin-up fermion from the empty band by increasing the magnetic field, $h > 0$, i.e., $\mu + h = E(1,0)$.

ED-FP boundary corresponds to flipping a single spin on fully paired state by increasing the magnetic field: we compare the energies of states with ($N_\uparrow > 0, N_\downarrow = 0$) particles and ($N_\uparrow - 1, N_\downarrow = 1$). Approximating the derivatives, Eq. (2), by finite differences, we find

$$h = \frac{E(N_\uparrow - 1, 1) - E(N_\uparrow, 0)}{2}, \tag{3}$$

$$\mu = \frac{E(N_\uparrow + 1, 1) - E(N_\uparrow, 0)}{-2}. \tag{4}$$

On the h-μ plane, the phase boundary is thus implicitly parameterized by $N_\uparrow$, or equivalently by the filling fraction, $n_\uparrow \equiv N_\uparrow / WL$.

ED-PP boundary is similar to the ED-FP boundary, only the "reference" state is $N_\uparrow = N_\downarrow > 0$ and we flip a single spin to obtain the effective magnetic field h and add a pair of particles to compute the chemical potential μ. This way, we find

$$h = \left.\frac{E(N_\uparrow + 1, N_\downarrow - 1) - E(N_\uparrow, N_\downarrow)}{2}\right|_{N_\uparrow = N_\downarrow}, \tag{5}$$

$$\mu = \left.\frac{E(N_\uparrow + 1, N_\downarrow + 1) - E(N_\uparrow, N_\downarrow)}{2}\right|_{N_\uparrow = N_\downarrow}. \tag{6}$$

On the h-μ plane, the phase boundary is parameterized by the filling fraction of the majority component $n_\uparrow \equiv N_\uparrow / WL$.

3   Numerical Simulations

We simulate the model (1) via numerically exact DMRG method [21,22], using the open-source implementations, ALPS [30] and iTensor [31]. The advantage of the ALPS implementation is that it provides precompiled binaries and Python wrappers for the Anaconda distribution. All user interaction—defining quantum operators and models, definitions of the lattices, handling simulation parameters and output is handled via XML files, which can be constructed and parsed by standard means. However, the ALPS package is unmaintained and should by considered a legacy reference implementation by now. Using the iTensor implementation is strongly preferred going forward.

The iTensor package [31] implements a collection of computational tools for simulations using matrix-product states (MPS), which includes DMRG simulations of quantum models. The package is implemented in C++ and provides optional `Julia` wrappers, so that orchestration of simulations and driver routines can be implemented in either C++ or Julia.

DMRG simulations are computationally intensive for quasi-1D models, because time complexity for calculating the ground-state energy of a single point, $E(N_\uparrow, N_\downarrow)$, scales exponentially with the transverse system size W [31] and linearly with the planar system size L. This is due to the fact that the value of the bond dimension (i.e., the matrix size used in the construction of an MPS) needed to capture the entanglement properties of the quantum state also grows exponentially with W [23,25]. The use of HPC facilities is thus dictated by two reasons. First, CPU time and memory requirements both grow with the system size, especially with the ladder width W (equivalently, with the bond dimension): a single simulation of a $W = 4, 5$ already requires about 11 Gb of memory; the CPU time for a single $W = 5$ and $L = 40$ run on Intel Xeon Gold 6152 2.1-3.7 GHz system of the HSE HPC system [33] takes 96 CPU-hours to converge. Second, the full grand-canonical phase diagram for a system of $W \times L$ sites $\sim 3WL$ runs with varying numbers of spin-up and spin-down particle numbers $N_\uparrow$ and $N_\downarrow$. Two reasons combined make the construction of grand-canonical phase diagrams for wide ladders inaccessible with the use of a PC only. Further scaling of the ladder widths, $W > 5$, is clearly out of reach of desktop-class systems.

We used a Macbook Pro with 2.6 GHz 6-core Intel Core i7, Turbo Boost up to 4.5 GHz, with 12 MB shared L3 cache for testing, and the computational resources of HPC facilities at HSE University for numerical simulations. HPC cluster at HSE University utilizes 46 computation nodes with 92 processors Intel Xeon Gold/AMD EPYC, 2584 cores and 40 Tb RAM in total.

Performance characteristics and parallelization of MPS type simulations strongly depend on the underlying linear algebra library layer, but there are also promising parallel realizations of DMRG algorithm itself reporting sublinear scaling in the number of nodes [24]. We used reference LAPACK for testing and the OpenBLAS package for main simulation runs. Parallelization is handled by OpenBLAS and we used up to 32 threads. By now we haven't observed any speedup by parallelizing linear algebra and this part of work is for further study.

We simulate ladders of up to $W = 5$ legs, with typical lengths $L = 40$. For testing, we used system sizes of up to 2×200 sites. For the coupling constant $U/t = -7$, we take the DMRG bond dimension of up to 2×10^3 states, which leads to the truncation error below 10^{-8} for $W \leqslant 3$ and below 10^{-6} for $W = 4$ and $W = 5$.

4   Results and Discussion

Figure 1 shows the ground-state phase diagrams of the model (1) for the 1D chain (W=1) and ladder widths from $W = 2$ to $W = 5$, which are computed from DMRG simulations using Eqs. (3)–(6). Our numerical results for $W = 1$ agree with the Bethe Ansatz calculations of Ref. [15]. For $W = 2$ and $W = 3$ our results agree with previous DMRG simulations of Refs. [18] and [32]. Several features stand out in Fig. 1. *First*, the region of stability of the PP phase—the FFLO candidate—is large for all values of W. This is in contrast to expectations for the 3D case, where the FFLO state is likely only stable in a narrow region of the phase diagram.

Second, multiple phase boundaries for ED, PP and FP phases, meet for each W at a single multicritical point, O. The location of the point O is fixed by the crossing between the V-ED boundary, $\mu = E(1,1)/2$, and the V-FP boundary,

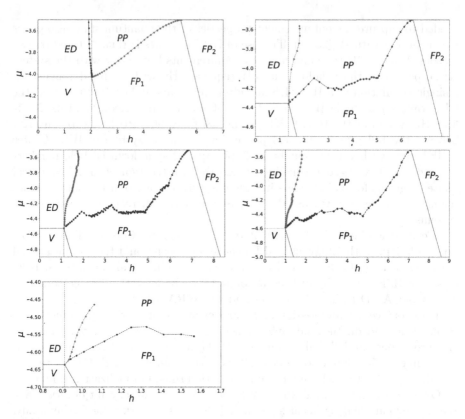

Fig. 1. Ground-state phase diagrams of the attractive Hubbard model (1) for various W and open boundary conditions in the perpendicular directions: top row, $W = 1$ (left) and $W = 2$ (right); second row: $W = 3$ and $W = 4$; bottom row: $W = 5$. For all runs, $L = 40$ and $U/t = -7$. Filled dots are DMRG results, and lines are to guide an eye. We denote by FP_2 the fully polarized phase where the majority band is filled, $N_\uparrow = WL$ and the minority component is absent, $N_\downarrow = 0$. See text for discussion.

$h + \mu = E(1, 0)$. This behavior should be contrasted with the MFA approximate calculations [19, 20] where the uncontrollable MF approximation leads to splitting of the multicritical point. This splitting is a clear artifact of the MF approximation, which thus becomes unreliable in the strong-coupling quasi-1D regime—in contrast to numerical DMRG simulations, which are applicable in this regime.

Third, the FP-PP boundary for $W > 1$ becomes non-monotonic, with cusps and sharp turns, and develops seemingly chaotic oscillations. This behavior can be traced to the structure of the single-particle spectrum of $W \geqslant 2$ ladders. Indeed, a single-particle spectrum of a W-leg ladder has W branches, and kinks and sharp turns of the FP-PP phase boundary corresponds to the filling fractions where multiple branches start filling from the bottom of a band (this behavior was first observed in Ref. [18] for $W = 2$). Small-scale chaotic oscillations, however, are a finite-size effect due to a finite level spacing at $L < \infty$.

Fourth, a qualitative difference between a strictly 1D chain, $W = 1$, and quasi-1D geometries, $W > 1$, is seen in Fig. 1 for the ED-PP boundary for small filling fractions, i.e. close to the multicritical point O. Namely, for $W = 1$ the slope, $d\mu/dh$, is negative, while for $W > 1$, the slope is positive, $d\mu/dh > 0$. Whether the phase boundary is to the right or to the left of the vertical line passing through the point O defines the spatial structure of the atomic cloud in an external potential. Indeed, in the local density approximation, the structure of the cloud can be read off a vertical cut in the h-μ plane, Fig. 1. For the ED-PP boundary located to the left of O, this leads to the PP phase occupying the center of the trap and surrounded by the ED wings. For the ED-PP boundary located to the right of the point O, the prediction of Fig. 1 is a three-layer structure: the center of the trap is ED, the next outside layer is PP, and the outer wings are FP. This change of the cloud structure was observed experimentally (e.g., in a recent work of Ref. [5]) by varying the exchange integrals between adjacent tube-shaped traps—and our numerical simulations capture the main features of the phenomenon. We note that this change of the behavior was previously observed in simulations of [32] for $W = 2$ and $W = 3$. The main conclusion we are able to draw from simulations of $W = 4$ and $W = 5$ is that the change of the sign of $d\mu/dh$ is not numerical artifact, but instead a robust effect which appears immediately upon departure from a strict 1D limit.

To further investigate the effect of the geometry in the perpendicular direction, we consider $W = 3$ and $W = 4$ ladders with periodic boundary conditions in the perpendicular direction ("cylinders"). Figure 2 shows a comparison of phase diagrams with open and periodic boundary conditions. For clarity of comparison, we shift the diagrams so that their respective multicritical points coincide, and we only show the ED-PP and PP-FP boundaries. It is clear from Fig. 2 that qualitatively the structure of the phase diagrams is the same and that the low filling fraction behavior is insensitive to the boundary conditions. For larger filling fractions, quantitative differences start to appear, which reflects the difference in the single-particle spectra.

Conclusions and Outlook. In this work, we study the ground state properties of polarized two-component superfluids in quasi-one-dimensional geometries. Specifically, we consider the attractive Hubbard model on ladders of widths of up to $W = 5$ with open and periodic boundary conditions in the perpendicular direction. Performing large-scale DMRG simulations, we construct ground state phase diagrams which feature polarized and unpolarized ground states, and obtain phase boundaries by comparing energies of the ground states. In the vicinity of the multicritical point—where mean-field based approximations become unreliable—we find a clear-cut difference between a strict 1D limit of a single chain and multichain ladders. This allows us to trace a difference in spatial structures of density profiles due to external potential, and our simulations capture qualitative features observed in experiments with ultracold gases.

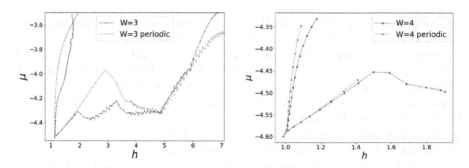

Fig. 2. Ground state phase diagrams of the attractive Hubbard model (1) for $W = 3$ (left-hand panel) and $W = 4$ (right-hand panel) for open and periodic boundary conditions in the perpendicular directions. On both panels, green (magenta) symbols show the open (periodic) BCs. We only show the ED-PP and PP-FP boundaries and shift the plots so that their respective multicritical points coincide, for clarity. Simulations are performed for $L = 40$ and $U = -7t$. See text for discussion.

For future work, two directions are most promising. First is to allow for unequal overlap integrals along the ladder and in the perpendicular direction. This would allow one to make more direct comparison with experiments, which engineer arrays of "tubes" with tunable intertube hopping amplitude. This way, the hopping ratio serves as a control parameter which governs the dimensional crossover. Second, it would be interesting to consider single-particle and two-particle correlation properties for multi-leg ladder geometries, to trace the evolution of the correlations from strict 1D to higher dimensions.

Acknowledgments. We are thankful to R. Mondaini, Th. Jolicoeur and G. Misguich for illuminating discussions. We acknowledge financial support through the RFBR and NSFC, project number 21-57-53014. Numerical simulations were performed using the computational resources of HPC facilities at HSE University [33].

References

1. Mazurenko, A., et al.: A cold Fermi-Hubbard antiferromagnet. Nature **545**, 462 (2017)
2. Hart, R.A., et al.: Observation of antiferromagnetic correlations in the Hubbard model with ultracold atoms. Nature **519**(7542), 211 (2015)
3. Baier, S., et al.: Science **352**, 201 (2016)
4. Hu, M.-G., van de Graaff, M.J., Kedar, D., Corson, J.P., Cornell, E.A., Jin, D.S.: Bose polarons in the strongly interacting regime. Phys. Rev. Lett. **117**, 055301 (2016)
5. Revelle, M.C., Fry, J.A., Olsen, B.A., Hulet, R.G.: 1D to 3D crossover of a spin-imbalanced Fermi gas. Phys. Rev. Lett. **117**, 235301 (2016)
6. Hirthe, S., et al.: Magnetically mediated hole pairing in fermionic ladders of ultracold atoms. arXiv:2203.10027
7. Fulde, P., Ferrell, R.A.: Superconductivity in a strong spin-exchange field. Phys. Rev. **135**, A550 (1964)

8. Larkin, A.I., Ovchinikov, Y.N.: Nonuniform state of superconductors. Sov. Phys. JETP **20**, 762 (1965)
9. Shin, Y., Zwierlein, M.W., Schunck, C.Y., Schirotzek, A., Ketterle, W.: Observation of phase separation in a strongly interacting imbalanced Fermi gas. Phys. Rev. Lett. **97**, 030401 (2006)
10. Liao, Y., et al.: Spin-imbalance in a one-dimensional Fermi gas. Nature **467**, 567 (2010)
11. Dobrzyniecki, J., Sowiński, T.: Simulating artificial 1D physics with ultra-cold fermionic atoms: three exemplary themes. Adv. Quantum Technol. 2000010 (2020). https://doi.org/10.1002/qute.202000010
12. Kinnunen, J.J., Baarsma, J.E., Martikainen, J.-P., Törmä, P.: Rep. Prog. Phys. **81**, 046401 (2018)
13. Agterberg, D.F., et al.: The physics of pair-density waves: cuprate superconductors and beyond. Annu. Rev. Condens. Matter Phys. **11**, 231 (2020)
14. Yang, K.: Inhomogeneous superconducting state in quasi-one-dimensional systems. Phys. Rev. B **63**, 140511 (2001)
15. Orso, G.: Attractive Fermi gases with unequal spin populations in highly elongated traps. Phys. Rev. Lett. **98**, 070402 (2007)
16. Gukelberger, J., Lienert, S., Kozik, E., Pollet, L., Troyer, M.: Fulde-Ferrell-Larkin-Ovchinnikov pairing as leading instability on the square lattice. Phys. Rev. B **94**, 075157 (2016)
17. Wolak, M.J., Grémaud, B., Scalettar, R.T., Batrouni, G.G.: Pairing in a two-dimensional Fermi gas with population imbalance. Phys. Rev. A **86**, 023630 (2012)
18. Feiguin, A.E., Heidrich-Meisner, F.: Pair correlations of a spin-imbalanced fermi gas on two-leg ladders. Phys. Rev. Lett. **102**, 076403 (2009)
19. Dutta, S., Mueller, E.J.: Dimensional crossover in a spin-imbalanced Fermi gas. Phys. Rev. A **94**, 063627 (2016)
20. Sundar, B., Fry, J.A., Revelle, M.C., Hulet, R.G., Hazzard, K.R.A.: Spin-imbalanced ultracold Fermi gases in a two-dimensional array of tubes. Phys. Rev. A **102**, 033311 (2020)
21. White, S.R.: Density matrix formulation for quantum renormalization groups. Phys. Rev. Lett. **69**, 2863 (1992)
22. Schollwöck, U.: The density-matrix renormalization group. Rev. Mod. Phys. **77**, 259 (2005)
23. Schollwöck, U.: The density-matrix renormalization group in the age of matrix product states. Ann. Phys. **326**, 96 (2011)
24. Stoudenmire, E.M., White, S.R.: Real-space parallel density matrix renormalization group. Phys. Rev. B **87**, 155137 (2013)
25. Eisert, J., Cramer, M., Plenio, M.B.: Area laws for the entanglement entropy - a review Rev. Mod. Phys. **82**, 277 (2010)
26. Bollmar, G., Laflorencie, N., Kantian, A.: Dimensional crossover and phase transitions in coupled chains: DMRG results. Phys. Rev. B **102**, 195145 (2020)
27. Kantian, A., Dolfi, M., Troyer, M., Giamarchi, T.: Understanding repulsively mediated superconductivity of correlated electrons via massively parallel density matrix renormalization group. Phys. Rev. B **100**, 075138 (2019)
28. Huang, K.S., Han, Zh., Kivelson, S.A., Yao, H.: Pair-Density-Wave in the Strong Coupling Limit of the Holstein-Hubbard model. arXiv:2103.04984
29. Chung, C.-M., Qin, M., Zhang, S., Schollwöck, U., White, S.R.: Plaquette versus ordinary D-wave pairing in the t'-Hubbard model on a width 4 cylinder. Phys. Rev. B **102**, 041106 (2020)

30. Bauer, B., et al.: (ALPS collaboration), The ALPS project release 2.0: open source software for strongly correlated systems. J. Stat. Mech. P05001 (2011)
31. Fishman, M., White, S.R., Miles Stoudenmire, E.: The ITensor Software Library for Tensor Network Calculations. arxiv:2007.14822
32. Burovski, E., Ikhsanov, R.S., Kuznetsov, A.A., Kagan, M.Y.: J. Phys: Conf. Ser. **1163**, 012046 (2019)
33. Kostenetskiy, P.S., Chulkevich, R.A., Kozyrev, V.I.: HPC resources of the higher school of economics. J. Phys.: Conf. Ser. **1740**, 012050 (2021)

Sintering Simulation Using GPU-Based Algorithm for the Samples with a Large Number of Grains

Dmitriy Prokhorov$^{(\boxtimes)}$ [ID], Yaroslav Bazaikin [ID], and Vadim Lisitsa [ID]

Sobolev Institute of Mathematics SB RAS,
4 Koptug Ave., 630090 Novosibirsk, Russia
dm.ig.prokhorov@gmail.com, bazaikin@math.nsc.ru, lisitsavv@ipgg.sbras.ru

Abstract. The sintering simulation is an actual problem in computational mathematics since computer simulation allows performing much more experiments than can be performed using chemical or physical techniques, especially in the case of studying the material's intrinsic structure. The most perspective approach for the sintering simulation is a phase-field method. Usually, this approach requires solving the system of the Cahn-Hilliard and Allen-Cahn equation. The main difficulty is that number of Allen-Cahn equations is equal to the number of different grains in the sample. It causes requirements in computational resources to increase not only with increasing the grid size but with increasing the number of grains in the sample; if finite differences are used for solving the system. The paper presents the sintering simulation algorithm, which tracks the individual grains. This feature allows solving each of the Allen-Cahn equations only in a small subdomain corresponding to the current grain. The algorithm is implemented using Graphic Processor Units.

Keywords: Sintering · Porous materials · Phase-field

1 Introduction

Sintering is a typical manufacturing process, which becomes widespread because it allows obtaining materials with predefined parameters. One of the important examples of such properties and materials is sorbent production. The key properties of sorbent are strength and capacity, which is related to the surface area [3,4,9]. Measurements of these properties using chemical and physical techniques, especially if the question is about a large number of samples, is a highly resource-intensive task. But such experiments can be conducted for digital representation of the sample in a more convenient way. Therefore, computer simulation of sintering is a point of interest for both: industry and computational mathematics [5].

Mathematically, the sintering problem is the Stefan problem or moving-boundary problem. There are several ways to solve Stefan's problem. In particular, when considering phase temperature transitions, the enthalpy statement

V. Voevodin et al. (Eds.): RuSCDays 2022, LNCS 13708, pp. 313–327, 2022.
https://doi.org/10.1007/978-3-031-22941-1_23

is used, in which the presence of a transition zone is assumed. The temperature and state of matter in this zone are determined by empirical relations. In particular, when considering phase temperature transitions, the enthalpy statement is used, in which the presence of a transition zone is assumed. The temperature and state of matter which is determined based on empirical relations [7,30]. In the problems of modeling multiphase fluid flows, front-tracking methods are common in combination with the finite volume method with truncated cells [19,27]. However, it is difficult to implement this approach since it requires solving many geometric problems at each time step to determine the position of the boundary, which is especially complicated when the topology of each of the phases changes. Another approach for solving the Stefan problem is the level-set method [15,20], which is used together with the immersed boundary method [21,25] in modeling the multiphase fluid flows and chemical interaction of a fluid with a porous material matrix [13,23]. This method is not widely used in sintering simulation because surface diffusion flow, which is one of the mass transport mechanisms in the sintering process, requires a very accurate approximation [22,24].

The most perspective and rapidly developing approach for solving Stefan problem is a phase-field method [17]. Phase-field method is often used in simulation of microstructural evolution in processes such as solidification [11], solid state sintering [12,31], grain growth [18], etc. The general principle of the phase-field method is to describe physical quantities by a set of phase fields that take constant values in specific domains and vary smoothly through interfaces between them. In the case of sintering, the distinct grains are these specific domains. One of the possible models is the system consisting of the one Cahn-Hilliard [6] equation and I Allen-Cahn Eq. [2], where I is the number of grains. The Cahn-Hilliard equation controls the evolution of mass density. Allen-Cahn equations describe the behavior of the order parameters. To allow the simulation of large samples consisting of thousands of grains, in [14] is presented locally reduced order parameter approach. This approach is implemented in the Pace3D solver [10]; its key feature is that every grid node stores only $I_c = const$ maximal values of the order parameters.

We introduce another method for simulation of the large samples. In our approach, each of the Allen-Cahn equations is solved in a small subdomain corresponding to the current grain. This method is described in Sect. 3; simulation results are presented in Sect. 4. Also, we provide a short description of the model and finite difference scheme in Sect. 2.

2   Model

In the current research, we use the model described in [29]. The set of phase-field parameters consists of one conservative field $\rho(\boldsymbol{x}, t)$ describing mass density and I non-conservative fields $\eta_i(\boldsymbol{x}, t)$ corresponding to the grains' order parameters. The evolution of mass density is described by the Cahn-Hilliard Eq. [6].

$$\frac{\partial \rho}{\partial t} = \nabla \cdot J; \quad J = -D\nabla\mu; \quad \mu = \frac{\partial f}{\partial \rho} - \beta_\rho \Delta\rho. \tag{1}$$

The set of Allen-Cahn equations describes the evolution of order parameters η_i [2].

$$\frac{\partial \eta_i}{\partial t} = -L\left(\frac{\partial f}{\partial \eta_i} - \beta_\eta \Delta \eta_i\right) \forall i. \tag{2}$$

In Eqs. 1-2, function f is the non-equilibrium bulk chemical free energy density.

$$f(\rho, \eta_1, ..., \eta_I) = A\rho^2(1 - \rho)^2 + B\left(\rho^2 + 6(1 - \rho)\sum_i \eta_i^2 - \right.$$
$$\left. - 4(2 - \rho)\sum_i \eta_i^3 + 3\left(\sum_i \eta_i^2\right)^2\right), \tag{3}$$

The diffusion coefficient D in Eq. 1 has the following form:

$$D = D_{vol}\phi(\rho) + D_{vap}(1 - \phi(\rho)) + D_{surf}\rho^2(1 - \rho^2) + D_{gb}\sum_{i<j} \eta_i \eta_j, \tag{4}$$
$$\phi(\rho) = \rho^3(10 - 15\rho + 6\rho^2).$$

The constants in Eqs. 2-4 can be divided into two groups. Parameters $A, B, \beta_\rho, \beta_\eta$ relate to the surface and grain boundary energies. Parameters L, D_{vol}, D_{vap}, D_{surf}, D_{gb} relate to the diffusivity in the different parts of grains.

We consider this system of equations in rectangular domain $\Omega = [X_1^{min}, X_1^{max}] \times [X_2^{min}, X_2^{max}] \times [X_3^{min}, X_3^{max}]$, in which are provided initial conditions 5 and periodical boundary conditions.

$$\eta_i(\boldsymbol{x}, 0) = \chi_i(\boldsymbol{x}), \forall i,$$
$$\rho(\boldsymbol{x}, 0) = max_i(\chi_1(\boldsymbol{x}), ..., \chi_I(\boldsymbol{x})). \tag{5}$$

In 5, χ_i is an indicator function of the i-th grain.

2.1   Finite Difference Scheme

For solving this equation system, rectangular grid G is defined in domain Ω. Let us define spatial steps h_m, $m = 1, 2, 3$ and denote integer and half-integer nodes as $(x_m)_j = h_m j$ and $(x_m)_{j+1/2} = h_m(j + 1/2)$. Assuming $X_m^{min} = j_m^{min} h_m$ and $X_m^{max} = (j_m^{max} + 1)h_m$, we have:

$$(x_m)_{j_m^{min}-1} = (x_m)_{j_m^{max}}; \quad (x_m)_{j_m^{max}+1} = (x_m)_{j_m^{min}}. \tag{6}$$

For simplicity, further, we use the following notation for the values of the solution components in the grid nodes:

$$g_{j_1 j_2 j_3} = g((x_1)_{j_1}, (x_2)_{j_2}, (x_3)_{j_3})$$
$$g_{j_1+1/2 j_2 j_3} = g((x_1)_{j_1+1/2}, (x_2)_{j_2}, (x_3)_{j_3}) \tag{7}$$

Spatial derivatives are approximated by a second-order finite difference scheme. Time derivative is approximated using the Euler rule. Taking the above into account, we obtain the following scheme for Eqs. 1–2:

$$\frac{\rho^{n+1}_{j_1j_2j_3} - \rho^n_{j_1j_2j_3}}{\tau} = -\left(\boldsymbol{D}^{c_2}_1[J_1]_{j_1j_2j_3} + \boldsymbol{D}^{c_2}_2[J_2]_{j_1j_2j_3} + \boldsymbol{D}^{c_2}_3[J_3]_{j_1j_2j_3}\right), \qquad (8)$$

$$(J_1)^n_{j_1+1/2j_2j_3} = -D^n_{j_1+1/2j_2j_3}\boldsymbol{D}^{c_1}_1[\mu]_{j_1+1/2j_2j_3}, \qquad (9)$$

$$\mu^n_{j_1j_2j_3} = \frac{\partial f}{\partial \rho}(\rho^n_{j_1j_2j_3}, (\eta_1)^n_{j_1j_2j_3}, ..., (\eta_I)^n_{j_1j_2j_3}) - \beta_\rho \boldsymbol{L}[\rho]^n_{j_1j_2j_3}. \qquad (10)$$

$$\frac{(\eta_i)^{n+1}_{j_1j_2j_3} - (\eta_i)^n_{j_1j_2j_3}}{\tau} = -L\left[\frac{\partial f}{\partial \eta_i}(\rho^n_{j_1j_2j_3}, (\eta_1)^n_{j_1j_2j_3}, ..., (\eta_I)^n_{j_1j_2j_3}) - \beta_\eta \boldsymbol{L}[\eta_i]^n_{j_1j_2j_3}\right],$$
$$(11)$$

$$1 \le i \le I, \ j^{min}_m \le j_m \le j^{max}_m,$$

where differential operators are approximated as:

$$\boldsymbol{L}[g]_{j_1j_2j_3} = \boldsymbol{D}^2_1[g]_{j_1j_2j_3} + \boldsymbol{D}^2_2[g]_{j_1j_2j_3} + \boldsymbol{D}^2_3[g]_{j_1j_2j_3}, \qquad (12)$$

$$\boldsymbol{D}^2_1[g]_{j_1j_2j_3} = \frac{g_{j_1+1j_2j_3} - 2g_{j_1j_2j_3} + g_{j_1-1j_2j_3}}{h^2_1} = \left.\frac{\partial^2 g}{\partial x^2_1}\right|_{j_1j_2j_3} + O(h^2_1), \qquad (13)$$

$$\boldsymbol{D}^{c_2}_1[g]_{j_1j_2j_3} = \frac{g_{j_1+1/2j_2j_3} - g_{j_1-1/2j_2j_3}}{h_1} = \left.\frac{\partial g}{\partial x_1}\right|_{j_1j_2j_3} + O(h^2_1), \qquad (14)$$

$$\boldsymbol{D}^{c_1}_1[g]_{j_1+1/2j_2j_3} = \frac{g_{j_1+1j_2j_3} - g_{j_1j_2j_3}}{h_1} = \left.\frac{\partial g}{\partial x_1}\right|_{j_1+1/2j_2j_3} + O(h^2_1), \qquad (15)$$

The rest of the parameters have the following approximation:

$$\left(\frac{\partial f}{\partial \rho}\right)^n_{j_1j_2j_3} = 2A\rho^n_{j_1j_2j_3}(1 - \rho^n_{j_1j_2j_3})(1 - 2\rho^n_{j_1j_2j_3}) +$$
$$+ B\left(2\rho^n_{j_1j_2j_3} - 6\sum_i((\eta_i)^n_{j_1j_2j_3})^2 + 4\sum_i((\eta_i)^n_{j_1j_2j_3})^3\right). \qquad (16)$$

$$\left(\frac{\partial f}{\partial \eta_i}\right)^n_{j_1j_2j_3} = 12B(\eta_i)^n_{j_1j_2j_3}\left(1 - \rho^n_{j_1j_2j_3} -\right.$$
$$\left. - (2 - \rho^n_{j_1j_2j_3})(\eta_i)^n_{j_1j_2j_3} + \sum_{\bar{i}}((\eta_{\bar{i}})^n_{j_1j_2j_3})^2\right) \qquad (17)$$

$$D^n_{j_1+1/2j_2j_3} = \frac{D^n_{j_1+1j_2j_3} + D^n_{j_1j_2j_3}}{2} \qquad (18)$$

$$D^n_{j_1 j_2 j_3} = D_{vol}\phi(\rho^n_{j_1 j_2 j_3}) + D_{vap}(1 - \phi(\rho^n_{j_1 j_2 j_3})) +$$
$$+ D_{surf}(\rho^n_{j_1 j_2 j_3})^2 (1 - (\rho^n_{j_1 j_2 j_3})^2) +$$
$$+ \frac{D_{gb}}{2}\left((\sum_i (\eta_i)^n_{j_1 j_2 j_3})^2 - \sum_i ((\eta_i)^n_{j_1 j_2 j_3})^2 \right). \tag{19}$$

Other operators and components in Eqs. 7, 9, 13—15 can be obtained from the presented ones by the permutation of spatial indices.

3   Algorithm

In the case of large I, $\eta_i = 0$ in most of the Ω. Computation of order parameters in the whole domain becomes redundant and expensive. Thus, we define $\Omega_i = [X_{i1}^{min}, X_{i1}^{max}] \times [X_{i2}^{min}, X_{i2}^{max}] \times [X_{i3}^{min}, X_{i3}^{max}], 1 \leq i \leq I$ such that $supp(\eta_) \subseteq \Omega_i \subseteq \Omega$. To compute the evolution of the Allen-Cahn equations in these subdomains, we need to introduce changes in the finite differences scheme.

3.1   Changes in the Finite Difference Scheme

Unlike Sect. 2.1, Dirichlet boundary conditions are defined for the Allen-Cahn equations.

$$\eta_i|_{\partial\Omega_i} = 0. \tag{20}$$

Let us assume that $\Omega_i, \forall i$ are chosen the same way as Ω, i.e. integer nodes lie on the boundary $X_{im}^{min} = (j_i)_m^{min} h_m$ and $X_{im}^{max} = (j_i)_m^{max} h_m$. Then, computation of the η_i is performed for nodes:

$$(j_i)_m^{min} + 1 \leq j_m \leq (j_i)_m^{max} - 1.$$

For all other nodes, $\eta_i = 0$ constantly. Further, the grid consisting of those nodes of G, which are in Ω_i, is denoted as $G_i \subseteq G$.

For simplicity, let us assume that nodes of grid G lie in the ranges:

$$0 \leq j_1 \leq k_1, \ \ 0 \leq j_2 \leq k_2, \ \ 0 \leq j_3 \leq k_3,$$

and nodes of grids $G_i, \forall i$ are in ranges:

$$k_{i1}^{min} \leq j_1 \leq k_{i1}^{max}, \ \ k_{i2}^{min} \leq j_2 \leq k_{i2}^{max}, \ \ k_{i3}^{min} \leq j_3 \leq k_{i3}^{max}.$$

Usually, in computer memory, the values of parameters are stored in arrays indexed from zero. The grid G has the same indexing as the corresponding array. The indexing in grid G_i starts with $k_{im}^{min}, m = 1, 2, 3$, i.e. it probably does not start from zero. The correspondence between array indexing (index with a tilde) and grid indexing is provided by the following formula:

$$\tilde{j}_1 = j_1 - k_{i1}^{min}, \quad \tilde{j}_2 = j_2 - k_{i2}^{min}, \quad \tilde{j}_3 = j_3 - k_{i3}^{min}, \quad 1 \le i \le I.$$

Or $\tilde{j} = j - k_i$ in vector form. In listings 1 and 2, this formula is used for the computation of $\sum_i \eta_i$ and the evolution of η_i.

Algorithm 1. Computation $\sum_i \eta_i$

---

for all j, j is the G node do
  $\tilde{j} \leftarrow j$
  $(\sum_i \eta_i)_{\tilde{j}} = 0$
end for
for $i = 1$ to N do
  for all j_i, j_i is the G_i node do
    $\tilde{j} \leftarrow j_i$
    $\tilde{j}_i \leftarrow j_i - k_i$
    $(\sum_i \eta_i)_{\tilde{j}} += (\eta_i)_{\tilde{j}_i}$
  end for
end for

The value of sums with other powers can be calculated in the same way as $\sum_i \eta_i$. The value of $\sum_{i<j} \eta_i \eta_j$ can be easily obtained by the formula:

$$\sum_{i<j} \eta_i \eta_j = \frac{1}{2} \left[(\sum_i \eta_i)^2 - \sum_i \eta_i^2 \right]$$

Algorithm 2. Evolution of η_i

---

for $i = 1$ to N do
  for all j_i, j_i is the G node do
    $\tilde{j} \leftarrow j_i$
    $\tilde{j}_i \leftarrow j_i - k_i$
    $(\eta_i)_{\tilde{j}_i}^{n+1} = (\eta_i)_{\tilde{j}_i}^{n} - \tau L(\frac{\partial f}{\partial \eta_i}(\rho_{\tilde{j}}^n, (\eta_i)_{\tilde{j}_i}^n) - \beta_\eta L[\eta_i]_{\tilde{j}_i}^n$
  end for
end for

3.2   Domains Tracking

The evolution of η_i goes with the grain growth process. Therefore we need to change the size of Ω_i.

Let us consider $\eta_i = 0.5$ as a grain boundary. Then, $mindist_i$ is a minimal distance between this boundary, and $\partial \Omega_i$ and $mindist_i$ is a maximal distance between the grain boundary and $\partial \Omega_i$.

At the beginning of the computation we chose Ω_i such that $mindist_i = maxdist_i = F_{start}$. Then, during the simulation, every T_r steps of model time, condition $mindist_i > F_{min}$ is checked for all i. If the condition failed for some i, this domain increases such that $mindist_i = F_{start}$. Also, every T_{fr} model time steps, all domains change such that $mindist_i = maxdist_i = F_{start}$. This allows eliminating of domains corresponding to the disappeared grains.

Algorithm depends on four parameters $F_{min}, T_r, F_{start}, T_{fr}$. F_{min} and T_r depend on model properties. F_{start} and T_{fr} allow us to control the balance between accuracy and performance. Decreasing F_{start} reduces memory usage. T_{fr} controls the frequency of memory reallocation. It is a very time-consuming operation, but on the other hand timely domain resizing reduces amount of computation. The parameter F_{min} should be at least wider than half of the phase-field interface. The parameter T_r depends on the grain boundary normal velocity, which is related to the grain boundary curvature κ_b and has the following evaluation [26]:

$$v_\eta = -L\beta_\eta \kappa_b, \tag{21}$$

For the spherical grains, we obtain the following evaluation:

$$T_r < \frac{F_{min}R^2}{L\beta_\eta}. \tag{22}$$

3.3   GPU-Based Implementation

In this section, we provide the main aspects of the GPU-based algorithm implementation. At every time step, the parameters μ, D, J, ρ are computed sequentially. The values in the nodes at the $n + 1$-th step do not depend on the values in other nodes; therefore, they can be computed independently using different GPU threads. All arrays are stored in the global memory, and different threads do not communicate with each other.

Separately, it is worth considering the calculation of $\sum_i \eta_i$ and the evolution of η_i. In the case of $\sum_i \eta_i$ in algorithm 1, the outer loop runs consequently since the data can be written in the same memory on different iterations. Iterations in the inner loop are independent. In algorithm 2, the outer loop can be computed in parallel, but for simplicity, it runs consequently. The inner loop in algorithm 2 is parallelized.

Our goal is fast sintering simulation; thus, we prefer to allocate memory for temporal parameters instead of recalculation for several grid nodes. To clarify the amount of memory required for the simulation, we provide a list of arrays used.

1. Two arrays, one for ρ^n and one for ρ^{n+1}.
2. Three arrays for sums.
3. One array for $\sum_{i<j} \eta_i \eta_j$
4. One array for μ

5. One array for D
6. Three arrays for components of J

If grid G has a size of $N_1 N_2 N_3$ nodes and double-precision arithmetic is used, these 11 arrays require $11 N_1 N_2 N_3 * 8$ bytes. Also, we need arrays for η_i^n and η_i^{n+1}, but their sizes depend on the sample configuration and algorithm parameters. Thus, the amount of memory required for storing the order parameters of the specific samples is presented in Sect. 4.

It is worth noting that due to the order of computation, some arrays can be reused. $\sum_i \eta_i$ necessary only for the computation of $\sum_{i<j} \eta_i \eta_j$. Therefore, one array can be used for both of them. Then, we do not need to store $\sum_i \eta_i^2$ and $\sum_i \eta_i^3$ after μ and η_i^{n+1} are computed. Similarly, an array for $\sum_{i<j} \eta_i \eta_j$ is not required after D is computed. Hence, three arrays for the J components are obtained. Finally, after the computation of flow components, the array for the chemical potential μ can be used for storing ρ^{n+1}. Assignment of the data between arrays is briefly shown in Table 1. As a result, only $6 N_1 N_2 N_3 * 8$ bytes are needed.

The tracking algorithm is developed for a single device (or node) with shared memory for all threads. Since grains move and their domains change, parallelization using several devices (or nodes) is not a trivial task and is currently unsupported.

Table 1. Data assignment between arrays

Array number	1	2	3	4	5	6
	ρ^n	$\sum_i \eta_i$	$\sum_i \eta_i^2$	$\sum_i \eta_i^3$	μ	D
		$\sum_{i<j} \eta_i \eta_j$	J_2	J_3	ρ^{n+1}	
		J_1				

4 Results

In this section, we present the results of the sintering simulation of the Y_2O_3. This material is chosen for the simulation because it can be used for the deactivation of CaO-based CO_2 sorbents. Therefore, we need to study its behavior during sintering. Since the Y_2O_3 crystallites have a rectangular shape [8], we consider the initial configuration as a regular package of randomly rotated cubes. The physical process that we want to simulate is the 2-hour calcination of the Y_2O_3 sample at $900°C$ in air. In all simulations, we use physical parameters from [28] with assumptions from [1,12] (Table 2). They are converted to model parameters and non-dimensionalized following [1] (Table 3).

Table 2. Physical parameters

Parameter	Parameter name	Parameter value	Units
γ_s	Surface energy	1.82	J/m^2
γ_{gb}	Grain boundary energy	1.43	J/m^2
D_{vol}	Volume diffusion coefficient	$6.14 \cdot 10^{-22}$	m^2/s
D_{vap}	Vapor diffusion coefficient	$3.07 \cdot 10^{-19}$	m^2/s
D_{surf}	Surface diffusion coefficient	$6.14 \cdot 10^{-19}$	m^2/s
D_{gb}	Grain boundary diffusion coefficient	$6.14 \cdot 10^{-19}$	m^2/s
D_a	Diffusion coefficient for atom mobility across grain boundary	$6.14 \cdot 10^{-19}$	m^2/s
$h_1 = h_2 = h_3 = h$	Spatial step	$1 \cdot 10^{-9}$	m
T	Temperature	1173	K
V_m	Molar volume	$45.1 \cdot 10^{-6}$	m^3/mol

Table 3. Simulation parameters

Parameter	A	B	β_ρ	β_η	L	D_{vol}
Value	11.85	1.43	41.49	26.74	$8.43 \cdot 10^{-2}$	$3.47 \cdot 10^{-4}$
Parameter	D_{vap}	D_{surf}	D_{gb}	h	τ	
Value	$1.73 \cdot 10^{-4}$	$3.47 \cdot 10^{-1}$	$3.47 \cdot 10^{-1}$	1	0.0026	

In all experiments, the parameters of the tracking algorithm take the following values:

$$F_{min} = 5h, \qquad T_r = 100\tau,$$
$$F_{start} = 10h, \quad T_{fr} = 1000\tau. \tag{23}$$

Computation node configuration is CPU Intel Xeon E5 2697 v3 and GPU NVIDIA K40.

4.1 Comparison of Solutions

In the first experiment, we create 10 samples consisting of 64 cubes. For each sample, the simulation is performed on the grid of size $83 \times 83 \times 83$ during 1000000 time steps (120 min of physical time) by two approaches. The first of them is the simulation explicitly as written in Sect. 2.1. The second one is the simulation using the algorithm described in Sect. 3. Let us denote the parameter related to the first approach by the index S. The index T is used for the second one. To compare obtained solutions, we compute the following values:

$$E_\rho(t) = \max_{x \in \Omega} |\rho_T(t, x) - \rho_S(t, x)|,$$
$$E_{SSA}(t) = \frac{|SSA_T(t) - SSA_S(t)|}{|SSA_S(t)|}. \tag{24}$$

The SSA parameter is computed by the Crofton formula [16] in the shrunk bounding box of the sample as described in [12]. This approach allows computing the surface area of intrinsic pores, which is more important for applications.

$$SSA = \frac{S_{bb}}{V_{bb}}, \tag{25}$$

where S_{bb} is the surface area of pores inside the shrunk bounding box, V_{bb} is the volume of the bounding box.

In Fig. 1 (left) E_ρ varies between 10^{-1} and 10^{-2} in most of the simulation. Since ρ is in the range $[0, 1]$, this difference is quite large. But as can be seen in Fig. 2, interfaces of two solutions are close to each other. It explains the large error; l_∞-norm is sensitive to shifts. Also, in Fig. 1 (right), we can see that the relative error of SSA is less than one percent.

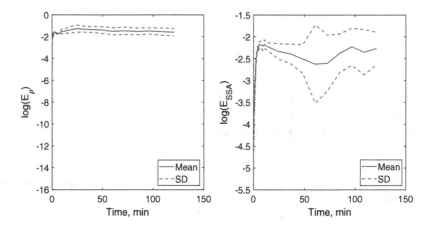

Fig. 1. Errors averaged across the ten samples.

Usage of the tracking algorithm decreases the computation time from 17.5 h to 1.2 h. Figure 2 shows the memory requirement for storing η_i averaged by samples. The explicit approach from Sect. 2.1 requires 292 MB, which is 10 times more than for the tracking algorithm. The plot named LROP corresponds to the locally reduced order parameters approach from [14] with $I_c = 6$. It is shown that tracking algorithms use fewer resources for most of the computational time.

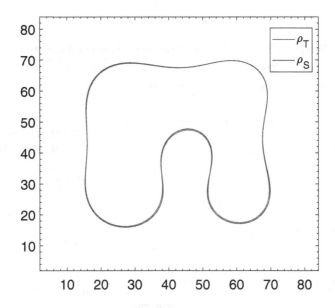

Fig. 2. Slice of the sample at the last time step for one of the experiments

4.2   Large Samples

In this section, we present the results of the sintering simulation for the two large samples (Table 4). They are created in the same way as in the previous section. The first of them, S_{16}, consists of 4096 cubes. Simulation for S_{16} is performed on the 294^3 grid during 1000000 iterations and takes 36.5 h. The second one

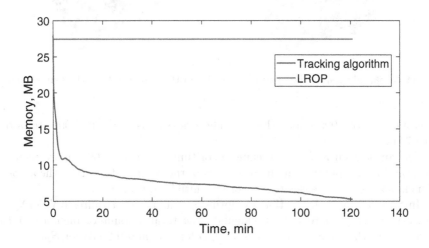

Fig. 3. Memory required for η_i storage

Table 4. Simulation of the large samples

Sample	Cubes	Grid size	Time steps	Computational time
S_{16}	4096	294^3	1000000	36.5 h
S_{20}	8000	358^3	1000000	74 h

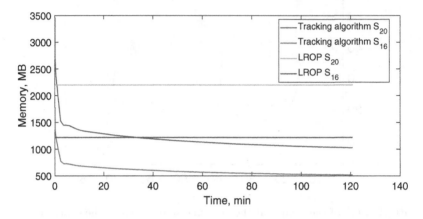

Fig. 4. Memory required for η_i storage

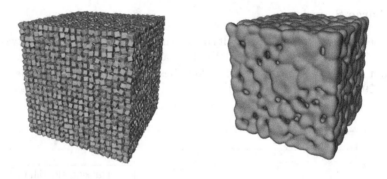

Fig. 5. Sample S_{20} at the beginning (left) and the end (right) of the simulation.

consists, S_{20}, of 8000 cubes (Fig. 5). The grid size is 358^3; 1000000 iterations take 74 h.

As can be seen in Fig. 4 tracking algorithm requires 50–60% more memory than the LROP approach at the beginning of the computation. But, the amount of memory fastly decreases to 40% of the initial requirements.

In Sect. 3.3, it is shown that excepting η_i, simulation requires $6N_1N_2N_3 * 8$ bytes of memory. Here we can calculate the total amount of memory at the beginning of the computation. It is 4.8 GB for S_{16}, and 9.2 GB for S_{20}.

4.3 Conclusion

According to the obtained results, we can conclude that tracking allows the sintering simulation without significant changes in sample properties such as SSA. Also, the usage of the algorithm decreases computation time and memory requirements in comparison with the explicit approach. The future work is to verify the possibility of changing the tracking algorithm parameters to decrease memory requirements without losing the quality. Another goal is to create a quantitative model of Y_2O_3 sintering.

Acknowledgements. The research is supported by the Russian Science Foundation grant no. 21-71-20003. Numerical simulations were performed using "Polytechnic RSC Tornado" (SPBSTU, Russia).

References

1. Ahmed, K., Pakarinen, J., Allen, T., El-Azab, A.: Phase field simulation of grain growth in porous uranium dioxide. J. Nucl. Mater. **446**, 90–99 (2014). https://doi.org/10.1016/j.jnucmat.2013.11.036
2. Allen, S., Cahn, J.: Ground state structures in ordered binary alloys with second neighbor interactions. Acta Metallurgica **20**(3), 423–433 (1972). https://doi.org/10.1016/0001-6160(72)90037-5, https://www.sciencedirect.com/science/article/pii/0001616072900375
3. Bazaikin, Y., Derevschikov, V., Malkovich, E., Lysikov, A., Okunev, A.: Evolution of sorptive and textural properties of cao-based sorbents during repetitive sorption/regeneration cycles: Part ii. modeling of sorbent sintering during initial cycles. Chem. Eng. Sci.**199**, 156–163 (2019). https://doi.org/10.1016/j.ces.2018.12.065, https://www.sciencedirect.com/science/article/pii/S0009250919300971
4. Bazaikin, Y., Malkovich, E., Derevschikov, V., Lysikov, A., Okunev, A.: Evolution of sorptive and textural properties of cao-based sorbents during repetitive sorption/regeneration cycles. Chem. Eng. Sci. **152,** 709–716 (2016). https://doi.org/10.1016/j.ces.2016.06.064, https://www.sciencedirect.com/science/article/pii/S000925091630361X
5. Bordia, R.K., Kang, S.J.L., Olevsky, E.A.: Current understanding and future research directions at the onset of the next century of sintering science and technology. J. Am. Ceram. Soc. **100**(6), 2314–2352 (2017). https://doi.org/10.1111/jace.14919
6. Cahn, J.W., Hilliard, J.E.: Free energy of a nonuniform system. I. interfacial free energy. J. Chem. Phys. **28**(2), 258–267 (1958). https://doi.org/10.1063/1.1744102
7. Tarwidi, D., Pudjaprasetya, S.R.: Godunov method for stefan problems with enthalpy formulations. East Asian J. Appl. Math. **3**(2), 107–119 (2018). https://doi.org/10.4208/eajam.030513.200513a
8. Derevschikov, V.S., Veselovskaya, J.V., Kardash, T.Y., Trubitsyn, D.A., Okunev, A.G.: Direct co2 capture from ambient air using k2co3/y2o3 composite sorbent. Fuel **127**, 212–218 (2014). https://doi.org/10.1016/j.fuel.2013.09.060, https://www.sciencedirect.com/science/article/pii/S0016236113009034
9. Florin, N., Fennell, P.: Synthetic cao-based sorbent for co2 capture **4**, 830–838 (2011). https://doi.org/10.1016/j.egypro.2011.01.126, https://www.sciencedirect.com/science/article/pii/S1876610211001287

10. Hötzer, J., Reiter, A., Hierl, H., Steinmetz, P., Selzer, M., Nestler, B.: The parallel multi-physics phase-field framework pace3d. J. Comput. Sci. **26**, 1–12 (2018). https://doi.org/10.1016/j.jocs.2018.02.011, https://www.sciencedirect.com/science/article/pii/S1877750317310116

11. Hötzer, J., et al.: Large scale phase-field simulations of directional ternary eutectic solidification. Acta Mater. **93**, 194–204 (2015). https://doi.org/10.1016/j.actamat.2015.03.051, https://www.sciencedirect.com/science/article/pii/S135964541500227X

12. Hötzer, J., Seiz, M., Kellner, M., Rheinheimer, W., Nestler, B.: Phase-field simulation of solid state sintering. Acta Mater. **164**, 184–195 (2018). https://doi.org/10.1016/j.actamat.2018.10.021

13. Gadylshina, K.A., Khachkova, T.S., Lisitsa, V.V. : Numerical modeling of chemical interaction between a fluid and rocks. Numer. Methods Programm. (Vychislitel'nye Metody i Programmirovanie) **20**(62), 457–470 (2020). https://doi.org/10.26089/NumMet.v20r440, https://en.num-meth.ru/index.php/journal/article/view/1035

14. Kim, S.G., Kim, D.I., Kim, W.T., Park, Y.B.: Computer simulations of two-dimensional and three-dimensional ideal grain growth. Phys. Rev. E 74, 061605 (2006). https://doi.org/10.1103/PhysRevE.74.061605, https://link.aps.org/doi/10.1103/PhysRevE.74.061605

15. Li, X., Huang, H., Meakin, P.: A three-dimensional level set simulation of coupled reactive transport and precipitation/dissolution. Int. J. Heat Mass Transf. **53**(13), 2908–2923 (2010)

16. Liu, Y.S., Yi, J., Zhang, H., Zheng, G.Q., Paul, J.C.: Surface area estimation of digitized 3d objects using quasi-monte carlo methods. Pattern Recogn. **43**, 3900–3909 (2010). https://doi.org/10.1016/j.patcog.2010.06.002

17. Moelans, N., Blanpain, B., Wollants, P.: An introduction to phase-field modeling of microstructure evolution. Calphad **32**, 268–294 (2008). https://doi.org/10.1016/j.calphad.2007.11.003

18. Moelans, N., Wendler, F., Nestler, B.: Comparative study of two phase-field models for grain growth. Comput. Mater. Sci. **46**, 479–490 (2009). https://doi.org/10.1016/j.commatsci.2009.03.037

19. Molins, S., et al.: Pore-scale controls on calcite dissolution rates from flow-through laboratory and numerical experiments. Environ. Sci. Technol. **48**(13), 7453–7460 (2014)

20. Osher, S., Fedkiw, R.P.: Level set methods: an overview and some recent results. J. Comput. Phys. **169**(2), 463–502 (2001)

21. Peskin, C.S.: Flow patterns around heart valves: a numerical method. J. Comput. Phys. **10**, 252–271 (1972)

22. Pino, D., Julien, B., Valdivieso, F., Drapier, S.: Solid-state sintering simulation: surface, volume and grain-boundary diffusions. In: ECCOMAS 2012 - European Congress on Computational Methods in Applied Sciences and Engineering, e-Book Full Papers (2012)

23. Prokhorov, D., Lisitsa, V., Khachkova, T., Bazaikin, Y., Yang, Y.: Topology-based characterization of chemically-induced pore space changes using reduction of 3d digital images. J. Comput. Sci. **58**, 101550 (2022). https://doi.org/10.1016/j.jocs.2021.101550, https://www.sciencedirect.com/science/article/pii/S1877750321002052

24. Smereka, P.: Semi-implicit level set methods for curvature and surface diffusion motion. J. Sci. Comput. **19**, 439–456 (2003)

25. Sotiropoulos, F., Yang, X.: Immersed boundary methods for simulating fluid-structure interaction. Prog. Aerosp. Sci. **65**, 1–21 (2014)

26. Spears, M., Evans, A.: Microstructure development during final/intermediate stage sintering-ii. grain and pore coarsening. Acta Metall. **30**(7), 1281–1289 (1982). https://doi.org/10.1016/0001-6160(82)90146-8, https://www.sciencedirect.com/science/article/pii/0001616082901468

27. Trebotich, D., Adams, M.F., Molins, S., Steefel, C.I., Shen, C.: High-resolution simulation of pore-scale reactive transport processes associated with carbon sequestration. Comput. Sci. Eng. **16**, 22–31 (2014)

28. Triantafyllou, G., Angelopoulos, G., Nikolopoulos, P.: Surface and grain-boundary energies as well as surface mass transport in polycrystalline yttrium oxide. J. Mater. Sci. **45**, 2015–2022 (2009). https://doi.org/10.1007/s10853-009-4013-7

29. Wang, Y.U.: Computer modeling and simulation of solid-state sintering: a phase field approach. Acta Materialia **54**(4), 953–961 (2006). https://doi.org/10.1016/j.actamat.2005.10.032, https://www.sciencedirect.com/science/article/pii/S135964540500635X

30. White, R.E.: An enthalpy formulation of the stefan problem. SIAM J. Numer. Anal. **19**(6), 1129–1157 (1982). http://www.jstor.org/stable/2157200

31. Zhang, R.J., Chen, Z.W., Fang, W., Qu, X.: Thermodynamic consistent phase field model for sintering process with multiphase powders. Trans. Nonferrous Metals Soc. China **24**, 783–789 (2014). https://doi.org/10.1016/S1003-6326(14)63126-5

Software Package for High-Performance Computations in Airframe Assembly Modeling

Nadezhda Zaitseva$^{(\boxtimes)}$ and Tatiana Pogarskaia

Peter the Great St. Petersburg Polytechnic University, St. Petersburg, Russia
zaitseva.n.i@mail.ru, pogarskaya.t@gmail.com

Abstract. Airframe assembly modeling is a complex problem that includes computations for large-scale compliant parts, variation analysis, optimization of fastening procedures and many other problems that occur in manufacturing process. At the same time the majority of these problems involve solving similar contact problems. It is often the most time-consuming part of computations needed to determine stress state of the assembled parts for further analysis. To overcome the problem and provide computations for serial production in reasonable time a special parallel software package called ASRP (Assembly Simulation of Riveting Process) was developed. The paper is devoted to the description of the software, problems and approach that combines variation simulation and HPC for aircraft assembly simulation. The main focus of this work is made on the analysis of temporary fastener patterns used during assembly. To demonstrate the efficiency of high-performance computing, we provide several industrial examples of the analysis for the fastening patterns in aircraft assembly processes.

Keywords: Assembly process · Optimization · Contact problem · Variation analysis · High-performance computing

1 Introduction

One of the prior tasks in the aircraft industry is to ensure the high quality of assembly at all production stages. Any decrease in quality leads to an appropriate decrease in the reliability of final products and can cause catastrophic consequences. Enormous financial resources have been invested in the development and equipment of technological lines for high-quality serial production [1]. The usage of computation software helps to predict the quality of production at any design stage and, thus, reduces the cost of assembly process development.

One of the key factors that influence the quality of assembly is random variations which can be caused by defects in the manufacturing and inaccuracies in the assembly process [2]. Because of these variations, the technical requirements for reliability and functionality of the final product can be violated [3]. Therefore, it is important to consider these variations in the mathematical modeling of the assembly process. In addition, for aircraft construction it is also essential to take into account deformations of parts during assembly.

V. Voevodin et al. (Eds.): RuSCDays 2022, LNCS 13708, pp. 328–341, 2022.
https://doi.org/10.1007/978-3-031-22941-1_24

The standard method for assembly analysis considering variations and deformations is the Direct Monte Carlo method [4] when the modeling of the assembly process is carried out by the finite element analysis and variations are generated from random distributions. This method is used both in research studies [5–7] and in commercial software products (3DCS [8], Tecnomatix [9]). However, the usage of the finite element method for large and complex structures makes it very time-consuming.

In order to reduce computational time, the MIC (Method of Influence Coefficients) was proposed in [2]. It significantly reduces the time for analysis but models contact only at predefined points. In [10] the MIC is combined with the algorithms of the direct contact points search. As a result, the accuracy of contact modeling increases. Therefore, this combination of approaches is widely used for analysis of assembly processes [11, 12] and for software tool development [3]. However, such methodology is difficult to implement for sufficiently detailed models.

Another way to reduce simulation time is proposed in [13]. The assembly modeling is based on the variational formulation of the reduced contact problem [14]. It provides an accurate and fast solution for aircraft assembly modeling. This approach is used is ASRP software (Assembly Simulation of Riveting Process). Additional decrease of computational costs in ASRP is achieved by using specialized numerical methods [15]. This paper describes how the high-performance computing (HPC) techniques are implemented in ASRP to provide fast aircraft assembly simulation. The industrial examples, included in this paper, show the effectiveness and practical use of developed approach.

2   Temporary Fastening

In the aerospace industry the flexible structures should be assembled with high accuracy. Hence, specialized assembly methods are used to meet the accuracy requirements [16]. Thus, the most common type of joining methods is fastening. The number of fasteners installed during aircraft assembly can reach up to 2 million pieces [17]. Despite persistent attempts to automate production [18], most fastening operations are still done manually. The mechanical installation of fasteners gives about 60% of the total aircraft assembly cost and provides 80% of all detected defects [19]. Therefore, the optimization of the fastening procedures can greatly affect the efficiency of production [20].

One of the stages of fastening is the installation of *temporary fastener elements* (TFE) in a predefined set of holes. These fasteners join parts together to minimize the gap between parts and to avoid defects during further operations (drilling, reaming etc.). This procedure is important as about 75%–85% of all failures happen around holes with fasteners [17]. After the end of drilling operations, the TFE are replaced by final rivets.

For serial assembly lines it is impossible to adjust the TFE installation for individual characteristics of an incoming parts. Therefore, a single TFE pattern is used for each joint. This pattern should reduce the gap between all the incoming parts. Therefore, the quality of TFE pattern is determined by its ability to minimize the gap with respect to possible assembly variations. Figure 1 shows two examples of TFE patterns: the colored circles are the TFE, the gray circles are empty holes that will be drilled. The first pattern includes 110 TFE and the second has only 80. This decrease in TFE number reduces the time for manual fastener installation. However, when we develop an assembly technology, it is important to know how this decrease in TFE number affects the gap between joined parts. The development of effective TFE patterns that provide a time/quality balance is one of the present methods for optimizing the assembly process in aircraft manufacturing [19].

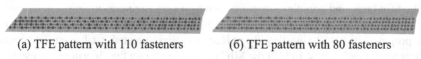

(a) TFE pattern with 110 fasteners   (б) TFE pattern with 80 fasteners

Fig. 1. Two different TFE patterns for wing-to-fuselage joining

3 Variation Analysis

The assembly variations are caused by random deviations in parts (manufacturing defects and deviations in part shapes) and deviations in the assembly process (inaccuracies and deviations in positioning, fastening, and other operations) [2, 21]. Variation analysis is a large area of research devoted to modelling and analysis of those variations both for aviation [5, 7] and automotive [2, 3, 12] industries.

The statistical modeling based on the Monte Carlo method (MCM) is the main approach in variation analysis. It consists of multiple simulations of the assembly process with random initial variations. Based on the obtained data, the required probabilistic characteristics of the analyzed process are determined.

When applying MCM to the analysis of assembly process, the main problem is to build the exact relationship between initial deviations in parts and the final variations in assembled structure. For flexible parts, the desired ratio can be affected by nonlinear effects associated with the deformations and contact interactions.

In ASRP the contact interaction of flexible parts is modeled through the gap between the parts [14]. The gap is a scalar function that specifies the distance between the surfaces to be joined. The presence of random assembly variations provides an *initial gap* between parts, that is the gap before parts contact interaction and fastening. The gap that remains between parts after their contact interaction and fastening is called the *residual gap*. In this approach, the initial gap conveys the effect of assembly variations and the residual gap determines the quality of the TFE pattern.

The residual gap is calculated by solving the contact problem. The corresponding contact problem with non-penetration condition can be reduced to a quadratic programming problem [15]:

$$\min_{g_{res}=g-u\geq0}\left(\frac{1}{2}u^{T}Ku-f^{T}u\right),\tag{1}$$

where u is the desired vector of relative normal displacements of parts; K is a positive-definite matrix that are determined through the stiffness matrix and defined pairs of contact nodes; f is a vector that specifies the external forces from fasteners; g is the vector of the initial gap; g_{res} is the vector of the residual gap after parts joining.

3.1 Verification of Fastening Pattern

The analysis of the TFE pattern with account of possible assembly variations is called *verification*. Verification is a practical tool for fastener pattern optimization as it helps to analyze, compare and modify patterns with respect to quality requirements. In this subsection we provide a detailed description of the proposed procedure for TFE pattern analysis based on statistical modeling [22].

For a given TFE pattern the developed verification procedure consists of three stages:

Stage 1. Generate a cloud of initial gaps. A large set of the initial gaps is generated. This set is called *a cloud of initial gaps*. The number N^{gen} gaps in the cloud is chosen so that statistical analysis gives stable results. Typically, $N^{gen} \geq 100$.

Stage 2. Model the assembly process. For each initial gap from the cloud, the joining of the parts is simulated: solving the contact problem the corresponding values of the residual gap are calculated.

Stage 3. Estimate the pattern quality. Based on the obtained set of residual gaps, the statistical characteristics of this gap are estimated. Thus, the quality of the analyzed TFE pattern considering assembly variations is evaluated.

The scheme of verification procedure is shown in Fig. 2. The contact problems at Stage 2 can be solved independently, so it is possible to use task parallelization on this stage. In ASRP two versions of the verification are implemented: *serial* version performs sequential calculations for contact problems and can be run on a PC and *parallel* version performs contact problem solving in parallel on separate processes and can be run on a supercomputer. The computation time for one contact problem solving for parts with complex three-dimensional geometry can reach up to 10 min. Therefore, usage of the parallel version significantly reduces the analysis time.

To analyze the TFE pattern quality, the probabilistic characteristics of the residual gap are used. For example, the probability that the residual gap exceeds a given tolerance δ for each point (x, y) of the area between the parts:

$$P_{loc}(x, y; \delta) = \text{Prob}\{g_{res}(x, y) > \delta\}, (x, y) \in \Omega. \tag{2}$$

This statistical characteristic shows the problem areas between the parts (where the residual gap will be bigger than tolerance δ). Thus, in such areas the modification of the TFE pattern is usually required.

3.2 Initial Gap Modeling

To carry out verification procedure, it is necessary to have a cloud of initial gaps (large set of possible initial gaps between parts). However, for a real assembly process it can be difficult to obtain a sufficient number of measured initial gaps. Therefore, the required number of samples should be generated artificially through modeling.

For the aircraft assembly, it can be assumed that the *junction area* between the joining parts (the area where parts can come in contact) can be represented as a continuous area $\Omega \subset \mathbb{R}^2$ with a local coordinate system. At each point of this junction area, the gap can

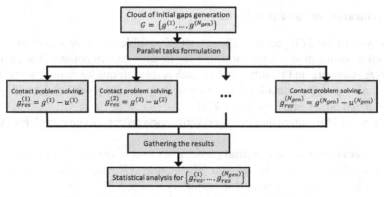

Fig. 2. Verification procedure with task parallelization

be defined as the distance between the parts in the normal direction to the surface of the parts. As the initial gap is a combination of random assembly variations, it can be presented as a random function $g(x, y)$, where $(x, y) \in \Omega$ are local coordinates in the junction area Ω. Based on this representation, two methods of initial gap modeling have been developed for ASRP software [23].

Modeling of Initial Gap as a Gaussian Random Field

Since all parts are manufactured the same way, a random deviation on the part's surfaces can be modeled as a Gaussian random field. Thus, the initial gap, as the sum of parts deviations, can be represented as some Gaussian random field. Accordingly, in [14] it is proposed to model the initial gap as:

$$g_{RF}(x, y) = \mu(x, y) + \xi(x, y), (x, y) \in \Omega, \tag{3}$$

where $\mu(x, y)$ is a deterministic function that models the regular component of the initial gap due to systematic deviations (similar deviations that can be observed for each manufactured parts), and $\xi(x, y)$ is a random field that presents a random component of the initial gap (occurs due to random assembly deviations). This approach is convenient since it does not require taking into account all the physical and technical reasons for the appearance of this random initial gap.

The regular component $\mu(x, y)$ is defined as the average value of the initial gap at each point of the junction area. The random field $\xi(x, y)$ is assumed to be a smooth, Gaussian, homogeneous and anisotropic field with zero mean value, variance σ^2 and exponential covariance function:

$$K(\overrightarrow{r}; \alpha, \beta) = \sigma^2 \exp\left(-\frac{\alpha^2 r_x^2}{2} - \frac{\beta^2 r_y^2}{2}\right), r_x = |x_2 - x_1|, r_y = |y_2 - y_1|, \tag{4}$$

where $\overrightarrow{r}$ is the distance between pair of points in junction area (x_1, y_1) and (x_2, y_2). Two parameters (α, β) define the correlation properties of this random field in the direction of the X and Y axes respectively. The parameters $(\mu, \sigma^2, \alpha$ and $\beta)$ can be estimated based

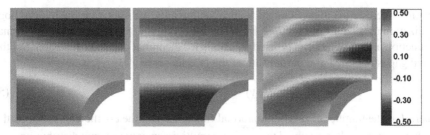

Fig. 3. Initial gaps for splice-to-fuselage joint, generated from model (3).

on the available measured initial gaps [24]. In the Fig. 3 the examples of generated initial gaps between splice and fuselage parts for fuselage assembly process are shown.

Since in most cases the set of available measurements is limited, it is important to evaluate the efficiency of the proposed initial gap model. To do so, it is studied how the number of available measurements N_s affects the accuracy of the model (3) parameter estimations. Some examples of the mean relative errors for model parameter estimates are shown in Fig. 4. The performed study shows that with the increase in the number of available measurements N_s, the estimation error decreases. This indicates that the proposed estimates are consistent. However, for small N_s, the estimation error is quite large, so in these cases it is better to use another method of initial gap modeling.

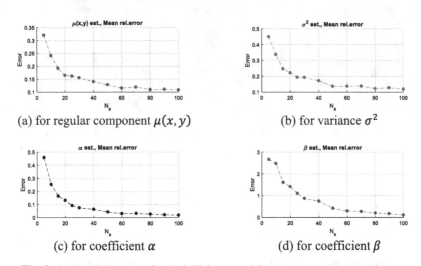

(a) for regular component $\mu(x, y)$

(b) for variance σ^2

(c) for coefficient α

(d) for coefficient β

Fig. 4. Mean relative error for the initial gap model $g_{RF}(x, y)$ parameter estimates

Modeling of Initial Gap Based on Mode Shapes

The modal analysis with finite element method can provide a set of natural frequencies and corresponding natural forms (*mode shapes*) of the free vibrations of each joining part. This set of mode shapes correspond to possible displacements of the parts. Since we are only interested in displacements in the junction area, we use Gram-Schmidt orthogonalization to get a set of functions $\{e_1(x, y), e_2(x, y), \dots\}, x \in \Omega$ that are orthonormal in junction area. This set can be used as a basis for the initial gap representation. So, the initial gap is regarded as a partial sum of the Fourier series [23]:

$$g_{MD}(x, y) = \sum_{i=1}^{L} \lambda_i e_i(x, y), \qquad (5)$$

where L is the number of used orthonormal functions, and the coefficients λ_i forms the random vector $\vec{\lambda}$. It is assumed that $\vec{\lambda}$ has a multidimensional normal distribution with mean $\vec{m} \in \mathbb{R}^L$ and covariance matrix $\mathcal{K} \in \mathbb{R}^{L \times L}$. To estimate parameters $\vec{m}$ and $\mathcal{K}$ the measured gaps decomposed in series (5) to get the sample for coefficients. To select the optimal number of functions L, a special procedure is proposed in [24] based on comparing of the total variations of the initial gaps. An example of the generated initial gaps is shown in Fig. 5.

Performed study of the model g_{MD} efficiency in case of limited set of measurements showed that for a small number of available measurements N_s the parameter estimation errors for the second model g_{MD} are smaller than for the g_{RF} (see Fig. 6). A full comparison of the practical use of these models in [25] proved that initial gap modeling based on mode shapes better reproduces the characteristics of the real initial gap in the case of a limited set of measurements.

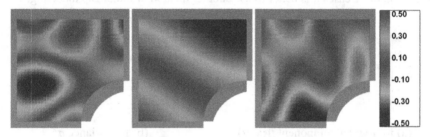

Fig. 5. Initial gaps for splice-to-fuselage joint, generated from model (4).

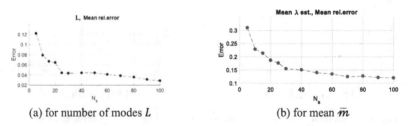

(a) for number of modes L (b) for mean $\vec{m}$

Fig. 6. Mean relative error for the initial gap model $g_{MD}(x, y)$ parameter estimates

3.3 Efficiency of Task Parallelization for Verification

In this subsection we provide the results of verification procedure and show the efficiency of its parallelization on the example of A350 fuselage section S19 assembly process. The verified TFE pattern is shown in Fig. 7a. This pattern consists of 76 temporary fastening elements.

For this assembly process the number of available initial gap measurements was not enough for statistical analysis, so at Stage 1 the cloud of 200 initial gaps was generated using the initial gap model (5). At Stage 2, the corresponding contact problems were solved using *"serial"* or *"parallel"* versions of verification procedure. At Stage 3, the statistical characteristic (2) of the residual gap was estimated.

The results of verification for the analyzed pattern are shown in Fig. 7b. It shows that in some areas the probability of tolerance violations is relatively big. Thus, the analyzed TFE pattern should be modified to meet quality requirements.

To examine efficiency and scalability of the parallelization, we conducted the verification procedures for different number N^{gen} of the initial gaps in cloud. The resulting time for serial and parallel procedures was compared. In the parallel version the number of processes was the same as the number of initial gaps in the cloud: $p = N^{gen}$. For parallel computations, the capacities of the Polytechnic supercomputer center were used.

The computation time for one contact problem solving varies from 2.5 to 4 min for different initial gaps. For serial procedure the verification time increases in proportion to the number of initial gaps in the cloud. For parallel procedure the verification time is slightly higher than the longest contact problem computation due to gathering results. For typical initial gap cloud with $N^{gen} = 200$ gaps the verification time for serial procedure is 490 min and for parallel procedure is 5 min. As expected the use of the parallel version gives a significant gain in time. Accordingly, such a variant of parallelization (task parallelization for contact problem solving) turns out to be very effective for solving the described assembly problems.

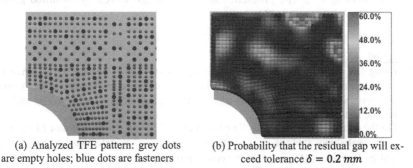

(a) Analyzed TFE pattern: grey dots are empty holes; blue dots are fasteners

(b) Probability that the residual gap will exceed tolerance $\delta = 0.2\ mm$

Fig. 7. Verification of TFE pattern for A350 fuselage section S19

4 Fastener Pattern Optimization

During the assembly process of aircraft structures, it is often necessary to optimize the TFE pattern. For example, when the verification procedure shows that the currently used pattern does not provide the desired quality of contact or when the number of TFE is to be reduce without losing quality of joining.

Let us describe notation for TFE pattern optimization. Let us introduce the set of holes $H = \{h_i\}_{i=1,n_h}$ numbered in ascending order where, n_h is the total number of holes. Each hole has a given diameter that determines the fastening load of a temporary fastener to be installed into this hole. The vector of normal fastener loads $F_n = (f_i)_{i=1,n_h}$ is associated with set of holes H. The fastener pattern $H^o = \{h_i^o\}_{i=1,n_f}$ is described as a set of occupied holes, where $n_f = |H^o|$ is the number of installed fasteners, $H^o \subset H$ (see Fig. 8).

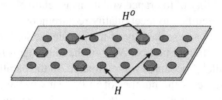

Fig. 8. Empty holes and a TFE pattern

4.1 Fastener Number Optimization

The optimization problem was fully described in [25] and here we just briefly formulate it. Find the pattern H^0 of the smallest possible size n_{f*} that yields a probability of defect for g_* smaller or equal to a given value P^* for all initial gaps in the gap cloud G (the residual gap after fastening H^0 supposed to exceed g_* with probability no larger than a predefined value P^*). The problem can be efficiently solved by modified geodesic algorithm (GA) proposed in [26]:

Optimization Algorithm 1
1 Using GA obtain a pattern of the maximum possible size (number of fasteners is equal to number of holes). GA defines TFE to be included in the pattern one by one. It means that a pattern of size one less that the regarded can be achieved by excluding the last added element;
2 For the pattern of each size calculate the vector $\{P(H_k^*, g_*)\}$, where value $P(H_k^*, g_*)$ is the probability that the value of the residual gap after installation of pattern H_k will be less or equal to g_* in all the computational nodes.
3 Find pattern $H_{n_*}^*$ of the minimal size in set $\{H_k^*\}$ providing maximum probability able satisfy the demands on the residual gap.

4.2 Fastener Order Optimization

At first glimpse, the determination of the assembly deformation on the base of minimization of functional (1) does not imply the dependence of results on order of fastener installation. Indeed, the displacement field is obtained as a unique minimizer of convex functional on convex set, that is determined only by matrix K, initial gap g and the vector of current fastening forces f with no history of fastener installation. Meanwhile in aircraft assembly practice it is very important to choose the temporary fastener order properly. Here we briefly describe this effect and update the model based on (1) in order to take it into account.

Presently the standard airframe assembly technology involves the drilling of parts already fixed in the assembly jig. The temporary fasteners are installed to the holes immediately after drilling. As the fastener diameter matches the diameter of hole, the installed fasteners fix the relative tangential displacements of parts (g_{res}^{τ}), that took place during drilling (see Fig. 9).

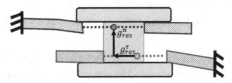

Fig. 9. Relative tangential displacements in a fastened hole.

Mathematicaly it corresponds to supplement the admissible set U_A by the additional constraints after installation of each fastener. These additional constraints have the similar form as given in relation (1). But presently the matrix A, and initial gap g contain the information on the history of fastener installation. It means that we cannot simulate the isntallation of several fasteners in one run, but need sequentially simulate one by one. That dramatically increases computational time. Such complication is justified only if the considered effect is significant (relatively flexible parts with high curvature as the fuselage panels).

Optimization Problem. Let us denote the set of all possible orders for pattern H^0 as J_{n_f}

$$J_{n_f}\left(H^0\right) = \{S(H^o)\}, \tag{6}$$

where S describes the fastening sequence as a permutation of indexes:

$$S = S(H^o) = (j_m)_{m=1,n_f} : \forall m \in \{1, .., n_f\} \exists! k \in \{1, .., n_f\} : i_k = j_m, \tag{7}$$

Then the optimization problem can be formulated, as follows: for a given TFE pattern H^o of n_f size and initial gap g^n find the fastener installation order $S^* \in J_{n_f}(H^o)$ minimizing maximal residual gap after the installation of all TFE in the pattern, i.e.

$$S^* = arg\left(\min_{S \in J_{n_f}(H^o)} \|Rg\left(g^n, S\right)\|\right). \tag{8}$$

The following algorithm is proposed to solve the stated problem:

Optimization Algorithm 2

1   Set $F_n = (f_i)_{i=1,n_h}$; $f_k = \{ \begin{array}{ll} f_k, & k \in \{i_1,..,i_{n_f}\} \\ 0, & \text{otherwise} \end{array}$,

where $\{i_m\}_{1,n_f}$ is the set of indexes of occupied holes;

2   Minimize functional (1) with empty tangential constraints;
3   Compute the tangential offsets of the parts in the occupied holes;
4   Arrange the vector of tangential offsets in ascending order (by absolute value);
5   Set the required sequence as $S := S(H^o) = (j_m)_{m=1,n_f}$,

where $\{j_m\}_{1,n_f}$ is the resulting permutation of indexes obtained from step 4.

The main idea of the algorithm is to define order of fastener installation up to already computed tangential displacements sorted in ascending order. It is a simple non-iterative way to find an appropriate solution quickly (no contact problem recalculations).

5   Application Examples for Fastener Pattern Optimization

5.1   Optimization of A350 Fuselage Section Manufacturing Process

Let us demonstrate several most typical applications of the developed software. As the first example, we consider a problem of a real aircraft when it is necessary to improve current TFE pattern and to decrease number of TFE but to keep the residual gap in a given range. Fasteners can be installed to any empty hole, except the ones to be reamed. Let us consider the model of the A350 fuselage Sect. 19 "S19" (see Fig. 10).

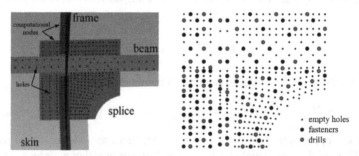

Fig. 10. The junction area (left): holes for fasteners (black) and computational nodes (red); The area for optimization (right): the positions of drilled holes and TFE (Color figure online).

The modeled assembly stage involves 48 reaming operations that are done one-by-one with the same 76 pre-installed TFE (see left side on Fig. 10). The other 283 holes remain empty and valid for the fasteners to be moved to. According to the current technology, the gap between parts while reaming must be no large than predefined value $\alpha = 0.3$ mm.

The problem was solved by GA and Local Variations algorithm which has already been successfully implemented for the type of problems [25, 26]. Both algorithms allowed to reduce number of TFE from 76 to 50 and 53 respectively.

Using parallelization in the kind of problems allows to perform optimization over a set of initial gaps and take into account measurements available from real aircrafts. It is a very important feature of the software as it allows to meet the needs of the industry.

5.2 Fuselage-to-Fuselage Joint

Let us consider a quite flexible joint where the effect of fastener order installation is significant. The model of fuselage to fuselage junction (see Fig. 11), that was previously used to verify contact problem solving methodology by comparison with physical exper-iments [13]. Each part of the joint is forced by seven stringers. Provided experiments show that the order of installation of fasteners for this joint can lead to bending of parts and a critical increase in the gap between parts after installation of fasteners.

For a TFE pattern H^o of 6 elements installation order is obtained by Algorithm 2. It is compared to the global optimum found by the exhaustive search. The obtained order provides only 0.052 mm (3.8%) higher maximal residual gap value than the global optimum and the residual gaps fields are very similar (see Fig. 12). The simulation results confirm that the correct order of installation of fasteners leads to a decrease in the gap between the parts. Moreover, the proposed algorithm for optimizing the fastening order allows one to get a result significantly faster and without much loss of accuracy.

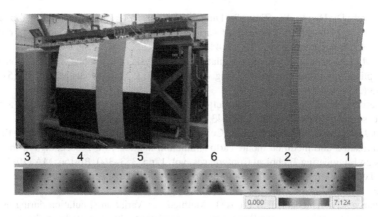

Fig. 11. Fuselage to fuselage joint. The test bench (left) and the computational model (right) and TFE pattern (down)

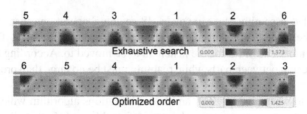

Fig. 12. Residual gap fields

6 Conclusion

The ASRP software is developed to model and analyze assembly processes in the aircraft industry. It supports analysis and optimization for serial production in reasonable time through specially developed numerical approaches and procedures. In particular, ASRP provides a wide range of methods and procedures for temporary fastener patterns analysis. The verification procedures supply the prediction of the quality of the pattern, taking into account random assembly variations. The developed optimization methods help to solve the problem of optimizing the fasteners pattern to speed up the assembly. In the numerical implementation of the proposed methods, parallelization by tasks is used, which significantly reduces computation time. As a result, the ASRP complex can be used in engineering practice for solving a wide range of tasks related to the development and optimization of aircraft assembly processes.

Acknowledgements. The research was supported by Russian Science Foundation (project No. 22–19-00062, https://rscf.ru/en/project/22-19-00062/).

References

1. Ceglarek, D., Huang, W., Zhou, S., Ding, Y., Kumar, R., et al.: Time-based competition in multistage manufacturing: stream-of-variation analysis (SOVA) methodology – review. J. Flexible Manufacturing Syst. **16**, 11–44 (2009)
2. Hu, M., Lin, Z., Lai, X., Ni, J.: Simulation and analysis of assembly processes considering compliant, non-ideal parts and tooling variations. Int. J. Mach. Tools Manuf **41**(15), 2233–2243 (2001)
3. Söderberg, R., Lindkvist, L., Wärmefjord, K., Carlson, J.S.: Virtual geometry assurance process and toolbox. Procedia CIRP **43**, 3–12 (2016)
4. Gao, J., Chase, K.W., Magleby, S. P.: Comparison of assembly tolerance analysis by the direct linearization and modified monte carlo simulation methods. In: Proceedings of the ASME Design Engineering Technical Conferences, vol. 1, pp. 353–360. Boston, MA (1995)
5. Saadat, M., Cretin, L., Sim, R.: Deformation analysis of large aerospace components during assembly. Int. J. Adv. Manuf. Technol. **41**, 145–155 (2009)
6. Falgarone, H., Thiebaut, F., Coloos, J., Mathieu, L.: Variation simulation during assembly of nonrigid components. Realistic assembly simulation with Anatoleflex software. In: 14th CIRP CAT 2016 – CIRP Conference on Computer Aided Tolerancing, 43, pp. 202–207 (2016)
7. Wang, H., Si, S.: A FEA simulation model for thin-walled C-section composite beam assembling with R-angle deviation. In: ASME International Mechanical Engineering Congress and Exposition, Proceedings (IMECE), vol. 2 (2014)

8. DCS Software Solutions. http://www.3dcs.com Accessed 09 Sept 2022
9. Tecnomatix Variation Analysis. https://www.plm.automation.siemens.com/global/ru/pro ducts/tecnomatix/. Accessed 09 Sept 2022
10. Wärmefjord, K., Lindkvist, L., Söderberg, R.: Tolerance simulation of compliant sheet metal assemblies using automatic node-based contact detection. In: ASME 2008 International Mechanical Engineering Congress and Exposition, vol. 14, pp. 35–44 (2008)
11. Jareteg, C., Wärmefjord, K., Cromvik, C., Söderberg, R., Lindkvist, L., et al.: Geometry assurance integrating process variation with simulation of spring-in for composite parts and assemblies. In: ASME 2014 International Mechanical Engineering Congress and Exposition, vol. 2A (2014)
12. Lorin, L., Lindkvist, L., Söderberg, R.: Variation simulation of stresses using the method of influence coefficients. J. Computing Inf. Science in Eng. **14**(1) (2014)
13. Lupuleac, S., Kovtun, M., Rodionova, O., Marguet, B.: Assembly simulation of riveting process. SAE Int. J. Aerosp. **2**, 193–198 (2010)
14. Lupuleac, S., Zaitseva, N., Stefanova, M., Berezin, S., Shinder, J., et al.: Simulation and optimization of airframe assembly process. In: ASME International Mechanical Engineering Congress and Exposition, vol. 2A (2018)
15. Stefanova, M., Minevich, O., Baklanov, S.: Convex optimization techniques in compliant assembly simulation. Optim. Eng. (2020)
16. Dmitriev, A.Y., Vashukov, Yu.A., Mitroshkina, T.A.: Robust design and technological preparation for the production of aircraft products. Samara: Publishing House of SSAU (2016)
17. Guseva, R.I. Features of aircraft airframe assembly technology. Komsomolsk-on-Amur: FGBOU VPO "KnAGTU" (2013, in Russian)
18. Mueller, R., Vette, M., Masiak, T., Duppe, B.: Intelligent real time inspection of rivet quality supported by human-robot-collaboration. SAE Int. J. Adv. Curr. Prac. in Mobility **2**(2), 811–817 (2020)
19. Assembly Automation Takes Off in Aerospace Industry (2015). https://www.assemblymag. com/articles/92790-assembly-automation-takes-off-in-aerospace-industry. Accessed 09 Sept 2022
20. Weber, A.: Assembling the super jumbo. Assembly **48**(9), 66–77 (2005)
21. Lorin, S., Cromvik, C., Edelvik, F., Lindkvist, L., Söderberg, R.: Variation Simulation of welded assemblies using a thermo-elastic finite element model. J. Computing and Information Science in Eng. **14**(3) (2013)
22. Zaitseva, N., Pogarskaia, T., Minevich, O., Shinder, J.: Simulation of Aircraft Assembly via ASRP Software. SAE Technical Paper (2019)
23. Zaitseva, N., Lupuleac, S., Khashba, V., Shinder, J., Bonhomme, E.: Approaches to initial gap modeling in final aircraft assembly simulation. In: ASME International Mechanical Engineering Congress and Exposition, vol. 2B (2020)
24. Zaitseva, N.: Part deviation modeling and variation analysis for aircraft assemblies. Dissertation, SPbPU (2021)
25. Lupuleac, S., Pogarskaia, T., Churilova, M., Kokkolaras, M., Bonhomme, E.: Optimization of fastener pattern in airframe assembly. Assem. Autom. **40**(5), 723–733 (2020)
26. Pogarskaia, T., Lupuleac, S., Bonhomme, E.: Novel approach to optimization of fastener pattern for airframe assembly process. Procedia CIRP **93**, 1151–1157 (2020)

State-of-the-Art Molecular Dynamics Packages for GPU Computations: Performance, Scalability and Limitations

Vsevolod Nikolskiy[1,2,3]($\boxtimes$) (ID), Daniil Pavlov[1,3] (ID), and Vladimir Stegailov[1,2,3] (ID)

[1] Joint Institute for High Temperatures of RAS, Moscow, Russian Federation
[2] National Research University Higher School of Economics,
Moscow, Russian Federation
[3] Moscow Institute of Physics and Technology (National Research University),
Dolgoprudny, Russian Federation
thevsevak@gmail.com

Abstract. Modern molecular dynamics (MD) packages have GPU support to provide the maximum spatial and temporal scales of the tasks being solved. To date, there is no standard approach to developing performance portable applications, and GPU programming is about overcoming limitations and balancing conflicting requirements. In this paper we focus on generic MD systems (water and Lennard-Jones liquid) and explore the limitations of state-of-the-art MD modeling packages LAMMPS and OpenMM running on Nvidia and AMD graphics accelerators. The packages include completely different solutions for the implementation of efficient computing.

Keywords: Performance portability · Heterogeneous parallelization · Hybrid computing · CUDA · ROCm

1 Introduction

Classical molecular dynamics (MD) simulations method is a key research tool in many areas of science and engineering. MD is one of the major consumers of supercomputer resources worldwide. The development of MD tools that enable ultra-long MD trajectories and extreme MD system sizes is one of the important vectors of development for high performance computing methods [1,2]. Shortly after the Nvidia CUDA technology had been introduced in 2007, hybrid MD algorithms appeared and showed their promising performance. Nowadays, GPU-accelerated hardware provides the most efficient and affordable way for doing MD studies [3–5] and makes various applied MD studies feasible [6–9].

The emergence of parallel distributed memory supercomputing systems stimulated the development of parallel codes for MD calculations. Among others, LAMMPS [10] and GROMACS [11] are two MD codes that have developed into

V. Voevodin et al. (Eds.): RuSCDays 2022, LNCS 13708, pp. 342–355, 2022.
https://doi.org/10.1007/978-3-031-22941-1_25

complex simulation packages and are widely used nowadays. Since the emergence of general-purpose computing on graphics processing units (GPGPU), both codes have been supplemented with GPU offloading capabilities [12–15]. Newer MD codes like HOOMD [16,17] and OpenMM [18,19] use GPU-oriented MD algorithms that are designed in a way to keep the amount of CPU-GPU communication to an absolute minimum.

Porting MD algorithms to hybrid architectures is a cumbersome endeavor that requires a lot of effort. Recently, such experience has been described for the HPC systems based on Sunway CPUs [20–23]. Another example is the porting of the MD algorithm to Adapteva Epiphany architecture [24]. Such efforts are unique since algorithms for these architectures have been programmed in an absence of an established software ecosystem.

At the moment, the best software ecosystem for GPU computing is based on Nvidia CUDA technology. CUDA is a platform for writing applications for GPGPU. It has mature driver and runtime support, great debugging and profiling tools, detailed documentation and samples. Almost every algorithm that has high computational complexity and parallelization possibility was implemented in CUDA. Unfortunately, CUDA is a closed-source technology that limits portability. The OpenCL standard is aimed to be a cross-platform alternative to CUDA but such a portability comes at a cost of much more complicated performance tuning for a particular GPU type. Currently, the SYCL standard of parallel programming is being actively developed and it can be considered "a reinvention of OpenCL".

In contrast, AMD HIP technology is aimed at CUDA-style development of portable GPU software both for new AMD GPU architectures and for Nvidia GPUs (without performance implications).

The strong driving force for the development of CUDA-based HPC software has been the development of the CORAL hybrid pre-exascale supercomputers Summit and Sierra [25] by IBM and Nvidia. The next exascale supercomputers Frontier and El Capitan that are developed within the CORAL-2 program are going to be built with AMD GPUs. Therefore, porting HPC software to HIP is an important part of numerical tools development.

In this work, we describe three prominent frameworks of GPU-accelerated molecular dynamics: GPU and KOKKOS GPU-backends in LAMMPS and the OpenMM project that can be regarded as a library of building blocks for efficient molecular dynamics calculations on GPUs. We present the benchmarks of these codes on novel GPU hardware and consider different types of interconnects for multi-GPU calculations.

2   Software

2.1   LAMMPS

LAMMPS software package [26] is one of the most popular supercomputing simulation codes. It is used to solve problems at the cutting edge of the science that require the application of record-breaking simulation scales in time and space. Among the breakthrough launches, the following can be noted:

1. Full load of the petascale Titan machine with about 16000 nodes at Oak Ridge National Laboratory [27];
2. One of the longest simulations in the world to the 2017 [28] at LLNL on the Sequoia Blue Gene Q machine with petascale performance;
3. Simulation using over 100,000 processor at Los Alamos National Laboratory on the Trinity machine [29];
4. Simulation using 4,650 nodes (27,900 NVIDIA V100 GPUs) at Oak Ridge National Laboratory on the Summit machine that was #1 supercomputer in 2018-2020 [30].

Efficient use of graphics accelerators plays a big role in such launches. LAMMPS performance is one of the targets that Nvidia developers consider for their solutions [31]. The optimized container has been published [32]. The project of development of the largest supercomputers at Lawrence Livermore, Oak Ridge, and Argonne national laboratories consider LAMMPS performance as one of key figures of merit, including the GPU variant. The Exascale Atomistic Capability for Accuracy, Length, and Time (EXAALT) project uses LAMMPS in combination with other programs for modeling with the prospect of efficient use of exascale scale capacities. At the SC21 conference, the related work [30] was nominated for the Gordon Bell Prize.

It is interesting that the LAMMPS achieves such high levels of scalability while being very flexible, versatile and extensible among other MD packages. The LAMMPS maintainers adhere to the position that the package should remain available for compilation under the widest range of systems. This enables one to build the package on supercomputers with conservative Linux distributions, non-standard systems, and even on minicomputers [33,34]. For this reason, all code related to hybrid computing is optional and is made in the form of modules and libraries.

GPU Backend for CUDA, OpenCL and HIP. Historically, the first approach to GPU support in LAMMPS was the GPU package [14,35,36] and it remains viable. It has basic support for GPU portability implemented at the preprocessor level. To do this, he uses the Geryon library, which allows one to write code using only common functionality for the CUDA, OpenCL and ROCm platforms [37]. Before compilation, this code is processed for the specific platform. This package follows the principles of the offload model. Only the hottest parts of the code are accelerated on the GPU — calculation of potentials, PPPM, neighbors lists. The data transfers occur before (host-to-device) and after (device-to-host) corresponding kernel calls and data moves back and forth on each timestep. The timestep and integration is controlled by the generic LAMMPS logic.

Kokkos Backend for CUDA, HIP and SYCL. Kokkos [38] is an open-source performance portability parallel programming library and the LAMMPS module of the same name. The core of the library is mainly based on headers, as templates are actively used. The library actively uses the capabilities of modern C++. A compiler with support for the C++ 14 standard is required to compile the module. Since the code is designed as a separate module, this requirement does not apply to the entire LAMMPS and C++ 11 is enough for the main package.

Compared to the GPU package, KOKKOS implements a much wider set of classes. While the GPU package only speeds up potential calculation and part of PPPM and building neighbor lists, KOKKOS speeds up other components such as Fix, Compute, etc. To do this, KOKKOS provides its own implementation of the main program loop in the Verlet integrator (or minimizer), which calls the available components. Components that do not have a KOKKOS implementation remain compatible and their classic CPU versions are called. Thus, in the long term, the entire LAMMPS can be accelerated on the GPU, but this can be done gradually.

2.2   OpenMM

OpenMM [19] is an open source toolkit for molecular dynamics. With its main focus being computational biology, it still performs remarkably well on other systems. This is achieved because unlike the high-level OpenMM Application Layer Python API [39], which is built around domain-specific constructs such as force fields, residue chains and topologies, OpenMM Library Level C++/Python API [40] is completely divorced from such constructs and provides a lower-level access to the underlying structures that can be used in a broader range of applications.

OpenMM supports four platforms: Reference, CPU, CUDA, OpenCL. There's also an ongoing effort [41] to add HIP to the list. Both CUDA and OpenCL are GPU-oriented platforms, and they provide the best performance. The underlying algorithms that are used in these platforms are almost identical, with most of the code having been merged into a meta-platform called Common Compute. In this work we are going to focus on the CUDA platform, implying that OpenCL and HIP operate in mostly the same way.

When parallelizing over a big amount of processing units, there are three wide classes of approaches [10]: atom-decomposition, force-decomposition and domain-decomposition. For distributing workload *inside* a GPU OpenMM uses a force-decomposition-like algorithm [42]: for N atoms, the NxN force matrix is divided into 'tiles' of size 32×32. Then, only the tiles that might contain non-zero forces are marked as 'interacting' based on comparing the tiles' coordinate bounds. Then, the list of interacting tiles is traversed to calculate forces and energy. Once the tiles' bounds change to a point that new interactions might appear, the list of interacting tiles is rebuilt.

There are a few important quirks of this algorithm that must be accounted for: first, due to the SIMT architecture of GPU execution, it does not matter whether there's only one pair of atoms interacting within a tile or all atoms are interacting with the other, the tile will take the same time to compute in either case. This suggests that the amount of interacting tiles should be brought to a minimum: either most atoms should interact within a tile, or none. Such an effect is achieved by making atoms 'spatially coherent': when atoms within a tile all lie close to each other, there are more interactions per tile and therefore fewer tiles. To achieve the 'spatial coherence', every 250 steps atoms are reordered along a Hilbert curve [43]. This does not eliminate the inherent possibility that there might still be tiles with only a few interactions, so the tiles that still are not "dense" are not processed as a whole, but split into individual atoms that are processed separately.

The second important quirk of the force-decomposition algorithm is its inherent complexity: traversing an NxN force matrix has the complexity of $\mathcal{O}(N^2)$. This means that this algorithm is not infinitely weakly scalable: at some point the rapidly increasing cost of finding interacting tiles would outweigh the benefits of being able to simulate bigger systems. The question is how soon. Current limitations restrict the use of OpenMM to systems with about $10^7 - 10^8$ atoms.

3 Hardware

The analysis presented in this work is based on the data obtained on three types of GPUs: Nvidia V100, A30 and A100, and AMD MI50. The following GPUs have been used for performance measurements:

- AMD MI50: 32 GB of GPU memory with 1 TB/s bandwidth, 13.3 TFlops/sec SP, 6.6 TFlops/sec DP.
- Nvidia A30: 24 GB of GPU memory with 0.9 TB/s bandwidth, 10.3 TFlops/sec SP, 5.2 TFlops/sec DP.
- Nvidia A100: 80 GB of GPU memory with 2 TB/s bandwidth, 19.5 TFlops/sec SP, 9.7 TFlops/sec DP.

Nvidia A100 have been accessed in the nodes of the cHARISMa supercomputer of HSE University [44]. Nvidia A30 and AMD MI50 GPUs were accessed in the nodes of the Desmos supercomputer of JIHT RAS.

The multi-GPU tests with A100 and MI50 presented below require the description of the architecture of the corresponding systems:

- The nodes of cHARISMa with 8 A100 GPUs have been used. Such a node has two AMD Epyc 7702 CPUs and the Nvidia Delta board with the assembly of 8 A100 connected by NVSwitch.
- The Desmos supercomputer consists of 32 nodes. Each node is a Supermicro 1018GR-T server with one Intel E5-1650v3 CPU and one AMD MI50 GPU. 32 nodes are connected by the Angara interconnect.

4 Results and Discussion

4.1 Comparison of GPU and KOKKOS Backends of LAMMPS

The Table 1 shows a comparison of the GPU kernels called during a run of the same model example that computes the SCP/E water model. The model is quite

Table 1. Comparison of the set of GPU kernels called when calculating the model with the SPC/E potential using LAMMPS-GPU and LAMMPS-KOKKOS

LAMMPS component	KOKKOS	GPU
Neighbor Lists	NPair	calc_neigh_list_cell
Pair Style	PairLJCutCoulLong	k_lj_coul_long
PPPM	PPPM	interp, make_rho, particle_map
Fix	FixShake	
Fix (integrator)	FixNVEInitialIntegrate FixNVEFinalIntegrate	
Compute	ComputeTemp	
Bond Style	BondHarmonic	
Angle Style	AngleHarmonic	
Other	View, Fill, Zero, etc	zero, etc

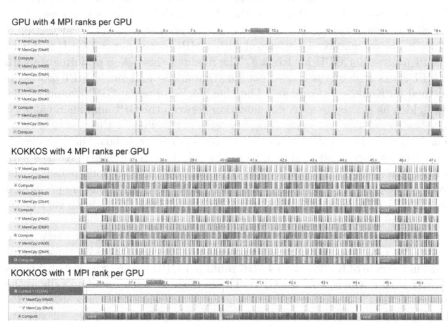

Fig. 1. LAMMPS GPU profile plotted with Nvidia visual profiler. The profile was built on a single node w/one Nvidia V100 GPU.

simple, but in addition to the pair potential, it includes long-range interaction and Fix (the SHAKE algorithm). Even in such a simple example, it can be seen that many more parts of the program are available for GPU acceleration in the case of Kokkos.

Table 2. Data transfer comparison for Kokkos w/4 MPI ranks per GPU, Kokkos w/single process per GPU and module GPU with 4 MPI ranks per GPU. Host-to-Device (H-to-D) and Device-to-Host (D-to-H) transfers are considered separately, the average value per process is specified.

	Kokkos (4 ranks / GPU)			Kokkos (1 rank / GPU)			GPU (4 ranks / GPU)		
	H-to-D	D-to-H	Overall	H-to-D	D-to-H	Overall	H-to-D	D-to-H	Overall
Session time, s			126.47			79.8			117.7
Copy time, s	28.7	10.5		2.32	2.95		4.55	0.763	
Invocations	10673	11418	89615	7469	6290	13759	392	430	3288
Total GB	95	48	572	11.8	17	28.9	14.74	4.791	78.2
Avg Gb/s	3.32	4.45		5.1	5.8		3.241	6.278	

Since the program alternates code fragments running on the GPU and the classic LAMMPS code, multiple intermediate data synchronization is required. The Fig. 1 shows the profiles when the above modeling task is performed with the SPC/E water model. The number of atoms are involved in the calculation is 972000. The calculation is performed with 4 MPI processes per 1 GPU and with 1 MPI process per GPU for Kokkos. The modules show close performance with 4 MPI ranks and this is convenient for comparison and single MPI process is optimal for Kokkos performance. The blue blocks represent GPU computations, the golden blocks represent communication between the GPU and main memory. The horizontal axis represents time, the scale of timeline for these cases is close. The larger blocks of calculations are the neighbor list rebuilds. One can clearly see a much higher density and number of calculations in the case of Kokkos with 4 MPI ranks per GPU, while for the GPU package there are long pauses in the work of the graphics accelerator while the rest of the calculations are performed on the CPU. The case of Kokkos with 1 MPI ranks per GPU shows very dense GPU computations and a moderate number of short data transfers.

The Table 2 shows the data transfer measurement results for these three cases. The total amount of data transferred and the time spent on these operations in the case of Kokkos with 4 MPI ranks per GPU is approximately 6.5 times greater than in the case of the GPU. The number of individual data calls in the case of Kokkos is more than 26 times higher. A different situation is observed for Kokkos with single process per GPU, it significantly reduces the amount of data transfers and becomes optimal for this parameter. The number of data transfer calls still remains higher than in the case of the GPU module.

Figure 2 compares the execution time of the above SPC/E model example by 100 steps. In the right plot, the acceleration of the PPPM method for calculating long-range interactions is disabled. One GPU accelerator is involved in the calculation with a various number of MPI processes.

For the GPU package, the use of many MPI processes per accelerator is preferred according to the documentation. This is clearly seen — the time for solving the problem decreases monotonically with an increase in the number of processes. A significant role here is played by the fact that with an increase in

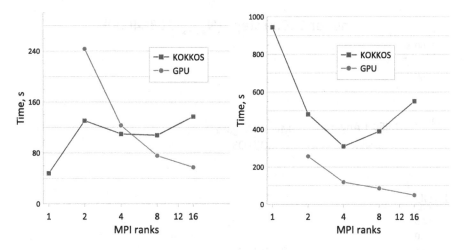

Fig. 2. MPI procs per GPU with PPPM acceration enabled (left) and disabled (right)

the number of processes, the time of calculations that are performed on the CPU decreases. It can also be noted that the acceleration of PPPM using the GPU package does not provide a significant acceleration on this task (however, this differs significantly for some models). Single process run is not presented on the plot since it failed with error.

For the Kokkos package, running with a single process per GPU is preferred — this can be seen in the left graph. With an increase in the number of processes, additional overhead costs and competition for accelerator resources arise. Therefore, for 2–16 MPI processes, a plot of the graph is observed that has a local minimum due to the balance of acceleration and overhead costs. In the right graph, the case with one process is not optimal due to the calculation of PPPM on the CPU, and more processes make a dominant contribution to the PPPM solution performance and, as a result, the total solution time. For the GPU package, the plot remains very close.

4.2 Efficiency of GPU Acceleration in the Largest System Size Limit

In order to explore the capabilities of LAMMPS and OpenMM to accelerate MD calculations in the largest system size limit, we consider generic Lennard-Jones liquid models with the same particle density but different number of atoms. The average number of neighbors in the interaction sphere of a give atom is ~ 180. LAMMPS have been used with 6 MPI ranks per node with the GPU backend on the Desmos supercomputer.

Figure 3 shows the strong scaling the model with 16 millions atoms (the largest size that fits into 32 GB of one AMD MI50). We see that the scalabitiy of this problem with GPU and KOKKOS backends does not differ. Surprisingly, the scalability over the Angara interconnect is not worse than the scalabiliy

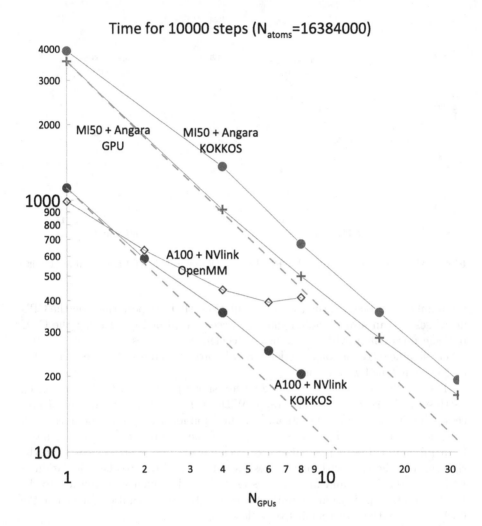

Fig. 3. Strong scaling for the Lennard-Jones liquid benchmark with 16384000 atoms. Circles show the data for KOKKOS on different number of A100 and MI50 GPUs. Crosses show the data for the GPU backend on Desmos. Diamonds show the data for OpenMM on different number of A100.

over NVLink that has much higher bandwidth and lower latency. The scalability of OpenMM over several GPUs is not very efficient. For multi-gpu processing OpenMM uses atom-decomposition, which requires copying the entire state of the system from master GPU to slave GPUs on every step. This incurs heavy delays which could be probably improved by fine-tuning of the overlapping computation and communication.

Figure 4 shows the weak scaling for the same Lennard-Jones model. Comparison of KOKKOS performance on MI50, A30 and A100 shows that the difference

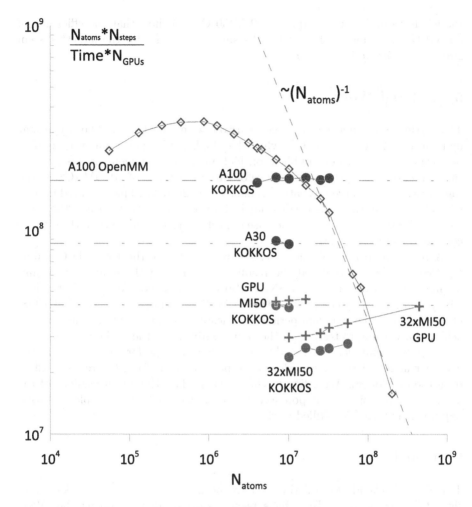

Fig. 4. Weak scaling for the Lennard-Jones liquid benchmark. The efficiency of MD calculations is shown as $N_{atoms}N_{step}$ per unit of time per GPU. Circles show the data for KOKKOS on different number of A100, A30 and MI50 GPUs. Crosses show the data for the GPU backend on Desmos and MI50.

between A100 and A30 is about 2x and can be explained by about 2x lower peak performance and 2x lower memory bandwidth of A30. However, there is practically no difference between A30 and MI50 in terms of peak performance and memory bandwidth. That is why their performance difference should be attributed to the lack of hardware support of fp64 atomic operations in MI50 (KOKKOS relies heavily on atomic operations).

OpenMM results for A100 obtained for mixed precision show its superiority over KOKKOS for system sizes up to 10 million particles. For larger system sizes the $\mathcal{O}(N^2)$ becomes the dominating factor. Data for the benchmarks for the whole Desmos supercomputer (32 MI50 GPUs) show that the efficiency of one GPU utilization tends towards the single GPU case for the largest system sizes (about 500 millions atoms).

5   Related Work

This article does not consider comparison with another popular molecular dynamics package GROMACS, which has high performance and was used in our work [37]. In a recent publication [45] on the development of this project, the results of testing the performance of various versions of GROMACS on the same testing setup were presented. Versions from 2016–2020 participated in testing, when active work was carried out to improve the performance of the GPU code. As a result, there was an increase of performance by more than three times compared to the entry level.

A recent preprint [46] and a related report [47] by the Exascale Computing Project (ECP) presented the results of optimizing the molecular dynamics machine-learning potential SNAP (Spectral Neighbor Analysis Potential). The potential is implemented in the LAMMPS package based on KOKKOS. Over a four-year development period, significant performance improvements were achieved according to testing on the same hardware — the authors claim a 22x speedup over that period, including more than 3.2x performance gains in the last year alone. Developing performance portable code for GPU requires effort from the developers. According to the above studies, the initial versions of the algorithms have significant potential for improvement, but its implementation requires long-term and skilled work.

6   Conclusions

Two GPU backends for LAMMPS have been tested: the GPU package and the KOKKOS package. Tests have been performed demonstrating the difference between the approaches in these two packages. The KOKKOS package accelerates many more LAMMPS components on the GPU, but it calls a lot of short data transfer. When using multiple processes with Kokkos, the amount of data transferred increases significantly. In the example with the SPC/E water model, data transfer in the case of KOKKOS is ~ 6.5 times larger in volume and time than in the case of GPU package. The modules show a comparable level of performance with a different number of MPI ranks. The overall performance of KOKKOS with a different number of MPI processes per accelerator is considered.

Strong scaling of LAMMPS for multi-node multi-GPU runs with Angara interconnect is not worse than the scaling over NVlink within the Nvidia Delta platform with NVSwitch. The lack of hardware support for fp64 atomic operations makes performance of AMD MI50 for KOKKOS twice less than the performance of the similar Nvidia A30 with the similar peak parameters.

OpenMM provides faster calculation speed than LAMMPS-KOKKOS for small system sizes. However, current multi-GPU scalability of OpenMM is quite limited and its performance for large systems is dominated by the $\mathcal{O}(N^2)$ traversal.

Acknowledgment. This research was supported in part through computational resources of HPC facilities at NRU HSE. The study was supported by the Russian Science Foundation (project no. 20-71-10127).

References

1. Shaw, D.E., et al.: Anton 2: raising the bar for performance and programmability in a special-purpose molecular dynamics supercomputer. In: SC '14: Proceedings of the International Conference for High Performance Computing, Networking, Storage and Analysis, pp. 41–53 (2014)
2. Tchipev, N., et al.: Twetris: twenty trillion-atom simulation. Int. J. High Perf. Comp. Appl. **33**(5), 838–854 (2019)
3. Kutzner, C., Páll, S., Fechner, M., Esztermann, A., de Groot, B.L., Grubmüller, H.: Best bang for your buck: GPU nodes for GROMACS biomolecular simulations. J. Comput. Chem. **36**(26), 1990–2008 (2015)
4. Kutzner, C., Páll, S., Fechner, M., Esztermann, A., de Groot, B.L., Grubmüller, H.: More bang for your buck: improved use of GPU nodes for GROMACS 2018. J. Comput. Chem. **40**(27), 2418–2431 (2019)
5. Stegailov, V., et al.: Angara interconnect makes GPU-based desmos supercomputer an efficient tool for molecular dynamics calculations. Int. J. High Perform. Comput. Appl. **33**(3), 507–521 (2019)
6. Kondratyuk, N.D., Pisarev, V.V.: Calculation of viscosities of branched alkanes from 0.1 to 1000 MPa by molecular dynamics methods using COMPASS force field. Fluid Phase Equilib. **498**, 151–159 (2019)
7. Pisarev, V., Kondratyuk, N.: Prediction of viscosity-density dependence of liquid methane+n-butane+n-pentane mixtures using the molecular dynamics method and empirical correlations. Fluid Phase Equilib. **501**, 112273 (2019)
8. Smirnov, G.S., Stegailov, V.V.: Formation free energies of point defects and thermal expansion of bcc U and Mo. J. Phys.: Condens. Matter **31**(23), 235704 (2019)
9. Antropov, A., Stegailov, V.: Nanobubbles diffusion in bcc uranium: theory and atomistic modelling. J. Nuclear Mater. **533**, 152110 (2020)
10. Plimpton, S.: Fast parallel algorithms for short-range molecular dynamics. J. Comput. Phys. **117**(1), 1–19 (1995)
11. Berendsen, H., van der Spoel, D., van Drunen, R.: Gromacs: a message-passing parallel molecular dynamics implementation. Comput. Phys. Commun. **91**(1), 43–56 (1995)
12. Brown, W.M., Wang, P., Plimpton, S.J., Tharrington, A.N.: Implementing molecular dynamics on hybrid high performance computers – short range forces. Comput. Phys. Commun. **182**(4), 898–911 (2011)
13. Brown, W.M., Kohlmeyer, A., Plimpton, S.J., Tharrington, A.N.: Implementing molecular dynamics on hybrid high performance computers – Particle-particle particle-mesh. Comput. Phys. Commun. **183**(3), 449–459 (2012)
14. Brown, W.M., Yamada, M.: Implementing molecular dynamics on hybrid high performance computers-three-body potentials. Comput. Phys. Commun. **184**(12), 2785–2793 (2013)

15. Abraham, M.J., et al.: Gromacs: high performance molecular simulations through multi-level parallelism from laptops to supercomputers. SoftwareX **1–2**, 19–25 (2015)

16. Anderson, J.A., Lorenz, C.D., Travesset, A.: General purpose molecular dynamics simulations fully implemented on graphics processing units. J. Comput. Phys. **227**(10), 5342–5359 (2008)

17. Glaser, J., et al.: Strong scaling of general-purpose molecular dynamics simulations on GPUs. Comput. Phys. Commun. **192**, 97–107 (2015)

18. Eastman, P., et al.: Openmm 4: a reusable, extensible, hardware independent library for high performance molecular simulation. J. Chem. Theory Comput. **9**(1), 461–469 (2013)

19. Eastman, P., et al.: Openmm 7: rapid development of high performance algorithms for molecular dynamics. PLOS Comput. Biol. **13**, 1–17 (2017)

20. Dong, W.: Implementing molecular dynamics simulation on Sunway TaihuLight system. In: 2016 IEEE 18th International Conference on High Performance Computing and Communications; IEEE 14th International Conference on Smart City; IEEE 2nd International Conference on Data Science and Systems (HPCC/SmartCity/DSS), pp. 443–450 (2016)

21. Dong, W., Li, K., Kang, L., Quan, Z., Li, K.: Implementing molecular dynamics simulation on the sunway TaihuLight system with heterogeneous many-core processors. Concur. Comput. Pract. Experience **30**(16), e4468 (2018)

22. Yu, Y., An, H., Chen, J., Liang, W., Xu, Q., Chen, Y.: Pipelining computation and optimization strategies for scaling gromacs on the sunway many-core processor. In: Ibrahim, S., Choo, K.-K.R., Yan, Z., Pedrycz, W. (eds.) ICA3PP 2017. LNCS, vol. 10393, pp. 18–32. Springer, Cham (2017). https://doi.org/10.1007/978-3-319-65482-9_2

23. Duan, X., et al.: Redesigning lammps for peta-scale and hundred-billion-atom simulation on Sunway TaihuLight. In: SC18: International Conference for High Performance Computing, Networking, Storage and Analysis, pp. 148–159 (2018)

24. Nikolskii, V., Stegailov, V.: Domain-decomposition parallelization for molecular dynamics algorithm with short-ranged potentials on epiphany architecture. Lobachevskii J. Math. **39**(9), 1228–1238 (2018). https://doi.org/10.1134/S1995080218090159

25. Hanson, W.A.: The CORAL supercomputer systems. IBM J. Res. Develop. **64**(3/4), 1:1-1:10 (2020)

26. Thompson, A.P., et al.: LAMMPS - a flexible simulation tool for particle-based materials modeling at the atomic, meso, and continuum scales. Comput. Phys. Commun. **271**, 108171 (2022)

27. Nguyen, T.D., Carrillo, J.M.Y., Matheson, M.A., Brown, W.M.: Rupture mechanism of liquid crystal thin films realized by large-scale molecular simulations. Nanoscale **6**(6), 3083–3096 (2014)

28. Zepeda-Ruiz, L.A., Stukowski, A., Oppelstrup, T., Bulatov, V.V.: Probing the limits of metal plasticity with molecular dynamics simulations. Nature **550**(7677), 492–495 (2017)

29. Wood, M.A., Kittell, D.E., Yarrington, C.D., Thompson, A.P.: Multiscale modeling of shock wave localization in porous energetic material. Phys. Rev. B **97**(1), 014109 (2018)

30. Nguyen-Cong, K., et al.: Billion atom molecular dynamics simulations of carbon at extreme conditions and experimental time and length scales (2021)

31. NVIDIA-Corporation: Nvidia HPC application performance. https://developer.nvidia.com/hpc-application-performance (2022)

32. NVIDIA-Corporation: Nvidia NGC LAMMPS container (2022). https://catalog. ngc.nvidia.com/orgs/hpc/containers/lammps
33. Nikolskiy, V., Stegailov, V.: Floating-point performance of ARM cores and their efficiency in classical molecular dynamics. J. Phys.: Conf. Series **681**(1), 012049 (2016). http://stacks.iop.org/1742-6596/681/i=1/a=012049
34. Nikolskiy, V.P., Stegailov, V.V., Vecher, V.S.: Efficiency of the Tegra K1 and X1 systems-on-chip for classical molecular dynamics. In: 2016 International Conference on High Performance Computing Simulation (HPCS), pp. 682–689 (2016)
35. Brown, W.M., Wang, P., Plimpton, S.J., Tharrington, A.N.: Implementing molecular dynamics on hybrid high performance computers - short range forces. Comput. Phys. Commun. **182**(4), 898–911 (2011)
36. Brown, W.M., Kohlmeyer, A., Plimpton, S.J., Tharrington, A.N.: Implementing molecular dynamics on hybrid high performance computers - particle-particle particle-mesh. Comput. Phys. Commun. **183**(3), 449–459 (2012)
37. Kondratyuk, N., Nikolskiy, V., Pavlov, D., Stegailov, V.: GPU-accelerated molecular dynamics: state-of-art software performance and porting from Nvidia CUDA to AMD HIP. Int. J. High Perform. Comput. Appl. **35**(4), 312–324 (2021)
38. Trott, C.R., et al.: Kokkos 3: programming model extensions for the exascale era. IEEE Trans. Parallel Distrib. Syst. **33**(4), 805–817 (2022)
39. OpenMM team: Openmm application layer python API. http://docs.openmm.org/ latest/api-python/app.html
40. OpenMM team: OpenMM library level C++/Python API. http://docs.openmm. org/development/api-c++/
41. Johar, A.: Final HIP Platform implementation for AMD GPUs on ROCm, 3338 (2021). https://github.com/openmm/openmm/pull/3338
42. Eastman, P., Pande, V.S.: Efficient nonbonded interactions for molecular dynamics on a graphics processing unit. J. Comput. Chem. **31**(6), 1268–1272 (2009)
43. Moon, B., Jagadish, H., Faloutsos, C., Saltz, J.: Analysis of the clustering properties of the hilbert space-filling curve. IEEE Trans. Knowl. Data Eng. **13**(1), 124–141 (2001)
44. Kostenetskiy, P., Chulkevich, R., Kozyrev, V.: HPC resources of the Higher School of Economics. In: Journal of Physics: Conference Series, vol. 1740, p. 012050. IOP Publishing (2021)
45. Páll, S., et al.: Heterogeneous parallelization and acceleration of molecular dynamics simulations in gromacs. J. Chem. Phys. **153**(13), 134110 (2020). https://doi. org/10.1063/5.0018516
46. Gayatri, R., et al.: Rapid exploration of optimization strategies on advanced architectures using testsnap and lammps (2020). https://arxiv.org/abs/2011.12875
47. Kothe, D.B., Perez, D.: Exascale computing project update. Technical report, HPC User Forum

Supercomputer Simulations of Turbomachinery Problems with Higher Accuracy on Unstructured Meshes

Alexey Duben[1]([✉]), Andrey Gorobets[1], Sergey Soukov[1], Olga Marakueva[1,2], Nikolay Shuvaev[1,2], and Renat Zagitov[1,2]

[1] Keldysh Institute of Applied Mathematics of Russian Academy of Sciences, Moscow, Russia
{aduben,gorobets}@keldysh.ru, {o.marakueva,n.shuvaev, r.zagitov}@rescent.ru
[2] LLC "Numerical Calculations Russia", Saint-Petersburg, Russia

Abstract. Numerical simulation is widely used while designing modern turbojet engines. However, it is computationally expensive to simulate multi-stage configurations. Turbines and compressors typically contain 8–14 stages and even more. Each stage consists of two rows, a rotor and a stator. In practice, the purpose of the simulation is mostly to obtain the averaged integral characteristics of the turbomachine. Therefore, the mixing plane interface (MP) between adjacent rows has become the most widely used. This approach assumes the absence of circumferential flow non-uniformity at the interface, thus allowing the use of periodicity conditions and including only one blade passage for each row in the calculations. The accuracy of the numerical scheme of the simulation algorithm also plays an important role in reducing the computational resource intensity, allowing the use of coarser meshes. A conservative low-reflection MP for higher-accuracy edge-based schemes on unstructured meshes will be presented. Details of its parallel implementation within the framework of a parallel heterogeneous simulation code will be considered. The results of the validation simulations and practical applications will be demonstrated.

Keywords: Turbomachinery · Mixing plane · Higher-accuracy scheme · Unstructured mesh · Parallel heterogeneous code

1 Introduction

One of the most challenging problems associated with the simulation of turbomachines is the presence of many closely spaced blade rows rotating relative to each other. Thus, the flow in turbomachines is fundamentally unsteady in nature and characterized by many interacting harmonics. The distance between adjacent rows is usually about 5–50% of the blade chord, so their interaction can be significant [1]. However, from the point of view of assessing the main aerodynamic characteristics of the turbomachine units (mass flow rate, total pressure ratio, efficiency), it is usually sufficient to consider only the steady component of the rows' interaction. The Mixing Plane (MP) technology

© The Author(s), under exclusive license to Springer Nature Switzerland AG 2022
V. Voevodin et al. (Eds.): RuSCDays 2022, LNCS 13708, pp. 356–367, 2022.
https://doi.org/10.1007/978-3-031-22941-1_26

[2] for matching the flows on the interfaces between rows was designed to meet these objectives. It assumes the absence of circumferential flow non-uniformity in one of the mating rows when determining characteristics in the other, and vice versa, thus making it possible to match the radial distributions of flow parameters between adjacent rotor and stator. The use of the MP leads to significant savings of computing resources, since it allows using only one vane channel (the vane wheel periodicity sector) per row for computation. In this case, on the surfaces limiting the computational domain in the circumferential direction, the classical periodicity conditions are used.

The MP method is a key element for aerodynamic simulations in commercial CFD software packages such as NUMECA FINE/Turbo or ANSYS CFX which are widely used by specialized industrial enterprises [3, 4]. The main disadvantage of commercial solvers is the use of low-accuracy (usually, basic 2nd order) numerical schemes. The problem of errors caused by using low-accuracy schemes is revealed in many studies [3, 5]. Traditional engineering approaches can yield a large error in the analysis of product parameters outside the design operating modes, when many complex and non-stationary phenomena of various nature appear [4].

We develop the MP technique in the in-house CFD code NOISette to simulate turbomachines on unstructured meshes. The code is based on higher-accuracy 2nd order numerical schemes of the EBR family [6, 7] that provide low computational error and can locally reach order of accuracy up to the 5th. The MP technique is implemented ensuring conservation and low-reflection properties. The latter is important, because mixing surfaces do not allow shocks, vortices, and other flow features to pass through the interface. Using reflective conditions on interfaces facilitates the distortion of the position and shape of such flow structures. The reflection from the interfaces is significantly enhanced [8] if the rotor and stator blades are located close to each other.

The paper is organized as follows. Section 2 briefly outlines the mathematical model and numerical method in use. Section 3 explains how the MP method works. The parallel algorithm is outlined in Sect. 4. Section 5 is devoted to comparing simulation results and evaluating parallel performance. Finally, conclusions are summarized in Sect. 6.

2 Mathematical Model and Numerical Method

The numerical algorithm realized in the NOISEtte code is based on the Navier-Stokes equations for a compressible ideal gas. In the present work, the Reynolds Averaged Navier-Stokes (RANS) approach with the SA [9] or SST [10] turbulence models is used to simulate the flow. As for the boundary conditions, the total pressure, temperature and velocity direction at the inlet and the static pressure at the outlet are specified for the considered computations. The periodicity boundary conditions are used for every blade row in the circumferential direction. Solid surfaces are considered as adiabatic no-slip walls.

The NOISEtte algorithm realizes a vertex-centered numerical scheme on mixed-element unstructured meshes for spatial discretization. So, the computational domain is split into control volumes, which are built around mesh nodes. The family of edge-based reconstruction schemes EBR [6] is used for the discretization of the convective fluxes. It provides higher accuracy (in terms of absolute numerical error) on unstructured meshes and can locally reach order of accuracy up to the 5th. The EBR schemes are equipped with the quasi-1D WENO techniques [7] to handle discontinuities and high gradients.

Time integration is carrying out using the 1st order implicit Newton-based scheme BDF1. The system of algebraic equations is solved using the preconditioned BiCGSTAB solver [11].

3 Mixing Plane

Turbines and compressors are formed of stages, stages consist of two rows, a rotor and a stator. In the simulation algorithm, the interfaces between rows are represented by the mixing-plane (MP) technique (as shown in Fig. 1). Each row is discretized using a mixed-element unstructured 3D mesh, which can be composed of tetrahedra, triangular prisms, quadrilateral pyramids, and hexahedra. However, in the present work, we use structured meshes in order to compare simulation results with those obtained using other codes that cannot work with unstructured meshes.

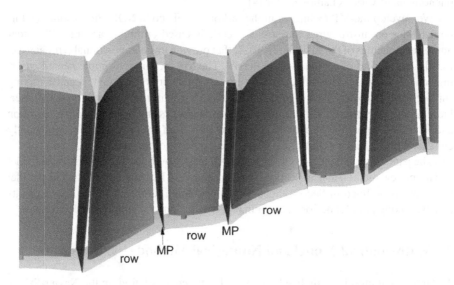

Fig. 1. Typical view of the computational domain

Each MP has two mesh boundary surfaces of the two incident rows assigned to it (Fig. 2). Let the axis of rotation be the z-axis. Consider a turbomachine in a cylindrical coordinate system (r, θ, z), where r, θ are the radial and azimuthal coordinates, respectively. The MP surface is not necessarily flat (despite called "plane"). In general, it is a revolution surface of a profile defined in the r-z plane. The profile of the MP surface between two adjacent rows is defined by a simple polygonal chain, or shortly a polyline, in the r-z plane. Revolution of this polyline around the z-axis gives us the MP surface in the 3D domain. Each line segment of the polyline corresponds to a "ribbon", a part of a conical surface between two circles passing through the nodes of the segment in the planes orthogonal to the axis of rotation (as shown in Fig. 3).

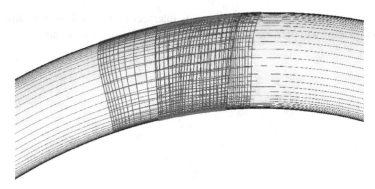

Fig. 2. Surface grids on both sides of the MP interface

Construction of each MP consists of two steps: forming the polyline given by a sequence of nodes in the r-z plane; finding for each boundary node at the mesh surface connected to the MP the "intersections" of its control volume (CV) boundary surface, or, in short, its trace, with the ribbons of the MP (Fig. 4).

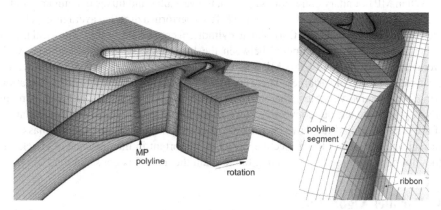

Fig. 3. Representation of the mixing plane interface on the example of a single-stage turbine

The MP polyline is automatically constructed on a base of the two incident mesh surfaces. Regarding the desired properties of the polyline, on the one hand, the fewer line segments, the better. On the other hand, the size of the segments must match the local mesh resolution at both sides. Therefore, all the surface nodes from both sides of the interface are projected to the r-z plane. For each node, its CV characteristic size is estimated from the sizes of the projections of its incident mesh edges to the r-z plane. The sizes of the ribbons are chosen so that each ring is as narrow as the minimal characteristic size of the nodes that fall on this ribbon.

Once the polyline is constructed, the MP is represented as set of ribbons, one for both sides. Then, on each side of the MP interface, each CV trace of boundary nodes is sliced into intersections with the ribbons (Fig. 4). Namely, each boundary node gets the list of ribbons its CV trace intersects with and knows the areas of the intersections.

Conversely, each ribbon knows the list of its intersecting nodes from both sides. This construction allows to perform azimuthal averaging of variables and fluxes.

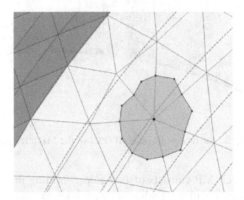

Fig. 4. Control volume trace around a boundary node at the mixing-plane interface

When MP boundary condition is applied, the variables and fluxes in boundary nodes need to be averaged from both sides of the MP. To perform azimuthal averaging, velocity vectors are transformed from Cartesian to cylindrical coordinate system. The local fluxes in boundary nodes are computed between the local CVs of nodes and ribbons with averaged values. Basically, this MP acts as an inlet or outlet boundary condition with a given radial profile of variables. There are many ways to implement this flux calculation using conservative variables, characteristic variables, etc., such as in [12–15]. Among other options, we use our convective flux calculation procedure based on the adaptation of the Lax–Fridrichs/Rusanov scheme [16]. It is conservative in terms of the mass flux through the MP and is low reflective, which is important in the presence of shocks. It does not need additional flow scaling to maintain the mass flux conservation.

4 Parallel Algorithm

The MP approach is implemented within the parallel framework of the NOISEtte supercomputer simulation code [17, 18]. It is primarily designed for time-accurate scale-resolving simulations of turbulent flows on hybrid supercomputers. Its multilevel MPI + OpenMP + OpenCL parallelization allows using both CPUs and GPUs of various vendors. Tens of thousands of CPU cores, hundreds of GPUs can be efficiently engaged in a single simulation, as was shown in our previous works [17–20]. In the present paper, stationary RANS simulations are considered, which is a rather different kind of application. The number of nodes in a mesh is usually several orders of magnitude smaller than in scale-resolving simulations due to the very high allowable mesh anisotropy. In contrast to large-scale supercomputer simulations, where parallel scalability is of high priority, in such stationary simulations, it is important to obtain solution quickly with minimal computing resources. Therefore, it would be especially interesting to evaluate performance in such unusual conditions for us.

The MP parallelization for CPUs is rather straightforward. Averaging procedure can be easily implemented using OpenMP loop-based parallelism, as well as the entire processing of boundary nodes on the MP. Distributed parallel processing requires only one group reduction exchange MPI_Allreduce among those MPI subdomains that have nodes on the MP interfaces. This communication is needed to perform averaging over the ribbons, which is typically several hundred values per interface. This communication is inexpensive due to its minor volume and does not have a significant impact on parallel efficiency (at least in typical operating conditions involving tens of processes, not thousands).

In terms of GPU computing, the situation is also simple. On the one hand, performing reduction of sums over small datasets (involving only surface nodes) for the MP averaging is not very suitable for GPUs that prefer big things. On the other hand, if the nodes are properly ordered, CPUs can do it very quickly due to the fact that such small datasets completely fit into the cache. Therefore, we cannot expect a noticeable acceleration of this operation on the GPU, and can leave it on the CPU side. When the simulation is performed on GPUs, the MP datasets are transferred to the CPU, all the calculations are performed there, while the GPU can be occupied with processing other boundary conditions. This approach (for now) allows us to simply avoid implementing rather complex kernels in OpenCL without a significant loss in performance.

5 Performance and Applications

Before studying parallel efficiency and performance, which are not much affected compared to the previous studies [17–20], it would be very curious to compare performance with a proper simulation code designed primarily for such applications. The NUMECA Fine/Turbo v. 15.1 code [21] was chosen for such a comparison since it is widely used in Russian turbomachinery industry and is considered the fastest simulation solution for this kind of applications. It uses a basic second-order numerical scheme and convergence acceleration based on a full approximation scheme multigrid. The latter makes it a very difficult opponent. The NOISEtte code has no such convergence acceleration since it is designed for scale-resolving simulations. However, it has fully implicit time integration schemes that will not let it give up so easily.

The fight between the codes took place on very similar dual-CPU servers with Intel Xeon Scalable CPUs. The test case is a model highly reactive transonic single-stage gas turbine. The nozzle assembly contains 24 blades, the wheel – 59 blades, rotor RPM is 12770 min^{-1}. There is no radial clearance between the wheel and the shroud. The flow conditions are following: the total pressure $P_0 = 310$ kPa, the total temperature $T_0 = 400$ K, the axial flow direction ($V_z/|V|=1$) and the turbulence intensity $Tu = 10\%$ are set at the inlet; the static pressure $P_2 = 65.8$ kPa is set at the outlet. We use the same computational mesh containing about 1 million nodes for simulation with both codes. The scheme of the computational domain is shown in Fig. 5, also this case was used above to illustrate the MP in Fig. 3.

To determine the point of convergence in equal conditions, we check when the difference in mass flow values between inlet and outlet becomes less than 0.01%. The timing results are shown in Table 1. To our surprise, the NOISEtte code somehow

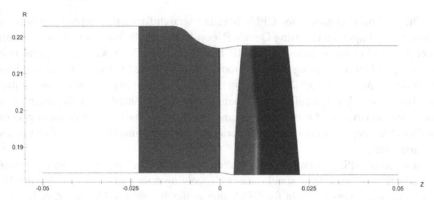

Fig. 5. Scheme of the computational domain of the single-stage gas turbine

managed to get a converged solution in almost the same time as the NUMECA code. This means that our implementation not only scales well (which is easy, especially for slow codes), but also computes fast. The same test case was computed on the NVIDIA A5000 GPU. This single GPU outperforms a dual-CPU server by almost two to one. Regarding parallel efficiency with MP + OpenMP on CPUs, we get a speedup of about 31 times when running 2 MPI processes with 32 threads each (2 threads per core) on two 16-core Intel Xeon Gold 5218 CPUs compared to sequential execution.

Table 1. Comparison of performance of NOISEtte and NUMECA FINE/Turbo for the single-stage gas turbine model case

Equipment	Code	Time, s
Two 24-core Intel Xeon Platinum 8268	NUMECA (MPI)	190
Two 16-core Intel Xeon Gold 5218	NOISEtte (MPI + OpenMP)	220
GPU NVIDIA A5000	NOISEtte (OpenCL)	130

Oh, yes, after proudly reporting that our implementation is about as fast as a specialized commercial industrial code, we almost forgot that it would be nice to make sure in one more thing. Indeed, another important issue, even more important than scalability and speed, more important even at a supercomputing conference, is the accuracy of the results. Comparison of the simulation results is shown in Table 2 and in Fig. 6. Table 2 contains integral characteristics: mass flow rate G (in kg/s), efficiency (η^*) and total pressure ratio (π^*). The following formulas are used:

$$\eta^* = \frac{1 - T_2^*/T_0^*}{1 - \left(P_2^*/P_0^*\right)^{(\gamma-1)/\gamma}}, \quad \pi^* = \frac{P_0^*}{P_2^*},$$

where subscripts 0 and 2 denote the inflow and outflow characteristics, respectively; P^* and T^* are the mass-averaged total pressure and temperature, respectively, $\gamma = 1.4$ is the heat capacity ratio.

Table 2. Comparison of integral characteristics for the single-stage gas turbine model case

	G, kg/s	π^*	η^*, %
Experiment	4.07	–	–
NUMECA	4.20	3.94	89.9
NOISEtte	4.21	3.94	90.01

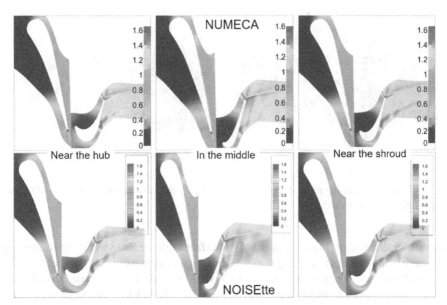

Fig. 6. Comparison of the relative Mach number field in different sections for the single-stage gas turbine case (NUMECA at the top, NOSEtte at the bottom)

Well, the comparison on a single model case is not so representative, the results could just coincide by chance. The second model test case represents an axial compressor stage. The number of blades in the inlet guide vane is 38, the rotor and stator of the first stage contain 25 and 40 blades, respectively, the rotor RPM is $15000\,\text{min}^{-1}$. The total pressure $P_0 = 101$ kPa, the total temperature $T_0 = 288.15$ K and the axial flow direction ($V_z/|V|=1$) are set at the inlet; the static pressure $P_2 = 106$ kPa is set at the outlet. We use the same computational mesh containing 1.24 million nodes for the simulation with both codes. Comparison of the stage simulation results is shown in Table 3 and Fig. 7. In contrast to the previous case, the efficiency is calculated as follows:

$$\eta^* = \frac{\left(P_2^*/P_0^*\right)^{(\gamma-1)/\gamma} - 1}{T_2^*/T_0^* - 1}.$$

The NOISEtte and NUMECA results seem to agree well. Finally, in order to somehow justify the completely unfounded statement that the introduction of the MP into the parallel algorithm did not affect much parallel efficiency, we need at least to demonstrate

Table 3. Comparison of integral characteristics for the axial compressor stage case

	G, kg/s	π*	η*, %
NOISEtte	11.6	1.25	91.36
NUMECA	11.74	1.25	91.67

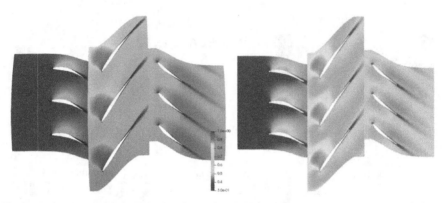

Fig. 7. Comparison of the relative Mach number field for the axial compressor case (NOISEtte on the left, NUMECA on the right)

a parallel speedup plot. In order for the MP interfaces to have more weight in computing time consumption, we use a configuration with a bigger number of rows. Parallel speedup with MPI on a cluster system is measured in simulation of the first 4 stages of the 12-stage axial compressor of the helicopter engine TV3–117 (8 MP interfaces between 9 rows: 8 rotor-stator plus inlet vane). This case was used above in Fig. 1 to illustrate what a typical computational domain looks like.

The computational mesh contains about 12 million nodes. The cluster nodes are dual-CPU computing servers with 24-core Intel Xeon Platinum CPUs, Intel Omni-Path interconnection. Parallel run configuration is 2 MPI processes per node, 24 threads per process. The resulting speedup plot is shown in Fig. 8. So, the code does reasonably well with a load of about 10 thousand nodes per core, reaching about a thousand cores with a parallel efficiency of 81%. When running on 20 nodes, the weight of the MP interfaces is within 10% of the total time.

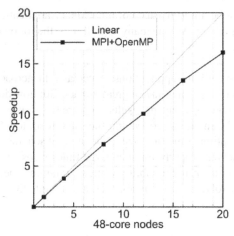

Fig. 8. Parallel speedup up to 960 cores on the TV3 4-stage test case (mesh contains 12 million nodes)

6 Conclusions

The present work is about how scientific computing gets its head out of the clouds and descend from heaven, where fairy tales about exaflops live, to industrial earth. At first, it really seems unusual when, instead of achieving extreme scalability and massively burning state-funded CPU time for the purpose of harvesting publication indicators, we have to run simulations quickly on minimal computing resources.

Specialized industrial applications, apart from the relevant set of RANS models, require the incorporation of additional technologies into the simulation code, such as the mixing plane technique for turbomachinery. Such extensibility is also rather challenging for the simulation code's software architecture.

In the present work we tried to start solving typical industrial turbomachinery applications using a simulation code primarily designed for high-fidelity scale-resolving supercomputer simulations. It was expected that without multigrid convergence accelerator we won't be able to compete with industrial commercial codes in small RANS simulations. As a result, the following conclusions can be outlined:

- even a bare implicit time integration method without any convergence acceleration can compete with a specialized multigrid-accelerated commercial code, at least in some particular applications;
- the mixing-plane approach is easy to parallelize and does not introduce significant overhead;
- in terms of the quality of the solution, the first results are in good agreement with the specialized commercial code;
- the parallel algorithm still plays a very important role even for small problems;
- yes, the GPU is a fast thing, even a cheap gaming/graphical one.

Since we have just begun to master turbomachinery applications, the further work plan looks frighteningly long. Among many other things, the following questions remain to be explored further.

- In our usual scale-resolving applications, especially in aeroacoustics of turbulent flows, higher-accuracy schemes have a great impact. But how does the use of a more accurate numerical scheme affect the results compared to a basic one in such stationary RANS simulations? Can we use coarser meshes, and if so, to what extent?
- How to choose the optimal time step size in the implicit scheme and how to configure the linear system solver properly for such large times steps (with CFL condition of order 10^3, 10^4)? How to ensure reliability while maintaining speed? If the time step is too big or the linear solver solution is not accurate enough, the simulation may break down.

Acknowledgements. This work has been funded by the Russian science foundation, project 21–71-10100. The research is carried out using the equipment of the shared research facilities of HPC computing resources at Lomonosov Moscow State University [22] and the equipment of Shared Resource Center of KIAM RAS (http://ckp.kiam.ru). The authors thankfully acknowledge these institutions.

References

1. Burgos, M.A., Contreras, J., Corra, R.: Efficient edge-based rotor/stator interaction method. AIAA J. **49**(1), 19–31 (2011). https://doi.org/10.2514/1.44512
2. Denton, J., Singh, U.: Time Marching Methods for Turbomachinery Flow Calculations. von Karman Institute Lecture Series 1979–7 (1979). https://doi.org/10.1115/1.3227444
3. Pinto, R.N., Afzal, A., D'Souza, L.V., Ansari, Z., Mohammed Samee, A.D.: Computational fluid dynamics in turbomachinery: a review of state of the art. Archives Comput. Methods Eng. **24**(3), 467–479 (2016). https://doi.org/10.1007/s11831-016-9175-2
4. Tyacke, J., Vadlamani, N.R., et al.: Turbomachinery simulation challenges and the future. Prog. Aerosp. Sci. **110**, 100554 (2019). https://doi.org/10.1016/j.paerosci.2019.100554
5. Desheng, Zhang & SHI et al.: Unsteady flow analysis and experimental investigation of axial-flow pump. Journal of Hydrodynamics **22**(1), 35–43 (2010). http://dx.doi.org/https://doi.org/10.1016/S1001-6058(09)60025-1
6. Bakhvalov, P.A., Abalakin, I.V., Kozubskaya, T.K.: Edge-based reconstruction schemes for unstructured tetrahedral meshes. Int. J. Numer. Methods Fluids. **81**(6), 331–356 (2016). https://doi.org/10.1002/fld.4187
7. Bakhvalov, P., Kozubskaya, T.: EBR-WENO scheme for solving gas dynamics problems with discontinuities on unstructured meshes. Comput. Fluids **157**, 312–324 (2017). https://doi.org/10.1016/j.compfluid.2017.09.004
8. Fritch, G., Giles, M.B.: An asymptotic analysis of mixing loss. ASME. J. Turbomach. **11**, 367–374 (1995). https://doi.org/10.1115/1.2835670
9. Spalart, P.R., Allmaras, S.R.: A one-equation turbulence model for aerodynamic flows. In: 30th Aerospace Science Meeting, AIAA Paper 92–0439 (1992)
10. Menter, F.R., Kuntz, M., Langtry, R.: Ten years of industrial experience with the SST turbulence model. Turbulence, Heat and Mass Transfer 4, ed: Hanjalic, K., Nagano, Y., Tummers, M.: Begell House, Inc., pp. 625–632 (2003)

11. Van der Vorst, H.A.: Bi-CGSTAB: a fast and smoothly converging variant of Bi-CG for the solution of nonsymmetric linear systems. SIAM J. Sci. Stat. Comput. **13**, 631–644 (1992)
12. Anker, J., Schrader, B., Seybold, U., Mayer, J., Casey, M.: A Three-dimensional non-reflecting boundary condition treatment for steady-state flow simulations. In: 44th AIAA Aerospace Sciences Meeting and Exhibit, Reno, Nevada, AIAA 2006–1275 (2006). https://doi.org/10.2514/6.2006-1275
13. Ray, S.R., Zangeneh, M.: A robust mixing plane method and its application in 3D inverse design of transonic turbine stages. In: Proceedings of the ASME Turbo Expo 2014: Turbine Technical Conference and Exposition, Volume 2B: Turbomachinery. Düsseldorf, Germany (2014). https://doi.org/10.1115/GT2014-26976
14. Holmes, D.G.: Mixing planes revisited: a steady mixing plane approach designed to combine high levels of conservation and robustness. In: Proceedings of the ASME Turbo Expo 2008: Power for Land, Sea, and Air, vol. 6, pp. 2649–2658, Berlin, Germany (2008). https://doi.org/10.1115/GT2008-51296
15. Hanimann, L., Mangani, L., Casartelli, E., Mokulys, T., Mauri, S.: Development of a novel mixing plane interface using a fully implicit averaging for stage analysis. ASME. J. Turbomach. **136**(8), 081010 (2014). https://doi.org/10.1115/1.4026323
16. Rusanov, V.V.: Calculation of interaction of non-steady shock waves with obstacles. J. Comput. Math. Phys. USSR **1**, 267–279 (1961)
17. Gorobets, A., Bakhvalov, P.: Heterogeneous CPU+GPU parallelization for high-accuracy scale-resolving simulations of compressible turbulent flows on hybrid supercomputers. Comput. Phys. Commun. **271**, 108231 (2022). https://doi.org/10.1016/j.cpc.2021.108231
18. Gorobets A., Duben, P.: Technology for supercomputer simulation of turbulent flows in the good new days of exascale computing. Supercomputing Frontiers and Innovations **8**(4), 4–10 (2021). https://doi.org/10.14529/jsfi210401
19. Gorobets, A., Soukov, S., Bogdanov, P.: Multilevel parallelization for simulating turbulent flows on most kinds of hybrid supercomputers. Comput. Fluids **173**, 171–177 (2018). https://doi.org/10.1016/j.compfluid.2018.03.011
20. Soukov, S., Gorobets, A.: Heterogeneous computing in resource-intensive CFD simulations. Dokl. Math. **98**, 472–474 (2018). https://doi.org/10.1134/S1064562418060194
21. NUMECA International: FINE/Turbo v15.1 Flow Integrated Environment Theoretical Manual (2020)
22. Voevodin, V., et al.: Supercomputer lomonosov-2: large scale, deep monitoring and fine analytics for the user community. Supercomputing Frontiers and Innovations **6**, 4–11 (2019). https://doi.org/10.14529/jsfi190201

Validation of Quantum-Chemical Methods with the New COSMO2 Solvent Model

Danil Kutov[1,2], Alexey Sulimov[1,2], Ivan Ilin[1,2], and Vladimir Sulimov[1,2(✉)]

[1] Dimonta, Ltd., Moscow 117186, Russia
dk@dimonta.com, sulimovv@mail.ru, ivan.ilyin@srcc.msu.ru,
vladimir.sulimov@gmail.com
[2] Research Computer Center, Lomonosov Moscow State University, Moscow 119992, Russia

Abstract. Quantum quasi-docking is carried out for 25 protein-ligand complexes. Quantum quasi-docking is the determination of a wide spectrum of low-energy minima of a protein-ligand complex when calculating the energy using a classical force field, and then recalculating the energies of these minima by a semiempirical quantum-chemical method. The goal is to compare quasi-docking accuracy when using the old COSMO and new COSMO2 implicit solvent models and two PM6-D3H4X and PM7 methods. The ligand position corresponding to the global minimum of recalculated energies is identified and compared with the position of the ligand in the crystallized protein-ligand complex. The combination of PM7 and the old COSMO model demonstrates the highest positioning accuracy. For successfully docked ligands, the enthalpy of protein-ligand binding is calculated. A high correlation coefficient of 0.74 between measured and calculated binding enthalpies was obtained for the PM7/COSMO energy calculation method.

Keywords: Generalized docking · Quasi-docking · Quantum chemistry · Global energy minimum · Binding enthalpy · PM6-D3H4X · PM7 · High-performance computing · Molecular modeling · Drug design

1 Introduction

The discovery of new medications against a given disease is based often on a paradigm: a molecule of the medication binds selectively to a biomolecule determining the disease development, and thereby pulls the disease over. Usually, proteins play a role of such therapeutic target biomolecules, and medication molecules bind to active centers of these proteins. For brevity, such molecules are referred to here as inhibitors, and inhibitor candidates are referred to as ligands. If spatial coordinates of atoms of the target protein are determined, the computer-aided search for inhibitors is usually performed using docking programs that carry out positioning of the ligand in the target protein and estimate the free energy of protein-ligand binding [1, 2]. The latter determines the effectiveness of the inhibitor: the greater the free energy of binding, the lower the concentration of the inhibitor gives the therapeutic effect. In recent years, docking is becoming a demanded computational method in the beginning of the drug development pipeline, for

V. Voevodin et al. (Eds.): RuSCDays 2022, LNCS 13708, pp. 368–381, 2022.
https://doi.org/10.1007/978-3-031-22941-1_27

example, see the recent reviews [2, 3]. And with the onset of the COVID-19 pandemic, an avalanche of publications appeared on the use of docking in the search for inhibitors for the development of antiviral drugs, for example, see a review [4]. The free energy of binding determines the binding constant, which can be measured experimentally. Many docking programs operate according to the docking paradigm [5–9], which assumes that the position of the bound ligand in the protein corresponds to or is close to the global energy minimum of the protein-ligand complex. Accuracy of the docking programs is still not high enough to play a main role in the hit-to-lead optimization [10, 11].

All docking programs use classical potentials, so-called force fields, to describe protein-ligand interactions. This is one of the main reasons for the low accuracy of docking, since a correct description of protein-ligand interactions can be obtained using only quantum-chemical or quantum-mechanical methods [11]. However, these methods require too much computational resources to be able to perform docking using the global energy optimization of the protein-ligand complex in a multidimensional space, where the number of dimensions is determined by the number of degrees of freedom of the molecular system. At best, quantum chemistry is used after docking to estimate the protein-ligand binding energy [12–18] (see also the corresponding section in the review [2]).

Recently, a new step towards the use of quantum-chemical methods in docking has been proposed in the form of a quantum chemical quasi-docking procedure, which can achieve the best ligand positioning accuracy [7, 8, 19], but requires, however, super-computing resources. This procedure is a combination of docking with a classical force field and recalculation of the energies of the found minima using the PM7 quantum-chemical semiempirical method [20] with the COSMO solvent model [21]. To take into account an aqueous solvent is very important due to strong screening of electrostatic interatomic interactions between atom charges by solvent due to high value of water permittivity [7, 8, 19]. The position of the ligand corresponding to the most negative PM7/COSMO energy of the protein-ligand complex, in accordance with the docking paradigm, must be close to the position of the ligand crystallized with the protein. It was recently shown [22] that the accuracy of quasi-docking when using PM7/COSMO is higher than the accuracy when using the PM6-D3H4X/COSMO method of the energy calculation, where PM6-D3H4X [23] is the quantum-chemical semiempirical method which is similar to PM7.

A new parameterization of the COSMO model has recently been presented in [24] and designated as COSMO2. COSMO2 has been parameterized specifically for PM6-D3H4X and PM7 methods. COSMO2 performs better than the old COSMO model on small molecules [24] and protein-ligand fragments [25] for both the PM6-D3H4X method and the PM7 method. COSMO and COSMO2 were also compared in the quasi-docking procedure for the PM7 method, and PM7/COSMO showed the best results in ligand positioning and protein-ligand binding enthalpy calculations [19]. However, an error was made in the COSMO2 model [19]: the radius of the sphere imitating a water molecule was 1.0 Å instead of 1.3 Å [24].

In the present study, two quantum-chemical methods, PM6-D3H4X and PM7, are compared in quasi-docking using the COSMO and COSMO2 solvent models, and in the latter the correct radius of water molecule of 1.3 Å [24] is used. For these methods, the accuracy of ligand positioning is determined. The ligand positions found in quasi-docking are used to estimate the enthalpy of protein-ligand binding, and the calculated values are compared to the measured binding enthalpies.

2 Materials and Methods

2.1 Quantum Quasi-docking

The quantum quasi-docking procedure [5, 7, 8, 19] is an approximation to quantum docking, which should be carried out by searching for the global minimum of the protein-ligand system energy calculated by a quantum-chemical or quantum mechanical method. Such methods require much more computational resources than force fields, so quantum docking has not yet been received software implementation. The idea of quantum quasi-docking arose from successful application of quantum-chemical semi-empirical methods for calculating scoring functions after docking with classical force fields [12, 14–16, 26, 27]. The quasi-docking consists of two stages. First, using the classical MMFF94 force field [28], a fairly wide spectrum of low-energy minima of the protein-ligand complex is determined. For this purpose the FLM supercomputer docking program is used [5, 29, 30], and for each test protein-ligand complex several thousand unique low-energy minima are determined. Second, energies of all these minima are calculated again using a semiempirical quantum-chemical method without energy optimization, and the best docking position of the ligand corresponds to the minimum with most negative quantum-chemical energy. This ligand position should be close to the position of the ligand in the corresponding crystallized protein-ligand complex.

An approach to the application of quantum chemical methods in docking, which is closest to our quasi-docking, was developed by a group of researchers from Czech Republic (Prague and Olomouc) and Germany (Leipzig and Berlin) [12]. However, their SQM/COSMO filter differs from our quasi-docking by two significant features. First, four popular docking programs were used in [12] to find a set of 2865 non-redundant ligand poses using seven different scoring functions; in our quasi-docking procedure, unique low energy minima and corresponding ligand poses are found by a massive parallel search using the MMFF94 force field without simplifications, in contrast to the SQM/COSMO procedure, where different force fields with simplifications and empirical scoring functions are used to find ligand poses. Second, in our quasi-docking, much more than 2865 ligand poses are found for the recalculating their energies by quantum chemical methods. The use of supercomputing for docking is becoming more and more demanded (see, for example, a review [31] and [32]), but in most cases supercomputer are used for virtual screening of large databases of ligand using classical docking programs, e.g. in [32], the popular but very simplified AutoDock Vina [33] docking program is used. In contrast, in our quasi-docking, supercomputers are used to increase the docking accuracy of a ligand.

In the present work, PM6-D3H4X and PM7 methods with COSMO or COSMO2 solvent models are used at the second stage of quasi-docking. For the validation, 25 protein-ligand complexes from Protein Data Bank [34] are used. The ligand positions are compared by the standard deviation, RMSD, calculated over all ligand atoms.

2.2 FLM Program

The FLM supercomputer docking program carries out a parallel multi-core search for spectra of low energy minima of protein-ligand complexes [5, 19, 29, 30]. The random search is done by massive parallel local energy optimizations from various initial positions of the ligand. During optimization, the Cartesian coordinated of the ligand atoms are varied, while the positions of the protein atoms remain fixed. The energy is calculated in the FLM-0.05 program [30] using the MMFF94 force field without solvent. Special attention is paid to the uniqueness of the found local energy minima. The uniqueness is determined by a sufficiently small RMSD between ligand poses corresponding to energy minima. As a result, a spectrum is determined that contains a preset number of unique low-energy minima. This spectrum has a global energy minimum and each subsequent minimum. For most of the test complexes, the spectrum contains 8192 unique energy minima, but for three complexes, 4CRC, 4CRD and 5CSD, many more low-energy minima were preserved, since among the first 8192 low-energy minima there is not a single minimum whose ligand position is close to the position of the ligand in the crystallized protein-ligand PDB complex. FLM can also be used to determine a spectrum of low-energy minima of the unbound ligand.

FLM-0.05 requires from 16 (for the 1C5P complex with a small ligand) to 47 (for the 1J84 complex with a large ligand) hours at 504 computing cores of the Lomonosov supercomputer per protein-ligand complex.

2.3 PM6-D3H4X and PM7 Methods

For quantum-chemical calculations of energies of protein-ligand complexes the MOPAC program [35] is used. MOPAC contains different semiempirical quantum-chemical methods and allows to calculate molecular systems consisting of many thousands of atoms due to the MOZYME module [36] where the localized molecular orbitals method is used. Note that neither *ab initio* nor DFT methods can be used for such large molecular systems. Various quantum-chemical semiempirical methods have been developed and widely used since early 70s of XX century, but energies of intermolecular interactions, i.e. dispersion and hydrogen bonds, were badly described by these methods. A renaissance of semiempirical methods has begun with creation of so-called enhanced methods [17]. Two of these enhanced methods, PM6-D3H4X [23, 37] and PM7 [20], are implemented in MOPAC. PM6-D3H4X and PM7 describe well not only dispersion interactions and hydrogen bonds, but also halogen bonds, and their accuracy is comparable to that of DFT methods [38].

2.4 COSMO Solvent Model

The COSMO model [21] belongs to a wide group of implicit solvent models for the calculation of electrostatic solute-solvent interactions. Besides COSMO, there are various realizations of the Polarized Continuum Model (PCM) [39, 40] and the Generalized Born model [41, 42] in these group. In these models, solvent is represented usually by a homogeneous isotropic dielectric medium surrounding the solute molecule. Non-electrostatic solute-solvent interactions [43] and a cavitation contribution [44] are much smaller for aqueous solvent and are either ignored or used in an extremely primitive but widely used form proportional to the Solvent Accessible Surface (SAS) area with a proportionality factor treated as a surface tension coefficient [45]. COSMO is an approximation of the PCM equation for the infinite case of permittivity $\varepsilon = \infty$, and the aqueous solvent is just right for this case with $\varepsilon = 74.8$ at $T = 300K$. Popularity of the COSMO model is due to the fact that it is faster than the PCM model [46]. The finite value of the permittivity is taken into account by multiplying the polarization energy obtained from COSMO equations, i.e. the energy of the Coulomb interaction of the solute atomic charges with polarized charges on the Solvent Excluded Surface (SES), by a factor $(\varepsilon - 1)/(\varepsilon + 1/2)$. The MOPAC program that is used for the semiempirical calculations in this article has only one implicit solvent model, and that model is COSMO, where COSMO equation for polarized charges is solved on a SAS surface. Main parameters of this model are radii of atoms of a solute molecule and the radius of the probe sphere representing a solvent molecule. SAS is built on the points of contact of the probe sphere, rolling around the solute molecule over the spheres representing its atoms. Radii of atoms are fitted to reproduce experimental values of solvation energy for a set of molecules. The default atomic radii of the COSMO model in MOPAC were obtained for the old semiempirical AM1 method shortly after the publication of COSMO in the mid-90s. When energy of the molecule in solvent is calculated using either PM6-D3H4X or PM7 methods the COSMO parameterization has been done again. Such COSMO parameters were recently found [24] using a large set of low molecular weight molecules and molecular ions, and this model was called COSMO2. A new feature of COSMO2 is to account for non-polar solute-solvent interactions. For this, the aforementioned simplest model is used: the energy of these interactions is calculated through the SAS area with a ξ factor, the latter is also a fitted parameter of the method. In the present work, COSMO and COSMO2 are used to compare quasi-docking accuracy when using PM6-D3H4X and PM7 methods with atomic radii and ξ presented in Table 1 of the article [24]. The radius of the probe sphere RSOLV is equal to 1.3Å.

2.5 Protein-Ligand Binding Enthalpy

The free energy of protein-ligand binding ΔG_{bind} consists of two contributions:

$$\Delta G_{bind} = \Delta H_{bind} - T\Delta S_{bind} \tag{1}$$

where ΔH_{bind} is the enthalpy contribution and $-T\Delta S_{bind}$ is the entropy contribution, T is temperature in energy units.

A negative value of ΔH_{bind} means that the bound state of the ligand is energetically more favorable than its unbound state and heat is released when the ligand binds to the protein. The entropy contribution, $-T\Delta S_{bind}$, is associated with the limitation of the conformational mobility of the ligand in the bound state and with the change in the entropy of solvent molecules. We use here the binding enthalpy ΔH_{bind} as a measure of protein-ligand binding energy, bearing in mind that in many cases protein-ligand binding is due to rather large negative values of ΔH_{bind} which can be calculated in the first approximation as follows:

$$\Delta H_{bind} = E_1(PL) - E_1(P) - E_1(L), \tag{2}$$

where $E_1(PL)$ and $E_1(L)$ energies of the protein-ligand complex and the unbound ligand in the conformations corresponding to the respective global energy minima, $E_1(P)$ is the energy of the unbound protein in the conformation that is used by the FLM program. The heat of formation from the corresponding MOPAC output file is used for each of these energies.

The $E_1(PL)$ is obtained as a result of the optimization of the energy of the protein-ligand complex by varying the positions of ligand atoms from the initial configuration found in the quasi-docking procedure and corresponding to the best ligand position. The solvent is taken into account only in the final optimized state. The global energy minimum $E_1(L)$ of the unbound ligand is calculated using the quasi-docking procedure applied to the unbound ligand, but in the second stage of quasi-docking, energy optimization is additionally performed by the PM6-D3H4X or PM7 methods by varying the coordinates of all ligand atoms.

The binding enthalpy with COSMO is calculated using Eq. (2), but for the calculation of the binding enthalpy with COSMO2 the following equation is used:

$$\Delta H_{bind} = E_1(PL) - E_1(P) - E_1(L) + E_{np}^S, \tag{3}$$

Here E_{np}^S is calculated as follows:

$$E_{np}^S = \xi \times \Delta S \tag{4}$$

where $\Delta S = S(PL) - S(P) - S(L)$, $S(X)$ is the SAS area of the molecule X, $X = PL, P$, and L, $\xi = 0.046$ or 0.042 kcal/mol/Å^2 for the PM6-D3H4X or PM7 method, respectively [24]. The SAS area is calculated in MOPAC using default atomic radii for COSMO, but for COSMO2 using atomic radii parameterized for either PM6-D3H4X or PM7 in [24].

2.6 Index of Near Native

If energy minima of the complex are ranked by their energies, then each minimum is assigned an integer energy index corresponding to its place in this ranked series. The energy index of the global minimum is equal to 1. Some of these minima may correspond to positions of the ligand close to its crystallized position in the complex. We define the closeness of two ligand positions as RMSD ≤ 2 Å, where RMSD is calculated over all ligand atoms. We introduce the notation INN for the energy index of such minimum (Index of Near Native) [5]. When ligand positions of more than one minimum are close to the crystallized ligand position, INN is attributed to the minimum with the lowest energy. INN $= 1$ indicates that the docking paradigm is fulfilled.

2.7 Test Set of Protein-Ligand Complexes

We use 25 high quality protein-ligand complexes [19, 22] from Protein Data Bank (PDB) [34] to validate quasi-docking accuracy. These complexes contain 12 different proteins and corresponding native ligands of varying flexibility and size (see Table 1). For each of these complexes, the protein-ligand binding enthalpy is known from experiments.

Table 1. Validation complexes from PDB. *Res* – resolution, Q_P and N_P – the protein charge and the number of protein atoms, Q_L and N_L – the ligand charge and the number of ligand atoms, respectively, N_{tor} is the number of internal rotational degrees of freedom of the ligand.

Protein	PDB ID	*RES*, Å	N_P	Q_P	N_L	N_{tor}	Q_L
GNB/LNB-binding protein	2Z8D	1.85	5897	– 21	51	6	0
	2Z8E	1.99	5897	– 21	51	6	0
α-fucosidase	2XII	1.8	7042	2	51	4	1
KIV-10 module of Apo(a)	3KIV	1.8	1206	1	20	5	0
BET protein	4MR5	1.63	1860	2	42	3	0
	4MR6	1.67	1860	2	49	6	0
CRP	1HW5	1.82	3284	1	33	1	– 1
Trypsin	1C5P	1.43	3220	6	18	1	1
	1K1J	2.2	3220	6	68	10	1
	2ZDM	1.93	3220	6	59	9	1
	2ZDN	1.98	3220	6	58	9	1
	2ZFS	1.51	3220	6	64	9	2
YKL-39	4P8V	1.64	5741	– 1	57	8	0
Factor XIa	4CRC	1.6	3711	2	60	11	0
	4CRD	2.1	3692	2	57	11	0
EngF	1J84	2.02	2642	– 7	87	10	0
Mp1p-LBD2	5CSD	1.45	2407	– 4	53	14	– 1
HIV-1 protease	1MRX	2	3140	6	74	11	0
	1MSM	2	3138	6	78	12	0
	2PYM	1.9	3100	2	86	12	1
	2PYN	1.85	3116	4	86	12	1
	3KDB	1.66	3138	6	86	13	0
	3NU3	1.02	3134	6	70	13	0
	4LL3	1.95	3134	4	75	13	0
Renin	2IKO	1.9	5144	– 8	46	5	1

3 Results

3.1 Positioning Accuracy

INN indexes for different methods of the energy calculation at the second stage of quasi-docking are presented in Table 2.

The table contains the comparison of results obtained with next methods of the energy calculation: the PM6-D3H4X method with the old parameterization of the COSMO

Table 2. INN indexes for different methods of the energy calculation at the second stage of quasi-docking. N_{min} is the number of unique energy minima determined at the first stage of quasi-docking by FLM. RMSD – a standard deviation between the native ligand positions in the crystal and in the global energy minimum.

PDB ID	N_{min}	PM6-D3H4X/ COSMO		PM6-D3H4X/ COSMO2		PM7/ COSMO		PM7/ COSMO2	
		INN	RMSD, Å	INN	RMSD, Å	INN	RMSD, Å	INN	RMSD, Å
1C5P	5349	1	0.44	1	0.44	1	0.43	1	0.43
1HW5	6848	1	0.48	1	0.48	1	0.48	1	0.48
1J84	8192	11	5.64	2	5.64	1	1.97	1	1.97
1K1J	8101	1	0.33	1	0.33	1	0.33	1	0.33
1MRX	3127	1	1.35	3	10.20	1	0.47	1	1.35
1MSM	6157	1	1.87	1	1.87	1	1.87	2	8.42
2KIO	2622	1	0.49	1	0.49	1	0.49	1	0.49
2PYM	4340	1	1.66	1	1.66	1	1.66	1	1.66
2PYN	4953	1	1.22	1	1.22	1	1.22	1	1.54
2XII	8192	1	0.58	2	5.67	1	0.58	1	0.58
2Z8D	8192	5	3.67	3	3.67	2	3.67	2	3.67
2Z8E	8192	1	1.11	1	1.11	1	1.11	1	1.11
2ZDM	5971	1	0.91	1	0.91	1	0.91	1	1.11
2ZDN	5645	8	2.12	1	0.68	1	0.68	1	0.68
2ZFS	5986	9	2.67	3	2.66	2	2.67	1	0.98
3KDB	5457	2	2.61	3	2.61	1	0.96	3	2.83
3KIV	5363	1	0.84	2	3.75	1	0.75	1	0.75
3NU3	4935	1	0.44	1	0.44	1	0.44	1	0.44
4CRC	11809	2	2.67	1	0.86	2	2.67	2	2.67
4CRD	20222	233	10.81	26	10.81	1	1.00	3	8.07
4LL3	5888	4	4.78	1	0.70	4	8.38	1	1.42
4MR5	5002	2	8.05	2	8.05	5	8.05	5	8.05
4MR6	4313	1	1.16	1	1.16	1	1.16	1	1.16
4P8V	8193	37	10.11	9	10.11	1	0.58	3	4.13
5CSD	29528	2576	10.33	8	11.34	993	10.33	3	11.92

solvent model, the PM6-D3H4X method with the new COSMO2 solvent model, PM7 with the COSMO solvent model, and PM7 with the new COSMO2 solvent model.

We see that the number of complexes (19) with INN = 1 is highest when the energy is calculated by PM7/COSMO. For PM6-D3H4X/COSMO, PM6-D3H4X/COSMO2, and

PM7/COSMO2 the numbers of complexes with INN = 1 are: 14, 14, and 17, respectively. Thus, for the PM7/COSMO method, the accuracy of quasi-docking to position the ligand in the active site of the protein is highest among other methods of energy calculation used in this work. As can be seen from Table 2, COSMO is slightly better than COSMO2 for both PM6-D3H4X and PM7.

If the requirement for the INN index is slightly loosen and it is determined at RMSD = 3Å, then the number of complexes with INN = 1 will increase to: 18, 16, 21, and 19 for PM6-D3H4X/COSMO, PM6-D3H4X/COSMO2, PM7/COSMO, and PM7/COSMO2, respectively.

For some cases with INN $\neq$ 1, a detailed analysis revealed reasons that could explain poor positioning results, and these observations were presented in [19].

3.2 Binding Enthalpy

For most of complexes from Table 1, except the 3KIV, 4CRC and 4CRD complexes, the experimental values of the enthalpy of protein-ligand binding can be found in the references presented in Protein Data Bank [34]. When choosing complexes for comparing the calculated and measured binding enthalpies, the following considerations were taken into account. First, INN = 1, that is, the quasi-docking demonstrates high positioning accuracy. Second, 2PYM and 2PYN were rejected because the formation of these complexes is energetically unfavorable and their binding enthalpy is positive. Third, complexes 1J84, 2Z8D, 2Z8E, and 4P8V were excluded, because carbohydrate ligands in them have a distorted pyranose rings in the bound and unbound states, which results in the "boat" or "twist-boat" conformations instead of the usual "chair" conformations.

The experimentally measured ΔH_{exp} and calculated ΔH_{bind} values of the protein-ligand binding enthalpy are shown in Table 3. We see that ΔH_{bind} is negative for all methods of the energy calculation in accordance with experiments. However, the absolute values of the binding enthalpy calculated by all methods significantly exceed the measured ones.

For PM6-D3H4X, the difference between the calculated and measured binding enthalpies is smaller than for PM7 with both COSMO models. The correlation coefficient R = 0.74 between the measured and calculated values is largest when the PM7/COSMO method is used for the energy calculation at the second stage of the quasi-docking procedure. The reason for the poor performance of COSMO2 may be related to the following. COSMO2 differs from COSMO by the last term in Eq. (3) describing non-polar solute-solvent interactions. This term contributes 25–50% to the value of the enthalpy of protein-ligand binding, and the too simplified form (4) can lead to poor performance of COSMO2.

3.3 Discussion of the Results

High correlation the measured and calculated binding enthalpies and high quasi-docking accuracy for the PM7/COSMO method of the energy calculation is an encouraging result. Possibly, poor performance of the COSMO2 solvent model for both considered

Table 3. Measured ΔH_{exp} and calculated ΔH_{bind} binding enthalpies.

The ligand pose is obtained by		PM6-D3H4X		PM7	
PDB ID	ΔH_{exp}, kcal/mol	ΔH_{bind}, COSMO, kcal/mol	ΔH_{bind}, COSMO2, kcal/mol	ΔH_{bind}, COSMO, kcal/mol	ΔH_{bind}, COSMO2, kcal/mol
1C5P	−4.52	− 27.7	−20.9	− 54.7	−56.6
1HW5	−0.97	− 37.0	−39.5	− 54.7	−41.6
1K1J	−9.46	− 29.6	−39.1	− 82.7	−98.3
1MRX	−2.10	− 9.4	−	− 54.9	−78.7
1MSM	−7.60	− 20.1	−34.1	− 67.9	−
2IKO	−9.50	− 33.8	−36.6	− 81.2	−91.8
2XII	−9.80	− 55.2	−	− 92.1	−84.6
2ZDM	−7.24	− 31.9	−39.6	− 82.2	−96.4
2ZDN	−5.09	−	−38.0	− 85.1	−76.9
2ZFS	−4.52	−	−	−	−101.6
3KDB	−1.55	−	−	− 54.7	−
3NU3	−7.30	− 6.8	−25.9	− 54.5	−68.7
4LL3	−16.40	−	−10.3	−	−55.8
4MR6	−4.04	− 15.3	−29.0	− 47.4	−66.1
The coefficient of correlation R between ΔH_{exp} and ΔH_{bind}		0.36	−0.53	0.74	0.16

quantum-chemical methods is connected to inadequate modeling of non-polar solute-solvent interaction, since the COSMO2 model takes into account the non-polar solute-solvent interaction, considering all solute atoms to be the same and using a single coefficient ξ describing this interaction in accordance with Eq. (4). An advanced model of non-polar solute-solvent interactions, such as the model described in [43], could possibly lead to improved performance of COSMO2. The reason of the large deviation of the calculated binding enthalpy from the measured values is not yet clear. A similar problem was faced in [25], where the energy of protein-ligand interaction "…is never smaller than 50 kcal/mol". Perhaps, the problem can be solved by improving the model. One such improvement could be the addition of mobility to some of the protein atoms. Our preliminary study of several protein-ligand complexes result in the larger decrease of the energy of unbound protein than the decrease in the energy of the protein-ligand complex when mobility of some protein atoms are taken into account. This should lead to less negative binding enthalpies. However, this conclusion needs broader confirmation.

4 Conclusions

The results presented in this study show high accuracy of the quasi-docking procedure with the PM7/COSMO method of the energy calculation. Other investigated methods of the energy calculation, PM6-D3H4X/COSMO, PM6-D3H4X/COSMO2 and PM7/COSMO2, demonstrate worse accuracy. The highest coefficient of correlation 0.74 between measured and calculated binding enthalpies is obtained for the PM7/COSMO method.

Further study of quasi-docking and improving the corresponding model is needed. The COSMO and COSMO2 parameterizations should be further improved.

The results presented in this study suggest that a future quantum docking program can be developed based on the PM7/COSMO energy calculation method.

Acknowledgements. The work was financially supported by the Russian Science Foundation, Agreement no. 21–71-20031. The research is carried out using the equipment of the shared research facilities of HPC computing resources at Lomonosov Moscow State University, including the Lomonosov-2 supercomputer [47].

References

1. Sulimov, V.B., Sulimov, A.V.: Docking: Molecular Modeling for Drug Discovery. AINTELL, Moscow (2017)
2. Sulimov, V.B., Kutov, D.C., Taschilova, A.S., Ilin, I.S., Tyrtyshnikov, E.E., Sulimov, A.V.: Docking paradigm in drug design. Curr. Top. Med. Chem. **21**(6), 507–546 (2021). https://doi.org/10.2174/1568026620666201207095626
3. Sulimov, V.B., Kutov, D.C., Sulimov, A.V.: Advances in docking. Curr. Med. Chem. **26**(42), 7555–7580 (2019). https://doi.org/10.2174/0929867325666180904115000
4. Macip, G., et al.: Haste makes waste: A critical review of docking-based virtual screening in drug repurposing for SARS-CoV-2 main protease (M-pro) inhibition. Med. Res. Rev. **42**(2), 744–769 (2022). https://doi.org/10.1002/med.21862
5. Oferkin, I.V., et al.: Evaluation of docking target functions by the comprehensive investigation of protein-ligand energy minima. Adv. Bioinformatics. **12**, 126858 (2015). https://doi.org/10.1155/2015/126858
6. Oferkin, I.V., Zheltkov, D.A., Tyrtyshnikov, E.E., Sulimov, A.V., Kutov, D.C., Sulimov, V.B.: Evaluation of the docking algorithm based on tensor train global optimization. Bull. South Ural State Univ. Ser. Math. Model. Program. Comput. Softw. **8**(4), 83–99 (2015). https://doi.org/10.14529/mmp150407
7. Sulimov, A.V., Kutov, D.C., Katkova, E.V., Sulimov, V.B.: Combined docking with classical force field and quantum chemical semiempirical method PM7. Adv. Bioinformatics. 6, 7167691 (2017). https://doi.org/10.1155/2017/7167691
8. Sulimov, A.V., Kutov, D.C., Katkova, E.V., Ilin, I.S., Sulimov, V.B.: New generation of docking programs: Supercomputer validation of force fields and quantum-chemical methods for docking. J. Mol. Graph. Model. **78**, 139–147 (2017). https://doi.org/10.1016/j.jmgm.2017.10.007
9. Sulimov, A.V., et al.: Evaluation of the novel algorithm of flexible ligand docking with moveable target-protein atoms. Comput. Struct. Biotechnol. J. **15**, 275–285 (2017). https://doi.org/10.1016/j.csbj.2017.02.004

10. Chen, Y.C.: Beware of docking! Trends Pharmacol Sci. **36**(2), 78–95 (2015). https://doi.org/10.1016/j.tips.2014.12.001

11. Yuriev, E., Holien, J., Ramsland, P.A.: Improvements, trends, and new ideas in molecular docking: 2012–2013 in review. J. Mol. Recognit. **28**(10), 581–604 (2015). https://doi.org/10.1002/jmr.2471

12. Pecina, A., et al.: The SQM/COSMO filter: reliable native pose identification based on the quantum-mechanical description of protein-ligand interactions and implicit COSMO solvation. Chem Commun. **52**(16), 3312–3315 (2016). https://doi.org/10.1039/c5cc09499b

13. Nikitina, E., Sulimov, V., Zayets, V., Zaitseva, N.: Semiempirical calculations of binding enthalpy for protein-ligand complexes. Int. J. Quantum Chem. **97**(2), 747–763 (2004)

14. Vasilyev, V., Bliznyuk, A.: Application of semiempirical quantum chemical methods as a scoring function in docking. Theor. Chem. Acc. **112**, 313–317 (2004). https://doi.org/10.1007/s00214-004-0589-9

15. Lepšík, M., Řezáč, J., Kolář, M., Pecina, A., Hobza, P., Fanfrlík, J.: The semiempirical quantum mechanical scoring function for in silico drug design. ChemPlusChem **78**(9), 921–931 (2013). https://doi.org/10.1002/cplu.201300199

16. Brahmkshatriya, P.S., et al.: Quantum mechanical scoring: structural and energetic insights into cyclin-dependent kinase 2 Inhibition by Pyrazolo[1,5-a]pyrimidines. Curr. Comput. Aided. Drug Des. **9**(1), 118–129 (2013)

17. Yilmazer, D.N., Korth, M.: Recent progress in treating protein-ligand interactions with quantum-mechanical methods. Int. J. Mol. Sci. **17**(5), 742 (2016). https://doi.org/10.3390/ijms17050742

18. Eyrilmez, S.M., Köprülüoğlu, C., Řezáč, J., Hobza, P.: Impressive enrichment of semiempirical quantum mechanics-based scoring function: HSP90 protein with 4541 inhibitors and decoys. ChemPhysChem **20**(21), 2759–2766 (2019). https://doi.org/10.1002/cphc.201900628

19. Sulimov, A., Kutov, D., Gribkova, A., Ilin, I., Tashchilova, A., Sulimov, V.: Search for approaches to supercomputer quantum-chemical docking. In: Voevodin, V., Sobolev, S. (eds.) RuSCDays 2019. CCIS, vol. 1129, pp. 363–378. Springer, Cham (2019). https://doi.org/10.1007/978-3-030-36592-9_30

20. Stewart, J.J.P.: Optimization of parameters for semiempirical methods VI: more modifications to the NDDO approximations and re-optimization of parameters. J. Mol. Model. **19**(1), 1–32 (2013). https://doi.org/10.1007/s00894-012-1667-x

21. Klamt, A., Schüürmann, G.: COSMO: a new approach to dielectric screening in solvents with explicit expressions for the screening energy and its gradient. J. Chem. Soc., Perkin Trans. **2**(5), 799–805 (1993). https://doi.org/10.1039/P29930000799

22. Sulimov, A., Kutov, D., Ilin, I., Sulimov, V.: Quantum-chemical quasi-docking for molecular dynamics calculations. Nanomaterials **12**(2), 274 (2022). https://doi.org/10.3390/nano12020274

23. Řezáč, J., Hobza, P.: Advanced corrections of hydrogen bonding and dispersion for semiempirical quantum mechanical methods. J. Chem. Theory Comput. **8**(1), 141–151 (2012). https://doi.org/10.1021/ct200751e

24. Kříž, K., Řezáč, J.: Reparametrization of the COSMO solvent model for semiempirical methods PM6 and PM7. J. Chem. Inf. Model. **59**(1), 229–235 (2019). https://doi.org/10.1021/acs.jcim.8b00681

25. Kříž, K., Řezáč, J.: Benchmarking of semiempirical quantum-mechanical methods on systems relevant to computer-aided drug design. J. Chem. Inf. Model. **60**(3), 1453–1460 (2020). https://doi.org/10.1021/acs.jcim.9b01171

26. Stewart, J.J.P.: A method for predicting individual residue contributions to enzyme specificity and binding-site energies, and its application to MTH1. J. Mol. Model. **22**(11), 1–19 (2016). https://doi.org/10.1007/s00894-016-3119-5

27. Ajani, H., et al.: Superior performance of the SQM/COSMO scoring functions in native pose recognition of diverse protein-ligand complexes in cognate docking. ACS Omega **2**(7), 4022–4029 (2017). https://doi.org/10.1021/acsomega.7b00503

28. Halgren, T.A.: Merck molecular force field. J. Comput. Chem. **17**(5–6), 490–641 (1996)

29. Sulimov, A., Kutov, D., Sulimov, V.: Parallel supercomputer docking program of the new generation: finding low energy minima spectrum. In: Voevodin, V., Sobolev, S. (eds.) RuSCDays 2018. CCIS, vol. 965, pp. 314–330. Springer, Cham (2019). https://doi.org/10.1007/978-3-030-05807-4_27

30. Kutov, D.C., Sulimov, A.V., Sulimov, V.B.: Supercomputer docking: Investigation of low energy minima of protein-ligand complexes. Supercomput. Front. Innov. **5**(3), 134–137 (2018). https://doi.org/10.14529/jsfi180326

31. Sulimov, A.V., Kutov, D.C., Sulimov, V.B.: Supercomputer docking. Supercomput. Front. Innov. **6**(3), 26–50 (2019). https://doi.org/10.14529/jsfi190302

32. Gorgulla, C., et al.: An open-source drug discovery platform enables ultra-large virtual screens. Nature **580**(7805), 663–668 (2020). https://doi.org/10.1038/s41586-020-2117-z

33. Trott, O., Olson, A.J.: AutoDock Vina: improving the speed and accuracy of docking with a new scoring function, efficient optimization, and multithreading. J. Comput. Chem. **31**(2), 455–461 (2010). https://doi.org/10.1002/jcc.21334

34. Berman, H.M., et al.: The protein data bank. Nucleic Acids Res. **28**(1), 235–242 (2000). https://doi.org/10.1093/nar/28.1.235

35. Stewart, J.J.P.: Stewart Computational Chemistry. MOPAC2016. http://openmopac.net/MOPAC2016.html

36. Stewart, J.J.P.: Application of localized molecular orbitals to the solution of semiempirical self-consistent field equations. Int. J. Quantum Chem. **58**(2), 133–146 (1996). https://doi.org/10.1002/(SICI)1097-461X(1996)58:2%3c133::AID-QUA2%3e3.0.CO;2-Z

37. Řezáč, J., Hobza, P.: A halogen-bonding correction for the semiempirical PM6 method. Chem. Phys. Lett. **506**(4), 286–289 (2011). https://doi.org/10.1016/j.cplett.2011.03.009

38. Hostaš, J., Řezáč, J., Hobza, P.: On the performance of the semiempirical quantum mechanical PM6 and PM7 methods for noncovalent interactions. Chem. Phys. Lett. **568–569**(Supplement C), 161–166 (2013). https://doi.org/10.1016/j.cplett.2013.02.069

39. Tomasi, J., Persico, M.: Molecular interactions in solution: an overview of methods based on continuous distributions of the solvent. Chem. Rev. **94**(7), 2027–2094 (1994). https://doi.org/10.1021/cr00031a013

40. Cramer, C.J., Truhlar, D.G.: Implicit solvation models: equilibria, structure, spectra, and dynamics. Chem. Rev. **99**(8), 2161–2200 (1999). https://doi.org/10.1021/cr960149m

41. Romanov, A.N., Jabin, S.N., Martynov, Y.B., Sulimov, A.V., Grigoriev, F.V., Sulimov, V.B.: Surface generalized born method: a simple, fast, and precise implicit solvent model beyond the coulomb approximation. J. Phys. Chem. A. **108**(43), 9323–9327 (2004). https://doi.org/10.1021/jp046721s

42. Aguilar, B., Onufriev, A.V.: Efficient computation of the total solvation energy of small molecules via the R6 generalized born model. J. Chem. Theory Comput. **8**(7), 2404–2411 (2012). https://doi.org/10.1021/ct200786m

43. Basilevsky, M.V., Leontyev, I.V., Luschekina, S.V., Kondakova, O.A., Sulimov, V.B.: Computation of hydration free energies of organic solutes with an implicit water model. J. Comput. Chem. **27**(5), 552–570 (2006)

44. Basilevsky, M.V., Grigoriev, F.V., Leontyev, I.V., Sulimov, V.B.: Excluded volume effect for large and small solutes in water. J. Phys. Chem. A. **109**(31), 6939–6946 (2005). https://doi.org/10.1021/jp051246z

45. Bordner, A.J., Cavasotto, C.N., Abagyan, R.A.: Accurate transferable model for water, n-Octanol, and n-hexadecane solvation free energies. J. Phys. Chem. B. **106**(42), 11009–11015 (2002). https://doi.org/10.1021/jp0264477

46. Katkova, E.V., Onufriev, A.V., Aguilar, B., Sulimov, V.B.: Accuracy comparison of several common implicit solvent models and their implementations in the context of protein-ligand binding. J. Mol. Graph. Model. **72**(Supplement C), 70–80 (2017). https://doi.org/10.1016/j.jmgm.2016.12.011
47. Voevodin, V.V., et al.: Supercomputer Lomonosov-2: Large scale, deep monitoring and fine analytics for the user community. Supercomput. Front. Innov. **6**(2), 4–11 (2019). https://doi.org/10.14529/jsfi190201

HPC, BigData, AI: Architectures, Technologies, Tools

Data-Based Choice of the Training Dataset for the Numerical Dispersion Mitigation Neural Network

Kirill Gadylshin, Vadim Lisitsa(✉)(iD), Kseniia Gadylshina,
and Dmitry Vishnevsky

Institute of Petroleum Geology and Geophysics SB RAS, 3 Koptug Avenue,
Novosibirsk 630090, Russia
lisitsavv@ipgg.sbras.ru

Abstract. The main way that numerical error in seismic modeling manifests itself is through numerical dispersion brought on by coarse grids. Refining the mesh has the potential to minimize it, but doing so will result in an unacceptably high computational cost. Numerical Dispersion Mitigation network (NDM-net), a new technique that was recently created, is applied to the full dataset computed using a coarse mesh after the network has been trained using a relatively small number of seismograms that were previously computed using a fine mesh. The creation of the training dataset is the component of the procedure that requires the greatest computation. Therefore, reducing the quantity of precomputed seismograms may help the approach perform better as a whole. In this article, we describe a method for building the training dataset so that the difference between it and the full dataset does not go above the allowed limit.

Keywords: Deep learning · Seismic modelling · Numerical dispersion

1 Introduction

The most computationally demanding step in seismic processing methods is the generation of the synthetic seismograms for a specific Earth interior model and acquisition system, also known as seismic modeling. Indeed, executing seismic modeling for all source positions for all taken model approximations is necessary to solve the full-waveform inversion problem, i.e., to reconstruct the model using the recorded seismic data. The simulation of the wavefield corresponding to a single source may demand up to dozens of Tb of RAM and several thousand node-hours, even in the most basic instance of isotropic elastic media. If the model becomes more complex, such as anisotropic [10,16], viscoelastic [3,18], or poroelastic [13] demand in the computational resources may increase significantly. Note also that the typical acquisition system includes thousands of shot points, leading to proportional growth in the computational intensity of the algorithms.

V. Voevodin et al. (Eds.): RuSCDays 2022, LNCS 13708, pp. 385–396, 2022.
https://doi.org/10.1007/978-3-031-22941-1_28

If wave propagation is considered, the spatial discretization and, thus, the size of the problem is governed by the number of grid points per wavelength which ensures an acceptable level of numerical dispersion if a particular method is used. Finite differences are common in seismic modeling due to their simplicity and the possibility of treating models of almost arbitrary complexity. However, their implementation may require three to ten grid points per minimal wavelength, which turns into 10^3–10^4 grid points in one spatial direction. Further grid coarsening leads to an unacceptable level of numerical dispersion. There are approaches to reduce numerical dispersion (increase the grid step) applying the discontinuous Galerkin method, pseudospectral methods, and others. However, a detailed analysis of these approaches reveals that they require more flops per grid point and, thus, do not improve algorithm efficiency [1,11].

On the other hand, a series of approaches were suggested to post-process noisy data simulated on a coarse mesh to reduce the numerical dispersion [6,14]. However, these approaches are mainly oriented toward the reduction of the dispersion caused by the discretization of the time derivative, whereas approximation of the spatial derivatives causes a major effect on the numerical error, and it can not be straightforwardly removed from the simulated data. A series of algorithms to remove the numerical dispersion based on machine learning methods were suggested recently [4,5,17]. In particular, in [4], the Numerical Dispersion Mitigation network (NDM-net) was suggested. It was developed to suppress numerical dispersion in seismic data recorded on a daylight surface, with the training dataset being wavefields simulated for a few source positions using a fine enough grid. However, in [4], the authors empirically choose the training dataset, i.e., using each tenth source position, which may not be the optimal choice because it does not take into account the data similarity. So, in this paper, we suggest the approach to generate the training dataset that preserves the "distance" (metric in the seismograms space) between the training dataset and the entire dataset.

The paper is organized as followed. We remind the NDM-net basis in Sect. 2. Analysis of the seismograms and two approaches to construct the training dataset are provided in Sect. 3.

2   NDM-net's Basic Aspects

2.1   Seismic Modelling

A standard seismic modelling problem statement can considered as mapping of the Earth interior model to the wavefield, corresponding to a particular source position and source wavelet function:

$$u(x, t) = A[M, x^s, f(t)], \tag{1}$$

where u is the vector velocity field inside the computational domain D, $M = M(x)$ is the model, which depends on the spatial coordinates. Vector x_s represents the is the spatial position of the source, and $f(t)$ is the source wavelet. We use $\boldsymbol{f}(t)$ to point out that the source can be an external force. In this research, we restrict considerations to isotropic media; thus, the model is defined by three parameters: λ and μ are the Lame parameters, and ρ is the mass density.

To construct the wavefield one needs resolve the linear elastic wave equation:

$$\begin{aligned}
\rho\frac{\partial u_1}{\partial t} &= \frac{\partial \sigma_{11}}{\partial x_1} + \frac{\partial \sigma_{13}}{\partial x_3} + \phi_1(t)\delta(\boldsymbol{x} - \boldsymbol{x}^s), \\
\rho\frac{\partial u_3}{\partial t} &= \frac{\partial \sigma_{13}}{\partial x_1} + \frac{\partial \sigma_{33}}{\partial x_3} + \phi_3(t)\delta(\boldsymbol{x} - \boldsymbol{x}^s), \\
\frac{\partial \sigma_{11}}{\partial t} &= (\lambda + 2\mu)\frac{\partial u_1}{\partial x_1} + \lambda\frac{\partial u_3}{\partial x_3} + \psi_{11}(t)\delta(\boldsymbol{x} - \boldsymbol{x}^s), \\
\frac{\partial \sigma_{33}}{\partial t} &= \lambda\frac{\partial u_1}{\partial x_1} + (\lambda + 2\mu)\frac{\partial u_3}{\partial x_3} + \psi_{33}(t)\delta(\boldsymbol{x} - \boldsymbol{x}^s), \\
\frac{\partial \sigma_{13}}{\partial t} &= \mu\frac{\partial u_1}{\partial x_3} + \mu\frac{\partial u_3}{\partial x_1} + \psi_{13}(t)\delta(\boldsymbol{x} - \boldsymbol{x}^s),
\end{aligned} \tag{2}$$

This equation can be rewritten as

$$L[\boldsymbol{u}] = \boldsymbol{f}(t)\delta(\boldsymbol{x} - \boldsymbol{x}^s), \tag{3}$$

where L is the linear differential operator. Having resolved this equation, one gets the wavefield inside the entire spatial domain D at all time instants $t > 0$, but for a fixed right-hand side, i.e., for fixed source position and source wavelet. In seismic modelling only the projection of the solution onto a surface $x_3 = 0$ is needed, but the problem 2 has to be solved for a large number of sources (right-hand sides) $\boldsymbol{x}_j^s$. Let us denote

$$\boldsymbol{u}_j = \boldsymbol{u}(\boldsymbol{x}_j^s, \boldsymbol{x}^r, t) = \boldsymbol{u}(\boldsymbol{x}_j^s, \boldsymbol{x}^o, t),$$

where $\boldsymbol{x}^r$ represents the coordinates of the receivers, and $\boldsymbol{x}^o = \boldsymbol{x}^r - \boldsymbol{x}_j^s$ is the source-receiver offset. Note that the seismograms are recorded for fixed offsets geometries, whereas the receiver's positions are adjusted to the source position to ensure fixed offsets. Thus, the seismograms can be considered as functions of two independent variables $\boldsymbol{x}^o$ and t. However, the seismograms depend on the source position $\boldsymbol{x}_j^s$ as a parameter.

In this paper, we perform numerical simulation to resolve Eq. (2) using the standard staggered grid finite difference scheme. We used the fourth-order accurate approximation in space and the second order accurate in time [9]:

$$\begin{aligned}
\rho D_t[u_1]_{i+1/2,j}^{n-1/2} &= D_1[\sigma_{11}]_{i+1/2,j}^{n-1/2} + D_3[\sigma_{13}]_{i+1/2,j}^{n-1/2} + (\phi_1)_{i+1/2,j}^{n-1/2}, \\
\rho D_t[u_3]_{i,j+1/2}^{n-1/2} &= D_1[\sigma_{13}]_{i,j+1/2}^{n-1/2} + D_3[\sigma_{33}]_{i,j+1/2}^{n-1/2} + (\phi_3)_{i,j+1/2}^{n-1/2}, \\
D_t[\sigma_{11}]_{i,j}^{n} &= (\lambda + 2\mu)D_1[u_1]_{i,j}^{n} + \lambda D_3[u_3]_{i,j}^{n} + (\psi_{11})_{i,j}^{n}, \\
D_t[\sigma_{33}]_{i,j}^{n} &= \lambda D_1[u_1]_{i,j}^{n} + (\lambda + 2\mu)D_3[u_3]_{i,j}^{n} + (\psi_{33})_{i,j}^{n}, \\
D_t[\sigma_{13}]_{i+1/2,j+1/2}^{n} &= \mu D_3[u_1]_{i+1/2,j+1/2}^{n} + \mu D_1[u_3]_{i+1/2,j+1/2}^{n} + (\psi_{13})_{i+1/2,j+1/2}^{n},
\end{aligned} \tag{4}$$

where finite-difference operators are

$$D_t[g]_{i,j}^{n} = \frac{g_{i,j}^{n+1/2} - g_{i,j}^{n-1/2}}{\tau},$$

and

$$D_1[g]_{i,j}^{n} = \frac{9}{8}\frac{g_{i+1/2,j}^{n} - g_{i-1/2,j}^{n}}{h_1} - \frac{1}{24}\frac{g_{i+3/2,j}^{n} - g_{i-3/2,j}^{n}}{h_1}.$$

In these notations, g is any smooth enough function. The permutation of the spatial indices can obtain an operator, approximating the derivatives with respect to x_3. Presented operators are defined in integer grid points but can be redefined in half-integer points by the corresponding shift of indices.

As it is follows from the general theory of finite differences if the scheme approximates the differential operator and it is stable, the numerical solution converges to the analytical solution and the following estimate takes place:

$$\|[u_j]_h - u_j^h\| = \varepsilon_h \leq C_1 h^4 + C_2 \tau^2 \leq Ch^2, \tag{5}$$

where u_j^h is the numerical solution, corresponding to the source position x_j^s, $[u_j]_h$ is the solution of the original differential problem projected onto the grid, C_1, C_2, and C are some constants. The last inequality is valid due to the stability condition of the explicit scheme 4.

2.2 NDM-net

It is clear that the decrease of the grid step can reduce the numerical error, according to the estimation (5). However, it would significantly increase the computational intensity of the algorithm. In particular, if the grid step is halved, the error will be reduced by the factor of four, whereas the size of the problem in terms of degrees of freedom will increase by the factor of eight, and the number of flops will increase by the factor of sixteen. It makes conventional approaches to accuracy improvement unacceptable for real-life simulations.

To overcome this contradiction, the NDM-net was suggested in [4]. The method's goal is to simulate all seismograms in the dataset using a mesh that is coarse enough to provide fast but an inaccurate result. The training dataset is then created by simulating a tiny fraction of the seismograms using a fine mesh. To transfer the coarse grid solution to the fine grid solution, a U-Net [15] is subsequently trained.

The NDM-net is implemented using the PyTorch machine learning framework. We employ the DataParallel Pytorch module to perform parallel DNN training using the batch size of 16. For training, we used a single GPU node with four Nvidia RTX 2080ti connected via NVlink. Exploiting this configuration led to a sublinear scaling using four GPUs.

Later on, NDM-net is applied to all seismograms to reduce the numerical error:

$$N[u_j^{h_c}] = u_j^{ML},$$

so that

$$\|u_j^{ML} - u_j\| \leq \|u_j^{h_c} - u_j\|,$$

where $u_j^{h_c}$ is the coarse grid solution and u_j^{ML} is the corrected solution.

According to the results presented in [4] the most computationally intense and time-consuming part of the presented approach is the generation of the training dataset. Indeed, even if the fine grid is half of the coarse grid step, simulation of a single shot seismogram by the fine grid would take 16 times more computational time and resources. Thus, It can be considered the bottleneck of the proposed algorithm, which requires optimization. Below we suggest a new strategy for training dataset construction and compare it with the previously described in [4].

3   Construction of the Training Dataset

3.1   Analysis of Seismogramms

The main assumption used to legitimate the NDM-net is that it is possible to construct a representative subset of seismograms that can be used as a training dataset. This assumption is based on the peculiarity of seismic modeling, where the model rapidly varies in x_3 direction but slowly changes in the x_1 direction. As an example we provide the BP model [2], which is presented in Fig. 1. The right part of the model smoothly varies in the horizontal direction. However, the changes are faster in the left part of the model. We simulated seismograms for a set of sources equidistantly placed in the daylight, with the step between the sources equal to 25 m. We used the Ricker pulse with a dominated frequency 30 Hz as the source wavelet function.

We considered the entire set of the seismograms and introduced a distance in the space of seismograms (not the distance between the sources) using the Normalized Root Mean Square reputability measure, commonly used in seismic monitoring [7,8,12] which is equivalent to a relative error in L^2 norm. We denote it as $d(\boldsymbol{u}_j, \boldsymbol{u}_i) = d_{i,j}$. Then, utilizing the pair-wise distances between the seismograms from the full dataset, we took into account the distance matrix. The considered acquisition system included 2696 sources in total. The distance matrix is presented in the Fig. 2. It can be seen that the distance $d_{i,j}$ in the seismogram space is well correlated with the physical distance between the sources. In addition to the entire distance matrix, we provide the plots of 14 rows, which are distances from 14 seismograms to all other seismograms. For the nearby sources ($|i - j| \leq i_0$), the distance $d_{i,j}$ rapidly grows if the physical distance increases. If the sources are well separated ($|i - j| \geq i_0$) distance between the seismograms remains almost constant; i.e., $d_{i,j} \approx const.$

3.2   Equidistantly Distributed Sources to Generate Training Dataset

This behavior of the seismograms discrepancy legitimates the previously suggested approach of choosing the training dataset as seismograms corresponding to the equidistantly distributed subset of the entire set of sources. To illustrate its applicability to the BP model, we performed wavefield simulations for the entire set of 2696 sources using a coarse ($h = 6$ m) and a fine ($h = 3$ m) grids. We used Ricker pulse with the dominated frequency 30 Hz as the source wavelet. After that, we constructed several datasets with equidistantly distributed sources. They are

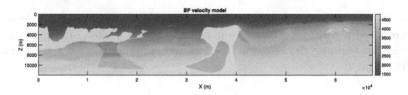

Fig. 1. Modified BP model

- D_{50} is the dataset composed of the 50% of the seismograms; i.e., each second seismogram was used, which is 1348 seismograms in total;
- D_{20} is the dataset with 20% of the total number of seismograms; i.e., 540 seismograms in total;
- D_{10} is the dataset with 10% of the total number of seismograms; i.e., 270 seismograms in total;
- D_5 is the dataset with 5% of the total number of seismograms; i.e., 135 seismograms in total;
- D_2 is the dataset with 2% of the total number of seismograms, i.e., 55 seismograms in total.

First, we estimated the distances in the seismogram space between a single seismogram and a dataset. Let us define the dataset D as a union of seismograms corresponding to the sources with indices $j_1, j_2, ..., j_N$. Let $J = \{j_1, j_2, ..., j_N\}$, than

$$d(\boldsymbol{x}_k^s, D) = \min_{j \in J} d(\boldsymbol{u}(\boldsymbol{x}_j^s), \boldsymbol{u}(\boldsymbol{x}_k^s)).$$

We provide the plots of the distances $d(\boldsymbol{x}_k^s, D)$ for all five considered datasets as the function of the source position in Fig. 4. Note that in the case of the densest dataset D_{50} where half of the total number of sources were used, the error is at the lowest possible limit varying within the interval of 30 to 60% of NRMS. Spacier datasets' use increases the NRMS discrepancy's maximal values between the entire dataset and the training dataset. The error increases rapidly if relatively dense datasets are compared, whereas there is almost no difference between the coarsest datasets D_2 and D_5.

We used five presented datasets to train the NDM-net. Training time varied from 700 to 2500 s. Having applied the NDM-net to the coarse-mesh solution, we compared the result with the precomputed fine-mesh solution for all source positions. The NRMS distance

$$\delta_j = d(\boldsymbol{u}_j^{h_f}, \boldsymbol{u}_j^{ML})$$

was computed for each position, and provided in Fig. 5. The mean values of the shot-by-shot NRMSs are provided in Table 1. Note that the use of a sparse

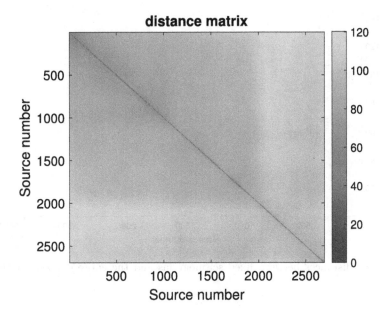

Fig. 2. Distance matrix for the BP model

training dataset leads to an unreasonably high discrepancy between the NDM-net predicted solution and the fine grid solution. On the contrary, extremely dense training datasets D_{50} and D_{20} do not ensure significant improvements but require much higher computational resources to generate them.

Table 1. Number of sources and average NRMS (error) for the training datasets constructed using equidistant sources distribution.

Dataset	Number of sources	Average NRMS
$D_{2\%}$	55	50.44%
$D_{5\%}$	135	44.16%
$D_{10\%}$	270	40.31%
$D_{20\%}$	540	36.89%
$D_{50\%}$	1348	30.8%

3.3 NRMS-Preserving Datasets

The approach to building the training dataset described above is predicated on the notion that the physical distance between the sources used in the training dataset should be kept to a minimum. However, the NRMS-based distinction

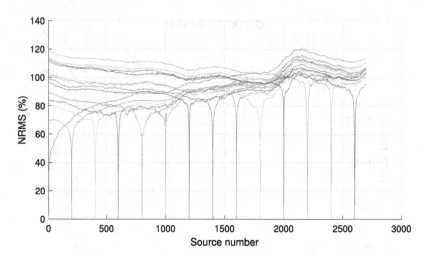

Fig. 3. The distances between fixed seismograms and the entire dataset for the BP model.

between the seismograms is used to assess the NDM-quality. net's The physical distance and this distance are somehow related, but they are not the identical. Thus, the NRMS-based distance between the seismograms and the training dataset varies in space, as seen by the plots in Fig. 4. The training dataset should be built as recommended in this section to maintain the NRMS-based distance between the seismograms and the training dataset. The distance between two datasets is presented by us as

$$d(D_K, D_J) = \max_{k \in \{k_1, \ldots, k_K\}} d(\boldsymbol{x}_k^s, D_J) = \max_{k \in \{k_1, \ldots, k_K\}} \min_{j \in \{j_1, \ldots, j_J\}} d(\boldsymbol{u}_j, \boldsymbol{u}_k),$$

where D_J and D_K are two datasets. To construct NRMS-based datasets, we require

$$d(D, D_t) \leq Q,$$

where D is the entire dataset, D_t is the training dataset, and Q is the maximally allowed seismogram discrepancy.

According to the distance matrix (Fig. 2 and 3) the NRMS-based distance varied from 40 to 100%. We constructed the NRMS-based datasets for a series of limits $Q = 40, 50, 60, 70, 80, 90$. The NDM-net was trained using each dataset. After that it was utilized to improve the entire dataset. Later, we computed the shot-by-shot discrepancy between the fine grid and the predicted solutions. The number of sources used in each training dataset as well as mean discrepancy are provided in Table 2. The pairwise NRMS between the accurate solution and NDM-net prediction are presented in Fig. 6. Note that, in general, the accuracy of the predictions based on the NRMS-preserving datasets are more accurate than those based on the equidistantly distributed sources. A detailed analysis of the data, provided in Tables 1 and 2 reveals that if the datasets generated by

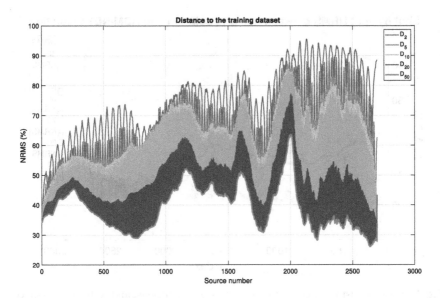

Fig. 4. Distances from the seismogramms to the training datasets constructed using equidistantly distributed sources.

the two methods contain approximately the same number of seismograms, the resulting discrepancy of the NRMS-preserving approach is about 1.5 lower than that of the equidistantly distributed sources approach. If considered the other way around, to get a similar NDM-net error, the NRMS-preserving technique allows using only one-third of the seismograms used by the first approach to generate a training dataset. Let us point out that the generation of a single-shot wavefield using a fine mesh is the most time-consuming procedure. Thus, the shot reduction leads to a significant overall speedup.

Table 2. NRMS-preserving datasets

Dataset	Number of sources	Average NRMS
$D_{40\%}^{NRMS}$	1672	24.36%
$D_{50\%}^{NRMS}$	794	27.04%
$D_{60\%}^{NRMS}$	425	30.76%
$D_{70\%}^{NRMS}$	216	35.45%
$D_{80\%}^{NRMS}$	90	40.54%
$D_{90\%}^{NRMS}$	27	46.35%

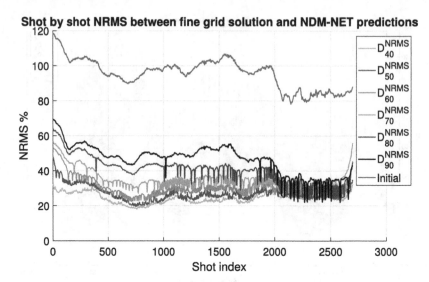

Fig. 5. Pairwise distances between fine, coarse grid solutions, and NDM-net predictions for different training dataset for equidistantly placed sources.

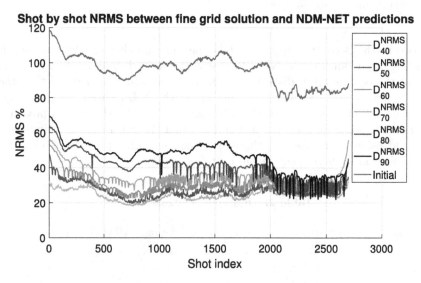

Fig. 6. Pairwise distances between fine, coarse grid solutions, and NDM-net predictions for different training dataset for NRMS-preserving method.

4   Conclusions

In this study, two methods for creating the training dataset for the Numerical Dispersion Mitigation neural network were provided (NDM-net). The goal of the NDM-net is to create a neural network that converts a simulation of an erroneous solution produced by a coarse enough grid into an accurate solution produced by a fine grid. The development of the training dataset takes the longest of all the steps in the NDM-net-based seismic modeling. Thus, cutting back on the seismograms in the training dataset enhances the effectiveness of the algorithm as a whole. To generate the training dataset, we proposed two methods for selecting the representative right-hand sides. The first method makes the supposition that the seismograms of the nearby sources are comparable. Therefore, we suggested using equally spaced sources to create a training dataset. We considered the cases of the use of 2, 5, 10, 20, and 50% of the total number of sources to form the training dataset. We noticed that when the training dataset gets sparser, the difference between the fine-grid solution and the NDM-net prediction grows. Second, we generated the training dataset with the NRMS-based distance between the seismograms directly in mind, ensuring that it does not exceed a certain limit. With an increase in the permissible separation between the seismograms, the number of sources in the training dataset decreases. We examined the two suggested ways and found that the second strategy only uses one-third of the first approach's sources to get a comparable discrepancy. Thus, NDM-net correction can be reasonably accurate by using as few as 3% of the total shots number if the NRMS-based distance approach is used to generate the training dataset.

Acknowledgements. The algorithm of optimal dataset construction was developed by Vadim Lisitsa, using the NKS-30T cluster of the Siberian Supercomputer Center, Dmitry Vishnevsky performed seismic modeling, while Kseniia Gadylshina carried out numerical experiments for NDM-net training with the help of RSCF grant number 22-11-00004. NDM-net hyperparameters were tuned by Kirill Gadylshin with the help of the grant for young scientists MK-3947.2021.1.5.

References

1. Ainsworth, M.: Dispersive and dissipative behaviour of high order discontinuous Galerkin finite element methods. J. Comput. Phys. **198**(1), 106–130 (2004)
2. Billette, F., Brandsberg-Dahl, S.: The 2004 BP velocity benchmark. In: 67-th EAGE Conference and Exibition, p. B035. EAGE (2005)
3. Blanch, J., Robertsson, J., Symes, W.: Modeling of a constant Q: methodology and algorithm for an efficient and optimally inexpensive viscoelastic technique. Geophysiscs **60**(1), 176–184 (1995)
4. Gadylshin, K., Lisitsa, V., Gadylshina, K., Vishnevsky, D., Novikov, M.: Machine learning-based numerical dispersion mitigation in seismic modelling. In: Gervasi, O., et al. (eds.) ICCSA 2021. LNCS, vol. 12949, pp. 34–47. Springer, Cham (2021). https://doi.org/10.1007/978-3-030-86653-2_3
5. Kaur, H., Fomel, S., Pham, N.: Overcoming numerical dispersion of finite-difference wave extrapolation using deep learning. In: SEG Technical Program Expanded Abstracts, pp. 2318–2322 (2019). https://doi.org/10.1190/segam2019-3207486.1
6. Koene, E.F.M., Robertsson, J.O.A., Broggini, F., Andersson, F.: Eliminating time dispersion from seismic wave modeling. Geophys. J. Int. **213**(1), 169–180 (2017)
7. Kragh, E., Christie, P.: Seismic repeatability, normalized RMS, and predictability. Lead. Edge **21**(7), 640–647 (2002)

8. Kragh, E., Laws, R.: Rough seas and statistical deconvolution. Geophys. Prospect. **54**(4), 475–485 (2006)
9. Levander, A.R.: Fourth-order finite-difference P-SV seismograms. Geophysics **53**(11), 1425–1436 (1988)
10. Lisitsa, V., Vishnevskiy, D.: Lebedev scheme for the numerical simulation of wave propagation in 3D anisotropic elasticity. Geophys. Prospect. **58**(4), 619–635 (2010). https://doi.org/10.1111/j.1365-2478.2009.00862.x
11. Lisitsa, V.: Dispersion analysis of discontinuous Galerkin method on triangular mesh for elastic wave equation. Appl. Math. Model. **40**, 5077–5095 (2016). https://doi.org/10.1016/j.apm.2015.12.039
12. Lisitsa, V., Kolyukhin, D., Tcheverda, V.: Statistical analysis of free-surface variability's impact on seismic wavefield. Soil Dyn. Earthq. Eng. **116**, 86–95 (2019)
13. Masson, Y.J., Pride, S.R.: Finite-difference modeling of Biot's poroelastic equations across all frequencies. Geophysics **75**(2), N33–N41 (2010)
14. Mittet, R.: Second-order time integration of the wave equation with dispersion correction procedures. Geophysics **84**(4), T221–T235 (2019)
15. Ronneberger, O., Fischer, P., Brox, T.: U-net: convolutional networks for biomedical image segmentation. In: Navab, N., Hornegger, J., Wells, W.M., Frangi, A.F. (eds.) MICCAI 2015. LNCS, vol. 9351, pp. 234–241. Springer, Cham (2015). https://doi.org/10.1007/978-3-319-24574-4_28 http://lmb.informatik.uni-freiburg.de/Publications/2015/RFB15a
16. Saenger, E.H., Gold, N., Shapiro, S.A.: Modeling the propagation of the elastic waves using a modified finite-difference grid. Wave Motion **31**, 77–92 (2000)
17. Siahkoohi, A., Louboutin, M., Herrmann, F.J.: The importance of transfer learning in seismic modeling and imaging. Geophysics **84**, A47–A52 (2019). https://doi.org/10.1190/geo2019-0056.1
18. Vishnevsky, D.M., Solovyev, S.A., Lisitsa, V.V.: Numerical simulation of wave propagation in 3D elastic media with viscoelastic formations. Lobachevskii J. Math. **41**(8), 1603–1614 (2020)

Deep Machine Learning Investigation
of Phase Transitions

Vladislav Chertenkov[1,2](✉) ⑩, Evgeni Burovski[1,2] ⑩, and Lev Shchur[1,2] ⑩

[1] Landau Institute for Theoretical Physics, 142432 Chernogolovka, Russia
satankow@yandex.ru
[2] HSE University, 101000 Moscow, Russia

Abstract. We explore the possibilities of using neural networks to study
phase transitions. The main question is the level of accuracy which can
be achieved for the estimates of the critical point and critical exponents
of statistical physics models. We generate data for two spin models in
two dimensions for which analytical solutions exist, the Ising model and
Baxter-Wu model, which belong to the different universality classes. We
applied six neural networks with three different architectures to the data
and estimated the critical temperature and the correlation length exponent. We find that the accuracy of estimation does depend on the neural
network architecture. The critical exponents of Baxter-Wu model are
estimated by the deep machine learning technique for the first time.

Keywords: Ising model · Baxter-Wu model · Deep learning ·
Finite-size scaling · Resnet

1 Introduction

Recent advances in deep learning—both algorithmic developments and efficient
utilization of novel high-performance hardware—revolutionize a variety of engineering practice and academic research areas. One notable development is an
observation that neural networks (NN) can successfully predict states of matter and phase transitions between them for both classical [1] and quantum [2]
many-body systems. Various network architectures, learning protocols and NN
observables are used [3–7] for several physical problems and using supervised or
unsupervised learning.

It is clear that NNs trained on an equilibrium ensemble of microscopic states
of a many-body system can learn and predict phase transitions between macroscopic states *in many situations*. The big open questions are "why" and "how".
A natural hypothesis is that a trained NN in some sense learns about the critical behavior of the model—if that is the case, some NN observables should
display a universal critical behavior and obey finite-size scaling governed by the
universality class of the learned many-body system.

To test this hypothesis, we consider two spin models, the two-dimensional Ising model [8] and two-dimensional Baxter-Wu (BW) model [9]. The models belong to different universality classes and their critical behavior is described by different sets of critical exponents. We apply a unified approach for both models. First, we generate ensembles of equilibrium spin configurations across a range of temperatures using conventional spin-flip Metropolis [10] Monte Carlo algorithms. We then train NNs on these datesets and extract critical exponents from the NN outputs. We consider several NN architectures (a fully connected network, a convolutional network and several members of the ResNet family) and compare their predictions to (i) the values of critical exponents extracted from the training data via conventional finite-size analysis, and (ii) the known values from exact solutions for these two models.

The rest of the paper is organized as follows. In Sect. 2 we define the spin models and briefly discuss the Monte Carlo process for generating the data sets. In Sect. 3 we detail the NN architectures and our training pipeline. In Sect. 4 we discuss the NN observables and our data analysis procedure, which results in estimates for the correlation length critical exponents ν for both Ising model and BW model. Finally, we discuss our results in Sect. 5.

2   Data Sets for Spin Models

In this section, we present briefly two spin models and describe some details of the data set generation.

Ising Model— The Ising model is defined on a square lattice. Each Ising spin $\sigma = \pm 1$ interacts with four of its neighbors (left, right, top, bottom). The Ising model Hamiltonian is $H_{\text{is}} = -J/2 \sum_{\langle i,j \rangle} \sigma_i \sigma_j$, where J is the coupling constant. The model belongs to the eponymous universality class and is described by the set of critical exponents presented in the second entry of Table 1.

BW Model— The Baxter-Wu model is defined on a triangular lattice. Each spin interacts with six of its neighbors. Summation is performed over 3 spins at the vertices of each triangular plaquettes (faces). Baxter-Wu Hamiltonian $H_{\text{bw}} = -J \sum_{\langle faces \rangle} \sigma_i \sigma_j \sigma_k$, $\sigma = \pm 1$. The arrangement of spins on a triangular lattice is stored as a two-dimensional array. The model belongs to the 4-state Potts [11] universality class [12–14].

We use periodic boundary conditions. Critical temperature $T_c = 2J/\log(1 + \sqrt{2}) \approx 2.269(1)$, where $J = 1$.

Monte-Carlo Simulations— We generate equilibrium spin configurations using the Metropolis single flip Monte Carlo algorithm. The data represents spin configurations on the lattice, which can be viewed as red and blue pixels at the $(L \times L)$ square grid, where L is the number of vertices at horizontal and vertical directions. Each image (snapshot) is an instant lattice spin configuration, represented as blue (spin-down, $\sigma_i = -1$) and red (spin-up, $\sigma_i = 1$) pixels (Fig. 1).

Table 1. Values of the critical exponents.

Model	Universality class	α	β	γ	ν	γ/ν
BW	4-state Potts	2/3	1/12	7/6	2/3	7/4
Ising	Ising	0	1/8	7/4	1	7/4

(a) $T = 1.8692$ (b) $T = 2.2697$ (c) $T = 2.7192$

Fig. 1. Ising spin configurations for $L = 216$ at different temperature T. (Color figure online)

To generate a set of snapshots at each temperature, we perform relaxation from an initial random state ("hot start") to the state of thermodynamic equilibrium and then take a series of snapshots. We consider as a unit of measurement of computational complexity the Monte Carlo step (MCS). One MCS is equivalent to L^2 Metropolis local spin flips. For each flip we determine whether to change the value of the single spin to the opposite value or not:

- If changing the value of the spin lead to energy decrease by the amount ΔE, we accept it with probability $p^{acc} = 1$.
- Otherwise, we accept it with probability $p^{acc} = \exp\left(-\Delta E/T\right)$, with a random number rnd taken from a uniform distribution on $[0, 1]$ is less than or equal to p^{acc}.

Uncorrelated Snapshots— It is known that Markov chain Monte Carlo methods generate configurations which may be correlated especially around the critical point of second order phase transitions. In order to take the uncorrelated snapshots, we adopt recommendations [15] and start taking snapshots after $20 \cdot t_{corr}$ MCS, where t_{corr} is correlation time of magnetization. We take snapshots every $2 \cdot t_{corr}$ MCS to avoid correlations of images. We estimate relaxation time dependence from the lattice size t_{corr} equal to $L^{2.15}$ MCS in our previous study [16].

Data sets were generated for both models in the temperature interval $[T_c - 0.5; T_c + 0.5]$ for the Baxter-Wu model and $[T_c - 0.4; T_c + 0.4]$ for the Ising model. The Baxter-Wu data set contains 171 000 snapshots for each lattice size (1500 images for each of 114 values of temperature). The maximum lattice size is $L = 243$. The Ising data set contains 189 000 images (1500 for each of 126 temperature points) and maximum lattice size is $L = 216$.

Generating data for lattice size 243 took approximately $3 \cdot 10^{15}$ spin flips. The total simulation time for each lattice size is given by formula:

$$N_{flips} = 20 \cdot L^2 \cdot t_{corr} \cdot N_{T_{points}} + L^2 \cdot 2t_{corr} \cdot N_{images}$$
$$= 20 \cdot L^{4.15} \cdot N_{T_{points}} + 2 \cdot L^{4.15} \cdot N_{images}$$

3 Machine Learning

In this section, we describe the deep learning approach we use for the analysis of data sets described in the previous section.

3.1 Basics

Neural network (NN) architectures differ in the sequence of layers and building blocks that form them. Each layer has an input, an output, and can contain linear and non-linear operators. To build our NNs we use essential blocks like fully connected layers, convolutional layers [17], poolings and activation functions.

The fully connected layer (fc) consists of neurons (perceptrons [18]). Each neuron applies the scalar product of the weight vector to the output vector of neurons from the previous layer. An activation function is applied to the result and the output of the neuron is passed to the connected neurons of the next layer. The most common activation functions are sigmoid, ReLU (rectified linear unit), and SoftMax (normalized exponential function) [19]. The latter is commonly used in the output layer to normalize output values if the NN output has more than one neuron. SoftMax output values have a Boltzmann distribution.

The convolutional layer (conv) is a set of sliding windows (kernels). Each kernel, given dimensions and adjustable weights, applies the dot product to the input matrix and moves along it with a fixed stride.

Pooling (pool) is similar to convolution moving windows with a fixed kernel size and step, but it uses a function to aggregate the values in the input matrix. We use pooling with the function of **max**imum to take the highest value - max pooling (max pool).

3.2 Architectures

FCNN— Our fully connected NN (FCNN) architecture takes images reshaped into a 1-dimensional array of size L^2. An input is forwarded to a hidden fully connected layer of 100 neurons and sigmoid activation function. The output of the network is two neurons with a SoftMax activation function.

ConvNN— Our convolutional neural network (ConvNN) takes images as a 2-dimensional array $(L \times L)$. An input is forwarded to 2-D convolutional layer (2×2) with 1 input channel and 64 output channels, stride 2 and padding 0. Convolutional layer output falls into max pooling with kernel size (2×2) and stride 2. After max pooling the array is reshaped into a 1-D vector of size $L/4 \cdot L/4 \cdot 64$. The vector is forwarded to a fully connected layer with the same number of neurons and ReLU activation function. The output of the network is two neurons with a SoftMax activation function.

ResNet— We use four types of deep convolutional residual network (ResNet) [20] architecture with different hidden layer depths. Our ResNet implementation has minor changes, as only one input channel is used in the first convolutional layer, unlike the classical ResNet designed for images with three color channels (RGB). ResNet takes images as a 2-dimensional array $(L \times L)$ as an input. The NN forwarding is the same for all types. The output is also two neurons with a SoftMax activation function. We have described used ResNet types in a Table 2.

Table 2. ResNet architecture configurations.

10-layer	18-layer	34-layer	50-layer
7×7, 64, stride 2			
3×3 max pool, stride 2			
$\begin{bmatrix} 3 \times 3, 64 \\ 3 \times 3, 64 \end{bmatrix} \times 1$	$\begin{bmatrix} 3 \times 3, 64 \\ 3 \times 3, 64 \end{bmatrix} \times 2$	$\begin{bmatrix} 3 \times 3, 64 \\ 3 \times 3, 64 \end{bmatrix} \times 3$	$\begin{bmatrix} 1 \times 1, 64 \\ 3 \times 3, 64 \\ 1 \times 1, 256 \end{bmatrix} \times 3$
$\begin{bmatrix} 3 \times 3, 128 \\ 3 \times 3, 128 \end{bmatrix} \times 1$	$\begin{bmatrix} 3 \times 3, 128 \\ 3 \times 3, 128 \end{bmatrix} \times 2$	$\begin{bmatrix} 3 \times 3, 128 \\ 3 \times 3, 128 \end{bmatrix} \times 4$	$\begin{bmatrix} 1 \times 1, 128 \\ 3 \times 3, 128 \\ 1 \times 1, 512 \end{bmatrix} \times 4$
$\begin{bmatrix} 3 \times 3, 256 \\ 3 \times 3, 256 \end{bmatrix} \times 1$	$\begin{bmatrix} 3 \times 3, 256 \\ 3 \times 3, 256 \end{bmatrix} \times 2$	$\begin{bmatrix} 3 \times 3, 64 \\ 3 \times 3, 64 \end{bmatrix} \times 6$	$\begin{bmatrix} 1 \times 1, 256 \\ 3 \times 3, 256 \\ 1 \times 1, 1024 \end{bmatrix} \times 6$
$\begin{bmatrix} 3 \times 3, 512 \\ 3 \times 3, 512 \end{bmatrix} \times 1$	$\begin{bmatrix} 3 \times 3, 512 \\ 3 \times 3, 512 \end{bmatrix} \times 2$	$\begin{bmatrix} 3 \times 3, 512 \\ 3 \times 3, 512 \end{bmatrix} \times 3$	$\begin{bmatrix} 1 \times 1, 512 \\ 3 \times 3, 512 \\ 1 \times 1, 2048 \end{bmatrix} \times 3$
avg pool, 2-d fc, SoftMax			

3.3 Training Pipeline

Our problem is a binary classification, and two classes represent ferromagnetic (low temperature) phase and paramagnetic (higher temperature) phase. The NN is trained using the backward propagation of errors algorithm (backprop) to update NN adjustable parameters (weights). We chose Adam optimizer (Adaptive Moment Estimation [21]) and fixed the learning rate at 10^{-4}. The binary cross-entropy (BCE) is a loss function to measure errors when training.

We divide data sets in two unequal parts: **2/3** of generated data used for training and validation and **1/3** used for testing. The validation data is 10% of the training. Training stage takes place in epochs. During training the data is divided into batches of size 36. We measure the mean loss function on the validation data for each epoch to make sure there is no overfitting. It took us 10 epochs to ensure we are not facing overfitting and the learning curve has plateaued. Additionally, we use augmentation heuristic to increase NN generalization ability by 4 times increasing training data size: each image is rotated by $\pi/2, \pi, 3\pi/2$ radians.

Before the test data inference, we choose the best NN parameters by the minimum loss function on the epoch for each lattice size. For all architectures, the BCE on the validation data does not exceed 0.36 (Ising), 0.4 (BW) and for the maximum lattice sizes it drops to the level of 0.16 (Ising), 0.05 (BW). The minimum value of the accuracy metric is 84% (Ising), 82% (BW) for lattice size 48 and reaches 92% (Ising), 98% (BW) for the maximum lattice sizes 216 and 243, respectively. The use of the accuracy metric is justified due to the balance of classes. With such values of the quality metric, we can conclude that the NN works better than random or constant (50% accuracy) classifier.

For input image at Fig. 1a the NN would output a correct prediction – 1 for ferromagnetic phase and 0 for paramagnetic phase. For image at Fig. 1c, the network is also output correct predictions but an opposite values 0 and 1 respectively.

All neural network models are implemented in Python using the Pytorch [22] library. NNs training was carried out on 1× NVIDIA Tesla V100-SXM2 32 GB configuration. The Table 3 summarizes the data on the training computational cost in seconds per epoch (*time*) and the quantity of NN adjustable parameters (*# parameters*) for Ising model with lattice size $L = 48$.

Table 3. Ising model computational summary.

NN type	# parameters	Time, s/ep
ConvNN	590 336	108(5)
FCNN	230 702	66.0(3)
ResNet-10	4 900 546	534(4)
ResNet-18	11 171 266	1200(72)
ResNet-34	21 279 426	2369(111)
ResNet-50	23 505 858	2590(145)

4   Exponents Estimation

We obtain critical exponents using the conventional method from Monte Carlo data and then compare them to the NN method.

MC Analysis— We evaluate the mean energy per spin E and magnetization per spin M to construct the heat capacity C and magnetic susceptibility χ. The set of equations used is as follows

Baxter-Wu model:

$$e = \frac{1}{L^2} H_{\text{bw}}(\{\sigma\})$$

$$m = \frac{1}{L^2} \sqrt{\sum_{lat=1}^{3} m_{lat}^2} \tag{1}$$

$$C = \frac{L^2}{T^2} \left(\langle e^2 \rangle - \langle e \rangle^2 \right)$$

$$\chi = \frac{L^2}{T} \left(\langle m^2 \rangle - \langle m \rangle^2 \right)$$

Ising model:

$$e = \frac{1}{L^2} H_{\text{is}}(\{\sigma\})$$

$$m = \frac{1}{L^2} \left| \sum_{i=1}^{L^2} \sigma_i \right| \tag{2}$$

$$C = \frac{L^2}{T^2} \left(\langle e^2 \rangle - \langle e \rangle^2 \right)$$

$$\chi = \frac{L^2}{T} \left(\langle m^2 \rangle - \langle m \rangle^2 \right)$$

We use finite-size analysis and extract exponents analysing dependence from the lattice size of the values of C_{max} and χ_{max}, the position of the maxima, and the width of the $C(T)$ and $\chi(T)$ curves.

NN Analysis— The NN output neurons return estimates of Bayesian posterior probability [23] that the input image belongs to ferromagnetic $p_i^f(T)$ and paramagnetic $p_i^p(T)$ phases, $p_i^f(T) + p_i^p(T) = 1$. The test data set consists with $N_{test} = 500$ snapshots at each value of temperature. The average value $F(T)$ and variance $V(T)$ of the NN ferromagnetic output neuron $p_i^f(T)$ for each temperature are

$$F(T) = \frac{1}{N_{test}} \sum_{i=1}^{N_{test}} p_i^f(T) \tag{3}$$

$$V(T) = \left(\frac{1}{N} \sum_{i=1}^{N_{test}} (p_i^f(T))^2 \right) - \left(\frac{1}{N} \sum_{i=1}^{N_{test}} p_i^f(T) \right)^2. \tag{4}$$

The critical exponents can be obtained by fitting the curve $V(T)$ using the probability density function (**pdf**) of the Gaussian distribution multiplied by k

$$V_{gauss}(k, \mu, \sigma) = k \cdot \text{pdf}(\mu, \sigma)$$

$$= \frac{k}{\sigma\sqrt{2\pi}} \exp\left(-\frac{1}{2}\left(\frac{x - \mu}{\sigma}\right)^2\right). \tag{5}$$

As a result, we obtain estimates of peak positions μ and standard deviation σ. We extract the critical exponent ν observing how the peak position $\mu(L)$ tends to the analytically known critical temperature $\mu(L) - T_c \sim L^{-1/\nu}$.

We found that the width $\sigma(L)$ of $V(T)$ changes as the lattice size increases $\sigma(L) \sim L^{-1/\nu}$.

One can expect that the width of the curve $V(T)$ in the low-temperature $V(T < T_c)$ and high-temperature $V(T > T_c)$ phases may not be the same. Therefore, we also fit separately the curves to the right and to the left of the $V(T)$ peak maximum with a power law.

We construct the dependencies of these parameters on the lattice size L.

Tables 5 and 4 summarize our results both using conventional finite-size analysis of Monte Carlo data and those obtained from the analysis of NN output.

Table 4. Estimates of exponents for the Baxter-Wu model with different methods.

Method	$\left(\frac{1}{\nu}\right)_\mu$	$\left(\frac{1}{\nu}\right)_\sigma$	$\left(\frac{\gamma}{\nu}\right)_{peak}$
MC (C)	1.54(2)	1.48(1)	−1.01(2)
MC (χ)	1.52(3)	1.30(6)	−1.83(3)
ConvNN	1.36(24)	1.49(2)	−0.22(2)
FCNN	1.49(6)	1.46(2)	−0.29(4)
ResNet-10	1.62(7)	1.49(1)	−0.32(3)
ResNet-18	1.48(14)	1.50(3)	−0.32(3)
ResNet-34	1.55(10)	1.50(2)	−0.30(3)
ResNet-50	1.35(7)	1.52(1)	−0.35(6)

Table 5. Estimates of exponents for the Ising model with different methods.

Method	$\left(\frac{1}{\nu}\right)_\sigma$	$\left(\frac{\gamma}{\nu}\right)_{peak}$
MC (C)	0.95(1)	–
MC (χ)	1.02(5)	−1.77(2)
ConvNN	1.10(9)	−0.025(126)
FCNN	0.71(5)	0.043(46)
ResNet-10	1.06(7)	0.087(85)
ResNet-18	1.03(7)	−0.324(354)
ResNet-34	1.07(8)	0.073(108)
ResNet-50	1.09(11)	0.098(142)

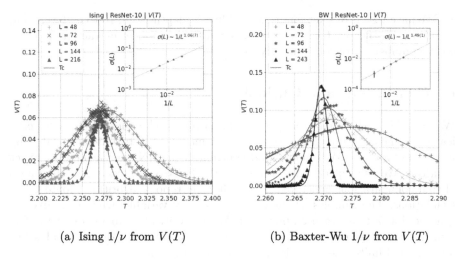

(a) Ising $1/\nu$ from $V(T)$ (b) Baxter-Wu $1/\nu$ from $V(T)$

Fig. 2. Estimating $1/\nu$ for Ising and BW models from $V(T)$, Eq. (4). See text for discussion.

5   Discussion

We are comparing two methods of extraction of critical exponents using finite-size scaling analysis—a FSS analysis of the Monte-Carlo data, and a FSS analysis of the fluctuations of outputs of trained neural networks. We find that the NN output fluctuations $V(T)$ contain an information about the exponent correlation length exponent, ν. We estimate the critical exponent ν using finite-size scaling from the NN output fluctuations. The best estimate of ν for the Baxter-Wu model is extracted (cf. Fig. 2b) with the same accuracy for both MC and NN approaches, and the results agree within the combined errorbars. Likewise, for the Ising model (cf. Fig. 2a) the MC and NN estimates have similar accuracy and are consistent within the combined errorbars.

While the width of the NN output fluctuation, $V(T)$, displays finite-size scaling consistent with the correlation length exponent ν, the scaling of the height of the peak of $V(T)$ is not clear. Specifically, the peak height for the BW model scales according to a power law $L^{0.30(3)}$ but the extracted values are not similar to any known combination of exponents for this model. The peak height for Ising model displays no finite-size scaling at all. Note that our results thus do not agree to the results of Ref. [3] which reported the ratio of exponents $\gamma/\nu = 1.78$ from the scaling of the peak height.

We obtain a smaller error bars and a smaller coefficient of variation for critical exponent ν on the level of 5% comparing with the result of paper [1] on the level of 30%. Our numerical results for the peak position for the Baxter-Wu model are roughly consistent with the $1/\nu$ scaling. Given that the Ising model does not display a shift at all, more work is needed to reliably assess whether the peak position is a reliable estimator for the critical exponent.

We have tested ResNet family with different depths from 10 to 50 layers and found no evidence that the quality of the critical exponent extraction depends on the number of convolutional layers.

6 Conclusions and Outlook

We investigate the applicability of deep learning techniques to studying critical phenomena. We consider two classical models, the two-dimensional Ising model, and a Baxter-Wu model, and benchmark the NN approach on the exact solutions. We use supervised learning, where the NNs are trained on ensembles of spin configurations generated by spin-flip Metropolis algorithm Monte Carlo simulations. The samples are labeled by a binary variable, whether a given is generated at a temperature above or below the critical temperature of the ferromagnetic phase transition. We also compare the results of the NN analysis to a traditional finite-size analysis of the Monte Carlo data sets.

We find that the fluctuation of the NN output as a function of temperature has a characteristic Gaussian shape. The parameters of the Gaussian depend on the lattice size. The width of the Gaussian displays a power-law dependence on the lattice size, which is consistent with the correlation length exponent ν of the corresponding spin model. We can thus conclude that the NN learns not only the location of the phase transition, but also (some) critical exponents of the universality class of the model.

We consider three different NN architectures: the fully connected network, a simple convolutional network and several members of the ResNet family. We find that for both models, the ResNet NNs achieve best accuracy of the estimates of the correlation length critical exponent. On the other hand, the quality of the ResNet estimates only weakly depends on the depth of the network: ResNet50 does not significantly improve on predictions of ResNet10. On the other hand, both reliability and accuracy of estimates of the critical exponent is clearly improved by ResNet NNs, as compared to both FCNN and a simple convolutional NN. This observation should be compared with Ref [5], which reported that shallow networks perform better than deep ones for the Ising model near criticality.

For future work, an important question is the accuracy and reliability of transfer learning: whether and to what accuracy an NN trained on one model, predicts critical properties of a different model in the same universality class. One other big question is whether NN learns only the correlation length exponent, or if other critical exponents can be extracted from the NN outputs.

Acknowledgements. This work is supported by the grant 22-11-00259 of the Russian Science Foundation. Simulations were done using the computational resources of HPC facilities at HSE University [24].

References

1. Carrasquilla, J., Melko, R.G.: Machine learning phases of matter. Nat. Phys. **13**(5), 431–434 (2017)
2. Carleo, G., Troyer, M.: Solving the quantum many-body problem with artificial neural networks. Science **335**, 602–606 (2017). https://doi.org/10.1126/science.aag2302
3. Bachtis, D., Aarts, G., Lucini, B.: Mapping distinct phase transitions to a neural network. Phys. Rev. E **102**(5), 053306 (2020)
4. Van Nieuwenburg, E.P., Liu, Y.H., Huber, S.D.: Learning phase transitions by confusion. Nat. Phys. **13**, 435–439 (2017)
5. Morningstar, A., Melko, R.G.: Deep learning the Ising model near criticality. J. Mach. Learn. Res. 18(163), 1–17 (2018). http://jmlr.org/papers/v18/17-527.html
6. Westerhout, T., Astrakhantsev, N., Tikhonov, K.S., Katsnelson, M.I., Bagrov, A.A.: Generalization properties of neural network approximations to frustrated magnet ground states. Nat. Commun. **11**, 1593 (2020)
7. Walker, N., Tam, K.M.: Infocgan classification of 2-dimensional square Ising configurations (2020). arXiv preprint arXiv:2005.01682
8. Onsager, L.: Crystal statistics. I. A two-dimensional model with an order-disorder transition. Phys. Rev. **65**(3–4), 117 (1944)
9. Baxter, R.J., Wu, F.Y.: Ising model on a triangular lattice with three-spin interactions. I. the eigenvalue equation. Aust. J. Phys. **27**(3), 357–368 (1974)
10. Metropolis, N., Rosenbluth, A.W., Rosenbluth, M.N., Teller, A.H., Teller, E.: Equation of state calculations by fast computing machines. J. Chem. Phys. **21**(6), 1087–1092 (1953)
11. Potts, R.B.: Some generalized order-disorder transformations. In: Mathematical Proceedings of the Cambridge Philosophical Society, vol. 48(1), pp. 106–109. Cambridge University Press (1952)
12. Den Nijs, M.P.M.: A relation between the temperature exponents of the eight-vertex and q-state Potts model. J. Phys. A Math. Gen. **12**(10), 1857 (1979)
13. Pearson, R.B.: Conjecture for the extended Potts model magnetic eigenvalue. Phys. Rev. B **22**(5), 2579 (1980)
14. Nienhuis, B.: Critical behavior of two-dimensional spin models and charge asymmetry in the Coulomb gas. J. Stat. Phys. **34**(5), 731–761 (1984)
15. Sokal, A.: Monte Carlo methods in statistical mechanics: foundations and new algorithms. In: DeWitt-Morette, C., Cartier, P., Folacci, A. (eds.) Functional Integration. NATO ASI Series, vol. 361, pp. 131–192. Springer, Boston (1997). https://doi.org/10.1007/978-1-4899-0319-8_6
16. Chertenkov, V., Shchur, L.: Universality classes and machine learning. In: Journal of Physics: Conference Series, vol. 1740(1), p. 012003. IOP Publishing (2021)
17. Fukushima, K., Miyake, S.: Neocognitron: a self-organizing neural network model for a mechanism of visual pattern recognition. In: Amari, S.I., Arbib, M.A. (eds.) Competition and Cooperation in Neural Nets. Lecture Notes in Biomathematics, vol. 45, pp. 267–285. Springer, Berlin (1982). https://doi.org/10.1007/978-3-642-46466-9_18
18. Rosenblatt, F.: The perceptron: a probabilistic model for information storage and organization in the brain. Psychol. Rev. **65**(6), 386 (1958)
19. Bishop, C.M., Nasrabadi, N.M.: Pattern Recognition and Machine Learning, vol. 4(4) Springer, New York (2006)

20. He, K., Zhang, X., Ren, S., Sun, J.: Deep residual learning for image recognition. In: Proceedings of the IEEE Conference on Computer Vision and Pattern Recognition, pp. 770–778 (2016)
21. Kingma, D.P., Ba, J.: Adam: a method for stochastic optimization (2014). arXiv preprint arXiv:1412.6980
22. Paszke, A., et al.: Pytorch: an imperative style, high-performance deep learning library. In: Advances in Neural Information Processing Systems, vol. 32 (2019)
23. Richard, M.D., Lippmann, R.P.: Neural network classifiers estimate Bayesian a posteriori probabilities. Neural Comput. **3**(4), 461–483 (1991)
24. Kostenetskiy, P.S., Chulkevich, R.A., Kozyrev, V.I.: HPC resources of the higher school of economics. In: Journal of Physics: Conference Series, vol. 1740(1), p. 012050. IOP Publishing (2021)

Educational and Research Project "Optimization of the Sugar Beet Processing Schedule"

Dmitry Balandin$^{(\boxtimes)}$ ⓘ, Albert Egamov ⓘ, Oleg Kuzenkov ⓘ,
Oksana Pristavchenko ⓘ, and Vadim Vildanov ⓘ

Lobachevsky University of Nizhny Novgorod, Nizhny Novgorod 603950, Russia
`dmitriy.balandin@itmm.unn.ru`

Abstract. This article is about of the experience of implementing the educational and research project "Optimization of the sugar beet processing schedule" by bachelors of "Fundamental Informatics and Information Technology" of the Nizhny Novgorod State University. In addition, the article is about of the analysis of project's significance as an effective tool for the formation of general professional competencies. The topic of the project is actual for the Nizhny Novgorod region in connection with the current modernization of the Sergachsky sugar plant, carried out by order of the Government of the Russian Federation, and the participation of the Nizhny Novgorod State University in the development of intelligent data processing systems and software for this modernization. The project is based on mathematical methods of discrete optimization, mathematical formalization of the problem of constructing an optimal schedule, available software tools and provided real data on sugar content. The results of the project allow us to conclude that the methodological approaches developed during the implementation of the project to the organization of design work have a high potential for modernizing the educational process of training bachelors in the area of information technology and improving the quality of their education.

Keywords: Project approach · Competence · Assignment problem · Hungarian algorithm

1 Introduction

The training of bachelors in the area of information technology should combine three main interrelated components: fundamental mathematical knowledge, software development skills and the ability to apply them in solving practical problems.

This approach is dictated by the current educational standards (both federal and self established by educational organizations [1]). These standards require the formation of the general professional competence system as a result of the bachelor educational program in IT-area. In particular, it contains general professional competencies-1 (GPC-1): "Able to apply fundamental knowledge obtained

V. Voevodin et al. (Eds.): RuSCDays 2022, LNCS 13708, pp. 409–422, 2022.
https://doi.org/10.1007/978-3-031-22941-1_30

in the area of mathematical and (or) natural sciences and use them in professional activities"; GPC-2: "Able to apply computer/supercomputer methods, modern software ... to solve problems of professional activity"; GPC-3: "Able to develop algorithmic and software solutions in the area of system and applied programming, mathematical, informational and simulation models..."

It should be noted that the curricula for the relevant educational programs are traditionally built from separate components (disciplines, modules) devoted to either mathematical or computer subjects. Possibly, such a division is justified by the specificity of the content, ensuring the necessary rigor in the study of mathematics. However, it often creates a misunderstanding among students of the role and place of mathematics for their future professional activities. Mathematical concepts are often divorced from the direct professional interests of students.

This reduces the motivation of students to study mathematical disciplines and negatively affects the overall performance, which leads to a general decrease in the quality of training. The situation is getting worse by the fact that the input level of applicants in the area of mathematics also decreases year by year. As a result, there is a decrease in students' knowledge of mathematical disciplines and an increase in the number of deductions [2].

These problems and the search for ways to solve them were the subject of research in a number of major international projects. As a result, a systematic approach was proposed to improve the quality of education [3–5]. Among the main means of solving problems was named the project method of teaching. The normative learning goals are achieved more effectively with the work on applied projects, the use of e-learning systems, and increased control of students' independent work by the teacher [6–10].

The project method of teaching can be implemented within a variety of disciplines. It can be used for organizing independent work on a subject, conducting laboratory work, etc. This method becomes an effective means of modernizing the educational process if the following necessary conditions satisfy, namely, the framework of the ongoing project is an actual practical problem; the solution of the problem requires a deep understanding of the corresponding mathematical basis and modern software tools. The project method involves a complete engineering solution to the problem. A mandatory requirement for the project is the practical use of software tools to solve the tasks. At the same time, the task contains an analytical study of applied importance in the area of computer technology. Here, the mathematical foundation becomes an organic part for the development of software algorithms and constructing a practically significant solution. Thus, the need for a deep mastery of mathematics becomes self-evident. Often, project tasks are carried out by small groups of students of 3–4 people, which contributes to the development of skills of professional interaction and teamwork.

The formulated principles became the basis for a number of educational and research works for bachelor students in the area "Fundamental informatics and information technologies" at the Nizhny Novgorod State University. The purpose of this article is to analyze the experience of implementing the educational and research project "Formation of the sugar beet processing schedule" carried out by 3rd year students within the course "Computational Methods".

The educational and research project involves three stages of implementation. The first stage is theoretical. Students get acquainted with the mathematical formulation of the problem and the mathematical foundations of its solution. For the successful implementation of the project, they must familiarize themselves with the recommended literature, as well as independently search for additional sources on the Internet. Familiarity with the sources provides an understanding of the techniques and methods underlying the algorithmic solution. It is supposed to master the mathematical justification of the chosen solutions and understand the mathematical theorems that ensure the effectiveness of these algorithms. To check the adequacy of understanding the theoretical material, a number of tasks were developed that show the degree of theoretical readiness of students to perform the main project research. The teacher controls the work of students at this stage, checking the tasks proposed by them. This stage is aimed at deepening the degree of formation of the GPC-1 competence, and control tasks are effective assessment tools for checking its formation.

The second stage of the educational and research project is aimed at mastering the software and computer facilities necessary for conducting research work. At this stage, students are acquainted with the software provided to them, using the recommended literature and expanding their knowledge by independently searching for additional sources on the Internet. Before starting to solve the main task of the project, students perform a number of exercises by using computer, which are necessary auxiliary elements of the project. This stage is aimed at deepening the degree of formation of the competence of GPC-2. The tasks performed at this stage serve as a means of assessing the level of formation of this competence.

Finally, the third stage is the solution of the main research problem. Students cannot be admitted to the third stage until they demonstrate an acceptable level of competency formation in the previous two stages. The main purpose of this stage is to conduct a numerical experiment and evaluate its results from the point of view of practical use. Based on the results of the study, students draw up a report. At this stage, the degree of formation of the competence of GPC-3 is deepened. The results of the study, presented in the students' written report, make it possible to assess the degree of formation of this competence.

2   Materials and Methods

2.1   Problem of Optimal Beet Processing Schedule

To create a training and research project, an important practical task was chosen to form an optimal schedule for the processing of various batches of sugar beets at a sugar plant.

The topic of the project is actual for the Nizhny Novgorod region in connection with the current modernization of the Sergach sugar plant, carried out by order of the Government of the Russian Federation, and the participation of the Nizhny Novgorod State University in the development of intelligent data processing systems and software for this modernization.

The significance of the problem of determining the best technological regime is explained by the fact that often a change in a certain processing strategy (schedule, plan) does not use large additional resources, but the result when choosing the optimal sequence of standard operations is sometimes comparable to the gain from equipment upgrades.

This problem is often touched upon in works devoted to the food industry and the industry processing agricultural products [11–13]. During storage, different grades of raw materials reduce their production value in different ways over time. Therefore, the optimal schedule for processing batches of raw materials can significantly increase the final yield of the final product [14–18].

This problem is relevant, in particular, for the production of sugar [19–22]. In this area, the raw material is sugar beet, which is harvested in the fall and stored for several months. During storage on the heap fields, the degradation of raw materials occurs, that is, the percentage of its sugar content decreases. The sugar industry needs software tools to make recommendations for building the optimal strategy for processing.

The yield of the finished product (sugar) depends on many variables, on the percentage of dirt on the beets, nitrate content, damage during transportation to processing, processing temperature, and so on, but the percentage of sucrose has the main influence on the yield of the final product [23].

An additional difficulty in resolving the issue of forming a beet processing schedule is the lack of complete information about the correct weather forecast in the current year for the period of beet storage and, accordingly, about the loss of sugar content of various beet varieties, etc.

To solve this important applied problem, it is necessary to have a deep knowledge of discrete optimization algorithms, mastery of modern software tools and the ability to evaluate the results obtained by numerical calculations in terms of their applied significance. Thus, this problem combines all the necessary components for the implementation of project work, it is a good material for teaching students in the area of IT and can serve as the basis for creating various projects within the academic discipline.

2.2   Mathematical Formalization of the Problem

Let there be n batches of sugar beets of equal weight, numbered from 1 to n. The mass of one batch of beets is the mass that the production facilities of the enterprise can process in a certain period (for example, in one day). Different batches differ in production value, the percentage of output of the finished product per unit mass (which corresponds to sugar content, the percentage of sugar in beets). Let us denote the production value, the proportion of sugar content in one kilogram of beets (sugar content) of the i-th batch of beets, a_i, $i = \overline{1, n}$. Thus, for the processing of n batches of raw materials, n stages are needed, let's number them from 1 to n. Let the i-th batch of beets lose some of their production value during storage at the j-th stage of processing (beets reduce their sugar content).

Let us designate b_{ij} is the degradation coefficient, which determines the wilting, loss of moisture, decrease in sugar content, etc., of the i-th batch of beets at the j-th stage of processing. For these coefficients, the inequality is true $0 < b_{ij} < 1$. It is assumed that during one stage of processing of a given batch of beets, its production value does not change.

Then, for the i-th batch of beets, the production value will change as follows: $a_i b_{i1}$ is after the first stage, $a_i b_{i1} b_{i2}$ is after the second, $a_{in} b_{i1} b_{i2} ... b_{in-1}$ is at the beginning of the last n-th stage of processing (unless, of course, this batch of beets is processed before this moment).

The yield of the finished product (sugar) depends on many variables: the percentage of dirt on the beets, the nitrate content, damage during transportation to processing, processing temperature, and so on, but the percentage of sucrose has the main influence on the yield of the final product.

We number the batches of raw materials in the order of their processing. Then the sugar yield after completion of all stages will be proportional to the objective function

$$S = a_1 + a_2 b_{21} + a_3 b_{31} b_{32} + ... + a_n b_{n1} b_{n2} ... b_{nn-1}$$

The task of constructing an optimal processing schedule in general terms is to choose such a sequence of raw materials processing for which the value of S will be maximum.

2.3   Solution Methods

Note that there are $n!$ different permutations (different processing schedules) of n batches of sugar beets, that is, when solving the problem by brute-force search, one should calculate and compare $n!$ objective function values.

We will show how it is possible to significantly reduce the number of calculations to find the optimal order for processing batches of raw materials with complete information about all parameters $b_{ij}, i = \overline{1, n}, \ j = \overline{1, n-1}$. Let's make the following transformations.

Denote $p_{i1} = a_i, \ p_{i2} = a_i b_{i1}, ..., p_{in} = a_i b_{i1} ... b_{in-1}, \ i = \overline{1, n}$. From the elements p_{ij} we form a square matrix $n \times n : P = (p_{ij})$. In this matrix, the column number determines the processing stage number, and the row number corresponds to the beet lot number. In this notation, the problem can be formulated as follows: select exactly one element from each row of the matrix P so that each column contains only one of the selected elements, and the sum of the selected elements is maximum.

From such a formulation of the problem, it follows that the problem of choosing the optimal processing schedule belongs to the class of discrete optimization problems, is a kind of analogue of the transport problem and can be solved, for example, by the simplex method previously studied by students on the subject of "Linear programming". The problem is represented as a linear programming problem with an objective function: $\sum_{i=1}^{n} \sum_{j=1}^{n} p_{ij} x_{ij}$ and restrictions: $x_{ij} \geq 0$,

$$\sum_{j=1}^{n} x_{ij} = 1, i = \overline{1, n}; \sum_{i=1}^{n} x_{ij} = 1, j = \overline{1, n}.$$

Moreover, there always exists an optimal solution with integer values under additional restrictions: $x_{ij} = 0$ or $x_{ij} = 1$.

It is more natural to solve this problem as a special case of the well-known "assignment problem" [24]. The assignment problem is a fundamental problem of combinatorial optimization. To solve it, in 1955, Harold Kuhn developed an algorithm called the "Hungarian algorithm" [25, 26], later it was proved that it has polynomial complexity $O(n^4)$. Sometime later, the Hungarian algorithm was modified to polynomial complexity $O(n^3)$. The Hungarian algorithm can find both the maximum and minimum value of the objective function, as well as the corresponding choice of matrix rows, that is, the extreme processing schedule.

2.4   Analytical Solutions

Under certain assumptions regarding the parameters a_i and b_{ij} in the problem formulated above, it is possible, without resorting to the use of the Hungarian algorithm, to obtain accurate analytical solutions for optimal raw material processing schedules.

Let the degradation coefficient not depend on the batch of raw materials, but depend only on the processing period, that is

$$b_{ij} = b_j, i = \overline{1, n}, j = \overline{1, n - 1}. \tag{1}$$

In the paper [14], based on the Karamata's inequality, it was proved that under the indicated assumption, the schedule (graph A) is optimal, assuming sequential processing of beet varieties in decreasing (non-increasing) order of the initial sugar content parameter a_i.

In another particular case, it is assumed that the parameters

$$b_{ij} = b_i, i = \overline{1, n}, j = \overline{1, n - 1}, \tag{2}$$

depend only on the batch number of the raw material and do not depend on the stage of processing. In addition, it is assumed that all varieties of beets have the same initial sugar content, that is

$$a_i = a, i = \overline{1, n}. \tag{3}$$

In the paper [15], the following assertion is proved, when conditions (2), (3) and $\beta \geq \frac{n-1}{n}$, where $\beta = \min_{i=\overline{1,n}} b_i$ are met, the optimal schedule (graph B) is the processing of beet batches in ascending (non-decreasing) order of the parameter. In other words, processing should be carried out starting with the variety with the lowest sugar content and then in increasing order.

2.5   Approximate Solutions

Despite the simplicity of the above optimal graphs A and B, their exact implementation in practice is impossible, due to the lack of reliable information on the degradation parameters b_{ij} at the beginning of the raw material processing season, which depend on a number of poorly predictable factors, primarily such as weather conditions and storage conditions of raw materials. In this regard, approximate solutions can be proposed, which will take into account the current information on the residual sugar content of beet varieties that have not yet been processed to this stage. Based on the optimal **plan A**, the following processing strategy can be proposed, at the next stage, raw materials with the highest residual sugar content are supplied for processing. This strategy will be called the **"greedy algorithm"** [27,28] in the future, meaning that the best of the remaining varieties of raw materials is sent to the next stage of processing. Another processing strategy can be associated with the optimal **plan B**: at the next stage, raw materials with the lowest residual sugar content enter the processing. Such a strategy can be called a **"thrifty algorithm"**, emphasizing by this name that the processing of the best varieties should be carried out to the last stages, and the processing of less valuable beet varieties (before they have completely lost their production value) should be carried out at the beginning of the season.

2.6   Software

As an algorithmic language for the implementation of algorithms for solving the problem, students are recommended to use the Python programming language. Python is a computer programming language that is optimized for programmer productivity and software quality. The Python programming language uses a number of standard libraries that allow you to work with various mathematical objects, in particular, functions of matrices [29]. This gives them an advantage over languages that do not use such libraries. The open source SciPy library is built to work with NumPy arrays and provides many convenient and efficient numerical routines designed to perform scientific and engineering calculations. NumPy and SciPy are among the seven major libraries commonly used in Python, they are "...easy to use, yet powerful enough to be relied upon by the world's leading scientists and engineers". The SciPy library has a section related to optimization, but the problem is not one of the standard ones included in this library. However, it includes the "Hungarian algorithm", you can also use the open source library "Munkres" to apply it. The NumPy library is considered one of the most popular in Python machine learning libraries. It is used to perform some operations not only with matrices, but also with tensors. The array interface is the best and most important feature of Numpy.

3   Content of the Project

3.1   Purpose of the Educational and Research Project

The aim of the educational and research project, set before the students, is to evaluate the possible loss of product yield when using the "greedy" and "thrifty" algorithms in relation to the optimal beet processing schedule for various values of sugar content and degradation parameters. Students sequentially in the course of three stages achieve the set goal: the stage of theoretical training, the stage of mastering software tools and the research stage. To control the passage of each stage by the teacher and check the degree of formation of the relevant competencies, the corresponding assessment tools were formed.

3.2   Tasks of the Theoretical Part

Evaluation tools of the first stage are tasks to test the theoretical readiness of students to perform research work.

1) Using the materials and sources presented by the teacher, analyze the formulation of the problem of the optimal beet processing schedule, the mathematical formulation of the assignment problem, as well as the Hungarian algorithm for finding the optimal solution. Using the Hungarian algorithm, analytically solve assignment problems given by the follow-ing matrices

$$P_1 = \begin{pmatrix} 7 & 6 & 5,1 & 4 \\ 6\,5,1 & 4 & 2 \\ 5 & 4 & 2 & 1 \\ 4 & 2 & 1 & 0,5 \end{pmatrix}, \quad P_2 = \begin{pmatrix} 7 & 6 & 5,5 & 4 \\ 6\,5,1 & 4 & 2 \\ 5 & 4 & 2 & 1 \\ 4 & 2 & 1 & 0,5 \end{pmatrix}.$$

The matrix P_1 differs from matrix P_2 by replacing the element $p_{13} = 5.1$ with $\tilde{p}_{13} = 5.5$.

2) Solve analytically the assignment problem for matrices:

$$P_3 = \begin{pmatrix} 4 & 2 & 2/3 & 1/6 \\ 15 & 7.5 & 2.5 & 5/8 \\ 6 & 3 & 1 & 1/4 \\ 12 & 6 & 2 & 1/2 \end{pmatrix}, \quad P_4 = \begin{pmatrix} 16 & 32/3 & 64/9 & 128/27 \\ 16 & 4 & 1 & 1/4 \\ 16 & 8 & 4 & 2 \\ 16 & 16/3 & 16/9 & 16/27 \end{pmatrix}.$$

When solving the assignment problem with matrices P_1 and P_2, students should pay attention to the fact that with a change of less than 8% from the initial value of only one element of the matrix p_{13} from 5.1 to 5.5, the optimal solution schedule and the corresponding maximum value of the objective function. It is equal to $p_{41} + p_{32} + p_{23} + p_{14} = 4 + 4 + 4 + 4 = 16$ for matrix P_1 and $p_{31} + p_{22} + \tilde{p}_{13} + p_{44} = 5 + 5.1 + 5.5 + 0.5 = 16.1$ for matrix P_2. When constructing the optimal algorithm for the matrix P_1, at the first step, the smallest element of the first column $p_{41} = 4$ is taken, and for the matrix P_2, only the third largest element of the first column $p_{41} = 5$ is taken as the first. This example demonstrates the high sensitivity of the optimal schedule to changes in the parameters of the problem, and additionally emphasizes the nontrivially of the assignment problem, as well as the need to use rigorous mathematical methods for studying and solving it.

The second task of the theoretical part allows students visually to see two important cases described in Sect. 2.4, in the case of a matrix P_3, plan A is used, and in the case of a matrix P_4, plan B is used. Besides the following additional tasks were formulated as follows.

1. Independently collect information about other known methods for solving the assignment problem (for example, the Mack method [24,26], etc.)
2. Prove the optimality of plan A under conditions (1).
3. Prove the optimality of plan B under conditions (2), (3) and $\beta \geq \frac{n-1}{n}$.

Performing additional tasks involves developing the ability to independently search for information from various sources, including the Internet, to conduct independent analysis, to critical and logical thinking. The construction of evidence shows the importance of mathematical justification for solving an applied problem. Evaluation tools of the first stage make it possible to assess the degree of formation of the GPC-1 competence.

3.3   Mastering the Software

The evaluation tools of the second stage are computational tasks and tasks for creating software that allow assessing the degree of formation of the GPC-2 competence.

1) Based on the Python algorithmic language and its mathematical libraries, write a program for solving the "assignment problem" given by the corresponding matrix.
2) Test the program using the matrices P_1 and P_2, P_3 and P_4 specified in Sect. 3.2.

3.4   Tasks for the Computational Experiment

The third part, research part of the project, involves the solution of the following tasks:

1) Write a program to calculate the values of the objective function S of sugar beet processing when implementing the optimal (S_0), "greedy" (S_A) and "thrifty" (S_B) algorithms for given values of the number of batches, the number of processing stages and a set of coefficients a_i and b_{ij}.
2) Provide calculation of relative losses in the implementation of "greedy" (R_A) and "thrifty" (R_B) algorithms as a percentage relative to the optimal algorithm according to the formulas $R_A = \frac{S_0 - S_A}{S} \times 100\%$, $R_B = \frac{S_0 - S_B}{S} \times 100\%$.
3) Perform 60 experiments described in tasks 1) and 2), calculate the average values of the objective function for the optimal $(\langle S_0 \rangle)$, "greedy" $(\langle S_A \rangle)$ and "thrifty" $(\langle S_B \rangle)$ algorithms and their averaged relative losses $(\langle R_A \rangle$ and $\langle R_B \rangle)$.

4) Develop a "friendly" program interface that provides convenient input of initial data and output of calculated values, as well as graphs of the dependence of the objective function on the number of processed batches.
5) Draw conclusions and write a report on the work done.

The presented tasks, including the preparation of the report, are evaluation tools for passing the third stage to assess the formation of the GPC-3 competence.

4   Project Results

There are presented the results of the project implementation by a group of four 3rd year students - Gleb Danshin, Andrey Kuklin, Karina Medvedeva and Mikhail Zarubin in the 2021–22 academic year. In the course of the project implementation, a program was created that provides the solution of research tasks; an interface has been created that allows for convenient input of initial data and output of the obtained graphs of the dynamics of objective functions. The initial data of the project corresponded to the estimates of sugar content and the rate of its loss by different batches of beets, which were recorded during many years of measurements carried out at the Sergachsky sugar plant.

Figures 1 and 2 show the resulting graphs of the dependence of the objective function S on the number of processed batches when implementing the optimal, "greedy" and "thrifty" algorithms for different input data.

The graphs in Fig. 1 correspond to the situation when the coefficients b_{ij} are uniformly distributed in the interval (0.97, 1), the coefficients a_i are uniformly distributed in the interval (0.16, 0.20). The graphs in Fig. 2 correspond to the situation when the coefficients a_i are uniformly distributed in the interval (0.16, 0.2), the coefficients b_{ij} are chosen from the interval (0.95, 1), with $|b_{ij} - b_{ik}| \leq 0.01$ and the distribution for each fixed i is uniform. The blue line marks the change in the objective function when implementing the optimal processing algorithm, the green line shows the change in the objective function when implementing the "thrifty" algorithm, and the orange dotted line shows the change in the objective function when implementing the "greedy" algorithm.

In addition, the value of relative losses was calculated in the implementation of the "greedy" and "thrifty" algorithms in relation to the optimal algorithm.

The results of the calculations shown in Fig. 1 allow us to conclude that in the considered situation, when the parameters are uniformly distributed over the given sections, when implemen-ting the "greedy" algorithm, the losses will be insignificant in relation to the implementation of the optimal algorithm. In this case, the "greedy" algorithm can be considered as a simple, convenient and efficient approximation of the optimal algorithm.

The calculation results shown in Fig. 2 allow us to conclude that in the case when there is a small scatter in the values of the degradation coefficients in each batch relative to the periods of processing and the scatter of the initial sugar content is also small, then the "thrifty" algorithm gives a better result than the "greedy" one. In this case, it is better to use the "thrifty" algorithm as an approximation of the optimal algorithm.

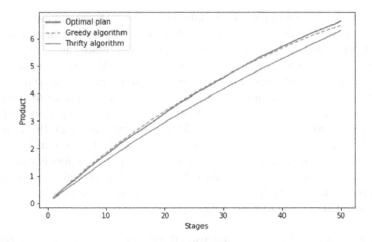

Fig. 1. Product dynamics versus the number of stages for three algorithms in the case when "greedy" algorithm is better than "thrifty" one.

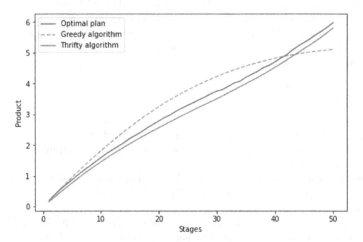

Fig. 2. Product dynamics versus the number of stages for three algorithms in the case when "thrifty" algorithm is better than "greedy" one.

5   Conclusion

The completed project shows the feasibility of using the project-based teaching method as the most effective way to achieve learning goals. The implementation of the project "Optimization of the sugar beet processing schedule" allows us to get significantly deepening the formation of the three general professional competencies GPC-1, GPC-2, GPC-3, and the formation is carried out in a complex, inextricably linked manner. This approach increases students' motivation to study the mathematical foundations of algorithmic and software solutions, turns

420 D. Balandin et al.

the studied mathematical methods into the same natural engineering design tool as computer tools. Of particular value for achieving learning goals is the fact that here students have a rare opportunity to evaluate the results obtained from the point of view of practical implementation, they see connections with actual production problems. This ensures the formation of the competence of the GPC-3. Involving a group of students in the implementation of the project ensures the development of teamwork skills, provides an opportunity to gain experience in professional interaction. Thus, the experience of the implementation of the presented educational and research project allows us to conclude that the methodological approaches developed during the implementation of the project to the organization of design work have a high potential to modernize the educational process of training bachelors in the field of information technology and improve the quality of their education.

Acknowledgments. The article was carried out under the contract No. SSZ-1771 dated 22.04.2021. On the implementation of R&D on the topic: "Creation of high-tech sugar production on the basis of JSC "Sergach Sugar Plant", within the framework of the Agreement on the provision of subsidies from the federal budget for the development of cooperation between the Russian educational organization of higher education and the organization of the real sector of the economy in order to implement a comprehensive project to create high-tech production No. 075-11-2021-038 of 24.06.2021. (IGC 000000S407521QLA0002).

References

1. Gugina, E.V., Kuzenkov, O.A.: Educational standards of the Lobachevsky State University of Nizhny Novgorod. Bull. Lobachevsky Univ. Nizhny Novgorod **3–4**, 39–44 (2014). (in Russian)
2. Kuzenkov, O.A., Zakharova, I.V.: Mathematical programs modernization based on Russian and international standards. Mod. Inf. Technol. IT-Educ. **14**(1), 233–244 (2018)
3. Kuzenkov, O.A., Zakharova, I.V.: The relationship between the METAMATH project and the ongoing reform of higher education in Russia. Educ. Technol. Soc. **20**(3), 279–291 (2017). (in Russian)
4. Shvetsov, V.I., Galeev, I.H., Zaitseva, K.K., Kuzenkov, O.A., Pozdnyakov, S.N., Fedosin, S.A.: Results of the project "modern educational technologies of teaching mathematics in engineering education in Russia". Educ. Technol. Soc. **22**(1), 51–60 (2019). (in Russian)
5. Petrova, I.Yu., et al.: Key guidelines for the development and implementation of educational programs in the subject area. In: Information and Communication Technologies, Bilbao (2013). (in Russian)
6. Kuzenkov, O.A., Kuzenkova, G.V., Kiseleva, T.P.: Computer support of educational and research projects in the field of mathematical modeling of selection processes. Educ. Technol. Soc. **22**(1), 152–163 (2019). (in Russian)
7. Kuzenkov, O.A., Ryabova, E.A.: Project approach in the study of mathematical analysis by engineering students. Educ. Technol. Soc. **22**(4), 225–232 (2019). (in Russian)

8. Kuzenkov, O.A., Kuzenkova, G.V., Kiseleva, T.P.: The use of electronic learning tools in the modernization of the course "mathematical modeling of selection processes". Educ. Technol. Soc. **21**(1), 435–448 (2018). (in Russian)

9. Kuzenkov, O.A., Kostromina, O.S.: The use of electronic means to verify the achievement of the minimum level of mastering the discipline "Mathematical analysis". Educ. Technol. Soc. **22**(4), 131–142 (2019). (in Russian)

10. Egamov, A.I., Pristavchenko, O.V.: Studying the discipline of computational methods using a design approach. Mod. Inf. Technol. IT-Educ. **17**(2), 404–414 (2021). https://doi.org/10.25559/SITITO.17.202102.404-414

11. Shirokov, E.P.: Technology of Storage and Processing of Fruits and Vegetables with the Basics of Standardization. Agropromizdat., Moscow (1988). (in Russian)

12. Manzhesov, V.I.: Technology of Storage, Processing and Standardization of Crop Production. Troitsky Bridge, St. Petersburg (2010). (in Russian)

13. Sumonsiri, N., Barringer, S.: Fruits and vegetables processing technologies and applications. In: Clark, S., Jung, S., Lamsal, B. (eds.) Food Processing: Principles and Applications. Wiley (2014). https://doi.org/10.1002/9781118846315.ch16

14. Balandin, D.V., Vildanov, V.K., Kuzenkov, O.A., Egamov, A.I.: Optimal schedule of sugar beet processing in conditions of uncertainty. In: Actual Problems of Applied Mathematics, Computer Science and Mechanics: Proceedings of the International Scientific Conference, Voronezh, pp. 328–334 (2022). (in Russian)

15. Balandin, D.V., Vildanov, V.K., Kuzenkov, O.A., Zakharova, I.V., Egamov, A.I.: Strategy of processing sugar beet batches with close parameters of its withering. In: The second All-Russian Scientific and Practical Seminar "Mathematical and Computer Modeling and Business Analysis in the Conditions of Digitalization of the Economy". Proceedings Lobachevsky University of Nizhny Novgorod, N. Novgorod, pp. 10–18 (2022). (in Russian)

16. Balandin, D.V., Kuzenkov, O.A., Vildanov, V.K.: A software module for constructing an optimal schedule for processing raw materials. Mod. Inf. Technol. IT Educ. **17**(2), 442–452 (2021). (in Russian)

17. Balandin, D.V., Kuzenkov, O.A.: Optimization of the schedule of processing of raw materials in the food industry. Mod. Eng. Innov. Technol. **17**(1), 59–66 (2021). (in Russian)

18. Balandin, D.V., Kuznetsov, Y.A.: The problem of optimizing the schedule of processing perishable agricultural products. Econ. Anal. Theory Pract. **20**(11), 2134–2150 (2021). (in Russian)

19. Sapronov, A.R.: Technology of Sugar Production. Koloss, Moscow (1999). (in Russian)

20. Anichin, V.L.: Theory and Practice of Production Resources Management in the Beet Sugar Subcomplex of the Agro-Industrial Complex. Publ. House of the Bel-GSHA, Belgorod (2005). (in Russian)

21. Jiao, Z., Higgins, A.J., Prestwidge, D.B.: An integrated statistical and optimisation approach to increasing sugar production within a mill region. Comput. Electron. Agric. **48**, 170–181 (2005)

22. Junqueira, R., Morabito, R.: Modeling and solving a sugarcane harvest front scheduling problem. Int. J. Prod. Econ. **231**(1), 150–160 (2019)

23. Kukhar, V.N., Chernyavsky, A.P., Chernyavskaya, L.I., Mokanyuk, Y.A.: Methods for assessing the technological properties of sugar beet using indicators of the content of potassium, sodium and α-amine nitrogen determined in beetroot and its processing products. Sugar **1**, 18–36 (2019). (in Russian)

24. Bunday, B.: Basic Linear Programming, London (1984)

25. Kuhn, H.: The Hungarian method for the assignment problem. Naval Res. Logist. Q. **2**, 83–97 (1955)
26. Sigal, I.H., Ivanova, A.P.: Introduction to Applied Discrete Programming: Models and Computational Algorithms. Textbook, Moscow (2002). (in Russian)
27. Asanov, M.O., Baransky, V.A., Racin, V.V.: Discrete Mathematics: Graphs, Matroids, Algorithms. Textbook, 2nd ed., St. Petersburg (2010). (in Russian)
28. Rafgarden, T.: Perfect Algorithm. Greedy Algorithms and Dynamic Programming, St. Petersburg (2020)
29. Harrison, M.: How Python Works. Guide for Developers, Programmers and Those Interested, St. Petersburg (2019)

Evaluation of the Angara Interconnect Prototype TCP/IP Software Stack: Implementation, Basic Tests and BeeGFS Benchmarks

Yuri Goncharuk[1], Yuri Grishichkin[2], Alexander Semenov[1,2,3]([✉]) [iD],
Vladimir Stegailov[2,3,4] [iD], and Vasiliy Umrihin[1]

[1] JSC NICEVT, Moscow, Russia
{goncharuk,semenov,umrihin}@nicevt.ru
[2] Joint Institute for High Temperatures of RAS, Moscow, Russia
gyg@jiht.ru
[3] National Research University Higher School of Economics, Moscow, Russia
[4] Moscow Institute of Physics and Technology, Dolgoprudny, Russia
stegailov.vv@phystech.edu

Abstract. In the paper, we present a prototype implementation of the TCP/IP software stack over the Angara high performance interconnect. Our approach is to use the standard TCP/IP stack implementation from the Linux kernel, while we implement in the Linux kernel an Ethernet network device driver for the Angara interconnect adapter. The paper presents the latency and bandwidth results and the results of the IO500 suite benchmarks of the distributed storage deployed with BeeGFS on 20 nodes of the Fisher supercomputer in JIHT RAS.

Keywords: Angara · TCP/IP · Ethernet · BeeGFS · IO500

1 Introduction

Parallel file system (PFS) is one of the most essential building blocks of the persistent storage in high performance computing (HPC) infrastructure. It provides fast global access to large volumes of data and ensures data persistence through a high number of distributed storage devices. One of the most critical components having a direct impact on the performance of HPC systems and PFSs is the interconnection network (interconnect). Parallel file system clients accessing data from the file system, communicate with the storage servers via any TCP/IP based connection or via remote direct memory access (RDMA) capable interconnects like InfiniBand [1], Omni-Path [2], Slingshot [3] and RDMA over Converged Ethernet (RoCE), which is a part the Infiniband specification [1].

Currently, the market is dominated by Infiniband. InfiniBand is an open standard for high performance network communications. The most commonly used InfiniBand implementations rely on NVIDIA Mellanox hardware, with switches

V. Voevodin et al. (Eds.): RuSCDays 2022, LNCS 13708, pp. 423–435, 2022.
https://doi.org/10.1007/978-3-031-22941-1_31

typically arranged in a fat tree topology. HDR 200 Gb/s is the sixth generation of the NVIDIA InfiniBand architecture. HDR has 0.6 us low-level latency
[4], the obtained MPI latency is 1 us [5]. Infiniband can support TCP/IP
protocol as IPoIB (IP over Infiniband), which implements regular networking
(through the Linux kernel stack) over Infiniband fabric by wrapping L3/L4
TCP/IP headers with Infiniband headers. Note that L2/L3/L4 layers correspond
to the 2nd/3rd/4th layers of the OSI model [6]. The second way is RoCE, which
implements RDMA over Ethernet fabric by wrapping Infiniband packets with
L2/L3/L4 headers.

Cray (HPE) released the Slingshot interconnection network [3]. Slingshot
uses an optimized Ethernet protocol, which allows it to be interoperable with
standard Ethernet devices while providing high performance to HPC applications. Slingshot switches have ports with 200 Gbit/s each and support arbitrary
network topologies, the default topology is Dragonfly [7]. The low-level latency
of Slingshot is 1.85 us between two nodes.

The focus of our work is the Angara interconnect. Angara [8,9] is the low-
latency, high bandwidth interconnect with 4D torus topology, the obtained MPI
latency between two adjacent nodes is 0.85 us. The Angara-C1 and Desmos [9]
cluster systems are based on the Angara interconnect. During the last several
years, the Angara interconnect has obtained a history of practical usage [9–13].

In this paper, we present a prototype implementation of the TCP/IP software
stack over the Angara high performance interconnect. For the sake of clarity, our
approach is to use the standard TCP/IP stack implementation from the Linux
kernel, while we implement in the Linux kernel the Ethernet device driver for
the Angara interconnect adapter. The goal is to support parallel file systems on
the Angara-based HPC systems.

PFS performance evaluation with network aspects are quite rare in computer science. Papers [14] and [15] with BeeGFS, Ceph, GlusterFS, OrangeFS
PFSs performance analysis should be highlighted. Performance improving of
large scale geophysical applications using BeeGFS is presented in [16]. Infiniband and TCP/IP software stack are used as a network transport. The emergence in 2017 of the IO500 list [17] played a big role in drawing attention to PFS
performance analysis. IO500 is a comprehensive benchmark suite to track storage performance and storage technologies of supercomputers, organized by the
Virtual Institute for I/O (VI4IO) [18]. Several works [19,20] address the IO500
performance on HPC systems.

The paper is structured as follows. In Sect. 2 the brief Angara interconnect
architecture is given, then the implementation of the Ethernet network device
over Angara is described. Section 3 presents the hardware configuration of the
Fisher supercomputer and software settings. Then the results of bandwidth,
latency and IO500 tests are given and discussed. Section 4 concludes the paper.

2   The Angara TCP/IP Implementation

The TCP/IP software stack for the Angara interconnect is supported by the standard TCP/IP implementation from the Linux kernel and three implemented in this work Linux kernel modules: angara_netdev, angara_rdma and angara_router. The main module is angara_netdev, which implements the Ethernet interface, i.e. the channel or second layer of the OSI model [6].

2.1   The Angara Interconnect Architecture

The Angara interconnect is a Russian-designed communication network with 4D torus topology. The interconnect ASIC was developed by JSC NICEVT and manufactured by TSMC with the 65-nm process. An Angara packet format provides a possibility to address 32K nodes.

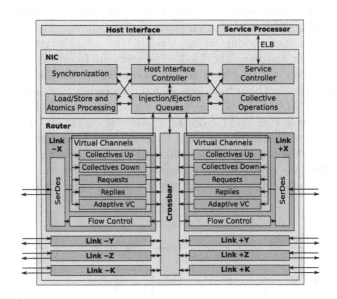

Fig. 1. The Angara ASIC architecture.

Figure 1 presents the Angara ASIC chip, which consists of an adapter and a router. The router contains 8 link blocks that are connected via a crossbar. The crossbar can simultaneously transmit flits (128 bits) from links if there are no conflicts.

The Angara chip supports simultaneous operations with multiple threads/processes of a user task; it is implemented as several injection channels available for use by independent packet buffers.

Each node has a dedicated memory region available for remote access from other nodes. The network adapter at the hardware level supports PIO and

RDMA modes. In PIO mode a processor creates network packets and sends them to the network using Angara PUT operation, thus consuming the resources of a processor core. On the contrary, RDMA (Remote Direct Memory Access) mode does not involve the CPU. Rather, the Angara adapter moves data directly to and from memory, bypassing the CPU altogether. Angara has RDMA write and read operations.

2.2   Ethernet Network Device Driver Implementation

The Ethernet network device for the Angara interconnect is implemented by three Linux kernel modules: angara_netdev, angara_rdma and angara_router. The main module is angara_netdev, which implements the Ethernet interface. The angara_netdev module uses functions that are exported by the angara_rdma and angara_router kernel modules. The angara_rdma module implements a native Angara network messaging interface with RDMA support in the kernel space. The angara_router module manages hardware resources of the Angara network adapter, including access to injection pipelines, control registers, etc.

The angara_netdev module is implemented as an Ethernet device driver with the following features. The Media Independent Interface (MII) [21] features, which include physical layer control and media access link layer control, are not implemented. These functions include managing the speed of the network adapter (10M/100M/1G/10G/40G), duplex mode (Full/Half), changing the Ethernet frame size (MTU) during the driver execution, monitoring the state of the physical link. The physical layer in the Angara network is custom designed, and at the moment there is no need to implement the standard Ethernet capabilities for managing the physical layer. In the future, these functions may be implemented. Also, the ARP protocol is implemented entirely in software.

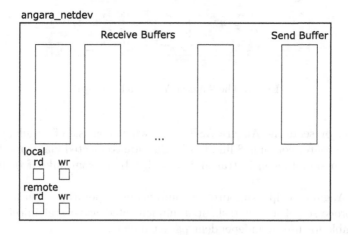

Fig. 2. The angara_netdev module memory scheme.

Receiving and sending data in the angara_netdev module corresponds to the implementation of the Ethernet layer. The angara_netdev module in memory on each node has a receive ring buffer for each other network node, the default buffer size is 8192 4 KB packets, see Fig. 2. There is a ring buffer for sending data to for all other nodes, its size is 8192 packets of a maximum 4 KB size. Local read and write counters and remote read and write counters are supported for each receive buffer. Also in the angara_netdev module there is a Forwarding Database (FDB) table with mapping MAC addresses and physical numbers (NODENUM) of nodes in the Angara network.

The message send consists of the following stages:

1. The angara_netdev module (angara0 interface) receives a socket buffer from the Linux kernel, which is represented by the structure sk_buff [22]. The IP address of the recipient is retrieved from the resulting structure.
2. Using the retrieved destination IP address, the ARP table is searched for MAC address by IP address.
3. The received MAC address of the recipient is used to search in the FDB table of the angara_netdev module for the corresponding physical NODENUM number of the destination node in the Angara network.
4. From the sk_buff structure data payload is retrieved, as well as its size. The received data is combined and transmitted as the first PUT sending over the Angara network to the node with the destination physical NODENUM number. The sending occurs with the requirement that the local write counter is less than the remote read counter.
5. The second PUT sending to the NODENUM node includes the incremented value of the local write counter and writes it to the corresponding memory location of the remote write counter on the remote NODENUM node. At the same time, the local read counter is also sent, which is written to the remote read counter of the remote NODENUM node to inform it about how many packets the current node has read.

If the recipient MAC address is missing, then the angara_netdev module perform a software broadcast ARP request to all possible physical nodes in the Angara network. The received ARP-request is processed by the angara_netdev module on a node, and sends a response, which eventually ends up in the system ARP table, and the NODENUM of the node goes into the FDB table of the angara_netdev module.

The message send can be performed in two modes:

1. Using the sending thread (parameter tx_threadless=0 of the angara_netdev module);
2. Without using the sending thread (parameter tx_threaless=1 of the angara_netdev module).

In the first mode, during the initialization of the angara0 network interface, a TX thread is created, it processes the send buffer. The module's send function adds data to this buffer, and the TX thread performs the described transmission.

In the second mode, the described transmission occurs immediately when the
sk_buff structure is received from the kernel, but this mode is the softirq interrupt handling mode [23], and long-term processing is undesirable. Since message
latency is higher for the first mode, the second mode is used in this paper. The
current implementation uses single injection channel of the Angara ASIC. Use
of several injection channel allows to improve network bandwidth.

The message receive is organized as follows. During the raising of the angara0
network interface, an RX thread is created, which permanently polls the remote
write counter of the receive ring buffer for each possible network node and compares it to the local read counter.

The polling discipline for receive buffers by the RX thread is round robin.
During each iteration of the RX thread, if a new buffer element is found, the
tasklet is launched. A tasklet [23] is a lightweight thread that does not have its
own context, it runs in a separate kernel thread and completely performs the
receive function for the specified sender node. The total number of launched
tasklets can not be more than the total number of nodes in the network. After
data processing, in the absence of new data the tasklet is destroyed.

The tasklet processes packets on each iteration of the receive loop for the
difference between the remote write counter and the local read counter. At each
iteration of this loop, the tasklet does the following:

1. Allocates memory for the sk_buff structure, write payload to this structure.
2. Sends the created structure using the netif_rx() to the kernel network stack,
   which corresponds to the 3rd layer of the OSI model.

The more participants in the data exchange, the longer delay between processing of each individual sender node. To speed up the processing of specific
sender nodes, the angara_parts parameter (short for Angara participants) has
been introduced. This parameter allows to set the list of active members of
the Angara network, note that messages from other network nodes will be processed with lower priority. At the same time, it is a disadvantage that the receive
buffers are created for all network nodes, and not only for active participants.
This shortcoming is planned to be eliminated in future work.

3   Experimental Evaluation

This section presents the performance evaluation of the proposed TCP/IP software stack for the Angara interconnect on the Fisher supercomputer.

3.1   Hardware and Software Setup

The main details about the Fisher supercomputer are given in Table 1 and illustrated in Fig. 3. Fisher has a segment with Infiniband FDR and air cooling and a
segment with Angara and immersion cooling [24]. The Angara segment is divided
into two equal size partitions, the first one is based on the first AMD EPYC processor microarchitecture generation called Naples, the second one is based on the

Table 1. The main characteristics of the segment of the Fisher supercomputer used for EoA testing.

Compute nodes	ang [1–20]
Chassis	Gigabyte H262-Z62
Processor/Memory	2 x Epyc 7301 16c/128 GB
Storage	Apacer AS2280P2 240 GB
Interconnect	Angara switch, 1 Gbit/s Ethernet
OS	openSUSE Leap 15.2
Kernel version	5.3.18-lp152.87-preempt
MPI	MPICH 3.2 for Angara

second AMD EPYC processor microarchitecture generation called Rome. Each Angara partition has an Angara ES8433 switch, each node of the Angara segment has a low-profile Angara ES8432 network adapter. ES8433 switches are connected by 4 links.

For the evaluation we have initialized Ethernet Angara interface on 20 nodes with AMD EPYC 7301 processers.

BeeGFS [25] is a parallel cluster file system. It was originally developed for High Performance Computing. BeeGFS transparently spreads user data across multiple servers. BeeGFS separates metadata from user file chunks on the servers. The metadata is the "data about data", such as access permissions, file size and the information about how the user file chunks are distributed across the storage servers. BeeGFS clients accessing data from the file system, communicate with the storage servers via any TCP/IP based connection or via RDMA-capable networks.

We use quick deploy with BeeGFS On Demand (BeeOND) option with default parameters that allows to run BeeGFS instances temporary exactly for the runtime of the compute job. BeeGFS version is 7.2.3.

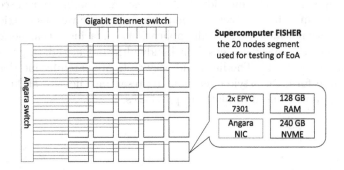

Fig. 3. The segment of the Fisher supercomputer used for EoA testing.

3.2 Benchmarks

We use the MPI-based osu_latency benchmark, version 5.9 for latency evaluation on 2 neighbouring nodes. For bandwidth evaluation we use iperf with 5 parallel client threads.

Table 2. IO500 benchmark suite components.

Component	Tests	Description
IOR 'easy'	ior_easy_write, ior_easy_read	Bandwidth for well-formed large sequential I/O patterns
IOR 'hard'	ior_hard_write, ior_hard_read	Bandwidth for unaligned (47001 bytes) operation from each client process to a single file
mdtest 'easy'	mdtest_easy_delete, mdtest_easy_stat, mdtest_easy_write	Metadata operations on 0-byte files, using separate directories for each MPI task
mdtest 'hard'	mdtest_hard_delete, mdtest_hard_stat, mdtest_hard_write, mdtest_hard_read	Metadata operations on small (3901 byte) files in a shared directory
Find	Find	Finding relevant files through directory traversals

IO500 [17] is a comprehensive benchmark suite to track storage performance and storage technologies of supercomputers. The IO500 benchmark suite consists of data (IOR) and metadata (mdtest) components as well as a parallel namespace scanning test (find), and calculates a single ranking score for comparison. Table 2 provides a list of IO500 tests. The tests represent the best and worst possible scenarios for bandwidth and metadata in the form of 'easy' and 'hard' use cases respectively. The individual IO500 tests are combined as a score using a geometric mean to find the central tendency among the various metrics. While a top score does not indicate that all applications can achieve that performance, the range from the 'hard' to 'easy' on bandwidth and metadata gives bounds for users can expect [19]. The hard and easy tests are carefully interleaved and timed to 5 min for create-style operations representing the typical 90% forward progress requirement used in platform purchases.

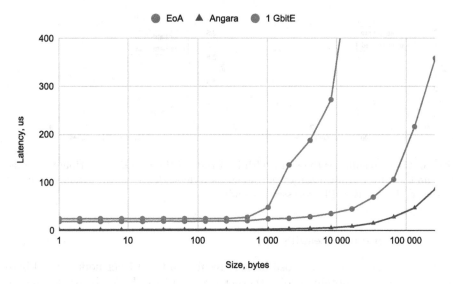

Fig. 4. The obtained osu_latency results on two Fisher nodes. EoA – Ethernet over Angara, Angara – native Angara protocol, 1 GbitE – 1 Gbit/s Ethernet network.

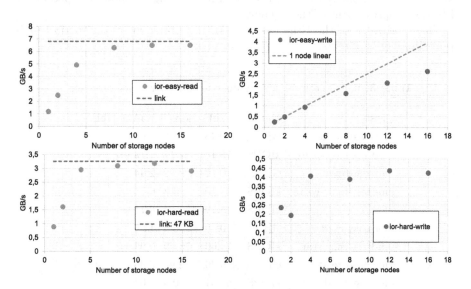

Fig. 5. IO500 results for the bandwidth IOR tests (at 4 client nodes with 16 client processes per node) as a dependence on the number of Fisher nodes that form the BeeOND distributed storage.

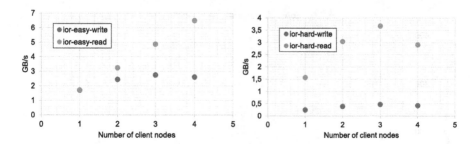

Fig. 6. IO500 results for the bandwidth IOR tests of the BeeOND distributed storage (16 nodes with 1 storage target per node) as a dependence on the number of client Fisher nodes (at 16 MPI processes per node).

3.3   Performance Results

Figure 4 shows the obtained osu_latency results on two Fisher nodes. For 0-byte message we have obtained for Ethernet over Angara (EoA) 19 us, for native Angara protocol (Angara) 1.7 us, for 1 Gbit/s Ethernet (1 GbitE) 25.4 us. Note that Angara interface is initialized on all 20 Fisher nodes. The large performance gap between for Ethernet over Angara and native Angara shows the possibility of further improvement of the latency.

The bandwidth of the Ethernet over Angara obtained by the iperf3 test is approximately 15 Gbit/s.

Table 3. IO500 performance results on the Fisher supercomputer.

Test	Metric	1 GbE	EoA	EoA/1 GbE
ior-easy-write	GB/s	0.46	2.61	5.69
mdtest-easy-write	kIOPS	15.18	17.17	1.13
ior-hard-write	GB/s	0.17	0.42	2.44
mdtest-hard-write	kIOPS	5.10	3.8	0.75
find	kIOPS	175.19	124.55	0.71
ior-easy-read	GB/s	0.45	6.5	14.5
mdtest-easy-stat	kIOPS	74.60	73.69	0.99
ior-hard-read	GB/s	0.46	2.91	6.38
mdtest-hard-stat	kIOPS	67.31	70.3	1.04
mdtest-easy-delete	kIOPS	14.20	10.18	0.72
mdtest-hard-read	kIOPS	14.59	15.03	1.03
mdtest-hard-delete	kIOPS	4.19	5.95	1.42
Total score		2.8	6.35	2.38

Figure 5 shows the dependence of the IOR tests results from the IO500 suite on the number of nodes that form the distributed storage using BeeOND. These tests have been performed for the fixed number of 4 client nodes with 16 client processes per node. We see that io-easy-read and io-hard-read saturate already for 8 and 4 storage nodes, respectively. This saturation can be explained by the limited aggregated bandwidth of 4 EoA links that come to 4 client nodes for large messages (io-easy-read) and 47 KB messages (io-hard-read). The bandwidth of the Angara link does not limit the io-easy-write performance, for 1–4 nodes the main bottleneck is the hard disk performance for write operation.

Figure 6 show the dependence of the same IOR tests results on the number of client nodes. These tests have been performed for the fixed number of 16 storage nodes with 1 storage target per node. We see that using 4 client nodes on io-easy-read one can not saturate the bandwidth of this distributed storage.

Table 3 shows IO500 performance results for the Fisher supercomputer. We have deployed BeeGFS storage on 16 Fisher nodes, including 1 metadata node. We use 4 client nodes, 16 processes are executed on each client node. The total number of client processes is 64. The advantage of Ethernet over Angara network (EoA) on large messages is approximately 15 times compared to 1 Gbit/s Ethernet (1 GbE). The relative read results for EoA are better than the write results, this can be explained by the bottleneck in the hard disk's poor write performance. For metadata and find tests the results are approximately the same on EoA and 1 GbE, except for mdtest-easy-write and mdtest-hard-write tests. The Angara's power is low latencies, which are important for small metadata requests, therefore detailed profiling is needed.

4 Conclusion

This work reports of a fully functional TCP/IP software stack implemented for the Angara interconnect using the prototype Ethernet over Angara driver implementation. The benchmarks of the distributed storage based on this EoA prototype do not show any evident performance limitations that could be attributed to the performance of the Angara interconnect within the EoA framework.

In our future work we plan to address the TCP/IP over Angara bandwidth, latency as well as a detailed profiling of IO500 results. The next Ethernet over Angara implementation will use multiple injection channels and RDMA operations, which will allow to improve the network bandwidth.

The study was carried out with a grant from the Russian Science Foundation (project no. 20-71-10127).

References

1. InfiniBand Trade Association. InfiniBand Architecture Specification. Release 1.0 (2000)
2. Birrittella, M.S., et al.: Intel® omni-path architecture: enabling scalable, high performance fabrics. In: 2015 IEEE 23rd Annual Symposium on High-Performance Interconnects, pp. 1–9. IEEE (2015)

3. De Sensi, D., Di Girolamo, S., McMahon, K.H., Roweth, D., Hoefler, T.: An in-depth analysis of the Slingshot interconnect. In: SC20: International Conference for High Performance Computing, Networking, Storage and Analysis, pp. 1–14. IEEE (2020)
4. Introducing 200G HDR InfiniBand Solutions. Mellanox Technologies (2019) http://mvapich.cse.ohio-state.edu/benchmarks/
5. Ruhela, A., Xu, S., Manian, K.V., Subramoni, H., Panda, D.K.: Analyzing and understanding the impact of interconnect performance on HPC, Big Data, and deep learning applications: a case study with Infiniband EDR and HDR. In: 2020 IEEE International Parallel and Distributed Processing Symposium Workshops (IPDPSW), pp. 869–878. IEEE (2020)
6. Zimmermann, H.: OSI reference model-the ISO model of architecture for open systems interconnection. IEEE Trans. Commun. **28**(4), 425–432 (1980)
7. Kim, J., Dally, W.J., Scott, S., Abts, D.: Technology-driven, highly-scalable dragonfly topology. In: 2008 International Symposium on Computer Architecture, pp. 77–88. IEEE (2008)
8. Simonov, A., Brekhov, O.: Architecture and functionality of the collective operations subnet of the Angara interconnect. In: Vishnevskiy, V.M., Samouylov, K.E., Kozyrev, D.V. (eds.) DCCN 2020. LNCS, vol. 12563, pp. 209–219. Springer, Cham (2020). https://doi.org/10.1007/978-3-030-66471-8_17
9. Stegailov, V., et al.: Angara interconnect makes GPU-based Desmos supercomputer an efficient tool for molecular dynamics calculations. Int. J. High Perform. Comput. Appl. **33**(3), 507–521 (2019)
10. Akimov, V., Silaev, D., Aksenov, A., Zhluktov, S., Savitskiy, D., Simonov, A.: FlowVision scalability on supercomputers with Angara interconnect. Lobachevskii J. Math. **39**(9), 1159–1169 (2018)
11. Khalilov, M., Timofeev, A.: Optimization of MPI-process mapping for clusters with Angara interconnect. Lobachevskii J. Math. **39**(9), 1188–1198 (2018)
12. Polyakov, S., Podryga, V., Puzyrkov, D.: High performance computing in multi-scale problems of gas dynamics. Lobachevskii J. Math. **39**(9), 1239–1250 (2018)
13. Tolstykh, M., Goyman, G., Fadeev, R., Shashkin, V.: Structure and algorithms of SLAV atmosphere model parallel program complex. Lobachevskii J. Math. **39**(4), 587–595 (2018)
14. Kunkel, J.M., Kuhn, M., Ludwig, T.: Exascale storage systems: an analytical study of expenses. Supercomput. Front. Innov. **1**(1), 116–134 (2014)
15. Mills, N., Feltus, F.A., Ligon III, W.B.: Maximizing the performance of scientific data transfer by optimizing the interface between parallel file systems and advanced research networks. Futur. Gener. Comput. Syst. **79**, 190–198 (2018)
16. Brzenski, J., Paolini, C., Castillo, J.E.: Improving the I/O of large geophysical models using PnetCDF and BeeGFS. Parallel Comput. **104**, 102786 (2021)
17. Kunkel, J.: IO500 (2020). https://www.vi4io.org/io500/start. Accessed 30 Apr 2022
18. Kunkel, J., Lofstead, G.F., Bent, J.: The virtual institute for I/O and the IO-500. Technical report, Sandia National Lab. (SNL-NM), Albuquerque, NM, USA (2017)
19. Liem, R., Povaliaiev, D., Lofstead, J., Kunkel, J., Terboven, C.: User-centric system fault identification using IO500 benchmark. In: 2021 IEEE/ACM Sixth International Parallel Data Systems Workshop (PDSW), pp. 35–40. IEEE (2021)
20. Hennecke, M.: DAOS: a scale-out high performance storage stack for storage class memory. Supercomput. Front. 40 (2020)

21. IEEE standards for local and metropolitan area networks: Supplement - media access control (MAC) parameters, physical layer, medium attachment units, and repeater for 100 Mb/s operation, type 100BASE-T (clauses 21–30). IEEE Std 802.3u-1995 (Supplement to ISO/IEC 8802–3: 1993; ANSI/IEEE Std 802.3, 1993 Edition), pp. 1–415 (1995)
22. Gonsalves, T.: Linux network device drivers: an overview (2020). http://students. iitmandi.ac.in/tag/csdoc/Linux_Network_Device_Drivers_Overview_2020.pdf
23. Rothberg, V.: Interrupt handling in Linux (2015)
24. Dlinnova, E., Biryukov, S., Stegailov, V.V.: Energy consumption of MD calculations on hybrid and CPU-only supercomputers with air and immersion cooling. In: PARCO, pp. 574–582 (2019)
25. Herold, F., Breuner, S.: An introduction to BeeGFS (2018). https://www.beegfs. io/docs/whitepapers/Introduction_to_BeeGFS_by_ThinkParQ.pdf. Accessed 01 May 2022

Fast Parallel Bellman-Ford-Moore Algorithm Implementation for Small Graphs

Alexei Vezolainen[1]([✉]) [ID], Alexey Salnikov[1,2] [ID], Artem Klyuchikov[1] [ID], and Sergey Komech[3] [ID]

[1] Huawei Russian Research Institute, Moscow, Russia
{alexei.v.vezolainen,klyuchikov.artem}@huawei.com
[2] Lomonosov Moscow State University, Moscow, Russia
salnikov@cs.msu.ru
[3] Institute for Information Transmission Problems, Moscow, Russia
komech@iitp.ru

Abstract. We present a practical multicore solution for a classical routing problem known as Single Source Shortest Path (SSSP), or the Shortest Path Tree (SPT) search. Most of the practical graphs are relatively small and a commodity hardware can be used though a synchronization overhead is relatively huge. Computing SPT for the large graphs is slow though the multicore synchronization overhead diminishes. We propose an enhancement of the classical Bellman-Ford-Moore algorithm with aligned in memory bit arrays for the next updating vertices in order to reduce the number of cache misses. We considered IPRAN, Fat Tree, and random networks with 2000 to 500000 nodes. For our optimized parallel Bellman-Ford-Moore implementation we obtained the performance improvement $\sim$4–9 times relative to the standard implementation of Dijkstra's algorithm (e.g. in Boost Graph Library). Performance improvement >10 times was also obtained for large, more than 50000 nodes, random graphs.

Keywords: Shortest path tree · Parallel single source shortest path · Multicore · Synchronization problem · Cache misses

1 Introduction

Routing in computer, datacenter, and HPC system networks is an important classical problem. Traditionally this problem is solved via a construction of the Shortest Path Tree (SPT) for a correspondent graph. The sizes of such graphs are relatively small; rarely a datacenter network, for example, consists of more than 5000–100000 nodes. Often network routers utilize multicore and possibly multiprocessor devices. In this paper we present an efficient approach based on multicore parallel processing to find the SPT for the networks of such relatively small size.

The original version of this chapter was revised: An error in the presentation of Sergey Komech's affiliation was corrected. The correction to this chapter is available at https://doi.org/10.1007/978-3-031-22941-1_51

V. Voevodin et al. (Eds.): RuSCDays 2022, LNCS 13708, pp. 436–449, 2022.
https://doi.org/10.1007/978-3-031-22941-1_32

Originally, parallel computing was utilized to make feasible, and sometimes accelerate, large-scale computations which otherwise were not fitting into the memory or took prohibitively large time to run. If some simulation code was running for several weeks, which was quite normal for global weather prediction or climate modeling for example, it was useful for the researchers to implement parallelization and make it run faster. Processors were relatively cheap and available; it was reasonable to use thousands of processors to improve running time from several weeks to several days or even hours. At the same time, it was not necessary to improve the code which was already fast. Such an ideology influenced parallel computing significantly.

Majority of scientific publications give O-notation style estimates for the running time. Researchers were struggling to lower the time complexity of their algorithms. Classical Dijkstra's Single Source Shortest Path (SSSP) algorithm time complexity $O(n^2)$, for example, was improved by using a binary heap priority queue to $O(n \log n)$, or even to $O(n)$ in Thorup's algorithm [25], where n is the number of nodes, and the number of links m is assumed to be of the order of n (i.e. average node degree <10) (Fig. 1).

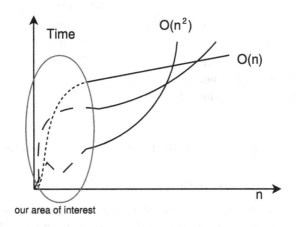

Fig. 1. Time complexity for different algorithms. $O(n)$ algorithm works faster than $O(n^2)$ for relatively large n.

Time complexity indicates that for a large n Thorup's algorithm work faster than classical Dijkstra's [25]. The problem exists, and many researchers are mentioning the fact, that it is rarely clear in advance how large is that "large n" and an extensive testing is required, e.g. [21]. For example, Thorup's algorithm becomes comparable with Dijkstra's at $n \sim 10^5$ nodes [21]. In addition, algorithm implementation performance strongly depends on the memory cache performance, e.g. [1,4,15,21]. The performance may and most probably will become significantly different if tested on a different hardware.

2 Current Approaches to SSSP in Parallel

When considering an implementation of parallel Single Source Shortest Path algorithm we can distinguish several kinds of strategies:

1. Parallelize the inner loop operations of a sequential SSSP algorithm.
2. Parallelize the outer loop operations of a sequential SSSP algorithm.
3. Perform several SSSP algorithms in parallel in disjoint subgraphs.

Table 1 summarizes a list of parallel solutions, classified according to the parallelization strategy implemented.

Table 1. SSSP algorithms parallel solutions.

Algorithm	Year	Parallelization
Fine-Grain Parallel SSSP [19]	1997	Inner
Coarse-Grane Parallel SSSP [19]	1997	Disjoint
Crauser [5]	1998	Outer
Delta-stepping [17]	2003	Outer
GPU Label-Correcting [10,11]	2007	Outer
Tang [24]	2008	Disjoint
GPU Label-Setting_F Delta = 0 [16]	2009	Outer
GPU Label-Setting_U Delta = 0 [16]	2009	Outer
GPU Parallel Bellman-Ford [14]	2011	Outer

In the following paragraphs we briefly overview these strategies.

2.1 Dijkstra's SSSP Algorithm

Dijkstra's algorithm [6] is one of the most famous algorithms for SSSP problem. It is very simple yet effective and is used in various applications. The key idea is to sustain a frontier that consists of the nodes for which a correct distance has not been calculated yet. At each step of Dijkstra's algorithm we take node from frontier with the lowest temporary distance and relax each outgoing edge (relax procedure is described a little bit further). After all outgoing edges were relaxed, we can delete this vertex with a guarantee that the current distance from source to this node is the lowest possible and thus is correct.

Runtime of Dijkstra's algorithm heavily relies on its implementation and on how exactly the nodes with the lowest temporary distance are chosen. Usually, a binary heap based priority queue is used, which brings the runtime asymptotic bound to $O((n + m) \log n)$. There are different ways to store and choose the required nodes from the frontier. For example one could use Fibonacci heap, although all its implementations work much slower than the implementaions of binary heap, e.g. [22].

The idea behind the parallelization of Dijkstra's inner loop is based on the parallel relaxation of outgoing edges, e.g. [19]. Indeed, we can relax each edge independently and it will not lead us to any contradiction when we merge all the information together before choosing new closing node. As for the outer loop, when we iterate over all vertices in the frontier, it can be parallelized, for example, by exploring in parallel several nodes grouped together according to different tentative distance ranges [5]. At each iteration, we can relax independently the outgoing edges from the nodes in the lowest range bucket [17]. As for the disjoint subgraphs processing, e.g. [19,24], it should be noted that most of the practical graphs, e.g. communication networks, hardly can be considered as disjoint.

2.2 Bellman-Ford Algorithm

Bellman-Ford algorithm [2,9] is a well known solution to SSSP problem (for the general case of weight function $w : E \to R$). It works as follows:

Algorithm 1. Bellman-Ford algorithm B-F(G, s)

Initialize d, π: $d[i] = +\infty$ for $i \in V(G)/\{s\}$; $d[s] = 0$; $\pi[i] = $ Null for $i \in V(G)$;
for $i \in [1 \ldots |V(G)| - 1]$ do
   for $e = (u, v) \in E(G)$ do:
      relax(u, v)
   end for
end for
return d, π

---

where the distance update procedure is

---

relax(u, v)

---

if $d[u] + w(u, v) < d[v]$ then
   $d[v] = d[u] + w(u, v)$
   $\pi[v] = u$
end if

This algorithm solves SSSP problem even in case of negative weights on edges without negative cycles (though one can easily modify this algorithm to check if graph G contains negative cycles). The complexity of the algorithm on graph G with the source node s is $\Theta(|V(G)| \cdot |E(G)|)$ or, to be precise, $\Theta((|V(G)| - 1)E(G))$. For the sake of simplicity we denote the number of nodes $V(G)$ as n and the number of edges $E(G)$ as m.

Due to its simplicity Bellman-Ford algorithm can be treated more as a framework rather than a solid algorithm. One can notice that in some cases the outer **for** loop of Bellman-Ford procedure will not update $d[\cdot]$ and $\pi[\cdot]$ arrays. Indeed, consider an undirected star graph $S_n = K_{1,n}$ with a center vertex s. In this case only one iteration of edge relaxation is needed to obtain desired $d[\cdot]$ and

$\pi[\cdot]$—lists of distances and predecessors respectively. After that, $d[\cdot]$, $\pi[\cdot]$ won't change. Thus, a very simple heuristic can be implemented. This trick reduces running time of Bellman-Ford algorithm down to $\Theta H(G,s) \cdot m$, where $H(G,s)$ is the depth of the shortest path tree in G rooted in s.

Algorithm 2. Bellman-Ford algorithm B-F(G, s) with convergence check

---
```
Iniitalize d, π: d[i] = +∞ for i ∈ V(G)/{s}; d[s] = 0; π[i] = Null for i ∈ V(G);
for i ∈ [1...|V(G)| − 1] do
    for e = (u, v) ∈ E(G) do:
        relax(u, v)
    end for
    if d[·] did not change then
        return d, π
    end if
end for
return d, π
```

Remark 1. The following inequality holds: $\Theta(H(G,s) \cdot m) \leq \Theta(D(G) \cdot m)$, where $D(G)$ is a diameter of graph G and $H(G,s)$ is height of the shortest path tree rooted at s.

2.3 Bellman-Ford-Moore Algorithm

The asymptotic bound obtained in the previous subsection is tight. However, we should note that many unnecessary operations are performed during the execution of Bellman-Ford algorithm. During the first iteration of edge relaxation we do not need to relax edges that are not outgoing from s simply because for such edges (u, v) $d[u] = d[v] = +\infty$ and relaxation won't be successful ($d[v]$ and $\pi[v]$ won't be updated). This leads to another simple heuristic where we do not relax unnecessary edges. If at some iteration $d[v]$ was not updated, there is no need to relax edges outgoing from v to subset $N(v)$ of $V(G)$, where $N(v)$ denotes the set of neighboring vertices of v. To keep track of such vertices we will maintain a set $Q = \{v | d[v]\}$, where $d[v]$ was changed on last iteration. This variation of Bellman-Ford algorithm was firstly published by Moore and known as Bellman-Ford-Moore algorithm [18]. This algorithm solves SSSP problem even in the presence of negative weights on edges without negative cycles (though it can be easily modified to check if graph G contains negative cycles).

The running time of Bellman-Ford-Moore algorithm is $O(H(G,s) \cdot m)$. It is easy to see that Θ asymptotics will not hold. Consider graph $G_{k,l}$ defined as follows. The define set of vertices $V(G_{k,l})$ as set of disjoint layers $\bigsqcup_{i=1}^{k} L_i$, where each layer $L_i = \{v_1^i, v_2^i, \dots, v_l^i\}$ for $i \in [1, k]$. The set of edges $E(G_{k,l}) = \{(v_\alpha^i, v_\beta^{i+1}) \mid i \in [1, k-1], 1 \leq \alpha, \beta \leq l\}$. One can easily verify that for any i after the first iteration the size of Q in B-F-M$(G_{k,l}, v_i^1)$ procedure will be exactly l and the number of iterations is equal to k. That leads us to the complexity of

---

Algorithm 3. Bellman-Ford-Moore algorithm B-F-M(G, s)

Iniitalize d, π: $d[i] = +\infty$ for $i \in V(G)/\{s\}$; $d[s] = 0$; $\pi[i] = $ Null for $i \in V(G)$;
$Q = \{s\}$
while $Q \neq \{\}$ **do**
    $Q' = \{\}$
    for $u \in Q$ **do**
        for $v \in N(u)$ **do**
            if relax(u, v) was successful **then**
                Add v to Q'
            end if
        end for
    end for
    $Q, Q' = Q', \{\}$
end while
return d, π

$\Theta(k \cdot l^2)$ because there are exactly l^2 edges between the layers L^j and L^{j+1} in the graph. If we rewrite it in terms of size of the graph, we would get $\Theta(m)$. Or, in other words, $\Theta(H \cdot \frac{m}{H})$, $H = H(G_{k,l}, v_1^1)$. To see more clearly that the upper bound actually decreases, let's consider graph $(k-1) = l$. Then time complexity will be $\Theta(H \cdot m^{2/3})$.

2.4 Performance Comparison

The performance of parallel SSSP implementation is usually compared with the performance of a sequential algorithm for the graphs of different sizes. GPU-based parallel solutions, e.g. [23], should not be considered for our purposes as their performance is bounded by relatively large CPU - GPU data transmission latency, which is rarely taken into account while comparing the published performance improvements due to the parallelization.

Table 2. Performance of parallel algorithms, p is the number of cores

Algorithm	Year	Nodes	Performance	Limitations
Parallel Bidirectional, e.g. [27]	2010	~100k	2–7 over A*	SSSD A*-like; 2 cores only
Parallel Ripple Search [3]	2011	~100k	2–10 over A*	SSSD A*-like;
Parallel Dial's [26]	1995	Theory	–	Large p
GPU based, e.g. [13]	2019	30k	~5	Large p, GPU
Δ-stepping [7]	2021			
ρ-stepping [7]	2021		1.3–2.6	

We collected some performance results for different algorithms in Table 2. The performance was normally measured on web, social, or road graphs of different sizes. A*-like algorithms, which use heuristics for the graphs embedded into coordinate plane [12], work relatively fast for the planar graphs of highways although they are not applicable to the real networks. Dial's algorithm provides the best possible theoretical running time $O(n)$, and a perfect parallelization $O(n/p)$, provided that the number of processors is large, i.e. $p = O(\sqrt{n}/\log n)$. Although the constant factor in O-notation appears to be significantly larger for Dial's than that of Dijkstra's algorithm. Our own Dial's algorithm implementations, for example, could not outperform an ordinary sequential Dijkstra's algorithm.

Δ-stepping is a promising candidate for a fast parallel algorithm. The main idea of is to explore independently the nodes grouped together according to different tentative distance ranges [5]. At each iteration, we can relax in parallel the outgoing edges from the nodes in the lowest range Δ-bucket [17]. Although we should take into account that the governing parameter Δ of the algorithm can significantly influence the performance of Δ-stepping and has to be chosen experimentally. The optimal value of the parameter Δ depends on the graph topology and the distribution of weights on the graph edges. The experiments with IP Radio Access Network (IPRAN) and Fat Tree topology graphs indicate that the larger the parameter Δ the faster the code runs. For very large Δ the algorithm mimics the behavior of the classical Bellman-Ford algorithm. Therefore we could use Bellman-Ford algorithm directly and possibly obtain an additional performance improvement due to the elimination of unnecessary in our case Δ-stepping specific operations.

Dijkstra's algorithm is faster, though Bellman-Ford's is better to paralellize. Taking into account relatively small graph sizes we are interested in, it may be beneficial to optimize the simplest algorithm for a specific topology.

3 Our Implementation of Bellman-Ford-Moore Algorithm

Our version of Bellman-Ford-Moore algorithm has been designed using the following optimizations:

1. We treat the edges at the frontier, where vertices distances are updated. This is basically the idea of Bellman-Ford-Moore algorithm.
2. We use bit arrays aligned in memory to track the next vertices to be updated. It reduces the number of cache misses for small graphs. With the growing of the number of vertices in the graph the bit arrays becomes large and more and more sparse. Large size of the arrays becomes the reason for the cache misses. So, starting from a certain size of graphs the advantage of bit arrays diminishes. For such a case we should use classical implementation of sets of hash tables instead of the bit arrays.
3. For the processor atomic operations we use builtin compiler function which implements hardware operation: *atomic bitwize or*.

A simplified version of C++ source code of our implementation of Bellman-Ford-Moore algorithm is presented at Fig. 2. We should note that the fast execution speed is mainly achieved due to the cache friendly usage of the aligned in memory bit arrays. It is quite possible that a different implementation might not provide a comparable performance.

```
flag=1;
while(true)
{
    uint64_t* current_edges_array  = edges_arrays[current_array];
    uint64_t* next_step_edges_array = edges_arrays[next_array];

    for(size_t block_number = 0; block_number < num_blocks; ++block_number)
    {
        register uint64_t block=current_edges_array[block_number];

        if(block == 0) continue;

        int end_pos = ((block_number << 6) < num_vertices) ? 64 : (num_vertices & 63);

        for(int block_pos=0; block_pos < end_pos; ++block_pos)
        {
            if(!(block & ((uint64_t)1 << block_pos))) continue;

            vertex_number_t source_vertex= (block_number << 6) + block_pos;

            const Vertex &vertex = (*adjacency_list)[source_vertex];

            size_t num_neighbours=vertex.num_edges();
            for(size_t i=0; i < num_neighbours; ++i)
            {
                Weight_vertex_pair dest = vertex.get_neighbour(i);
                vertex_number_t dest_vertex=dest.vertex;

                if(nodes_path[dest_vertex].distance > nodes_path[source_vertex].distance + dest.weight)
                {    // update the distance to the vertex
                    nodes_path[dest_vertex].distance = nodes_path[source_vertex].distance + dest.weight;
                    nodes_path[dest_vertex].previous=source_vertex;
                    next_step_edges_array[dest_vertex >> 6] |= ((uint64_t)1 << (dest_vertex & 63));
                    flag=1;
                }
            }// end of the loop through the neighbours
        }// end of the loop through the positons inside the block
    }// end of the loop through the blocks

    if(flag == 0) // finish the algorithm
        return;
    else
    {    // swap the auxiliary bit arrays
        memset(current_edges_array, 0, alloc_size);
        next_array     = current_array;
        current_array = (current_array+1) % 2;
        flag = 0;
    }
}
```

two auxiliary bit arrays "current" and "next":

allocated in blocks of size 64 bits

loop through the "current" bit array and try to update the distances for the nodes which bit is set to 1

list of neighbors for each node:

if some distance was updated, mark the correspondent bit in the "next" array and set the flag to continue

"current" ←→ "next"

Fig. 2. Simplified C++ source code of our implementation of the algorithm.

In order to speed up the algorithm while keeping its memory access pattern simple, in a multi-threaded system with a shared memory, we distribute the located in the shared memory auxiliary bit arrays among the threads. Namely, the blocks of size of 64 bits are distributed in a round robin fashion among a predefined number of threads. We use standard POSIX pthread library and GNU C++ compiler for our implementation. Synchronization is done after each Bellman-Ford-Moore outer loop iteration using pthread mutex primitives. Swapping of the auxiliary bit arrays happens after all the threads finish their outer loop iteration. Updates of the tentative distances in the inner loop of the algorithm are performed with __atomic_or_fetch built-in GCC function without inter-thread ordering constraints, i.e. using __ATOMIC_RELAXED memory order.

3.1   The Baseline for the Performance Comparison

We choose several baselines to compare our implementation with. First of all, we use single core implementation of the SSSP algorithm from the Boost Graph Library. In addition, as it is a usual practice, we measure a parallel algorithm performance relative to a single core implementation of the same algorithm. Finally, we have implemented Dijkstra's SSSP algorithm using C++ standard library priority_queue. It shows nearly the same performance as the Boost Graph Library SSSP algorithm implementation.

It should be noted that the parallel codes should create threads to run in parallel. For small graphs ($\sim$1000 nodes) the creation of the threads takes longer than Dijkstra's algorithm implementation runtime (Table 3). Even if some "perfect parallel algorithm" is ideally parallelizable, i.e. it runs 2 times faster with 2 cores, the running time for such an ideal algorithm would be $0.02 + 0.12/2 = 0.08$ ms and the maximum performance improvement for that ideal algorithm would be $0.12/0.08 = 1.5$. In reality, additional time is required for the communications between the threads, locks, etc., as well as for the calculations themselves. Clearly, parallelization cannot improve the performance for the small graphs. The creation of the threads takes too much time. Although if we assume that some SPT computing process has already started (and all the necessary threads are already created) we could ask whether it is beneficial to use parallel algorithm for small graphs. Thus, we modify our second baseline (standard library priority queue Dijkstra) so we could neglect the thread creation time. Namely, we run sequential Dijkstra's SSSP at the same amount of threads the parallel code does.

Table 3. Creation time of the threads in comparison with single thread Dijkstra's SSSP algorithm running time for IPRAN graph with 2200 nodes (Intel Core i7-8700 CPU @ 3.20 GHz processor with 6 cores)

Number of threads	Treads creation time, ms	SSSP time, ms
2	0.02	0.12
4	0.04	
8	0.12	

Thus, our baselines are:

1. Boost Library sequential SSSP
2. Single core version of our algorithm
3. Sequential SSSP running in multi-threaded environment.

3.2 Results

We test the performance of the optimized parallel Bellman-Ford-Moore algorithm implementation for IPRAN, generated according to the description below with the core structure taken from the NetworkX Python library Autonomous System network generator [8]; K-ary Fat Tree network, e.g. [20]; and for a random network topology, where the average node degree was set to 20. In all the above cases, the weights on the graph edges were uniformly randomly chosen in the range of 100–1000.

Figure 3 presents the basic structure of IPRAN topology. Generally, IPRAN has a closely connected structure of aggregation nodes and a lot of rings. Statistically, the number of aggregation nodes in the graph is about 10% while the number of access nodes is about 90%. Each ring generally has 20–40 nodes, although rings of size up to 200 nodes could also exist.

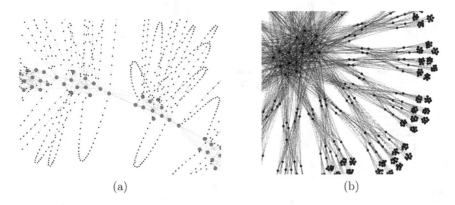

(a)   (b)

Fig. 3. (a) Typical fragment of IPRAN graph. Aggregation nodes are shown in red. (b) A fragment of a K-ary Fat Tree graph. (Color figure online)

For the tests we used a dedicated Intel(R) Core(TM) i7-8700 CPU @ 3.20 GHz with L1d/L1i/L2/L3 cache sizes: 192K/192K/1.5M/12M respectively.

Figure 4 presents the performance results of the optimized Bellman-Ford-Moore algorithm implementation for the graphs of size 2000–10000 nodes for IPRAN and Fat Tree topology respectively. In addition, we present the results for the large graphs of random topology of size 50000–500000 nodes (Fig. 5). Average node degree for our random graphs is ~20.

The tests show the performance improvement of 4 to 9 times for the networks of IPRAN and Fat Tree topology of size of 2000–10000 nodes respectively. It should be noted that the best possible performance improvement has been obtained for a single core optimized Bellman-Ford-Moore algorithm implementation. Network graphs with ~10000 nodes are too small for the parallelization to be useful (Fig. 4). From another hand, for the graphs of size more than 50000 nodes we can observe the performance improvement due to the parallelization (Fig. 5).

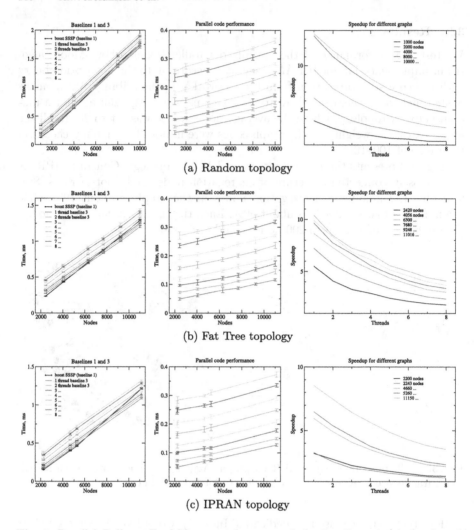

(a) Random topology

(b) Fat Tree topology

(c) IPRAN topology

Fig. 4. Parallel Bellman-Ford-Moore performance: Left: Baselines 1 (single thread Boost Graph Lib SSSP) and baseline 3 (Dijkstra's SSSP with thread creation time added). Center: Parallel code performance. Right: Parallel code performance improvement relative to the baseline 3 (sequential SSSP in multi-threaded environment) for the different number of threads.

4   Discussion

Asymptotic runtime superiority of Dijkstra algorithm over Bellman-Ford-Moore is not in doubt. However, the number of machine code instructions in Bellman-Ford-Moore implementation is less than that in Dijkstra. In addition, the structures used in the Bellman-Ford-Moore implementation use a significantly smaller amount of memory than those for Dijkstra. We believe that it is these arguments that should underlie the paradigm for developing parallel algorithms for the

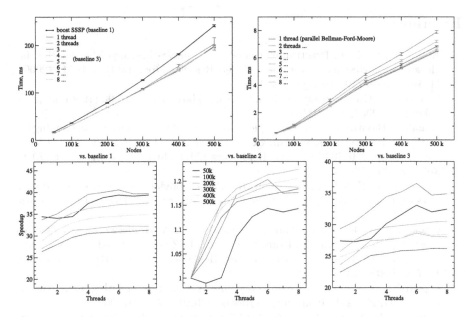

Fig. 5. Parallel Bellman-Ford-Moore performance for large graphs of 50000–500000 nodes. Speed up is shown relative to all three baselines: (1) Boost Library SSSP, (2) single thread version, and (3) sequential multi-threaded SSSP.

graphs of practical size. Although it should also be noted that multi-threading environment does not provide performance improvement for the already fast, if compared to standard Dijkstra's SSSP, and memory efficient Bellman-Ford-Moore parallel implementation.

5   Conclusion

The tests show the performance improvement of 4–9 times for our Bellman-Ford-Moore implementation over baseline Dijkstra's SSSP for the networks of IPRAN and Fat Tree topology of size of 2000–10000 nodes respectively. Thus, despite the theoretical superiority of Dijkstra's algorithm in terms of asymptotic behavior, hidden constants as well as implementation and execution features on modern processors lead to the fact that Bellman-Ford-Moore, as an algorithm which uses compact cache friendly data structures, works much faster for the graphs of practical size.

References

1. Asano, Y., Imai, H.: Practical efficiency of the linear-time algorithm for the single source shortest path problem. J. Oper. Res. Soc. Jpn. **43**(4), 431–447 (2000). https://doi.org/10.15807/jorsj.43.431
2. Bellman, R.: On a routing problem. Q. Appl. Math. **16**(1), 87–90 (1958). https://doi.org/10.1090/qam/102435
3. Brand, S., Bidarra, R.: Parallel ripple search – scalable and efficient pathfinding for multi-core architectures. In: Allbeck, J.M., Faloutsos, P. (eds.) MIG 2011. LNCS, vol. 7060, pp. 290–303. Springer, Heidelberg (2011). https://doi.org/10.1007/978-3-642-25090-3_25
4. Brodal, G.S., Fagerberg, R., Jacob, R.: Cache oblivious search trees via binary trees of small height. BRICS Rep. Ser. (36) (2001). https://doi.org/10.7146/brics.v8i36.21696
5. Crauser, A., Mehlhorn, K., Meyer, U., Sanders, P.: A parallelization of Dijkstra's shortest path algorithm. In: Brim, L., Gruska, J., Zlatuška, J. (eds.) MFCS 1998. LNCS, vol. 1450, pp. 722–731. Springer, Heidelberg (1998). https://doi.org/10.1007/BFb0055823
6. Dijkstra, E.W., et al.: A note on two problems in connexion with graphs. Numer. Math. **1**(1), 269–271 (1959). https://doi.org/10.1007/bf01386390
7. Dong, X., Gu, Y., Sun, Y., Zhang, Y.: Efficient stepping algorithms and implementations for parallel shortest paths. In: Proceedings of the 33rd ACM Symposium on Parallelism in Algorithms and Architectures. ACM (2021). https://doi.org/10.1145/3409964.3461782
8. Elmokashfi, A., Kvalbein, A., Dovrolis, C.: On the scalability of BGP: the role of topology growth. IEEE J. Sel. Areas Commun. **28**(8), 1250–1261 (2010). https://doi.org/10.1109/jsac.2010.101003
9. Ford, L.R., Jr.: Network flow theory. Technical report, Rand Corp Santa Monica Ca (1956)
10. Harish, P., Narayanan, P.J.: Accelerating large graph algorithms on the GPU using CUDA. In: Aluru, S., Parashar, M., Badrinath, R., Prasanna, V.K. (eds.) HiPC 2007. LNCS, vol. 4873, pp. 197–208. Springer, Heidelberg (2007). https://doi.org/10.1007/978-3-540-77220-0_21
11. Harish, P., Vineet, V., Narayanan, P.: Large graph algorithms for massively multi-threaded architectures. International Institute of Information Technology Hyderabad, Technical report IIIT/TR/2009/74 (2009)
12. Hart, P.E., Nilsson, N.J., Raphael, B.: A formal basis for the heuristic determination of minimum cost paths. IEEE Trans. Syst. Sci. Cybern. **4**(2), 100–107 (1968). https://doi.org/10.1109/tssc.1968.300136
13. Iacono, J., Karsin, B., Sitchinava, N.: A parallel priority queue with fast updates for gpu architectures. arXiv preprint arXiv:1908.09378 (2019)
14. Kumar, S., Misra, A., Tomar, R.S.: A modified parallel approach to single source shortest path problem for massively dense graphs using CUDA. In: 2011 2nd International Conference on Computer and Communication Technology (ICCCT-2011), pp. 635–639. IEEE (2011). https://doi.org/10.1109/iccct.2011.6075214
15. Ladner, R.E., Fortna, R., Nguyen, B.-H.: A comparison of cache aware and cache oblivious static search trees using program instrumentation. In: Fleischer, R., Moret, B., Schmidt, E.M. (eds.) Experimental Algorithmics. LNCS, vol. 2547, pp. 78–92. Springer, Heidelberg (2002). https://doi.org/10.1007/3-540-36383-1_4

16. Martín, P.J., Torres, R., Gavilanes, A.: CUDA solutions for the SSSP problem. In: Allen, G., Nabrzyski, J., Seidel, E., van Albada, G.D., Dongarra, J., Sloot, P.M.A. (eds.) ICCS 2009. LNCS, vol. 5544, pp. 904–913. Springer, Heidelberg (2009). https://doi.org/10.1007/978-3-642-01970-8_91

17. Meyer, U., Sanders, P.: δ-stepping: a parallelizable shortest path algorithm. J. Algorithms **49**(1), 114–152 (2003). https://doi.org/10.1016/s0196-6774(03)00076-2

18. Moore, E.F.: The shortest path through a maze. In: 1959 Proceedings of the International Symposium on Switching Theory, pp. 285–292 (1959)

19. Papaefthymiou, M., Rodrigue, J.: Implementing parallel shortest-paths algorithms. DIMACS Ser. Discrete Math. Theoret. Comput. Sci. **30**, 59–68 (1997). https://doi.org/10.1090/dimacs/030/04

20. Petrini, F., Vanneschi, M.: K-ary n-trees: high performance networks for massively parallel architectures. In: Proceedings of the 11th International Symposium on Parallel Processing, IPPS 1997, p. 87. IEEE Computer Society, USA (1997). https://doi.org/10.1109/ipps.1997.580853

21. Sakumoto, Y., Ohsaki, H., Imase, M.: Performance of thorup's shortest path algorithm for large-scale network simulation. IEICE Trans. Commun. **E95.B**(5), 1592–1601 (2012). https://doi.org/10.1587/transcom.E95.B.1592

22. Sneyers, J., Schrijvers, T., Demoen, B.: Dijkstra's algorithm with Fibonacci heaps: an executable description in CHR. In: Proceedings of the 20th Workshop on Logic Programming, vol. 1843, pp. 182–191. Technische Universität Wien, Austria (2006)

23. Surve, G.G., Shah, M.A.: Parallel implementation of bellman-ford algorithm using CUDA architecture. In: 2017 International Conference of Electronics, Communication and Aerospace Technology (ICECA), vol. 2, pp. 16–22. IEEE (2017). https://doi.org/10.1109/iceca.2017.8212794

24. Tang, Y., Zhang, Y., Chen, H.: A parallel shortest path algorithm based on graph-partitioning and iterative correcting. In: 2008 10th IEEE International Conference on High Performance Computing and Communications, pp. 155–161. IEEE (2008). https://doi.org/10.1109/hpcc.2008.113

25. Thorup, M.: Undirected single-source shortest paths with positive integer weights in linear time. J. ACM **46**(3), 362–394 (1999). https://doi.org/10.1145/316542.316548

26. Tsitsiklis, J.N.: Efficient algorithms for globally optimal trajectories. IEEE Trans. Autom. Control **40**(9), 1528–1538 (1995). https://doi.org/10.1109/9.412624

27. Vaira, G., Kurasova, O.: Parallel bidirectional Dijkstra's shortest path algorithm. Databases Inf. Syst. VI Front. Artif. Intell. Appl. **224**, 422–435 (2011)

Full-Scale Simulation of the Super C-Tau Factory Computing Infrastructure to Determine the Characteristics of the Necessary Hardware

Dmitry Wiens[1]([✉]) [iD], Igor Chernykh[1] [iD], and Ivan Logashenko[2] [iD]

[1] Institute of Computational Mathematics and Mathematical Geophysics of Siberian Branch of Russian Academy of Science, Novosibirsk, Russian Federation
vins@sscc.ru, chernykh@ssd.sscc.ru
[2] Budker Institute of Nuclear Physics of Siberian Branch Russian Academy of Sciences (BINP SB RAS), Novosibirsk, Russian Federation

Abstract. This paper presents the results of a full-scale simulation of the computing infrastructure for data storage and processing from the Super C-Tau Factory installation. The simulation model of the computing system implements models of the expected data flows and tasks, and also takes into account the characteristics of the modern hardware. The simulation of this system work in the mode of unlimited resources is carried out. The maximum amount of computing resources for processing experimental data is determined based on this simulation. There are also defined requirements for the data storage system – the required system bandwidth and its volume.

Keywords: C-Tau factory · HPC design · Simulation modeling

1 Introduction

Numerical simulation of high-energy physics experiments plays an important role in optimization of different parameters of experiment's hardware from detectors to high-performance storage and data analysis [1–6]. One of the most important role in modern high energy physics experiments plays high-performance data storage and data analysis facility. In our research, as for the ATLAS experiment, we describe a solution that enables execution of CPU intensive simulation workloads on HPC systems, addressing specifically the following challenges: workload management, input data provisioning and output data retrieval [7]. These challenges play the most important role in simulation of HPC system workload [8–10]. The Super-C-Tau Factory (SCTF) project was among the winners in the competition of Russian mega-science installations in 2011. The installation will be an electron-positron collider of ultra-high luminosity. The factory includes a unique acceleration and storage complex and a universal elementary particle detector. The letters C and Tau in the name means that precision measurements of the parameters of fundamental particles born in the energy range from 2 to 6 GeV will be carried out at the collider. Such particles primarily include the tau-lepton and the «charmed» quark (c-quark) [11].

To imagine the scale of the computing infrastructure of the future factory, one can imagine that in an experiment beams of electrons and positrons moving at great speed collide 100–200 million times every second, and particles born in these collisions are registered by a detector. During the experiments, hundreds of petabytes of raw data will be read from the elementary particle detector. They need to be preserved, processed, analyzed, highlighting in trillions of events a dozen that deserve close study.

In order to cope with the expected data flow, 10–100 thousand copies of the data modeling and analysis program are planned to work simultaneously at the Super-C-Tau factory. A feature of the computing system for storing and processing data from the Super S-Tau Factory detector is a very large volume of initial data, relatively low computational complexity of their reconstruction, but serious computational complexity of data modeling and analysis (Fig. 1). Huge volumes of raw data require significant investments in the creation of a localized computing infrastructure of the complex.

It is possible to carry out an appropriate design of such computing infrastructure using simulation modeling methods. The model of high-performance computing system (HPC system) will help to understand how processing tasks are started, what resources the system will consume, what data flows are needed. As a result of the simulation, it will be possible to estimate the structure and volumes of data in advance, as well as to determine the parameters and configuration of the computational infrastructure necessary to solve the problems of the experiment.

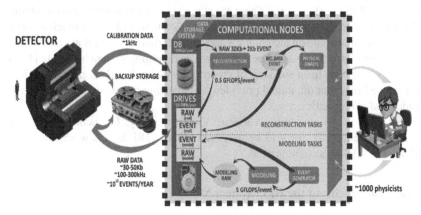

Fig. 1. Description of the project HPC system

2 Full-Scale Simulation of the Super C-Tau Factory Computing Infrastructure

A detailed process of developing and analyzing complex systems of large size, which in particular include modern computing systems, is impossible using only mathematical models. The complex nature of control algorithms and the stochastic nature of incoming data flows and jobs makes it necessary to perform simulation modeling of such systems [12].

Like any research method simulation modeling has advantages and disadvantages that manifest themselves in specific applications. The main advantages of the simulation modeling method in the study of complex systems include the following: a machine experiment with a simulation model makes it possible to investigate the features of the system functioning process in any conditions; using computer in a simulation experiment significantly reduces the duration of tests compared to a real experiment; the simulation model allows you to include real system tests results or its parts for further research; the simulation model has a known flexibility of varying the structure, algorithms and parameters of the simulated system, which is important from the point of view for finding the optimal variant of the system; simulation modeling of complex systems is often the only practically feasible method of studying the process of functioning of such systems at the stage of their design.

The main disadvantage of the simulation modeling method is that the solution obtained by analyzing the simulation model is always having a private nature, since it corresponds to fixed elements of the structure, behavior algorithms and system parameters values, initial conditions and environmental influences. Therefore, for a comprehensive analysis of the whole process of systems operation, and not obtaining only a single point, it is necessary to repeatedly reproduce the simulation experiment, varying the initial data. At the same time, as a consequence, there is an increase in the cost of machine time for conducting an experiment with a simulation model.

This approach to the HPC centers design and analysis for commercial and scientific projects is used all over the world. There are many approaches to simulation modeling of HPC systems: modeling to create energy-efficient systems [13, 14], modeling systems based on preliminary data on the volumes and characteristics of data flows and jobs [15], modeling to optimize the cost and performance of computing system hardware [16], etc. In our work, we start from the idea of creating a system based on previously known data flows and jobs, but the model provides for balancing resources, and ensuring fault tolerance and energy efficiency.

There are various simulation software tools for today, for example: for cluster computing systems [17], for grid systems and clouds [18]. In this work, the AGNES multi-agent modeling system is used.

2.1   General Scheme of the HPC System Model

There are multiple opportunities presented by the AGNES multi-agent system: not only it can be applied to develop an HPC system model, but it also turns out to be quite efficient for modeling telecommunication networks, running a distributed control system, and executing high-performance parallel programs [19, 20]. The previously developed computer system (CS) model described in [21] serves as a basis for the HPC system model for SCTF. It is comprised of several models: that of computing nodes (CN agents), that of a hierarchical control system (whose components are Commutator, Statistical analysis, Collector, and Controller agents), and, finally, that of a data storage system (Data storage agents). The multi-agent model of the HPC system is schematically illustrated in Fig. 2.

The entire set of objects presented in the schematic are intelligent agents having their own sets of parameters and behavior algorithms.

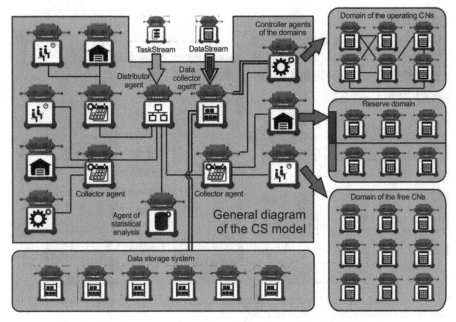

Fig. 2. Visual representation of the multi-agent model of the HPC system

During the modeling process, agents implement their specific tasks and exchange with each other through specialized messages (Fig. 3). To generate both data flows and tasks, the model has specialized agents of input currents. Their setup is always unique for each model experiment. Agents of computing nodes simulate the actions of real computing nodes, executing their thread of a parallel program or being in standby mode. Agents controllers organize the correct operation and control over the state of the hardware and software of the computational nodes under their control. The collector agent acts as a task scheduler for the HPC system. Collector, schedules the tasks received for execution, organizes their execution, and also participates in the load balancing process. Commutator agents distribute the flow of tasks that have come to solve between the clusters under its control, Statistical analyzes agents process and store statistics on already solved tasks. This statistic helps planning the execution of tasks. Data controller agents simulates work of data storage system.

This article [22] describes the operation and interaction algorithms of these intelligent agents in order to simulate the system operation.

2.2 Preparing for Modeling and Setting Up the Model

According to preliminary estimates of data flows and tasks, their models were set up as follows:

A stream of raw data (RAW) and calibration data (KALIBR) is sent from the SFTF detector to the storage. Calibration data is received at a frequency of 1 kHz. The typical raw data flow of detector is 100 kHz of events, but when operating at energies near J/psi

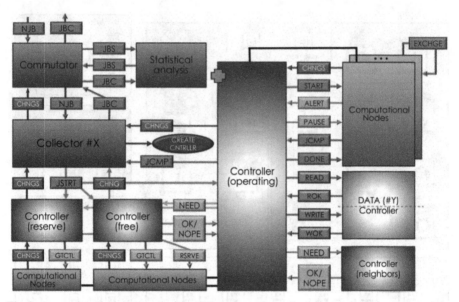

Fig. 3. Interaction between the intelligent agents occurring in the course of simulation of the operation of the computational infrastructure.

mesone (3.1 GeV), the flow can grow up to 300 kHz. The size of one «raw» event is 30 Kbytes.

The task queue receives tasks of event reconstruction (RECO), experimental data modeling (MOD) and data comparison (CMPR). Reconstruction tasks are started automatically when 100,000 events are set in the storage for their processing, have a computational complexity of 0.5 GFLOPs/event, and at the end they write the reconstructed events (RECO) into memory. The size of one reconstructed event is 2 Kbytes. Experimental data modeling tasks are run with a certain probability (Pmod), have no input data, generate «raw» model data (MRAW) and have a computational complexity of 5 GFLOPs/event. Data comparison tasks simulate reading and comparing RAW and MRAW sequences.

Previously, the processing of such data flows and tasks was simulated on the model of the existing NKS-1P cluster of the SSCC SB RAS [23], which showed that the resources of this cluster are insufficient for the project purposes.

This paper describes the results of modeling a full-scale computing infrastructure to assess the requirements for equipment from above, i.e. the maximum amount of computing resources and data storage that can be required for the operation of the SCTF was estimated. Therefore, when data or tasks entered the model that lacked resources for processing and storage, these resources were additionally created automatically.

2.3 Determination of Computing Hardware Parameters

It is necessary to configure the model in accordance with the flow of tasks and the current state of technology to determine the number and parameters of computing hardware.

Since the task flow is characterized by a high degree of parallelism with virtually no data exchanges between computing processes, a cluster architecture with homogeneous computing nodes was chosen for the HPC system. The tasks are also optimized for execution on a classical processor, so the models of computing nodes assume the absence of co-processors. A modern node with a capacity of 6.3 TFlops equipped with two scalable processors of the 3rd generation Intel Xeon 8368Q (2.6 GHz, 38 cores) is considered as a computational node. Considering that the amount of RAM of one node (DDR4–3200, up to 512 GB) can be expanded with Intel Optane Pmem up to 4 TB, we believe that it will contain data for the operation of any of the incoming tasks entirely.

Several model experiments simulating a month of the system operation were performed with different startup parameters. Two modes of operation of the detector were considered: with a frequency of 100 kHz and 300 kHz with different probabilities of tasks. Since it is assumed that reconstruction tasks are started automatically when a certain amount of data is accumulated, we need to determine the frequency of occurrence of the remaining tasks. The probability of comparison tasks appearing in the task stream at each second of the model time was set to 2%, for modeling tasks Pmod was selected as 5.10 and 20%, respectively. In the graph shown in Fig. 4 you can observe how the number of computing nodes changed for different startup parameters.

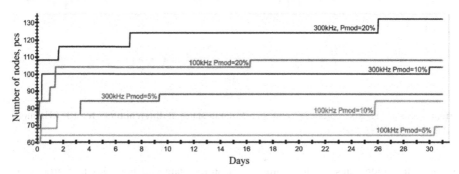

Fig. 4. Amount of computing nodes for different startup parameters

As can be seen on the graph, the required number of nodes directly depends on both the operating mode and the number of incoming modeling tasks. The maximum performance of the HPC system of SCTF at the same time is ~600 TFLOPs. However, as can be seen from the graphs of the average relative number of nodes in different states (Fig. 5), about half (in 300 kHz mode) or 70% (in 100 kHz mode) of the nodes are simply idle. Therefore, to determine the optimal number of computing nodes, it will be necessary to conduct additional model experiments with limited resources in a known range (70–110 nodes).

2.4   Determination of Data Storage System Parameters

A data storage system model is a set of Data storage agents/ Each of these agents simulates the process of recording a certain type of data (raw, calibration, reconstructed,

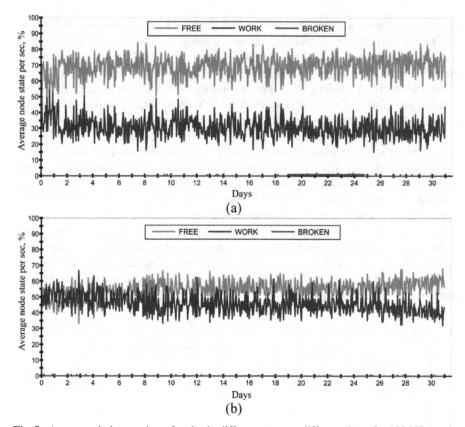

Fig. 5. Average relative number of nodes in different states at different times for 100 kHz mode (a) and for 300 kHz mode (b)

model, etc.), calculates the total amount of stored data and manages this process in accordance with a given bandwidth (Fig. 6). Since in these model experiments there are no limited resources, then in this case they just count the number of data read and written per second. And to configure the the storage system model, the characteristics of the programmatically defined Distributed Asynchronous Object Storage (DAOS) were used. DAOS servers store their metadata in permanent memory, whereas large data is written directly to NVMe SSD. Additionally, small-volume data of I/O operations can be accumulated in permanent memory, then aggregated and only then transferred to more capacious flash drives. Thus, the time to access data can be reduced several times and reach the order of microseconds instead of the usual milliseconds, and the speed of write/read operations is about 50 Gb/sec [24].

Figure 7 shows the information of various agents of the data storage system work for a model experiment for 100 kHz mode (Pmod = 20%). As you can see in the graphs presented, the required volume of data storage system will be 17 Pbytes to store the result of a month of installation work, while the bandwidth of such a system should be at least 8 Gb/s. It should be noted that most of the stored data is raw data.

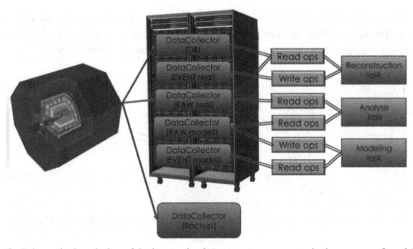

Fig. 6. Schematic description of the interaction between storage agents in the process of modeling the operation of storage systems

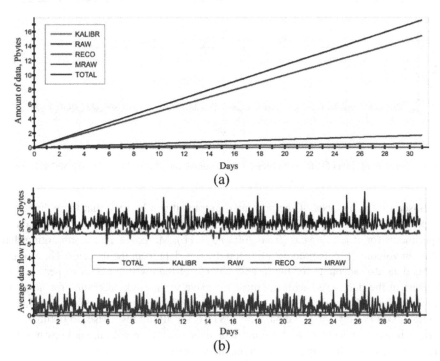

Fig. 7. Amount of data of different types (a) and average data flow per sec (b) for 100 kHz mode

Figure 8 shows the information of various agents of the data storage system work for a model experiment for 300 kHz mode (Pmod = 20%). As you can see in the graphs presented, the required volume of data storage system will be a colossal 48 Pbytes to store the result of an only month of installation work, while the bandwidth of such a system should be at least 20 Gb/s. As with the modeling of the previous mode, the main stored data remains raw data, but here this difference is more pronounced.

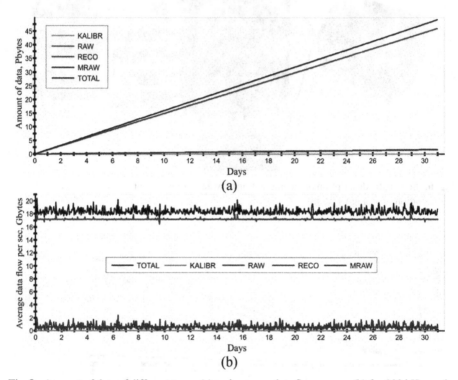

Fig. 8. Amount of data of different types (a) and average data flow per sec (b) for 300 kHz mode

Based on the analysis of the presented graphs, it can be seen that the volumes of the projected data storage system must be really huge in order to store all the data of experiments for at least a year (from 200 to 576 Pb). Moreover, it is worth noting that the main volume of the stored data falls on the raw data from the detector. The storage of this data also accounts for the largest volume of read/write operations per second. The rest of the data, even with the most intensive work mode, accounts for no more than 2–3 Gb/sec. Therefore, it may be worth using different systems for storing data, for example, DAOS only for raw data and LUSTRE for all the rest. Also, to optimize the storage, it may be necessary to store raw data in the storage only for the last few months, and store the rest in backup storage on magnetic tapes.

3   Conclusion

To determine the maximum amount of computing resources and the necessary characteristics of a data storage system for a high-performance computing system serving SCTF, a full-scale simulation of such a system with unlimited resources was carried out. In this simulation, the parameters of data flows and tasks received by the system, as well as the characteristics of modern hardware, were considered.

Model experiments have shown that from 70 to 100 modern computing nodes with performance of about 600TFLOPs are needed for the full operation of the system. However, with this approach, the system's performance is consumed inefficiently, because there is a large percentage of idle nodes. Therefore, in continuation of this work, additional modeling with a limited amount of resources is needed to determine the optimal number of computing nodes (with an acceptable execution latency).

The parameters for the data storage system were also defined. It is necessary to use solutions that allows to organize the storage of hundreds of petabytes of data and a bandwidth from 5 to 20 Gb/s. It is also reasonable to use a combination of different distributed data storage systems for the most efficient use of it.

Acknowledgements. The work was funded by the Russian Science Foundation (Grant No. 19-72-20114). Resources of the Siberian Supercomputer Center cluster (ICM&MG SB RAS, Novosibirsk) were used to conduct model experiments.

References

1. Morais, A.P., Moretti, S., Pasechnik, R.: Phenomena beyond the standard model: what do we expect for new physics to look like? Front. Phys. **8**, 209 (2020)
2. Beacham, J., et al.: Physics beyond colliders at CERN: beyond the standard model working group report. J. Phys. G: Nucl. Part. Phys. **47**(1), 010501 (2019)
3. Apollinari, G., Bejar Alonso, I., Bruning, O., Lamont, M., Rossi, L.: High-Luminosity Large Hadron Collider (HL-LHC): preliminary design report. CERN-2015- 005, FERMILAB-DESIGN-2015-02 (2015)
4. Wolfgang, L.: Fast simulation for ATLAS: Atlfast-II and ISF. J. Phys. Conf. Ser. **396**(2), 022031 (2012)
5. Hariri, A., Dyachkova, D., Gleyzer, S.: Graph variational autoencoder for detector reconstruction and fast simulation in high-energy physics. In: EPJ Web Conference, vol. 251, p. 03051 (2021)
6. Bird, I., et al.: Update of the computing models of the WLCG and the LHC experiments. CERN, Switzerland (2014)
7. Haug, S., Hostettler, M., Sciacca, F.G., Weber, M., ATLAS Collaboration: The ATLAS ARC backend to HPC. J. Phys. Conf. Ser. **664**, 062057 (2015)
8. Bird, I.: Computing for the large hadron collider. Annu. Rev. Nucl. Part. Sci. **61**, 99–118 (2011)
9. Robertson, L.: Computing service for LHC: from clusters to grids. In: Brun, R., Carminati, F., Carminati, G.G. (eds.) From the Web to the Grid and Beyond, Computing Paradigms Driven by High Energy Physics. Springer, Heidelberg (2012). https://doi.org/10.1007/978-3-642-23157-5_3
10. Bird, I., et al.: Update of the computing models of the WLCG and the LHC experiments. CERN-LHCC-2014-014 (2014)
11. Bondar, A.: Project of a super charm-tau factory at the Budker Institute of Nuclear Physics in Novosibirsk. Phys. At. Nucl. **76**, 1072–1085 (2013)

12. Law, A.M., Kelton, W.D.: Simulation Modeling and Analysis, 2nd edn. McGraw-Hill, New York (1991)
13. Forshaw, M., Thomas, N., McGough, A.S.: Trace-driven simulation for energy consumption in high throughput computing systems. In: Proceedings of the 2014 IEEE/ACM 18th International Symposium on Distributed Simulation and Real Time Applications (DS-RT) (2014)
14. Borghesi, A., et al.: Pricing schemes for energy-efficient HPC systems: design and exploration. Int. J. High Perform. Comput. Appl. **33**, 716–734 (2019)
15. Korenkov, V., Nechaevskiy, A., Ososkov, G., Priakhina, D., Trofimov, V.: A probabilistic approach to the simulation of data processing centers. In: EPJ Web Conference, vol. 226 (2020). Article Number 03012
16. Wienke, S.: Productivity and software development effort estimation in high-performance computing. Dissertation, RWTH Aachen University (2017)
17. Zheng, G., Kakulapati, G., Kalé, L.V.: BigSim: a parallel simulator for performance prediction of extremely large parallel machines. In: Proceedings of the 18th International Parallel and Distributed Processing Symposium, p. 78 (2004)
18. Korenkov, V.V., Muravev, A.N., Nechaevskij, A.V.: Pakety modelirovaniya oblachnyh infrastruktur. Sistemnyj analiz v nauke i obrazovanii, Dubna (2014). № 2
19. Glinskiy, B.M., Kulikov, I.M., Chernykh, I.G., Snytnikov, A.V., Sapetina, A.F., Weins, D.V.: The integrated approach to solving large-size physical problems on supercomputers. In: CCIS, vol. 793, pp. 278–289 (2017). https://doi.org/10.1007/978-3-319-71255-0_22
20. Wiens, D.: Analysis of the effectiveness of the task flow control system for the SCC in a multi-agent simulation model. Vestnik NSU **12**(2), 33–41 (2014)
21. Wiens, D., Glinskiy, B., Rodionov, A.: Investigation of control processes in supercomputer systems based on multi-agent modeling. Vestnik SibSUTI **4**(28), 35–44 (2014)
22. Weins, D., Vorobyev, V., Chernykh, I., Logashenko, I.: Development of simulation model of HPC system for Super Charm-Tau factory. J. Phys. Conf. Ser. **1336** (2019). Article Number 012025
23. Wiens, D., Chernykh, I., Logashenko, I., Kolpakov, F., Vorobiev, V.: Simulation model of HPC system for Super Charm-Tau factory. In: CEUR Workshop Proceedings, vol. 3041, pp. 568–572 (2021)
24. Liang, Z., Lombardi, J., Chaarawi, M., Hennecke, M.: DAOS: a scale-out high performance storage stack for storage class memory. In: Panda, D.K. (ed.) SCFA 2020. LNCS, vol. 12082, pp. 40–54. Springer, Cham (2020). https://doi.org/10.1007/978-3-030-48842-0_3

Overhead Analysis for Performance Monitoring Counters Multiplexing

Vadim Voevodin$^{(\boxtimes)}$, Konstantin Stefanov, and Sergey Zhumatiy

Lomonosov Moscow State University, Moscow, Russia
{vadim,cstef,serg}@parallel.ru

Abstract. To analyze the efficiency of supercomputer functioning, it is useful to collect information from performance monitoring counters available in all modern processors. However, the ability to obtain such data is very limited—usually no more than 4 counters can be accessed simultaneously. To overcome this, multiplexing technology can be used, which allows collecting more data thanks to switching between counters—at any time, data from a specific set of counters is collected, and such sets repeatedly alternate. However, the use of this technology comes at a price of growing overheads—the execution time of supercomputer applications increases. Unfortunately, this topic has not been sufficiently studied so far. In this paper, we have carried out a detailed analysis and comparison of overheads caused by three different variants of multiplexing implemented using PAPI and LIKWID libraries. The obtained results show that the average overhead is ∼3–5%, and manual multiplexing using LIKWID has the least impact.

Keywords: Supercomputing · Monitoring · Performance monitoring counters · Multiplexing · Overhead

1 Introduction

Modern supercomputers require constant monitoring and analysis of all its main components—compute nodes, service servers, file system, engineering infrastructure, etc. The lack of such control often leads to failures as well as a significant decrease in the overall performance of the supercomputer, therefore monitoring with varying degrees of detail is performed in all large supercomputing centers both in Russia [20] and around the world. One of the key solutions to provide such control is a system software for monitoring the state of compute nodes. And if the issue of basic monitoring of nodes reliability is generally solved in practice by existing monitoring systems like Zabbix [5] or Nagios [6], the efficiency of using computational resources is often not studied in detail.

To monitor the performance of compute nodes usage (which, in turn, is necessary to analyze the performance of supercomputer applications), data from various node sensors is most often collected, including performance monitoring

V. Voevodin et al. (Eds.): RuSCDays 2022, LNCS 13708, pp. 461–474, 2022.
https://doi.org/10.1007/978-3-031-22941-1_34

counters (PMC) available in all modern processors. These counters allow determining, for example, the frequency of memory accesses, L1 or LLC cache misses, the number of instructions executed, etc. At the same time, only a small number of such counters is usually collected in practice in most modern supercomputing centers. There are two reasons for this: 1) supercomputer administrators are far from always ready to pay great attention to the issues of application execution efficiency (which, in our opinion, is definitely worth doing), and therefore they do not need a lot of such data; 2) most processors allow simultaneously collecting a very limited number of counters (usually no more than 4).

However, the collection of a larger number of counters is possible through the use of multiplexing technology, and this allows you to get more useful information. For example, within the framework of the project aimed at creating a universal assessment system for analyzing the quality of supercomputer resources usage [18], estimates were proposed for analyzing the quality of using CPU and the memory subsystem. To calculate these estimates, 5 performance monitoring counters are needed (plus 3 more are needed for other metrics), and that requires multiplexing, which resulted in the study described in this paper. And these estimates, in our opinion, allow you to quickly and fairly accurately determine how efficient a particular job is, which is useful for the initial analysis of the job flow efficiency and allows identifying inefficient job launches even when the user himself is not yet aware that his job has a greatly reduced performance.

The main goal of this study is to organize constant PMC data collection in the multiplexing mode, in our case needed for analyzing the quality of supercomputer resources usage, for all jobs running on a supercomputer. One of the key challenges in this case is the evaluation and minimization of overheads that arise due to the use of multiplexing technology. We will evaluate overheads as an increase in the execution time of supercomputer applications.

The main contribution of this paper lies in the analysis of three different ways of implementing PMC multiplexing (using PAPI and LIKWID) and the evaluation of the resulting overheads. Such information is useful primarily for administrators and management of supercomputing centers who plan to implement detailed performance analysis of their systems. All work was carried out on the Lomonosov-2 supercomputer, however, the general idea and conclusions can be applied to other systems as well.

The rest of the paper is organized as follows. Section 2 briefly describes related works about collecting PMC data as well as studying accuracy and overhead of such collection process. In Sect. 3, details on the implementation of three different multiplexing variants are provided. Section 4 is devoted to the analysis and comparison of overheads caused in practice by these selected variants. Conclusions are made in Sect. 5.

2   Related Work

When performance monitoring counters were introduced in processors, an access to them required using low-level machine instructions. This approach was difficult to use and often required elevated (superuser) privileges. Moreover, it required using different commands or parameters for different processors, even in the same processor family like Pentium and Pentium Pro.

To ease using PMCs, several high-level libraries (and APIs) were introduced. One of the first was (now gone) Performance Counters Library [14]. It provided unified interface for using PMCs on several processors and OSes.

The PAPI (Performance Application Programming Interface [3]) is a well-known and widely used library for accessing PMCs and other sources of data related to the performance analysis. At the beginning it was a suite of user-level library and OS kernel modules to gain access to PMCs. Eventually most OSes used on HPC clusters got their own or borrowed interfaces, to access PMCs so PAPI authors could focus on user-level library only.

Another example of high-level library for accessing PMCs is LIKWID [17]. Its main distinction from PAPI is that PAPI first was aimed at getting performance data for the specific program and required inserting calls into the program. LIKWID, on the other hand, was designed for external monitoring, it reads PMCs from CPU cores regardless of which core the program runs on or whether it is running at all. Later PAPI got features to monitor all CPU cores and LIKWID got API to monitor a specific program only. But still the first design goals leave its mark on the way in which a specific library is easier to use.

The task of estimating overheads of performance monitoring is quite old. In paper [13] four different methods of obtaining information about a program performance are compared from the overhead viewpoint, and using PMCs was found as the least intrusive (having the least overhead) among all considered.

The fact that there is only a small number of registers that can be used for collecting PMCs leads to introducing multiplexing to overcome this restriction. At the best of our knowledge, first multiplexing implementation was described in [9]. It was a user-level implementation, in a sense that PMC switching was done in user space.

The next step to implement multiplexing was to make OS kernel to switch PMCs. Such approach was intruduced in [1] for K42 OS. At that moment PAPI was able to make multiplexing only in user space. One of the declared reasons for transferring multiplexing to kernel was reducing the overhead, but no overhead estimation is given in the paper. First mention of kernel-based multiplexing in Linux and support in user-level profiling tool Oprofile was given in [10].

The other related topic is estimating the accuracy and run-to-run variations of data obtained with PMCs. There are many papers on this topic, including the questions of obtaining PMC data in different modes and improving the accuracy, see [8,11,12,22].

There are several works that touch upon the overhead topic. An estimation of PMC monitoring overhead for three implementations in Linux was done in [21], where authors explore non-multiplexing modes. The paper [15] discusses LIK-WID overhead, which is measured in CPU cycles and compared to PAPI, but no comparison for multiplexing is given (which is not surprising because LIKWID did not support multiplexing at that moment).

The paper [4] discusses optimizations in counters scheduling in multiplexing modes. One of the declared goals of the work is reducing overhead, but the overhead itself is not measured. The paper discusses better (in particular, less resource consuming) scheduling algorithms, which helps to reduce overhead.

At the best of our knowledge, there are no works that compare overheads caused by collecting PMC data in multiplexing mode for different libraries or different modes.

3   Implementing Different Multiplexing Variants

We conducted our research on the Lomonosov-2 supercomputer [19]. This super-computer uses DiMMon [16] system for monitoring compute nodes. The general scheme for collecting and processing data in the DiMMon system is as follows (Fig. 1).

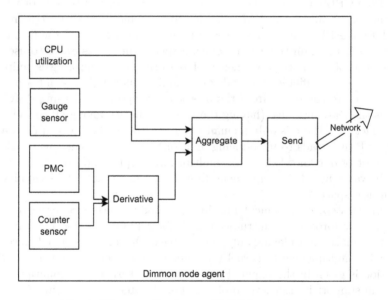

Fig. 1. The overall scheme of DiMMon node agent

Data collection is launched with a configured frequency (every 1 s as of now). At a certain moment all sensors (modules obtaining performance data) are called to acquire data. The output of modules which count events (like PMC) is sent to a module that counts time derivative. The output from the derivative module and gauge sensors (that give values ready to be consumed, like CPU utilization) is sent to the aggregation module. The output from the aggregation module is sent (e.g. every 1 min) over network to the central part of the monitoring system, which resides not on a compute node but on a dedicated server or virtual machine.

DiMMon is a modular solution, and collection of each data source is implemented within its own sensors module, which can be independently connected and configured. In this paper, we consider three different ways of multiplexing, which required implementation of three modules, while the rest of DiMMon remained virtually unchanged. The only thing that still needed to be done to implement each method of multiplexing (besides creating the module itself) was to edit the configuration file that specifies which modules to connect and how to transmit and process collected data.

Before proceeding to the description of the multiplexing methods themselves, several important remarks should be made:

- We need to collect data from 8 performance monitoring counters. The list of particular counters and their namings for PAPI and LIKWID are shown in Table 1. PAPI 5.6 and LIKWID 5.2.1 versions were used.
- All three DiMMon variants with different multiplexing methods work in the same way: they are started together with a job for which the overhead is evaluated (each job is launched in a standard way via Slurm), and they provide full and identical functionality in everything except the PMC module. Needed DiMMon variant is selected manually before the job launch.
- We measure the overhead as the percentage increase of application execution time, compared to using default DiMMon monitoring without multiplexing (data from only 4 PMCs are collected in this case). Our main goal is to keep the overhead as low as possible—the increase in execution time should be no more than a few percent.

Table 1. List of collected counters and their namings for PAPI and LIKWID

Counter description	PAPI naming	LIKWID naming
Number of instructions retired	PAPI_TOT_INS	INST_RETIRED_ANY_P
Core cycles when the thread is not in halt state	PAPI_TOT_CYC	CPU_CLOCK_UNHALTED_THREAD_P
L1D data line replacements	PAPI_L1_DCM	L1D_REPLACEMENT
Core-originated cacheable demand requests missed L3	PAPI_L3_TCM	LONGEST_LAT_CACHE_MISS
Retirement slots used	UOPS_RETIRED: RETIRE_SLOTS	UOPS_RETIRED_RETIRE_SLOTS
Core cycles when at least one thread on the physical core is not in halt state	CPU_CLK_UNHALTED:t=1	CPU_CLOCK_UNHALTED_THREAD_P_ANY
Execution stalls due to memory subsystem	CYCLE_ACTIVITY: STALLS_LDM_PENDING	CYCLE_ACTIVITY_STALLS_LDM_PENDING
Cycles stalled due to no store buffers available	RESOURCE_STALLS: SB	RESOURCE_STALLS_SB

It is important to mention that the experiments were conducted using our DiMMon monitoring system, however the overhead is not caused by the monitoring system itself but by the libraries for accessing PMC data (PAPI and LIKWID) as well as OS. Moreover, the overheads caused by default DiMMon version without multiplexing are very low [7]. So, the results achieved do not depend on the selected monitoring system and will be applicable when using other systems as well.

Next, we will describe how different multiplexing methods have been implemented.

3.1   Using PAPI with Automatic Multiplexing

First, we tried a variant using PAPI automatic multiplexing. In fact, this method is very simple to implement—it comes down to: 1) adding `PAPI_set_multiplex(EventSet)` call to the base module that implements PMC data collection without multiplexing; and 2) adding more events to the event set. After that PAPI (and Linux kernel `perf_event` subsystem) automatically starts to multiplex requested counters.

3.2   Using PAPI and LIKWID with Manual Multiplexing

Using PAPI and LIKWID with manual multiplexing involves changing event set which is acquired from the CPU on every data read. Generally, the frequency of event set change may not be equal to the frequency of data read, but we take them equal for simplicity. The pseudocode for manual multiplexing is given in Fig. 2.

In this code, on every data read we get the data for the current event set (which was started at previous data read). The values acquired for the event set are added to data accumulated since the start of the work. It is multiplied by the number of event sets as every event set is calculated only for the $1/n\_events$ part of time.

LIKWID and PAPI manual multiplexing modules differ only in the calls needed to configure an EventSet, to start/stop it and to acquire the data.

3.3   Comments on LIKWID Usage

Until the need of multiplexing, we always used PAPI for collecting processor counters, as it was enough for our purposes. But first experiments with PAPI multiplexing showed too high overheads, so we decided to try LIKWID as well. As mentioned before, LIKWID, unlike PAPI, was initially intended for HPC systems and for external monitoring, while PAPI was initially designed for the instrumentation-based analysis of a specific program. So there was an assumption that overheads should be generally lower in case of LIKWID.

We use LikwidAPI[1]—an API that enables simple usage of LIKWID from other applications. There are two major ways how you can access PMC data

---

[1] https://github.com/RRZE-HPC/likwid/wiki/LikwidAPI-and-MarkerAPI.

```
int n_eventset; // Number of eventsets
int n_event;    // Number of event in every set
uint64_t values[n_eventset][n_event];
uint64_t accum[n_events]; // accumulator for current eventset

values[][] = 0;

Start eventset0;

loop(on every data read) {
    Get data for current eventset to accum;
    Stop current eventset;
    for (e=0; e < n_event; ++e) {
        // Fix for every event is being accumulated
        // only 1/n_event of the overall time
        values[cur_eventset][e] += accum[e] * n_event;
    }
    Send values to output of the module;
    Start next eventset;
}
```

Fig. 2. Manual multiplexing pseudocode

from LIKWID—using daemon or direct access. It was decided not to use daemon since: 1) it brings additional overhead, as mentioned in LIKWID manual; 2) it uses synchronous calls, which is not suitable in our case due to DiMMon internal architecture (DiMMon requires all data source to return very quickly, which can't be guaranteed for an inter-process call to another daemon). But in case of direct access, LIKWID does not allow collecting PMC data without root privileges. That's why we had to use setuid in order to run DiMMon as root. Also, it is necessary to use setcap command to provide DiMMon rights for accessing MSR device files, as specified in LIKWID manual.

4   Evaluating Overheads from Multiplexing

This section describes in detail the experiments we conducted using different multiplexing variants and the overheads they introduce.

4.1   Experimental Conditions

We tested 8 NASA Parallel Benchmarks [2] (further referred as NPB) in our experiments—BT, CG, EP, FT, IS, LU, MG, SP. Fortran implementations were used, with MPI for parallelization. We studied different configurations of these benchmarks, changing the number of nodes used, the number of processes per nodes and the benchmark class that specifies problem size and parameters (classes C and D were used[2]). 11 configurations were studied, their list can be found in the header of Table 2. The following notation is used: <*number of nodes*>-<*number of processes per node*>-<*benchmark class*>. So, 4-1-C means that corresponding experiments were conducted using 4 nodes, with 1 process per node, and class C for each NPB benchmark were specified.

Four different DiMMon variants were compared:

1. No multiplexing (only 4 PMC collected)—as a reference variant to compare with;
2. PAPI with automatic multiplexing;
3. PAPI with manual multiplexing;
4. LIKWID with manual multiplexing.

All experiments were carried out on the Lomonosov-2 supercomputer, using standard launch procedure using Slurm. We used nodes equipped with Intel Xeon E5-2697 v3 and 64 GB of RAM, the OS is CentOS 7 with kernel 3.10.0. First three DiMMon variants use PAPI version 5.6, while the fourth one uses LIKWID version 5.2.1.

When comparing any specific benchmark and its launch configuration, the same compute nodes were used for all 4 DiMMon variants (except for configurations with class D, since they require too much time to run otherwise), but different sets of nodes were used when performing different comparisons. Each experiment was repeated 10 times in order to get more reliable results, the arithmetic mean and the confidence intervals are further used. Outliers showing significantly different execution time (4.8% of overall number of launches) were removed, since they happen due to external perturbations in the Lomonosov-2 behavior (e.g. issues with Lustre file system or impact of other jobs running in parallel) and therefore are considered invalid.

Before proceeding with the overhead analysis, it is important to notice that PAPI with automatic multiplexing provided invalid values for the last two metrics in Table 1—DiMMon monitoring system frequently reported that the absolute values of these counters were decreasing, although they should monotonically increase. We haven't investigated this issue in detail, but it resulted not only in local inaccuracies (which may possibly arise due to inaccuracies in multiplexing) but also in integral values for the whole job being invalid. However, we decided to continue studying this variant, since this problem presumably occurs only for a certain combination of versions of OS and PAPI as well as selected set of counters, i.e. it is not a general issue, and at the same time it does not affect the results of the overhead analysis.

4.2   PAPI with Automatic Multiplexing

Table 2 shows the overheads of using PAPI with automatic multiplexing, comparing to the default DiMMon (without multiplexing). Each value indicates the

---

[2] https://www.nas.nasa.gov/software/npb_problem_sizes.html.

percentage increase in the average execution time of the corresponding benchmark and its launch configuration. The last row (column) provides the arithmetic mean between all benchmarks for the selected configuration (between all
configurations for the selected benchmark). The green color indicates that the
overhead is not significant (more specifically, the upper bound of the confidence
interval for default DIMMon is greater than the lower bound of the confidence
interval for DIMMon with PAPI automatic multiplexing); we will further refer
to such values as "green values". The "—" indicates that the experiments were
not conducted, due to BT and SP requiring the number of processes to be a
square number, and memory issues in MG and FT with D class.

Table 2. Overheads caused by PAPI with automatic multiplexing

	1-1-C	1-4-C	1-16-C	2-2-C	4-1-C	4-4-C	8-1-C	8-8-C	16-1-C	4-1-D	1-16-D	avg.
BT	7.19	7.64	1.63	8.55	6.07	7.49	—	−0.61	5.21	6.90	1.47	5.15
CG	4.78	4.66	1.77	4.81	3.21	3.89	6.44	−2.98	−7.02	5.52	4.14	2.66
EP	8.74	4.98	0.82	−0.15	−2.01	6.42	−11.19	−0.55	−8.75	11.31	2.14	1.07
FT	6.66	5.64	1.49	6.74	4.45	5.17	4.65	−1.24	4.84	6.76	—	4.52
IS	7.42	4.46	0.88	6.05	6.36	2.56	6.51	0.00	5.17	5.05	−0.82	3.97
LU	7.36	7.36	1.35	5.82	6.53	4.92	4.69	0.85	2.92	15.38	1.71	5.36
MG	6.50	5.90	2.14	4.75	5.78	7.39	3.63	−4.07	7.18	—	1.88	4.11
SP	5.87	4.78	1.47	6.18	5.93	4.97	—	−3.07	6.31	6.73	0.96	4.02
avg.	6.81	5.68	1.44	5.34	4.54	5.35	2.46	−1.46	1.98	8.24	1.64	3.83

According to this table, overheads can vary significantly, from −11.19% to
15.38%. But there are some trends that can be seen. For example, the more
processes per node are used—the less overhead is: the average for 1-1-C is 6.81%,
for 1-4-C is 5.68%, for 1-16-C is 1.44% (with some overheads starting to be
statistically insignificant). It is even more noticeable when using 8 nodes: the
average overhead for 8-1-C is 2.46%, while for 8-8-C it is −1.46%, with almost
all benchmarks starting to execute even slightly faster (supposedly due to almost
no overheads and different levels of external influence). The average for 4-4-C is
a little higher than for 4-1-C, but here MG shows statistically insignificant high
value of 7.35%, and some external perturbations could intervene (as we will see
later, this is not observed in case of other two variants). The situation with class
D is similar to the class C—while 4-1-D shows high overhead of 8.24% (which is
also quite high for 4-1-C), overhead for 1-16-D is noticeably lower, resulting in
1.64% (overhead for 1-16-C is also low—1.44%).

The overall average overhead is 3.83%, being not too big but noticeable. It
should be noted here that the observed spread of execution times for similar or
even the exact same experiments suggests that external influence can be quite

significant. Moreover, it seems that this influence can be stable for days—you can run identical jobs many times during one day and get almost identical results, then run the same job series on another day and again get almost identical results, but these results will be different from the first ones. The main sources of such external influence are, in our opinion, the current state of the Lustre file system and the compute nodes on which the program is running (over time, noise on the node seems to accumulate, becoming minimal after node reboot). Given this information, we believe that the actual absolute overhead values may slightly differ, however the noted trends (as well as further conclusions regarding the comparison of three variants) should remain true.

4.3 PAPI with Manual Multiplexing

The overhead results for the same set of experiments, in case of using PAPI with manual multiplexing, are shown in Table 3. The general picture is similar, with the aforementioned trend being even more noticeable—the overheads decrease as the number of processes per node increases. In this case almost all overheads for 1-16-C, 4-4-C, 8-8-C and 1-16-D configurations are statistically insignificant or even negative (corresponding values are green).

It is also interesting to notice that the most number of "green values", both for PAPI variants, are shown for CG and EP benchmarks. But the reason for this seems to be different. CG shows the least overhead overall, resulting in CG being the most "overhead-resistant". And EP provides quite unstable results, leading to both confidence intervals being long enough and overheads jumping from -11.19% (PAPI auto, 8-1-C) to 14.63% (PAPI manual, 4-1-D). The least "overhead-resistant" is LU, showing the largest overhead in total.

The overall average overhead between all experiments is 4.47%, which is slightly higher than the average in case of automatic multiplexing.

4.4 LIKWID Multiplexing

As initially expected, LIKWID shows the least overall average overhead of 2.78% as well as the most number of "green values". The details are shown in Table 4. It can be seen that the assumptions made earlier are further confirmed here: increasing the number of processes per node leads to the overhead decrease, both CG and EP shows "green values" more often than others, and LU is the least "overhead-resistant" benchmark, showing the highest overhead.

Studying results for all three variants, we can also see that configurations that differ only in used benchmark class (4-1-C/D and 1-16-C/D) show similar overheads. This was expected, since the behavior of benchmarks does not change much when the class changes. But the execution time increases significantly, and these results help to ensure that the results obtained are correct for long-running jobs as well.

Table 3. Overheads caused by PAPI with manual multiplexing

	1-1-C	1-4-C	1-16-C	2-2-C	4-1-C	4-4-C	8-1-C	8-8-C	16-1-C	4-1-D	1-16-D	avg.
BT	10.54	3.94	0.22	7.08	9.61	3.43	—	−3.82	18.32	7.31	0.18	5.68
CG	3.10	0.15	0.41	1.64	1.60	0.94	4.56	−8.72	5.16	2.21	0.56	1.06
EP	14.11	4.25	0.11	4.77	8.51	5.84	10.44	−3.21	13.00	14.63	2.70	6.83
FT	9.07	2.88	0.24	5.99	5.18	1.52	7.23	−2.98	8.88	5.61	—	4.36
IS	10.81	2.85	0.16	7.01	9.10	1.71	9.57	0.00	7.99	7.63	−2.02	4.98
LU	12.37	5.51	−0.25	7.33	10.83	4.61	17.44	1.12	12.60	9.93	0.07	7.42
MG	9.58	3.39	0.48	4.68	10.02	−1.49	5.47	−13.73	7.27	—	−0.60	2.51
SP	6.81	1.49	0.26	3.61	5.79	0.29	—	−6.38	9.06	5.46	0.06	2.65
avg.	9.55	3.06	0.20	5.26	7.58	2.11	9.12	−4.71	10.29	7.54	0.14	4.47

Table 4. Overheads caused by LIKWID with manual multiplexing

	1-1-C	1-4-C	1-16-C	2-2-C	4-1-C	4-4-C	8-1-C	8-8-C	16-1-C	4-1-D	1-16-D	avg.
BT	10.38	3.96	0.04	5.82	8.12	2.69	—	−3.60	6.89	6.78	−2.08	3.90
CG	2.95	0.21	0.14	1.17	0.76	0.58	0.72	−6.73	−5.80	1.54	1.07	−0.31
EP	14.04	4.24	−6.49	1.00	4.33	4.47	−3.34	−2.01	−1.27	13.18	−2.68	2.32
FT	9.13	2.50	−3.66	5.58	2.04	2.07	0.52	−3.03	2.41	5.36	—	2.29
IS	10.87	3.51	1.91	5.95	9.43	0.53	9.47	0.00	7.99	7.16	−3.76	4.82
LU	12.44	4.59	−0.34	5.67	9.06	3.13	7.17	1.79	3.15	9.31	0.14	5.10
MG	9.44	3.06	−1.64	2.66	7.55	−1.16	4.99	−10.97	7.10	—	−0.31	2.07
SP	6.56	1.53	0.06	3.28	5.26	0.41	—	−6.96	4.98	5.44	−0.52	2.00
avg.	9.48	2.95	−1.25	3.89	5.82	1.59	3.25	−3.94	3.18	6.97	−1.16	2.78

4.5 Comparing Different Multiplexing Variants

In this section, we focus on the comparison of three multiplexing variants.
Figure 3 presents the average overheads introduced by three variants for different NPB benchmarks. The last two columns show the overall average and the overall maximum values between all benchmarks.

It can be seen that LIKWID shows the least overhead for all benchmarks, except EP and IS, resulting in the least total overhead of 2.78%. Both of PAPI variants show the highest overhead in half of cases (whereas LIKWID never), and due to the large gap on EP and LU, PAPI manual multiplexing variant results in the largest total overhead. Also, this variant reaches the largest overall maximum between all benchmarks and their configurations—18.32% overhead, obtained on BT benchmark with 16-1-C configuration.

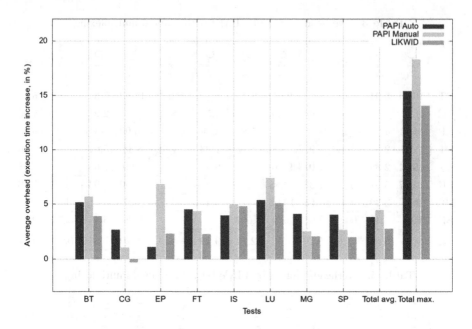

Fig. 3. Comparison of average overheads caused by three multiplexing variants

The results obtained allow us to conclude that LIKWID is the most appropriate variant for multiplexing. However, since the overhead caused by it is still noticeable, it was decided to run the selected DiMMon variant in sampling mode on the Lomonosov-2 supercomputer, only for a part of jobs, thus decreasing the average overhead to less than 1%.

It is also worth noting the following. Judging by the outliers (runs with significantly longer execution times) that we obtained and discarded from consideration for the purity of the experiments, in some cases the external influence of the HPC system can be much more noticeable than the influence of the considered multiplexing variants. This allows us to suggest that the transition to the selected DiMMon variant with PMC multiplexing will be generally imperceptible to supercomputer users.

5 Conclusions

In this paper, we have carried out a detailed comparison of the overheads caused by PMC data collection using three different multiplexing variants—automatic and manual multiplexing using PAPI, as well as manual multiplexing using LIKWID. For this, special modules were implemented within the framework of the DiMMon monitoring system; the choice of monitoring system is unimportant in this case, since overheads are caused by the libraries for PMC data collection as well as the OS. The experiments carried out on the Lomonosov-2 supercomputer show that the variant using LIKWID results in the least overhead (percentage increase in application execution time) of 2.78% on average. We have also observed some trends, showing, for example, that the overhead tends to decrease with the increase of the number of processes per node used in an application.

We believe that both the described overhead analysis process and the results obtained in general can be applicable in case of other supercomputers, and therefore can be useful to administrators of different HPC centers.

Acknowledgments. The results described in this paper were achieved at Lomonosov Moscow State University with the financial support of the Russian Science Foundation, agreement No. 21-71-30003. The research is carried out using the equipment of shared research facilities of HPC computing resources at Lomonosov Moscow State University.

References

1. Azimi, R., Stumm, M., Wisniewski, R.W.: Online performance analysis by statistical sampling of microprocessor performance counters. In: Proceedings of the International Conference on Supercomputing, pp. 101–110 (2005). https://doi.org/10.1145/1088149.1088163
2. Bailey, D., Harris, T., Saphir, W., Van Der Wijngaart, R., Woo, A., Yarrow, M.: The NAS parallel benchmarks 2.0. Technical report, Technical Report NAS-95-020, NASA Ames Research Center (1995)
3. Browne, S.V., Dongarra, J.J., Garner, N., Ho, G., Mucci, P.J.: A portable programming interface for performance evaluation on modern processors. Int. J. High Perform. Comput. Appl. **14**(3), 189–204 (2000). https://doi.org/10.1177/109434200001400303
4. Dimakopoulou, M., Eranian, S., Koziris, N., Bambos, N.: Reliable and efficient performance monitoring in Linux. In: SC16: International Conference for High Performance Computing, Networking, Storage and Analysis, pp. 396–408. IEEE (2016). https://doi.org/10.1109/SC.2016.33, http://ieeexplore.ieee.org/document/7877112/
5. Documentation on Zabbix software. http://www.zabbix.com/ru/documentation/
6. Infrastructure monitoring system Nagios. https://www.nagios.org/
7. Khudoleeva, A.A., Stefanov, K.S.: A study on the influence of monitoring system noise on MPI collective operations. In: Malyshkin, V. (ed.) PaCT 2021. LNCS, vol. 12942, pp. 132–142. Springer, Cham (2021). https://doi.org/10.1007/978-3-030-86359-3_10
8. Mathur, W., Cook, J.: Improved estimation for software multiplexing of performance counters. In: Proceedings of the IEEE Computer Society's Annual International Symposium on Modeling, Analysis, and Simulation of Computer and Telecommunications Systems, MASCOTS 2005, pp. 23–32 (2005). https://doi.org/10.1109/MASCOTS.2005.34
9. May, J.: MPX: Software for multiplexing hardware performance counters in multithreaded programs. In: Proceedings of the 15th International Parallel and Distributed Processing Symposium, IPDPS 2001, p. 8. IEEE Computing Society (2001). https://doi.org/10.1109/IPDPS.2001.924955, http://ieeexplore.ieee.org/document/924955/
10. de Melo, A.C.: The New Linux 'perf' tools. In: Linux Kongress, Nuremberg, Germany (2010). http://vger.kernel.org/~acme/perf/lk2010-perf-acme.pdf

11. Moore, S.V.: A comparison of counting and sampling modes of using performance monitoring hardware. In: Sloot, P.M.A., Hoekstra, A.G., Tan, C.J.K., Dongarra, J.J. (eds.) ICCS 2002. LNCS, vol. 2330, pp. 904–912. Springer, Heidelberg (2002). https://doi.org/10.1007/3-540-46080-2_95

12. Mytkowicz, T., Sweeney, P.F., Hauswirth, M., Diwan, A.: Time interpolation: so many metrics, so few registers. In: Proceedings of the Annual International Symposium on Microarchitecture, MICRO, pp. 286–298 (2007). https://doi.org/10.1109/MICRO.2007.27

13. Ojha, A.K.: Technique in least-intrusive computer system performance monitoring. In: Conference Proceedings - IEEE SOUTHEASTCON, pp. 150–154 (2001). https://doi.org/10.1109/SECON.2001.923105

14. PCL - The Performance Counter Library (1999). http://www.fz-juelich.de/zam/PCL/

15. Röhl, T., Treibig, J., Hager, G., Wellein, G.: Overhead analysis of performance counter measurements. In: Proceedings of the International Conference on Parallel Processing Workshops, May 2015, pp. 176–185 (2015). https://doi.org/10.1109/ICPPW.2014.34

16. Stefanov, K., Voevodin, V., Zhumatiy, S., Voevodin, V.: Dynamically Reconfigurable Distributed Modular Monitoring System for Supercomputers (DiMMon). Procedia Comput. Sci. **66**, 625–634 (2015). https://doi.org/10.1016/j.procs.2015.11.071. In: Sloot, P., Boukhanovsky, A., Athanassoulis, G., Klimentov, A. (eds.) 4th International Young Scientist Conference on Computational Science. http://www.sciencedirect.com/science/journal/18770509/66/supp/C, http://linkinghub.elsevier.com/retrieve/pii/S1877050915034201

17. Treibig, J., Hager, G., Wellein, G.: LIKWID: A lightweight performance-oriented tool suite for x86 multicore environments. In: Proceedings of the 2010 39th International Conference on Parallel Processing Workshops, pp. 207–216. IEEE (2010). https://doi.org/10.1109/ICPPW.2010.38., http://ieeexplore.ieee.org/document/5599200/

18. Voevodin, V., Zhumatiy, S.: Universal assessment system for analyzing the quality of supercomputer resources usage. In: Voevodin, V., Sobolev, S. (eds.) RuSCDays 2021. CCIS, vol. 1510, pp. 427–442. Springer, Cham (2021). https://doi.org/10.1007/978-3-030-92864-3_33

19. Voevodin, V.V., et al.: Supercomputer Lomonosov-2: large scale, deep monitoring and fine analytics for the user community. Supercomput. Front. Innovations **6**(2), 4–11 (2019). https://doi.org/10.14529/jsfi190201

20. Voevodin, V.V., et al.: Administration, monitoring and analysis of supercomputers in Russia: a survey of 10 HPC centers. Supercomput. Front. Innovations **8**(3), 82–103 (2021). https://doi.org/10.14529/jsfi210305

21. Weaver, V.: Linux perf event features and overhead. In: Fastpath 2013 - Second International Workshop on Performance Analysis of Workload Optimized Systems, Austin (2013). https://s3.us.cloud-object-storage.appdomain.cloud/res-files/1946-FastPath_Weaver_Talk.pdf

22. Weaver, V., Dongarra, J.: Can hardware performance counters produce expected, deterministic results. In: Proceedings of Third Workshop on Functionality of Hardware Performance Monitoring (2010). http://icl.cs.utk.edu/news_pub/submissions/fhpm2010_weaver.pdf, http://web.eece.maine.edu/simvweaver/projects/deterministic/fhpm2010.pdf

Regularization Approach for Accelerating Neural Architecture Search

Mikhail Nikulenkov[(✉)], Kamil Khamitov, and Nina Popova

Lomonosov Moscow State University, Moscow, Russia
mrrhayader@gmail.com, popova@cs.msu.ru

Abstract. Modern Artificial Neural networks utilizes vast topologies to become applicable to the vast majority of the ML problems. Such topologies have an enormous number of parameters nowadays, which make it easier to use, but harder to train and modify. With such a number of parameters, the usage of semi-automatic techniques for constructing or adjusting new models for topical problems is vital for the whole industry. It makes it essential to optimize such methods like Neural Architecture Search (NAS) to efficiently utilize computational resources of the GPU and whole cluster. Since modern NAS tools are commonly used to optimize models in different areas or make a combination of models from the past, they have to use a plenty of computational power to perform certain hyperparameters optimization routines. Many NAS methods are of a highly parallel nature, but still they need a lot of computational power and have an enormous convergence time. The key to increasing performance of many NAS methods is boosting performance of the training of the highly-depth and synthesized model, to evaluate the probe of the model and obtain the score for this epoch. It means that demands for parallel implementations need to be available in different cluster configurations and should utilize as many nodes as possible, showing high scalability. However, straightforward approaches where NAS solving does not consider previous results lead to wasteful utilization of computation power. In this article, we introduce a new method that can improve convergence in NEAT-based NAS method using L1/L2 regularization during the evolution step.

Keywords: Hyperparameters tuning · NNI · HPC · Neural architecture search · LASSO

1 Introduction

In modern Artificial neural networks (ANN) applications, the significant increase in complexity of the models was demonstrated. In production we can observe ANN which number hyperparameters exceeded the 100M [1]. For large natural language processing (NLP) models, the number can even exceeds the 200M [1]. Which leads to the problem of hardware utilization. Even for single node unit with modern GPU's/TPU' the computation power is not enough for the effective training and inference. In most cases the pre-trained model is enough, but if you want to build something new from scratch you have to spend hours training it on the one node. Especially if you provide some custom layers or blocks to the ANN that correspond only to your specific domain problem. In the study [3] it was observed that new, fully automatically synthesized architecture may beat existing state-of-the art models in the some specific domain problems. The key problem with such an approach is how to reduce computation power to efficiently perform searches for this architecture with the highest speedup and a certain degree of parallelism to effectively reduce computation time. Some methods like DARTS [2] tries to increase level of parallelism using some assumptions on some certain properties of the source models, which limits applicability of such methods to the certain type of the models. It leads us to generalizations in Neural Architecture Search and so-called hyperparameters tuning. This task can be put together by performing optimization in an extensive search space with a great number of parameters. But since ANNs do not compose a simple graph, such peculiar Hyperparameters optimization (HPO) (the result of optimization should be a valid ANN graph) should be considered. It means that our requirement is a certain set of large-scale optimization problems with specific constraints: the NAS (Neural Architecture search) problem and a problem of updating a particular network topology. We are obliged to use algorithms with prebuilt constraints in order to limit search space [3]. At the other hand such generic approaches usually utilize a lot of computational power, but demonstrate remarkable results [4,5]. Another approach is not to limit the search space to improve performance of the key step of the search method – trial on and test micro-batches of the test data, which costs a lot if you have different model candidates in such an approach. Some approaches to reduce such limits are to perform light-transforming of the model before moving to the next generation, but it requires some complicated work. Another approach to remove some connections and use techniques like dropout in order to keep models as smallest as possible. And some novel approach in this field is to use some kind of regularization, either L1 or L2, to restrain model and build some kind model-aggregate that resembles original model and it's behavior and than test it in the trial, which leads to reducing time on the step.

2   Neural Architecture Search Problems

This article mainly focuses on two neural architecture search problems:

– updating existing topology by applying it to new particular task,
– building new topology from scratch (Neural Architecture search).

Due to the increased resource utilization of actual deep neural networks (DNN), topology adaptation of neural networks has become a noteworthy problem. In this case, the process resembles the approach of best model development for the particular task that can be utilised to tune multiple sets of hyperparameters and then construct a "purified" model that fits the resource limitations on the device of interest. In this article, we take advantage of both steps from the process. Hyperparameters tuning requires a lot of computational resources, thus it's significant to provide an efficient way to perform such tuning on HPC clusters.

Adaptation Problem. The adaptation problem is formulated as updating the pre-existing model $min_\theta L(\theta_n), \theta_n = X(\theta_{n-1}, ...\theta_{n-k})$, where L – loss function, θ – hyperparameters set, θ_0 – initial hyperparameters(initial model) that are used as a core of method, X – the iterative process of new model construction that is based on previous hyperparameters.

Neural Architecture Search Definition. The neural architecture search problem does not imply setting the initial value of hyperparameters. It limits potentiality of methods that rely on the initial approximation quality. Search process can be described as follows: $L(\theta_n), \theta_n = X(\theta_{n-1}, ...\theta_{n-k}), \theta_0 = \mathbf{0}$.

Distributed Hyperparameters Optimization. Both problems that we consider in this article are large-scale hyperparameters optimization problems that usually utilize a lot of computational powers. Distributed technologies and HPC are essential for tackling such problems in a meaningful time. Moreover, since CoDeepNEAT makes use of evolution-based techniques, it has a build-in potential for parallel computations. Other methods, even those which are not meant to use parallel computations, can benefit from distributed optimization that can be achieved by parallel running of different tuners. The system we've chosen is NNI (Neural Network Intelligence) [6]. It provides an adjustable interface that makes it possible to easily integrate bindings to different HPC schedulers into rather large cluster configurations. Integrating SLURM/LSF into this method can be done via plugins system of NNI and other appliances.

3   Techniques for Tuning Hyperparameters

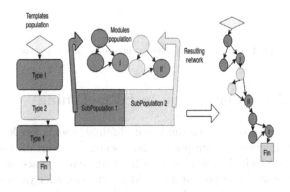

Fig. 1. Evolution scheme of CoDeepNEAT [3]

CoDeepNEAT Method. Co-Evolution version of DeepNEAT (Deep Neural Evolution of Augmenting Topologies) is a evolutionary method for tuning structure-based hyperparameters of ANN. Like the NEAT, this method utilizes an evolutionary approach to build from scratch or modify architectures. The main step of the methods consists of the evolution process in both modules, that represents the building blocks for the resulting networks and blueprints, that represents the graph of how modules should be connected with each other. On each step we build combinations of modules and blueprints; perform certain iterations of training, and then propagate back the score through both populations, and, according to the score, perform selection and other necessary things, important for the evolutionary process. During the step we may perform mutating of the module and blueprints independently which allows to perform it in a parallel manner. Specific mutations like change edges, add links can be represented in both cases, but some mutations like linking blocks or merging recurrent connections can be block-specific. Before evaluation of the specific network the specific builder process [3] resolves differences in the connected models via inserting specific layers and provides resulting network without any weights. After that it trains the resulted network on a certain number of epochs to obtain the resulting accuracy and then uses its accuracy as measurement for the scoring elements of both populations. CoDeepNEAT surpasses its predecessors in terms of convergence rate and applicability, since this method has more meaningful mutation possibilities. The most negligible mutations applied to populations of templates or modules resulted in a major change in final networks.

The CoDeepNEAT evolution scheme is demonstrated in Fig. 1.

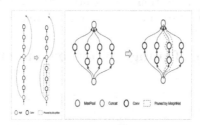

Fig. 2. MorphNet scheme for ResNet-style and Inception-style networks. [7]

4   Usage of Regularization in HPO-Tuning

In our approach we provide a method that eliminates some CoDeepNEAT drawbacks like high demand of computational resources in certain tasks and areas. Another approach, which utilize idea of limiting search space was described in [5]. Here we present the approach for building some smaller variants of networks from the original one during the initial step of the algorithm. The idea is to perform regularization process on each step of the CoDeepNEAT. The original idea belongs to MorphNET [7]. The method is based on altering tensors dimensions of some categories of layers (in convolutional layers for the most part) and on optimization of convolution sizes in order to minimize the considered regularizer loss. The main step can be understood as shrinking and sparsifying convolution layers based off regularizer values. MorphNet doesn't start trying vast number of architectures across a large design space, instead it starts with an pre-existing architecture for an adjacent problem and, optimizes it for the task at hand, attempting to zero out some outputs of the layer by using resource-dependent penalties. In the Fig. 2 the right side shows how residual connections are removed in ResNet-style and Inception-style networks. The main idea is to modify a loss function with a resource-dependent penalty. Penalty is added to loss (with weight factor λ) and is shaped like $\sum_{all_w} |cost_w * Y_w|$ where $cost_w$ is the cost in terms of the optimized metrics of the channel and Y_w is the scaling factor associated with the channel in the succeeding batch normalization layer (prunning criterion). L1 regularization (LASSO) is designed to handle problems where layers which are combined by skipping connections are required to have the same number of channels. Here it is used it to lessen the quantity of nonzero weights without or just with little penalty on model performance (e.g. accuracy). Proposed method is mainly used for network distillation in this article. This implies that we consider it as the post-processing tool, which comes in handy where there is a task of optimizing inference time with no significant changes in model loss. Since the resulting network, if we add FLOPS regualizer requires much less power for inference time, we may significantly reduce the training time using the regualrized method for scoring the elements of population. So the step of the method can be described as follows:

- Obtain original resulting network
- Perform the L1 regularization process
- Train regularized model on the training set and propagate the score to the unmodified network

5   Automatic System Architecture

The brief architecture of the NAS system with support of tuning problems execution via HPC cluster was described in [5]. It consists of four main parts

1. HPO-Tuners, or HPO-methods – kernels that runs on a host and tune the particular model, can be configured independently (CoDeepNEAT, PetriDish, TreeParzenEstimation, Naive Evolution etc.)
2. Search space constraints part
   - Storage for modules classifications and corresponding classes in each part of the "benchmarking suite".
   - Classifier that acquires specific set of available modules for executing trials.
3. Problems storage – predefined presets for the certain amount of problems, that allows limit search space [5].

4. Post-processors – regularization methods that can be run on the final generation of population in order to change topology and fit certain constraints of L1/L2 regularization. (MorphNet, modified Morphnet)

The scheme of such system briefly described in Fig. 3. So now, it is possible to run NAS in two different modes: making use of the previous information from storage or making new benchmarking data for it. Before applying NAS, we execute our classifier and after that choose the limited set of modules obtained after problem reclassification process during mini-benchmark [5]. So the classifier is executed after the choose of tuners and cluster configuration. The actual optimization problem starts after the classifier execution. Post-processing is unaffected for the tuners selection. It is worth mentioning, that we provided supplementary workflow for integrating such data with model-dependent post-tuners. The integration was described in [4]. Since system supports variety of limitations for search space and tuners that utilize such conditions for better convergence we allow user to tune hyperparameters in the semi-automatic mode with predefined sets of the search spaces or "detected" search space via classification model. Automatic usage of regularization in (Co)DeepNEAT method supported in the configuration files via option. And can be enabled by default parameter for certain classes of problems.

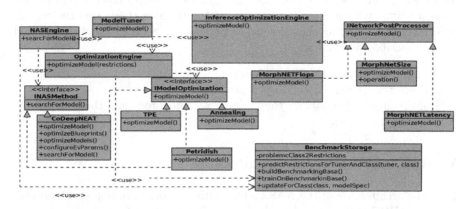

Fig. 3. Unified modelling language (UML) class diagram, that briefly describe system's architecture with Tuners [6].

6   Experiments

6.1   An Approach to Comparing Neuroevolution Methods

In order to minimize the impact of randomness, which is a built-in feature of evolution algorithms, each group of experiments uses the same pre-generated populations of modules, blueprints and individuals as a starting point of evolution. Given that the number of generations in evolution is fixed and the same in corresponding experiments, a comparison of the proposed approach with regular CoDeepNEAT can be done via analyzing the average accuracy of the last individual generation.

Two groups of the same dataset experiments are compared, the first one using the proposed approach and the second one using the regular CoDeepNEAT method. Populations of individuals belonging to the same group are merged into one mixed population; an average accuracy over the mixed population is calculated. An average time required for evolving a series of generations is calculated over each group of experiments.

Key values for estimating the performance of a proposed method are speedup and accuracy degradation. A speedup is calculated as $\frac{t_a}{t_b}$, where t_a is an average time over a group of CoDeepNEAT experiments and t_b is an average time over a group of experiments of proposed approach. An accuracy degradation is calculated as $acc_a - acc_b$, where acc_a is an average accuracy over a mixed population of CoDeepNEAT experiments and acc_b is an average mixed population accuracy over a group of experiments on proposed approach. A negative value for accuracy degradation means that the proposed method generated better results than the original CoDeepNEAT.

6.2   Experimental Setup and Configuration

Clusters Configuration. The following cluster configuration was used for the experimental study of the proposed approach

- 2 nodes of Polus cluster with $2 \times$ IBM POWER8 processors with up to 160 threads, 256 GB RAM and $2 \times$ Nvidia Tesla P100 [8].

Datasets. Following datasets were used:

- MNIST
- CIFAR-10
- CIFAR-100 (3 times augmented)
- Tiny ImageNet (100 classes, 4 times augmented)

Evolution Configuration. MNIST and CIFAR-10 experiments were done over 7 generations, CIFAR-100 and Tiny ImageNet experiments were done over 4 generations. Each group consists of 5 experiments with a population of 12 individuals.

MorphNet Configuration. One epoch of full training set shrinking of each individual was performed, with regularization coefficient set as $\frac{1}{init\_flopn}$, where $init\_flopn$ is a pre-shrinking number of individual's floating point operations required to calculate the result of the input data by the neural network (FLOPN stands for floating points operations number). The FLOPN values of the considered networks vary as $8 \cdot 10^6 - 10^9$. MorphNet alive threshold parameter is used for determining when an activation is alive: the smaller connection weight is considered dead; neurons with all-dead connections are considered redundant and are proposed for removal. This parameter was set to 0.1 for MNIST and CIFAR-10 and to 0.05 for CIFAR-100 and Tiny ImageNet.

Search Space. Search space configuration was performed by hand with a trial-and-error method, given the authors' previous experience in solving adjacent problems. Search space for MNIST and CIFAR-10 is composed of: Conv2D layers with 16–68 filters (kernel sizes vary as $[1, 3, 5]$) with possible adjacent Max-Pooling2D (pool size is 2) or dropout layers (dropout rate varies as 0–0.5); a pre-output Dense layer of size 32–256 (with ReLu activation). Search space for CIFAR-100 and Tiny Imagenet is composed of: Conv2D layers with 16–128 filters (kernel sizes vary as $[1, 3, 5]$) with possible adjacent MaxPooling2D (pool size is 2) or dropout layers (dropout rate varies as 0–0.5); a pre-output two layer perceptron with Dense layers of size 32–128 (with ReLu activation).

6.3   Experimental Results

Average time and accuracy on each dataset are presented in Fig. 4: diagrams show compared time and accuracy of proposed method and original CoDeep-NEAT over considered datatests. Time and accuracy of original CoDeepNEAT method can be compared with those of the proposed method: Fig. 4 shows that proposed method requires less computation time and shows comparable accuracy results.

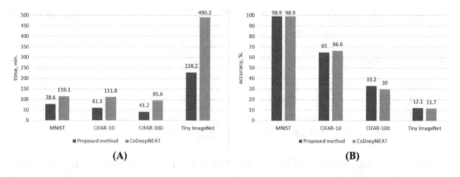

Fig. 4. (A) – time comparison on different datasets. (B) – accuracy comparison on different datasets

Speedup and accuracy degradation on each dataset are presented in Table 1. Average speedup of the proposed method relative to CoDeepNEAT is more than 1.9, while accuracy degradation is negligible or even does not take place (in case of negative accuracy degradation values).

Table 1. Speedup and accuracy on different datasets.

	MNIST	CIFAR-10	CIFAR-100	Tiny ImageNet
Speedup	1.48	1.82	2.31	2.14
Acc. degradation, %	0.02	1.61	−3.16	−0.38

Training process of each dataset best architecture is presented in Figs. 5, 6, 7 and 8. Validation set loss and accuracy change as number of epochs grows is shown.

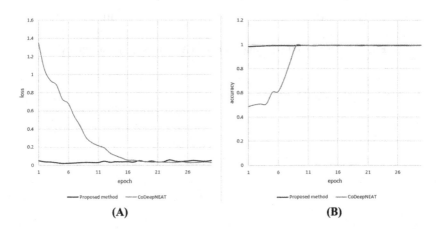

Fig. 5. MNIST training process. (A) – loss, (B) – accuracy.

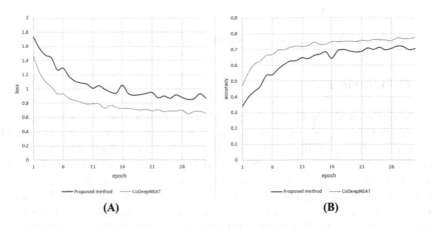

Fig. 6. CIFAR-10 training process. (A) – loss, (B) – accuracy.

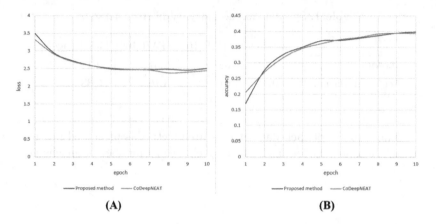

Fig. 7. CIFAR-100 training process. (A) – loss, (B) – accuracy.

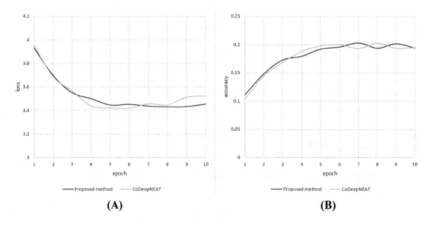

Fig. 8. Tiny ImageNet training process. (A) – loss, (B) – accuracy.

7   Conclusion

We developed and implemented a new type of optimization for Neuroevolution techniques that enables us to reduce the demands of computational power. The proposed technique utilizes L1 regularization for model simplification and distributing loss through this simplified model. In the terms of power reduction, it leads to the more than 1.9 speedup in average Table 1. In some complex image classification tasks it grows better than some small one like MNIST. Such an effect can be explained by different search spaces and complexity of the resulting networks (in MNIST/CIFAR-10 the resulting networks have much less graph nodes and types of nodes than in Tiny ImageNet). Such an approach was analyzed via parallel experiments on Polus clusters and in image classification problems we obtained not only negligible results in the terms of accuracy degradation, but also significant in the terms of FLOPS/iteration. At some points like in Tiny ImageNet and CIFAR-100, the overall accuracy degradation is negative it means the resulting networks is better after augmentation than original one.

Acknowledgements. Reported study was funded by RFBR according to research project №20-07-01053. The research is carried out using the equipment of the shared research facilities of HPC computing resources at Lomonosov Moscow State University.

References

1. Devlin, J., et al.: BERT: pre-training of deep bidirectional transformers for language understanding. arXiv preprint arXiv:1810.04805 (2018)
2. Liu, H., Simonyan, K., Yang, Y.: DARTS: differentiable architecture search. arXiv preprint arXiv:1806.09055 (2018)
3. Miikkulainen, R., Liang, J., Meyerson, E., et al.: Evolving deep neural networks. In: Artificial Intelligence in the Age of Neural Networks and Brain Computing, pp. 293–312. Elseiver (2019). https://doi.org/10.1016/B978-0-12-815480-9.00015-3
4. Khamitov, K., Popova, N., Konkov, Y., Castillo, T.: Tuning ANNs hyperparameters and neural architecture search using HPC. In: Voevodin, V., Sobolev, S. (eds.) RuSCDays 2020. CCIS, vol. 1331, pp. 536–548. Springer, Cham (2020). https://doi.org/10.1007/978-3-030-64616-5_46
5. Khamitov, K., Popova, N.: "Mini-benchmarking" approach to optimize evolutionary methods of neural architecture search. In: Voevodin, V., Sobolev, S. (eds.) RuSCDays 2021. CCIS, vol. 1510, pp. 352–364. Springer, Cham (2021). https://doi.org/10.1007/978-3-030-92864-3_27
6. Neural Network Intelligence, April 2020. https://github.com/microsoft/nni
7. Poon, A., Narayanan, D.: MorphNet: towards faster and smaller neural networks. Google AI Perception (2019)
8. Polus cluster specifications, April 2020. http://hpc.cs.msu.su/polus

RICSR: A Modified CSR Format
for Storing Sparse Matrices

Roman Kuprii$^{(\boxtimes)}$, Boris Krasnopolsky$^{(\boxtimes)}$ ⓘ, and Konstantin Zhukov$^{(\boxtimes)}$

Lomonosov Moscow State University, Moscow, Russia
roman.kupry@gmail.com, krasnopolsky@imec.msu.ru, zhukov_k@cs.msu.ru

Abstract. Improving the efficiency of solving systems of linear algebraic equations is an actual problem arising in various applications of mathematical physics. Iterative methods typically used for solving large sparse systems combine vector operations together with the matrix-vector multiplications. Both types of operations are characterized by low computational intensity, and their efficiency is limited by the memory bandwidth of the compute system. The current paper deals with the problem of improving the efficiency of methods for solving sparse linear systems, and specifically optimizing the basic arithmetic operation, matrix-vector multiplication. The paper proposes the Row Incremental Compressed Sparse Row format, a lightweight modification of the popular Compressed Sparse Row data storage format. The modified format focuses on reducing the amount of memory for storing the column indices of matrix nonzero elements by storing row-wise increments instead of basic values. The theoretical efficiency estimates and an applicability criterion are formulated for the modified format. The proposed data storage format is implemented in the XAMG library. The corresponding implementation is tested in detail for matrix-vector multiplication and solving a system of equations using a set of matrices from the SuiteSparse Matrix Collection. The acceleration of the matrix-vector multiplication by 17% and 28% for double and single precision calculations, respectively, for the matrices meeting the applicability criterion has been achieved. Finally, the use of proposed format allows to speed up the linear system solution time by 15% and 25% when operating with matrices in double and single precision.

Keywords: Matrix storage format · Sparse matrix-vector multiplication · Systems of linear algebraic equations · Compressed sparse row format

1 Introduction

Solving sparse systems of linear algebraic equations (SLAEs) is among the common questions when modeling mathematical physics problems. One of these problems is the modeling of incompressible turbulent flows within the framework of eddy-resolving approaches. When carrying out such calculations, a significant

V. Voevodin et al. (Eds.): RuSCDays 2022, LNCS 13708, pp. 486–500, 2022.
https://doi.org/10.1007/978-3-031-22941-1_36

portion of time is spent on solving the SLAE obtained as a result of discretizing the pressure Poisson equation. Therefore, the realization of computationally efficient algorithms, as well as the improvement of their software implementation, is an urgent problem. It also requires constant attention due to the ongoing development of the architecture of computer systems.

Iterative methods, e.g. Krylov subspace and/or multigrid methods, are often used to solve large sparse SLAEs. A significant portion of time for these methods falls on the execution of the basic operation of multiplying a sparse matrix by a vector (SpMV), $y = Ax$, where $A \in \mathbb{R}^{n \times n}$ is a sparse matrix with n rows/columns and nnz nonzero elements, $(nnz \ll n \cdot n)$, and $x, y \in \mathbb{R}^n$ are the dense vectors. A sparse matrix is a matrix with only few nonzero elements per each row. For example, in many mathematical physics applications this value varies in the range of 5–30, while the size of the matrix can be 10^6–10^8. Therefore, the only nonzero elements with some additional information about their location in the matrix are stored to reduce the memory requirements.

The SpMV operation is characterized by low computational intensity: for each addition or multiplication operation, several operations of reading and writing data to the memory are required, producing the traffic of about 10 bytes per each floating point operation. As a result, a large data traffic prevails over the calculations. Thus, the execution time of SpMV and hence the efficiency of the numerical methods used depends primarily on the bandwidth of the computer system's memory bus [14]. Several basic optimization approaches to increase the corresponding algorithms performance are known in the literature, e.g. the calculations with reduced precision [6] or cache usage optimizations [10]. Adopting the data storage formats to reduce the traffic with the memory is also a popular research direction.

The choice of the storage format for sparse matrices is the key issue when implementing numerical methods for solving SLAEs with sparse matrices. Despite the abundance of available formats, most of mature libraries of numerical methods such as hypre [4] or PETSc [2] use the Compressed Sparse Row (CSR) [11] format. The universality and simplicity of implementing the basic mathematical operations used in the numerical methods of linear algebra are among the advantages of this format for the matrices of general form.

The CSR format is simple and versatile, but in many cases not optimal. Several variations based on this format have been constructed, e.g. [5,9,12] to name but a few. The CSR5 [9] format is aimed at efficient execution of the SpMV operation by creating a uniform loading of processes for sparse matrices with any structure. The nonzero elements are packed into 2D tiles, for which the calculations can be performed in parallel. The height and width of the tiles are the configurable parameters. Two additional arrays are required to index these tiles. Matrix elements that cannot be effectively included in any tile are stored separately. The key disadvantage of this modification is the need for time-consuming preprocessing and reordering the data for efficient block processing. Another modification, Block Based CSR [12] format, utilizes the specific vector processor instructions. The sparse matrix is divided into vertical blocks. Each block is stored in six arrays, two − for storing the values of nonzero elements and their column indices, and four − for storing special 1-bit flags. For this format to work effectively, a significant change in the SpMV algorithm is also required.

The more general modifications, such as CSR Delta Unit, CSR Value Indexed, aimed at data compression, are also exist. The first modification packs two arrays with row and column information into one array of units. Each unit contains 4 byte fields of different sizes, which are determined when packing the data into a unit. Therefore, the size of the resulting array is not known in advance, and it is necessary to implement a dynamically growing array structure. The last modification is aimed at compressing the array of values of non-zero elements of the matrix. The modification is based on the assumption that there are many duplicate values in the matrix nonzero elements. Therefore, an array of unique non-zero matrix elements and an array of pointers to these values can be used to reduce the amount of memory consumed to store a sparse matrix. These modifications are not universal and may slow down the execution of the SpMV operation for some matrices [5].

The current paper provides alternative lightweight modification of the CSR data storage format. The key advantages of the proposed data storage representation is the simplicity of implementation and the low costs to convert the data from the original CSR format. Specifically, the required data objects can supplement the CSR format and the corresponding matrix operations may be performed with original CSR or the proposed RICSR data format representation. The formulated applicability criterion simplifies the choice of using the modified format, and the basic theoretical estimates highlight the potential calculation speed up of the SpMV operation for the specific matrix.

The rest of the paper is organized as follows. The second section introduces the modified Row Incremental CSR format. The third section demonstrates theoretical efficiency estimates for the proposed modification when performing the SpMV operations. The efficiency evaluation methodology is discussed in fourth section. The corresponding testing results are summarized in fifth section. Finally, the conclusion section summarizes the results presented in the paper.

2   Row Incremental CSR Format

2.1   CSR Format

The CSR data storage format assumes that information about nonzero matrix elements is stored in three arrays: Val, Row and Col. The size of the Val and Col arrays is equal to the number of nonzero elements, nnz. The Val array stores the values of matrix nonzero elements, and the Col array contains the column indices of these elements. The third array, Row, consists of $n + 1$ elements. Its i-th value indicates the offset in the Val and Col arrays for the elements, corresponding to i-th matrix row. Accordingly, the difference $row[i + 1] − row[i]$ is equal to the number of nonzero elements in the i-th row. The size of the integer data types used in the Row and Col arrays generally is determined by the size of the matrix and the number of nonzero elements, respectively.

$a_{0,0}$			$a_{0,3}$		
	$a_{1,1}$			$a_{1,4}$	$a_{1,5}$
		$a_{2,2}$			
			$a_{3,3}$		
$a_{4,0}$		$a_{4,2}$		$a_{4,4}$	
		$a_{5,2}$			$a_{5,5}$

$$n = 6, nnz = 12$$

Fig. 1. An example of the sparse matrix.

Let us consider the matrix shown in Fig. 1. The following values would be stored in the Val, Row, and Col arrays:

$$Val[nnz] : \{a_{0,0}, a_{0,3} | a_{1,1}, a_{1,4}, a_{1,5} | a_{2,2} | a_{3,3} | a_{4,0}, a_{4,2}, a_{4,4} | a_{5,2}, a_{5,5}\}$$
$$Row[n+1] : \{0, 2, 5, 6, 7, 10, 12\}$$
$$Col[nnz] : \{0, 3|1, 4, 5|2|3|0, 2, 4|2, 5\}$$

2.2 RICSR Format

The current paper proposes the Row Incremental CSR format (RICSR), a lightweight modification of the basic CSR data storage format. The essence of the modification is that instead of single array containing the column indices of nonzero matrix elements, two arrays Col_0 and Col_i of size n and nnz-n are used respectively. The Col_0 array stores the column index of the first nonzero element in each row, and the Col_i array contains offsets of the column indices of subsequent nonzero elements from the first element. This representation requires the presence of at least one nonzero element per each matrix row. An example of representing the matrix (Fig. 1) in the RICSR format is shown below:

$$Val[nnz] : \{a_{0,0}, a_{0,3} | a_{1,1}, a_{1,4}, a_{1,5} | a_{2,2} | a_{3,3} | a_{4,0}, a_{4,2}, a_{4,4} | a_{5,2}, a_{5,5}\}$$
$$Row[n+1] : \{0, 2, 5, 6, 7, 10, 12\}$$
$$Col\_0[n] : \{0, 1, 2, 3, 0, 2\}$$
$$Col\_i[nnz - n] : \{3|3, 4|||2, 4|3\}$$

Reducing the memory used is achieved by reducing the integer data type bitness. The bitness of the array Col_0 remains the same as the bitness of the array Col in the CSR format. Bitness of the Col_i, however, can be lower than the Col. It is determined by the maximum offset of the last element of the string from the first element, δ, unlike the original Col array, whose bit depth is determined by the number of matrix columns.

Since the number of nonzero elements in the sparse matrix row is significantly less than the number of columns, such an optimization can be practically significant. In the worst case, when the Col_i array uses the same data type as the CSR format Col array, the new arrays consume the same amount of memory as Col.

The key feature of the proposed format is its simplicity and compatibility with the original CSR. The algorithm for multiplying a sparse matrix by a vector does not undergo significant changes, except for single additional arithmetic operation for calculating array indices (Figs. 2 and 3). It takes little time to convert from the CSR format, and the corresponding computational cost is equal to a single read of arrays Row and Col. Additionally, this modification can be used alongside the base CSR format by loading and using the two new arrays Col_0 and Col_i instead of Col.

```
for (i = 0; i < n; i++) {
  y[i] = 0;
  for (j = Row[i]; j < Row[i+1]; j++)
    y[i] += x[Col[j]] * Val[j];
}
```

Fig. 2. Pseudocode of the SpMV operation for CSR data storage format.

```
for (i = 0; i < n; i++) {
  y[i] = x[Col_0[i]] * Val[Row[i]];
  for (j = Row[i]+1; j < Row[i+1]; j++)
    y[i] += x[Col_0[i] + Col_i[j-i-1]] * Val[j];
}
```

Fig. 3. Pseudocode of the SpMV operation for RICSR data storage format.

3   Theoretical Estimates

The theoretical performance gain estimates for the matrix-vector multiplication are proposed based on the amount of memory traffic. The amount of data to perform the SpMV operation for the considered formats can be expressed as:

$$\Sigma_{CSR} = F \cdot (2nnz + n) + P(nnz) \cdot (n+1) + P(n) \cdot nnz,$$
$$\Sigma_{RICSR} = F \cdot (2nnz + n) + P(nnz) \cdot (n+1) + P(n) \cdot n + P(\delta) \cdot (nnz - n).$$

These formulas include reading/writing the matrix elements and dense vectors x, y. Here F is the size of the floating point data type for the arrays Val, x, and y; $P(s)$ is the size of the minimum integer data type that can hold the number s, refers to the arrays Row, Col, Col_0, Col_i.

Table 1. Reducing the amount of data when performing the SpMV operation with floating point data in single (K^{32}) and double (K^{64}) precision.

Col_i array bitness	C	K^{32}	K^{64}
1	5	1.21	1.12
2	5	1.13	1.08
4	5	1	1
1	30	1.31	1.17
2	30	1.19	1.1
4	30	1	1

The corresponding estimate of the SpMV operation speed up can be represented as a ratio of the transferred amount of data when using CSR and RICSR formats. Thus, the following formula is proposed:

$$K = \frac{\Sigma_{CSR}}{\Sigma_{RICSR}} \approx \frac{(2\,F + P(n)) \cdot C + F + P(nnz)}{(2\,F + P(\delta)) \cdot C + F + P(nnz) + P(n) - P(\delta)}, \quad (1)$$

where $C = nnz/n$ is the mean number of nonzero elements per matrix row and δ is the maximum offset between the first and last elements per row. Despite the fact that expression (1) does not take into account the differences in the number of arithmetic operations when calculating array element indices (Figs. 2 and 3), it allows to estimate the potential benefit of using the proposed RICSR format.

Let us consider a matrix with $P(nnz)$ and $P(n)$ equal to 4 bytes, and F equal to 4 or 8 bytes. Using the formula (1) one can obtain the typical SpMV operation speed up depending on the parameter C, which practically varies within a fairly wide range, from 5 to 200. The corresponding results with two reference values $C = 5$ and $C = 30$ are summarized in Table 1. The speed up by about 10% is expected when switching to 2-byte integer data types to store the Col_i array for $C = 5$, and this value increases to about 10–20% when increasing C to 30. These values remain constant with further increasing the parameter C. In ideal case when the column offsets can be stored using the 1-byte integer array, an additional 10% speed up can be expected.

Based on these estimates, the simple applicability criterion for the RICSR format can be proposed: the acceleration can be achieved when the data type for Col_i array takes less than 4 bytes. This means that the maximum distance between the first and last occurrence of a nonzero element in a row must not exceed $2^{16} - 1$.

4 Testing Methodology

The current section describes the configuration of computing resources used for testing, the corresponding software, and the list of test matrices and testing scenarios, performed to evaluate the efficiency of the RICSR format.

4.1 Hardware

The two compute systems were used to evaluate the performance and provide reliable testing results. The first one is a workstation with a 6-core Intel Core i7-8700 processor and 2-channel DDR4 memory operating with 2667 MHz frequency. The second one is the single node of the cluster containing two 14-core Intel E5-2680v4 processors with 6-channel DDR4 2400 MHz memory; the single processor was used for the tests. All the tests were performed using all available processor physical CPU cores, i.e. 6 and 14 cores respectively.

4.2 Software

The proposed RICSR data storage format is implemented in the XAMG library of iterative methods for solving systems of linear algebraic equations [7,8]. This library is designed to solve large sparse SLAEs, including those with multiple right-hand sides. It contains a set of numerical methods including the algebraic multigrid method, Krylov subspace methods (CG, BiCGStab), Jacobi and Gauss-Seidel iterative methods, Chebyshev polynomial method, and others. The XAMG library reuses the open-source hypre library at the initialization stage to construct the multigrid matrix hierarchy when using the algebraic multigrid method. The library provides hierarchical three-level parallelization with a hybrid MPI+POSIX shared memory parallel programming model. This parallelization approach introduces three logical data distribution levels, which can be configured in accordance with the specific hardware architecture: the node layer, the numa-node layer, and the computing core layer. The basic MPI library functionality is used to spawn and pin the computational processes (the per core pinning is used and ensured during the tests), and the POSIX shared memory functionality with atomics is used to implement fast data exchange and processes synchronization over intra-node shared memory. Some details on the XAMG library and the hierarchical parallelization approach can be found in [6]. The library also contains several specific optimizations, such as various scenarios of using the mixed precision calculations, data alignment, vectorization, and different matrix storage formats including the CSR and RICSR discussed in this paper.

The results presented below also include the comparison of the efficiency of SpMV operation with Intel Math Kernel Library [1] when using the basic CSR format. The MKL 2021.1 is used for the corresponding tests. The Intel C/C++ compilers v2021.1 and v2021.5 together with the Intel MPI library were used to compile the code on workstation and cluster node respectively. The XAMG library was configured to perform the calculations using the hybrid component of the parallelization model, i.e. the parallelization of the calculations was performed with the POSIX shared memory (single node, single numa-node, and multiple computing cores).

Several tests have been performed to evaluate the efficiency of the proposed RICSR data storage format. The corresponding tests include the comparison of the standalone SpMV operation execution time as well as solving the systems of linear algebraic equations with iterative methods.

4.3   Test Matrices and Testing Scenario

A subset of the sparse matrices from the SuiteSparse Matrix Collection [3] was used for testing. The square matrices ranging in size form 500 thousand to 2 million unknowns were sorted in descending order by the number of non-zero elements, and the first 40 matrices were included in to the test set. The details of the test matrices selected are summarized in Appendix A.

The step-by-step performance evaluation is performed to demonstrate the efficiency of the RICSR data storage format. The results presented below include the comparison of SpMV operations with basic CSR matrix in XAMG and MKL, comparison of CSR and RICSR SpMV operations with single and double precision floating point operations in XAMG library, and the same comparison for preconditioned linear solvers used for solving large sparse SLAEs. The calculations were limited to a fixed number of iterations; the convergence of the method was not monitored. The number of iterations was selected for each method in such a way that the order of measurement times ranged from one to several tens of seconds.

5   Performance Evaluation Results

5.1   Comparison with MKL

Most of results presented below compare the performance of various formats in the XAMG library. To demonstrate relevance of the corresponding results with the other state of the art libraries, preliminary comparison of the SpMV operations in XAMG and MKL with basic CSR format is performed. The MKL comparison tests were performed on workstation with 6 OpenMP threads, and the inspector-executor sparse BLAS API was used to increase the MKL routines performance.

The obtained SpMV execution time results in the form of MKL to XAMG relative time are shown in Fig. 4. The values higher than 1 indicate advantage of the XAMG library; the lower values show the benefit of MKL. Most of the cases demonstrate comparable results within the range of ±5%. MKL outperforms XAMG by 25% with only three matrices, #23, #28, and #29. The detailed analysis has shown that these matrices have very irregular distribution of the nonzero elements and may require some additional specific optimizations to improve the SpMV operation performance. These optimizations, however, are out of topic of the current paper, and such matrices – out of the area of interest for the XAMG library. The averaged comparison results demonstrate about 2.5% performance gain for the MKL library if accounting all 40 matrices, and this value decreases to 0.06% if excluding three matrices with specific data distribution structure. These results allows to conclude that the XAMG library SpMV performance results with CSR format are comparable with the ones implemented in the well known MKL library.

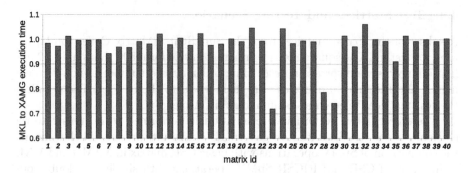

Fig. 4. Comparison of the SpMV operation execution time for the CSR matrix storage format in XAMG and MKL.

5.2   SpMV Performance for CSR and RICSR

The performance of the SpMV operation with CSR and RICSR formats in the XAMG library has been investigated for 4 ("Fp32") and 8 bytes ("Fp64") floating point numbers on both workstation and cluster node. The obtained results presented as the reference of the CSR to RICSR execution times is summarized in Fig. 5; results for both hardware platforms coincide within 1–2%. The speed up when using the RICSR format is observed for 17 out of 40 matrices. The average execution time reduction for these matrices by a factor of 1.28 and 1.17 for "Fp32" and "Fp64" test modes is achieved. It should be noted that for the other 23 matrices the execution time when using the RICSR is within 1–2% of the CSR one, i.e. the minor overhead to accululate indices, expectedly, does not affect the performance of memory bound SpMV operation.

The applicability criterion indicating the matrices which have the distance between the first and last nonzero elements per row lower than $2^{16} - 1$, fully correlates with the execution time results: the speed up is observed for exactly the same matrices, that meet the formulated criterion. The measured speed up also complies with the theoretical estimates, discussed in Sect. 3, and even slightly exceed the theoretical predictions.

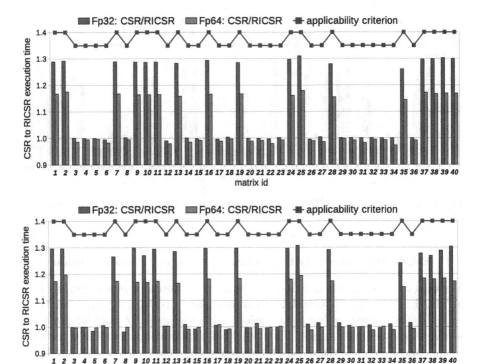

Fig. 5. Comparison of the SpMV operation execution time for the CSR and RICSR matrix storage formats with single and double precision floating point data; top − workstation, bottom − cluster node.

5.3 BiCGStab Solver

The next step of efficiency evaluation includes comparison of the BiCGStab solver [13] execution time when performing the calculations with CSR and RICSR matrix formats. The BiCGStab method combines matrix-vector multiplications together with vector operations, and thus efficiency of the method strongly depends on the efficiency of the SpMV operations. The corresponding test series for solving SLAEs with the matrices from the SuiteSparse Matrix collection and constant right-hand sides is calculated on workstation.

The results of corresponding experiments performed on workstation, demonstrate direct correlation with the matrix-vector multiplication results (Fig. 6). The absolute performance gain values slightly decrease due to the contribution of vector operations in the total solver execution time, however, this decrease is of only about 2–3%. Thus, for the "Fp32" mode the average execution time reduction decreases from 1.28 to 1.25, and for "Fp64" − from 1.17 to 1.15.

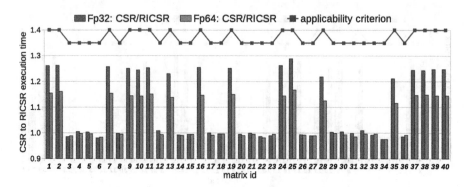

Fig. 6. Acceleration of the BiCGStab method when using RICSR format compared to CSR.

5.4   BiCGStab Solver with Algebraic Multigrid Preconditioner

The final test configuration includes estimating the potential of accelerating solving SLAEs using the BiCGStab method preconditioned with algebraic multigrid method. The corresponding combination of the methods is a popular choice for solving elliptic equations, and this result has practical impact. These tests are performed for both workstation and cluster node, investigate results for "Fp32" and "Fp64" modes and demonstrate the potential performance gain compared to the basic CSR data storage format. The fixed number of iteration of the numerical method are calculated to estimate the execution time, the convergence aspects are not considered in these tests.

The tests performed have shown that the use of RICSR can also be advantageous for solving SLAEs with robust iterative method configurations (Fig. 7; results for matrices #23, #26, #28, and #35 are missing on the plot due to the fact of failing the multigrid method to construct the corresponding matrix hierarchy). For the cluster node the calculations speed up on average by about a factor of 1.15 for "Fp32" mode and 1.10 for "Fp64" mode is observed. These values are slightly lower than for the SpMV tests, which can be explained by the presence of a significant portion of vector operations. Meanwhile, the workstation tests demonstrate better average results with the corresponding performance increase by a factor of 1.24 and 1.14, which comply with the values for the unpreconditioned BiCGStab solver.

It should be noted that the multigrid matrix hierarchy uses a set of matrices, and the RICSR applicability criterion is applied to each matrix. Thus, the information on fulfillment of the corresponding criterion is provided for the basic SLAE matrix (top level hierarchy matrix), which covers only single matrix but

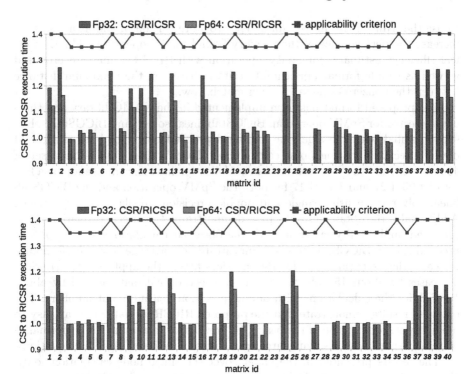

Fig. 7. Comparison of the execution time for the BiCGStab method with algebraic multigrid preconditioner using the CSR and RICSR matrix storage formats with single and double precision floating point data; top − workstation, bottom − cluster node. Missing data indicates the matrices for which the multigrid solver failed to construct a matrix hierarchy.

not the whole hierarchy. Even not satisfying this criterion some of the lower level matrices, however, may utilize the benefits of using the RICSR data storage format. This explains the observed minor speed up even for the matrices not satisfying the RICSR applicability criterion.

6 Conclusions

The paper presents row incremental CSR data storage format, which is a lightweight modification of the popular CSR format used for storing sparse matrices. It implements a more efficient storage of column indices of nonzero matrix elements by storing their offsets in a row instead of the base values. This allows to use the reduced size integer data types to store this data, and as a result, to increase the performance of the memory bound SpMV operation. The theoretical efficiency estimates for SpMV operation with RICSR format are proposed as well as simple format applicability criteria based on the maximum distance between the nonzero elements in each matrix row.

The proposed format has been implemented in the XAMG library and thoroughly tested for SpMV operation, BiCGStab linear solver, and BiCGStab solver supplemented with the algebraic multigrid preconditioner for both single and double precision floating point calculations. The obtained results for a set of 40 matrices from the SuiteSparse Matrix Collection have shown speedup by a factor of 1.25–1.27 and 1.15–1.17 for both the SpMV operation and the BiCGStab linear solver when using single and double precision calculations, respectively. Additionally, the obtained results have demonstrated the direct correlation of the proposed applicability criterion with the observed calculations speed up. The preconditioned BiCGStab solver demonstrates on average lower performance increase: the execution time for the matrices fitting the applicability criterion, decreases by about 15–20% for the single precision calculations and by about 10–15% for the calculations with double precision floating point numbers. The obtained results demonstrate that the proposed RICSR format can be an easy-to use lightweight extension of the basic CSR format for increasing the performance of iterative methods for solving large sparse systems of linear algebraic equations.

The results presented in the paper cover the single node calculations only. However, the same principle can be applied for multi-node calculations, when the matrix is distributed over the processes and segmented by blocks. Each block is stored as a separate submatrix and the RICSR format can be used to store each of them.

Acknowledgements. The current work is supported by the Russian Science Foundation Grant No. 18-71-10075. The research is carried out using the equipment of the shared research facilities of HPC computing resources at Lomonosov Moscow State University.

Appendix A. The List of Test Matrices

The performance evaluation tests were performed in this paper using a subset of matrices from SuiteSparse Matrix Collection. The details of the matrices used for testing are summarized in the Table 2. The columns of the table correspond to the ordinal numbers of the matrices, original matrix names, the number of rows, nonzero elements and the average number of nonzero elements per matrix row, and the maximal distance between the first and last nonzero elements in the matrix rows.

Table 2. A subset of sparse matrices from SuiteSparse Matrix Collection used for RICSR format efficiency evaluation.

Matrix id	Matrix name	Number of rows	Number of nonzeros	C	δ
1	Flan_1565	1564794	117406044	75	40994
2	ML_Geer	1504002	110879972	73.7	9317
3	dielFilterV3real	1102824	89306020	81	1036506
4	Long_Coup_dt0	1470152	87088992	59.2	71727
5	Long_Coup_dt6	1470152	87088992	59.2	71727
6	audikw_1	943695	77651847	82.3	928967
7	bone010	986703	71666325	72.6	25952
8	Serena	1391349	64531701	46.4	159833
9	Geo_1438	1437960	63156690	43.9	51839
10	Hook_1498	1498023	60917445	40.7	57845
11	boneS10	914898	55468422	60.6	17912
12	nv2	1453908	52728362	36.3	1128330
13	af_shell10	1508065	52672325	34.9	5259
14	dielFilterV2real	1157456	48538952	41.9	948112
15	ldoor	952203	46522475	48.9	687560
16	Emilia_923	923136	41005206	44.4	34475
17	dgreen	1200611	38259877	31.9	989317
18	RM07R	381689	37464962	98.2	310041
19	PFlow_742	742793	37138461	50	14256
20	inline_1	503712	36816342	73.1	502406
21	ss	1652680	34753577	21	1603068
22	vas_stokes_1M	1090664	34767207	31.9	1078014
23	nlpkkt80	1062400	28704672	27	550481
24	Fault_639	638802	28614564	44.8	39494
25	ML_Laplace	377002	27689972	73.4	4665
26	cage14	1505785	27130349	18	976037
27	F1	343791	26837113	78.1	343781
28	bone010_M	986703	23888775	24.2	25950
29	Transport	1602111	23500731	14.7	103362
30	CoupCons3D	416800	22322336	53.6	166723
31	gsm_106857	589446	21758924	36.9	589350
32	StocF-1465	1465137	21005389	14.3	73188
33	msdoor	415863	20240935	48.7	291414
34	bundle_adj	513351	20208051	39.4	510044
35	boneS10_M	914898	18489474	20.2	17910
36	Ga41As41H72	268096	18488476	69	69927
37	af_shell1	504855	17588875	34.8	9484
38	af_shell2	504855	17588875	34.8	9484
39	af_shell3	504855	17588875	34.8	9484
40	af_shell4	504855	17588875	34.8	9484

References

1. Intel Math Kernel Library (2020). https://software.intel.com/content/www/us/en/develop/tools/math-kernel-library.html. Accessed 27 Dec 2020
2. Balay, S., et al.: PETSc Web page (2018). http://www.mcs.anl.gov/petsc
3. Davis, T.A., Hu, Y.: The university of Florida sparse matrix collection. ACM Trans. Math. Softw. **38**(1), 1–25 (2011). https://doi.org/10.1145/2049662.2049663
4. Falgout, R.D., Yang, U.M.: *hypre*: a library of high performance preconditioners. In: Sloot, P.M.A., Hoekstra, A.G., Tan, C.J.K., Dongarra, J.J. (eds.) ICCS 2002. LNCS, vol. 2331, pp. 632–641. Springer, Heidelberg (2002). https://doi.org/10.1007/3-540-47789-6_66
5. Kourtis, K., Goumas, G., Koziris, N.: Optimizing sparse matrix-vector multiplication using index and value compression. In: Proceedings of the 5th Conference on Computing Frontiers, CF 2008, pp. 87–96. Association for Computing Machinery, New York (2008). https://doi.org/10.1145/1366230.1366244
6. Krasnopolsky, B., Medvedev, A.: Evaluating performance of mixed precision linear solvers with iterative refinement. Supercomput. Front. Innov. **8**(3), 4–16 (2021). https://doi.org/10.14529/jsfi210301
7. Krasnopolsky, B., Medvedev, A.: XAMG: a library for solving linear systems with multiple right-hand side vectors. https://doi.org/10.1016/j.softx.2021.100695
8. Krasnopolsky, B., Medvedev, A.: XAMG: Source code repository (2022). https://gitlab.com/xamg/xamg. Accessed 22 June 2022
9. Liu, W., Vinter, B.: CSR5. In: Proceedings of the 29th ACM on International Conference on Supercomputing. ACM (2015). https://doi.org/10.1145/2751205.2751209
10. Nishtala, R., Vuduc, R.W., Demmel, J.W., Yelick, K.A.: When cache blocking of sparse matrix vector multiply works and why. Appl. Algebra Eng. Commun. Comput. **18**, 297–311 (2007). https://doi.org/10.1007/s00200-007-0038-9
11. Saad, Y.: Iterative Methods for Sparse Linear Systems, 2nd edn. SIAM, Philadelpha (2003)
12. Vassiliadis, S., Cotofana, S., Stathis, P.: Block Based Compression Storage Expected Performance. Kluwer International Series in Engineering and Computer Science, vol. 657 (2001). https://doi.org/10.1007/978-1-4615-0849-6_26
13. van der Vorst, H.A.: BI-CGSTAB: a fast and smoothly converging variant of BI-CG for the solution of nonsymmetric linear systems. SIAM J. Sci. Stat. Comput. **13**(2), 631–644 (1992). https://doi.org/10.1137/0913035
14. Williams, S., Waterman, A., Patterson, D.: Roofline: an insightful visual performance model for multicore architectures. Commun. ACM **52**(4), 65–76 (2009). https://doi.org/10.1145/1498765.1498785

Root Causing MPI Workloads Imbalance Issues via Scalable MPI Critical Path Analysis

Artem Shatalin[✉], Vitaly Slobodskoy, and Maksim Fatin

Huawei, Computing Application Acceleration Technology Center, Nizhny Novgorod, Russia
{artem.shatalin,vitaly.slobodskoy}@huawei.com

Abstract. Analyzing performance of MPI application usually requires non-trivial approaches. Classical hotspot-based analysis is often misleading for such applications because hotspots optimization might not actually cause any speedup, but just increase the time ranks spent on waiting for each other.

One of the solutions is representing MPI program as a graph (known as Program Activity Graph) and perform only analysis of activities on Critical Path of this graph (the longest path containing computation and communication, but not waiting). Reducing computing time on Critical Path obviously reduces elapsed time of the whole application. While there are many papers in this area, Critical Path analysis representation in well-known performance tools is still quite limited. First of all, real-life HPC applications running on large scale produce huge Program Activity Graphs and scalability of classical graph algorithms is quite poor to calculate Critical Path reasonably fast. Moreover, using timing information only performance tools based on Critical Path provide limited capabilities. This paper describes an algorithm of building Program Activity Graph and calculating Critical Path which naturally scales to the same amount of CPU cores as profiled MPI application uses. We also show how to combine the Critical Path analysis with the hardware-level performance data available on all the modern CPUs to enable efficient root causing of MPI imbalance issues even on very high scale.

Keywords: MPI · Imbalance · HPC · Program Activity Graph · Critical path · Performance analysis · Hardware sampling · Tracing · Performance Monitoring Unit

1 Introduction

Development of scalable parallel applications is a very challenging task and its complexity grows significantly with the growth of target environment scale. One of the reasons of poor scaling is imbalance of work assigned to the hardware resources. Using MPI [6, 11] parallel programming standard, load imbalance can be detected by various tools measuring amount of time spent within MPI API functions. However it is very hard to root cause the exact reason of imbalance between various reasons candidates – for example, different MPI ranks might execute different amount of job, the slowdown might be caused by specific CPU Microarchitecture issues happening within dedicated ranks only, the communication path between particular ranks takes longer than for others, etc.

© The Author(s), under exclusive license to Springer Nature Switzerland AG 2022
V. Voevodin et al. (Eds.): RuSCDays 2022, LNCS 13708, pp. 501–521, 2022.
https://doi.org/10.1007/978-3-031-22941-1_37

All these cases cause increase of the time spent within MPI API functions waiting on implicit barriers.

The traditional performance analysis methodology is based on statistical sampling [14–18] providing the list of so-called "hotspot" functions (or modules, threads, etc.) – the list of the most frequently executed places in the profiling application using statistical measurement. This analysis usually provides quite detailed and precise information about places in the code where CPU spent its time. However, collecting performance data from the whole HPC cluster for MPI workload, often results in MPI runtime spin locks within top hotspot functions. This happens due to MPI ranks imbalance resulting to additional wait time. Meanwhile the real root cause of imbalance can be easily hidden by ineffective CPU utilization accumulated from the majority of ranks.

Another common approach in performance analysis is tracing [19–23]. Tracing is based on ability to hook particular events or function calls within application, parallel runtime, operating system, etc. using static source level or dynamic runtime instrumentation. The primary idea is to inject profiling code into the relevant point of application execution in order to measure various characteristics – e.g. number of function calls, function duration, capture call stack, etc.

Tracing all the MPI runtime functions, MPI program can be represented as a graph (known as Program Activity Graph [9]) to analyze only activities on Critical Path [8] of this graph (the longest path containing computation and communication, but not waiting). Reducing computing time on Critical Path obviously reduces elapsed time of the whole application.

In order to simplify the analysis of MPI workloads, we propose to combine traditional performance analysis methodologies with MPI Critical Path analysis to characterize application execution on Critical Path only naturally representing the root causes of imbalance and minimize amount of useless data (e.g. there is no wait time on the Critical Path by definition). We show how to find Critical Path in a fast and reliable way performing scalable calculation right on the MPI cluster used for the application execution. We demonstrate the usefulness of data retrieved as a result of this performance tuning approach.

The paper is organized as follows: Sect. 2 introduces the terms Program Activity Graph and Critical Path, lists works related to finding the longest path in the graph and known methodologies to apply Critical Path analysis in understanding imbalance issues of parallel applications. Section 3 describes hardware sampling approach and hotspots representation. Section 4 explains how combination of Critical Path analysis and sampling-based hotspots helps in triaging of parallel application imbalance issues. Section 5 describes an algorithm of Program Activity Graph creation for MPI applications and finding Critical Path in the graph. Section 6 provides results of Critical Path analysis and compares regular hotspots with hotspots on Critical Path only. Section 7 evaluates the performance of the proposed solution. The conclusion is in Sect. 8.

2 Prior State of the Art

An approach to finding the Critical Path on the execution graph of parallel programs in order to root cause imbalance issues has been exposed in the literature since 1980s. Graph that represents program activities during the program's execution has been called Program Activity Graph (PAG) [9]. Program Activity (PA) is a non-overlapping individual job which has duration. A precedence relationship exists among the PAs – some PAs must be finished before others can start. PAG is a directed, weighted, acyclic graph, whose vertices represent beginnings and endings of PAs associated with particular communication events (e.g. send/receive) in a program and whose edges represent the duration of PA.

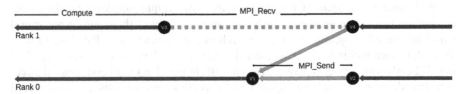

Fig. 1. Part of program activity graph.

On the Fig. 1 the example of typical PAG segment, for better understanding of events occurrence, we'll represent PAG on the timeline. Horizontal axis is a time (from left to right), vertical axis represents MPI ranks. Green lines represent PAG edges (Program Activities). Yellow lines are communication edges connecting endings and beginnings of PAs (graph vertices, marked as v#) with precedence relationship. If there is more than 1 outgoing communication edge possible, only the shortest one is marked as solid yellow line, others are marked as dotted yellow lines (not considered to be edges of graph). The direction of PAG is from right to left (from the ending of application execution to the beginning).

The Critical Path is the longest path in the graph. The typical way to find the longest path in the directed acyclic graph is to use shortest path algorithms with negative weights [24]. A well-known sequential algorithm to solve this problem for directed acyclic graphs is Dijkstra's algorithm which complexity linearly depends on the number of edges. It has various modifications like A* algorithm [25] efficiently operating under particular assumptions, or parallel Delta-stepping [26] and its modifications [27, 28] with reasonable performance on large clusters and supercomputers. Another approach is based on the knowledge of incoming edges for any vertex and shows up to 46% better performance in single-thread implementation comparing with Dijkstra's algorithm, while also compares favorably to Delta-stepping in parallel implementation [29].

A first attempt to apply Critical Path analysis methodologies for the parallel programs was presented in [9] with parallel version of longest path algorithm based on [30]. Later, an online algorithm for finding the critical path has been proposed [10]. Their approach is based on the idea to combine instrumentation messages into the application messages achieving ~5% of analysis overhead on synthetic benchmarks.

By the 2000s, Critical Path analysis targets MPI workloads. In [1] researches described an algorithm for finding the Critical Path based on tracing of MPI calls. While they report just 8% of overhead on 64 nodes (ranks) on particular case, the scalability of their approach is questionable, because it is based on merging local subgraphs into a single graph with further critical path analysis done on a single node. Graph reduction steps are introduced in order to reduce processing time. They also suggest capturing call stacks of MPI functions associated with each graph node to simplify analysis of imbalance root causes. One of the significant limitations mentioned in the paper is inability to handle long-running applications due to potentially huge amount of data captured on every rank and the need to store local subgraphs.

A similar to [10] online approach to find Critical Path for MPI workloads has been explored in [31] with just 1% overhead per 10000 MPI calls per rank on synthetic benchmark.

While the performance of Critical Path analysis can be quite impressive under particular circumstances (e.g. synthetic benchmark, small scale, etc.), the results on real-world workloads were less optimistic. In [2] researchers explained a Critical Path based analysis implemented within Scalasca toolset [5]. Their approach is based on capturing of all the MPI calls with further replay of relevant calls in both backward and forward directions in order to exchange data required for the performance analysis at each recorded synchronization point using a communication operation similar to the one originally used by the program. There is only one benchmark result mentioned in the paper which leads to 148% of overall critical path analysis overhead. A backward replay might also potentially cause stability issues leading to hangs of the analysis process.

An approach for automatic search of optimization suggestions using Critical Path analysis of task graph built on top of GASPI [7] applications was considered in [3]. The Critical Path detection method is based on backward traversal of the extended task graph where it is assumed that the whole graph is present on the single node and parallel version of critical path analysis algorithm is not considered. However, this is probably the first approach where critical path data has been combined with memory access analysis.

Critical path analysis has been used for performance modelling in [4] introducing the concept of critical-path candidates (group of paths that could potentially be the critical path). However, instead of using execution time as a primary metric for critical path construction, instruction and communication counts are used in order to perform precise microarchitecture-independent modelling.

One of the most recent papers [32] underlines the importance of Critical Path for the efficient performance analysis of the real-world HPC workloads. A new metric called "Workflow Critical Path" is defined to characterize distributed workloads. A cloud-based infrastructure has been developed for Critical Path analysis using algorithm proposed in [28], however, the performance of their implementation hasn't been fully uncovered.

In this paper we propose a highly scalable MPI calls replay based solution for constructing the Critical Path with less than 5% of collection overhead and less than 5% of application elapsed time spent on post-processing independently on the number of ranks. Our approach has been tested on various real-world workloads and stays within performance targets even on relatively high scale (available to us for testing). Moreover, we suggest combining critical path data with hardware sampling data in order to:

1) Represent the most critical information for the further optimization (any reduction of Critical Path will lead to application elapsed time reduction).
2) Limit the amount of performance data analyzed to the size equal to performance data size collected from a single MPI rank only due to Critical Path relates to just a single rank at any moment of application execution time. This naturally supports

any scale since the amount of performance data to be analyzed is always limited and depends on the application execution time only.

3 Hardware Sampling Based Hotspots

Performance profiling efficiency hardly depends on the analysis intrusiveness. The techniques based on static [19, 20] or dynamic [35–38] instrumentation usually add significant overhead (2–100x) growing with increase of details level. Our experiments show that using default settings of Score-P [33] source level instrumentation system leads to more than 5× (500%) of collection runtime overhead on LAMMPS [34] workload using Scalasca toolset [5] on single node with 2 × 64 core Hisilicon Kunpeng 920 CPU (2.6 GHz). The primary root cause of the overhead is instrumentation of all the function calls in order to provide proper source-level attribution.

Non-intrusive approach to the performance analysis is based on the hardware sampling [14, 15]. All modern CPUs have Performance Monitoring Unit (PMU) [39] providing hardware counters with the ability to trigger hardware interrupt (Performance Monitoring Interrupt, PMI) when counter reaches programmable threshold value. Performance tools can capture operating system (thread ID, process ID) and hardware context (timestamp, counter ID, counter value, instruction pointer, physical/logical core) within PMI handler providing detailed analysis level using statistical measurement. All the data captured within a single PMI is a *sample*.

Moreover, combining instruction pointer information with dynamic module load/unload events, using symbol and debug information from the module binary, it is possible to attribute every sample to the function, source file and source line. Since function and source level resolution can be done after data collection, source-level attribution for the hardware sampling can be achieved with less than 5% of collection overhead primarily depending on the event threshold value only.

Let S be the set containing all the samples captured during performance analysis data collection with set of counters $C = \{c_1, c_2, \ldots, c_p\}$, $|C| = p$. Every sample $s \in S$ has a timestamp *time* (s), counter identifier $c(s) \in C$, counter value *value* (s) and a set of attribute values $a_i(s) \in A_i, A_i \in A, |A| = k, i \in 1..k$, A_i is a set containing all the possible attribute i values, it also can be called as *sample attribute* assuming attribute type (or name). Attributes represent all the characteristics retrieved directly within PMI handler (e.g. instruction pointer, CPU core PMI happened on, etc.) or after post-processing analysis (e.g. module, function, source file, etc.).

Aggregation is an accumulation of sample values:

$$t = \{v_j | j \in 1..p\}, v_j = \sum_{s \in S, c(s) = c_j, j \in 1..p} value(s) \tag{1}$$

Grouping is one or more sample attributes:

$$G = \left(A^1, A^2, \ldots, A^l\right), A^j \in A, j \in 1..l, 1 \leq l \leq k \tag{2}$$

Grouping value for sample s is defined as: $g(s, G) = (a_1(s), a_2(s), \ldots, a_l(s))$. Consider all the possible combinations of grouping values for grouping G and set of samples

S:

$$U(S, G) = \left\{ u = (a_1, a_2, \ldots, a_l) \,\middle|\, u \in \prod_{j=1}^{l} A^j, \exists s \in S : a_j(s) = a_j, j \in 1..l \right\} \quad (3)$$

Aggregation of samples S by grouping G is:

$$T = \left\{ (u, v_1, v_2, \ldots, v_p) \right\} \quad (4)$$

Every item of T contains grouping attribute values and aggregated values of counters $c_1, c_2, \ldots c_p \in C$.

$M_\theta = F_\theta\left(v_{i_1}, v_{i_2}, \ldots, v_{i_{q(\theta)}}\right), 1 \le i_j \le p, j \in 1..q(\theta)$, where F_θ is any function $N^q \to R$ depending on values $v_{i_1}, v_{i_2} \ldots, v_{i_q}$ of counters $c_{i_1}, c_{i_2}, \ldots, c_{i_q}$, is called *metric definition* or just *metric*. Let $M = \{\}$ is a set of metric definitions and M_0 is a definition of *primary metric*. For each item in aggregation of samples S by grouping G vector of values $\{m_0, m_1, \ldots, m_\tau\}$ of corresponding metrics can be calculated from the counter values $v_1, v_2, \ldots, v_p$. Table $H(S, G, M)$ with rows representing items of aggregation of samples where $v_1, v_2, \ldots, v_p$ is replaced with $\{m_0 \ldots m_\tau\}$, sorted by the value m_0 of primary metric M_0 in descending order is called *hotspots*.

Example: Let $c_1 = Cycles$ – one of the most frequently used PMU counters incrementing cycle of CPU; $c_2 = Instruction$ s – another popular PMU counter incrementing on each instruction retired from the CPU pipeline. Then $CPU\ Time = \frac{Cycles}{CPU\ frequency}$, $CPI = \frac{Cycles}{Instructions}$ – the most popular metrics in performance analysis.

Let $G = (Function, Module)$, $M = \{M_0 = CPU\ Time, M_1 = CPI\}$, CPU frequency is constant and equals to 2.6 GHz. S contains 1000 samples of counter *Cycles* and 300 samples of counter *Instruction* s with *Function* = main and *Module* = main, 200 samples of counter *Cycles* and 500 samples of counter *Instruction* s with.

Function = memset and *Module* = libc.so,

Hotspots $H(S, G, M)$ will be (Fig 2):

Function	Module	CPU Time(s)	CPI
main	main	0.769	0.300
memset	libc.so.0.0.0	0.154	2.500

Fig. 2. Hotspots example

CPU time is a primary metric representing places in the code where CPU spent most of the cycles. CPI metric indicates efficiency of CPU Microarchitecture usage (smaller value is better). It also can be represented as Instructions Per Cycle (IPC). A Top-Down Analysis is a set of other metrics based on hardware counters enabling methodological root causing of CPU Microarchitecture efficiency issues [40]. The accuracy of PMU metric values depends on the event threshold (smaller value gives better accuracy, however, too small value might cause much higher collection overhead due to frequent PMI handling negatively affecting application execution) and the number of samples contributed to the hotspots entry (higher – better).

Various popular tools use hardware sampling for the lightweight performance analysis: HPCToolkit [41], Tau [42]. On Linux hardware counters can be accessed through PAPI [43], Linux perf [16] or custom drivers.

Hotspots is a basic performance data for the CPU compute-intensive applications, however, later in the paper we'll show that using only hotspots data for analyzing MPI application is often not enough and, in some cases, can be even misleading. But combining hardware samples with the Critical Path analysis will lead directly to the functions which are the most important for optimization.

4   Root Causing MPI Imbalance Issues

There are many tools which measure MPI Imbalance Time for the application execution [44, 45], however they usually do not provide any clues about the reasons of imbalance. Consider the following list of hotspots:

Function	Module	CPU Time(s)
hmca_bcol_basesmuma_bcast_k...	hmca_bcol_basesmuma.so	2838.6540
uct_dc_mlx5_iface_progress_ll	libuct_ib.so.0.0.0	2795.7913
uct_mm_iface_progress	libuct.so.0.0.0	2327.4292
opal_progress	libopen-pal.so.40.30.1	2090.3369

Fig. 3. Hotspots with MPI Imbalance Time

Figure 3 lists a set of typical hotspots functions for the application using Open-MPI runtime. Functions within modules hmca_bcol_basesmuma.so, libuct*.so, libopen-pal.so and other dynamic libraries related to the OpenMPI software stack, represent spinning/waiting within MPI runtime. If these functions take the leading position in the hotspots data, it is usually a sign for the significant MPI Imbalance Time in the application. However, analyzing spinning functions is a wrong way since we have to determine why there is so much waiting in the ranks.

Using only PMU samples belonging to the time intervals on Critical Path as a source for hotspots data allows to naturally filter out all the spinning (since there is no wait time on critical path by definition) and get only meaningful information (Fig. 4):

Function	Module	CPU Time(s)
__mapz_module_MOD_ppm2m	cesm.exe	1977.2391
__clubb_intr_MOD_clubb_tend...	cesm.exe	1969.3700
memcpy	libc-2.28.so	1342.6702
__physics_types_MOD_physics...	cesm.exe	1200.6958

Fig. 4. Hotspots on critical path

In general, hotspots on critical path can highlight the most critical performance problems to be solved – either computing hotspots related to the algorithm, CPU

Microarchitecture issues (if various Microarchitecture hardware counters are sampled) or communication issues.

5   Finding Critical Path in Program Activity Graph

Program Activity Graph is a graph reconstructed from the MPI calls traced during application execution. Let define Program Activity Graph construction rules:

1. Graph vertex is a beginning or ending of MPI call on a particular rank.
2. Graph vertex gets weight, which equals to the elapsed time from the beginning of the application execution to the beginning/ending of corresponding MPI call.
3. Every vertex has only one outgoing edge. All the edges are directed from the node having bigger weight to the one having smaller weight. Edge representing communication time goes to the vertex with the highest weight (rank with the latest further MPI call start time).
4. Everything executed outside of MPI call is treated as a useful compute job (Program Activity).
5. Program Activity edges stay on the same rank.

Program Activity Graph is a weighted acyclic graph for which Critical Path finding complexity linearly depends on the number of edges [24]. However, we'll show below that the graph constructed such a way allows very efficient and scalable algorithm for finding the Critical Path.

The core idea of the Critical Path analysis is a replay of all the MPI calls in order to exchange call timings between relevant ranks. The basic structure of the algorithm is the following:

- Runtime:

  - Trace all the relevant MPI calls with arguments capture for enabling further replay.

- Post-processing (done within MPI_Finalize call of the application):

  - Reconstruction of MPI communicators used by application.
  - Exchange timings information between P2P senders and receivers via MPI P2P calls replay (from sender to receiver) and further collective-based exchange (from receiver to sender).
  - Graph edges creation, replay of MPI collective calls.
  - Finding Critical Path: retrieve time intervals of the path within the corresponding ranks via traversing Program Activity Graph from the rank with the latest MPI_Finalize call time.

Lemma 1. There is only one path on the last step of the algorithm.

Proof: As every node has only one outgoing edge and graph is acyclic (graph construction rule 3), there is only one path in the graph from every node representing MPI_Finalize.

Since only a single start node is chosen based on MPI_Finalize start time, there is only one path found.

The features of the proposed algorithm:

1) Efficiently utilizes all the available computing resources naturally inheriting the cluster topology knowledge from the application.
2) Every rank keeps and maintains information about its own graph nodes and edges only.
3) Post-processing elapsed time depends on the application elapsed time and is supposed to be less than 5% of elapsed time of the application in general case. This conclusion comes out from the replay-based nature of the algorithm – MPI calls from the application are replayed only without computing portion of the application, the amount of data transferred within replay has small fixed amount for every MPI call. The post-processing overhead depends on the frequency of MPI calls done by the application.

As a result, the proposed algorithm for the critical path analysis allows to maintain perfect scalability and reliably works for the high scale environment.

5.1 Data Collection

In order to build Program Activity Graph, it is required to trace all the MPI calls within every rank of the target application. We use PMPI [12] and LD_PRELOAD mechanisms for tracing, which does not require target application recompilation. It allows to intercept all the relevant MPI calls and capture required arguments. There are 2 groups of MPI calls requiring dedicated handling:

1) MPI calls related to communicators management (e.g. MPI_Comm_create, MPI_Comm_dup, etc.). In order to enable replay of MPI calls on the post-processing stage, it is required to reconstruct all the MPI communicators, because communicators can be destroyed during application execution. Communicators reconstruction involves some challenges related to proper handling of pointer and array arguments, as well mapping of communicators on analysis stage.
2) Other synchronous and asynchronous MPI calls related to communication between ranks. In order to successfully replay (re-execute) all the relevant MPI calls, all the required arguments are preserved for every MPI call (e.g. communicator, root, source, tag, etc.). In order to build Program Activity Graph, the required timing information is also captured (start/end time using MPI_Wtime). Since the replay transfers timing information only, the original data, transferred within MPI calls, is not preserved. Special handling of MPI_ANY_SOURCE and MPI_ANY_TAG is required in order to know the actual sender information.

All the traced data can be stored on the local (for the rank) file system (preferred) or, in case of lacking local file system space, can be kept within memory of rank process (since post-processing stage executes within application processes). Storing data to the shared file system is possible, but less preferred due to potential network bandwidth issues.

5.2 MPI Communicators Reconstruction

Communicators reconstruction is required because communicators can be destructed using MPI_Comm_free. Communicator management MPI calls are executed in the same order as during the application execution using an arguments captured during data collection. Mapping between preserved and reconstructed communicators is carefully maintained during further replay of MPI calls.

5.3 Exchange Timings Information Between P2P Senders and Receivers

The purpose of this step is building graph edges between nodes related to P2P MPI calls in a scalable way. In order to support this, every P2P call has to retrieve a timing information about its pair call. This happens in 2 stages:

1) Replay of P2P calls and Wait/Waitall calls related to asynchronous P2P calls. Receivers get information about senders on this stage.
2) Use MPI collective calls in order to distribute information about receivers to every sender.

Let's consider a simple example (Fig. 5):

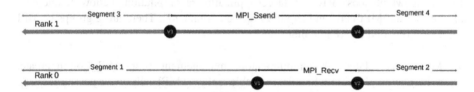

Fig. 5. Typical MPI send/receive pattern

Here, MPI_Ssend is used to send a message, MPI_Recv is used to receive the message. During the first stage, MPI_Ssend sends the following information:

- Time points v3, v4
- Previous computing segment (Segment 3)

Rank 0 receives and preserves this information together with its own timings v1, v2 and previous computing segment (Segment 1).

On the second stage the sequence of MPI_Alltoallv calls is used in order to send similar data from receivers to senders. Every MPI_Alltoallv invocation can send information about up to 200000 calls.

5.4 Graph Edges Creation

This step is responsible for edges creation in Program Activity Graph. The logic for edge construction depends on the type of MPI call node relates to (collective or P2P). One important property is that ranks preserve outgoing edges only, they don't know about incoming edges.

The primary edge creation rule is based on the Program Activity Graph construction rule 3: consider k time intervals of related MPI calls $[b_i; e_i]$, $i \in 1..k$, for every e_i create an edge $(e_i \rightarrow b)$ where $\exists j : b = b_j, e_i > b_j, \nexists l : b_l > b_j, j \in 1..k, l \in 1..k$.

Let's take a look on the following example of how it is done for P2P calls (Fig. 6):

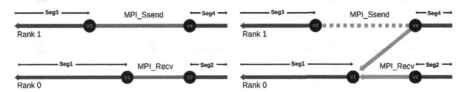

Fig. 6. Creating graph edges for P2P calls

There are two MPI calls in the example: MPI_Ssend and MPI_Recv, create an edge to the rank with the latest MPI call start time: from v4 to v1 for rank 1, from v2 to v1 for rank 0.

While time intersection between pair of P2P calls looks like a natural requirement, in reality MPI runtime can execute some optimizations and place the data in a buffer for more effective transfer. In this case time intervals of P2P calls might not intersect. Consider the following example (Fig. 7):

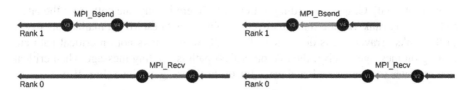

Fig. 7. Caching is involved within P2P calls

When this happens, there is no actual wait between both parties (sender and receiver), so no cross-rank edges are created: v4 → v3 for rank 1, v2 → v1 for rank 0.

When asynchronous MPI calls are used, both asynchronous call and corresponding MPI_Wait are included in the related time intervals ([v1; v2], [v3; v4], [v5; v6]) (Fig. 8):

All the synchronous collective MPI calls during replay are replaced to the call of MPI_Allreduce in order to find the highest begin time for every end point (Fig. 9):

Asynchronous collective calls follow the same rule taking into account that corresponding MPI_Wait calls are also included into the related intervals list.

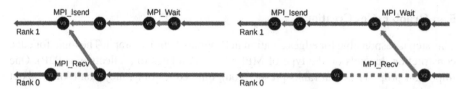

Fig. 8. Asynchronous P2P calls. Left picture: v3 is the highest begin point for v4 and v2 (v5 > v4, v5 > v2), v5 is the highest begin point for v6. Right picture: v3 is the highest begin point for v4, v5 is the highest begin point for v6 and v2.

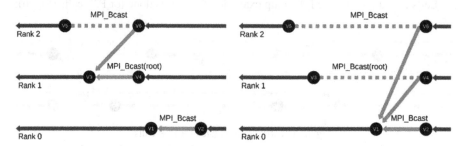

Fig. 9. Synchronous collective calls

5.5 Finding the Critical Path

As result of previous steps, Program Activity Graph satisfying graph construction rules has been created. Every MPI rank has information about graph vertices related to MPI calls executed on this rank. Every graph vertex has information about a single outgoing edge potentially going to the vertex in another rank.

In order to find the Critical Path we need to traverse through edges of the whole Program Activity Graph. According to Lemma 1, there is only one path from the latest node on every rank. So, the starting traversal point is the latest MPI_Finalize call across all the ranks. Traversing is done using P2P calls where ranks not on critical path are waiting on message receive, the one on critical path is sending message when critical path migrates to another rank and waits for further message receive (Fig. 10):

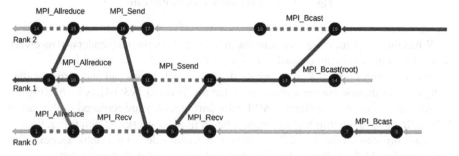

Fig. 10. Critical path example

When rank receives message, it stores locally Critical Path time intervals going through this rank. At the end, every rank gets its own Critical Path time intervals locally, some ranks may have this list empty. The accumulated duration of Critical Path intervals is always less than application elapsed time.

6 PMU Samples Aggregation on the Critical Path

While Critical Path intervals can be used in analysis of imbalance issues [13], we propose combination of Critical Path data with PMU samples, which can effectively highlight algorithmic and CPU Microarchitecture issues. Since every PMU sample can have hardware and software context associated to it (time, event, sample count, core, instruction pointer, process, thread, etc.), it is possible to aggregate PMU samples on Critical Path intervals and filter out samples with the time out of any interval on Critical Path. As every rank has information about its own Critical Path intervals, PMU samples aggregation can natively be parallelized across the ranks on Critical Path, and the amount of time required to perform this action is always equal or less than the time needed to process PMU samples collected on a single rank only (Fig. 11).

There are two primary advantages on analyzing hotspots on Critical Path only:

1. Hotspots on the Critical Path naturally highlight activities having the most significant influence on the application elapsed time. Optimization of the hotspots on Critical Path obviously leads to the reduction of application elapsed time. Various situations are easily handled with Hotspots on Critical Path:

   - Load imbalance due to the difference in the code flows (e.g. amount of load) within ranks.
   - CPU Microarchitecture Issues happening in particular ranks only.
   - Communication problems (e.g. improper MPI stack configuration).

2. It brings natural scaling capability for the performance analysis tool, because aggregation of PMU samples on Critical Path always limits the amount of aggregating samples to the number of samples collected from within just a single node:

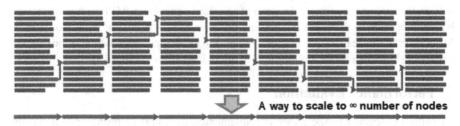

A way to scale to ∞ number of nodes

Fig. 11. Scaling of PMU data analysis with critical path

6.1 Hotspots on Critical Path – Examples

By Top Hotspots here we mean first 5 rows of hotspots list where PMU samples from all the ranks are aggregated. By Top Hotspots on MPI Critical Path we mean hotspots aggregated from the samples falling to the time intervals of Critical Path only (all the ranks).

```
Top Hotspots on MPI Critical Path
Function               Module        CPU Time(s)  Inst Retired    CPI
--------------------------------------------------------------------
zgemm_                 pw.x          15.1443      42899112983     0.9179
ztrsm_                 pw.x           3.2306       7691043444     1.0921
dlaebz_                pw.x           2.8353       2478888508     2.9738
zher2k_                pw.x           2.7822       8033314443     0.9005
zgemv_                 pw.x           2.1234       5357958074     1.0304

Top Hotspots
Function                    Module                CPU Time(s)   Inst Retired       CPI
-------------------------------------------------------------------------------------
hmca_bcol_basesmuma_bcast_k... hmca_bcol_basesmuma.so  13383.5000  93319394951143  0.3729
ucp_worker_progress         libucp.so.0.0.0       12456.9659    69298900225456   0.4674
hmca_bcol_basesmuma_barrier... hmca_bcol_basesmuma.so  10216.3521  79180406179086  0.3355
uct_mm_iface_progress       libuct.so.0.0.0        4788.1269    28096224988430   0.4431
zgemm_                      pw.x                   4519.1347    12829183732610   0.9159
```

Fig. 12. Hotspots on MPI critical path comparing to non-filtered hotspots, QuantumEspresso benchmark

```
Top Hotspots on MPI Critical Path
Function       Module CPU Time(s)  Inst Retired    CPI
------------------------------------------------------
compute_rhs_   bt.C.x   0.2853      801341496    0.9257
binvcrhs_      bt.C.x   0.2664     1646724591    0.4206
x_solve_cell_  bt.C.x   0.2565      951072004    0.7013
z_solve_cell_  bt.C.x   0.2408      900313343    0.6953
y_solve_cell_  bt.C.x   0.2329      942058909    0.6428

Top Hotspots
Function                      Module            CPU Time(s)   Inst Retired      CPI
----------------------------------------------------------------------------------
uct_dc_mlx5_iface_progress_ll libuct_ib.so.0.0.0  295.3117   1400019640511   0.5484
binvcrhs_                     bt.C.x             182.3859    862089470040    0.5501
compute_rhs_                  bt.C.x             164.1930    372248709623    1.1468
x_solve_cell_                 bt.C.x             137.2237    454555473911    0.7849
y_solve_cell_                 bt.C.x             136.8946    516508431287    0.6891
```

Fig. 13. Hotspots on MPI critical path comparing to non-filtered hotspots, NAS Parallel benchmark (NPB) BT

On both examples Top Hotspots are misleading because contain MPI runtime internals on the top, whereas the real reason of the slow-down is not MPI runtime slowness, but spinning due to the ranks are waiting others who are on critical path. Hotspots on MPI critical paths lead to the compute-intensive part of application which is the primary reason of slowdown by the definition of Critical Path (Figs. 12 and 13).

7 Performance Evaluation

Algorithm described in the paper is implemented as a part of profiling tool. In this section we provide performance characteristics of this tool. The results are collected on the clusters with Huawei Taishan 2280v2 compute nodes. The data on 1-4 nodes is in Table 1, 2, 3 and Fig. 14, 15. The data from 8-64 nodes is in Table 4:

- 2×64 core Hisilicon Kunpeng 920 CPU, 2.6 GHz
- 256 GB DRAM, DDR4
- Storage: PCI-e NVME SSDs
- Interconnect: NVIDIA® (Mellanox) Infiniband Connect X6 100 Gb adapters, 100 Gb switch
- Operating system: CentOS 8
- Compiler: gcc/gfortran 11.2
- MPI: OpenMPI 4.1.4

Benchmarks used for tool performance characteristics evaluation:

- NAS Parallel Benchmark BT (NPB BT): solver for synthetic system of nonlinear partial different equations using block tridiagonal algorithm [46]
- NAS Parallel Benchmark LU (NPB LU): solver for synthetic system of nonlinear partial different equations using Lower-Upper symmetric Gauss-Seidel algorithm [46]
- MiniFE: sparse linear system solver using a simple un-preconditioned conjugate-gradient algorithm [47]
- WRF: Weather Research and Forecasting Model – a numerical weather prediction and atmospheric simulation system [48]

Columns description:

- Nodes: number of compute nodes used.
- Ranks: total number of MPI ranks.
- Problem size: in all the examples below computation is done on 3-dimension grid. Computation complexity of the benchmark linearly depends on the size of each dimension. Size on each dimension is provided.
- Elapsed time(s) – wall time of the slowest rank. Either reported by benchmark itself (NPB) or measured by time command for MPI launcher.
- Elapsed time under collector (s) – elapsed time of application running under the tool, not including post-processing time.
- Overhead – elapsed time difference with and without tool. Value in percent is normalized by application elapsed time.
- Postprocessing – wall time spent on post-processing (including Critical Path analysis), measured by the tool. Value in percent is normalized by application elapsed time.
- MPI Calls total and average per-rank average number of MPI calls. Measured by the tool.

Table 1. Runtime collection overhead and data post-processing time for NPB BT

Nodes	Ranks	Problem size	Elapsed time (s)	Elapsed time under collector (s)	Overhead		Postprocessing		MPI calls	
					s	%	s	%	Total	Per rank
1	121	224× 224× 224	137.611	138.945	1.334	0.97	0.529	0.38	8,005,118	66,158
2	256	320× 320× 320	130.621	132.071	1.450	1.11	0.545	0.42	24,631,808	96,218
4	400	384× 384× 384	132.891	134.741	1.850	1.39	0.537	0.40	48,103,628	120,259
4	484	408× 408× 408	114.041	115.439	1.398	1.23	0.522	0.46	64,028,360	132,290

Table 2. Runtime collection overhead and data post-processing time for NPB LU

Nodes	Ranks	Problem size	Elapsed time (s)	Elapsed time under collector (s)	Overhead		Postprocessing		MPI calls	
					s	%	s	%	Total	Per rank
1	128	256× 256× 256	67.834	70.361	2.527	3.73	3.261	4.81	71,235,432	556,527
2	256	320× 320× 320	61.425	63.811	2.386	3.88	2.823	4.60	184,370,232	720,196
3	384	384× 384× 384	70.071	72.321	2.250	3.21	3.129	4.47	335,724,808	874,283
4	512	408× 408× 408	68.320	70.837	2.517	3.68	2.872	4.20	478,295,000	934,170

The data shows that runtime overhead and post-processing time is less than 5% of application elapsed time. It is stable and doesn't grow with increasing number of ranks. Also on the benchmarks with small number of MPI calls per rank post-processing time is close to zero (Fig. 15).

We also performed evaluation and comparison of performance with Scalasca toolset [5] on the same hardware configuration:

Table 3. Runtime collection overhead and data post-processing time for miniFE benchmark

Nodes	Ranks	Problem size	Elapsed time (s)	Elapsed time under collector (s)	Overhead		Postprocessing		MPI calls	
					s	%	s	%	Total	Per rank
1	128	1024× 512× 512	120.074	122.522	2.448	2.04	0.044	0.04	899,008	7,024
2	256	1024× 1024× 512	122.572	124.886	2.314	1.89	0.046	0.04	1,977,536	7,725
3	384	1024× 1024× 768	121.861	124.084	2.223	1.82	0.048	0.04	2,912,448	7,585
4	512	1024× 1024× 1024	124.244	126.113	1.869	1.50	0.043	0.04	4,350,016	8,496

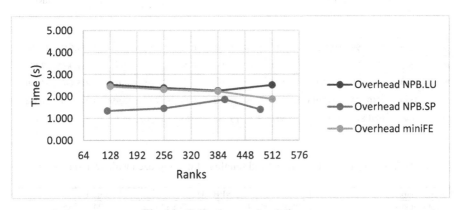

Fig. 14. Collection overhead diagram

The difference in performance with Scalasca is up to 30× Table 5. We also met with a set of stability issues with Scalasca: miniFE benchmark wasn't able to compile with Score-P instrumentation, Scalasca tool post-processing wasn't able to finish on NPB LU benchmark with 384×384×384 grid size. Our tool has no stability issues on such workloads.

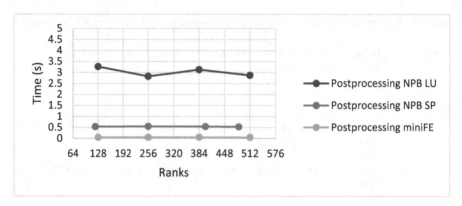

Fig. 15. Post processing time diagram

Table 4. Collection of overhead and data post-processing time for WRF benchmark

Nodes	Ranks	Elapsed time (s)	Elapsed time under collector (s)	Overhead		Postprocessing		MPI calls		Overhead per call (us)
				s	%	s	%	Total	Per rank	
8	256	5992.799	6037.222	44.423	0.74	6.831	0.11	386,975,194	1,511,622	29.388
16	512	3032.759	3075.891	43.132	1.42	7.236	0.24	812,547,288	1,587,006	27.178
32	1024	2079.178	2125.290	46.112	2.22	7.254	0.35	1,859,041,028	1,815,470	25.399
48	1536	1210.573	1247.913	37.340	3.08	7.102	0.59	2,684,833,958	1,747,939	21.362
64	2048	1091.817	1127.626	35.809	3.28	7.447	0.68	3,833,675,393	1,871,912	19.129

Table 5. Comparison the overhead and stability of our approach with Scalasca toolset

Benchmark		NPB LU		miniFE
Problem size		384x384x384	320x320x320	1024x512x512
Scale (nodes x ranks)		1x128	1x128	1x128
Elapsed time (s)		195.24	121.85	120.08
Under collection	Our tool	199.95 (+2.41%)	122.64 (+0.64%)	125.52 (+2.04%)
	Scalasca	255.38 (+30.80%)	147.25 (+21.41%)	Failure
Post-processing (s)	Our tool	3.29 (1.69%)	2.89 (2.37%)	0.044 (0.04%)
	Scalasca	Out of memory after 96s	86.45 (60.52%)	Failure
Collected data size	Our tool	4.1GB	3.3GB	57MB
	Scalasca	96GB	64 GB	Failure

8 Conclusion

In order to improve efficiency of MPI parallel applications performance analysis, we have created a novel scalable and robust approach for root causing MPI Imbalance issues in the MPI applications. New algorithm for building Program Activity Graph and finding the Critical Path in the Program Activity Graph of the MPI application has been developed, which scales well and doesn't require any complex operations on data collection. A novel approach of PMU data aggregation to the hotspots on Critical Path has been proposed. It supports ideal analysis scalability due to the limitation of analyzed PMU data to the amount of data collected from a single rank.

The runtime and post-processing cost of the analysis is negligible which has been confirmed by experiments involving real-world parallel workloads. The runtime overhead of the proposed approach stays within just 5% related to wrapping of all the relevant MPI calls and capturing required data for further replay. Critical Path analysis overhead also stays within just 5% of application elapsed time and doesn't depend on the number of ranks. Overall, Critical Path analysis stays within 5% of runtime overhead which is much less than any existing solution working on the real-world applications.

References

1. Schulz, M.: Extracting critical path graphs from MPI applications. In: Proceedings of the 7th IEEE International Conference on Cluster Computing (2005)
2. Bohme, D., Wolf, F., Geimer, M.: Characterizing load and communication imbalance in large-scale parallel applications. In: Parallel and Distributed Processing Symposium Workshops Ph.D. Forum (IPDPSW), 2012 IEEE 26th International, pp. 2538–2541 (2012)
3. Herold, C., Krzikalla, O., Knüpfer, A.: Optimizing one-sided communication of parallel applications using critical path methods. IEEE Int. Parallel Distrib. Process. Symp. Workshops (IPDPSW) **2017**, 567–576 (2017)
4. Chen, J., Clapp, R.M.: Critical-path candidates: scalable performance modeling for MPI workloads. IEEE Int. Symp. Perform. Anal. Syst. Softw. (ISPASS) **2015**, 1–10 (2015)
5. Geimer, M., Wolf, F., Wylie, B.J.N., Abraham, E., Becker, D., Mohr, B.: The scalasca performance toolset architecture. Concurr. Comput.: Pract. Exper. **22**(6), 702–719 (2010)
6. Gropp, W., Lusk, E., Doss, N., Skjellum, A.: A high-performance, portable implementation of the MPI message passing interface standard. Parallel Comput. **22**(6), 789–828 (1996)
7. Grunewald, D., Simmendinger, C.: The GASPI API specification and its implementation GPI 2.0. In: 7th International Conference on PGAS Programming Models, vol. 243 (2013)
8. Cedell, A.A., Lambert, A.B., Reese, D.S., Harden, J.C., Brightwell, R.B.: Near-critical path analysis: a tool for parallel program optimization. In: Proceedings of the First Southern Symposium on Computing (1998)
9. Yang, C.-Q., Miller, B.P.: Critical path analysis for the execution of parallel and distributed grams. In: 8th International Conference on Distributed Computing Systems, San Jose, California, pp. 366–375 (1988)
10. Hollingsworth, J.K.: Critical path profiling of message passing and shared-memory programs. In: EEE Transactions on Parallel and Distributed Systems, vol. 9, no. 10 (1998)
11. Gabriel, E., et al.: Open MPI: goals, concept, and design of a next generation MPI implementation. In: Kranzlmüller, D., Kacsuk, P., Dongarra, J. (eds.) Recent Advances in Parallel Virtual Machine and Message Passing Interface, pp. 97–104. Springer Berlin Heidelberg, Berlin, Heidelberg (2004). https://doi.org/10.1007/978-3-540-30218-6_19
12. MPI: A Message-Passing Interface Standard. Version 4.0. 9 June 2021
13. Lorenz, D., Böhme, D., Mohr, B., Strube, A., Szebenyi, Z.: Extending scalasca's analysis features. In: Cheptsov, A., Brinkmann, S., Gracia, J., Resch, M.M., Nagel, W.E. (eds.) Tools for High Performance Computing 2012, pp. 115–126. Springer Berlin Heidelberg, Berlin, Heidelberg (2013). https://doi.org/10.1007/978-3-642-37349-7_8

14. Dean, J., Waldspurger, C.A., Weihl, W.E.: Transparent, low-overhead profiling on modern processors. In: Workshop on Profile and Feedback-Directed Compilation, Paris, France (1998)
15. Lessard, J.: Profiling Concurrent Programs Using Hardware Counters (2005)
16. Carvalho de Melo, A.: The new linux 'perf' tools. In: Slides from Linux Kongress (2010)
17. Ren, G., Tune, E., Moseley, T., Shi, Y., Rus, S., Hundt, R.: Google-wide profiling: a continuous profiling infrastructure for data centers. IEEE Micro 30(4), 65–79 (2010)
18. Kanev, S., et al.: Profiling a warehouse-scale computer. In: ACM SIGARCH Computer Architecture News (2015)
19. Graham, S.L., Kessler, P.B., Mckusick, M.K.: Gprof: a call graph execution profiler. SIGPLAN Not. 17(6), 120–126 (1982)
20. Shende, S., Malony, A.D., Cuny, J., Beckman, P., Karmesin, S., Lindlan, K.: Portable profiling and tracing for parallel, scientific applications using C++. In: Proceedings of the SIGMETRICS Symposium on Parallel and Distributed Tools (SPDT '98). Association for Computing Machinery, New York, NY, USA, pp. 134–145 (1998)
21. Shende, S.: Profiling and tracing in linux. In: Dans Extreme Linux Workshop 2, Monterey CA (1999)
22. Shende, S., Cuny, J.E., Malony, A.D.: The role of instrumentation and mapping in performance measurement (2001)
23. Anjoy, R.G., Chakraborty, S.: Efficiency of LTTng as a Kernel and Userspace Tracer on Multicore Environment (2010)
24. Uehara, R., Uno, Y.: Efficient algorithms for the longest path problem. In: Fleischer, R., Trippen, G. (eds.) ISAAC 2004. LNCS, vol. 3341, pp. 871–883. Springer, Heidelberg (2004). https://doi.org/10.1007/978-3-540-30551-4_74
25. Zeng, W., Church, R.L.: Finding shortest paths on real road networks: the case for A. Int. J. Geogr. Inf. Sci. 23(4), 531–543 (2009)
26. Meyer, U., Sanders, P.: Δ-stepping: a parallelizable shortest path algorithm. J. Algorithms 49(1) 114–152 (2003). ISSN: 0196-6774
27. Chakaravarthy, V.T., Checconi, F., Murali, P., Petrini, F., Sabharwal, Y.: Scalable single source shortest path algorithms for massively parallel systems. In: IEEE Transactions on Parallel and Distributed Systems, vol. 28, no. 7, pp. 2031–2045 (2017)
28. Kranjčević, M., Palossi, D., Pintarelli, S.: Parallel delta-stepping algorithm for shared memory architectures. In: 19th International Workshop on Software and Compilers for Embedded Systems (SCOPES 2016) (2016)
29. Alves, D.R., Krishnakumar, M.S., Garg, V.K.: Efficient parallel shortest path algorithms. In: 2020 19th International Symposium on Parallel and Distributed Computing (ISPDC), pp. 188–195 (2020)
30. Chandy, K.M., Misra, J.: Distributed computation on graphs: shortest path algorithms. Commun. ACM 25(11), 833–837 (1982)
31. Dooley, I., Kale, L.V.: Detecting and using critical paths at runtime in message driven parallel programs. In: 2010 IEEE International Symposium on Parallel & Distributed Processing, Workshops and Ph.D. Forum (IPDPSW), Atlanta, GA, 19–23 April 2010
32. Nguyen, D.D., Karavanic, K.L.: Workflow critical path: a data-oriented critical path metric for holistic HPC workflows. BenchCouncil Trans. Benchmarks Stan. Evaluations 1(1), 100001 (2021)
33. Mey, D.A., et al.: Score-P: a unified performance measurement system for petascale applications. In: Bischof, C., Hegering, H.G., Nagel, W., Wittum, G. (eds.) Competence in High Performance Computing 2010. Springer, Berlin (2011). https://doi.org/10.1007/978-3-642-24025-6_8
34. Thompson, A.P., et al.: LAMMPS - a flexible simulation tool for particle-based materials modeling at the atomic, meso, and continuum scales. Comput. Phys. Commun. 271, 108171 (2022)

35. Gorgovan, C., d'Antras, A., Luján, M.: MAMBO: a low-overhead dynamic binary modification tool for ARM. ACM Trans. Archit. Code Optim. **13**(1), 1–26 (2016)
36. Bruening, D.L.: Efficient, transparent, and comprehensive runtime code manipulation. Ph.D. Dissertation. Massachusetts Institute of Technology, Cambridge, MA (2004)
37. Luk, C.-K.: Pin: building customized program analysis tools with dynamic instrumentation. In: ACM Conference on Programming Language Design and Implementation, pp. 190–200, Chicago, IL (2005)
38. Nethercote, N., Seward, J.: Valgrind: a program supervision framework. Electron. Notes Theor. Comput. Sci. **89**(2), 44–66 (2003)
39. Lei, M., Yin, T.Y., Zhou, Y.C., Han, J.: Highly reconfigurable performance monitoring unit on RISC-V. In: 2020 IEEE 15th International Conference on Solid-State & Integrated Circuit Technology (ICSICT), pp. 1–3 (2020)
40. Yasin, A.: A top-down method for performance analysis and counters architecture. IEEE Int. Symp. Perform. Anal. Syst. Softw. (ISPASS) **2014**, 35–44 (2014)
41. Adhianto, L., et al.: HPCToolkit: tools for performance analysis of optimized parallel programs. Concurrency Comput.: Pract. Experience **22**(6), 685–701 (2010)
42. Shende, S.S., Malony, A.D.: The TAU parallel performance system. Int. J. High Perform. Comput. Appl. **20**(2), 287–311 (2006)
43. London, K., Dongarra, J., Moore, S., Mucci, P., Seymour, K., Spencer, T.: End-user tools for application performance analysis using hardware counters, pp. 460–465 (2001)
44. Skinner, D.: Performance monitoring of parallel scientific applications, United States (2005)
45. Knüpfer, A., et al.: The vampir performance analysis tool-set. In: Resch, M., Keller, R., Himmler, V., Krammer, B., Schulz, A. (eds.) Tools for High Performance Computing, pp. 139–155. Springer Berlin Heidelberg, Berlin, Heidelberg (2008). https://doi.org/10.1007/978-3-540-68564-7_9
46. Bailey, D.H., et al.: The NAS parallel benchmarks summary and preliminary results. In: Supercomputing '91: Proceedings of the 1991 ACM/IEEE Conference on Supercomputing, pp. 158–165 (1991). https://doi.org/10.1145/125826.125925
47. Crozier, P.: Improving performance via mini-applications. Technical report SAND2009-5574, Sandia National Laboratories (2009)
48. Skamarock, W.C., et al.: A description of the advanced research WRF version 3. NCAR Technical note NCAR/TN4751STR, p. 125 (2008)

Rust Language for GPU Programming

Andrey Bychkov[1] and Vsevolod Nikolskiy[1,2]([email]) [iD]

[1] National Research University Higher School of Economics, Moscow, Russia
abychkov@hse.ru, thevsevak@gmail.com
[2] Joint Institute for High Temperatures of RAS, Moscow, Russia

Abstract. Rust is a promising compiled programming language that
has gained in popularity in recent years, as well as support from cor-
porations. It allows one to create efficient code, but it also provides
a higher level of security and predictability. However, its GPU programming ecosystem is quite young and may be inferior to the classical
C/C++ ecosystem in both performance and programmer friendliness, as
well as in the range of features provided. Nevertheless, the Rust language
model theoretically allows extensive optimization capabilities available
to functional programming languages in particular, and the semantics of
the language simplifies and secures code when properly applied. In this
paper, we will explore the theoretical capabilities of the Rust language
in GPU programming and compare the performance of Rust with C++
in the CUDA ecosystems using benchmarks.

Keywords: Rust language · CUDA · GPGPU · Benchmarking ·
Metaprogramming · Declarative macros · Language extension

1 Introduction

General Purpose computing on Graphics Processing Unis (GPGPU) is commonly used as accelerators in computation demanding areas such as computational biology, material sciences, machine learning and etc. Even a single GPU
can accelerate a program drastically if the algorithm and the size of the problem
are suitable for GPU computing. However, such specialization requires specific
programming models. Thus, GPU programming requires splitting out into two
different kinds of subprograms: (1) a host program that manages general tasks
and memory transfers and (2) a GPU device kernel that manages its computations. Both of these subprograms are commonly written in system programming
languages, C/C++ in particular. This choice is motivated by the need for complete control over the work with memory and a narrow specialization of GPUs.
Moreover, there languages have gather a rich GPGPU ecosystem around them,
including educational courses, detailed documentation, tools for debugging and
profiling, and some support in IDEs and code editors. However, the semantics
of C/C++ itself usually restricts programmers with only simple data structures,
weak static analysis, and complex and therefore error-prone memory management. Moreover, this can be a limiting factor for higher-level programming languages, since they must either compile into a C-based solution or drop the C level

V. Voevodin et al. (Eds.): RuSCDays 2022, LNCS 13708, pp. 522–532, 2022.
https://doi.org/10.1007/978-3-031-22941-1_38

and compile directly into bytecode or machine code to avoid the restrictions of C/C++. On the other hand, as shown in [1], describing GPU kernel with high-level data structures and operations can be beneficial for performance, especially in the multiplatform case. Also, high-level semantics can be descriptive enough to naturally fit in many models and algorithms used in supercomputing applications. Thus, the languages of interest are high-level languages that can compile both subprograms of type (1) on the host side and GPU kernels (2).

One such language is the Rust programming language. As it have been shown in [2] Rust programming language can be successfully applied in supercomputing modeling. Also, the primary compiler of Rust exists in the LLVM infrastructure, which allows to select intermediate GPU languages such as PTX and SPIR as targets for compilation. Also, [3] illustrates that GPU kernels written even in the old version of Rust support its high-level semantics. There are also many details around Rust that can enrich GPGPU ecosystem in general such as great building tools and invariant preserving semantics (i.e. memory safety) which can help scientists and researchers who do not specialize in GPGPU computing to develop, enhance and deploy their projects.

In this study, we want to answer the question of whether Rust is currently ready for use of GPUs and what difficulties may arise. We also want to describe promising ways of developing GPGPU computing in Rust by exploring its theoretical possibilities and the experience of similar programming languages. In addition we will show how much performance overhead the Rust language has compared to the solutions in C in CUDA and OpenCL ecosystems.

The paper is organized as follows:

- In Sect. 2 we will consider theoretical background of using GPUs in high-level languages and possibilities of Rust in this field.
- In Sect. 3 we will describe and setup benchmark experiments to compare GPU ecosystems of Rust and C/C++.
  - In Subsects. 3.2 we will discuss implementation of the naive matrix multiplication algorithm in Rust-CUDA and compare its performance with nvcc.
  - In Subsect. 3.3 we will compare the performances of more optimized tiled matrix multiplication algorithm for Rust-CUDA and nvcc.
  - In Subsect. 3.4 we will discuss Rust's semantic ability to extend its syntax using the example of the shared memory declaration in the kernel.
- In Sect. 4 we will describe our results and discuss the future work.

2 Related Work

In [3] the authors used the LLVM backend to generate GPU kernels directly from Rust. They used very low-level features but Rust was used to build higher-level abstractions. Since that time, there have been many changes in both Rust and GPU programming, but the article demonstrates the technical capabilities and high expressiveness of the language Unfortunately, there is currently no established way to program GPUs in Rust.

In [1] the authors used the compilation of high-level algorithmic primitives to generate performance-portable OpenCL code, which is also sometimes outperforms state-of-the-art solutions. The generalization of this technique is a common performance optimization in functional programming languages such as Haskell, even in GPGPU [4].

There are also multiple papers which tackle the memory transfer problem. In [5] the authors utilize the *arenas* - the regions in memory which manages the objects inside it and can act as an atomic for memory transfers. The notable result is that the authors managed to significantly optimize memory transfers and used Harlan - a high-level programming language based on Scheme, to inject rich data structures such as Algebraic Data Types and graphs into a computation model. In [6] the authors also suggest the Dynamic Kernel Scheduler - a software layer between the host application and the hardware accelerator which is also notably optimizes memory transfers by using platform-specific optimizations. Similar approach is used in [7] where the software is automatically schedules data transfers, but suffers from the need of transferring entire data structures. However, aforementioned region-based technique [5] could be helpful. As [3] mention, Rust has does not have as fast memory transfers as C, and these approaches can diminish the problem significantly.

It is also useful to consider the experience of the other languages similar to Rust. There is a notable ecosystem around OCaml. The authors have also implemented rich data structures in GPU kernels [8,9], and also have reached a certain progress in amortization of data transfers and working with multiplatform-heterogeneous systems (Rust utilized the same approach in multithreaded programming [2,10]). Even though the solution has open problems with branching divergence and describing recursive types, aforementioned approaches, i.e. [5] could fix them. The authors also made an application of the framework in browser [11] which is also useful in visualizing scientific results. We believe that the experience of the language of the same programming language family as Rust could be used in enhancing Rust's solutions and could also act as a practical implementation of theoretical results.

In [12] the author successfully used Rust's verification capabilities to make a statically checked neutral biodiversity simulation by using GPU programming.

3   Becnhmarking

In this section we will compare performances of Rust and C/C++ GPGPU ecosystems, CUDA and OpenCL in particular. As effects we want to track, we will note the possible slowness of Rust in transferring data [3] and the possible differences between PTX code compiled by Rust-CUDA and the native nvcc compiler.

3.1   Benchmark Characteristics

For this and further sections we will use a laptop for numerical experiments with the following parameters:

- Intel(R) Core(TM) i7-8750H CPU. The upper frequency limit in turbo boost mode is at 4.10 GHz. Despite dynamic CPU frequency is widely used in modern HPC [13], but it can significantly complicate the correct interpretation of the microbenchmarks. In this regard, we fix the frequency of our CPU to 3.90 GHz.
- NVidia GTX 1060 with the frequency fixed on 139 MHz;
- CUDA 11.6 drivers;
- Windows 10 operating system.
- We compile C++ by using Visual Studio 2019 compiler and Rust by nightly-2021-12-04 toolchain.

For C++ benchmarks we use Google-benchmark framework. Each function is repeated at least 100 times. To remove artifacts, we run the tests 10 times and calculate the average. For Rust benchmarks we use Criterion framework. The setup is similar to C++ benchmarks.

3.2 Naive Matrix Multiplication

We will compare Rust-CUDA [14] with the nvcc compiler by using a simple linear algebra problem - matrix multiplication. We also show the main features of Rust with code examples. First, let's look at the matrix multiplication kernel itself in the Listing 1.1.

```
#[kernel]
pub unsafe fn matmul(a: &[f32], b: &[f32], c: *mut f32, n: usize){
    let row = (block_idx_y() * block_dim_y() + thread_idx_y())
        as usize;
    let col = (block_idx_x() * block_dim_x() + thread_idx_x())
        as usize;
    if row < n && col < n {
        let mut sum = 0.0f32;
        for i in 0..n {
            sum += a[row * n + i] * b[i * n + col];
        }
        *c.add(row * n + col) = sum;
    }
}
```

Listing 1.1. Naive matrix multiplication kernel in Rust-CUDA

The kernels in Rust-CUDA are written in Rust, which allows you to use the capabilities of the language, albeit limited. Rust-CUDA provides this with a pipeline, the main elements of which are compiling the code into NVVM IR, and then obtaining and optimizing the PTX code. In this implementation, matrices a and b are multiplied and the result is written in matrix c. Although it is currently not possible to prove many of the invariants used by Rust, we can nevertheless establish that the arrays a and b are not nullptr, have a certain fixed length (i.e. the parameter n is only left here for C compatibility in the benchmarks), and there is a type check between the kernel and the passed arguments in the calling code, as will be shown below.

As Fig. 1 show, code generated by Rust has only about 1/3 of nvcc performance. The analysis by nvvp showed that the algorithm compiled with nvcc was more L2-cache aware than the one compiled with Rust-CUDA, having 3 times more L2 Read transactions and 3 times less L2 Write transactions, respectively. This can be explained by the fact that the Rust-CUDA project is rather new at the moment, and it has not implemented all the optimizations available in nvcc.

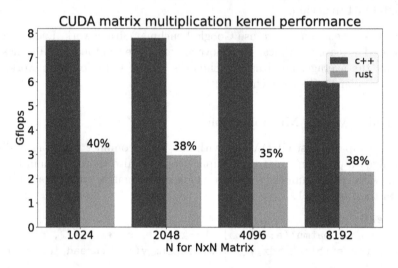

Fig. 1. Time spent comparison of naive matrix multiplication only for kernels written by Rust-CUDA and CUDA C.

Now we will look at an example of using the kernel in external Rust code and measure the data transfers.

On the first lines of Listing 1.2 we define the function that will work with the kernel and manage data transfers. A distinctive feature of the declaration of this function is the return type: Result<...>, which is the sum of two types - Vec<f32>, which we expect when the function completes successfully, and Box<dyn Error>, which encapsulates all types of errors the function can return. This declaration transfers some of the responsibility for error handling to the programmer calling the function and prevents the code from being compiled if errors are not handled explicitly.

Lines 4–6 are responsible for initializing and configuring the work with CUDA code, as well as reading kernels from the file in the PTX variable. This is also the first time we encounter a question mark construct "?" at the end of an expression, which passes the handling of errors that may occur in the expression to the calling code. Nevertheless, we can also manually handle errors, as in Line 32.

```
1  pub(crate) fn matmul_gpu(lhs: &Vec<f32>, rhs: &Vec<f32>)
2      -> Result<Vec<f32>, Box<dyn Error>> {
3
4      let _ctx = cust::quick_init()?;
5      let module = Module::from_ptx(PTX, &[])?;
6      let stream = Stream::new(StreamFlags::NON_BLOCKING, None)?;
7
8      let lhs_gpu = lhs.as_slice().as_dbuf()?;
9      let rhs_gpu = rhs.as_slice().as_dbuf()?;
10
11      let mut out = vec![0.0f32; N*N];
12      let out_gpu = unsafe { DeviceBuffer::uninitialized(N*N) }?;
13
14
15      let block_size = 32;
16      let grid_size = (N as u32 + block_size - 1) / block_size;
17      let dim_block = (block_size, block_size, 1);
18      let dim_grid = (grid_size, grid_size, 1);
19
20      let func = module.get_function("matmul")?;
21      unsafe {
22          launch!(
23              func<<<dim_grid, dim_block, 0, stream>>>(
24                  lhs_gpu.as_device_ptr(),
25                  lhs_gpu.len(),
26                  rhs_gpu.as_device_ptr(),
27                  rhs_gpu.len(),
28                  out_gpu.as_device_ptr(),
29                  N
30              )
31          ).expect("Launch was wrong");
32      }
33
34      stream.synchronize()?;
35
36      out_gpu.copy_to(&mut out)?;
37      Ok(out)
38  }
```

Listing 1.2. Using matrix multiplication kernel from the external Rust code

Lines 8–12 are responsible for initialization and data transfer to the GPU. lhs_gpu and rhs_gpu are created by explicitly copying the lhs and rhs vectors to the GPU. At the same time, out_gpu we create by allocating raw memory on the GPU to avoid unnecessary copying. This is a more dangerous operation and is placed as unsafe, just like in CPU code, due to the fact that the Rust compiler cannot prove a number of errors.

In lines 22–33, we start the kernel according to the semantics described beforehand in Rust-CUDA, namely by explicitly passing the size of the lhs_gpu and rhs_gpu buffers. In the same way, the compiler will explicitly check that the types of arguments and their number correspond to the kernel.

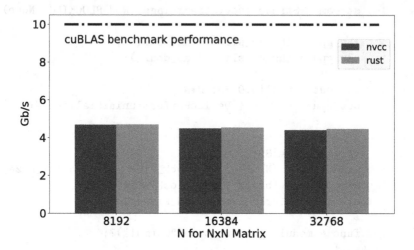

Fig. 2. Memory Read throughput of matrices for native CUDA compiler marked as 'nvcc' and Rust-CUDA compiler marker as 'rust'

Using the nvvp profiler, we found no significant differences in the data transfer between programs generated by nvcc and Rust-CUDA as shown in Fig. 2. Thus, working with CUDA can eliminate the possible negative effects described in [3].

3.3   CUDA Tiled Matrix Multiplication

In order to evaluate the more advanced capabilities of the GPU and to compare implementations of more efficient algorithms, we will look at the tiled matrix multiplication algorithm as the example. Before presenting the results of the benchmark, we note that the current version of Rust-CUDA does not implement multidimensional shared memory, due to which the obtained kernels will be different. Nevertheless, we have implemented it ourselves [15] based on the one-dimensional approach, and thus we will compare two different implementations of the algorithm in Rust.

Figure 3 shows that on small sizes the algorithms do not diverge much. However, it is noticeable that for the example nvcc produces more stable code in terms of performance, since it does not degrade performance at the maximum matrix size.

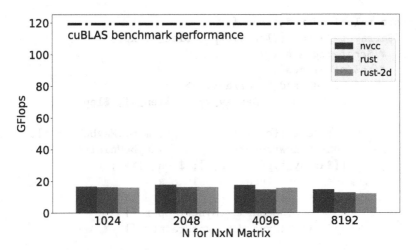

Fig. 3. Performance comparison of tiled matrix multiplication with tile size = 16. 'nvcc' represents the native CUDA compiler, 'rust' - one-dimensional algorithm in Rust, 'rust-2d' - the two-dimensional one

3.4   Implementation of 2D Shared Memory Syntax

In pure Rust, you cannot reserve new keywords, which prevents you from creating shared memory variables the way you are used to in CUDA. However, the Rust language provides the ability to extend its syntax using the *macro* mechanism. This example shows how to create a one-dimensional shared memory buffer for the tiled algorithm.

```
let mut tile_a = shared_array![f32; TILE_SZ * TILE_SZ];
```

However, initially the initialization of the 2D shared memory was not implemented. However, we were only able to add one line to the macro definition to be able to handle 2D cases as shown in the lines 2–4 in Listing 1.3. Syntactically, the macro definition works like pattern matching, allowing us to use arbitrary syntax, from SQL queries to writing mathematical expressions. In Listing 1.3 we use pattern $array_type:ty; [$len_x:expr; $len_y:expr] where array_type is a type variable of the array and len_x and len_x are arbitrary expression as TILE_SIZE constant in our example or 32*32*32 expression for instance.

```
1  macro_rules! shared_array {
2    ($array_type:ty; [$len_x:expr; $len_y:expr]) => {{
3      #[$crate::gpu_only]
4      #[inline(always)]
5      unsafe fn shared_2d_array() ->
6          &'static mut [[$array_type; $len_y]; $len_x] {
7
8          use ::core::{cell::UnsafeCell, mem::MaybeUninit};
9          struct SyncWrapper(UnsafeCell<MaybeUninit<
10           [[$array_type; $len_y]; $len_x]>>);
11          // We cannot fundamentally check
12          // shared memory usage for soundness
13          unsafe impl Send for SyncWrapper {}
14          unsafe impl Sync for SyncWrapper {}
15
16          #[$crate::address_space(shared)]
17          static SHARED: SyncWrapper =
18          SyncWrapper(UnsafeCell::new(MaybeUninit::uninit()));
19
20          &mut *SHARED.0.get()
21              .as_mut().expect("Conversion to mut broke")
22              .as_mut_ptr()
23      }
24      shared_2d_array()
25    }};
26    ($array_type:ty; $len:expr) => {{
27      // Rust CUDA implementation for 1D case
28      // with altered return type logic
29    }};
30  }
```

Listing 1.3. Developed macro extension for natural use of 2D shared memory

Lines 8–18 contain the declaration of a memory area in the address space and a description of its properties. Unfortunately, proving the invariants that Rust requires for memory on CPU programs is currently impossible and requires special fundamental work. Also note that the allocation itself may end up with an error, which we decided to handle in the line 21. An alternative solution would be to return the Result<..., Err> type to the user, which would contain the error of type Err, and enforce the programmer to include error handling in the architecture.

Thus, we can set the 2D shared memory in a more familiar way using the macros in the Listing 1.3:

```
let mut tile_a = shared_array![f32; [TILE_SZ; TILE_SZ]];
```

4   Conclusion

In this work, we have provided an overview of Rust in the area of General Purpose computing on Graphics Processing Unis and the performance comparison between C/C++ and Rust in context of CUDA ecosystem. The optimized code generated by the Rust-CUDA package has performed close to CUDA C results. The hypothesis is that the overhead also comes from the slower data transfer on the Rust's side and provided benchmarks could be treated as the experiment which results decline the hypothesis for the Rust-CUDA in particular. The shared memory allocation macro in Rust-CUDA has been extended to the two-dimensional case for more natural writing of GPU kernels in Rust. The benchmarks of the proposed code are provided. We also considered the ways to diminish effect of slower data transfer in general that were successfully used in similar languages and situations.

In the benchmarks, CUDA tests were compiled by nvcc, Nvidia's mature proprietary tool, while Rust uses the less developed but open source LLVM for GPU compilation as a backend. In one of the tests in this work, the advantage of CUDA was observed, and in the other test there were close results. The development of optimizations in LLVM and the library itself can significantly reduce the number of cases in which the code shows lower performance. The methods [5,6,9], considered in the Sect. 2 could significantly narrow the efficiency gap between C and Rust in CUDA.

In Rust, one can write GPU kernels in the same language, which enable additional security guarantees that are not available in conventional CUDA programming. Such guarantees are consist of solving buffer initialization and forgotten deallocation problems, forcing a programmer to handle every error explicitly, introducing a strong type system that can handle such problems as overflows, mismatching kernel parameters, and many more. Some particular guarantees and invariants are discussed in Sect. 3.2. On the other hand, calling kernels is a tricky part of CUDA and the programmer is still required to manually enforce certain invariants.

By taking advantage of the expressiveness of the Rust language as shown in Sect. 3.4, one can expand the language quite a lot. It would be possible to integrate methods for static analysis and verification of GPU code into existing tools. In the context of the use of graphics accelerators in the Rust language and the use of the expressive power of this language for security and optimization, it is of interest for further research to experiment with Rust in the OpenCL environment since it can be used specifically to get optimized code [1]. Note, however, that in all the Rust software we examined, the OpenCL kernels could only be written in C, which reduces the potential for Rust to work with OpenCL at this point.

Acknowledgment. Support from the Basic Research Program of the National Research University Higher School of Economics is gratefully acknowledged.

References

1. Steuwer, M., Fensch, C., Lindley, S., Dubach, C.: Generating performance portable code using rewrite rules: from high-level functional expressions to high-performance OpenCL code. In: Proceedings of the 20th ACM SIGPLAN International Conference on Functional Programming, ICFP 2015, pp. 205–217. Association for Computing Machinery, New York (2015). https://doi.org/10.1145/2784731.2784754
2. Bychkov, A., Nikolskiy, V.: Rust language for supercomputing applications. In: Voevodin, V., Sobolev, S. (eds.) RuSCDays 2021. CCIS, vol. 1510, pp. 391–403. Springer, Cham (2021). https://doi.org/10.1007/978-3-030-92864-3_30
3. Holk, E., Pathirage, M., Chauhan, A., Lumsdaine, A., Matsakis, N.D.: GPU programming in rust: implementing high-level abstractions in a systems-level language. In: 2013 IEEE International Symposium on Parallel Distributed Processing, Workshops and Phd Forum, pp. 315–324 (2013)
4. Svensson, J., Claessen, K., Sheeran, M.: GPGPU kernel implementation and refinement using obsidian. Procedia Comput. Sci. 1(1), 2065–2074 (2010). https://www.sciencedirect.com/science/article/pii/S1877050910002322. iCCS 2010
5. Holk, E., Newton, R., Siek, J., Lumsdaine, A.: Region-based memory management for GPU programming languages: enabling rich data structures on a spartan host. SIGPLAN Not. 49(10), 141–155 (2014). https://doi.org/10.1145/2714064.2660244
6. Adelmann, A., Locans, U., Suter, A.: The dynamic kernel scheduler-part 1. Comput. Phys. Commun. 207, 83–90 (2016). https://www.sciencedirect.com/science/article/pii/S0010465516301370
7. Ashcraft, M.B., Lemon, A., Penry, D.A., Snell, Q.: Compiler optimization of accelerator data transfers. Int. J. Parallel Prog. 47(1), 39–58 (2017). https://doi.org/10.1007/s10766-017-0549-3
8. Bourgoin, M., Chailloux, E., Lamotte, J.-L.: Efficient abstractions for GPGPU programming. Int. J. Parallel Prog. 42(4), 583–600 (2013). https://doi.org/10.1007/s10766-013-0261-x
9. Bourgoin, M., Chailloux, E., Lamotte, J.-L.: High level data structures for GPGPU programming in a statically typed language. Int. J. Parallel Prog. 45(2), 242–261 (2016). https://doi.org/10.1007/s10766-016-0424-7
10. Matsakis, N.: Rayon: data parallelism in Rust. https://smallcultfollowing.com/babysteps/blog/2015/12/18/rayon-data-parallelism-in-rust/
11. Bourgoin, M., Chailloux, E.: High-level accelerated array programming in the web browser. In: Proceedings of the 2nd ACM SIGPLAN International Workshop on Libraries, Languages, and Compilers for Array Programming, ARRAY 2015, pp. 31–36. Association for Computing Machinery, New York (2015). https://doi.org/10.1145/2774959.2774964
12. Langenstein, M.: Communication-free and parallel simulation of neutral biodiversity models. CoRR abs/2108.05815 (2021). https://arxiv.org/abs/2108.05815
13. Calore, E., Gabbana, A., Schifano, S.F., Tripiccione, R.: Evaluation of DVFS techniques on modern HPC processors and accelerators for energy-aware applications. Concurr. Comput. Pract. Exp. 29(12), e4143 (2017). https://onlinelibrary.wiley.com/doi/abs/10.1002/cpe.4143
14. D'Ambrosio, R.: The Rust CUDA project. https://github.com/Rust-GPU/Rust-CUDA
15. The Rust-CUDA 2D shared memory implementation. https://github.com/AndreyBychkov/Rust-CUDA/commit/8f6fce6e26f693780dc7de1fbf628932c58fd329

Study of Scheduling Approaches for Batch Processing in Big Data Cluster

Ilya Timokhin[1(✉)] and Aleksey Teplov[2]

[1] HSE University, Moscow, Russia
is.timokhin@hse.ru
[2] Advanced Software Technologies Laboratory of Huawei Moscow Research
Center,Moscow, Russia
aleksey.teplov@huawei.ru

Abstract. Different approaches for batch scheduling in multiprocessors system presented in this paper. In the experimental big data processing framework authors used a novel graph-based strategy for optimal data locality usage in HDFS and several data-driven heuristics concepts to define the order of tasks execution in batch and to allocate resources optimally. The authors explained key principals of building the graph and its optimization with Dinic's algorithm and bi-criteria linear search. The model of real network topology (distributed storage, switches, system cores) was designed and developed. Described the set of metrics for evaluating the efficiency of each strategy (time metrics, CPU metrics, idle metrics). Performance on the real test case and cores utilization comparison with other scheduling approaches (greedy and non-historical based) are also provided. Visualization for current processing was designed and implemented in algorithms to analyze bottlenecks (idle time, efficiency capacity). There is also an explanation of parametrization tuning process for data-driven heuristics and how to achieve the best performance with the presented approach.

Keywords: Scheduler · Heuristics · Max-flow · CPU utilization · Multiprocessing · Resource scheduling · Data locality · Network · Resource management

1 Introduction

Scheduling is a basic operation for distributed systems. The main concept of the scheduling approach is to share processing between available hardware resources and do it according to scheduling priorities, cluster parameters and complexity for each operation (see [1] for detailed description of such operations).

Applications in the distributed environments for Big Data processing for many reasons use static resource allocation from cluster resource schedulers like YARN and start an internal job, task, process or worker scheduling upon allocated resources using internal mechanisms and strategies. This provides a flexible scheduling strategy usage for many specific cases like telecom data processing or any specific scenarios.

According to the application usage scenario processing strategies also can vary and use different approaches to schedule tasks and allocated resources for internal logic.

For the data processing in batch processing style (where batch is a set of SQL-like queries), it can be used more efficient SQL-query engine and during execution utilize different optimization hints to reduce computation overheads and resource idleness.

One of the fundamental approaches, that can be very effective in the case of data distributed file systems, is the data locality principle when resource scheduling for computations is allocated concerning data topological location in the cluster. The locality principle can reduce the amount of data to transfer between nodes from the physical location to the computation resource allocated node.

During scheduling strategy efficiency study in the distributed computing environment of the Big Data type two different impacts were compared: resource scheduling data locality concept implementations and different resource utilization metrics.

The first one means compliance between the theoretical approach of data locality principles and its hardware implementation, and the second one means comparison between the utilization of CPU resources after execution of the whole batch with certain queries.

This paper presented single-task and multi-task static schedulers which are based on the data locality concept and provides data computing on transport network with heuristics information.

2   Related Works

There are a lot of different approaches to schedule tasks and calculate CPU utilization ([9] contains a brief description of them).

Different systems meet different requirements according to input data and the design of the specific cluster. Some of them use a weighted "deadline" approach to prune time of execution (see [3]) and some schedulers are strongly based on CPU resources and dynamic information from system monitoring [2]. This paper described several methods to provide a full pipeline of scheduling in the batch of analytical tasks.

Other schedulers use different scheduling strategies (see [1] with defined priority-driven and table-driven approaches) to reduce job batch execution time.

See [2,4] to learn about CPU scheduling metrics and certain unobvious approaches to measure it. Some basic methods of monitoring and simple time scheduling are described in [6].

At [7] it was provided real-time dynamical scheduling procedure for supercomputers. It's interesting to note that differences between static and non-static processing are small and based on the same adaptive mechanism provided in such an article.

Also there is a no-scheduling approach provided in [10]. Authors described the certain concept of interconnection without any heuristics optimization of a cluster, but with parametrization in the Hadoop ecosystem. There are defined several principles for IoT computing that applies to large-scale systems.

Mathematical basis and optimization problem for resource allocating and some fundamental tasks were considered in [11]. This book contains not only HPC and multiprocessing formulations, but theoretical differential metaheuristics view on the famous problems (backpack problem, hybridization, memetic algorithms).

3   Single Task and Multi-task Scheduling

3.1   Data Locality in HDFS and Framework's Design

In the testing environment, HDFS used to store all the analytical data (see [10] to find Hadoop basic concepts). The cluster executes batch of SQL queries and mapped HDFS files with data used for these. It also contains one table file which stores historical statistics for each query. Set of queries (tasks) described in the table file calls **Job**.

The whole query processing pipeline is designed in Fig. 1.

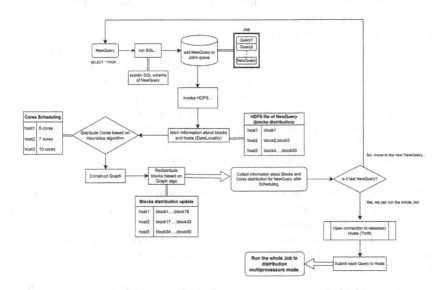

Fig. 1. Framework's flowchart

3.2   Graph Block Scheduler

Assume that considered file contains B blocks of data and is located at H hosts, each block is stored with replica factor R (same for all blocks). The main task is to redistribute blocks to be processed on each specific host in such a way that the blocks are most evenly distributed. For this task was proposed the max-load value L which means that *each host can process no more than L blocks*. The transport network $G = (V, E, C, F)$ is a model of file in HDFS, where V is a set of vertices, E is a set of edges, C is a set of capacities between edges, F is a set of flows between edges.

Problem. *What is the minimum of maximum host-load L value? How many blocks can be processed by single job on the host with the condition of each block is available?*

Function **MaxFlow** : $G_L \to \mathbb{Z}$ returns the maximum flow in graph G with max-load value L (capacity between hosts related edges and sink) via Dinic's algorithm.

Binary search algorithm based on Dinic's approach will find the optimal L value with the next complexity: $O(|V| + |B| \times k) + O(|V|^2 \times |E|) \log |B|$

The idea of such a method is following: it defines left and right bounds as $\frac{B}{H}$ and B respectively, and recalculates $F = \textbf{MaxFlow}(G_L)$ for each new L value which is a median between left and right bounds. Then it moves bounds (as it is done in classic binary search) and repeat the procedure while $F \geq B$ or the left bound is less than the right bound.

Denote such Algorithm as **BinSearch**(G), where **BinSearch** : $G \to \mathbb{Z}$, returns minimal host-load L value for graph G with condition $F = B$ (maximum flow of graph G equals to number of blocks B).

A similar approach with maximum flow calculations and the graph representation was described at [8], but results were published only for two processors and weights were used as the inner scheduler's metric. Moreover, there is no optimization via Dinic's algorithm and binary search, only flow's network model.

Assume that process requires to transfer some blocks from one host to another. For this case, it's more efficient to use a switch engine for connection between hosts. Note that switch has its capacity with the ability to transfer m blocks of data, receiving l_1 blocks of data from host i and sending to L_2 blocks to host j.

Switch engine based on the two vertices: switch receiver S_R and switch transceiver S_T, the capacity of edge (S_R, S_T) equals m. Assume that new graph G^* (updated graph G) consists switch engine.

The computing of blocks and transferring between hosts are two operations with different costs and complexity. Denote the cost of blocks computing as τ_c and blocks transmission cost as τ_t.

Let the coefficients $\tau_c, \tau_t \in \mathbb{R}$ be given and the next **cost function** is defined:

$$C(x, y) = \tau_c x + \tau_t y \tag{1}$$

Now the function **MaxFlow** : $G^*_{L,m} \to \mathbb{Z}$ returns maximum flow in graph G^* (via Dinic's algorithm) with max-load value L and switch capacity m.

Problem. *What is the minimum of maximum host-load L value and minimum of transmissions count m with respect to cost function $C(L,m)$ with τ_c and τ_t fixed values?*

So the problem is to find an optimal (L,m)-pair with a minimal $C(L,m)$ value. **Forward search** algorithm will find the trade-off solution with complexity like $O(|V| + |B| \times k) + O(|V|^2 \times |E|)(\log_2 |B|)^2$

It contains **BinSearch** procedure to iteratively update L value and recalculate m value with binary optimization. Therefore, it uses a binary search to find the value m in an external binary algorithm that searches for the value L.

The forward search contains a significant disadvantage – it tries to find out the optimal m via binary search and that's why it can returns only local optimum on the $(\frac{r-l}{2}, r)$ interval, where l and r are the left and right bounds respectively.

$$V(L,m) = \{\mathbf{MaxFlow}(G_{L,m}) = B\} \in \{0,1\}, \tag{2}$$

where $G_{L,m}$ – graph G with max-load value L and switch capacity m.

Algorithm 1 (further – **Optimal area search**) consists of two steps (area optimization and optimum values search in the pruned area) and it will find the trade-off global optimal value.

Algorithm 1. Optimal area search: Bi-criteria optimization

1: Provides an area optimization via searching through L values verification condition $V(L-1,m) = 1$ and then searching through m values with verification $V(L,m-1) = 1$ to found pruned L and m bounds;

2: Calculate $L_B = \lfloor \frac{C(L,m)}{\tau_c} \rfloor - 1$ value and found the minimal m' value via **BinSearch** method.

3: Finish algorithm if $\frac{C(L,m')-\tau_t m'}{\tau_c} < C(L,m)$. Otherwise $L_B = C(L_B, m')$ and go to previous step of L_B recalculating.

There is a concept of another approach to calculating optimal blocks calculating distribution on HDFS. Hosts with unique blocks shuffle first: if there is a host which stores only one block, it should select the block of this host in the priority since other machines' calculations may finish the computing of this block, i.e., this host will lose the unique local block. Hosts with fewer blocks should be a priority: if there are several hosts with the same minimal number of blocks, it should further consider which one will affect other machines less. Further, we will call such an algorithm, which realized described greedy logic, an **Equilibrium**.

Several test cases were executed on real data via Graph, Equilibrium, and Baseline methods (this is a modified inner HDFS mechanism to choose blocks uniformly according to replica factor). Different cases were tested with the same system and data configuration: 200 hosts, 30000 blocks, replica factor $R = 3$. Since one block in HDFS has a size of 128 MB, this test describes a file with $128 * 30000 \approx 3.5$ TB of data (Table 1).

Table 1. Distribution of blocks for big data

Case	Graph (no switch)		Equilibrium		Baseline	
	L	Time (secs)	L	Time (secs)	L	Time (secs)
0	155	0.154	156	164.06	170	0.136
1	155	0.149	155	169.36	165	0.132
2	156	0.156	156	172.76	169	0.135
3	154	0.153	154	170.12	166	0.139
4	153	0.154	153	165.00	163	0.131
5	153	0.140	153	165.97	168	0.133
6	155	0.159	155	172.54	164	0.131
7	154	0.155	154	170.87	165	0.136
8	154	0.140	154	170.17	165	0.133
9	155	0.147	155	172.43	168	0.132

Baseline implementation works faster but is not so accurate as Graph and Equilibrium approaches. On another hand, the Graph algorithm executes much faster than the Equilibrium. The equilibrium approach works for x iterations until the target block metric is reached. That's why for a large number of hosts it selects nodes in the most greedy way and doesn't terminate (can't find the best metric). Poor performance is a consequence of such a strategy.

In previous cases (with no switch engine) Graph alg. didn't achieve bound value for L (optimal theoretical value for such data is 150). In the next case linear functions $C(L,m) = 1000L + m$ was applied with switch mechanism and $S_T = m = const = 100$ (Table 2).

Table 2. Results for bi-criteria optimization with $\tau_c = 1000, \tau_t = 1$

Case	Optimal area search				Forward search			
	L	m	C(L,m)	Time (secs)	L	m	C(L,m)	Time (secs)
0	150	34	150034	1.0365	150	34	150034	0.5301
1	150	50	150050	1.0536	150	50	150050	0.6891
2	150	57	150057	1.3422	151	28	151028	0.5992
3	150	46	150046	1.0632	150	46	150046	0.7385
4	150	45	150045	1.0314	150	45	150045	0.7191
5	150	60	150060	1.0072	151	12	151012	0.6977
6	150	50	150050	1.4023	150	50	150050	0.8845
7	150	45	150045	1.2511	150	45	150045	0.7673
8	150	64	150053	1.3352	151	23	151023	0.8266
9	150	62	150062	1.4827	151	31	151031	0.7256

Optimal Area algorithm calculates better L-values (Cases #2, 5, 8, 9), but works slower because of an accurate searching process for (L, m)-optimization. Thereby, forward search obtains worse target value and returns $L = 151$ for such cases, but optimal value is $L = 150$. Calculation of one block costs $\tau_c = 1000$ in this model, in real systems it obtained more "penalty" for block's calculation.

Also, the Forward algorithm is faster than the OptimalArea approach, so it should choose between less τ_c-penalty and searching algorithm performance. If $\tau_c \gg \tau_t$, the forward strategy works faster. The choice is following: distribute all jobs most uniformly with a pedantic approach according to the relation between τ_c and τ_t or just distribute them fast and approximately evenly, but receive poor performance on real-time calculations.

First of all, it's necessary to understand how to modify the bi-criteria approach to achieve optimized (L, m) values with complexity and performance similar to the Forward search, but with an accuracy of the OptimalArea algorithm. For some cases high complexity is critical, but for other cases distribution should be even for all blocks because of the high penalty.

Another question is the structure of the $C(L, m)$ function. Tests for nonlinear function are still non-optimized in terms of switch capacity m.

It's obvious that in real systems there are some complex dependencies between blocks calculations and transmissions, that's why a linear function is not applicable for clusters. Summarizing, there is no investigation on bi-criteria optimization for the common case.

The last field to research is multi-criteria optimization. The goal is not to optimize only (L, m), (S_R, S_T) or (L, S_R) pairs for different scenarios, but the whole set of parameters (L, S_R, S_T, m). The problem of an optimal trade-off between minimal max-load, switch capacity, receiver, and transceiver values is still unresolved.

3.3   Data-Driven Heuristics Approach: Cores Scheduler

This strategy describes the method to allocate resources based on task sizes, number of blocks and scoring metric. As was described in Fig. 1, before HDFS-blocks will be distributed between several nodes in the system, it should schedule cores (workers) for each task. Let τ_c be the computation time for a single block (different for each task in Job) and τ_t is transfer time for a single block (same for all of the tasks in Job, system configuration parameter). The Job contains of Y tasks in batch and h hosts, C described a maximum number of cores **per host**.

Firstly it's necessary to fix the order in which tasks are processed. It will be used sequentially ordering. Then for each new task, it will select which cores will do the computation (very similar although not completely equivalent is to selecting how many cores on each node will do the computation without specifying which ones). Finally, the method decides which blocks are processed on which of the selected cores via single task scheduling (see Graph scheduler part).

The basic data-driven method has the highest complexity over all of the solutions considered in this paper. So it uses several loops with extremely high labor intensity for cores selection. Also, it spend too many memory resources to store maps with difficult historical substructures with all scores for different cores set.

After some simplification heuristics approach was redesigned and presented as Algorithm 2.

Algorithm 2. Simplified data-driven description

1: Assume there are N tasks in batch Δ and array W of weights for task sizes' labels from 0 to 4 (according to aliases "empty", "small", ..., "large") for each task in Δ, $|W| = N$; Set the batch cardinality parameter λ and the σ-density parameter as well.
2: Reorder tasks based on block sizes (descending order);
3: Create new batch: choose 1 task from "head" of the queue and x tasks from "tail", where $\sum W(x) \approx \sigma$ and repeat it until the end of batch;
4: Calculate mean number of blocks M for all tasks;
5: **for each** task q in Job **do**
6: $\quad Cores = \frac{NumBlocks(q)}{M} \times \frac{C}{H} + \tau_c(q)\frac{W(q)}{\tau_t(q)}$;
7: $\quad$ **if** $Cores > \frac{C}{\sigma}$ **then**
8: $\quad\quad Cores = \frac{C}{\sigma}$;
9: $\quad$ **end if**
10: $\quad$ Assign $Cores$ for task q and distribute them uniformly between all h nodes;
11: $\quad$ Do a single task scheduling for q (Graph strategy);
12: **end for**

3.4 Other Scheduling Strategies

This part considered several approaches to reorder tasks and calculate an efficient number of cores for current tasks. Further, it will be compared data-driven approach implementations with other competitive scheduling strategies. Note that it was considered not some specific implementations, but the class of realizations (strategy), so in this subsection, the definitions of "strategy" and "algorithm" will be equated for convenience. Was chosen the other different popular scheduling strategies to discuss them in terms of our contribution and compare examples of strategies implementations, that use its approach to schedule tasks in the Job. Implementations are marked with some alias to show the association with the related class of scheduling approaches (for instance, **Annealing** means the class of simulated annealing methods [11]).

- **Annealing.** This approach is based on heuristics data, but it uses only the historical execution time of each task (without τ_c, τ_t and size of the task). The purpose of scheduling is how to make the "box" fit the tightest, that is, the shortest horizontal coordinate. One very intuitive idea is the greedy method, for each case, putting this case down will make the current horizontal coordinate shortest. However, for practical scenarios, the greedy method is easy to fall into the local optimal problem. The simulated annealing class is an optimization paradigm that can avoid the local minimum and eventually global optimal serial structure by endowing the search process with a time-varying probability jump property that tends to zero.

- **Dynamic Annealing.** The basic annealing class contains a significant disadvantage. It obtained a theoretically optimal task queue, but only theoretically because it was constructed the queue with historical task execution times, but the actual execution times may differ slightly from historical value for various reasons. Such a situation can be avoided by using dynamic forecasting of tasks order: before each task is calculated, it was found the optimal permutation based on its historical execution time. After the task calculation is complete, it computes an optimal permutation based on the actual time of the task (it updates time's metric).

- **Multiple Batch.** This strategy uses an optimal stacking mechanism and is most applicable for several batches (Jobs) execution. Moreover, it uses no historical or heuristics information to proceed with scheduling. For an unknown task, an estimation can be performed only from certain dimensions of the task. The more dimensions, the better the estimation results. Measurements in a single dimension may not be accurate. Clustering based on multi-dimensional measures—different classes are in different scheduling queues. Queues are sorted based on the centroid of the cluster in advance.

- **Greedy Division.** This is a single-thread scheduling concept with no usage of historical data. It sorts all tasks by file size in descending order, the maximum number of cores occupies by 50% of the maximum task and for other tasks the number of allocated cores based on the ratio of the file size to the first task. Whenever there are remaining cores, it tries to select the tasks that can occupy these cores to perform, i.e., select the tasks that are just right from large to small.

4 Scheduling Measurements

4.1 Review of Existing Approaches

To date, there is a sufficient number of ways to analyze the obtained data after performing batch execution. Some of them are related to consider in testing environment cases (see [6,9]), but a reliable way is to develop custom metrics to evaluate the overall state of the schedulers. As described at [1], the scheduler needs to "achieve timeliness" and time is the priority metric for all types of schedulers. However, since this paper described a statical scheduler with historical information, it's important to choose the correct metrics (for instance, for statical approaches there is no need to use system response and delays, because it's unnecessary in a non-dynamical approach).

At [3] authors describe a deadline (guarantee ratio) metric based on critical-ness level and related weight, but such an approach is incompatible because of the same priority of executions for all tasks in the testing system, so it is based only on inner historical values.

Some metrics and parameters updated dynamically on the flow (evolutionary class of schedulers) and recalculates from task to task (see [4]), but there is no option to get current values in runtime because of the static approach. Another method to measure the efficiency of the scheduler is based on a linear differential equation which assumes as the model of tasks processing [5]. Multiprocessors system is too complex for linear approximation and differential analysis is out of scope for the current paper. For some systems [7] there is an ability to balance metrics before the scheduler's launch (define bounds for metrics values and execute scheduler's model which achieves such parameters). The case described in this paper is not suitable for this approach by the architecture of the cluster.

None of the metrics described above can be applied to the paradigm of current research because it is based on statical information about the system in states before execution and after execution, but considered values driven by another system information. Therefore efficiency metrics (related to the problem's definition and measured resource usage in a cluster) were developed and applied in real cases.

4.2   Scheduling Metrics: Diagrams, Resources, Efficiency

For a current model of multiprocessing system, it was decided to develop metrics to measure the efficiency of each strategy's implementations.

An optimal way to make such metrics is to answer the next questions: *How can it indicate the batch execution process and its troubles? How can it measure the idle part and non-idle part? What is the target resource for the cluster?*

As a result, there was constructed two types of data visualization: Gantt chart and CPU usage diagram. The first one is based on time distribution for each task in batch. It's pretty easy to see what's the "largest" task in batch and where are the most not parallelized places in the whole Job. The second one comes from cores and hosts usage information and consists of many parameters (not only tasks order with execution time). CPU diagram can represent the "weak" place with idle workers and how much space it can fill with another worker. Another advantage of the second diagram is the ability to provide accurate measurements for the idle part of Job execution. It can smoothly divide tasks into two groups according to "wasting" space which is visually defined on the CPU usage diagram.

Definition 1. *Tail part is a part of the whole execution progress which starts after the minimum end-time of the last task among all of cores.*

Statement. *The whole batch can be divided into two parts: the main part and the tail part. Each of them represents a useful and idle proportion of execution.*

To measure schedulers' efficiency there were considered the next metrics:

- **Execution Time:** the whole time of scheduler work (basic metric);
- **Main part Time:** execution time without tail part (from $0\,s$ to $\widehat{t}$);
- **Tail Time:** execution time of tail part (from $\widehat{t}$ to the end);

- **Pure CPU Usage:** square of the diagram in the main part;
- **Tail CPU Usage:** square of the diagram only on the tail (starts from $\hat{t}$);
- **Tail Overhead:** the ratio between tail time and median time value among all of the tasks;
- **Efficiency Capacity:** summation of the execution time of each task multiplied by the total used cores for current tasks.

Based on such metrics it's easy to make conclusions about different scenarios of schedulers execution. For example, if the whole execution time is large and tail time is more than main part-time, but tail CPU usage is pretty small, it can add another batch with different tasks to fill the tail part. On the other side, if CPU usage is high in the tail as well as in the main part then it's obvious that the batch executes efficiently, because it fills all the batches with certain tasks and definition of a tail is irrelevant for the current case.

Tail overhead metrics represent penalties for large tasks which were scheduled at the end of the batch's execution. It's better to start from large tasks and minimize the tail part, but if tail tasks larger than the median task in the main part, it got the highest value for tail overhead which means that there is a need to reschedule some tasks.

The idealistic situation is when the execution time is small, tail time tends to 0, CPU usage for the tail and main part tends to 100% and tail overhead tends to 1.

4.3   Experiments Conduction in Real Environment

Previously it was described flowchart of the cluster's framework in Fig. 1. The log dispatcher launches after the HDFS invoking step. It provides us the ability to measure time for the scheduler part.

So after the execution of the batch, it was obtained the log which contains task detalization: start time, end time, the real execution time for a task, the distribution between cores and blocks, an ID of using cores for current task processing.

For testing it was prepared the Job with tasks (which consists of HDFS-data, SQL-query, and real execution plan). In such a way it finishes (on average) 20 tests per each scheduler strategy. Data-driven approaches use the Graph strategy to schedule the blocks as well, but other schedulers work with Equilibrium and baseline HDFS strategies.

5   Summary of the Results

In this section, the authors provide results for different schedulers in one test batch including 71 tasks. The total size of the batch is 584 GBs and it contains ≈3.6 billions of data rows. After applying certain SQL operations (filter, select, group by...) it was obtained 38 GBs of output data with ≈0.3 rows. The testing environment contains the next hardware configuration: 6 nodes at the cluster,

CPU with *Intel Xeon Gold 6230N* (2.30 GHz/20cores), RAM: *8*32G DDR4 ECC*. An experiment was carried out under such conditions. Note that it was used not for the whole set of cores in the system, but its subset (the mean value for cores per host is 10).

5.1 Performance and Runtime Comparisson

After the execution of this Job, the performance results presented at Table 3. Multi-batch scheduler has the worst performance as well as the worst efficiency capacity. Annealing class of algorithms is the best solution with approximately the same performance, but a simplified version of the data-driven approach shows the best capacity result.

Table 3. Performance test for different schedulers

Strategy	Time (secs)	Efficiency capacity
MultiBatch	996.851594	33792.451026
Greedy	520.334221	30531.777603
Data-driven	482.04614	25617.325310
Dyn.annealing	442.392825	24944.507181
Annealing	445.535692	25340.807954
Simple d.-driven	428.740834	22410.507381

5.2 Metrics Comparison and Improvements

Gantt charts show us the runtime process of each scheduler (see Fig. 2). Also, it was provided a table with CPU and "tail" metrics (see Table 4 and Fig. 3).

Table 4. Different metrics for the scheduling strategies

Method	Main part time	Tail time	Pure CPU usage (%)	Tail overhead	Tail CPU usage (%)
Annealing	417.083	28.452	79.54	2.82	36.70
Dyn. Annealing	321.111	121.281	76.17	6.81	68.67
MultiBatch	567.060	429.790	96.07	129.69	2.64
Greedy	485.182	35.151	82.96	1.87	64.92
Data-driven	413.250	68.795	75.62	10.38	27.55
Simple d.-driven	377.707	51.033	84.01	20.52	78.77

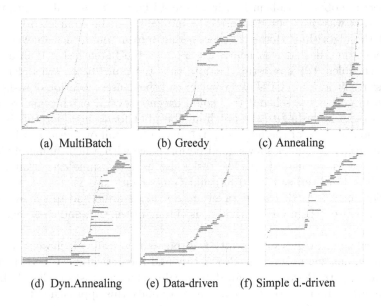

(a) MultiBatch   (b) Greedy   (c) Annealing

(d) Dyn.Annealing   (e) Data-driven   (f) Simple d.-driven

Fig. 2. Gantt charts for different strategies

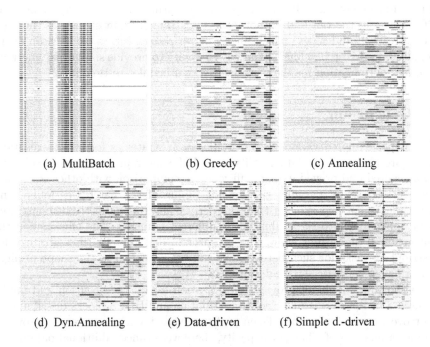

(a) MultiBatch   (b) Greedy   (c) Annealing

(d) Dyn.Annealing   (e) Data-driven   (f) Simple d.-driven

Fig. 3. CPU diagrams for different strategies

There are obvious tails in Fig. 2(a, b) and Fig. 3(a, b) as well. It means that certain task was distributed incorrectly and could not be completed before the end of the algorithm. However, even taking into account such unevenness in execution time, data-driven heuristics executes the batch faster than a multi-batch scheduler. It's interesting to note that the multi-batch scheduler shows the best result for pure CPU usage because of the densest location of tasks. This is a feature of such a scheduler: it could execute several batches and relocates tasks in them according to the batch number, but for a single job this is a bad application because of the huge long tail inside (the tail overhead is ≈129.69).

The greedy scheduler shows good performance with a high filling of the tail part as well as the main part. Tail tasks also have the same execution time as others (the tail overhead is ≈1.87) and Gantt chart also visualizes sequential execution of tasks with high parallelism. So this is a method to achieve a tidy trade-off between high CPU usage, dense filling of the tail, and small execution time.

Annealing strategies work pretty fast, but fair annealing is more stable than dynamical one: the tail part is always tiny and theoretically can be transferred to the main part. Performance for dynamically relocated tasks is slightly better, but the huge tail and lower efficiency capacity make this approach not so reliable as the basic annealing one.

After analyzing efficiency metrics and calculating CPU values, it was chosen the best (λ, σ)-parameters as 3 and 15 values respectively for simplified data-driven implementation. It was improved by optimization of performance and CPU usage in the tail and it shows the best result overall of metrics, but this method is still under research. It shows better results with a comparison of the default data-driven baseline, so there is an ability to provide similar parametrization and optimization for the basic heuristics scheduler to tune it.

6   Conclusion

This paper explored various resource allocation strategies for batch execution. An approach based on data locality and HDFS-file representation feature was implemented and proved its high efficiency in comparison with other strategies. The optimal set of parameterization for tuning of the batch was found, and it was shown in experiments that the derived metrics perfectly demonstrated their applicability to the evaluation of different launches. The efficiency of the implemented algorithms shows the prospect of developing such a strategy for distributing tasks for such batches and will be developed in the shape of high-performance heuristics strategies in future work.

Although, this paper provides optimization for query execution and implemented a two-part scheduler (cores distribution and HDFS-blocks distribution). Moreover, measures for the efficiency of the current solution were also provided and after analysis of efficiency capacity, there were tuned additional parameters to increase performance and to make cores usage denser.

There is still a field to improve such methods and reduce historical information volume, because heuristics are still not flexible with other systems where it doesn't know predefined information about each task.

Also, performance analysis can help us to change some parts of algorithmic implementation and simplify complex scoring for cores distribution. It's necessary to keep a balance between the reasonable detailed solution to allocate resources and the ability to prune some extra-scoring with high complexity.

References

1. Ramamritham, K., Stankovic, J.: Scheduling algorithms and operating systems support for real-time system. Proc. IEEE **82**(1), 55–67 (1994). https://doi.org/10.1109/5.259426
2. Shakor, M.-Y.: Scheduling and synchronization algorithms in operating system: a survey. J. Stud. Sci. Eng. **2**(1), 1–16 (2021). https://doi.org/10.53898/josse2021121
3. Biyabani, S.-R., Stankovic, J., Ramamritham, K.: The integration of deadline and criticalness in hard real-time scheduling. In: Proceedings of Real-Time Systems Symposium, Huntsville. IEEE Press (1988). https://doi.org/10.1109/REAL.1988.51111
4. Peng, Z., Ting-lei, H.: Research of multi-resource dynamic job-shop scheduling based on the hybrid genetic algorithm. In: 2009 Third International Conference on Genetic and Evolutionary Computing, Guilin. IEEE Press (2009). https://doi.org/10.1109/WGEC.2009.31
5. Wen-qiang, L., Zhi-qiang, Z.: Robust gain-scheduling controller to LPV system using gap metric. In: IEEE International Conference on Information and Automation, Zhangjiajie. IEEE Press (2008). https://doi.org/10.1109/ICINFA.2008.4608054
6. Shah, S.-N.-M., Mahmood, A.-K.-B., Oxley, A.: Hybrid scheduling and dual queue scheduling. In: 2009 2nd IEEE International Conference on Computer Science and Information Technology, Beijing, pp. 539–543. IEEE Press (2009). https://doi.org/10.1109/ICCSIT.2009.5234480
7. Tang, W., Dongxu, R., Lan, D., Desai, N.: Adaptive metric-aware job scheduling for production supercomputers. In: 41st International Conference on Parallel Processing Workshops, Pittsburgh, pp. 107–115. IEEE Press (2012). https://doi.org/10.1109/ICPPW.2012.17
8. Stone, H.: Multiprocessor scheduling with the aid of network flow algorithms. IEEE Trans. Soft Eng. **3**(1), 85–93 (1977)
9. Omar, H.-K., Jihad, K., Hussein, S.-F.: Comparative analysis of the essential CPU scheduling algorithms. Bull. Electr. Eng. Inform. **10**(5), 2742–2750 (2021). https://doi.org/10.11591/eei.v10i5.2812
10. Al-Hami, M., Maabreh, M., Taamneh, S., Pradeep, A.: Apache Hadoop performance evaluation with resources monitoring tools, and parameters optimization: IoT emerging demand. J. Theor. Appl. Inf. Tech. **99**(11), 2734–2750 (2021)
11. Sahab, M., Toropov, V., Hossein, M., Gandomi, A.: Metaheuristic Applications in Structures and Infrastructures. Elsevier Print (2013). https://doi.org/10.1016/B978-0-12-398364-0.00002-4

System for Collecting Statistics on Power Consumption of Supercomputer Applications

Evgeniy Kiselev[1], Anton Baranov[1]([✉]) [ID], Pavel Telegin[1] [ID],
and Egor Kuznetsov[2]

[1] Joint Supercomputer Center, Russian Academy of Sciences, Moscow, Russia
{kiselev,abaranov,ptelegin}@jscc.ru
[2] MIREA - Russian Technological University, Moscow, Russia

Abstract. The basic data for power consumption monitoring in supercomputers is statistics on electric energy use by user applications. As a
rule, within a single R&D supercomputer center there are simultaneously
running several HPC systems of different generations and architecture.
This article researches the software methods for measuring power consumption of such computers. The goal of the work is to develop a consistent approach to collecting, processing, and storing power consumption
statistics for user applications that can be run on different supercomputers at one center. Basing on specifications data and public documentation, the article studies the capabilities of hardware platforms of modern commodity (Intel, AMD) and graphics (Nvidia, AMD) microprocessors, as well as compatible software, to get access to power consumption
data. New statistical indicators are proposed that enable to evaluate the
impact of user applications on supercomputer power consumption. The
extension of the well-known monitoring system Prometheus for obtaining those indicators is explored. The results of applying the developed
software on JSCC RAS computing resources are presented, and the values of the proposed indicators are estimated using the example of NAS
Parallel Benchmarks tests.

Keywords: HPC systems · Energy monitoring · RAPL ·
Prometheus · Job management · Job scheduling

1 Introduction

The increase of supercomputers power consumption is one of the vital problems in the high-performance computing. Simultaneous launch of several energy-
consuming applications can lead to increase of the load on supercomputer center
(SCC) power grids up to peak values. Under such conditions the risk of computing nodes partial emergency shutdown and, consequently, shutdown of the
running user applications is increased. Maintaining the unfailing operating of
SCC computing resources and minimizing the impact of their failure on the

V. Voevodin et al. (Eds.): RuSCDays 2022, LNCS 13708, pp. 548–561, 2022.
https://doi.org/10.1007/978-3-031-22941-1_40

computation process requires continuous control for power consumption permissible exceedance during running user parallel programs.

Users normally get access to SCC resources submitting their jobs in a queue. By the term "job" we hereby understand a parallel program (application) with described input arguments and launch parameters (runtime, number of required processors or computing nodes, computing resource type or queue name, etc.). Jobs are managed by special software like Slurm, PBS, and similar. In the Joint Supercomputer Center of the Russian Academy of Science (JSCC RAS) a domestic system of parallel jobs management called SUPPZ [1] is used. One of important functions of SUPPZ is the supercomputer resources accounting that is assigned to the subsystem of collecting and processing statistics. The information on the user jobs that came through the queue, their launch parameters, completion codes and the resources allocated for them is stored in the statistics database (DB).

Monitoring systems are automated tools and techniques to ensure the operating health of a SCC resources. To enable the computing resources billing and accounting for the user applications impact on the supercomputer power consumption, it is required to bind the monitoring information to the user jobs. In this study we solve the problem of the supercomputers power consumption statistics collecting, processing, and accounting.

This study continues the work [2] and develops the idea of software methods of power consumption measuring in HPC systems. For different architectures and generations of commodity (Intel, AMD) and graphics (Nvidia, AMD) microprocessors those methods may vary. Our work aims at developing and testing a consistent approach to collecting, processing, and storing the statistics information on supercomputer applications impact on SCC power consumption.

2   Software-Based Measuring of Commodity Microprocessors Power Consumption

Different approaches can be used to measure power consumption. Some of them require measurement hardware. Others can be implemented using only software. Table 1 demonstrates some of the most popular tools for software and hardware power consumption measuring approaches. The advantage of the hardware approach is high measurement accuracy. However, the hardware approach is poorly scalable, because it requires the measurement hardware on each computing node. The software approach is usually implemented using sensors and counters built into the microprocessor and often provides results comparable with the hardware approach. Some software approaches are based on energy consumption models. These models allow calculating power consumption based on microprocessor usage and other characteristics provided by the operating system through API and SDK. The disadvantage of software approaches compared to hardware ones is less accuracy. Due to scalability and independence from additional measuring devices software approaches have become widespread in HPC.

The listed in Table 1 measurement tools are focused on real-time use on a single node. In this case, the user needs to independently collect power consumption data from all nodes for their processing. The user has to run copies of measurement tools on a set of nodes allocated for a job. In addition, it is often necessary to change the format of the displayed information, to calculate new values or statistical indicators based on existing ones. This is not always possible using only the mentioned tools. In our research we focus on software methods for measuring power consumption which can be integrated into a supercomputer monitoring system and allow collecting statistical data on power consumption.

Table 1. Software and hardware approaches for power consumption measurement.

API	SDK and framework	Software	
Software measurement			Hardware measurement
PowerAPI [3], PAPI [4], Hwmon [5], perf_events [4], perfmon [4], HPM [4]	Intel Energy Checker [3], Power Capping Framework (powercap) [6]	pTop [3], PowerTop [3], Joulemeter [3]	PowerScope [3], Powermeter [3], PowerPack [4], PowerMon2 [4], PowerInsight [4]

In modern processors, hardware performance counters are used to provide power consumption data. Hardware performance counters are special function registers located directly in the processor. They are used to gather different metrics of computation system status. Compared to software profilers, hardware counters provide access to data for a shorter time and with less overhead costs. Because the number of such registers in a microprocessor is limited, and the same register can be used for calculation of different data, it is necessary to perform several measures to collect all needed metrics. Each vendor defines their own APIs to access the performance counters, and these APIs can vary in different CPU generations even of the same vendor. In such conditions, we need a common tool of power consumption measurement compatible with different processors. The Running Average Power Limit (RAPL) interface [7] became such tool. Modern CPUs contain microcode implemented the RAPL interface.

RAPL microcode applies a power consumption prediction model basing on the data acquired from the hardware performance counters. According to RAPL terminology, a processor is divided into domains. By RAPL domain a microprocessor component is understood that is physically meaningful for power management. The contents and the number of RAPL domains differ depending on the microprocessor architecture, but in most cases, power consumption data on the following domains can be acquired [6] (Fig. 1):

- Package domain—management of power consumption for all microprocessor cores, integrated graphics, cache memory, and memory controller;
- DRAM—management of RAM power consumption;
- PP0—management of power consumption for all cores (power consumption management for separate cores is not provided);

– PP1—management of power consumption for the integrated graphics;
– PSys—chip-integrated power consumption management of the whole system (available starting from Intel Skylake microprocessors series).

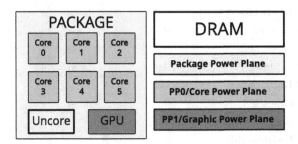

Fig. 1. RAPL domains.

RAPL support was initially applied in Intel microprocessors only, but in time it was implemented in the latest generations of AMD microprocessors, starting from Zen series. In AMD microprocessors RAPL superseded Application Power Management interface. Table 2 contains the overview of power consumption data availability for various RAPL domains in different generations of Intel and AMD microprocessors. With Linux operation systems, one of the following methods can be used to access RAPL domain power consumption data.

1. Using MSR registers accessible through a driver integrated in the Linux kernel that is compatible with modern Intel and AMD microprocessors.
2. Using sysfs virtual file system accessible through powercap [8] software interface that is available for Intel microprocessors only.
3. Using perf_event [9] software interface that is available for Intel microprocessors only.
4. Using hwmon [5] software interface compatible with modern microprocessors Intel and AMD. For old generations of AMD processors (ancestors of Zen series without RAPL support) the interface enables to determine the thermal design power only.

The work [7] presents the results of accuracy estimation of power consumption data measurement using MSR driver. According to the results, the accuracy is 99% while the overhead costs do not exceed 1%.

It is notable that this study did not cover the methods of collecting data for power consumption of ARM-based microprocessors due to their relatively rare usage within supercomputer systems. However, due to ever-growing use of ARM architecture in wearable and portable microelectronic products, ARM microprocessors contain power consumption management tools similar to RAPL. The methods of collecting data on Power microprocessors power consumption are overviewed in work [10].

Table 2. RAPL domains supported by different generations of Intel and AMD microprocessors.

Name	Package domain	PP0	PP1	DRAM
Intel Sandy Bridge	+	+	+	−
Intel Ivy Bridge	+	+	+	−
Intel Haswell	+	+	+	+
Intel Broadwell	+	+	+	+
Intel Skylake	+	+	+	+
Intel Kaby Lake	+	+	+	+
Intel Cascade Lake	+	+	+	+
Intel Knights Landing	+	−	−	+
Intel Knights Mill	+	−	−	+
AMD Bulldozer	−	−	−	−
AMD Piledriver	−	−	−	−
AMD Piledriver/Trinity	−	−	−	−
AMD Steamroller "Kaveri"	−	−	−	−
AMD Excavator "Carrizo"	−	−	−	−
AMD Jaguar "Mullins"	−	−	−	−
AMD Zen	+	+	−	−
AMD Zen+	+	+	−	−
AMD Zen2	+	+	−	−

3 Methods of Power Consumption Measuring for Graphics Microprocessors

Due to widespread use of graphics coprocessors (accelerators) in modern computers, power consumption monitoring of the CPU alone does not provide the general idea of the whole computer power consumption. We shall review Nvidia and AMD GPU power consumption control tools compatible with Linux. Nvidia Management Library (NVML) [11] is an API for collecting data on NVIDIA graphic power consumption that is part of NVIDIA driver. It provides for acquiring the following information:

- utilization of graphics processor and memory;
- list of active processes along with the name/identificator and the allocated graphics processor memory;
- graphics cores frequency in MHz and frames per second;
- cores temperature and fan rpm;
- GPU board current power consumption and allowable power limits;
- information on the board serial number, PCI identificator, BIOS version.

For AMD graphics accelerators (starting from Ryzen series) a sensor tool is implemented on the level of Linux driver (starting from 4.11 kernel version) for acquiring data similar to NVML. Currently, the open source code is available of lm-sensor [12] software that implements GPU power consumption data collection.

4   Software Stack for Collecting Data on Computers Power Consumption

Because there is no off-the-shelf technology for getting simultaneous access to power consumption data for both commodity and graphics microprocessors, it is practical to use the reviewed software tools as part of a unified SCC infrastructure monitoring system. Notably, for each computing resource type a separate software tool for power consumption data collection is used that is compatible with SCC monitoring system. The data accumulated in the monitoring system can further be processed and stored in the SCC statistics DB.

To solve the problem of power consumption data collection, we analyzed the best practices for high-load systems monitoring. We mainly focused on monitoring systems with the possibility of introducing self-developed extension modules in different programming languages, integrated data storage subsystem, and a broad dev community. The analysis resulted in choosing Prometheus monitoring system that is successfully applied in supercomputer centers as well. Works [8,9,13] note that Prometheus provides necessary characteristics for its components scaling at supercomputer resources and processing speed of queries for monitoring data reading and recording. Experience of Prometheus application on Fugaku [13] supercomputer proved that Prometheus enabled to gather up to 1 mil metrics per second from more than 150,000 heterogenic computing nodes, and to record them in the persistent store within 20 s. Popular scenarios of Prometheus application within a supercomputer software are:

- load estimation of the supercomputer resources, network infrastructure, and file system;
- control of the SCC services health and user job queue state;
- software license provisioning;
- IT security audit, etc.

Based on Prometheus, we developed a software stack for collecting data on user jobs power consumption. The application diagram of Prometheus is displayed in Fig. 2.

For Prometheus DB interoperability with SUPPZ statistics DB, a data aggregation module was developed (see Fig. 3). The module functions on the head node of supercomputer and SUPPZ calls this module from epilog script (close_nodes_local) at the moment of user job completion. The aggregation subsystem receives the supercomputer or its partition name, the list of allocated

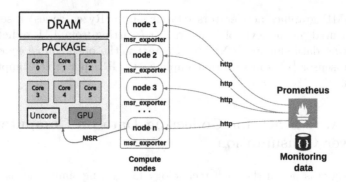

Fig. 2. Prometheus application diagram for power consumption data collection.

nodes, the job start and completion time, and forms the query to Prometheus DB. The fetched data is stored in the SCC statistics database for further analysis.

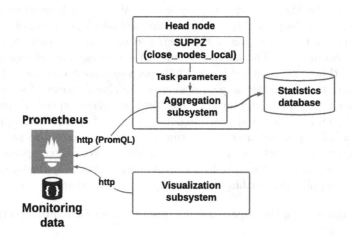

Fig. 3. Diagram of statistics data recording from Prometheus to SCC Statistics DB.

Because the existing Prometheus module for power consumption data collection uses perf_event interface, which is incompatible with AMD microprocessors, a self-developed module msr_exporter [14] was set up. This module enables to acquire power consumption data from msr registers of Intel and AMD microprocessors. The example of RAPL domains power consumption graph acquired by the developed msr-exporter module is shown in Fig. 4.

To study the capabilities of NVML interface, we developed a software module nvidia_gpu_exporter for Prometheus monitoring system. The module acquires data on power consumption in Nvidia microprocessors. This module enables to acquire information on current power consumption in J/s, and GPU load in

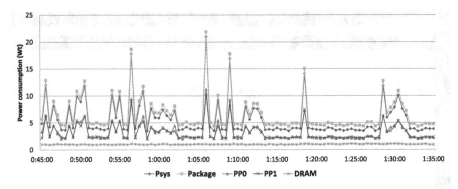

Fig. 4. Example of RAPL domains power consumption graph acquired with `msr_exporter` module.

%. The example of information display on power consumption and GPU load acquired with `nvidia_gpu_exporter` module is shown in Fig. 5 and 6 correspondently. These results demonstrate the graphical interface and the possibility to extract and collect data on NVidia GPU power consumption and load using Prometheus. However, it is necessary to separately evaluate the accuracy of the results obtained using NVML on different jobs.

Due to PromQL [15] query language integrated in Prometheus, the following statistics indicators can be calculated in the back-end.

E_{max} (J/s) is maximum total power consumption of all allocated computing nodes during job runtime. Power consumption peak values accounting enables to evaluate the possibility of exceeding the allowable limits for SCC power consumption during simultaneous launch of several power-consuming user jobs.

E_{med} (J/s) is median value of allocated nodes power consumption. Let current power consumption during a job runtime be measured n times at moments $1, 2, \ldots, n$. Let us indicate the value of the current power consumption measured at moment i as x_i. Let us grade the number series $x_1, \ldots, x_n$ in ascending order and obtain a new series $x'_1, \ldots, x'_n$. Then the median value of power consumption is calculated as follows:

$$E_{med} = x'_{(n+1)/2} \text{ for odd } n, \quad E_{med} = \frac{x'_{n/2} + x'_{(n+1)/2}}{2} \text{ for even } n$$

The need for calculating the median value is reasoned by the fact that for power consumption statistics a distribution with a large number of local "outliers" considerably different from average value is typical. Accounting for the median and the maximum power consumption values enables to evaluate the SCC power grid loading conditions.

E_{sum} (J) is the total value of power consumption of all allocated nodes during a job runtime. It enables to estimate power usage for a user job runtime.

To determine the load of computing resources during a job runtime, the following statistical indicators are calculated.

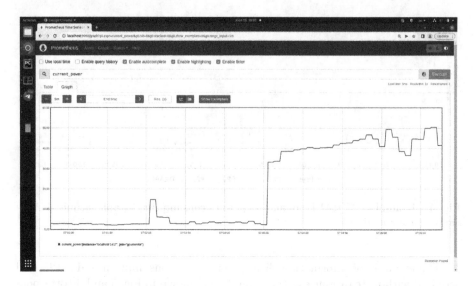

Fig. 5. Example of displaying the data on Nvidia GPU power consumption acquired with `nvidia_gpu_exporter` module.

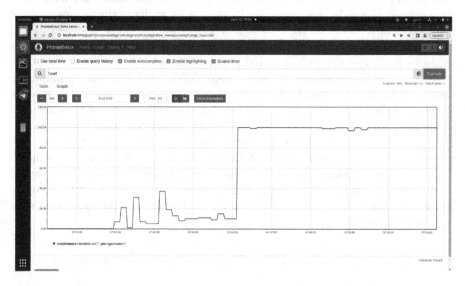

Fig. 6. Example of displaying the data of Nvidia GPU current load acquired with `nvidia_gpu_exporter` module.

$C_{med}(U)$ (cores number) is median value of the number of cores with load per cent exceeding the set limit value U. The limit value is set by the system administrator basing on resources usage statistics during user jobs runtime, e.g., 50%. It enables to estimate the number of intensively used processor cores during user job runtime.

U_{med} (%) is median value of the computing node cores load per cent. It enables to estimate the % of processor cores load during user job runtime.

The statistics data acquired from Prometheus DB are entered into the SUPPZ statistics DB.

For data visualization, a web application Grafana is often used together with Prometheus [16]. This application enables to build various diagrams that display the monitoring data and SCC infrastructure statistics. The visualization subsystem not only makes it possible to evaluate the calculated statistical indicators of power consumption (maximum, median, total values of power consumption), but also provides for displaying the instantaneous values of power consumption for each computing node. The power consumption data can be presented either in text format in the form of a report after the user job completion or in graphic format with diagrams and graphs displayed in Grafana. To create dashboards in Grafana one needs to form a query to Prometheus in PromQL language. For example, to display the power consumption of the supercomputer nodes once in 2 s, the query will appear as follows

```
irate(msr_rapl_joules_total{job=\"msr_exporter\"}[2s])
```

where `msr_exporter` is the name of the developed module for power consumption data collection, and `2s` is the frequency of data update.

Similarly, to display the power consumption data of a GPU, one has to change the module name `msr_exporter` for `nvidia_gpu_exporter`.

5 Experimental Study of NPB Tests Power Consumption

With the purpose of checking the proposed solutions efficiency, we performed a series of experiments that involved standard NAS Parallel Benchmarks tests (NPB). To reach the maximum load of the computing nodes allocated for the experiment, the size class D test was performed. The list and the parameters of the used NPB test jobs are shown in Table 3.

Table 3. NPB test jobs run parameters.

Test name	Required number of cores	Number of allocated computing nodes			
		Broadwell	Cascade Lake	KNL	Skylake
BT	144	5	3	2	4
EP	144	5	3	2	4
IS	256	8	6	4	8
LU	256	8	6	4	8
SP	256	8	6	4	8

NPB tests were launched on 4 partitions of MVS-10P OP supercomputer installed at JSCC RAS [17]: Broadwell, Skylake, KNL, and Cascade Lake. MVS-10P OP partitions have different CPU architecture, performance, and power consumption. For each test, we performed 10 repetitions with the same parameters. The number of repetitions was determined experimentally and proved to be sufficient to reduce the measurement error and the possible impact of clock frequency changes on the power consumption. For each test, the same set of computing nodes of each partition was used. To do this, a test script was created, which, after allocating computing nodes, performed 10 consecutive runs of each test and saved the results in the service directory. The results of the experiment series are presented in Table 4.

While analysing the presented results one can note that each NPB test has its own typical E_{max} and E_{med} values. The largest E_{max} and E_{med} values were obtained on Broadwell and KNL during LU test, while on Cascade Lake and Skylake—during SP test. The obtained values show that one and the same algorithm can have different impact on different computers power consumption.

E_{max} and E_{med} difference value does not always correlate with U_{med} and C_{med} values. During BT, EP, LU, and SP tests the difference between E_{max} and E_{med} reached from 0.5% to 5.1% for BT, from 0.4% to 4% for EP, from 0.3% to 0.9% for LU, and from 0.3% to 1.1% for SP depending on the used partition, while U_{med} and C_{med} had maximum possible values (i.e. the load per cent and the number of the used cores were close to maximum values). During IS test the increase of the difference between E_{max} and E_{med} from 1.2% to 11.07% correlated with the decrease of U_{med} value from 99.8% to 78.3% and C_{med} value from 236 cores to 13 cores of 256 available. Hence, the difference between the maximum and the median values of power consumption is not always related to the load of the processor cores.

The results of comparing E_{max}, E_{med}, U_{med} and C_{med} values demonstrate the need to examine them in a bundle to determine the impact of a user application on energy consumption.

E_{sum} is affected by the job runtime. Even if E_{max} and E_{min} are very small, the low performance of microprocessors leads to longer job runtime and higher power consumption. When running LU and EP benchmarks with intensive computation, less productive KNL consumed more energy. For other jobs with less computation, the difference in execution time did not have a significant impact on the total energy consumption. Thus, it can be assumed that there is a computation time limit at which less productive, but energy-efficient systems can reduce total energy consumption. However, if it is exceeded, the use of such microprocessors does not reduce the total energy consumption, but rather increases it. This fact requires further investigation.

Table 4. Results of NPB tests.

MVS-10P OP partition	BT	EP	IS	LU	SP
E_{max} (J/s)					
Broadwell	1257.31	1242.06	1665.8	2259.55	2101.64
Cascade Lake	1407.69	1327.63	2259.09	2437.02	2582.92
Skylake	1698.96	1668.48	2447.07	2949.48	3233.33
KNL	417.45	308.01	622.39	727.29	792.04
E_{med} (J/s)					
Broadwell	1234.385	1237.64	1645.6	2243.83	2080.74
Cascade Lake	1336.78	1274.32	2008.72	2416.16	2555.56
Skylake	1683.2	1656.01	2398.48	2937.6	3206.13
KNL	397.755	306.82	599.9	709.58	775.16
E_{sum} (J)					
Broadwell	265769	30765.86	15783.49	172417.16	335122.6
Cascade Lake	227116.15	31585.87	17115.27	172090.65	294234.58
Skylake	282044.02	37303.34	13217.98	188012.64	364193.15
KNL	85568.39	39289.36	7765.45	222308.9	235798.77
C_{med} (number of cores)					
Broadwell	144	144	236	256	256
Cascade Lake	144	144	179	256	256
Skylake	144	144	163	256	256
KNL	144	144	192	254	255
U_{med} (%)					
Broadwell	100	100	99.8	100	100
Cascade Lake	100	100	78.3	100	100
Skylake	100	100	96.3	100	100
KNL	100	100	93.7	99.6	99.8

It is notable that for a total the values of E_{max}, E_{med}, U_{med} and C_{med} allow for the conclusion of the workload character during a parallel algorithm execution. If E_{max} and E_{med} have close values, and U_{med} and C_{med} are reaching their maximum values, the major time of the parallel algorithm accrues to computation operations. In opposite case, when the median power consumption value E_{med} for the computing nodes is considerably lower than the maximum E_{max}, and the values U_{med} and C_{med} approach the minimum possible values, it can be concluded that the major time accrues to communication traffic or I/O operations. Thus, for IS test meant for the performance evaluation of the supercomputer interconnect, we observed the greatest difference between the maximum and the median power consumption values on all partitions, and the smallest U_{med} and C_{med} values. Therefore, accounting for E_{max}, E_{med}, U_{med} and

C_{med} values allows for identifying the user job energy profiles. A particularly it is possible to identify jobs not fully loading the available computation capacities of the partition, and for further assigning such jobs to less productive but more power efficient partitions.

6 Conclusion

To solve the problem of power consumption statistics collecting, processing, and accounting at supercomputer jobs runtime, the needed software stack, as well as the list of statistical indicators necessary for parallel applications power consumption description were determined. Using the example of MVS-10P OP supercomputer installed at JSCC RAS the feasibility of power consumption data aggregation using the Prometheus monitoring system and the developed modules `msr_exporter` and `nvidia_gpu_exporter` was demonstrated.

The information on the available tools for power consumption collecting data for contemporary commodity and graphics Intel and AMD microprocessors was summarized. The results of using RAPL and NVML interfaces were presented.

In this paper, we propose statistical indicators that allow us to evaluate the impact of the user application execution on the energy consumption of the computer system.

The results show the practicability of accounting and control of the impact that parallel applications execution has on computers power consumption. Controlling this impact enables both tracking instantaneous and peak power consumption loads in computers and analyzing the statistics of using the computing resources by the SCC users to identify user jobs energy profiles. The information on the energy profiles will allow implementing energy efficient job scheduling at a supercomputer center.

Through experimentation, we determined that the use of microprocessors with minimal power consumption does not always reduce the total power consumption. For computationally intensive jobs, the use of less powerful but more energy efficient microprocessors can lead to increase in total power consumption. In the further work, it is necessary to determine conditions under which it is possible to allow an increase in the job runtime to reduce energy consumption, and under what conditions it is pointless.

Acknowledgements. The research was carried out at JSCC RAS as part of government assignment on the topic FNEF-2022-0016.

References

1. Savin, G.I., Shabanov, B.M., Telegin, P.N., Baranov, A.V.: Joint supercomputer center of the Russian Academy of sciences: present and future. Lobachevskii J. Math. 40(11), 1853–1862 (2019). https://doi.org/10.1134/S1995080219110271
2. Kiselev, E.A., Telegin, P.N., Shabanov, B.M.: An energy-efficient scheduling algorithm for shared facility supercomputer centers. Lobachevskii J. Math. 42(11), 2554–2561 (2021). https://doi.org/10.1134/S1995080221110147

3. Noureddine, A., Rouvoy, R., Seinturier, L.: A review of energy measurement approaches. ACM SIGOPS Oper. Syst. Rev. **47**(3), 42–49 (2013). https://doi.org/10.1145/2553070.2553077

4. Wu, X., Taylor, V.: Utilizing hardware performance counters to model and optimize the energy and performance of large scale scientific applications on power-aware supercomputers. In: IEEE International Parallel and Distributed Processing Symposium Workshops (IPDPSW), pp. 1180–1189 (2016). https://doi.org/10.1109/IPDPSW.2016.78

5. Linux Hwmon Documentation: The kernel development community. https://www.kernel.org/doc/html/latest/hwmon/index.html. Accessed 21 Jun 2022

6. Cesarini, D., Bartolini, A., Benini, L.: Benefits in relaxing the power capping constraint. In: 1st Workshop on Autotuning and Adaptivity Approaches for Energy Efficient HPC Systems, pp. 1–6 (2017). https://doi.org/10.1145/3152821.3152878

7. Khan, K., Hirki, M., Neimi, T., Nurminen, J.: RAPL in action: experiences in using RAPL for power measurements. ACM Trans. Model. Perform. Eval. Comput. Syst. **3**(2), 1–26 (2018). https://doi.org/10.1145/3177754

8. Na, H., et al.: HPC software tracking strategies for a diverse workload. In: 2020 IEEE/ACM International Workshop on HPC User Support Tools (HUST) and Workshop on Programming and Performance Visualization Tools (ProTools), pp. 1–9 (2020). https://doi.org/10.1109/HUSTProtools51951.2020.00008

9. Sukhija, N., et al.: Event management and monitoring framework for HPC environments using ServiceNow and Prometheus. In: 12th International Conference on Management of Digital EcoSystems (MEDES 2020), pp. 149–156. Association for Computing Machinery, New York (2020). https://doi.org/10.1145/3415958.3433046

10. Gschwandtner, P., Knobloch, M., Mohr, B., Pleiter, D., Fahringer, T.: Modeling CPU power consumption of HPC applications on the IBM POWER7. In: 22nd Euromicro International Conference on Parallel, Distributed, and Network-Based Processing, pp. 536–543 (2014). https://doi.org/10.1109/PDP.2014.112

11. NVML. https://developer.nvidia.com/nvidia-management-library-nvml. Accessed 21 Jun 2022

12. Lm-sensors. https://github.com/lm-sensors. Accessed 21 Jun 2022

13. Terai, M., Yamamoto, K., Miura, S., Shoji, F.: An operational data collecting and monitoring platform for Fugaku: system overviews and case studies in the prelaunch service period. In: Jagode, H., Anzt, H., Ltaief, H., Luszczek, P. (eds.) ISC High Performance 2021. LNCS, vol. 12761, pp. 365–377. Springer, Cham (2021). https://doi.org/10.1007/978-3-030-90539-2_24

14. EScheduler. https://github.com/ekuznetcov/escheduler. Accessed 21 Aug 2022

15. Sabharwal, N., Pandey, P.: Working with Prometheus query language (PromQL). In: Sabharwal, N., Pandey, P. (eds.) Monitoring Microservices and Containerized Applications, pp. 141–167. Apress, Berkeley (2020). https://doi.org/10.1007/978-1-4842-6216-0_5

16. Getting started with Grafana and Prometheus. https://grafana.com/docs/grafana/latest/getting-started/getting-startedprometheus/. Accessed 15 Apr 2022

17. JSCC RAS computing resources. https://www.jscc.ru/resources/hpc/. Accessed 21 Jun 2022

Teaching Advanced AI Development Techniques with a New Master's Program in Artificial Intelligence Engineering

Andrey Sozykin[1,2]([✉])[iD], Evgeniy Kuklin[1,2][iD], and Irina Iumanova[1][iD]

[1] Ural Federal University, Yekaterinburg, Russia
{Andrey.Sozykin,Evgeny.Kuklin,Irina.Iumanova}@urfu.ru
[2] N.N. Krasovskii Institute of Mathematics and Mechanics, Yekaterinburg, Russia

Abstract. The paper presents a new Master's program *Artificial Intelligence Engineering* at Ural Federal University created in cooperation with IT companies and partner universities. The aim of the program is to teach engineers who are able to develop complex large-scale software solutions that use artificial intelligence and put the solutions into production. The students study in detail not only the theoretical foundations and practical applications of artificial intelligence for various areas (natural language processing, computer vision, time series analysis, information security) but also contemporary methods and software engineering tools for machine learning operations (MLOps). The students acquire soft skills through project-based learning by solving research or real-world problems provided by partner companies, universities labs and Institutes of Russian Academy of Science. In addition to Ural Federal University, the program was implemented at six partner universities.

Keywords: AI engineering · MLOps · ML education · Master's program

1 Introduction

Machine learning is a very rapidly developing area in the industry. In a decade, we have gone from the first attempts to apply newly created models in business to the creation of industrial complexes based on AI. Such an impressive result was achieved, among other things, with the help of machine learning specialists and data scientists trained in special programs, who gradually began to close the long-term shortage of researchers in this area. Universities around the world have launched educational programs that teach various methods of machine learning (like statistics or neural networks) and how they can be applied to solve business problems.

However, the progress goes on: machine learning projects in industry are scaling, total number of the projects and potential applications are growing every year. Therefore, at the moment, the industry lacks engineers who are able

V. Voevodin et al. (Eds.): RuSCDays 2022, LNCS 13708, pp. 562–573, 2022.
https://doi.org/10.1007/978-3-031-22941-1_41

not only to train a model, which can solve a business problem, but also to make the model ready for production usage with the help of advanced software development methods and tools. Such tasks began to be solved by specialists in the field of AI Engineering or Machine Learning Operations (MLOps), which are basically two different names for the same: building production-ready machine learning systems.

In this paper we present our experience in developing a Master's program *Artificial Intelligence Engineering* at Ural Federal University based on modern trends and technologies. Students study in detail not only the theoretical foundations and practical application of artificial intelligence for several areas, but also modern methods and tools of software engineering. Students acquire soft skills through project-based learning, solving research or real-world problems provided by partner companies, university labs or Institutes of Russian Academy of Science. Thus, the Master's program was created with the aim of obtaining all the necessary skills for the learners to create complex large-scale production-ready software systems based on AI.

2   Background

2.1   A Demand for AI Engineers

The complexity of software systems with embedded machine learning features is growing up tremendously recent years. Often the ML model, which can be the core of the application, became just a small part of the entire software system [1], so the interplay between the model and the rest of the software and context is essential. Therefore, it was only a matter of time to bring the best practices from software development to the creation of AI systems. Continuous software engineering practices, such as DevOps, have been rapidly adopted by software development organizations in their operations and became the standard. This has resulted in an ability to deploy new features to use whenever their development is completed, which in turn means that systems are updated frequently. The practice of continuous delivery of ML is called MLOps [2].

The term *MLOps* (stands for Machine Learning Operations) came from the industry as a subfield or extension of DevOps [3]. It enables data scientists to collaborate and increase the pace of delivery and quality of model development through monitoring, validation, and management of machine learning models. MLOps supports the data science life cycle just as DevOps supports the application development life cycle with CI/CD pipelines, source and version control, testing, and other concepts. Machine learning operations mean advocating automation and monitoring at all steps of ML system development, including integration, testing, releasing, deployment and infrastructure management.

In order to analyze the difficulties data scientists are having in their daily work, the authors of the paper [2] created a survey consisted of a number of questions, addressing the background and the activities performed by the target audience. To understand the goals of the work, they asked a detailed question about short-term activities to be completed within next 3 months. In general, the answers to this question show that the top goals are "developing models for production use" and "deploying models to production". Looking at respondents roles, it seems that the skills of a data scientist are expanding from data science and models to other domains, in particular ML infrastructure and deployment.

Meesters et al. conducted the research to study the requirements from the job market for the position of AI engineer [4], by retrieving job ad data between April 2018 and April 2021 from a job ad database. The part of this work was the analysis of the job ads for focusing on data science or software engineering. The results were the following: about forty percent of the job ads did not have a specific focus on either data science or engineering tasks, but instead required a mix of them. Also, the research shows that the number of AI engineering related vacancies will continue to grow in the nearest future.

Thus, we see that the industry is in need of AI engineers who are skilled enough in several machine learning areas and are able to bring ML models to production using MLOps practices. The training of such specialists should become a priority in education in the coming years.

2.2 Related Work

In the leading universities of the world, more and more areas of study are emerging, covering not only data science, but also AI engineering. For example, the paper [5] describes experience with the bachelor level educational program for software engineers to specialize as AI engineers, being held in Fontys University of Applied Sciences, Eindhoven, Netherlands. As soon as the first students studying this program have been graduated, the authors shared the lessons they learned during educating process. Among them are intensive training in data engineering and collaborating with practitioners in MLOps to achieve the efficient and effective engineering of high-quality AI systems. Their experience confirms the strategy we chose when creating our curriculum.

University of Chicago provides Master's of Science in Analytics program [6], where future data scientists acquired advanced programming and data engineering architecture skills to be ready to tackle automated machine learning, big data, cloud computing platforms, and all the large-scale engineering challenges that come with parallel processing and real-time AI solutions. Along the classic machine learning-related subjects, the students here are provided with elective courses, where they can choose some AI Engineering courses like Real Time Intelligent Systems or Machine Learning Operations.

Department of Engineering Cybernetics of National University of Science and Technology MISIS implements the Master's program *Artificial Intelligence and Machine Learning* [7]. Similar with the previous example, students learn basic ML courses and can chose supplementary subjects like Modern software development tools for AI or ML-DevOps.

In addition, there is a growing number of various online courses. Coursera offers several ones related directly to machine learning in production. These can be either standalone courses, introducing participants to MLOps tools and best practices, or entire specializations like Machine Learning Engineering for Production (MLOps) [8]. This specialization includes the study of data life cycles, modeling pipelines, and deploying machine learning models to make them available to end-users.

Another example: one of the courses by Simplilearn [9] is dedicated to training AI engineers. According to the authors from Simplilearn, an AI Engineer can work with machine learning algorithms, neural networks, and other techniques in various types of business worldwide. Also, the AI Engineers can build, test, and deploy Artificial Intelligence models and are responsible for maintaining the Artificial Intelligence infrastructure. This role can have many responsibilities in an organization, such as:

- Coordinating between Data Scientists and Business Analysts.
- Automating infrastructure used by the data science and engineering teams.
- Testing, deploying, and converting machine learning models and algorithms into APIs so that other applications can access them, and develop viable products based on machine learning.

3   The Master's Program Description

3.1   Mandatory Courses

The program is aimed at bachelors of IT, engineering, mathematics, natural sciences and economics.

Students master academic disciplines for three semesters according to the curriculum (see Fig. 1). In the last semester, they undergo industrial and educational practice, as well as defend their final qualifying work.

The academic program includes a detailed study of the application of artificial intelligence for several subject areas: computer vision, natural language processing, information security, predictive analytics. Considerable attention is paid to automating the creation and deployment of machine learning systems, including DevOps, MLOps and data engineering. The main programming language studied and used in the program is Python.

The studied mandatory disciplines are described below.

The *Linux Operating System* and *Python Programming* courses are kind of preliminary ones, propaedeutic in nature, and are designed to give students a tool for mastering further professional courses.

The purpose of studying the discipline *Mathematical Foundations of Artificial Intelligence* is to master the apparatus of higher mathematics, which is most in demand in the field of data science and artificial intelligence applications: linear algebra, optimization methods, probability theory and applied statistics.

Since students learned the basics of linear algebra in the undergraduate program, they deepen their knowledge in this program. Particular attention is paid to the application of concepts to machine learning problems. For example, it is shown how pseudo-inversion of degenerate and non-square matrices arises in regression problems, approximation of large matrices by matrices of lower rank

1st semester	2nd semester	3rd semester	4th semester
Mathematical Foundations of Artificial Intelligence			Educational practice
Machine Learning			Industrial Practice, Research Work
Foreign Language in the Field of Business and Professional Communication			
Software Engineering		Computer Vision	
Linux Operating System	Deep Learning in Python	Natural Language Processing	
Python Programming	Machine Learning Operations		
Data Engineering	Data access methods (Elective Course)	AI Project Management (Elective Course)	Master Thesis
Philosophy and Methodology of Science	Introduction to SQL (Elective Course)	Technical Communications (Elective Course)	
	Data Science Competitions (Elective Course)	Data Science Competitions (Elective Course)	
	Time Series Analysis (Elective Course)	Artificial Intelligence for Information Security (Elective Course)	
Project Development Workshop	Project Development Workshop	Project Development Workshop	

Fig. 1. The curriculum of the Master's program in Artificial Intelligence Engineering at Ural Federal University

– in image compression problems. Various types of matrix decompositions are studied, their advantages are discussed depending on the problem being solved. Iterative methods of linear algebra and ways of speeding up convergence are studied. The concept of ill-conditioned systems of linear algebraic equations and methods for their regularization are given. Time for the study of these applied issues can be allocated due to the fact that we completely abandoned manual calculations "on a piece of paper", assigning them to Python.

From the course of mathematical analysis, only topics related to differentiation are repeated to the extent necessary to study numerical methods for minimizing functions of many variables. This knowledge is expanded by studying regularization issues, due to the instability of numerical differentiation. When studying gradient methods, attention is paid to the problems of slowing down convergence (for example, the Rosenbrock-like function) and ways to overcome them.

In the classes on probability theory and mathematical statistics, we tried, if possible, to abandon the solution of problems from the textbook, and fill the courses with analysis of real world cases.

As part of the discipline *Machine Learning*, students study methods of data processing and feature generation, get acquainted with the sklearn library. Further, clustering, regression, classification, support vector machine, Bayesian methods, decision trees and ensemble methods are studied. In the end, the issues of applied application of machine learning methods are discussed: task development methodology, definition of business requirements, data collection and preparation, model development, model testing and implementation.

Within the framework of the discipline *Deep Learning in Python*, the following topics are considered: measuring forecast error, time series analysis, visualization for time series analysis, statistical time series models, comparing the performance of various statistical models for time series analysis, time series analysis using convolutional and recurrent neural networks.

Within the discipline *Computer Vision*, students learn how to use deep neural networks for image classification, segmentation, and object detection by considering a special type of neural network architecture suitable for image analysis – convolutional neural network. Students are given the opportunity to get a comprehensive view of pre-trained neural networks for image analysis.

The discipline *Natural Language Processing* introduces students to modern natural language processing methods based on deep neural networks and machine learning. The content of this course allows students to learn how to use deep neural networks for text classification, sentiment analysis, and automatic text generation. Within the discipline, special types of neural network architectures suitable for text processing will be considered: recurrent neural networks, including LSTM and GRU, and one-dimensional convolutional networks.

The discipline *Data Engineering* is dedicated to preparing data for machine learning models. The features of working with data in various formats in the Python language are considered. Attention is paid to tools and technologies for downloading data from the Internet and social networks. Data cleaning methods and corresponding libraries in Python are studied in detail as well.

As the part of the discipline *Software Engineering*, the students study the following topics: team development tools and the Git version control system, methods and types of software testing, Continuous Integration tools, approaches to developing software architecture, design patterns and anti-patterns using machine learning applications as an example, organizing the work of a machine learning application through the API, reusing the program code, the life cycle of a software product. It also discusses code quality issues, the concept of clean code, refactoring and code review. Students learn how to build machine learning application pipelines from data collection and preparation to model training and deployment.

The questions studied in *Software Engineering* are developed in the second semester in the classes on *Machine Learning Operations*.

First, students are introduced to DevOps administration automation, the Infrastructure as Code approach, the machine learning application lifecycle, and MLOps automation. Next, an overview of Continuous Integration and Continuous Delivery is given. The Docker container technology is studied, in particular, information security in Docker and the creation of containers with machine learning applications.

Further, students study cloud technologies and distributed computing: tools for automating the management of server clusters using the examples of Ansible and Terraform, ensuring information security in a server cluster. The topic of managing containers in a cluster deals with technologies and tools for managing containers (Kubernetes, Docker Swarm), automation of deployment and management of containers in Kubernetes, information security, microservice architecture applications in a Kubernetes cluster.

Next, students learn how to automate the learning process of artificial intelligence models using tools such as creating machine learning pipelines, learn how to use CI/CD in conjunction with machine learning pipelines, and monitor the quality of machine learning applications using Graphana and Prometheus. Students use Kubeflow, MLFlow, and TensorFlow Extended as machine learning automation tools.

3.2   Elective Courses

Along with the mandatory courses, curriculum also includes elective courses that are described below.

The *Introduction to SQL* discipline is devoted to the study of the language for working with SQL databases. Everything needed to get started with SQL is covered: creating tables, filling them with data, and writing queries to retrieve data from tables. The sections of SQL that cause the greatest difficulties are studied in detail: combining data from several tables in the database, including using different types of joins, using subqueries, grouping data and using aggregation functions. In addition, practical mechanisms of database management systems are considered, such as transactions and integrity constraints that are needed to maintain the database in a consistent state, and indexes that can improve the performance of SQL queries.

The discipline *Data Access Methods* is closely related to the previous one and is devoted to technologies for storing and processing information using examples from the PostgreSQL RDBMS core. At first, students study DBMS architecture concepts and general algorithms: main ideas and source code organization, tools for development query and kernels, memory paging. Then, they study common algorithms and data structures: B-tree, concepts of requests analysis, write-ahead log and the concept of disaster recovery, generalized tree index. Also addresses issues specific algorithms specific to PostgreSQL: PostgreSQL extensions, cube and smlar, full text search, inverse index, PostgreSQL development cycle, mailing lists, commitfests.

The purpose of mastering the discipline *Data Science Competitions* is to familiarize students with the modern platform for holding competitions Kaggle.com. Students will learn how to use various algorithms and data analysis methods to solve specific application problems. In practice, all types of data analysis tasks are considered: tabular data analysis, time series analysis, natural language processing, image processing. The course discusses methods for analyzing basic trained models, selecting and testing new features, optimal methods for finding the best algorithm problem solving.

The aim of the *Time series analysis* course is to develop skills in applying the methods of analysis and forecasting of time series based on statistical analysis and machine learning. In the beginning, students get acquainted with the tasks where time series arise, some types of time series and their models. In the topic

Statistical analysis of time series, students study the main statistical characteristics of time series, perform residual analysis and stationarity tests, perform filtering and linear regression analysis of time series, get acquainted with robust statistics and adaptive regression models. Next, they study autoregressive analysis and extraction, selection methods and feature processing. Finally, students are introduced to modern ML-methods of time series analysis and apply them to find anomalies in time series, clustering and classifying time series. They also study the features of using deep learning methods as applied to time series analysis.

The course *AI Project Management* provides students with a general understanding of IT project management in the field of artificial intelligence using common methodologies and approaches. Here, students learn who a Project Manager is, what are his areas of responsibilities and capabilities, and get an idea about the types of projects and their specifics in different areas. Further, students learn how to collect and prioritize requirements, evaluate their complexity and determine the readiness criteria in the project, get an idea of the main stages of work. Also, they learn how to develop a plan and determine the purpose of the project, plan the scope, deadlines, budget, share responsibility with the customer.

3.3   Project Development Workshop

An important part of the educational process is the Project Development Workshop. The students participate in the real-world projects in collaboration with the partner IT companies (Sect. 4), university labs and Russian Academy of Sciences (N.N. Krasovskii Institute of Mathematics and Mechanics, Institute of Immunology and Physiology UrB RAS [10]).

A more detailed description of the project-based learning can be found in the article [11].

4   Cooperation with IT Industry

The *Artificial Intelligence Engineering* program was developed in tight cooperation with IT industry. IT companies developed educational courses and provided topics for student projects.

The following companies are the main partners of the program:

- **Kontur**, one of the biggest Russian IT companies, the leader among Russian SaaS-providers. The company creates cloud services for automation of business everyday work. Kontur became the partner of the *AI Engineering* Master's program because it recruits AI practitioners who will be able to improve the quality of the cloud services using artificial intelligence.
- **NAUMEN**, a big Russian software vendor and cloud service provider, which offers software solutions for customer communications, digital infrastructure management and other services based on artificial intelligence, predictive analytics and big data processing. The company collaborates with Ural Federal University in the area of AI-powered dialog systems, which require advanced

research in natural language processing for developing new algorithms and a large number of skilled AI engineers who will implement the algorithms in production-ready software.
- **Ural Center of Security System**, a big cyber security company. The company is interested in applying artificial intelligence to tackle information security problems.

Headquarters of all companies are located in Ekaterinburg, which had a positive impact on cooperation with Ural Federal University. The companies hire a large number of the university graduates and several founders of the companies graduated from the university.

Two courses of the *AI Engineering* Master's program were developed by the Ural Center of Security System company:

- **Artificial Intelligence for Information Security.** The students study possible ways of using artificial intelligence in the field of information security. By applying machine learning methods, students detect spam, injection in requests and DDoS attacks, find malicious malware, analyze anomalies in user activity.
- **Machine Learning Operations (MLOps).** The course aimed at teaching students the methods and techniques of automation of routing machine learning operations. The course materials are developed by the Ural Center of Security System employees based on their experience of building production-ready machine learning pipelines with the help of modern MLOps tools, which are popular in industry. The full description of the course is presented in Sect. 3.

The most valuable contribution from the companies are tasks for the student projects. Such tasks are based on the real world problems that companies are working on. Moreover, the companies provide the datasets for the tasks. Well-prepared data set paves the way to good machine learning model and AI solution for the problem.

The examples of the projects include detecting the attacks on the cyber physical systems [12], finding various secrets (passwords, keys, etc.) in open GitHub repositories, developing the knowledge graphs for legal documents and information security systems, improving the algorithms of multi-language dialog systems.

5 Partnership with the Universities

Ural Federal University developed the *AI Engineering* Master's program in collaboration with six Russian Universities who launched the Master's program for their students.

The list of the partner universities is as follows:

- Altai State University,
- Vladimir State University,

- Kazan State Power Engineering University,
- Samara Polytech,
- Siberian Federal University,
- University of Tyumen.

The partner universities were provided with our online courses that cover the part of *AI Engineering* Master's program topics. The list of the online courses is presented in the Table 1 (all courses are in Russian). We recommend to conduct courses in a flipped format: students watch lectures on online platform and participate in classroom offline workshops with a teacher's guidance. The additional online courses are being developed.

Table 1. Online courses for the AI Engineering Master's program

Online course name	Course link
Python Programming	https://openedu.ru/course/urfu/PYAP/
Linux Operating System	https://courses.openedu.urfu.ru/course-v1:UrFU+ASTROLINUX+spring_2022
Deep Learning in Python	https://openedu.ru/course/urfu/PYDNN/
Data Access Methods	https://openedu.ru/course/urfu/DATAINF/
Philosophy and Methodology of Science	https://openedu.ru/course/urfu/PHILSCI/

For the staff of the partner universities, two advance educational programs for professional retraining were created (Table 2). The programs cover two major topics of the *AI Engineering* Master's program: artificial intelligence and machine learning (deep learning, computer vision, natural language processing) and professional complex software development (Python programming, Linux operating system, software engineering). After graduating from the programs the university staff will be able to teach students of the *AI Engineering* Master's program implemented at their university.

6 Conclusion

We presented a new Master's program *Artificial Intelligence Engineering* developed by Ural Federal University in cooperation with the IT companies and Russian Universities. In contrast to popular existing Master's programs [7,13–15], which are devoted to mathematics and research methods in artificial intelligence, our program is focused on the engineering and building large complex software systems that uses machine learning and artificial intelligence.

Collaboration with the IT companies allowed us to create the Master's program that combine both strong theoretical foundation of machine learning and

Table 2. Educational programs for teachers from the partner universities

Program name	ECTS credits
Artificial Intelligence Application	**9**
- Deep Learning in Python	3
- Natural Language Processing	3
- Computer Vision	3
AI-powered Software Development	**11**
- Python Programming	3
- Linux Operating System	3
- Software Engineering	6

artificial intelligence (provided by the university) and practical skill acquisition by attaining courses created by the IT companies and participating in the student projects that are based on real-world problems. In addition, participating in the real-world projects during the Master's training positively affects the students employability.

Nowadays, artificial intelligence engineering is actively forming as a field of study. University professors lack the experience in developing topics such as Machine Learning Operations. Hence, the high quality courses on such topics could be created only in cooperation with the IT companies that have the required expertise.

The *AI Engineering* Master's program was launched in the six Russian partner universities. The first admission to the program will take place in Fall 2022. The expected number of students (including Ural Federal University and six partner universities) is 200 people. Hence, collaboration with the university partners allowed us to create a scalable Master's program and contribute to reducing the artificial intelligence developers shortage.

The partner universities are able to use online courses developed by Ural Federal University for the *AI Engineering* Master's program. The recommended approach is to use blended learning: students watch online lectures from Ural Federal University and participate in offline workshops with the partner university professor. In order to help the professors to teach the new courses, two advanced educational programs were created. More then 100 people from the partner universities study the programs.

Our program is open to new partners, both for IT companies and universities.

References

1. Sculley, D., Holt, G., Golovin, D., et al.: Hidden technical debt in machine learning systems. In: Proceedings of the 28th International Conference on Neural Information Processing Systems, vol. 2, pp. 2503–2511. MIT Press, Cambridge (2015)
2. Mäkinen, S., Skogström, H., Laaksonen, E., Mikkonen, T.: Who needs MLOps: what data scientists seek to accomplish and how can MLOps help? In: IEEE/ACM

1st Workshop on AI Engineering - Software Engineering for AI (WAIN), pp. 109–112 (2021). https://doi.org/10.1109/WAIN52551.2021.00024

3. Ebert, C., Gallardo, G., Hernantes, J., Serrano, N.: DevOps. IEEE Softw. **33**(3), 94–100 (2016). https://doi.org/10.1109/MS.2016.68

4. Meesters, M., Heck, P., Serebrenik, A.: What is an AI engineer? An empirical analysis of job ads in The Netherlands. In: 1st Conference on AI Engineering - Software Engineering for AI (CAIN 2022), Pittsburgh, PA, USA, 16–24 May 2021, 9 p. ACM, New York (2022). https://doi.org/10.1145/3522664.3528594

5. Heck, P., Schouten, G.: Lessons learned from educating AI engineers. In: IEEE/ACM 1st Workshop on AI Engineering - Software Engineering for AI (WAIN), pp. 1–4 (2021). https://doi.org/10.1109/WAIN52551.2021.00013

6. University of Chicago: Master of Science in Analytics. https://professional. uchicago.edu/find-your-fit/masters/master-science-analytics. Accessed 1 May 2022

7. National University of Science and Technology MISIS: Artificial Intelligence and Machine Learning. https://misis.ru/applicants/admission/magistracy/faculties/ prikladnayainformatikamag/iskintel/#program-details. Accessed 14 June 2022

8. Machine Learning Engineering for Production (MLOps). https://ru.coursera.org/ specializations/machine-learning-engineering-for-production-mlops/#courses. Accessed 1 May 2022

9. Simplilearn: Artificial Intelligence Engineer Course in San Francisco. https:// www.simplilearn.com/artificial-intelligence-training-courses-san-francisco-city/# what-does-an-ai-engineer-do. Accessed 1 May 2022

10. Sozykin, A., Chernoskutov, M., Koshelev, A., Zverev, V., Ushenin, K., Solovyova, O.: Teaching heart modeling and simulation on parallel computing systems. In: Hunold, S., et al. (eds.) Euro-Par 2015. LNCS, vol. 9523, pp. 102–113. Springer, Cham (2015). https://doi.org/10.1007/978-3-319-27308-2_9

11. Sozykin, A., Koshelev, A., Ustalov, D.: The role of student projects in teaching machine learning and high performance computing. In: Voevodin, V., Sobolev, S. (eds.) RuSCDays 2019. CCIS, vol. 1129, pp. 653–663. Springer, Cham (2019). https://doi.org/10.1007/978-3-030-36592-9_53

12. Goh, J., Adepu, S., Junejo, K.N., Mathur, A.: A dataset to support research in the design of secure water treatment systems. In: Havarneanu, G., Setola, R., Nassopoulos, H., Wolthusen, S. (eds.) CRITIS 2016. LNCS, vol. 10242, pp. 88–99. Springer, Cham (2017). https://doi.org/10.1007/978-3-319-71368-7_8

13. Digital Technologies and Artificial Intelligence Master's Program at Moscow State University. https://ai-in-msu.ru. Accessed 14 June 2022

14. Methods and Technologies of Artificial Intelligence Master's Program at Moscow Institute of Physics and Technology. https://mipt.ru/education/departments/ fpmi/master/methods-technologies-ai. Accessed 14 June 2022

15. Data Science Master's Program at Higher School of Economics. https://www.hse. ru/ma/datasci. Accessed 14 June 2022

Teragraph Heterogeneous System for Ultra-large Graph Processing

Aleksey Popov[✉], Stanislav Ibragimov, and Egor Dubrovin

Department of Computer Systems and Networks, Bauman Moscow State Technical University, Moscow, Russia
{alexpopov,sibragimov,dubrovinen}@bmstu.ru

Abstract. The interest to the complex data models analysis has grown significantly in the last decade. Graphs are known as the most adequate form of the real data representation in social networks, computer program's structure, the topology of integrated circuits, to the bio-informatics and knowledge databases and other areas. As the size of datasets increases, the need to find more efficient computer architecture and software tools for analyzing and visualization of large graphs, including improved hardware, becomes obvious.

Modern CPUs and GPUs have a great parallelism and performance level, but cannot resolve the fundamental architectural flaws of the graphs processing: the data dependency, the distribution of irregular graphs computing workload on multiple processing devices, as well as memory access conflicts for multiple cores.

We introduce the new version of multicore Leonhard x64 microprocessor based on the Discrete mathematics Instruction Set Computer (DISC) instruction set for an ultra-scale graph processing. We show some advantages of DISC and compare the efficiency of universal computing systems with Leonhard x64 based system. Also, we introduce the Teragraph supercomputer architecture based on multiple heterogeneous Graph Processing Cores.

Keywords: Discrete mathematics instruction set computer · Leonhard microprocessor · Graph processing core · Teragraph · Graph operations · Data structure · Graph theory

1 Introduction

A new stage of information technology improvement has led to the explosive growth of accumulated data that need to be analyzed in order to acquire knowledge. The Internet of Things, biology, personalized medicine and social media are able to generate Exabytes of unstructured data, which are extremely difficult to store and analyze with commonly used computing technology.

Since a simple heuristics are no longer provides the required decision quality, it is required to apply more complex data models and processing algorithms to

© The Author(s), under exclusive license to Springer Nature Switzerland AG 2022
V. Voevodin et al. (Eds.): RuSCDays 2022, LNCS 13708, pp. 574–590, 2022.
https://doi.org/10.1007/978-3-031-22941-1_42

understand the causes of the observed phenomena. Therefore, the search for effective computing technologies to process over complex models, such as graphs (i.e. graph structures), should be continued with increasing efforts. Such initiatives as heterogeneous architecture, AMD Alveo technology, OpenPOWER, or HSA Foundation are promising to create high-performance system architecture with different types of accelerators. However, the set of widespread acceleration cores is almost limited by cryptography processing and matrix/vector operations.

In this work we focus on the important challenge of discrete optimization and graphs processing, which are widely used in most computational challenges in applied science (e.g., bioengineering, chemistry, statistics, physics, economics) and in industries (telecommunication, manufacturing, retail, banking, and others). Therefore, it is important to note the disadvantage of universal computing, where discrete optimization can only be processed through multiple calls of primitive arithmetic operations. There are still no discrete mathematics acceleration units that could perform a set of basic discrete mathematics operations in hardware.

The purpose of our work is to improve the fundamental principles of discrete optimization processing, including the new approach to the microprocessor instruction set. In this work, we will show performance of a system with discrete mathematics instructions set, which can be the basis for further highly parallel solutions. We use this experience to build a highly parallel Teragraph system, developing at the Bauman Moscow State Technical University.

2   Challenges of Graph Processing and Related Works

Nowadays, computers use universal microprocessors, which are not only the main processing devices in terms of computer architecture, but also determine the specifics of the program development and execution. In the case of well-predictable iterative variables and looped pieces of code, the microprocessor is able to rhythmically deliver the requested operands for execution, and the long pipeline is therefore effective. It is precisely on such tasks that we can observe the high performance of universal microprocessors.

Problems of data dependencies, however, are very common for graph algorithms. As a result of such dependencies, the rhythmic execution is disrupted, as well as the efficiency of hardware prefetching decreases and the number of pipelines penalties increases due to incorrectly predict transitions [20] Moreover, the instructions execution statistics show [13] that arithmetic and logical processing commands are only about 30% of all instruction stream, and such service instructions as operand moving takes not less than 50% of the stream. Considering that this data was obtained on a microprocessor with a Complex Instruction Set Computing (CISC), in which memory access is encoded together with processing operations, we can state a large percentage of non-arithmetic commands in the instruction stream, and as a result, a low-efficiency of the general purpose microprocessors for the computational workload.

A significant problem of generic microprocessors follows from the virtual memory subsystem, which leads to a stream of multiple accesses to the physical

RAM due to the address translation mechanism [5]. In this case, there is a slowdown in the data exchange between the processor and the memory subsystem due to the opening and closing of a large amount of RAM and virtual memory pages, while the pipeline is idle due to data dependencies. The batch mode adopted for modern DDR DRAM types also reduces the efficiency of graph processing, since it contributes to incomplete use of the system bus and processor resources (cache lines, buffers and so on). It can be assumed that the architectural principles incorporated into generic computers are aimed to accelerate vector and matrix operations, but, on the contrary, slow down the dependent data structures processing. At the same time, the processing of complex data models, such as graphs, is difficult due to the large graphs into RAM placement issues.

The development of computing tools for graph processing turned out to be a complex problem, requiring the creation of new hardware and software solutions at all system levels. Research is focused on the following system aspects: the top level is the CPU and graph storage or graph accelerator interactions (i); multi-threading level (ii); graph processing with a thread (iii); optimization of the memory subsystem (iv). Our project is focused on the (iii) level, and we are going further to cover (i) and (ii) levels using our results.

Graph processing is a task involving intensive, irregular and non-local memory access [11]. In this regard, the performance of graph processing can be improved using accelerators implemented directly in the storage cell array [4,6,7,27,33]. In [30] graph acceleration is based on a set of finite automata implemented directly inside the dynamic memory matrix. Another useful way to solve this problem is to modify the DDR SDRAM memory interface to adapt it to random non-regular access to small portions of data [10,25].

An additional problem of speeding up graph processing is the large dependencies between parallel branches of graph algorithms: most optimization algorithms on graphs, perform one iteration, after which data in the main memory are corrected. For example, in the classical Dijkstra algorithm, it is necessary to change the queue of vertices. This leads to frequent execution of map-reduce actions and the flow of small transactions on the data bus. Thus, the use of bus designed for streaming data becomes inefficient. Some researches focused on the efficient communication between the CPU and the accelerator. This works [16] proposes a solution to this problem based on stream files. Taking this into account, we use the most reasonable way to speed up communication between the control processor (such as a conventional central processor) and the discrete mathematics acceleration unit: to place them on the same chip. A fairly simple way to implement this approach is to use hardware micro-kernels, such as RISCV cores, for example.

Another way how the graph processing can be accelerated is an any kind of parallel processing on distributed systems using customized algorithms [18]. A commonly used formal approach to describe the computational model for this processing method is the Pregel, which assumes sending messages to vertices and processing the messages sent in the previous step [8,19,34].

For an efficient graph processing on GPU, the whole task should be divided into independent computational streams with minimal dependencies, as well as data should be separated between stream processors local memory [14]. Various options for accelerating graph processing on GPU [15,34] are considered. When GPU is involved, the graph is most often stored in the form of a CSR - an optimized adjacency list [28]. Emulation on the GPU of the so-called STAR machine is also described, which is an associative SIMD processor well suited for processing graphs [26]. An extra difficulty appears when graphs cannot be not fitted into the RAM or GPU memory. To solve this issue, streaming methods are often used, which involve dividing the graph into parts that can fit into the RAM. Proper partitioning helps pipeline processing, loading data, and saving data to SSD [15,23].

The parallel nature of many graph algorithms allows using FPGAs as an acceleration technology. There are various approaches to building specialized GPUs by this way. Multi-threading based [3] approaches are used, including using thread migration between processors to ensure local memory handling [10], multiprocessing [9], based on events [35] that speed up operations with sparse matrices [28] or use tree structures [21,24]. It is noted that architectures with explicit multi-threading are used for processing graphs, which are executed using the [1] in-order pipeline, which leads to better performance on graph tasks than the superscalar out-of-order execution that dominates today in general-purpose processors. A detailed description of the various computing architectures used for graph processing can be found in [12].

3   Discrete Mathematics Instruction Set

In [21] we initially presented eight fundamental principles of heterogeneous DISC system operations. It was shown that such a system executes several instruction streams over the one data stream, i.e. it belongs to the MISD class of the Flynn's taxonomy. Further research required some architecture improvements and principles refinement to achieve higher system performance. Thus, in this article, we improve our arguments and generalize some principles of Discrete mathematics Instructions Set Computer (DISC) execution. In this work, we present a complete 64-bit DISC instruction set and its correspondence to the operations and quantifiers of discrete mathematics (see Table 1). The computing system with Discrete mathematics Instruction Set consists of two different microprocessors: the well known Central Processing Unit (CPU) for working with the generic workload and the Structure Processing Element (SPE) for discrete math operations. For this reason, the SPE instructions corresponds to the discrete mathematics operations and quantifiers.

We have upgraded SPE with important opcodes NGR and NSM for the searching of nearest greater or nearest smaller, as well as GRLS double slice command, which significantly speed up many algorithms. Every instruction includes up to three operands: key, value and data structure number. As of now, the instruction set consists of more than twenty high-level operation codes, which are listed below.

Table 1. Implementation of discrete mathematics operations

Discrete math operations	Description	DISC instructions
$A = \langle A_1, \ldots, A_n \rangle$	- store function of n sets as an A tuple	Insert
$R(A_i, x, y), x \in A_i, y \in A_i$	- relationship between the x and y in the set A_i	Next/Previous/Neighbors
$|A_i|, i = 1, n$	- cardinality of the A_i set	Cardinality
$x \in A_i, x \notin A_i, i = 1, n$	- check the inclusion/exclusion of the x in the set	Search
$A_i \cup x, i = 1, n$	- inserting the x into the set	Insert
$A_i \backslash x, i = 1, n$	- removing an element x from the set	Delete, Delete structure
$A \backslash A_i$	- removing the set A_i from the tuple A	Delete structure
$A_i \subset A_j$	- inclusion relation of the set A_i in A_j	Slices
$A_i \equiv A_j$	- equivalence relation operation	Slices
$A_i \cup A_j$	- union operation of two sets	OR
$A_i \cap A_j$	- intersection operation of two sets	AND
$A_i \backslash A_j$	- difference operation	NOT
$A_i \triangle A_j$	- symmetric difference	–
A	- complement of the A_i	NOT
$A_i \times A_j$	- Cartesian product operation	–
2^{A_I}	- Boolean operation	–

- **Search (SRCH):** starts the exact search for the value related to the key.
- **Insert (INS):** key-value pair inserting into the structure. SPE renews volume if the key is already stored.
- **Delete (DEL)** operation performs the exact search for the specified key and removes it from the data structure.
- **Smaller and Greater Neighbors (NSM, NGR)** instructions searches for the smallest (greatest) key that is a neighbor to the key given, and return its value. The neighbor operation can be applied for heuristic computing, where interpolation is used instead of exact calculations (e.g. clustering or aggregation).
- **Maximum and Minimum (MAX, MIN)** instructions search for the first or last keys in the data structure.
- **Cardinality (CNT)** operation defines the count of keys stored in the structure.
- **AND, OR, NOT** instructions perform union, intersection, and complement operations on two data structures.
- **Slices (LS, GR, LSEQ, GREQ, GRLS)** extract a subset of one data structure into another.
- **Search next and previous (NEXT, PREV)** instructions find keys in the data structure that are neighbors (next or previous) to the key stored. This instruction differs from the NSM/NGR instructions. It is mandatory to store the key in the data structure before calling this instruction.
- **Delete all structure (DELS)** clears all resources used by the given structure.
- **Squeeze (SQ)** instruction compresses the memory blocks used by the data structure (used timely to lower DSM memory fragmentation).
- **Jump (JT)** instruction branches the SPE code in order to give the CPU control and is available only in the MISD mode.

The performance level shown in [21] are well promising for further DISC system implementation in many important areas. In this work, we improve this system by adding a RISCV arithmetic microprocessor named Computing Processing Element (CPE) as an on-chip pair with the SPE, and then extend the key and value to 64 bit word.

4   Leonhard x64 Microarchitecture

Data structures are commonly used in program engineering to represent complex data models (such as sets, graphs, etc.) in the computer memory. Formally, the data structure combines two types of information: information about the data stored (i) and information about the structuring relations themselves (ii) The duality of data structures allows sharing the workload between two threads: the first computes the relational part, and the second - the informational part. Due to this, we can divide the optimization algorithm which using data structures, into at least two types of instruction threads: arithmetic instructions over numbers; and discrete mathematics operations over relational sets (ii).

We will show an example of how the discrete optimization algorithm can be implemented in the DISC system. The well known Dijkstra algorithm helps to find the shortest path from the starting vertex to all other vertices in the graph and uses two data structures: graph data structure himself and the priority queue to store an ordered sequence of unresolved vertices. To understand which microprocessor should perform an algorithm's operation in the DISC heterogeneous system, we will accept the following remarks in pseudocode Algorithm 1: D - this action based on the discrete mathematical operation and should be executed on the SPE; M - this is a memory (or register) read/write operation and can be initiated by any processor in the DISC system; A - this is an arithmetic operation which can be executed by the Host CPU or CPE.

Algorithm 1. Dijkstra's algorithm (Graph; Q; source).

```
for all vertices v in Graph^(D) do
    dist[v] ← infinity^(M)
    previous[v] ← undefined^(M)
end for
dist[source] ← 0^(M)
Q ← the set of all nodes in Graph^(D)
while Q is not empty^(D) do
    u ← node in Q with the smallest dist[ ]^(D)
    remove u from Q^(D)
    for all neighbor v of u do^(D)
        alt ← dist[u] + dist_between(u, v)^(A)
        if alt < dist[v]^(A) then
            dist[v] ← alt^(M)
            previous[v] ← u^(M)
        end if
    end for
end while
```

As we can see, the most complex and time-expensive operations are related to the discrete mathematics logic, not arithmetic. Therefore, all hardware improvements to perform these parts of the workload are able to significantly increase the overall system performance. Thus, we use some new hardware principles to partially resolve hardware limitations fixed above:

- We implemented a new and optimized version of the highly parallel lnh64 microprocessor to perform DISC instructions. This microprocessor includes a special B+tree cache, does memory management with the control unit, and all data structures accessing was implemented only by hardware.
- We use an extremely short pipeline in the lnh64 microarchitecture (see Fig. 1), which significantly reduces the latency for dependent data operations. Such a pipeline cannot be used for generic arithmetic, but is well suited for data sets and graphs.
- We separate the computation workload between the Host subsystem (which can be Intel or ARM-based microprocessors), and on-chip heterogeneous cores with dedicated arithmetic microprocessors.
- We use closely connected pairs of lnh64 Structure Processing Element and tiny RISCV Computing Processing Elements as a heterogeneous Graph Processing Core or GPC (see Fig. 2, a), which allow us to reduce interconnect latency, simplify programming and reduce hardware resources.

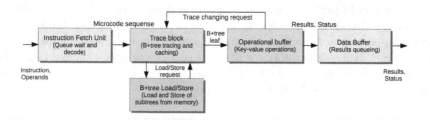

Fig. 1. lnh64 structure processing element pipeline

The lnh64 SPE accesses Local Structure Memory (LSM) in order to store and load data structures for the active job. The SPE's operation results are forwarded to the CPE and (if necessary) to the Host CPU for further use in the computations. Local Structure Memory is the DDR4 SDRAM based associative key-value storage, accessed by SPE using B+tree data structure. The last one also stored inside the LSM and used to convert 64-bit unique key to the memory address.

A helpful feature of the knowledge graphs, like a human memory, is that processing occurs closely to the memory in which the graph is stored, and not vice versa, when it is necessary to transfer the graph to the place where it will be processed. So graphs are formed in the LSM and stored there for a long time, as long as there is a need for their processing. Therefore, there is no need to transfer large amounts of data every time to run a task for a short job. This is a significant advantage of our approach, in contrast to the shared main memory ideology of the host system and the use of DMA mechanisms for the GPGPU.

At the same time, there is a problem of an ultra-scale graph operations, when we cannot load it all into the LSM. To be able to process ultra-large graphs, we use external Main Graph Memory of sufficient size (up to 30 Terabytes per node). This allows us to load graph clusters into the Local Structure Memory when needed.

The lnh64 SPE stores information in LSM as key-value pairs in the form of non-overlapping B+ trees. To provide the tree leaves execution, the SPE has a pipeline parallel microarchitecture, and not only performs the search in subtrees and provides insertion and deletion operations through the tree structure, but also allocates and frees memory for nodes and leaves.

We divide the tree's processing into "tree tracing" and "leaf operation" stages (see Fig. 1). This allows us to speed up the computing process over the keys and to store the search path in the internal B+ tree cache. The sequence of tree nodes on the path from the root to the target leaf is called "trace", and is always ready for immediate access by the so-called Trace Block.

After the tree tracing has finished, the second stage is started by the Operational Buffer (OB) to operate keys and values on the bottom leaf level. To perform this for large data structures, the lnh64 SPE memory subsystem includes multilevel storage devices, described below. The first-level is the register memory that stores nodes and leaves inside the Trace Block and OB. It is organized as an associative memory to perform key searching, shifting, union, and other low level operations. The second-level is the boundary addressable memory (Internal Structure Memory, ISM), accessed by the Trace Block to define the physical addresses for the next tree level. The third memory level is the Local Structure Memory, described above.

After the full path becomes known for the Trace Block, the target leaf loading to the Operational Buffer from the ISM. After the leaf is processed in the OB, it uploads results back to the ISM. If any further processing is needed, then the Trace Buffer loads the new trace and OB processes the new leaf again. At the end of execution, the OB puts the result into the output queue and since CPE can read it.

Graph Processing Cores are grouped by 6 cores into Core Group to share the same Local Structure Memory and Global Memory (see Fig. 2,b). The Leonhard x64 microprocessor consists from 12 up to 24 GPC interconnected with Host subsystem through the Global Memory.

5   Teragraph Architecture

The high-performance computer system named "Teragraph" is being developed at the Department of Computer Systems and Networks of the Bauman Moscow State Technical University and is funded under the Priority 2030 government program. The main application of the Teragraph system is to store and process over ultra-large graphs. In its development, the main emphasis is on hardware and architecture optimization in order to speed up the work with graphs. The

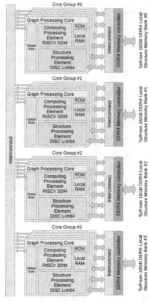

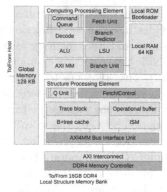

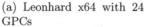

(a) Leonhard x64 with 24 GPCs

(b) Graph Processing Core

Fig. 2. Leonhard x64 microprocessor architecture

system includes tree heterogeneous computing nodes of the same type that interact with each other to extend graph size and parallelism. The block diagram of one node is shown in Fig. 3.

Each node consists of a Host subsystem, a Graph Main Memory, an interconnection unit, and a Graph Processing subsystem. The Host subsystem initializes all the system and perform network connection to other such nodes and external agents (user browsers, sensors, storage, data sources, JavaScript programs etc.). The Host is connected to the graph processing subsystem via a high-speed PCIe x16 bus, through which the initial graph is loaded into the GPC, as well as data exchange with the SPE and CPE. For that purpose we are using Host2GPC and GPC2Host FIFO buffers for 512 words for each GPC, and addressable Global Memory shared between GPC and Host. Every GPC has a significant amount of local structure memory (up to 16 GB for one GPC), which is organized as an associative memory (Local Structure Memory). In addition, every GPC can use DMA access to the Main Graph Memory to load and store the huge graph parts.

The Host subsystem includes two CPU blocks with 26 cores each, 8 TB non-volatile storage and the main memory of 1 TB, where we temporarily store graph vertices, edges and their attributes. The Host subsystem uses now an x86 processor, but can be rebuilt with ARM or MIPS microprocessors as well. The Host system role is to initiate interconnection over the internal and external 100 Gb Ethernet networks, distribute job between Leonhard x64 v4 accelerator cards

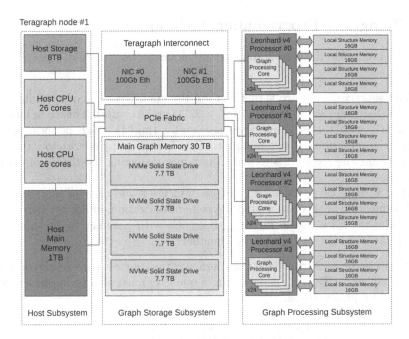

Fig. 3. Teragraph node architecture

and collect information from external data sources, i.e. it controls the interaction of all graphs processing resources with the world.

Two parts of software interact with each other to share task between Host and graph processing resources. Host kernel - is a central piece of software that interacts with the accelerator software core via the PCIe bus, queues and Global Memory. Accelerator kernel - is a RISCV based software that is assembled on the host, but transferred to the GPC during the initialization process (like a shader program in modern graphic accelerator cards).

The Graph Storage subsystem for one node includes a 30 TB Main Graph Memory, consisting of four NVMe SSD drives of 7.7 TB each. NVMe (Non-Volatile Memory Express) technology provides a communication interface and driver that takes advantage of the increased bandwidth provided by PCIe. It improves productivity and efficiency of the large-scale graph processing.

The Teragraph interconnection block consists of two 100Gb Ethernet modules and provides interaction between heterogeneous nodes and external resources. The Graph Processing Subsystem consists of some Leonard x64 v4 cards (we are using three or four cards versions), each card including up to 4 Core Groups, each of them consists of up to 6 Graph Processing Cores (up to 24 GPC per card).

All GPCs of the Core Group use the same Global Memory and DDR memory, connected through the AXI buses. Thus, each Core Group connected to 16 GB of DDR4 memory, which stores the graphs as a sequence of 64 bit key-value records. Thus, each GPC use dedicated 2.5 GB of Local Structure Memory.

6   Teragraph Programming Techniques

Programming for the Teragraph system requires two "vis-a-vis" parts of the code:

- The *sw_kernel* software kernel is a uni-threaded C/C++ code running on a CPE hardware micro-kernel (RISCV 32IM architecture). This code interacts directly with the SPE hardware accelerator (lnh64) which perform parallel B+tree operations. Programming consists in generating queries to structures, analyzing the received keys and values, and managing the thread of calculations.

- *Host kernel* - this code is also written in C/C++ and runs on an x86 system. The function of this part includes system initialization, sw_kernel distribution among the GPC cores, running sw_kernels with parameters, and data and results messaging with sw_kernel handlers.

Below is the sw_kernel code that performs the shortest path search on graph G. To implement Dijkstra's algorithm, a queue Q must also be implemented to store the graph's vertices.

```
 1  void dijkstra() {
 2    unsigned int start_virtex = mq_receive(); //get start virtex from MQ
 3    unsigned int stop_virtex = mq_receive(); //get stop virtex
 4    lnh_del_str_async(Q); //Clear Q from previous run
 5    //Insert start virtex to Q with zero shortest path
 6    lnh_ins_async(Q,INLINE(q_record,{.u=start_virtex,.index=0}),0);
 7    //Get btwc to store it again
 8    lnh_search(G,INLINE(u_key,{.index=PTH_IDX,.u=start_virtex}));
 9    btwc = (*(u_index*)&lnh_core.result.value).__struct.btwc;
10    //Save du for start virtex
11    lnh_ins_async(G,INLINE(u_key,{.index=PTH_IDX,.u=start_virtex}),
12    INLINE(u_index,{.du=0,.btwc=btwc}));
13    while (lnh_get_first(Q)) { //Iterate all vertices in order of Q
14        u = (*(q_record*)&lnh_core.result.key).__struct.u;
15        du = (*(q_record*)&lnh_core.result.key).__struct.index;
16        lnh_del_async(Q,lnh_core.result.key); //Delete it from Q
17        lnh_search(G,INLINE(u_key,{.index=BASE_IDX, .u=u}));
18        pu = (*(u_attributes*)&lnh_core.result.value).__struct.pu;
19        eQ = (*(u_attributes*)&lnh_core.result.value).__struct.eQ;
20        adj_c = (*(u_attributes*)&lnh_core.result.value).__struct.adj_c;
21        // Clear eQ flag
22        lnh_ins_async(G,lnh_core.result.key,
23          INLINE(u_attributes,{.pu=pu, .eQ=false, .non=0, .adj_c=adj_c}));
24        for (i=0;i<adj_c;i++) {  //Fore ach Adj
25            lnh_search(G,INLINE(u_key,{.index=i,.u=u})); //Get Adj[i]
26            wu = (*(edge*)&lnh_core.result.value).__struct.w;
27            adj = (*(edge*)&lnh_core.result.value).__struct.v;
28            //Get information about adjacency
29            lnh_search(G,INLINE(u_key,{.index=BASE_IDX,.u=adj}));
30            eQc=(*(u_attributes*)&lnh_core.result.value).__struct.eQ;
31            count=(*(u_attributes*)&lnh_core.result.value).__struct.adj_c;
32            lnh_search(G,INLINE(u_key,{.index=PTH_IDX,.u=adj}));
33            dv=(*(u_index*)&lnh_core.result.value).__struct.du;
34            btwc=(*(u_index*)&lnh_core.result.value).__struct.btwc;
35            if (dv>(du+wu)) { //If shortest path changed
36              if (eQc) {
37                if (dv!=INF) //if not a loopback, push it to Q
38                    lnh_del_async(Q,INLINE(q_record,{.u=adj, .index=dv}));
39                lnh_ins_async(Q,INLINE(q_record,{.u=adj, .index=du+wu}),0); }
40              //Update the shortest path
41              lnh_ins_async(G,INLINE(u_key,{.index=PTH_IDX,.u=adj}),
```

```
42              INLINE(u_index,{.du=du+wu,.btwc=btwc}));   //change du
43              lnh_ins_async(G,INLINE(u_key,{.index=BASE_IDX,.u=adj}),
44              INLINE(u_attributes,{.pu=u, .eQ=eQc, .non=0, .adj_c=count}));
                }}}
45  //send shortest path to the Host
46  lnh_search(G,INLINE(u_key,{.index=PTH_IDX, .u=stop_virtex}));
47  mq_send((*(u_index*)&lnh_core.result.value).__struct.du);
48  }
```

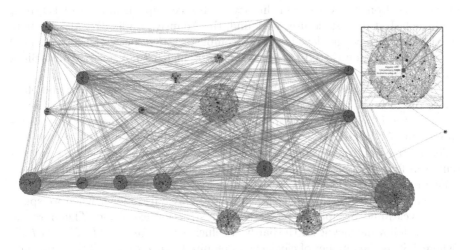

Fig. 4. Betweenness centrality visualization made on a single GPC (oriented weighted graph with 4011 vertices; 16M shortest paths; betweenness centrality metric displayed as vertices color and size; communities defined using the modularity metric).

As it shown on listing above, we use various C++ macros to simplify programming, taking the small RAM into account. The *INLINE* macro allows, for example, to create a composite structure and form 64-bit keys/values from it. The most important part of workload, as discussed earlier, performed by SPE as DISC instructions calls, asynchronous, synchronous, queued or mail boxed (lnh_del_str_async, lnh_ins_async, lnh_search, lnh_get_first, lnh_del_async, lnh_del_async). This operation takes $O(1)$. Source code can be found here: https://gitlab.com/alexpopov366/leonhard-x64-xrt-v2. We tested this programming techniques on various algorithms, including betweenness centrality, community finding and graph visualization (see Fig. 4).

7 Efficiency Tests and Comparison

The Leonhard x64 microprocessor was implemented on the AMD Alveo acceleration platform (Ultrascale+ FPGA) with a relatively low frequency from 180 to 267 MHz. In spite of this, we reached the high-performance level for multicore DISC in comparing with software discrete mathematics operations on Intel x86. This shows the high adequacy of the DISC architecture to the graph problem's requirements and the significance of further frequency and micro-architecture improvements. Experiments were done to understand the productivity of the implemented Leonhard x64 micro-architecture and compare it with generic CPUs-based systems (see Table 2).

We compared Leonhard x64 performance for basic discrete mathematics instructions with their software counterparts. Three types of software data structures were used to carry out key-value: red-black tree (we are used the standard MAP class from the C++ STL library), software implementation of B+trees, and the fastest data structures we found: the Adaptive Radix Tree [17]. Despite the low frequency and low hardware complexity, the speed of the sequential search operation on the GPC turned out to be higher than software Red-Black or B+ trees.

To clearly understand the efficiency of the developed architecture and eliminate the technological factor, we also compared the hardware efficiency for it. Most of the DISC instructions require $O(log_8 n)$ load/store memory operations (excluding AND/OR/NOT and slice operations). However, due to the high parallel B+ tree implementation to store key-value pairs, lnh64 instructions are executed in fewer clock cycles compared to universal processors. It should also be taken into account the CPUs hardware complexity (transistors or gates count).

The micro-architecture efficiency have to be assumed higher when we spend fewer cycles and occupies fewer gates for instruction execution. Therefore, we used the following metric for the hardware efficiency: $E_{HW} = 1/(TSC \cdot GATES)$, where TSC is the number of clock cycles required to execute; GATES is the gate count for the hardware implementation. As a result, it turned out the hardware efficiency of Xeon Platinum 8168 CPU is from 160,2 times lower (sequential search for the ART) to 12,75 times lower (random insert for the ART) if compare it with the Leonhard x64 hardware B+tree. However, the Adaptive Radix Tree (ART) high performance follow us to implement the ART tree data structures in the next versions of the DISC microprocessors.

Table 2. Performance comparison for basic discrete mathematics instructions

Characteristic	Leonhard v4	Intel Xeon Platinum 8168		
Data structure type	B+ tree	Red-Black tree	B+ tree	ART
DISC instructions execution	Hardware	Software	Software	Software
Used cores	1	1	1	1
Clock frequency (MHz)	267	2700	2700	2700
Gate count per core (millions)	2.5	83	83	83
Average sequential insert rate (ops./sec.)	1179495	719948	2463484	7356619
Average random insert rate (ops./sec.)	200607	667519	1358625	5278771
Average sequential search rate (ops./sec.)	7570905	1168116	6354895	15860176
Average random search rate (ops./sec.)	329867	614191	1341165	4812921
Average sequential delete rate (ops./sec.)	1649342	788151	2689176	11228889
Average random delete rate (ops./sec.)	313392	491050	941129	3903154

The Leonhard v4 microprocessor was completely developed in RTL and does not contain any proprietary IP cores. To communicate with out-of-chip mem-

Table 3. Implementation of discrete mathematics operations

Characteristic	Value			
Graph Processing Cores count (instances)	1	6	12	24
Leonhard x64 clock frequency (MHz)	190	190	190	180
Average sequential insert rate (ops./sec.)	875007	5221048	10471506	19840700
Average random insert rate (ops./sec.)	159625	917561	1834893	3476651
Average sequential search rate (ops./sec.)	5427726	32566360	65135016	123413715
Average random search rate (ops./sec.)	267749	1546293	3093292	5860974
Average sequential delete rate (ops./sec.)	1240522	7257526	14510883	27494305
Average random delete rate (ops./sec.)	253154	1441458	2883251	5463000
LSM 1M keys traversing time (msec.)	271	45	23	13
Average neighbours search rate (ops./sec.)	271284	1553684	3104482	5882176
1M dataset AND time (msec.)	377	64	32	17
1M dataset OR time (msec.)	401	68	34	18
1M dataset NOT time (msec.)	396	68	34	18

ory, a DDR3 memory controller core has been developed as well. The benchmarks shown, however, using the Xilinx MIG memory controller core for the Ultrascale+ FPGAs, as development of the own DDR4 controller core has not yet been completed. The RTL hardware complexity in equivalent gate count is based on the methodology presented in [32]. The gate count measurement of the Intel Xeon Platinum 8168 microprocessor is based on the known number of transistors [29] with taken into account that one gate is equivalent NAND2 and occupies 4 transistors [31]. We tested the performance of the multicore GPC on basic DISC operations and found linear scalability even on most complex random insert operations (see Table 3).

8 Teragraph Applications

We have considered several Leonhard x64 microprocessor implementations [2,21, 22]. The first one aimed to create a hardware-based software-defined networks (SDN) controller. The SDN control unit is software, which collects transaction information by the OpenFlow protocol and controls routing resources to improve total network productivity. Most of SDN management algorithms are based on graph models and discrete optimization. In this regard, the hardware support for SDN controllers based on the Leonhard x64 microprocessor is relevant.

The Leonhard x64 microprocessor has also been implemented for the k-nearest algorithm, which is usually associated with machine learning. The DISC system showed higher performance levels and quality results for the Space Shuttle telemetry data classification problem (99.7% accuracy achieved). This allows us to use the Leonhard x64 microprocessor as an intellectual decision subsystem inside dynamic control systems.

Ultra-large graphs also need to be stored and processed to model biological systems, to analyze banking transactions in real time, to accumulate and analyze knowledge graphs for artificial intelligence, to prevent financial and tax crime. Another important area of and ultra-scale knowledge graphs we are researching is to improve the safety of citizens in the urban environment, such as safe car driving and driving incident prevention. The Leonhard x64 microprocessor and Teragraph system should make it possible to increase the productivity and processing volumes for domestic general-purpose computing systems, reduce power consumption, and reduce the size and cost of computer equipment for such important implementations.

9   Conclusions and Future Works

The presented version of the Leonhard v4 microprocessor is completely tested, ready for operation and already using for graph processing and visualization. Graph processing core based on lnh64 and RISCV cores is suitable for common programming practice and has comparable performance to the multicore Intel Xeon Platinum 8. We have found ART as a very efficient data structures that promising for implementing associative graph storage in the future version of the lnh64 microarchitecture.

The presented principles of Teragraph system operations involve the processing of multiple computational threads over multiple graphs, which requires the development of effective mechanisms for load distribution and the direct GPC access to the graph storage. The principles for increasing the efficiency of these mechanisms will be explored in the future works through the real workload test on a Teragraph system.

References

1. Aananthakrishnan, S., Ahmed, N.K., Cave, V., et al.: PIUMA: programmable integrated unified memory architecture. arXiv:2010.06277 (2020)
2. Abdymanapov, C., Popov, A.: 2019 IEEE Conference of Russian Young Researchers in Electrical and Electronic Engineering (EIConRus) (2019)
3. Adamov, A.N., Pavlukhin, P., Bikonov, D., et al.: Modern GPGPU alternative perspective universal and specialized processors-accelerators. Voprosy kiberbezopasnosti, **4**, 13–21 (2019)
4. Ahn, J., Hong, S., Yoo, S., et al.: A scalable processing-in-memory accelerator for parallel graph processing. SIGARCH Comput. Archit. News **43**(3S), 105–117 (2015)
5. Alam, H., Zhang, T., Erez, M., Etsion, Y.: Do-it-yourself virtual memory translation. SIGARCH Comput. Archit. News **45**(2), 457–468 (2017)
6. Angizi, S., Fan, D.: GraphiDe: a graph processing accelerator leveraging in-dram-computing. In: Proceedings of the 2019 on Great Lakes Symposium on VLSI (2019)
7. Angizi, S., Sun, J., Zhang, W., et al.: GraphS: a graph processing accelerator leveraging SOT-MRAM. In: Proceedings of the 2019 Design, Automation and Test in Europe Conference and Exhibition, DATE 2019, pp. 378–383. Institute of Electrical and Electronics Engineers Inc., May 2019. https://doi.org/10.23919/DATE.2019.8715270
8. Chen, L., Huo, X., Ren, B., et al.: Efficient and simplified parallel graph processing over CPU and MIC. In: 2015 IEEE International Parallel and Distributed Processing Symposium, pp. 819–828 (2015). https://doi.org/10.1109/IPDPS.2015.88

9. Dadu, V., Liu, S., Nowatzki, T.: PolyGraph: exposing the value of flexibility for graph processing accelerators. In: 2021 ACM/IEEE 48th Annual International Symposium on Computer Architecture (ISCA), pp. 595–608 (2021)

10. Dysart, T., Kogge, P., Deneroff, M., et al.: Highly scalable near memory processing with migrating threads on the Emu system architecture. In: 2016 6th Workshop on Irregular Applications: Architecture and Algorithms (IA3), pp. 2–9 (2016). https://doi.org/10.1109/IA3.2016.007

11. Eisenman, A., Cherkasova, L., Magalhaes, G., et al.: Parallel graph processing: prejudice and state of the art. In: Proceedings of the 7th ACM/SPEC on International Conference on Performance Engineering (2016)

12. Gui, C., Zheng, L., He, B., et al.: A survey on graph processing accelerators: challenges and opportunities. J. Comput. Sci. Technol. **34**, 339–371 (2019). https://doi.org/10.1007/s11390-019-1914-z

13. Huang, I.J., Peng, T.C.: Analysis of x86 instruction set usage for dos/windows applications and its implication on superscalar design. IEICE Trans. Inf. Syst. **E85-D**(6), 929–939 (2002)

14. Kasmi, N., Mahmoudi, S.A., Zbakh, M., et al.: Performance evaluation of sparse matrix-vector product (SpMV) computation on GPU architecture. In: 2014 Second World Conference on Complex Systems (WCCS), Agadir, pp. 23–27 (2014)

15. Kim, M.S., An, K., Park, H., et al.: GTS: a fast and scalable graph processing method based on streaming topology to GPUs. In: Proceedings of the 2016 International Conference on Management of Data (2016)

16. Lee, J., Kim, H., Yoo, S., et al.: ExtraV: boosting graph processing near storage with a coherent accelerator. Proc. VLDB Endow. **10**(12), 1706–1717 (2017)

17. Leis, V., Kemper, A., Neumann, T.: The adaptive radix tree: artful indexing for main-memory databases. In: 2013 IEEE 29th International Conference on Data Engineering (ICDE), pp. 38–49 (2013). https://doi.org/10.1109/ICDE.2013.6544812

18. Lumsdaine, A., Gregor, D.P., Hendrickson, B., et al.: Challenges in parallel graph processing. Parallel Process. Lett. **17**, 5–20 (2007)

19. Malewicz, G., Austern, M.H., Bik, A.J., et al.: Pregel: a system for large-scale graph processing. In: Proceedings of the 2010 International Conference on Management of Data, New York, NY, USA, pp. 135–146 (2010). https://doi.org/10.1145/1807167.1807184

20. Patel, G.R., Kumar, S.: The effect of dependency on scalar pipeline architecture. IUP J. Comput. Sci. **11**(1), 38–50 (2017)

21. Popov, A.: An introduction to the MISD technology. In: Proceedings of the 50th Hawaii International Conference on System Sciences, HICSS50, pp. 1003–1012 (2017)

22. Rasheed, B., Popov, A.Y.: 2019 IEEE Conference of Russian Young Researchers in Electrical and Electronic Engineering (EIConRus) (2019)

23. Roy, A., Mihailovic, I., Zwaenepoel, W.: X-stream: edge-centric graph processing using streaming partitions. In: Proceedings of the Twenty-Fourth ACM Symposium on Operating Systems Principles (2013)

24. Scheevel, M.: NORMA: a graph reduction processor. Association for Computing Machinery, New York (1986)

25. Seshadri, V., Mullins, T., Boroumand, A., et al.: Gather-scatter DRAM: in-DRAM address translation to improve the spatial locality of non-unit strided accesses. In: 2015 48th Annual IEEE/ACM International Symposium on Microarchitecture (MICRO), pp. 267–280 (2015)

26. Snitnikova, T.: Implementation of an associative-computing model on GPU: a basic procedure library of the star language. Numer. Methods Program. (Vychislitel'nye Metody i Programmirovanie) **19**(55), 85–95 (2018)

27. Song, L., Zhuo, Y., Qian, X., et al.: GraphR: accelerating graph processing using ReRAM (2017). https://doi.org/10.48550/ARXIV.1708.06248. arxiv.org/abs/1708.06248

28. Song, W.S., Gleyzer, V., Lomakin, A., et al.: Novel graph processor architecture, prototype system, and results. In: 2016 IEEE High Performance Extreme Computing Conference (HPEC), pp. 1–7 (2016). https://doi.org/10.1109/HPEC.2016.7761635

29. TechPowerUp: Intel Xeon Platinum 8180 (2018). https://www.techpowerup.com/cpu-specs/xeon-platinum-8180.c2055. Accessed 14 Aug 2022

30. Wang, K., Angstadt, K., Bo, C., et al.: An overview of micron's automata processor. Association for Computing Machinery, New York (2016)

31. Wikipedia contributors: Transistor count – Wikipedia, the free encyclopedia (2022). https://en.wikipedia.org/w/index.php?title=Transistor_count&oldid=1104295960. Accessed 14 Aug 2022

32. Xilinx Client Support Forum: Equivalent asic gate count (2020). https://support.xilinx.com/s/question/0D52E00006hplYMSAY/equivalent-asic-gate-count?language=en_US. Accessed 14 Aug 2022

33. Zhang, J., Khoram, S., Li, J.: Boosting the performance of FPGA-based graph processor using hybrid memory cube: a case for breadth first search. Association for Computing Machinery, New York (2017)

34. Zhong, J., He, B.: Medusa: simplified graph processing on GPUs. IEEE Trans. Parallel Distrib. Syst. **25**(6), 1543–1552 (2014). https://doi.org/10.1109/TPDS.2013.111

35. Zhou, S., Kannan, R., Prasanna, V.K., et al.: HitGraph: high-throughput graph processing framework on FPGA. IEEE Trans. Parallel Distrib. Syst. **30**(10), 2249–2264 (2019). https://doi.org/10.1109/TPDS.2019.2910068

Towards OpenUCX and GPUDirect Technology Support for the Angara Interconnect

Mikhail Khalilov[1,2]([envelope]) [ORCID], Alexei Timofeev[1,2,3] [ORCID], and Dmitry Polyakov[4]

[1] HSE University, Moscow, Russia
mkhalilov@hse.ru
[2] JIHT RAS, Moscow, Russia
timofeev@jiht.ru
[3] MIPT, Moscow, Russia
[4] JSC NICEVT, Moscow, Russia

Abstract. Modern supercomputers consist of thousands of GPUs interconnected by high-speed HPC fabric. Angara interconnect supports Remote Direct Memory Access (RDMA) semantic, hence making it promising fabric solution for GPU-based supercomputers with a large amount of high-bandwidth RAM. Within this work we extend Angara interconnect low-level API allowing one transparently register (pin) GPU and user-space memory, hence enabling zero-copy approach and GPUDirect RDMA support. We present our implementation of Angara interconnect support within the state-of-the-art OpenUCX and OpenMPI communication stack. Memcpy function optimized for AMD GPU achieves up to 10× bandwidth speed up for medium to large MPI messages. With the help of Rendezvous protocol and our memory registration API the MPI bandwidth is increased by up to 68×.

Keywords: Angara interconnect · RDMA · MPI · GPUDirect · OpenUCX

1 Introduction

With the development of computing technologies on GPU accelerators, an increasing part of computational algorithms is transferred to GPU [1,2]. In this situation, the CPU begins to play a supporting role and the need to store data in the CPU's memory almost disappears.

Technologies for optimized data-transfer between MPI ranks using GPUs memory are being developed [3–5], which allow transferring data from GPU memory to GPU memory without intermediate copying to CPU memory (the so-called GPU-aware MPI).

Within this work we present new MPI software stack for the Angara interconnect [6,7]. Our stack supports GPUDirect RDMA technology to minimize the latency between GPU-GPU data transfers. Our design based on the OpenMPI

© The Author(s), under exclusive license to Springer Nature Switzerland AG 2022
V. Voevodin et al. (Eds.): RuSCDays 2022, LNCS 13708, pp. 591–603, 2022.
https://doi.org/10.1007/978-3-031-22941-1_43

[8] and OpenUCX [9] libraries allows to tightly integrate Angara interconnect with the AMD GPU and helps to achieve significant MPI latency reduction.

The paper is organized as follows. Section 2 provides a brief overview of MPI point-to-point communication, Angara interconnect and GPUDirect technology. Section 3 present details of UCX-Angara and Memory Registration API implementation. Section 4 provides the experimental results of UCX-Angara performance benchmarking. Section 5 consists of related work overview. Section 6 outlines main results of our study and point out main directions of our future work.

2   Background

2.1   Angara Interconnect API

Angara interconnect [10] support RDMA [11,12] data transfer semantic. Alongside with the traditional CPU-based blocking operations (ANGARA_PUT()), Angara API support the non-blocking (ANGARA_GET()) operation.

ANGARA_GET() operation allows one to transfer data in the zero-copy fashion. Within this paper we propose a memory registration API to support non-blocking zero-copy data transfers to non-contiguous memory physical locations, hence supporting truly RDMA semantic. We discuss our proposal for Angara memory registration API in the later section.

2.2   OpenMPI and OpenUCX Libraries

OpenMPI [8] library is the state-of-the-art implementation of the MPI standard for supercomputers. The development of OpenMPI is actively supported by a number of academic institutions and companies, including NVIDIA, IBM, Intel, Huawei, and others.

Both OpenMPI [8] and MPICH [13] support point-to-point communication middlewares, such as OpenUCX and OpenFabrics Interfaces [26,27], in order to transparently implement point-to-point transfers between host and GPU memory.

The OpenUCX (UCX) [9] library is the middleware of choice for efficient support of AMD and NVIDIA GPU memory. UCX implements a unified point-to-point operation interface for InfiniBand, Cray GNI and TCP/IP interconnects with support for the Eager, Segmentation-and-Reassembly (SAR) and pipelined Rendezvous protocols [14], connection management, tag-matching, atomic operations, GPU-aware memcpy, etc. Within this work we implemented Angara interconnect support within the OpenUCX, UCX-Angara, using described Angara interconnect API.

2.3   Conventional MPI Point-to-Point Communication Protocols

Efficient transmission of data between MPI ranks over the network assumes that, depending on the size of the transmitted message, the most appropriate data exchange protocol is selected. Traditionally, MPI communication stacks [14], including OpenUCX, implement 3 main protocols:

1. **Eager protocol** for a small message transmission (usually less than 1024 Bytes). For this protocol to work, the receive side allocates buffers in advance for receiving messages. This approach eliminates the connection establishment and meta-data exchanging overheads between MPI ranks, but requires intermediate copying of from intermediate eager buffers to user buffers, thereby using the CPU on the critical path.
2. **Segmentation-and-Reassembly (SAR) protocol** for a medium to large (1024 Byte — 128 KBytes) message transmission. On the sending side, the SAR protocol divides the original message into blocks, which are then transmitted via the previously described Eager protocol. The receiving side restores the original message from the received blocks. The SAR protocol is used when the message size exceeds the maximum message size of the Eager protocol.
3. **Rendezvous protocol** for transferring large messages [14]. We denote Rendezvous protocol as a Large Message Transfer (LMT) protocol throughout the text. Within LMT the sending and receiving parties exchange service messages (Ready-to-Receive (RTR)/Ready-to-Send (RTS) packet) via the Eager protocol with the information about pinned user buffers for sending/receiving messages in memory. After that, one of the parties (the active size) initiates a non-blocking operation Remote Direct Memory Access operation (`Put()` or `Get()`), and the network interface card (NIC) starts data transmission. After the completion of the non-blocking operation, the active side notifies the opposite side about the completion of the data transfer via the Eager protocol by sending an appropriate message (ACK/FIN packet). Through the use of non-blocking Put/Get operations, which are supported by modern interconnects, the LMT protocol allows one to send user data without using the CPU and intermediate buffering in a zero-copy fashion.

2.4 GPUDirect Technology

GPUDirect is a family of technologies introduced by NVIDIA to support optimized data transfers from/to GPU memory by NIC.

Efficient support the Eager and SAR protocols when transferring data between GPUs over the interconnect is done using the optimized `memcpy` function for copying data between device-/host-memory. OpenUCX library supports optimized `memcpy` operation for both NVIDIA and AMD GPUs.

To support transfers with the LMT protocol between GPUs, a support for non-blocking Put/Get operations directly from/to device memory by the NIC, so called GPUDirect RDMA, is required. Ideally, an efficient implementation of the GPUDirect RDMA for transfers between GPUs should not slow down transfers between host-memory nodes. We describe our implementation of this functionality for the Angara interconnect in the next section.

3 UCX-Angara

Within the framework of this project, support for the OpenUCX library [9] for the Angara network, UCX-Angara, was implemented (Fig. 1). The implementation of the Eager and SAR protocols is inherited from the MPICH 3.2 Angara library, but is supplemented by the built-in support for optimized `memcpy` operation in UCX, optimized for AMD GPUs.

At the moment, the UCX-Angara layer features connection management and establishment between Angara network enpoints, called processing elements (PEs). We implement support for the Eager/SAR protocols as well as zero-copy operations to bootstrap the LMT protocol and GPUDirect RDMA support.

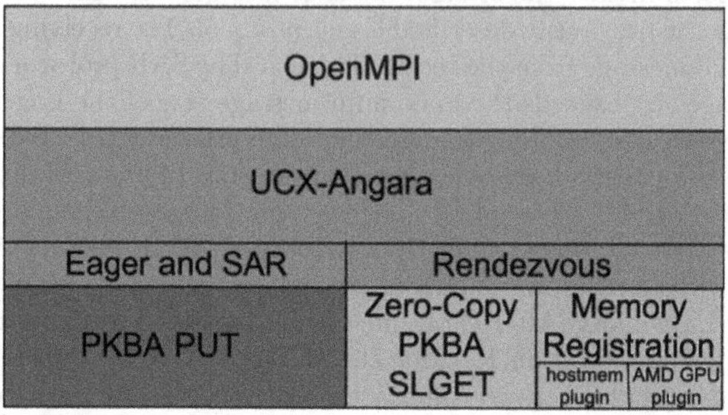

Fig. 1. Angara interconnect software stack based on OpenMPI and OpenUCX.

3.1 Connection Management

Connection Establishment functionality is required to allocate networking resources (ring buffers, pinned memory, etc.) before communication between MPI ranks [15]. Within the UCX-Angara we implement lazy connection management approach:

1. During the first data transfer between a pair of PEs (MPI ranks), the sending PE sends a Connection Request to the receiving PE;
2. After receiving the setup request, the receiving PE allocates a buffer for receiving short messages via the Eager protocol (ring buffer) and sends an acknowledgment (ACK) with the offset of this buffer to the sender PE;
3. The sender PE can then send data to the receiver PE using the eager protocol.

The implementation of a PE-to-PE lazy connection establishment protocol allows for future support of dynamic connection management. Withing this approach, only active PE consume CPU resources and RAM polling ring buffers for new incoming packets in these buffers.

3.2   Eager, SAR and LMT Protocols Support

The internal UCX am_short() operation is used to send small messages using the Eager protocol. When the Eager protocol limit is exceeded, the Segmentation and Reassembly (SAR) protocol is enabled, within which the am_bcopy() function is used. In UCX-Angara both operations are supported using the ANGARA_PUT() blocking operation synchronized via a ring buffer.

put_zcopy() and get_zcopy() operations are used in the LMT protocol to trigger non-blocking Put()/Get() operations done by NIC without intermediate copying of user data on the sender/receiver side. These operations are supported using the adapted ANGARA_SLGET() operation and the memory registration mechanism described below.

3.3   Designing Angara Interconnect Memory Registration API

To support the LMT protocol implemented in UCX [9,14], we propose an extension of the system-level Angara network API. By analogy with the leading interconnects in the industry we leverage Memory Registration/Pinning functionality of the Linux operating system and AMD GPU driver in order to allow RDMA data-transfers from non-contiguous memory locations.

Implemented for both host (hostmem_plugin) and AMD GPU memory (rocm_plugin), the Memory Registration operation allows one to fix the location of the user-space buffer in physical memory (memory pinning) and generate a memory registration key (MR key) containing an offsets withing the Angara NIC PCIe Base Address of the user buffer in the physical memory of Host/GPU RAM.

The MR key is sent with the rest of the information in RTR/RTS messages in the Rendezvous protocol as described in the Sect. 2. Upon receipt of the RTR/RTS packet, the active side initiates the non-blocking data-transfer using the MR key pair (local and obtained from RTR/RTS packet) of send/receive user buffers to generate a sequence of non-blocking ANGARA_GET operations.

Memory Registration design has significant advantage [11] in comparison to custom memory allocation, since working with the host and GPU memory buffers becomes transparent from the NIC API point-of-view. Within the MR there is no intermediate copying from/to a contiguous memory region allocated using the function. It is also possible to implement caching of registered buffers (memory registration cache) technique.

It is also worth to note that the task of implementing the GPUDirect RDMA technology for the Angara NIC is reduced to implementing the GPU memory registration mechanism at the OS kernel level.

In the future, it is also possible to simplify the software stack of the Angara network by offloading the user-space memory fragmentation to the DMA engine of the NIC by analogy with the InfiniBand interconnect and Intel OPA [19].

Our memory registration mechanism is implemented as the Linux kernel module (angara_memreg) and has the following API:

mr_key_t *angara_reg_mr(void *buf, size_t len, uint32_t flags);

The Memory Registration process can be divided into several key stages:

1. allocate space for a memory descriptor (mr_key_t) in the user-space;
2. call the kernel level memory registration functionality (module angara_memreg) via the ioctl() interface:
3. call the copy_from_user() function to obtain information about the registered memory region (pointer to the user buffer, its size and access flags), copying this data to the memory descriptor in allocated in the kernel-space. This memory descriptor will contain information about the location of the user buffer in physical memory;
4. add a kernel memory descriptor to the hash-table of the angara_memreg module;
5. search for a *plugin* that can pin the user buffer in physical memory:
   - use the get_uset_pages() OS kernel function, if the user buffer is located in the host memory, to pin the Host memory pages in the physical memory and return pinned pages list;
   - call a similar operation using the AMD GPU driver interface (rdma_interface::get_pages) if user-space buffer is allocated within the GPU and return page offset list;
6. calculate the offset of each page relative to the Angara NIC DMA base address and generate a list of fragments forming MR key. Contiguous pages are combined into one fragment of the appropriate length with 64-bit word alignment;
7. copy fragment list (MR key) to the user-space memory descriptor using the copy_to_user() function.

A pair of memory keys - the key of the message buffer to send (lkey) and the key of the buffer to receive this message (rkey) - are used to invoke non-blocking ANGARA_GET() operation in the LMT protocol in UCX-Angara. This function invokes a series of non-blocking operations between contiguous chunks of physical memory whose location is computed from the pair of keys lkey and rkey.

4   Experimental Results

4.1   Hardware and Software Testbed

JIHT RAS Desmos supercomputer [6,7] was used to carry out the experiments. The main partition of Desmos consists of 32 computing nodes, interconnected by the Angara network in a 3D-torus topology. Each compute node includes an Intel Xeon E5-1650v3 CPU, 32 GB of RAM, and an AMD Radeon Instinct MI50 accelerator GPU with 32 GB of memory. Each node runs SLES 15SP1 based on Linux 4.12 kernel and ROCm v3.7.

8 nodes were equipped with an Infiniband FDR [18] to support parallel file system and be able to compare interconnects performance in apple-to-apple fashion [16]. The Infiniband software stack is based on the MOFED 4.9 LTS.

Additional BIOS settings were performed on the nodes to enable correct AMD GPU memory interaction with NIC driver:

- Above 4G Decoding was enabled;
- MMIOHBase was decreased to 1 TB;
- MMIO High Size was reduced to 128 GB.

4.2 Experiment Policy

We tested UCX-Angara using Ohio-State University (OSU) benchmark suite [28]. Our performance study presented in the subsequent sections were performed in several modes (these modes are similarly marked on the legends of the corresponding figures):

1. **OpenMPI 4.1.1, UCX, IB:** data transfer was performed via the InfiniBand network, for small and medium size messages in the Eager and SAR protocols, an optimized version of the memcpy function for AMD GPUs was used, large messages were transmitted using the LMT protocol based on the RDMA_READ operation;
2. **OpenMPI 4.1.1, UCX, IB, GDR:** same as 1) with explicitly enabled GPUDirect RDMA
3. **OpenMPI 4.1.1, UCX, IB, no GDR:** same as 1) with explicitly disabled GPUDirect RDMA
4. **MPICH 3.2 Angara, SAR:** old MPICH-Angara implementation [10] with disabled LMT mode; MPICH-Angara lacks of GPUDirect RDMA support;
5. **MPICH 3.2 Angara, LMT:** old MPICH-Angara implementation with enabled LMT mode;
6. **OpenMPI 4.1.1, UCX-Angara, SAR:** Eager and SAR protocols were used with all message sizes. When transferring between GPUs, these protocols used an optimized version of the memcpy function for AMD GPUs (the rocm_copy component from the UCX library);
7. **OpenMPI 4.1.1, UCX-Angara, LMT (MR):** same as 6) with enabled LMT protocol and GPUDirect RDMA support thorough Memory Registration API

4.3 Performance of MPI P2P Operations with Host and GPU Memory

Figures 2a, 3a, and 4a present the results of performance testing of the OpenMPI and UCX-Angara communication stack using the OSU point-to-point benchmarks between two compute nodes. Data was transferred between host-memory in these experiments.

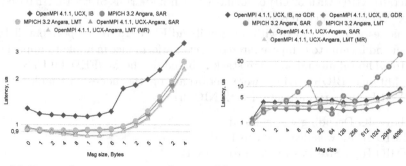

(a) Host-to-host memory transfers   (b) Device-to-device memory transfers

Fig. 2. Ping-pong latency between two MPI ranks on different nodes

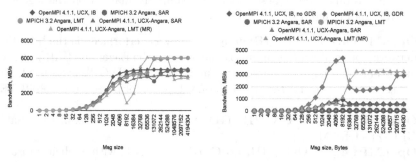

(a) Host-to-host memory transfers   (b) Device-to-device memory transfers

Fig. 3. Uni-directional bandwidth between two MPI ranks on different nodes

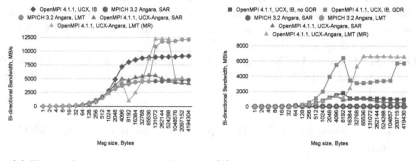

(a) Host-to-host memory transfers   (b) Device-to-device memory transfers

Fig. 4. Bi-directional bandwidth between two MPI ranks on different nodes

Latency tests (Fig. 2a) show that the UCX-Angara stack has comparable performance to the MPICH-Angara on small message-size transfers and achieves latency of nearly 850 nanoseconds.

Bandwidth tests in uni-/bi-directional (Figs. 3a, 4a) modes show the same trend. The SAR mode in UCX-Angara is close in performance to the MPICH-Angara and has a bandwidth spread of 150 MB/s depending on the size of the message being sent. It is assumed that this effect is due to different maximum message size thresholds in the Eager protocol in MPICH-Angara and UCX-Angara.

Bandwidth tests with UCX-Angara and enabled with LMT protocol and MR mechanism show unstable performance in the message size range of $8 - 65$ KB, but allow to reach the peak bandwidth of the Angara interconnect link on larger messages ($128 - 256$ KB range). Such a significant slowdown in the range of $8 - 65$ KB is due to significant fragmentation of the user buffer, which leads to an increase in the number of fragmented non-blocking operations within the ANGARA_GET() operation as describes in previous section.

Further improvements suggest the implementation at the UCX library level of support for registering memory in blocks, the fragmentation of which will allow writing all fragment offsets into one memory key. The possibility of supporting memory keys of arbitrary size at the level of the UCX library is also being considered.

Meanwhile, using the UCX-Angara allows one to achieve a significant increase in point-to-point data transfer performance between AMD GPUs over the Angara network. Thanks to the AMD GPU-optimized memcpy function the UCX-Angara stack shows up to 4× lower latency on small message sizes (2b), up to 10× lower latency on large message sizes, and up to 11× lower latency within the large transfers. Usage of the LMT protocol and the Memory Registration mechanism in the UCX-Angara make it possible to reduce the latency in the transmission of large messages up to 144×.

The increase in bandwidth (Figs. 3b and 4b) due to the use of the memcpy function optimized for the AMD GPU in UCX-Angara for medium-large messages is up to 10×. Enabling of LMT protocol and the Memory Registration mechanism in UCX-Angara helps to increase the bandwidth by 68× in comparison to MPICH-Angara(Fig. 6).

4.4 Performance of MPI Collectives with Host and GPU Memory

The current internal limitations of the UCX-Angara library and the memory registration mechanism make it impossible to use the LMT protocol on a large number of MPI ranks. For this reason, this and the following sections present the results of an evaluation of the OpenMPI stack and UCX-Angara, where the SAR protocol was used to send medium-large MPI messages within the collective operations.

600   M. Khalilov et al.

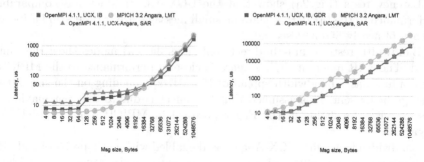

(a) Host-to-host memory transfers   (b) Device-to-device memory transfers

Fig. 5. MPI_Allreduce latency on 8 nodes

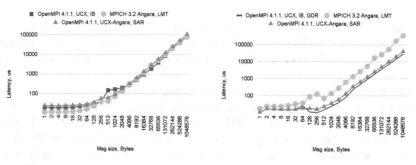

(a) Host-to-host memory transfers   (b) Device-to-device memory transfers

Fig. 6. MPI_Alltoall latency on 8 nodes

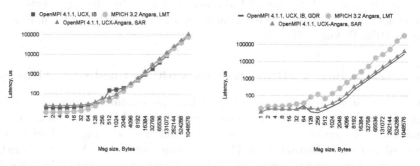

(a) Host-to-host memory transfers   (b) Device-to-device memory transfers

Fig. 7. MPI_Bcast latency on 8 nodes

Figures 5a, 5a and 7a show the results of benchmarking MPI collective operations latencies on 8 nodes with 6 MPI processes per node. Within these tests the Host memory was used for data transfers. It can be seen from the graphs that OpenMPI with UCX-Angara back-end exhibits higher latency in comparison to conventional MPICH-Angara implementation. For small-medium messages we observe nearly 3× MPI_Allreduce latency degradation.

The graphs 5b, 5b and 7b show the significant latency gain from using OpenMPI and UCX-Angara compared to MPICH-Angara in collective communication between GPU memory on 8 nodes. Latency improvement in all message ranges is nearly 5× for the MPI_Allreduce test, 8× for the MPI_Alltoall traffic pattern, 5× times for the MPI_Bcast collective operation.

We see a such significant gain in latency due to the use of an optimized version of the `memcpy` function to move data between the AMD GPU and host memory during the above operations.

5   Related Work

Performance gains from the GPUDirect RDMA technology are discussed in numerous of works [3,17,20].

GPU-aware MPI support is currently available in the several modern molecular dynamics packets. GPU-aware MPI is supported by LAMMPS [21], GROMACS [22] and HOOMD-Blue [23]. Works [24,25] also show significant performance gain from GPUDirect enabling in their codes.

6   Conclusion and Future Work

Within this work the open-source OpenUCX library is ported to the Angara interconnect. UCX-Angara allows to use OpenMPI library on systems with the Angara network. The UCX-Angara stack is adapted for efficient use with the AMD GPUs ROCm infrastructure and the GPUDirect RDMA technology. An optimized memory copy mechanism is used and a prototype of the memory registration interface is developed to implement an optimized version of the LMT protocol. Usage of UCX-Angara helps to achieve up to 70× speedup for GPU-GPU data transfers.

Acknowledgments. The study was carried out with a grant from the Russian Science Foundation (project no. 20-71-10127).

References

1. Ghorpade, J., Parande, J., Kulkarni, M., Bawaskar, A.: GPGPU processing in CUDA architecture. arXiv preprint arXiv:1202.4347 (2012)
2. Sanders, J., Kandrot, E.: CUDA by Example: An Introduction to General-Purpose GPU Programming. Addison-Wesley Professional, Boston (2010)

3. Rossetti, D., Team, S.: GPUDIRECT: integrating the GPU with a network interface. In: GPU Technology Conference (2015)
4. Potluri, S., Hamidouche, K., Venkatesh, A., Bureddy, D., Panda, D. K.: Efficient inter-node MPI communication using GPUDirect RDMA for InfiniBand clusters with NVIDIA GPUs. In: 2013 42nd International Conference on Parallel Processing, pp. 80–89. IEEE (2013)
5. Hamidouche, K., Venkatesh, A., Awan, A.A., Subramoni, H., Chu, C.H., Panda, D.K.: Exploiting GPUDirect RDMA in designing high performance OpenSHMEM for NVIDIA GPU clusters. In: 2015 IEEE International Conference on Cluster Computing (CLUSTER), pp. 78–87. IEEE Computer Society (2015)
6. Stegailov, V., et al.: Angara interconnect makes GPU-based Desmos supercomputer an efficient tool for molecular dynamics calculations. Int. J. High Perform. Comput. Appl. **33**(3), 507–521 (2019)
7. Stegailov, V., et al.: Early performance evaluation of the hybrid cluster with torus interconnect aimed at molecular-dynamics simulations. In: Wyrzykowski, R., Dongarra, J., Deelman, E., Karczewski, K. (eds.) PPAM 2017. LNCS, vol. 10777, pp. 327–336. Springer, Cham (2018). https://doi.org/10.1007/978-3-319-78024-5_29
8. Graham, R.L., Woodall, T.S., Squyres, J.M.: Open MPI: a flexible high performance MPI. In: Wyrzykowski, R., Dongarra, J., Meyer, N., Waśniewski, J. (eds.) PPAM 2005. LNCS, vol. 3911, pp. 228–239. Springer, Heidelberg (2006). https://doi.org/10.1007/11752578_29
9. Shamis, P., et al.: UCX: an open source framework for HPC network APIs and beyond. In: 2015 IEEE 23rd Annual Symposium on High-Performance Interconnects, pp. 40–43. IEEE (2015)
10. Zhabin, I.A., Makagon, D.V., Polyakov, D.A., Simonov, A.S., Syromyatnikov, E.L., Shcherbak, A.N.: First generation of Angara high-speed interconnection network. Naukoemkie Tekhnol **1**, 21–27 (2014)
11. Kalia, A., Kaminsky, M., Andersen, D.G.: Design guidelines for high performance RDMA systems. In: 2016 USENIX Annual Technical Conference (USENIX ATC 16), pp. 437–450 (2016)
12. Woodall, T.S., Shipman, G.M., Bosilca, G., Graham, R.L., Maccabe, A.B.: High performance RDMA protocols in HPC. In: Mohr, B., Träff, J.L., Worringen, J., Dongarra, J. (eds.) EuroPVM/MPI 2006. LNCS, vol. 4192, pp. 76–85. Springer, Heidelberg (2006). https://doi.org/10.1007/11846802_18
13. Thakur, R., Rabenseifner, R., Gropp, W.: Optimization of collective communication operations in MPICH. Int. J. High Perform. Comput. Appl. **19**(1), 49–66 (2005)
14. Sur, S., Jin, H.W., Chai, L., Panda, D.K.: RDMA read based rendezvous protocol for MPI over InfiniBand: design alternatives and benefits. In: Proceedings of the Eleventh ACM SIGPLAN Symposium on Principles and Practice of Parallel Programming, pp. 32–39 (2006)
15. Yu, W., Gao, Q., Panda, D.K.: Adaptive connection management for scalable MPI over InfiniBand. In: Proceedings 20th IEEE International Parallel & Distributed Processing Symposium, pp. 10-pp. IEEE (2006)
16. Shamsutdinov, A., et al.: Performance of supercomputers based on Angara interconnect and novel AMD CPUs/GPUs. In: Balandin, D., Barkalov, K., Gergel, V., Meyerov, I. (eds.) MMST 2020. CCIS, vol. 1413, pp. 401–416. Springer, Cham (2021). https://doi.org/10.1007/978-3-030-78759-2_33
17. Shainer, G., et al.: The development of Mellanox/NVIDIA GPUDirect over InfiniBand-a new model for GPU to GPU communications. Comput. Sci. Res. Dev. **26**(3), 267–273 (2011). https://doi.org/10.1007/s00450-011-0157-1

18. Pfister, G.F.: An introduction to the InfiniBand architecture. High Perform. Mass Storage Parallel I/O **42**(617–632), 102 (2001)
19. Birrittella, M.S., et al.: Intel® Omni-path architecture: enabling scalable, high performance fabrics. In: 2015 IEEE 23rd Annual Symposium on High-Performance Interconnects, pp. 1–9. IEEE (2015)
20. Li, A., et al.: Evaluating modern GPU interconnect: PCIe, NVLink, NV-SLI, NVswitch and GPUdirect. IEEE Trans. Parallel Distrib. Syst. **31**(1), 94–110 (2019)
21. Thompson, A.P., et al.: LAMMPS - a flexible simulation tool for particle-based materials modeling at the atomic, meso, and continuum scales. Comput. Phys. Commun. **271**, 108171 (2022)
22. Van Der Spoel, D., Lindahl, E., Hess, B., Groenhof, G., Mark, A.E., Berendsen, H.J.: GROMACS: fast, flexible, and free. J. Comput. Chem. **26**(16), 1701–1718 (2005)
23. Anderson, J.A., Glaser, J., Glotzer, S.C.: HOOMD-blue: a Python package for high-performance molecular dynamics and hard particle Monte Carlo simulations. Comput. Mater. Sci. **173**, 109363 (2020)
24. Matsumoto, K., Hanawa, T., Kodama, Y., Fujii, H., Boku, T.: Implementation of CG method on GPU cluster with proprietary interconnect TCA for GPU direct communication. In: 2015 IEEE International Parallel and Distributed Processing Symposium Workshop, pp. 647–655. IEEE (2015)
25. Otten, M., et al.: An MPI/OpenACC implementation of a high-order electromagnetics solver with GPUDirect communication. Int. J. High Perform. Comput. Appl. **30**(3), 320–334 (2016)
26. Grun, P., et al.: A brief introduction to the OpenFabrics interfaces-a new network API for maximizing high performance application efficiency. In: 2015 IEEE 23rd Annual Symposium on High-Performance Interconnects, pp. 34–39. IEEE (2015)
27. Pritchard, H.P.: Comparison of Open UCX and OFI Libfabric. No. LA-UR-16-26499. Los Alamos National Lab. (LANL), Los Alamos, NM, United States (2016)
28. Bureddy, D., Wang, H., Venkatesh, A., Potluri, S., Panda, D.K.: OMB-GPU: a micro-benchmark suite for evaluating MPI libraries on GPU clusters. In: Träff, J.L., Benkner, S., Dongarra, J.J. (eds.) EuroMPI 2012. LNCS, vol. 7490, pp. 110–120. Springer, Heidelberg (2012). https://doi.org/10.1007/978-3-642-33518-1_16

Wiki Representation and Analysis of Knowledge About Algorithms

Alexander Antonov[1,2]([✉]) [iD]

[1] Lomonosov Moscow State University, Moscow, Russian Federation
asa@parallel.ru
[2] Moscow Center of Fundamental and Applied Mathematics,
Moscow, Russian Federation

Abstract. As part of the project to create an AlgoWiki Open encyclopedia of parallel algorithmic features, many properties of computational algorithms are described, primarily related to parallelism. For this, wiki representation is used, which allows the entire computing community to participate in the description of such properties. At the moment, a large number of algorithms from different fields of science have already been described using a single universal scheme. But gradually the project becomes something much more than just a library of algorithms. The logical development of the AlgoWiki project extends the analysis of specific algorithms by expert evaluation of the quality of possible approaches to solving individual problems. Further expansion within the framework of the Algo500 project allows for each implementation of the algorithm from the AlgoWiki encyclopedia to build its own independent rating list, which provides new opportunities for analyzing the quality of mapping problems to computer architecture.

Keywords: AlgoWiki · Algorithms information structure · Supercomputers · High-performance computing · Parallel programming · Wiki encyclopedia · Algo500

1 Introduction

The fundamental scientific problem, the solution of which is aimed at creating the AlgoWiki Open encyclopedia of parallel algorithmic features [1], is the creation of methods for the efficient use of computer systems with a parallel architecture. Depending on what the emphasis is on, different formulations of this problem can be used. In particular, we can talk about solving the problem of mapping the structure of programs and algorithms to the architecture of parallel computing systems.

With such a mapping, it is necessary to carefully coordinate the structure of algorithms and programs with the features of computer architecture. The capabilities of modern computers are great, but if there is no matching at least at one of the stages of the process of solving the problem 1, then computer

V. Voevodin et al. (Eds.): RuSCDays 2022, LNCS 13708, pp. 604–616, 2022.
https://doi.org/10.1007/978-3-031-22941-1_44

performance will be close to zero. And this is true for every parallel program, and it is all the more true for every program oriented towards supercomputer systems.

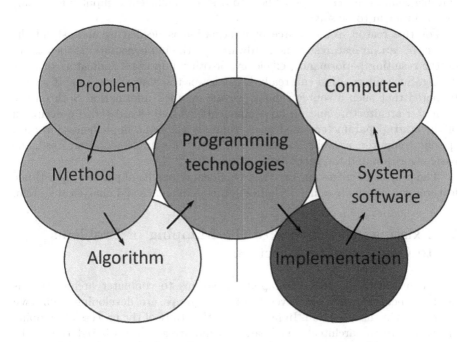

Fig. 1. A typical scheme for mapping tasks to computer architecture

The formulated problem is significantly complicated by the fact that it is complex. Here, there is a variety of parallelism features in the architecture of modern computers, and the complication of their memory subsystems, the complexity of determining and describing a parallel structure in algorithms, insufficient support from parallel programming technologies and run-time systems. In addition to the fact that parallel programs are generally more difficult to write than their serial counterparts, the efficiency also falls catastrophically. If in the mid-70s of the XX century the efficiency of program execution in 30–50% was considered the norm, then today fractions of a percent of peak performance have already become commonplace, and average efficiency indicators continue to decrease rapidly.

Despite the orientation of this project towards powerful supercomputer systems, the formulated problem is relevant for all computer platforms, up to mobile phones and tablets, which also became parallel a long time ago.

There are a large number of computationally intensive problems in almost all spheres of human activity, for which many algorithms have been developed, which, in turn, can have different software implementations. At the same time, a wide range of computing platforms are available for solving these problems, differing in architecture, scale, supported functions, etc. The question may be how to choose the best implementation for a given algorithm and computing platform, or, on the other hand, how to match a given algorithm with the most suitable computing resources, or how to design an efficient computer for a particular problem to be solved.

For this reason, some source of information is needed to understand the impact of certain features of the hardware and the implementations themselves on the resulting performance, efficiency, or other important indicators of computing. Such information can really help answer the above questions. It should be noted that such a source should provide detailed information both on the computer architecture and on its components, as well as a detailed description of the startup parameters used when running a specific implementation on a specific computer, as well as information about this implementation itself, the basic algorithm and the problem being solved.

The project to create an AlgoWiki Open encyclopedia of parallel algorithmic features was originally aimed at building such a reference and analytical system.

2   Existing Approaches to the Mapping of Problems to Computer Architecture

At the moment, the task of mapping problems to computer architecture is far from being solved, but several research groups are developing their own approaches in this direction. In many cases, the study of the process of mapping algorithms to the architecture of parallel computing systems is reduced to the study of the so-called *typical algorithmic structures*, on the basis of which a significant number of problems from various subject areas are built. The main idea is that the study of the process of mapping a small number of these structures will allow us to draw conclusions about the mapping of a set of real problems built on their basis. And such knowledge can be used both for more efficient implementation of such problems, and for more accurate design of the architecture of future computing systems.

For example, a group of researchers at Berkeley use a concept called *motifs*, or *dwarfs*, to refer to algorithmic methods that highlight some common pattern of computing and communication [2]. A set of motifs was chosen, which are not specific algorithms, but designate classes of algorithms with a similar computational and communication profile, which makes it possible to accurately identify their distinctive characteristics and describe their behavior. These motives, according to the authors of the study, will be the basis of the absolute majority of real applications from various fields.

The SNL (Sandia National Laboratories) laboratory is working on the Mantevo project, which is aimed at studying the so-called *mini-applications* [3]. Mini-applications are computational cores of various research and engineering real-world applications. In a huge application of hundreds of thousands and millions of lines in size, the main computational part is allocated, which is usually much smaller than the application itself, but on which most of the time of its operation is spent. In this study, it is assumed that a small number of such computational cores covers many real-world problems. The mini-application has the same properties and behavior as the original real app, but is much easier to learn. Unlike motifs, mini-applications are complete programs — benchmarks that can be run on the target computer system to collect real data about their behavior and execution dynamics.

In the above studies, the authors use a fairly holistic approach to solving the problem. However, many other teams are engaged in related areas, such as: development of program execution support (T. Sterling, Indiana University), development of parallel program execution models (W. Gropp, University of Illinois Urbana-Champaign), development of methods for studying scalability (T. Hoeffler , ETH Zurich), development of prototyping applications (S. Matsuoka, Technology University of Tokyo), automatic program tuning (G. Fursin, INRIA). Interesting research is being conducted by a group led by V.A. Kryukov (IPM RAS) on creating tools for automatic parallelization of programs.

In our project, the study of the process of mapping tasks to computer architecture was carried out on the basis of the concept of an *algorithm graph* [4] — the only graph model of programs and algorithms that contains complete information about their structure. Orientation to the use of the algorithm graph guarantees the completeness of the definition of the parallelism resource. Two fundamentally important properties that determine the quality of implementation are analyzed: the resource of parallelism and work with data. An additional complication lies in the fact that these two properties must be consistent both across the stages of the mapping process, and among themselves at each stage. For each stage, features are highlighted that affect both other stages of the mapping process and the efficiency of the resulting program. For each, invariants are allocated that do not change when moving from platform to platform, when replacing one algorithm with another, which just become the basis for simplifying the process of programming parallel computers. An extremely important issue is also the completeness of the description of the mapping process, which determines the control over efficiency both in the development of new parallel programs and in their transfer from one computer platform to another. All fundamentally important features that affect the efficiency of the resulting programs are reflected in the descriptions of the AlgoWiki encyclopedia.

The created AlgoWiki Open encyclopedia of parallel algorithmic features has no direct analogues in the world practice. There are a number of projects on classifying, describing properties, and writing implementations of algorithms (for example, [5–7]), but none of them describes all the necessary properties of algorithms and their implementations for various target architectures in a single predefined unified scheme. Only in the AlgoWiki project, in contrast to previous studies by various teams, the solution of this problem has been brought to a truly logical conclusion. The development of the fundamental foundations and the formalization of the process of mapping algorithms to the architecture of parallel computing systems ended not only with a detailed description of the stages of the mapping process, not only with the technology for describing the properties of algorithms and with a description of the first set of real algorithms. Most importantly, the work ended with a workable encyclopedia of the properties of algorithms, available to everyone on the Internet and filled by the forces of the entire computing community.

3   Description of Algorithm Properties and Structure

Based on the developed methods and approaches, a technology for describing the properties and features of algorithms has been formed. The proposed structure for describing the properties of algorithms consists of two parts. The first part describes the algorithms themselves and their properties, and the second part is devoted to describing the features of their software implementations, taking into account specific software and hardware platforms. The third section is also explicitly highlighted for the list of literature on the described algorithm, which the authors used in preparing a specific description, and links to primary sources and classic works in this area are also provided here. The developed structure for describing the properties of algorithms has the following form Fig. 2.

1. Properties and structure of the algorithm
   1.1 General description of the algorithm
   1.2 Mathematical description of the algorithm
   1.3 Computational kernel of the algorithm
   1.4 Macro structure of the algorithm
   1.5 Implementation scheme of the serial algorithm
   1.6 Serial complexity of the algorithm
   1.7 Information graph
   1.8 Parallelization resource of the algorithm
   1.9 Input and output data of the algorithm
   1.10 Properties of the algorithm
2. Software implementation of the algorithm
   2.1 Implementation peculiarities of the serial algorithm
   2.2 Locality of data and computations
   2.3 Possible methods and considerations for parallel implementation of the algorithm
   2.4 Scalability of the algorithm and its implementations
   2.5 Dynamic characteristics and efficiency of the algorithm implementation
   2.6 Conclusions for different classes of computer architecture
   2.7 Existing implementations of the algorithm
3. References

Fig. 2. Description of algorithm properties and structure

This description structure allows revealing all fundamentally important properties of the studied algorithms and their implementations.

At the beginning of the description, an algorithm card is placed, in which the main properties that characterize this algorithm are taken out. The information from the algorithm card should allow the reader to quickly assess how this algorithm can be useful to him. In the future, it is planned to supplement the information in the algorithm card with expert assessments (for example, "implemented well only on computers with shared memory", "allows efficient use of graphics accelerators", etc.) as well as data on the efficiency of the most popular implementations.

Also, in all articles, the authorship of the people who carried out this description is indicated.

4 Wiki Encyclopedia

The AlgoWiki Open encyclopedia of parallel algorithmic features algorithms is available on the Internet at http://algowiki-project.org [8,9]. The MediaWiki [10] software engine was chosen as the basis for the implementation, which implements a content management system in the style of the so-called wiki technology. MediaWiki is free and open source software written in PHP and distributed under the GNU license. MySQL database is used for data storage.

The MediaWiki engine was developed specifically for the Wikipedia [11] project and is also used by many of the Wikimedia Foundation [12] projects and other projects on the Internet. The server part of the engine can be installed on top of any modern web server, such as Apache [13]. The Apache web server is cross-platform — there are versions for both Windows and Linux. To work with clients, the engine, which is a web application, uses the http protocol, which is supported by all modern browsers, both on desktop devices running Windows, Linux, MacOS, and on mobile devices running Android and iOS. Thus, users can work with the AlgoWiki encyclopedia using any of their preferred devices.

The MediaWiki engine supports simultaneous work of many users — by changing some information in the AlgoWiki encyclopedia, users create their own copy of this document and work with it. Subsequently, new information can be automatically or manually added to the main version. All history and authorship of changes is retained, allowing the administrator to easily correct any acts of vandalism or spam, as well as unintentional errors.

Wiki technology provides an opportunity to create an Internet site, the structure and content of which can be independently changed by users using the provided tools. For formatting text and inserting various objects, a special markup is offered. MediaWiki offers a text markup format called wikitext, which supports hyperlinks to create links between pages, and is simpler, cleaner, and safer than HTML. Its use allows users who are not familiar with technologies such as XHTML and CSS to create and edit pages. All variants of the page edited by the user are recorded in the MySQL database.

For some special purposes (displaying formulas, generating pdf, special formatting, etc.) special extensions are used, written in PHP by independent developers. A large number of such extensions have been developed, their use allows administrators and users to be able to adapt the site to their own needs.

The MathJax extension is used to present mathematical formulas on the site. It allows you to display formulas in TEX and MathML formats by calling the MathJax JavaScript toolkit.

To support other languages (the current version supports two languages, Russian and English), the Interwiki extension is installed — a tool for organizing links between different wiki sites on the Internet. It provides an opportunity to avoid inserting the full page address into the text, limiting itself to an internal link. In this case, the link is formed from two parts: the name of the remote page is added to the prefix of the remote wiki site.

The main part of AlgoWiki encyclopedia is in the "Algorithm classification" section. In this section, all descriptions of algorithms are accessed by groups corresponding to the types of operations performed. In order for all users to unambiguously understand the terms used in the descriptions of algorithms, a special "Glossary" section has been introduced. By current convention, a reference to a term in the Glossary is inserted on the first occurrence of that term in the page being edited.

In order to fill in all sections of the description of properties of different algorithms according to one scheme, the formation of the section "Guidelines for filling in description sections" began, where step-by-step instructions for obtaining data for the corresponding sections of descriptions are entered.

The "Help with editing" section contains the materials necessary to ensure that external users work with the project.

5   Hierarchical Representation of Knowledge About Algorithms

The logical development of the AlgoWiki project [14] extends the analysis of specific algorithms by expert evaluation of the quality of possible approaches to solving individual problems.

The AlgoWiki Open encyclopedia of parallel algorithmic features takes the description of an *algorithm* as the basic unit of description. But computational algorithms are needed not by themselves, but to solve *problems* that arise in various fields of science and industry. On the other hand, many practical problems can be solved using various *methods* — this is how another basic concept arises, intermediate between the concepts of a problem and an algorithm. As a rule, several different methods can be used to solve each problem. Each method has its own characteristics, and those algorithms that are well suited for one class of computers are far from always suitable for another. On the other hand, any algorithm assumes the presence of its various *implementations* both in relation to one computing platform and when using different platforms. The "Problem–Method–Algorithm–Implementation" chain is the basis for describing any subject area within the AlgoWiki encyclopedia [15] and implements the concept of a linked representation of different algorithmic approaches to solving the same problem. In essence, new dimensions appear in the AlgoWiki project, allowing you to move from the level of analysis of individual algorithms to the analysis of various algorithmic methods for solving problems.

For inexperienced developers, an attempt to take into account the features of the computer architecture often occurs only at the very last stage of the computations when analyzing the results already obtained. However, the best result in terms of efficiency and scalability of the program can be achieved at the highest levels even when choosing a method for solving the problem. One of the main goals of creating the AlgoWiki encyclopedia is precisely the ability to provide the user with the opportunity to present in advance in all details the entire described chain from the problem to the implementation 1, and choose those methods and algorithms that will lead to the most effective solutions.

The *Problem* level can correspond to the description of both specific practical problems being solved, and problems in a purely mathematical formulation.

The *Method* level describes different approaches to problem solving. Each method has its own characteristics and features and in certain conditions it may be advantageous to use one of them.

The *Algorithm* level is the base level of the AlgoWiki encyclopedia. Each method of solving a problem may provide for the possibility of using one or another algorithm. The properties of the algorithms described in detail make it possible to choose the most suitable one in each specific situation.

Finally, the *Implementation* level provides for the possibility of using different implementations for the same algorithm. Implementations may differ both in the features of using the properties of the implemented algorithms themselves, and in the features of the computing platforms used.

To be able to analyze the effectiveness of various problem solving options, this chain must be supplemented directly with a description of *Computer* systems, resulting in an extended chain "Problem–Method–Algorithm–Implementation–Computer" [16]. In the future, fixing various fragments of such chains, within the framework of the Algo500 project, it will be possible to choose the most effective solutions for the remaining stages, obtaining effective solutions to many emerging problems.

6   Algo500 Project

The problem of developing a methodology for evaluating the performance of computers has existed for a long time, but its satisfactory solution has not yet been proposed. Supercomputer ratings are an important component in the world of supercomputing. They allow assessing the current state in this area, observing development trends, which can be important when designing and creating new systems. The generally accepted approach for assessing the performance of supercomputers is to analyze data from the Top500 list of the most powerful supercomputers in the world [17]. In this list, all computers are ranked by the performance they achieve when solving systems of linear equations with a dense matrix based on the Linpack [18] benchmark. The list has existed since the beginning of the 90s, contains a lot of interesting information, but is strongly criticized for a completely understandable reason — if in a particular application the solution of systems of linear equations is not a computational core, then it is practically impossible to draw meaningful conclusions for this application based on the data from the list. Several attempts were made to remedy the situation, resulting first in the Graph500 [19,20] list and then HPCG [21,22] list. Graph500 shows the computer's ability to process large graphs, and the properties of the HPCG test determine the conjugate gradient method and work with sparse matrices.

Undoubtedly, these three lists together characterize computing systems much better than one Top500 list. At the same time, of course, it is impossible to call it a full-fledged solution to the problem of evaluating the performance of computers. The main drawback has been preserved — if the application's computational core is not the basic Top500, Graph500 or HPCG algorithm, then it is extremely difficult to draw meaningful conclusions for this application based on the data from these lists.

Existing supercomputer ratings use completely different performance tests and their corresponding different metrics to rank systems, i.e. each of them evaluates the ability of the computing system to cope with its own specific class of problems. To some extent, this reflects the real picture in the field of HPC — supercomputers are designed taking into account real applications that are planned to run on them after commissioning. The variety of ratings of supercomputers helps to evaluate the performance of computing systems from fundamentally different angles and introduce an understanding of which specific computing systems and architectures can better and more efficiently solve certain problems.

At the same time, almost all supercomputer ratings are conducted independently, which makes it difficult to collect data and analyze them to form a single current picture in the field of high-performance computing. Here, the disparity in the presentation of descriptions of the computing systems participating in the ratings is of great importance, which makes it difficult, and in some cases impossible, to qualitatively compare supercomputers with each other.

However, within the framework of this project, a much larger task is being solved — combining within a single platform not two or three, but a significant set of benchmarks and tests implemented on the basis of the algorithms described in the Algowiki encyclopedia for heterogeneous software and hardware platforms. The design of the functional and technological architecture of the Algo500 digital platform [23] was carried out, containing four main blocks:

1. AlgoWiki — description of algorithmic approaches for solving problems;
2. PerfData — source code repository and run results;
3. CompZoo — description of computer systems;
4. Algo500 engine — building selections, custom ratings, etc.

Now, in addition to the built rating, any user will be able to immediately get acquainted with detailed information about the algorithm used in ranking systems. And vice versa, having become familiar with some algorithm, the user of the encyclopedia will be able to see on which computing systems and architectures this algorithm is implemented most efficiently. The traditional ratings of supercomputers tied to specific benchmarks, which are implementations of well-defined algorithms, also fit into the scheme.

At the same time, this approach allows you to go beyond the existing ratings of supercomputers and provides ample opportunities for further development of the platform, combining in a single system more and more ratings that arise on the basis of the most relevant and currently interesting algorithms.

The AlgoWiki encyclopedia contains descriptions of many algorithms, and their number is constantly growing. One section of the description of each algorithm in AlgoWiki involves an analysis of the dynamic properties [24], including a presentation of the performance and efficiency of implementations of a given algorithm obtained for different numbers of processors and different task sizes. Within the framework of the project, a technology has been developed that allows, in the description of each AlgoWiki algorithm, to form its own independent top list, showing the quality of the implementation of this particular algorithm on various computing platforms. Instead of three lists of Top500, Graph500 and HPCG representing only three points on the whole set of algorithms, AlgoWiki's advanced version helps you understand the capabilities of any computer in terms of any described algorithm. Among the algorithms from AlgoWiki, for detailed analysis and comparison, we can take not any, but choose only those that are of interest in the first place. If the required algorithm is not available in AlgoWiki, it can be added by starting the formation of a new rating corresponding to it.

Such an extension of the Top500 methodology within AlgoWiki has a number of additional important nuances. We can not only see the result of comparing the features of the work of various algorithms on different computers, but also analyze and understand the reasons for the results. Detailed descriptions of all algorithms are presented here in AlgoWiki and are always at hand. It is also important that within AlgoWiki it is possible to save not only the results obtained on record-breaking computer configurations and on very large amounts of input data, the range of medium and small values is of considerable interest in practice and is also available for analysis. From this point of view, Top500 ratings for any of the algorithms presented in AlgoWiki will be just the tip of the iceberg of the entire set of data stored in AlgoWiki for each algorithm.

Since the quality of mapping a problem onto a computer architecture largely depends on the specific implementation of the algorithm, each new rating is associated precisely with the concept of "implementation of the algorithm" — a specific source code of a program in some programming language that implements a given algorithm.

An algorithm is a basic building block that can be used to solve many problems. If an algorithm is selected, then its properties and features can be described in the AlgoWiki encyclopedia. But to solve each problem, as a rule, several different algorithmic approaches can be used. Each approach has its own characteristics, and those algorithms that are well suited for one class of computers are far from always suitable for another. Calculation of a definite integral, finding eigenvectors, finding the minimum spanning tree of a graph — for each problem, many algorithms for solving them can be proposed, and each algorithm has its own properties that can be decisive for obtaining an effective implementation on a particular computer system. If even for such familiar problems it is difficult to make an informed choice, it is not easy, what can we say about truly non-trivial options?

When data on the execution of an algorithm on a certain computing system is entered into the AlgoWiki encyclopedia, information about the entire chain from the problem to the computing platform is stored. This gives additional freedom for comparison and analysis. In particular, having data structured in this way, it is possible to form queries to AlgoWiki that allow you to compare:

- computer performance achieved by using different methods for solving the same problem;
- computer performance achieved by using different methods for solving a given problem of a fixed size;
- time to solve a problem of a fixed size when using different methods for solving it;
- computer performance achieved by using different implementations of a given method for solving a given problem;
- time to solve a problem of a fixed size when using different methods for solving it on clusters containing, for example, no more than 128 nodes;
- methods on which this class of computers shows the maximum/minimum/ given efficiency, and many others.

In addition to the analysis based on such parameters as time, performance, efficiency, it is possible to conduct a qualitative analysis of another kind, in particular to find:

- algorithms that are used to solve this problem;
- problems for which this algorithm is used;
- algorithms that are used to solve this problem and have sequential complexity no higher than $O(n^2)$;
- all pairs of method-computer solutions to this problem, in which the method has serial complexity no higher than $O(n^2)$ and parallel complexity no higher than $O(n)$, and the method implementation efficiency on this computer exceeds 40%.

In any links of the above chain "Problem–Method–Algorithm–Implementation –Computer", we can fix the desired values, and change the rest, and build new ratings on this basis or find those combinations that satisfy the specified conditions.

7   Conclusions

The scientific articles presented in AlgoWiki approach papers from scientific journals, which is confirmed by numerous publications with the results of research in the proceedings of Russian and foreign conferences, as well as in articles published in peer-reviewed journals.

The descriptions of the algorithms presented in the AlgoWiki encyclopedia demonstrated the enormous potential of this technology. The described algorithms represent a variety of science areas: linear algebra algorithms, algorithms for working with large graphs, algorithms for modeling quantum systems etc. Despite such significant differences in algorithmic approaches and in the properties of the algorithms themselves, the universal scheme for their description allows us to present a detailed mathematical description of the algorithm, describe its information structure and properties (primarily related to the use of the parallelism resource), analyze the features of its implementation on various architectures, explore its dynamic properties, including locality, scalability, efficiency, and many others, as well as provide specific computation results for various software and hardware platforms.

The development of the project significantly expands the scale of application of the results. This fully applies both to the development of different algorithmic approaches to solving problems, a new approach to estimation, and to the study of methods for analyzing the performance of computing systems (in the Algo500 project). The significance of the tasks set is determined by the fact that for their solution the most significant properties inherent in both algorithms and computer architectures are identified, on the basis of which methods for their joint analysis are developed, which is in demand in many related fields of science and industry.

Acknowledgements. The work on the development of the functionality of the Algo-Wiki system is carried out at Lomonosov Moscow State University with the financial support of the Russian Science Foundation, agreement No. 20-11-20194. The work on the description of implementations of algorithms is supported by Russian Ministry of Science and Higher Education, agreement No. 075-15-2022-284. The research is carried out using the equipment of the shared research facilities of HPC computing resources at Lomonosov Moscow State University [25].

References

1. Open encyclopedia of parallel algorithmic features. http://algowiki-project.org
2. Asanovic, K., Bodik, R., Catanzaro, B.C., et al.: The Landscape of Parallel Computing Research: A View from Berkeley, Report UCB/EECS-2006-183. University California, Berkeley (2006)
3. Heroux, M.A., et al.: Improving performance via Mini-applications. Sandia National Laboratories, Report SAND2009-5574 (2009)
4. Voevodin, V., Voevodin, Vl.: Parallel computing. BHV-Petersburg, St. Petersburg, p. 608(2002)
5. Thrust – parallel algorithms library. https://thrust.github.io/
6. Parallel algorithms of the standard template library – modernescpp.com. https://www.modernescpp.com/index.php/parallel-algorithm-of-the-standard-template-library
7. List of algorithms – Wikipedia. https://en.wikipedia.org/wiki/List_of_algorithms
8. Voevodin, V., Antonov, A., Dongarra, J.: AlgoWiki: an open encyclopedia of parallel algorithmic features. Supercomput. Front. Innov. 1(2), 4–18 (2015). https://doi.org/10.14529/jsfi150101

9. Voevodin, V.: An open AlgoWiki encyclopedia of algorithmic features: from mobile to extreme scale. Numer. Methods Program. 16(1), 99–111 (2015). https://doi.org/10.26089/NumMet.v16r111
10. MediaWiki. https://www.mediawiki.org
11. Wikipedia. https://wikipedia.org
12. Wikimedia foundation. https://wikimediafoundation.org
13. Welcome! – The Apache HTTP Server Project.
14. Antonov, A.S., Maier, R.V.: A new representation of algorithmic approaches in the AlgoWiki encyclopedia. Lobachevskii J. Math. **42**(7), 1483–1491 (2021). https://doi.org/10.1134/S1995080221070039
15. Antonov, A., Frolov, A., Konshin, I., Voevodin, V.: Hierarchical domain representation in the AlgoWiki encyclopedia: from problems to implementations. In: Sokolinsky, L., Zymbler, M. (eds.) PCT 2018. CCIS, vol. 910, pp. 3–15. Springer, Cham (2018). https://doi.org/10.1007/978-3-319-99673-8_1
16. Popov, A., Nikitenko, D., Antonov, A., Voevodin, Vl.: Formal model of problems, methods, algorithms and implementations in the advancing AlgoWiki open encyclopedia. In: CEUR Workshop Proceedings, vol. 2281, pp. 1–11 (2018)
17. Home – — TOP500. https://top500.org
18. Dongarra, J.J., Bunch, J.R., Moler, G.B., Stewart, G.W.: LINPACK Users' Guide. Society for Industrial and Applied Mathematics (1979–1993)
19. Graph 500 — large-scale benchmarks. https://graph500.org
20. Murphy, R.C., Wheeler, K.B., Barrett, B.W., Ang, J.A.: Introducing the Graph 500. Cray User's Group (CUG). 5 May 2010, vol. 19, pp. 45–74 (2010)
21. HPCG Benchmark. https://www.hpcg-benchmark.org
22. Heroux, M., Dongarra, J.: Toward a new metric for ranking high performance computing systems. UTK EECS Technical report and Sandia National Labs Report SAND2013-4744 (2013)
23. Antonov, A.S., Nikitenko, D.A., Voevodin, V.V.: Algo500—a new approach to the joint analysis of algorithms and computers. Lobachevskii J. Math. **41**(8), 1435–1443 (2020). https://doi.org/10.1134/S1995080220080041
24. Antonov, A., Voevodin, Vad., Voevodin, Vl., Teplov, A.: A study of the dynamic characteristics of software implementation as an essential part for a universal description of algorithm properties. In: 24th Euromicro International Conference on Parallel, Distributed, and Network-Based Processing Proceedings, 17th-19th February, pp. 359–363 (2016). https://doi.org/10.1109/PDP.2016.24
25. Voevodin, V., et al.: Supercomputer Lomonosov-2: large scale, deep monitoring and fine analytics for the user community. Supercomput. Front. Innov. 6(2), 4–11 (2019). https://doi.org/10.14529/jsfi190201

Distributed and Cloud Computing

BOINC-Based Volunteer Computing Projects: Dynamics and Statistics

Valentina Ivashko[1(✉)] and Evgeny Ivashko[1,2]

[1] Laboratory for Digital Technologies in Regional Development, KRC of RAS,
Petrozavodsk, Russia
va.lentina97@yandex.ru, ivashko@krc.karelia.ru
[2] Petrozavodsk State University, Petrozavodsk, Russia

Abstract. Citizen science brings together civil crowd resources to help
the scientific community. It is widely recognized as a scientific approach
with huge and global potential with the ability to involve individual volunteers and community groups in tackling large global challenges. In
this way, volunteer computing is a shining example of citizen science. It
is characterized by ease of participation, indifferentiation to geography,
understandable contribution, and many other magnetic issues promoting permanent interest of volunteers. The BOINC community offers a
number of scientific volunteer computing projects to participate, both
fundamental and applied. In this paper we analyze changes in the number and structure of volunteer computing projects, share of fundamental
and applied science, number of volunteers and the role of the Russian
community. This study can help to understand current trends in the
evolution of volunteer computing.

Keywords: Distributed computing · Volunteer computing · Desktop
grid · Citizen science · BOINC

1 Introduction

Citizen science brings together civil crowd resources to help the scientific community. It is widely recognized as a scientific approach with huge and global
potential with the ability to involve different local community groups in tackling
large global challenges.

The past decade has seen a massive growth in the number of citizen science activities and participant volunteers [6]. This growth reflects a number of
phenomena [7]:

1. demand to make research societally relevant,
2. to develop large-scale and long-term monitoring datasets to underpin science
   and planning decisions,
3. increased public awareness of environmental issues,
4. 'enabling' of both technology, (e.g., low cost sensor networks, smartphones)
   and citizen scientists.

V. Voevodin et al. (Eds.): RuSCDays 2022, LNCS 13708, pp. 619–631, 2022.
https://doi.org/10.1007/978-3-031-22941-1_45

In recent years, pandemia of COVID-19 has totally changed the world. Millions of people have turned their minds and views on science. In early 2020, more than 700,000 new participants joined the Folding@home to help in developing an antiviral agent against SARS-CoV-2. The project performance exceeded one exaflops, making Folding@home the first world's exascale system, more powerful than the top 100 supercomputers combined [21].

Paper [4] defines four levels of citizen science participation from 'crowdsourcing' (Level 1, low) through to 'extreme citizen science' (Level 4, high). Under this typology, participatory levels start from data gathering (i.e., Level 1) to fully collaborative (with professional scientists) research involvement which may include defining the research question and scope, data collection and data analysis (Level 4).

Volunteer computing is a shining example of citizen science. It is easy to participate, indifferent to geography, provides understandable of contribution, and many other magnetic issues promoting permanent interest of volunteers. BOINC (Berkeley Open Infrastructure for Network Computing) is the most used software platform for volunteer computing. Many of the world's leading research institutions run large-scale computational projects based on BOINC (e.g., Washington University: Rosetta@home; CERN: LHC@home; University of Oxford: Climateprediction.net and others). In this paper we use terms 'volunteer computing' and 'BOINC-project' as synonyms, since BOINC is standard de-facto for volunteer computing. Unfortunately, this excludes from the consideration the largest non-BOINC volunteer computing project Folding@HOME. This project stays apart since use of its own developed volunteer computing software platform.

In this paper we analyze changes in number and structure of volunteer computing projects, share of fundamental and applied science, number of volunteers and role of Russian community. This study can help in understanding of the current trends in evolution of volunteer computing.

A number of research papers were devoted to studying of BOINC volunteers community (see [11,13–16,20]). However, to the best of our knowledge there are no available systematic reviews of volunteer computing projects.

2 Citizen Science and Volunteer Computing

Citizen science is defined as scientific activities in which the general public participate to some degree in data collection, analysis, and dissemination. Citizen science could make a great contribution to certain domains of science. Meanwhile, it involves broad public participation in research activities, volunteers receive new skills and knowledge. Volunteering of this kind solves the problems of educating the population, popularizing science, and drawing attention to research.

Historically, the application of citizen science is well established within the fields of conservation and environmental monitoring. These mass participation projects have been predominantly in the fields of ecology (e.g., wildlife surveys) and astronomy (e.g., searching for new planets); these two disciplines were the first to identify the potential for significantly increasing the quantity and frequency of observational data by utilizing enthusiastic amateurs [3]. In [18] the authors show that Citizen science is proliferating in the water sciences with increasing public involvement in monitoring water resources, climate variables, water quality, and in mapping and modeling exercises.

In 1990, the National Audubon Society launched its annual Christmas Bird Count project[1]. It is the longest running civilian science project in North America. Another citizen science project, Stardust@home[2], is calling on volunteers to search for images of small interstellar dust collisions. The largest citizen science project of this kind in Russia is *Flora of Russia*[3]. A non-profit Internet project was launched in 2019 by the Herbarium of Moscow State University to prepare an atlas of the Russian flora. More than 25,000 people have uploaded about 1.8 mln observations (as of May 2022) of wild vascular plants from around the country.

Volunteer computing is a good example of citizen science. It is a type of distributed computing in which volunteers donate unused resources of their personal computers to a research project. According to [4], volunteers can be distributed across all the levels of participation. At the most basic level (Level 1), participation is limited to the provision of resources, and the cognitive engagement is minimal. Volunteer computing relies on large number of participants that are engaged at this level. Meanwhile, participants that become committed to the project might move to the second level and assist other volunteers when they encounter technical problems. Highly committed participants might move to the top level (Level 4) and communicate with the scientists who coordinate the project to discuss the results of the analysis and suggest new research directions or even develop a highly effective computing software.

Volunteer computing gives huge computing capacity (potentially on the order of hundreds of ExaFLOPS) at low cost [1]. Volunteer mobile phones, laptops and desktops can be connected to form the equivalent of one huge and powerful virtual supercomputer. By pooling all the idle resources, it is possible to process much faster calculations that would take decades to complete.

BOINC community proposes a wide range of volunteer computing projects to participate. Volunteer computing projects are ranged from searching for signs of extraterrestrial intelligence (SETI@HOME [5]) to crowdsourced drug discovery (SiDock@Home [10]). Among them are both fundamental and applied science. Fundamental volunteer computing projects are aimed at studying the laws governing the behavior and interaction of the basic structures of nature, society and

---

[1] https://www.birdscanada.org/bird-science/christmas-bird-count/.

[2] https://stardustathome.ssl.berkeley.edu/.

[3] https://www.inaturalist.org/projects/flora-rossii-i-kryma-flora-of-russia-and-the-crimea.

thinking. Applied projects aimed at the practical solution of technical and social problems. The purpose of applied projects is the application of fundamental sciences to solve not only cognitive, but also social and practical problems.

The peculiarities of fundamental volunteer computing projects are:

- tasks and results are usually understandable only by experts;
- difficult to connect results with real life;
- difficult to motivate volunteers to participate.

Peculiarities of applied science are:

- tasks and results are understandable for everybody;
- easy to trace results with real life;
- ease of actualization;
- attracts more interest of volunteers.

Our experience shows that applied volunteer computing projects motivate volunteers and attract more new participants, who later contribute their resources to other projects – not only applied, but also to fundamental ones (see, for example, [15]).

The purpose of this work is to analyze the existing projects of volunteer computing based on BOINC. The rest of the paper is organized as follows: in Sect. 3 we describe applied and fundamental volunteer computing projects, their topical areas, number of projects year by year, shortly describe the most popular projects; in Sect. 4 we analyze dynamics in the number of volunteers; finally, Sect. 5 refers to analysis of the statistics of projects originated from Russia. In Sect. 6 we give the conclusion and the final remarks.

3   Volunteer Computing Projects

BOINC was originally developed at University of California, Berkeley for the largest volunteer computing project SETI@home and published in 2002[4]. Later, the developers made the platform available to third-party projects under an Open Source license. Meanwhile, the SETI@Home project, which is one of the first distributed computing projects on the BOINC platform, had shut down its work on March 31, 2020, after more than 20 years of continuous work.

By now, according to the information from the website BOINCstats[5], the total number of BOINC-projects is 118. However, this number shows not only active, working projects, but also inactive – finished, abandond, etc. Figure 1 shows the number of active projects since 2005.

The number of BOINC-projects shows clear dynamics. As one can see, the peak in number of projects was reached in 2014. It took eleven years to reach the peak since BOINC initial release, and today the number of BOINC-projects is rolled back to the level of 2009. This can witnessing lack of interest to volunteer computing among academia and researchers.

---

[4] https://wikipedia.org/wiki/BOINC.
[5] https://www.boincstats.com/.

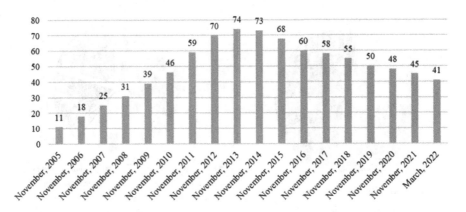

Fig. 1. Number of active projects by year.

For the further analysis we separated applied and fundamental projects (see Fig. 2). Fundamental volunteer computing projects are aimed at studying the laws governing the behavior and interaction of the basic structures of nature, society and thinking. Applied projects are aimed at the practical solution of technical and social problems; the purpose of applied projects is the application of fundamental sciences to solve not only cognitive, but also social and practical problems. Among the BOINC-projects we also distinguish three 'other' (not applied or fundamental) projects: BOINC@TACC[6] – general umbrella project, T.Brada Experimental Grid[7] – serves as a development system for the project administrator, and WUProp@Home[8]. – a non-intensive project that uses Internet-connected computers to collect workunits properties of BOINC projects such as computation time, memory requirements, checkpointing interval or report limit.

As one can see, the BOINC-projects are almost equally shared between fundamental and applied projects. This holds both for active and inactive projects (see Fig. 2).

The BOINC-projects have been implemented in various fields of science. Let us consider topical areas of volunteer computing projects. Figure 3 shows topical areas of applied and fundamental projects. Biology is the main interest for applied projects. Other popular topics are applied mathematics, climate prediction, and materials research. Among the fundamental projects, the main areas of research are astrophysics and mathematics.

The largest BOINC-project is Rosetta@home[9], which studies 3-dimensional shapes of proteins in the hopes of curing diseases [2]. The project also aims to develop at designing new proteins to fight such diseases as HIV, malaria, cancer,

---

[6] https://boinc.tacc.utexas.edu/.
[7] https://boinc.tbrada.eu/.
[8] https://wuprop.boinc-af.org/
[9] https://boinc.bakerlab.org/rosetta/rah/rah_about.php.

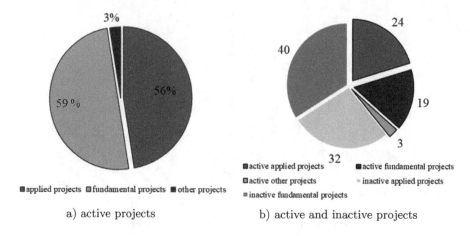

a) active projects   b) active and inactive projects

Fig. 2. Applied and fundamental projects shares.

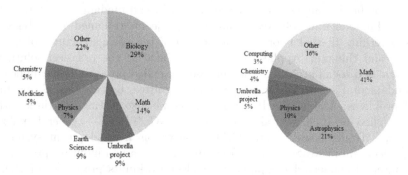

a) topical area of applied projects   b) topical area of fundamental projects

Fig. 3. Topical areas.

and Alzheimer's. The project has been active since October 2005 with more than 1.3 mln volunteers by now.

The World Community Grid[10] is the other largest applied project. Being an umbrella project, it mostly supports research developing better treatments fighting cancer, HIV/AIDS, and understudied tropical diseases. The project has five active studies:

- search for potential treatments for COVID-19;
- forecasting rainfall in Africa;
- search for better treatments to more types of childhood cancer;
- modeling the behavior of molecules called mycolic acids to better understand how they provide protection for tuberculosis bacteria;
- Mapping Cancer Markers.

---

[10] https://www.worldcommunitygrid.org/about/.

4   Volunteers and Performance

Let us consider the dynamics of volunteers number. Quick growth ended by a big fall (possibly, due to the pandemic) and stagnation for the last couple of years (see Fig. 4). The biggest victims of the fall are LHC@home, Einstein@home, Climate prediction and World Community Grid.

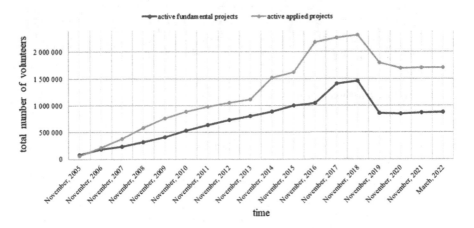

Fig. 4. Dynamics of the total number of volunteers.

The current distribution of volunteers among the projects is given in Fig. 5. We give this distribution in two versions: with and without Rosetta@home to make it possible to compare different projects.

The absolute leader is Rosetta@home, which attracted more than 53% (1.3 mln) of volunteers all over the world. Totally, seven active BOINC-projects accumulates about 90% of all the volunteers (see Fig. 6).

5   Volunteer Computing in Russia

In February 2008, the first Russian volunteer computing project Gerasim@Home was launched. Among all the 118 projects, eleven were organized by Russian scientists. Let us take a look at these projects in more detail:

– _Sidock@home_[11] - launched in Dec, 2020; organizers are:
   • Federal Research Center "Karelian Research Center" of the Russian Academy of Sciences (Petrozavodsk);
   • Faculty of Chemistry and Chemical Technology, University of Maribor (Maribor, Slovenia);
   • University of Ljubljana (Ljubljana, Slovenia);

---

[11] https://www.sidock.si/sidock/.

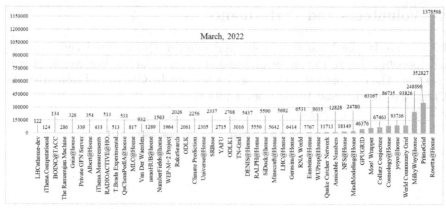

a)with the Rosetta@home project

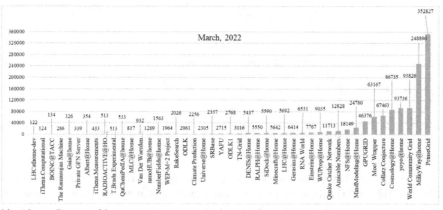

b)without Rosetta@home project

Fig. 5. Number of users in March 2022.

- Internet portal BOINC.Ru (Moscow);
- Federal Research Center "Computer Science and Control" of the Russian Academy of Sciences (Moscow).

An international volunteer computing project aimed at drug discovery. The first mission of the project is to search for potential drugs against the SARS-CoV-2 virus. It started as an extension of the COVID.SI project, designed to engage the BOINC community in drug discovery [10].

– *RakeSearch*[12] - launched in Sep, 2017; organized:
  - Federal Research Center "Karelian Research Center" of the Russian Academy of Sciences (Petrozavodsk);
  - Internet portal BOINC.Ru (Moscow).

---

[12] https://rake.boincfast.ru/rakesearch/.

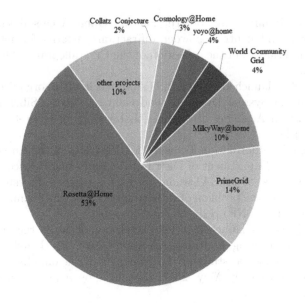

Fig. 6. Distribution the volunteers among the projects.

The project implements an application that selects individual pairs of mutually orthogonal DLSs, which makes it possible to reconstruct their complete orthogonality graphs [8].

- *Acoustics@home*[13] - launched in Mar, 2017, finished in 2020; organizers are:
  - Institute of System Dynamics and Control Theory, Siberian Branch of the Russian Academy of Sciences (Irkutsk);
  - Federal Research Center "Computer Science and Control" of the Russian Academy of Sciences (Moscow);
  - Computing Center of the Russian Academy of Sciences (Moscow).

  The project is aimed at solving inversion problems in underwater acoustics [19].

- *Amicable Numbers*[14] - launched in Jan, 2017; organized by a private person Sergei Chernykh.

  Amicable Numbers is an independent research project to find new friendly numbers. The current goal of the project is to find all friendly pairs with the smallest member $< 10^{20}$.

- *XANSONS for COD*[15] - launched in Nov, 2016, finished in 2020; organizers are:
  - Kurchatov institute (Moscow);
  - Institute for Information Transmission Problems (Kharkevich Institute) (Moscow).

---

[13] https://www.boincstats.com/stats/175/project/detail.

[14] https://sech.me/boinc/Amicable/.

[15] https://www.boincstats.com/stats/169/project/detail.

The project is aimed at construction the Open Access database of simulated x-ray and neutron powder diffraction patterns for nanocrystalline phase of materials from the collection of the Crystallography Open Database (COD) [9].

- *SAT@home*[16] - launched in Oct, 2011, finished in 2016; organizers are:
  - Institute of System Dynamics and Control Theory, Siberian Branch of the Russian Academy of Sciences, Laboratory of Discrete Analysis and Applied Logic (Irkutsk);
  - Institute for Information Transmission Problems of the Russian Academy of Sciences, Department of Distributed Computing (Moscow).

  The scientific goal of the SAT@home project is to solve discrete problems by reducing them to the problem of satisfiability of Boolean formulas in conjunctive normal form (CNF) [12].

- *Gerasim@Home*[17] - launched in Feb, 2008; organized by the Department of Computer Engineering, Southwestern State University (Kursk).

  The project is aimed at studying the properties of diagonal Latin squares [17].

- *ODLK*[18] - launched in May, 2017; organized by a private person Natalia Makarova.

  The project generates a database of canonical forms (CF) of diagonal Latin squares (DLS) of order 10 having orthogonal diagonal Latin squares (ODLS).

- *ODLK1*[19] - launched in Nov, 2017; organized by a private person Natalia Makarova.

  The project ODLK1 continues to solve the problem of BOINC-project ODLK.

- *Optima@home*[20] - launched in Jun, 2011, finished in 2015; organized by Institute for System Analysis RAS.

  The project aimed at researching the effective implementation of optimization methods.

- *USPEX@home*[21] - temporarily stopped; organized by Institute for Information Transmission Problems RAS.

  The project adapted for the search for polymers, nanoclusters, reconstruction of crystalline surfaces.

The very first Russian volunteer computing projects were Gerasim@Home, SAT@home and OPTIMA@HOME (see Fig. 7). The current most popular active fundamental Russian project is Amicable Numbers, which holds more than 12 thousand volunteers (see Fig. 8). The most recent applied project SiDock@home is launched at the end of 2020.

---

[16] https://www.boincstats.com/stats/123/project/detail.
[17] https://gerasim.boinc.ru/.
[18] https://boinc.progger.info/odlk/.
[19] https://boinc.multi-pool.info/latinsquares/.
[20] https://boinc.berkeley.edu/wiki/OPTIMA@HOME.
[21] https://boinc.ru/proekty/proekt-uspexhome/.

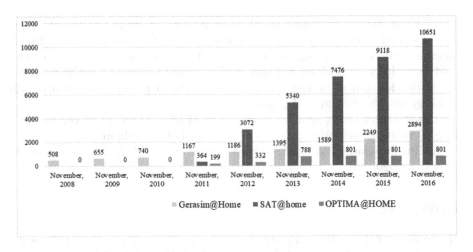

Fig. 7. Number of volunteers of Russian projects (2008–2016).

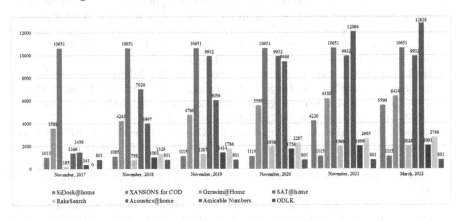

Fig. 8. Number of volunteers of Russian projects (2017–2022).

6 Conclusion and Discussion

Citizen science is a great resource for different domains of science as well as a great resource for science popularization. Volunteer computing is a shining example of citizen science which is able to gather huge resources to solve computationally intensive scientific problems.

This paper presents a quick analysis of volunteer computing development over the years. We were based on BOINCstats website since it is the last working aggregator of BOINC projects' statistics. So, we had to follow its restrictions, such as lack of information about the projects (we noticed missing information on Folding@home project) and performance. Still, available information shows us a rough picture.

The statistics shows significant loss in number of project. Since its tops BOINC-based volunteer computing lost about a half of the projects. This disappointing statistics is a strong trend for the last seven years. The active projects hold parity between fundamental and applied projects. The most active projects are in the domains of biology and math (for applied projects) and math and astrophysics (for fundamental projects).

The statistics shows great changes in size of BOINC volunteer community. In 2019 volunteer computing lost about one third of the volunteers.

In Russia volunteer computing keeps its numbers. There is a new project started in 2020.

References

1. Anderson, D.P.: BOINC: a platform for volunteer computing. J. Grid Comput. **18**(1), 99–122 (2019). https://doi.org/10.1007/s10723-019-09497-9
2. Cusack, C.A., Peck, E., Riolo, M.: Volunteer computing games: merging online casual gaming with volunteer computing. Comput. Sci. **3**(1), 78–83 (2008)
3. Dickinson, J., Zuckerberg, B., Bonter, D.: Citizen science as an ecological research tool: challenges and benefits. Annu. Rev. Ecol. Syst. **41**, 149–172 (2010). https://doi.org/10.1146/annurev-ecolsys-102209-144636
4. Haklay, M.: Citizen science and volunteered geographic information: overview and typology of participation. In: Sui, D., Elwood, S., Goodchild, M. (eds.) Crowdsourcing Geographic Knowledge, pp. 105–122. Springer, Netherlands, Dordrecht (2013). https://doi.org/10.1007/978-94-007-4587-2_7
5. Korpela, E., Werthimer, D., Anderson, D., Cobb, J., Leboisky, M.: SETI@ home-massively distributed computing for SETI. Comput. Sci. Eng. **3**(1), 78–83 (2001)
6. Kosmala, M., Wiggins, A., Swanson, A., Simmons, B.: Assessing data quality in citizen science. Front. Ecol. Environ. **14**, 551–560 (2016). https://doi.org/10.1002/fee.1436
7. Lee, K.A., Lee, J.R., Bell, P.: A review of citizen science within the earth sciences: potential benefits and obstacles. Proc. Geol. Assoc. **131**(6), 605–617 (2020). https://doi.org/10.1016/j.pgeola.2020.07.010, https://www.sciencedirect.com/science/article/pii/S0016787820300730
8. Manzyuk, M., Nikitina, N., Vatutin, E.: Start-up and the results of the volunteer computing project RakeSearch. In: Voevodin, V., Sobolev, S. (eds.) RuSCDays 2019. CCIS, vol. 1129, pp. 725–734. Springer, Cham (2019). https://doi.org/10.1007/978-3-030-36592-9_59
9. Neverov, V., Khrapov, N.: XANSONS for COD: a new small BOINC project in crystallography. Open Eng. **8**, 102–108 (2018). https://doi.org/10.1515/eng-2018-0014
10. Nikitina, N., Manzyuk, M., Jukić, M., Podlipnik, Č, Kurochkin, I., Albertian, A.: Toward crowdsourced drug discovery: start-up of the volunteer computing project SiDock@home. In: Voevodin, V., Sobolev, S. (eds.) Supercomputing, pp. 513–524. Springer International Publishing, Cham (2021). https://doi.org/10.1007/978-3-030-92864-3_39
11. Nov, O., Anderson, D., Arazy, O.: Volunteer computing: A model of the factors determining contribution to community-based scientific research, pp. 741–750 (2010). https://doi.org/10.1145/1772690.1772766

12. Semenov, A., Zaikin, O., Kochemazov, S.: Finding effective SAT Partitionings via black-box optimization. In: Pardalos, P.M., Rasskazova, V., Vrahatis, M.N. (eds.) Black Box Optimization, Machine Learning, and No-Free Lunch Theorems. SOIA, vol. 170, pp. 319–355. Springer, Cham (2021). https://doi.org/10.1007/978-3-030-66515-9_11

13. Tishchenko, V.: Models of patterns of behavior of the participants of BOINC.RU community (in Russian) (2016). https://ceur-ws.org/Vol-1787/468-475-paper-81.pdf

14. Tishchenko, V., Prochko, A.: Statistical analysis of communications of participants of virtual community BOINC.RU (in Russian) (2018). https://doi.org/10.14357/20718632180308, https://doi.org/10.14357/20718632180308

15. Tishchenko, V.: Coopetition strategy in volunteer computing: the example of collaboration online in BOINC.RU community. Comput. Sci. Inf. Technol. **6**(3), 31–39 (2018). https://doi.org/10.13189/csit.2018.060301

16. Tishchenko, V., Prochko, A.: Russian participants in BOINC-based volunteer computing projects the. activity statistics (in Russian). Comput. Res. Model. **7**, 727–734 (2015)

17. Vatutin, E., Belyshev, A., Nikitina, N., Manzuk, M.: Evaluation of efficiency of using simple transformations when searching for orthogonal diagonal Latin squares of order 10. In: Jordan, V., Filimonov, N., Tarasov, I., Faerman, V. (eds.) HPCST 2020. CCIS, vol. 1304, pp. 127–146. Springer, Cham (2020). https://doi.org/10.1007/978-3-030-66895-2_9

18. Walker, D., Smigaj, M., Tani, M.: The benefits and negative impacts of citizen science applications to water as experienced by participants and communities. Wiley Interdisc. Rev.: Water **8**, e1488 (2020). https://doi.org/10.1002/wat2.1488

19. Zaikin, O., Petrov, P., Posypkin, M., Bulavintsev, V., Kurochkin, I.: Using volunteer computing for sound speed profile estimation in underwater acoustics. In: Proceedings of the Third International Conference BOINC:FAST 2017, vol. 3(1), pp. 43–48 (2017)

20. Zhukova, T., Tishchenko, V.: Volunteer computing in Russia: the empirical model of motivation factors for participation in VC-projects. Obshchestvennye nauki i sovremennost **5**, 86–96 (2019). https://doi.org/10.31857/s086904990006564-2

21. Zimmerman, M.I., et al.: SARS-CoV-2 simulations go exascale to capture spike opening and reveal cryptic pockets across the proteome. bioRxiv (2020). https://doi.org/10.1101/2020.06.27.175430, https://www.biorxiv.org/content/early/2020/10/07/2020.06.27.175430

Desktop Grid as a Service Concept

Evgeny Ivashko[1,2]([✉])

[1] Institute of Applied Mathematical Research, Karelian Research Center
of the Russian Academy of Sciences, Pushkinskaya 11, 185910 Petrozavodsk, Russia
ivashko@krc.karelia.ru
[2] Petrozavodsk State University, Lenina 33, 185035 Petrozavodsk, Russia

Abstract. Cloud Computing brings a lot of benefits to its consumers. Adoption of Cloud Computing technologies to Desktop Grid-based high-throughput computing promises better usability and flexibility, on-demand scalability, improved control and higher performance. In this paper a Desktop Grid as a Service concept is presented. We propose the Desktop Grid as a Service definition, describe three main services related to SaaS, PaaS and IaaS, and present a high-level architecture.

Keywords: Distributed computing · Desktop grid · BOINC · Cloud computing · Software as a service

1 Desktop Grid and Cloud Computing

Cloud Computing has become a huge step in the evolution of Information Technologies. It brings a lot of benefits to its consumers with virtually unlimited computing and storage resources, extremely high flexibility and reliability, and on-demand scalability at low cost.

National Institute of Standards and Technology (abbr. NIST, USA) defines Cloud Computing as a model for enabling convenient, on-demand network access to a shared pool of configurable computing resources (e.g., networks, servers, storage, applications, and services) that can be rapidly provisioned and released with minimal management effort or service provider interaction[1].

The following inherent characteristics of Cloud Computing are employed to serve its stakeholders:

- Provision of on-demand self-service: multiple computing capabilities such as server time, storage or network bandwidth can be unilaterally automatically provisioned as needed.
- Broad network access: services are accessible through various heterogeneous platforms (such as workstations, tablets, mobile phones, and laptops) using Internet or LAN.
- Capabilities of resources pooling: accessible computing resources (such as memory, processing, storage, and bandwidth) are pooled together to serve multiple clients. The resources are dynamically assigned and/or reassigned as needed according to demands.

---

[1] https://www.nist.gov/programs-projects/nist-cloud-computing-program-nccp.

© The Author(s), under exclusive license to Springer Nature Switzerland AG 2022
V. Voevodin et al. (Eds.): RuSCDays 2022, LNCS 13708, pp. 632–643, 2022.
https://doi.org/10.1007/978-3-031-22941-1_46

- Rapid elasticity: computing resources (such as memory, processing, storage, and bandwidth) can be elastically provisioned and released according to demands; computing resources are seemed to be unlimited.
- Measured value of service: metering capabilities are employed for automatic resources control and optimization, appropriate to the type of used service.

There are three main types of cloud service (or referred sometimes as cloud service models or cloud computing service models)[2]:

- SaaS, or software as a service, is on-demand access to ready-to-use, cloud-hosted application software.
- PaaS, or platform as a service, is on-demand access to a ready-to-use, complete, cloud-hosted platform for applications development, running, management and maintaining.
- IaaS, or infrastructure as a service, is on-demand access to cloud-hosted physical and virtual servers, storage and networking - the backend IT infrastructure for running applications and workloads in the cloud.

One of the most valuable benefits of cloud services is employing of Service Level Agreements (abbr. SLA). SLA is the key agreement between the consumer and cloud service provider; it binds them for a specific time period with the commitment of used services. Service Level Agreement guarantees Quality of Service (abbr. QoS), QoS is one of the SLA's main parameters to perform a trusted relationship. QoS parameters such as trust, security, privacy, resource management, risk management etc. are combined together to form a viable SLA between a consumer and service provider.

In this paper we aimed at hybridization of Cloud Computing and Desktop Grid technologies to develop a Desktop Grid as a Service concept. Growing computing power of personal computers (common computer nodes in volunteer computing) and speeding up regular Internet connection, high-throughput computing with use of Desktop Grid technologies more and more raises its potential.

Bu definition, Desktop Grid is referred to as a distributed high-throughput computing system which uses idle resources of non-dedicated geographically distributed computing nodes connected over regular network. The regular computing nodes of a Desktop Grid are desktop and laptop computers of volunteers, which are connected over the regular Internet (this concept is called Volunteer computing) or organizational workstations connected over local area network (this concept is called Enterprise Desktop Grid) [9].

Desktop Grid computing gives huge computing capacity with low costs, but raises new challenges related to high computing nodes heterogeneity, their low reliability and availability, etc. The potential accessible computing power of Volunteer computing is on the order of hundreds of ExaFLOPS [1]. There are a number of middleware software systems implementing Desktop Grid technologies: BOINC, Condor, XtremWeb, and others (see [19] for the deeper analysis). Defacto, BOINC (Berkeley Open Infrastructure for Network Computing) is the standard and the most popular platform for volunteer computing.

---

[2] https://www.ibm.com/cloud/learn/iaas-paas-saas.

One can enumerate the following advantages of Desktop Grid:

- ease of deployment, running, management and support,
- low costs,
- huge scalability and potential peak performance,
- ease of software development, management and support,
- etc.,

and disadvantages:

- low speed connection between the computing nodes and the server,
- low computational power of separate nodes,
- high software and hardware heterogeneity,
- no availability and computing status information,
- lack of trust to computing nodes,
- and low reliability of computing nodes.

Desktop Grids are limited by "bag-of-tasks" problems, which have independent parallelism and low data/compute ratio (the examples are combinatorics, parameter sweep optimization and Monte-Carlo simulations,). That is why Desktop Grids are less widespread than computing clusters (supercomputers) and Computational Grids. Still, Cloud Computing promises to improve some of the Desktop Grid characteristics and eliminate some of its disadvantages.

Both Cloud Computing and Desktop Grid concepts are beneficial to their stakeholders. Combination of these technologies promises additional benefits such as better usability and flexibility, on-demand scalability, improved control and higher performance. The most natural way of Desktop Grid and Cloud computing paradigms combination is to provide high-throughput computing as a cloud service.

In this paper a 'Desktop Grid as a Service' concept is presented. First, we give a summary of the approaches of Desktop Grid and Cloud Computing hybridization. Then, we propose the Desktop Grid as a Service definition and describe three main services of cloud high-performance computing (see Subsect. 3.1). We also present a high-level architecture (see Subsect. 3.2) and provide an extended description of Desktop Grid as a Service stakeholders (see Subsect. 3.3). This concept could become the next step in the evolution and advancement of Desktop Grids.

2 Desktop Grid and Cloud Computing Hybridization Approaches Review

Both computing tools – Desktop Grid and Cloud Computing – have their own advantages, so there are a number of works aimed at hybridization of the approaches. The guiding idea is to construct a flexible, reliable and user-friendly Cloud service employed powerful and cheap Desktop Grid computing resources.

In paper [10], based on analysis of existing research works, we presented a short comparative survey on Desktop Grid and Cloud Computing hybridization approaches. There are four main ways are considered: (1) extension of a Cloud by Desktop Grid's nodes; (2) extension of a Desktop Grid by Cloud nodes; (3) implementation of Cloud services on top of Desktop Grid's nodes; and (4) implementation of a high-throughput computing service based on Cloud Computing principles:

1. Extension of a Desktop Grid using a Cloud. This first approach tries to extend a Desktop Grid using Cloud resources. The background idea is following. Desktop Grid computing nodes are unreliable and could leave without announcing this to the server. This raises a huge problem, especially in case of the second phase of computation (completion of the last tasks of a computing experiment, see [10,11]). One could use Cloud resources to improve reliability and speedup the computations, even to provide a high level SLA with low costs.

2. Extension of a Cloud using a Desktop Grid resources. Cloud resources are much more expensive than the Desktop Grid's ones. Therefore, one could use Desktop Grid' computing nodes to grow up a Cloud, improving economics of provide services still keeping high level of SLA. The papers used this approach are [2,20] and [12].

3. Implementation of a Cloud basing on Desktop Grid resources. This is the direct evolution of the Desktop Grid concept and one of the most attractive ideas. One implements a Cloud basing on Desktop Grid' unreliable computing infrastructure. For example, a Desktop Cloud platform can run bundles of virtual machines using idle resources of non-dedicated workstations. The platform of such type executes virtual machines along with the applications running by the users in their desktops. This requires reconstruction of internal Cloud subsystems (such as billing subsystem, auditing, etc.) to dynamic and unreliable computing network. UnaCloud is on of the most advanced platforms (see [3,8,16–18]) and Cloud@Home[3] [4–7] is another. Another example is cuCloud presented in [13] which is based on virtual machines. One more example presents Volunteer Computing as a Service (VCaaS) based Edge Computing infrastructure [14]. In the paper the authors proposed and discussed a three layer Volunteer Computing as a Service based Edge Computing infrastructure. The proposed volunteer Edge computing architecture is a blend of Volunteer Computing, Mobile Computing, IoT, and Cloud Computing.

4. Implementation of a high-throughput computing Cloud service. The most natural way of Desktop Grid and Cloud computing paradigms hybridization is to provide high-throughput computing as a cloud service.

5. Other ways, such as extension of Desktop Grids to mobile devices basing on Cloud Computing principles [15] and development of mobile cloud computing model (Mobile Computing).

Among the described approaches, we consider providing high-throughput computing as a Cloud service as the most promising and beneficial. We use this approach to develop a Desktop Grid as a Service concept.

---

[3] seems to be nondeveloping.

3   Desktop Grid as a Service

In this section we describe a Desktop Grid as a Service concept, its workflow, implementation of three main services (SaaS, PaaS and IaaS) based on Desktop Grid as a Service, and its stakeholders.

3.1   Desktop Grid as a Service Concept

The Desktop Grid as a Service concept is aimed at adoption of the best practices in Cloud Computing to use with high-throughput computing based on Desktop Grid. This concept we build around high-throughput computing projects running with help of Desktop Grid as a Service.

The name "Desktop Grid as a Service" reflects combination of Desktop Grid and Cloud Computing technologies. As a Desktop Grid, it is aimed at high-throughput computing using idle resources of non-dedicated geographically distributed computing nodes connected over regular network. From the other side, as a Cloud Computing, it provides convenient on-demand access to a shared pool of configurable computing resources (computing nodes).

Thus, in coordination with NIST Cloud Computing definition, we define Desktop Grid as a Service as a model for enabling convenient, on-demand network access to a shared pool of configurable computing resources (computing nodes) gathered from idle resources of non-dedicated geographically distributed computing nodes connected over regular network that can be rapidly provisioned and released with minimal management effort or service provider interaction. We define three main services provided by Desktop Grid as a Service:

- Software as a Service (SaaS): providing high-throughput computing software to an end user. A user deploys a pre-defined project than runs on top of Desktop Grid as a Service. This software includes application for supported platforms, input files, work generator, assimilator, scheduler, validator, transitioner, and file deleter, as well as preprocessing and visualization tools if needed. A special type of software, such as high-throughput virtual screening, for example, together with necessary additional resources (databases of ligands), are provided to a user. Use of the software is restricted by running the application with user-specific input data. All the workflow related to high-throughput computing, task scheduling, interaction with computing nodes, etc. is hidden from the user.
- Platform as a Service (PaaS): gives to a user capabilities of implementation a Desktop Grid application, provides a needed network of computing nodes, solves the problems of tasks scheduling, and infrastructure control. A user employs the pre-defined project infrastructure (computing nodes, scheduler) to develop and implement an own project. This includes the need to develop and maintain an application for all the supported platforms, but eliminates the need to develop and support an own computing network.
- Infrastructure as a Service (IaaS): gives a user capabilities of a distributed computing network construction, control of tasks scheduling and other low-level issues of Desktop Grid. Still, a Desktop Grid as a Service implements

rights differentiation, accounting, information security, and control. A user employs the service' resources and control panel to implement a Desktop Grid. This includes the need to construct a computing nodes network as well as develop an application, scheduler, etc. This way is the most similar to development of an own Desktop Grid but also gives unified access to a Desktop Grid control (including opportunities to use pre-defined resources scheduler, monitoring, statistics visualization, runtime estimation tools and so on).

Figure 1 depicts the pyramid of services.

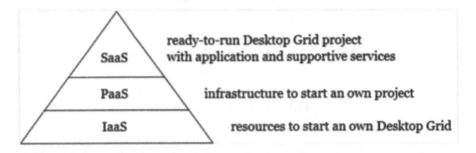

Fig. 1. Pyramid of services

One more issue related to Cloud Computing is SLA (Service Level Agreement): Desktop Grid as a Service should have internal tools to provide quality control: records keeping on resources availability, computing complexity, computing infrastructure usage, and so on.

Finally, one more analogy to Cloud Computing is deployment models related to the sources of computing power, i.e. a Desktop Grid as a Service project could use one of the models:

- *public*: use of Volunteer Computing resources, provided by volunteers and therefore use of computing nodes of low reliability, availability and trust. Also, the project owner needs to make publicity to the project, publish notes on the initial problem and the final results.
- *private*: similar to Enterprise Desktop Grid, use of computing nodes with high availability, reliability and trust, controlled by the project owner.
- *community*: use of resources delegated to a community of any kind, such as "umbrella projects" sharing the same computing resources to support different, for example, biomedical projects.
- *hybrid*: hybrid approach which uses two or more different approaches.

Figure 2 depicts the summary of deployment models.

Being a project owner, one can also be the same time an owner (administrator or manager) of computing nodes. In this case, one should connect its computing nodes to private (Enterprise Desktop Grid) or public/community use.

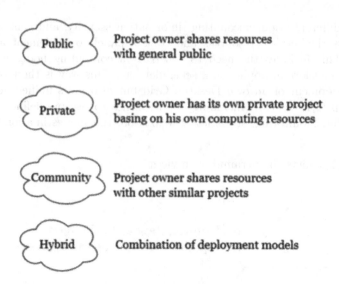

Fig. 2. Deployment models

The concept described above allows to make a combination of advantages both Desktop Grid and Cloud Computing, provide to a project owner low barrier of entry into high-throughput computing.

3.2 Architecture

Figure 3 presents an overview of the Desktop Grid as a Service architecture, which identifies the main subsystems of the service. The diagram depicts a generic high-level architecture and is intended to facilitate the understanding of the requirements, uses, characteristics and standards of Desktop Grid as a Service.

On the top level Desktop Grid as a Service supports use of heterogeneous computing resources by project owners over network, which is Internet or LAN (the latter in some cases of Enterprise Desktop Grid).

An entry point of a project owner is a *Project management subsystem*. It gives access to services of different types (SaaS, PaaS, IaaS) and available computing resources, management of the current projects, their statistics, visualization tools, scheduler, work generator, validator, etc.

Work with heterogeneous distributed computing nodes is hidden by the *Resource abstraction and control layer*. This subsystem is in charge of employing different types of nodes: from regular personal computers to Clouds, computing clusters and service Grids, other Desktop Grids, including Enterprise Desktop Grid, and even other implementations of Desktop Grid as a Service. This layer also collects the data related to reliability and availability of computing nodes, their performance and other characteristics.

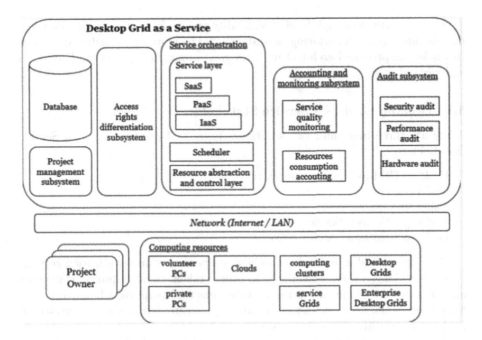

Fig. 3. Desktop Grid as a Service architecture

Service orchestration subsystem performs all the work needed to organize heterogeneous computing nodes into high-level services SaaS, PaaS and IaaS. With it, the service-level scheduler balances the load on the whole pool of computing nodes between the different projects. On the next stage, project-level schedulers distribute the tasks among their available nodes. Such a hierarchical model provides high level of abstraction and independence of different service-level and project-level subsystems and modules.

The two other subsystems – *Accounting and monitoring subsystem* and *Audit subsystem* – play important role in providing needed level of quality of service (QoS) and compliance with possible Service Level Agreement (SLA). QoS and SLA are not commonly used in the domain of scientific computing or high-throughput computing. But this is a mandatory step towards predictable service meeting business needs which could be used to extend widespread of high-throughput computing usage in applied science.

Accounting and monitoring subsystem gathers information on resources consumption. While *Resource abstraction and control layer* gathers node-level information on availability and reliability, *Accounting and monitoring subsystem* performs service-level analysis on resources consumption (including usage effectiveness) and service quality.

Finally, *Audit subsystem* performs extended audit of security, performance and hardware status. This subsystem gives valuable information needed to ensure sustainability of Desktop Grid as a Service.

In order to provide high-level of scalability and performance, *Audit subsystem* and *Accounting and monitoring subsystem* could be moved to distributed servers. In whole, the proposed architecture gives great opportunities to both horizontal and vertical scaling.

3.3   Desktop Grid as a Service Stakeholders

There are three main and two additional types of Desktop Grid as a Service stakeholders:

- Desktop Grid as a Service provider,
- project owner,
- computing node owner,
- Desktop Grid as a Service auditor,
- Desktop Grid as a Service broker.

A Desktop Grid as a Service provider is a person or an organization responsible for making a service available to other stakeholders. A provider acquires and manages the computing infrastructure, runs the operating software required for providing the services, and makes arrangement to deliver the services to the project owners through network access.

For Software as a Service, the provider deploys, configures, maintains and updates the software applications on an infrastructure and related input files or auxiliary utilities so that the services are provisioned at the expected service levels to project owners. The provider of SaaS is responsible for managing and controlling the applications and the infrastructure, while the project owners have limited administrative control of the applications.

For PaaS, the provider manages the computing infrastructure for the platform and runs the Desktop Grid software that provides the components of the system, such as runtime software execution stack (Desktop Grid middleware), databases, and other middleware components. The PaaS project owner has control over the applications and possibly some hosting environment settings, but has no or limited access to the infrastructure underlying the project such as Desktop Grid middleware, computing nodes, operating system, or storage.

For IaaS, the provider controls the physical computing resources underlying the service, including the servers, networks, storage and hosting infrastructure as well as operating system. The provider can give to an IaaS project owner some access to operating system environments and a Desktop Grid middleware or a virtual machine to deploy individual middleware instance for a separate Desktop Grid deployment.

The project owner is the principal stakeholder for the Desktop Grid as a Service. A project owner represents a person or organization that with help of provider uses resources of computing node owners to perform high-throughput computing. A project owner browses the service catalog from a provider, requests the appropriate service, sets up service contracts with the provider, and uses the service. In case of commercial relationship the project owner may be billed for the service provisioned, and needs to arrange payments accordingly.

Project owners of SaaS run their projects with provided applications. Their responsibility is for configuring application and auxiliary utilities, provide input data. Project owners of PaaS employ the Desktop Grid middleware and execution resources provided by a provider to develop, test, deploy and manage the applications hosted in a Desktop Grid as a Service environment. Project owners of IaaS have access to underlying Desktop Grid middleware to setup and configure or even can deploy a separate Desktop Grid on a virtual machine of a provider.

A computing node owner is a person or organization which provides computing power having all the control over hardware and system operating software. A computing node owner has to install client Desktop Grid software which uses sandboxing to run an application.

A Desktop Grid as a Service auditor is an optional stakeholder, which appears in case of business-relations in Desktop Grid as a Service to verify conformance to standards (SLA) in terms of security controls, privacy impact, performance, etc.

A Desktop Grid as a Service broker is one more optional stakeholder which manages the use, performance and delivery of services and negotiates relationships between providers and project owners or computing node owners. A broker can provide services of two types:

– Service Intermediation and Arbitrage: a broker enhances a given service by improving some specific capability and providing value-added services to other stakeholders. The improvement can be in providing more advanced applications or auxiliary utilities, managing access to services, identity management, performance reporting, enhanced security, etc. This includes flexibility to choose services from multiple agencies. The broker, for example, can use a credit-scoring service to measure and select an agency with the best score.
– Service Aggregation: a broker combines and integrates multiple services into one or more new services with providing data integration and ensuring the secure data movement between the project owner and multiple providers.

4 Conclusion

Cloud Computing brings a lot of benefits to its consumers. Adoption of Cloud Computing technologies to Desktop Grid-based high-throughput computing promises better usability and flexibility, on-demand scalability, improved control and higher performance.

In this paper we propose a Desktop Grid as a Service concept, which is based on drawing analogies with the best practices of Cloud Computing. We give the formal definition of Desktop Grid as a Service and describe a pyramid of three main services: SaaS, PaaS and IaaS. Each service type endows a project owner specific capabilities, responsibilities and control level. There are four deployment types related to the sources of computing power: private, public, hybrid, and community. They are also draws analogy to Cloud Computing and cover Volunteer computing and Enterprise Desktop Grid as well as their combinations. We identify five types of stakeholders with their specific roles and responsibilities.

We believe the proposed Desktop Grid as a Service concept could serve evolution and advancement of Desktop Grid.

References

1. Anderson, D.P.: BOINC: a platform for volunteer computing. J. Grid Comput. **18**(1), 99–122 (2019). https://doi.org/10.1007/s10723-019-09497-9
2. Andrzejak, A., Kondo, D., Anderson, D.: Exploiting non-dedicated resources for cloud computing. In: 2010 IEEE Network Operations and Management Symposium, NOMS 2010, pp. 341–348 (2010). https://doi.org/10.1109/NOMS.2010. 5488488
3. Chavarriaga, J., Forero-González, C., Padilla-Agudelo, J., Muñoz, A., Cáliz-Ospino, R., Castro, H.: Scaling the deployment of virtual machines in UnaCloud. In: Mocskos, E., Nesmachnow, S. (eds.) CARLA 2017. CCIS, vol. 796, pp. 399–413. Springer, Cham (2018). https://doi.org/10.1007/978-3-319-73353-1_28
4. Cunsolo, V.D., Distefano, S., Puliafito, A., Scarpa, M.: Volunteer computing and desktop cloud: the cloud@home paradigm. In: 2009 Eighth IEEE International Symposium on Network Computing and Applications, pp. 134–139 (2009). https:// doi.org/10.1109/NCA.2009.41
5. Cuomo, A., Di Modica, G., Distefano, S., Rak, M., Vecchio, A.: The cloud@home architecture - building a cloud infrastructure from volunteered resources, pp. 424–430 (2011)
6. Distefano, S., Puliafito, A.: Cloud@home: toward a volunteer cloud. IT Prof. **14**, 27–31 (2012). https://doi.org/10.1109/MITP.2011.111
7. Distefano, S., et al.: QoS management in cloud@home infrastructures, pp. 190–197 (2011). https://doi.org/10.1109/CyberC.2011.40
8. Garcés, N., et al.: Analysis of Gromacs MPI using the opportunistic cloud infrastructure UnaCloud. In: 2012 Sixth International Conference on Complex, Intelligent, and Software Intensive Systems, pp. 1001–1006 (2012). https://doi.org/10. 1109/CISIS.2012.142
9. Ivashko, E.: Desktop grid and cloud computing: short survey. In: Voevodin, V., Sobolev, S. (eds.) RuSCDays 2021. CCIS, vol. 1510, pp. 445–456. Springer, Cham (2021). https://doi.org/10.1007/978-3-030-92864-3_34
10. Ivashko, E., Nikitina, N.: Replication of "Tail" computations in a desktop grid project. In: Voevodin, V., Sobolev, S. (eds.) RuSCDays 2020. CCIS, vol. 1331, pp. 611–621. Springer, Cham (2020). https://doi.org/10.1007/978-3-030-64616-5_52
11. Kovács, J., Marosi, A., Visegradi, A., Farkas, Z., Kacsuk, P., Lovas, R.: Boosting gLite with cloud augmented volunteer computing. Future Gener. Comput. Syst. **43**, 12–23 (2015). https://doi.org/10.1016/j.future.2014.10.005
12. Marshall, P., Keahey, K., Freeman, T.: Improving utilization of infrastructure clouds. In: 2011 11th IEEE/ACM International Symposium on Cluster, Cloud and Grid Computing, pp. 205–214 (2011). https://doi.org/10.1109/CCGrid.2011.56
13. Mengistu, T.M., Alahmadi, A.M., Alsenani, Y., Albuali, A., Che, D.: cuCloud: Volunteer computing as a service (VCaaS) system. In: Luo, M., Zhang, L.-J. (eds.) CLOUD 2018. LNCS, vol. 10967, pp. 251–264. Springer, Cham (2018). https:// doi.org/10.1007/978-3-319-94295-7_17

14. Mengistu, T.M., Albuali, A., Alahmadi, A., Che, D.: Volunteer cloud as an edge computing enabler. In: Zhang, T., Wei, J., Zhang, L.-J. (eds.) EDGE 2019. LNCS, vol. 11520, pp. 76–84. Springer, Cham (2019). https://doi.org/10.1007/978-3-030-23374-7_6

15. Noor, T.H., Zeadally, S., Alfazi, A., Sheng, Q.Z.: Mobile cloud computing: challenges and future research directions. J. Netw. Comput. Appl. **115**, 70–85 (2018). https://doi.org/10.1016/j.jnca.2018.04.018. https://www.sciencedirect.com/science/article/pii/S1084804518301504

16. Ortiz, N., Garcés, N., Sotelo, G., Méndez, D., Castillo-Coy, F., Castro, H.: Multiple services hosted on the opportunistic infrastructure UnaCloud. In: Proceedings of the Joint GISELA-CHAIN Conference (2012)

17. Osorio, J.D., Castro, H., Brasileiro, F.: Perspectives of UnaCloud: an opportunistic cloud computing solution for facilitating research. In: 2012 12th IEEE/ACM International Symposium on Cluster, Cloud and Grid Computing (CCGRID 2012), pp. 717–718 (2012). https://doi.org/10.1109/CCGrid.2012.14

18. Plazas Montañez, L.F., et al.: Opportunistic IaaS platform based on containers. B.S. thesis, Uniandes (2019)

19. Rahmany, M., Sundararajan, A., Zin, A.: A review of desktop grid computing middlewares on non-dedicated resources. J. Theor. Appl. Inf. Technol. **98**(10), 1654–1663 (2020)

20. Sukhoroslov, O.: Integration of Everest platform with BOINC-based desktop grids. In: CEUR Workshop Proceedings of the Conference BOINC: FAST 2017, pp. 102–107 (2017)

Distributed Computing for Gene Network Expansion in R Environment

Diana Dolgaleva[1,2]($\boxtimes$) (ID), Camilla Pelagalli[4], Enrico Blanzieri[3,4] (ID),
Valter Cavecchia[3], Sergey Astafiev[1,2] (ID), and Alexander Rumyantsev[1,2] (ID)

[1] Institute of Applied Mathematical Research, Karelian Research Centre of RAS,
Petrozavodsk, Russia
ar0@krc.karelia.ru
[2] Petrozavodsk State University, Petrozavodsk, Russia
abcdi_do@mail.ru
[3] CNR-IMEM, Trento, Italy
{enrico.blanzieri,valter.cavecchia}@unitn.it
[4] DISI, University of Trento, Trento, Italy
camilla.pelagalli@studenti.unitn.it

Abstract. In this paper we discuss preliminary results of experiments of distributed gene network expansion. As a proof of concept, we use the celebrated PC algorithm together with the novel RBOINC package within R environment, which turns out to be a convenient way of massively parallel numerical experiments conduction. Data parallelism at the distributed computing level, and integrated multicore computations on the host level altogether provide significant speedup for the in-silico causal relationship analysis.

Keywords: Distributed computing · RBOINC · Causal relationship · Gene network expansion

1 Introduction

Causal relation discovery from observational data is a research topic that has recently attracted attention in the artificial intelligence and machine learning [10] communities. Finding direct causal relationships between variables of interest [19] can impact the analysis of the data originated in scientific and industrial practice. The PC-algorithm [12] infers causal relationships between variables by means of Conditional Independence (CI) tests. PC-algorithm application permits to discover direct causal relationships between correlated variables and it has been applied to a wide range of domains including Yeast gene expression data [13] and QSAR/QSPR analyses [18]. This comes, however, at the price of a computationally consuming task which does not allow to perform analysis over relatively large genes. To overcome the computational limitations of the PC algorithm, a few capabilities are used, including usage of the distributed computing platforms.

V. Voevodin et al. (Eds.): RuSCDays 2022, LNCS 13708, pp. 644–656, 2022.
https://doi.org/10.1007/978-3-031-22941-1_47

The causal relation discovery is one step in the gene regulatory network study, which allow to analyze in-silico the important processes of cell functioning. In the present paper, we address a specific problem that appears in the gene network expansion post-processing phase which requires to run PC algorithm in order to obtain causal relationships between the genes in the network. This phase requires a large amount of computational resources and needs to be performed in parallel way. Moreover, in order to equip the bioinformatics specialists with necessary tools for subsequent analysis, the results may be made available in R environment, which contains a significant amount of useful packages in the `Bioconductor` package distribution system. As such, this research is a case-study that demonstrates the capabilities of distributed computing available for researchers with BOINC [1] framework and `RBOINC` software [6] within R environment, which is the main contribution of the present paper.

The structure of the paper is as follows. In Sect. 2 we introduce the application side of the problem. Gene expansion is discussed in Sect. 2.1 and details on the `gene@home` project established for local gene network analysis is described in Sect. 2.2. The main object of the present study, i.e. the post-processing of the gene expansion list, is discussed in Sect. 2.3. In Sect. 3 we discuss the distributed computing software used for the present study (Sects. 3.1 and 3.2) and we present the results of the numerical experiments in Sect. 3.3. We finalize the work with a conclusion and discussion of some future research directions.

2   Distributed Computing for Gene Network Expansion

In this section, we briefly outline the gene expansion problem, in-silico methods of its solution, and state the specific post-processing problem related to the local gene network expansion, which is the focus application of the distributed computing methods for the present paper.

2.1   Gene Expansion Problem

Since the successful sequencing of the genome of complex organisms, biology has moved into a phase in which the comprehension and understanding of the function of each single gene is of fundamental importance. This phase is called post-genomics era and it is characterised by the fact that the measurements that the biologists perform, in some cases, extend to the whole genome. The so called high-throughput methods such as RNAseq permit to measure the expression level of genes which correspond to the concentration of mRNA that has been transcripted and ready to be translated into proteins. The expression levels of the genes are different in different tissues which is essential to have the differentiation of the cells since every cell of a complex organism in fact shares the same DNA. As such, understanding the relationship between the expression level of different genes is of fundamental importance in order to shed a light to the functioning of the cell.

The transcription of a gene is a phenomenon that takes course inside the nucleus of a cell. The result of the process of the transcription is a strand of messenger RNA that eventually leaves the nucleus. The transcription is realised by a complex called *RNA polymerase* that copies a strand of DNA into a strand of RNA. The process is initiated by the presence of transcription factors that bind on an area of the DNA called promoter. The strands of mRNA are then edited and divided into introns and exons. The introns are removed whereas the exons are eventually used for being translated into proteins. The translations are operated by complexes called ribosomes that actually translate the triplets of nucleotides present in the strands of mRNA into sequence of amino acids following the genetic code. Some proteins can act as transcription factors for other genes or even for the same gene that encodes the protein itself. The cascade of processes that connect the transcription of DNA into mRNA, the translation of mRNA into proteins and the fact that the proteins can factor as a transcription factors establish a *causal relationship* between the transcription of two different genes.

The causal relations between the transcription of different genes can be usefully represented by the graph called *gene regulatory network* (GRN). In a GRN the nodes correspond to the genes and the edges corresponded to the causal relationship between the transcription of the genes. The edges are usually directed and the direction of the arrow represent the causal direction between the transcriptions of the two genes. The determination of the relationships and of their direction is done in the wet lab by doing experiments in which one of the two genes is controlled for example by knocking it off. However the knocking-off of genes can be done only for simple organisms, as a consequence it is necessary to devise techniques that use the data obtained by the high-throughput measurements in order to reconstruct the GRN in silico. A common way to perform this task is modelling the problem with Bayesian networks and reducing the problem to the problem of Bayesian network reconstruction. One of the techniques that are used is the so-called PC algorithm [12] that reconstructs a Bayesian network from observational data (in this case the Bayesian network is considered to model causal relationship which is not so in general). The PC algorithm has exponential complexity in the number of variables, in this case genes, in the worst case. But under some assumptions, essentially the fact that the network to be reconstructed follows the so-called power law, the complexity reduces to polynomial. A common implementation of the PC-algorithm is provided by the `pcalg` package [11] for R language [17]. The computational characteristics of the PC algorithm prevent its usage for reconstructing GRN that spans the whole genome where the number of genes is usually in the order of the tens of thousands.

The impossibility of reconstructing directly the complete GRN of the genome led to the definition of the task of gene network expansion. In this task the input is given by a relatively small GRN, called Local Gene Network (LGN), and the goal is to determine which other genes in the genome are possibly connected to the LGN. The strategy that we adopted in our algorithms NESRA [2],

NES^{2}RA [3] and OneGenE [4] is to perform computations by subsetting the genes into the so-called tiles and running the PC algorithm on each single tile. This subsetting is repeated in a randomised way for several times and a statistic of the number of times a gene is connected to a gene of the LGN is computed. In this way, given an LGN, is possible to obtain a list of genes the are putatively connected to it, however the heavy computations that are required on the tiles are such as that it is not possible to keep track of the information needed in order to draw the *direction of the relationships*. In the case of OneGenE the expansions are done on single genes instead of LGN. In principle is possible to think that each single gene of a whole genome can be expanded in a systematic way, the obtained expansion lists, that do not include the direction of the relationships, can be integrated, compared or in different ways post-processed. As we will see below, the computation of the direction of the relationship can be done in a *post-processing phase*. In the following, details about the distributed computing system that performs the GNE are given.

2.2 Gene@home

The TN-Grid platform (https://gene.disi.unitn.it/test) is a joint project between the National Research Council of Italy (CNR), the Fondazione Edmund Mach (FEM), S. Michele all'Adige, Trento, Italy and the Department of Information Engineering and Computer Science (DISI) of the University of Trento, Italy. It uses the BOINC platform (discussed in Sect. 3.1) to provide high computing power for local research activities. The project currently running on TN-Grid is called **gene@home** and currently runs the OneGenE experiments. OneGenE has been successfully applied to *Vitis vinifera* [16] organism and it is currently working on the *Homo sapiens* FANTOM5 dataset (discussed in Sect. 2.3). This dataset, in a reduced version called FANTOM-full, contains 87554 gene isoforms. Any single expansion using the NES^{2}RA algorithm (with a tile size of 1000 transcripts, 2000 iterations and 0.05 as the conditional-independence significant-test alpha threshold) is divided into 294 computational workunits sent by BOINC to the volunteers participating in TN-Grid. This computation is intensive, as a reference a single workunit takes $\approx$11.500 s ($\approx$3.2 h), per thread, to be successfully computed on a recent CPU like the AMD Ryzen™ Threadripper 3970X 32-Core Processor.

The current computational power provided by TN-Grid is currently at around 32 teraFLOPS, expanding an average of $\approx$85 isoforms/day (of the FANTOM-full dataset). This is our theoretical computing limit, given our hardware and software resources. The performance history of the system is depicted in Fig. 1 (courtesy of https://www.boincstats.com), where the BOINC credits are proportional to teraFLOPS. The low peaks observed around the mid and end of February 2022 are due to a failure of the storage system used by the project. A snapshot of the server status, including the users and computers participating is also available in Fig. 2. The number of users and computers joining the project is constantly rising, the main contribution obviously comes, as expected, from the

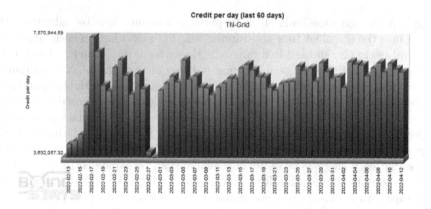

Fig. 1. BOINC credits history as of 2022-04-13

more industrialized countries, see Fig. 3, but please notice that the nationality is just an optional user information given while registering to the system.

The results of gene expansion problem solved by the `gene@home` project require further post-processing to obtain the gene expansion networks in the form of graph objects which may be interesting for further consideration by specialists in bioinformatics. In the next section we discuss the structure of the post-processing required and outline the main computational issue considered in the present paper.

2.3   Expansion Lists Post-processing

The expansion list post-processing consists in the application of the *MPC-stable* algorithm (available in `pcalg` package) [11], which is a modified version [9] of the *original* PC algorithm [20], to gradually larger subsets of genes belonging to a candidate gene expansion list, until the subset size coincides with the whole expansion list. The candidate gene is included in every subset.

The expansion list provides a ranking of genes for which a correlation is found with the candidate gene used as input to the OneGenE method [4]. The relative frequency is also listed next to the gene identification. The list follows a decreasing order: the first ranking gene has the highest relative frequency and the strongest correlation with the candidate gene. As the relative frequency increases, the correlation between the candidate gene and the genes belonging to the upper part of the expansion list cannot be explained in terms of other genes. This condition provides evidence of a putative *direct* causal relationship [7]. In this context, direct is intended as *without the intermediation of other genes*. It should not be confounded with *directed* which, in graph theory, stands for oriented.

Figure 4 (obtained using Cytoscape version 3.9.1) is a graphical representation of the direct relationships found by OneGenE between the candidate gene

Computing status

Work	#
Tasks ready to send	11
Tasks in progress	45336
Workunits waiting for validation	5
Workunits waiting for assimilation	5
Workunits waiting for file deletion	0
Tasks waiting for file deletion	8
Transitioner backlog (hours)	0.00

Users	#
With credit	3050
With recent credit	834
Registered in past 24 hours	1

Computers	#
With credit	60037
With recent credit	5987
Registered in past 24 hours	3
Current GigaFLOPS	32260.54

Tasks by application				
Application	Unsent	In progress	Runtime of last 100 tasks in hours: average, min, max	Users in last 24 hours
gene@home PC-IM	11	45336	4.35 (0.64 - 81.42)	428

Task data as of 13 Apr 2022, 10:37:23 UTC

Fig. 2. gene@home server status snapshot

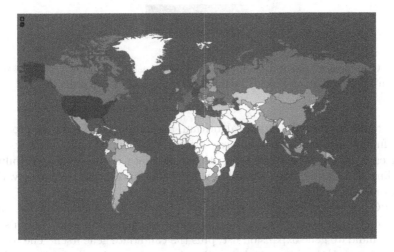

Fig. 3. gene@home world credits distribution as of 2022-04-13

and the first thirty genes of its expansion list. Here, as an example, the candidate gene is human MFSD2A (Major Facilitator Superfamily Domain Containing 2A) [21]. The edge color reflects the relative frequency between the candidate gene (p1@MFSD2A, centered) and the first thirty genes of its expansion list. Relative frequency ranges from 1 to 0.9809.

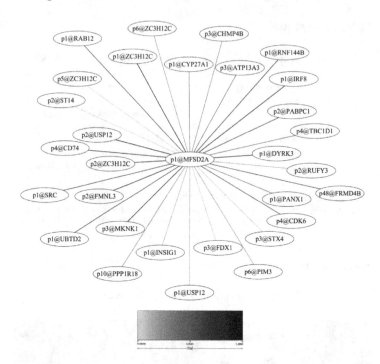

Fig. 4. Graphical representation of the direct relationships found by OneGenE project between the candidate gene and the first thirty genes of its expansion list.

By applying the MPC-stable algorithm, the main goal of the post-processing is to further explore and test these direct relationships and, possibly, orient them causally. Note that the algorithm takes into account the possibility of sampling errors and hidden variables, which is not uncommon with observational expression data [9].

MPC-stable receives a text matrix as its input. The columns of the matrix correspond to the variables, in this case these are genes from the chosen subset of the candidate gene expansion list, plus the candidate gene itself. The rows are observations [11], in this case observational gene expression data, retrieved from the FANTOM5 project [14] available at https://fantom.gsc.riken.jp/5/. The raw FANTOM5 dataset has been organized and filtered in a coherent normalized data matrix by the gene@home project [5]. The version of the FANTOM dataset used as input for the MPC-algorithm is called FANTOM-full [7].

The order of genes is irrelevant to the modified algorithm, since it is fully order-independent, in contrast to the original PC-algorithm, whose output may change in response to a different ordering of the input variables [9]. However, order is relevant to expansion list subsetting, since genes are ranked in decrescent relative frequency order. So, the subsetting is done by adding to the candidate gene the first thirty genes in the ranking and a fixed number of the subsequent genes of the list. At every run of the algorithm this number is increased until it coincides with all the genes of the candidate gene expansion list.

The algorithm starts by building the complete undirected graph, connecting every pair of genes with each other. In the first step the graph *skeleton* is computed: undirected edges are cut according to the conditional independence test, performed on all couples. If gene X and gene Y pass the test, the edge between them is cut and the subset S of genes, conditioned on in the independence test, is included in their *separation set*. If X and Y fail the test, the edge is preserved [9,20]. Note that since $S \subseteq adj(G, X) \backslash \{Y\}$, the S cardinality increases from zero to $|adj(G, X) \backslash \{Y\}|$ [12].

Given the separation sets, the second and third steps of the algorithm apply orientation rules to the remaining edges. If an edge between two genes X and Y is oriented in the graph, as X→Y, X is interpreted as *direct cause* of Y [20]. The output should be a completed partially directed acyclic graph (CPDAG) [9,12]. Further parameter settings allow for bi-directed edges X↔Y, which may lead to an invalid CPDAG as output. Note that bi-directed edges reflect conflicting orientations, not causal relationships [9].

Figure 5 represents the MPC-stable output for the candidate gene MFSD2A and the first thirty genes of its expansion list. The algorithm was applied to a MFSD2A expansion list subset of size 40 genes, plus the candidate gene (p1@MFSD2A, highlighted).

Multiple runs of the MPC-stable algorithm with an increasing input of genes is a useful tool of comparison: the resulting graphs make every change in edge directions and node connections clear and visible. Keeping track of the candidate gene, and the first thirty genes of its expansion list, allows for pattern detection and consistency checking of the output graphs. The retrieved directed or undirected edges could shed light on gene functional interactions. This part of the post-progressing is still a work in progress and lacks biological validation.

Since the research within the possible graphs requires to perform iterative runs of the aforementioned algorithm over a large set of the input data, and each iteration produces a time and resource consuming computation, there is a need to utilize parallel and distributed computing resources. We discuss an implementation of such a process in Sect. 3, where preliminary experimental results are also reported.

3   BOINC in R Environment

In this section we discuss the capabilities of BOINC-based distributed computing and RBOINC package [6] to equip the post-processing phase of the GNE algorithm with necessary computational resources and report preliminary results of numerical experiments.

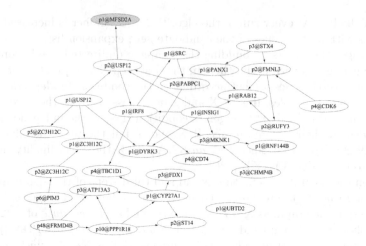

Fig. 5. The graph representation of the MPC-stable algorithm output for the candidate gene MFSD2A and the first thirty genes of its expansion list.

3.1 BOINC

A few methodologies exist which allow to obtain large computational resources, ranging from highly specialized and expensive ones, such as the supercomputers, to the distributed networks of conventional computers such as the *desktop grids*. The latter are commonly used for such problems that can be solved in split-merge way, i.e. the large computational problem is split into a (large number of) small independent subproblems (*workunits*) and the results of the latter are merged in some way into the result of the original problem.

BOINC is one of the standard frameworks to organize a desktop grid. The BOINC middleware is responsible for workunit distribution among the clients (hosts) which perform computations and return the *results* upon completion. A few parameters such as redundancy configuration (the so-called *replication* and *quorum*) and result processing are to be configured in such a way to deliver optimal performance while taking into account unreliable resources. Open problems of such type of resources are summarized in [8,15].

Being essentially limited in terms of the class of tasks that can be solved with, the desktop grid nevertheless allows to obtain significant computational power out of the idle resources of the hosts, which are contributed by volunteers to the project organizers as in case of the BOINC grid. As such, this framework is a good technical media for the post-processing of LGN problem introduced in Sect. 2.3. It remains to describe the technical details on using the pcalg package in BOINC environment which is done in the following section.

3.2 RBOINC Software

The RBOINC software [6] is used for running R code in BOINC environment. Since BOINC is a type of desktop grid with centralized server, large number of clients (hosts), (relatively) slow network connection and no host-to-host interaction, the package is suitable for performing massively parallel tasks with relatively large calculation time.

The RBOINC software consists of several components. The server part must be installed on the BOINC server. It equips the RBOINC.cl package with interfaces for workunit initialization and validation, including job upload capabilities and file/job names generation, as well as templates for creating tasks and BOINC applications.

Tasks are performed on the computers of volunteers in specific virtual machines. The standard BOINC client downloads all the necessary files and launches the application that controls the virtual machine. VirtualBox executes the task and sends its result to the BOINC client via the global shared folder.

Connection to the BOINC server is established by the RBOINC.cl package for the R language (http/ssh interfaces are supported). The update_jobs_status function retrieves the jobs results, and the connection to BOINC server can be opened/closed at any time required. In addition, the package includes functions for canceling and debugging jobs on the local machine.

3.3 PCALG in RBOINC: A Case Study

To perform the post-processing of the LGN lists, we use the RBOINC.cl package described in the previous section.

Based on the expansion lists supplemented by the candidate gene, we construct correlation matrices, which are then placed in the list of data for processing in BOINC environment by the hosts. A function for processing one expansion list is then described locally in R environment, then a connection to the BOINC server is created. The batch of tasks is created, which includes the processing function, the prepared list of data (each list item is a separate task), and a list of additional R-packages required for installation on a volunteer machine. This information is archived and transmitted to the BOINC server. After receiving the archive, the server unpacks it and registers the tasks. Volunteer machines periodically access the server and, having received the next task, begin to perform it. Tasks on volunteer machines are performed independently of each other, and as they are completed, the corresponding status obtained and, if necessary, failed workunits are re-processed by the hosts automatically. The results of calculations are returned to the server, where they can be picked up one by one or all together into the R environment of the researcher.

For test runs, several small datasets with extension lists truncated to 20 genes were used. Subsequently, a large list of about 1800 genes was processed, which took about 48.7 CPU hours in a single-core regime on a conventional host. The graph constructed by the first 30 vertices of this list is shown in Fig. 6.

In order to reduce the calculation time, we decided to use a parallel version of the PC algorithm from the ParallelPC package, which (slightly) differs from a conventional PC in the way the skeleton is built. This algorithm offers multicore computing, providing the ability to specify the number of cores to use. By distributing the intermediate calculations for the task between the cores, the overall calculation time of a workunit is significantly reduced.

Finally, the parallel PC algorithm was run over a number of truncated expansion lists leaving the first 1000 genes (ordered by the relative frequency of the relation with the candidate gene descending). The data parallelization was done by means of the input data in a single-instruction-multiple-data way, i.e. the same algorithm was run over multiple input files which were the results of gene@home project. Due to a diversity in the host machines computation capabilities as well as usage statistics (by design, BOINC uses the idle resources in order to minimize the effect on the user of the host machine), such computation times were ranging approx. from 10 to 160 CPU hours, respectively.

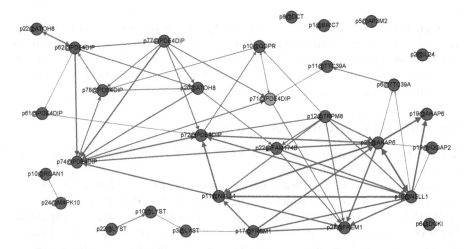

Fig. 6. Graph of causal relationships with a selected gene and 30 other genes ordered in the relative frequency (descending). The relative frequency is indicated as the width of the edge.

4 Conclusion

In the present paper, we discussed the capabilities of distributed computing for bioinformatics researchers available with BOINC framework and RBOINC software within R environment. It might be interesting to further study such capabilities by addressing other cases within the same research field. Moreover, a lengthy experiment is planned to post-process the set of results of the gene@home project, however, these possibilities are left for future research.

Acknowledgements. The paper was published with the financial support of the Ministry of Education and Science of the Russian Federation as part of the program of the Moscow Center for Fundamental and Applied Mathematics under the agreement №075-15-2022-284.

References

1. Anderson, D.P.: BOINC: a system for public-resource computing and storage. In: Proceedings of the 5th IEEE/ACM International Workshop on Grid Computing, GRID 2004, Washington, DC, USA, pp. 4–10. IEEE Computer Society (2004). https://doi.org/10.1109/GRID.2004.14

2. Asnicar, F., et al.: Discovering candidates for gene network expansion by distributed volunteer computing. In: 2015 IEEE Trustcom/BigDataSE/ISPA, vol. 3, pp. 248–253, August 2015

3. Asnicar, F., et al.: NES^2RA: network expansion by stratified variable subsetting and ranking aggregation. Int. J. High Perform. Comput. Appl. **32**(3), 380–392 (2016)

4. Asnicar, F., Masera, L., Pistore, D., Valentini, S., Cavecchia, V., Blanzieri, E.: OneGenE: regulatory gene network expansion via distributed volunteer computing on BOINC. In: 2019 27th Euromicro International Conference on Parallel, Distributed and Network-Based Processing (PDP), Pavia, Italy, pp. 315–322. IEEE, February 2019. https://ieeexplore.ieee.org/document/8671629/

5. Asnicar, F., et al.: TN-Grid and gene@home project: volunteer computing for bioinformatics. In: Proceedings of the Second International Conference BOINC-Based High Performance Computing: Fundamental Research and Development (BOINC:FAST 2015), vol. 1502, pp. 1–15. CEUR-WS (2015). http://ceur-ws.org/Vol-1502/paper1.pdf

6. Astafiev, S., Rumyantsev, A.: R-Forge: RBOINC (2022). https://r-forge.r-project.org/projects/rboinc/

7. Blanzieri, E., et al.: A computing system for discovering causal relationships among human genes to improve drug repositioning. IEEE Trans. Emerg. Top. Comput. **9**(4), 1667–1682 (2021) https://ieeexplore.ieee.org/document/9224179/

8. Chernov, I., Nikitina, N., Ivashko, E.: Task scheduling in desktop grids: open problems. Open Eng. **7**(1), 343 (2017). https://www.degruyter.com/view/j/eng.2017.7.issue-1/eng-2017-0038/eng-2017-0038.xml

9. Colombo, D., Maathuis, M.H.: Order-independent constraint-based causal structure learning. J. Mach. Learn. Res. **15**, 3741–3782 (2014)

10. Geffner, T., et al.: Deep end-to-end causal inference (2022). arXiv:2202.02195

11. Kalisch, M., Mächler, M., Colombo, D., Maathuis, M.H., Bühlmann, P.: Causal inference using graphical models with the R package pcalg. J. Stat. Softw. **47**(11), 613–636 (2012). https://www.jstatsoft.org/article/view/v047i11

12. Kalisch, M., Bühlmann, P.: Estimating high-dimensional directed acyclic graphs with the PC-algorithm. J. Mach. Learn. Res. **8**, 613–636 (2007)

13. Maathuis, M.H., Colombo, D., Kalisch, M., Bühlmann, P.: Predicting causal effects in large-scale systems from observational data. Nat. Methods **7**(4), 247–248 (2010). http://www.nature.com/articles/nmeth0410-247

14. Noguchi, S., et al.: FANTOM5 CAGE profiles of human and mouse samples. Sci. Data **4**(1), 170112 (2017). http://www.nature.com/articles/sdata2017112

15. Durrani, M.N., Shamsi, J.A.: Volunteer computing: requirements, challenges, and solutions. J. Netw. Comput. Appl. **39**, 369–380 (2014). http://linkinghub.elsevier.com/retrieve/pii/S1084804513001665

16. Pilati, S., et al.: Vitis OneGenE: a causality-based approach to generate gene networks in Vitis vinifera sheds light on the laccase and dirigent gene families. Biomolecules **11**(12), 1744 (2021). https://www.mdpi.com/2218-273X/11/12/1744

D. Dolgaleva et al.

17. R Core Team: A language and environment for statistical computing. R Foundation for Statistical Computing, Vienna, Austria (2021). https://www.R-project.org
18. Sizochenko, N., Gajewicz, A., Leszczynski, J., Puzyn, T.: Causation or only correlation? Application of causal inference graphs for evaluating causality in nano-QSAR models. Nanoscale 8(13), 7203–7208 (2016). http://xlink.rsc.org/?DOI=C5NR08279J
19. Spirtes, P., Glymour, C.: An algorithm for fast recovery of sparse causal graphs. Soc. Sci. Comput. Rev. 9(1), 62–72 (1991). http://journals.sagepub.com/doi/10.1177/089443939100900106
20. Spirtes, P., Glymour, C.N., Scheines, R.: Causation, Prediction, and Search. Adaptive Computation and Machine Learning, 2nd edn. MIT Press, Cambridge (2000)
21. Ungaro, F., et al.: MFSD2A promotes endothelial generation of inflammation-resolving lipid mediators and reduces colitis in mice. Gastroenterology 153(5), 1363–1377.e6 (2017). https://linkinghub.elsevier.com/retrieve/pii/S0016508517359887

Distributed Simulation of Supercomputer Model with Heavy Tails

Alexander Golovin[1,2]($\boxtimes$) (iD), Alexander Rumyantsev[1,2] (iD),
and Sergey Astafiev[1,2] (iD)

[1] Institute of Applied Mathematical Research, Karelian Research Centre of RAS,
Petrozavodsk, Russia
{golovin,ar0}@krc.karelia.ru
[2] Petrozavodsk State University, Petrozavodsk, Russia

Abstract. In this paper we apply the distributed regenerative estimation of the steady-state performance to the supercomputer queueing model with heavy-tailed distributions. Discrete-event simulation by generalized semi-Markov processes is the key tool for the analysis. Based on extensive numerical simulation used, we illustrate the approach by delivering some basic though important properties of the model.

Keywords: Distributed regenerative simulation · Steady-state performance · Supercomputer model · Generalized semi-Markov process

1 Introduction

Among the multiserver queueing models, the simultaneous service multiserver queue is an example of a simplistic description which results in sophisticated analysis. Dating back to the works of R. Evans [6], S. S. Kim [18], P. Brill and L. Green [4] (treating the model in the context of e.g. social service systems), this model had recently experienced a spike of interest due to a new application in the context of supercomputers, see e.g. [1,13,16,20], to name a few. Several interesting open problems in the model (hereinafter referred to as supercomputer model) are named in a very recent paper [15].

Due to a rather sophisticated machinery, the model (to the best of our knowledge) permits analysis only in rather restrictive cases such as exponential interarrival/service times, or a small number of servers. Thus, in realistic environment, the study needs to be performed numerically e.g. by simulation, whereas the known analytical solutions can be used for simulation model validation.

In the present paper, we address the simulation supercomputer model. One of the specific observations made in [8] based on the analysis of the supercomputer workload logs are heavy-tailed distributions of the key random variables such as interarrival/service times. It is well known that the presence of heavy tails may dramatically affect the system performance [14]. Thus, we restrict our attention to several specific effects induced by heavy tails in the supercomputer model, and perform numerical study to illustrate these effects. Due to the parallelization capabilities of the methods used for simulation, we selected BOINC-based

V. Voevodin et al. (Eds.): RuSCDays 2022, LNCS 13708, pp. 657–669, 2022.
https://doi.org/10.1007/978-3-031-22941-1_48

Desktop Grid as a natural venue to conduct the simulation, and the R environment to perform the modeling.

The key contribution of our research is the empirical evidence of the effects of heavy-tailed distributions on the performance of a simulation supercomputer model which was studied by means of regenerative simulation on a distributed computing system.

The structure of the paper is as follows. Firstly we introduce the simulation methodology and discuss a few complications that appear when dealing with heavy-tailed distributions in simulation. Then we introduce the discrete event simulation models of a supercomputer and describe the necessary performance metrics. Numerical results are then reported and discussed. We finalize the paper with a conclusion.

2   Discrete-Event Simulation

In this section we briefly recall the basics of discrete-event simulation (DES) and performance estimation of the model in steady state. One of the powerful DES methodologies is based on the so-called Generalized Semi-Markov Processes (GSMP) [10,12]. The GSMP is a multidimensional process

$$\Theta = \{\boldsymbol{X}(t), \boldsymbol{T}(t)\}_{t \geq 0}, \tag{1}$$

possessing a discrete, $\boldsymbol{X}(t) = (X_1(t), \ldots, X_n(t)) \in \mathcal{X}$, component representing the system *state* and the continuous, $\boldsymbol{T}(t) = (T_1(t), \ldots, T_m(t)) \geq \boldsymbol{0}$, component known as timers or clocks. The set of active timers $A(\boldsymbol{x}) \neq \varnothing$ as well as the timer decay *rate* vector $\boldsymbol{r}(\boldsymbol{x}) = (r_1(\boldsymbol{x}), \ldots, r_m(\boldsymbol{x})) \geq \boldsymbol{0}$ depend on the system state $\boldsymbol{x} \in \mathcal{X}$. It is assumed that the speed is positive only for the active timers,

$$r_i(\boldsymbol{x}) > 0 \text{ if and only if } i \in A(\boldsymbol{x}).$$

The timers decay linearly with given rates and the i-th type event epoch is the time t of i-th timer expiration $T_i(t-) = 0$, $i \in A(\boldsymbol{X}(t))$. Upon event, state transition may happen which are driven by probabilities $\boldsymbol{P}^{(i)} = ||P_{\boldsymbol{x},\boldsymbol{x}'}^{(i)}||_{\boldsymbol{x},\boldsymbol{x}' \in \mathcal{X}}$, where

$$P_{\boldsymbol{x},\boldsymbol{x}'}^{(i)} = \mathrm{P}\{\boldsymbol{X}(t) = \boldsymbol{x}' | \boldsymbol{X}(t-) = \boldsymbol{x}, T_i(t-) = 0\}. \tag{2}$$

Upon transition, the timers corresponding to the new active events $i' \in A(\boldsymbol{x}') \setminus (A(\boldsymbol{x}) \setminus \{i\})$ are initialized from some given density

$$f_{i'}(u, \boldsymbol{x}, \boldsymbol{x}', i) = \mathrm{P}\{T_{i'}(t) \in du | \boldsymbol{X}(t-) = \boldsymbol{x}, \boldsymbol{X}(t) = \boldsymbol{x}', T_i(t-) = 0\}, \tag{3}$$

while other timers are left unmodified.

Assume some performance measure $\chi(\boldsymbol{X}_e)$ of the system in steady state is to be estimated, where $\boldsymbol{X}_e$ has the limiting distribution of the state $\boldsymbol{X}(t)$. Then if the process Θ is regenerative, i.e. there exists some sequence of the time epochs $\{\tau_k\}_{k \geq 1}$ with i.i.d. time intervals, such that the random elements $\{\boldsymbol{X}(t), \boldsymbol{T}(t)\}_{\tau_i \leq t < \tau_{i+1}}$ are i.i.d., then the steady-state (time average) performance estimate is obtained by using the integral estimate on the corresponding regeneration cycles,

$$Y_j = \sum_{k=\beta_{j-1}}^{\beta_j - 1} \chi(\boldsymbol{X}^{(k)})(t_{k+1} - t_k), \quad j \geq 1, \tag{4}$$

where $\{t_k\}_{k\geq 0}$ is the sequence of event epochs, $\boldsymbol{X}^{(k)} = \boldsymbol{X}(t_k)$, while the regeneration epochs in discrete time β_j (starting from $\beta_0 = 0$) are obtained from

$$t_{\beta_j} = \tau_j, \quad j \geq 1.$$

The pointwise estimate is then obtained as

$$\bar{r}_n = \frac{Y_1 + \cdots + Y_n}{\tau_n} = \frac{S_{Y_n}}{S_{R_n}}, \tag{5}$$

where partial sums used in the fraction are given as

$$S_{Y_n} = Y_1 + \cdots + Y_n, \quad S_{R_n} = R_1 + \cdots + R_n = \tau_n, \quad n \geq 1. \tag{6}$$

Assuming $\mathrm{E}(Y_1 + \tau_1)^2 < \infty$, regenerative central limit theorem allows one to obtain $(1 - 2\gamma)\%$ confidence estimate for the true mean $r = \mathrm{E}Y_1/\mathrm{E}\tau_1$ as follows [5]:

$$\bar{r}_n \pm \frac{h_\gamma \sqrt{\mathrm{Var}(n)}}{\sqrt{n} S_{R_n}}, \tag{7}$$

where the unbiased estimator $\overline{\mathrm{Var}}(n)$ of the value $\mathrm{Var}(Y_1) - 2r\mathrm{cov}(Y_1, \tau_1) + r^2\mathrm{Var}(\tau_1)$ is obtained as

$$\overline{\mathrm{Var}}(n) = \frac{nS_{Y_n^2} - (S_{Y_n})^2 - 2\bar{r}_n(nS_{YR_n} - S_{Y_n}S_{R_n}) + \bar{r}_n^2(nS_{R_n^2} - (S_{R_n})^2)}{n(n-1)}, \tag{8}$$

and corresponding partial sums are given in (6) and by

$$S_{Y_n^2} = Y_1^2 + \cdots + Y_n^2, \quad S_{YR_n} = Y_1 R_1 + \cdots + Y_n R_n, \quad S_{R_n^2} = R_1^2 + \cdots + R_n^2. \tag{9}$$

The constant $h_\gamma = \Phi^{-1}((1 - \gamma)/2)$ is the corresponding quantile of the standard normal distribution and $\Phi(x)$ is the Laplace function. It is important to stress that, due to additive way of computations in (5) and (7) which are based on partial sums (6) and (9) of i.i.d. elements, it is natural to use the time-parallel computations [9,11,17]. Moreover, since such computations are embarrassingly parallel, the desktop grid seems to be the naturally suitable computing facility. As such, we use the simulato[1] package for R language to implement the model and the RBOINC[2] R package to conduct the experiments on a self-hosted BOINC desktop grid facility. Both packages are available at R-Forge package distribution system.

---

[1] https://r-forge.r-project.org/projects/simulato.
[2] https://r-forge.r-project.org/projects/rboinc.

2.1 Heavy-Tailed Distribution Sampling

The moments, including the expected value and standard deviation of a heavy-tailed distributed random variable can be infinite [7]. This effect is hard to be observed in simulation environment. An important special case of a heavy-tailed distribution is Pareto distribution. It is a two-parameter distribution with scale x_0 and shape α parameters having the distribution function

$$F(x) = P(X \leq x) = 1 - \left(\frac{x_0}{x}\right)^{\alpha}, \quad x > x_0. \tag{10}$$

The parameter x_0 gives the minimum value that can theoretically be generated (the support of a Pareto distribution is $[x_0, +\infty)$). The shape parameter α determines how likely large values are to be generated. Its estimation is always difficult and different methods can give markedly different estimates [8].

Using inverse function method for generation random value we obtain:

$$x = \frac{x_0}{\sqrt[\alpha]{u}}, \tag{11}$$

where u is a random variable uniformly distributed on $(0, 1]$. Note that if u is uniformly distributed on $[0, 1]$, then $1 - u$ is also uniformly distributed on $[0, 1]$. Additionally, we must exclude the point 0 when generating to avoid numerical inconsistency. Thus, to sample from Pareto distribution, it is enough to generate a number from standard uniform distribution and perform small arithmetic transformation. Since random and pseudo-random generators on modern computers return discrete values, there is a strictly defined $\epsilon > 0$ smaller than which the numbers with standard uniform distribution can't be generated.

Consider the case where $\alpha = 1, x_0 = 1$. Then standard deviation and expected value are infinity, and the random number can be generated like this:

$$x = \frac{1}{u}, \tag{12}$$

where u is a random variable uniformly distributed on $(0, 1]$. Note that in this case the maximum possible number that can be generated is ϵ^{-1}. However, it should be noted that the probability of generating such a large number is of the order of ϵ.

One of the problems with using such distributions in simulations is that the system is in transient mode for the entire duration of the simulation, no matter how long it lasts. This is true since extremely large values continue to be generated. In [7] it is proposed to set a threshold depending on the length of the simulation and discard values that exceed it to solve this problem.

Another problem with such distributions is that a very large number can be generated, which is unattainable in practice. For example, in real data networks, the maximum packet size is always upper bounded by some value. Thus, when generating, we may need to limit the maximum possible value.

There are two groups of distribution truncation methods [8]. The first group of methods is the selection of the maximum point beyond which the random variable cannot take values. This method leads to many problems. If we take as a limit the maximum of the data measured in the experiment, then in reality the distribution can very rarely go beyond this limit. If we take the maximum theoretically possible value as the right boundary, then we can get too large values in the sample that are unattainable in practice.

The second group of methods is dynamic distribution truncation. Here, the right boundary of the distribution is determined depending on the size of the generated sample. For example, if we need to generate n values, then we can choose a value as the right border for which [8]:

$$\overline{F}(x) \approx \frac{1}{2n}, \tag{13}$$

where $\overline{F}(x)$ is a cumulative distribution function for truncated distribution. Obviously, this approach does not solve the problem, but it allows one to get some horizon characterized by a sample size n. The larger the sample size, the higher the probability of sampling ever larger values, and this method allows one to delve into the tail of the distribution.

3   Supercomputer Model

Let us describe the GSMP model of a supercomputer. Consider a queueing system with c identical servers receiving input of customers of c classes, where the (random) class N_i of a customer i corresponds to the number of servers required to serve the customer. All servers dispatched to the customer are seized and released simultaneously for the same random amount of time S_i. Customers are waiting for service in a single unbounded queue working on a first-come-first-served basis. The distinctive feature of the supercomputer model compared to the classical multiserver queue is the simultaneous service of a customer by a random number of servers, which makes the discipline non-work-conserving and complicates the analysis [20]. Thus, simulation is required to study the model under realistic assumptions.

Firstly we define the state vector with $c + 2$ components $X_1, \ldots, X_{c+2}$ where

- $X_1, \ldots, X_c$ are the classes of not more than c customers being served (some elements may be zero),
- X_{c+1} is the class of the customer at the head of the queue,
- X_{c+2} number of customers in the queue (after the first one, if any).

Let us now define the timers:

- $T_1, \ldots, T_c$ are the remaining service times of the customers being served (corresponding to the nonzero state components),
- T_{c+1} is the remaining interarrival time.

It remains to note that the timer speed is unit for the nonzero timers.

Due to space limitation, we do not describe the transitions which can be defined straightforwardly, but note instead that upon departure, multiple customers may enter service.

Let us define the sequence $\{\beta_j\}_{j\geqslant 1}$ of regeneration points in discrete time as follows,

$$\beta_{j+1} = \min\{k > \beta_j : X_1^{(k)} = \cdots = X_{c+2}^{(k-1)} = 0, T_{c+1}(t_k-) = 0\}. \qquad (14)$$

This means that the regeneration epoch corresponds to arrival of a customer into an empty system. It is now easy to define the performance measure of the system e.g. for the average steady-state number of customers in the system,

$$\chi_1(\boldsymbol{x}) = \sum_{i=1}^{c+1} 1_{x_i>0} + x_{c+2}, \qquad (15)$$

or the average queue in steady state,

$$\chi_2(\boldsymbol{x}) = 1_{x_{c+1}>0} + x_{c+2}, \qquad (16)$$

where 1_A is the logical indicator of condition A. Note that multiple performance measures can be estimated in parallel using the same GSMP trajectory. The GSMP model of a supercomputer is implemented e.g. in the simulato package for R language.

The χ_1 and χ_2 allow one to obtain count performance measures of the system (mean number of customers in the system/queue). However, by using the celebrated Little's law (see e.g. [3]), the time measures can also be obtained, e.g. the sojourn time/waiting time in the system. The Little's law is formulated in the form of relation between the average count characteristic, say H, and average time characteristic, say V, of the system or its part in the following way

$$H = \lambda V,$$

where λ is the input rate. This allows one to obtain time-based performance measures of the system indirectly by using count-based measures and vice versa.

Another important simulation mechanism is based on the stochastic recurrent relations between the driving sequences $\{\tau_i, S_i, N_i\}_{i\geq 1}$ and the c-dimensional system workload vector $\boldsymbol{W}_i$ (with components in ascending order) observed just before arrival of customer i. In a classical multiserver queue this mechanism is given by the celebrated Kiefer–Wolfowitz recursion, which, after appropriate modification, can be used to model a supercomputer. Specifically, the workload before arrival of customer $i + 1$ is given as

$$\boldsymbol{W}_{i+1} = \mathrm{R}\left(\boldsymbol{e}_{1:N_i}(W_{i,N_i} + S_i) + (\boldsymbol{1} - \boldsymbol{e}_{1:N_i}) \circ \boldsymbol{W}_i - \boldsymbol{1}\tau_i\right)^+, \qquad (17)$$

where $(\cdot)^+ = \max(0, \cdot)$, R orders the components ascendingly, $\circ$ is Hadamard (componentwise) product and $\boldsymbol{e}_{1:N_i}$ is the vector with N_i (first) unit components. As such, the customer i's delay is given by the workload W_{i,N_i} of N_i-th least busy server. It is straightforward to derive a continuous-time analog of the recursion (17) that gives the workload at arbitrary time t as follows

$$\boldsymbol{W}(t) = \mathrm{R}\left(\boldsymbol{e}_{1:N_i}(W_{A(t),N_{A(t)}} + S_{A(t)}) + (\boldsymbol{1} - \boldsymbol{e}_{1:N_{A(t)}}) \circ \boldsymbol{W}_{A(t)} - \boldsymbol{1}\bar{\tau}(t)\right)^+,$$
(18)

where $\bar{\tau}(t) = t - \tau_{A(t)}$ is the time since most recent arrival, and $A(t)$ is the counting process giving the number of most recent arrival before time $t \geq 0$.

Both the continuous time process $\{\boldsymbol{W}(t)\}_{t \geq 0}$ and the discrete-time sequence $\{\boldsymbol{W}_i\}_{i \geq 0}$ (with $W_0 \equiv \boldsymbol{0}$) regenerate at the arrival epochs into an empty system, which is, when an arriving customer observes a zero workload vector. However, the stationary limits of these processes do not necessarily coincide. The conditions for such a coincidence are given by the celebrated PASTA property (Poisson Arrivals See Time Average) [3], which hereby can be guaranteed by the input process to be memoryless and independent of the system state. In such a case, the following stochastic relation is obtained,

$$\boldsymbol{W}(\infty) =_d \mathrm{R}\left(\boldsymbol{e}_{1:N}(W_{\infty,N} + S + (\boldsymbol{1} - \boldsymbol{e}_{1:N}) \circ \boldsymbol{W}_\infty - \boldsymbol{1}\tau\right)^+ =_d \boldsymbol{W}_\infty,$$
(19)

where $\boldsymbol{W}(\infty)$ is the continuous-time, and $\boldsymbol{W}_\infty$ is the discrete-time limit (this relation follows from (18) since in steady state the limit of $\bar{\tau}(t)$ is τ due to the memoryless property of exponential distribution). Hereinafter the generic random variables are given without subindex. However, it may also be possible to modify this equality into (stochastic) inequality for specific classes of distributions having the new-better-than-used (NBU) or new-worse-than-used (NWU) distribution. A random variable τ with distribution function F_τ is NBU if for any $x, y \geq 0$ the following inequality holds good,

$$\overline{F}_T(x + y) \leq \overline{F}_T(y)\overline{F}_T(x).$$
(20)

Define the remaining interarrival time

$$\hat{\tau}(t) = t_{A(t)+1} - t.$$

Note that $\bar{\tau}(t) + \hat{\tau}(t) = \tau_{A(t)}$. Assume that $\bar{\tau}(t) = x$, then $\hat{\tau}(t)$ has the following conditional distribution [2]

$$\mathrm{P}\{\hat{\tau}(t) > y | \bar{\tau}(t) = x\} = \frac{\overline{F}_\tau(x + y)}{\overline{F}_\tau(x)}.$$
(21)

Then if τ is NBU, it follows from (20) and (21) that

$$\tau \geq_d \hat{\tau}(t).$$
(22)

(The NWU property requires to invert the inequality signs.) Since in the limit, as $t \to \infty$, both $\hat{\tau}$ and $\bar{\tau}$ have the same limiting random variable $\tilde{\tau}$, the same inequality (22) holds good for $\tilde{\tau}$ as well.

Using this order in recursion (18) and letting $t \to \infty$, the following inequality is obtained, hereinafter referred to as PASTA inequality

$$\boldsymbol{W}(\infty) =_d \text{R}\left(\boldsymbol{e}_{1:N}(W_{\infty,N} + S + (\boldsymbol{1} - \boldsymbol{e}_{1:N}) \circ \boldsymbol{W}_\infty - \boldsymbol{1}\tilde{\tau}\right)^+$$
$$\geq_d \text{R}\left(\boldsymbol{e}_{1:N}(W_{\infty,N} + S + (\boldsymbol{1} - \boldsymbol{e}_{1:N}) \circ \boldsymbol{W}_\infty - \boldsymbol{1}\tau\right)^+ =_d \boldsymbol{W}_\infty. \qquad (23)$$

Note that in case of NWU, the inverted inequalities are obtained in similar way.

A specific example when the NBU/NWU property holds in parametric way is the Weibull distribution

$$\text{P}\{\tau \leq x\} = 1 - e^{-(x/b)^a}, \quad a, b > 0, x \geq 0. \qquad (24)$$

The shape parameter a is responsible for the aforementioned property, with $a \geq 1$ corresponding to NBU and $a \leq 1$ to the NWU case, with the mean interarrival time given by [19]:

$$\text{E}\tau = b\Gamma(1 + 1/a). \qquad (25)$$

Note also that if $a = 1$, the Weibull distribution reduces to the classical exponential. Thus, Weibull input is a flexible model to study PASTA inequality.

To conclude this section we note that time-based performance measures may be obtained both directly by using the modified Kiefer–Wolfowitz recursion (17), and indirectly by using Little's law and GSMP model. Thus, it may be interesting to numerically study the obtained confidence estimates from the point of view of efficiency (in terms of the width of the interval obtained for a given configuration). These issues are addressed in the following section.

4 Numerical Experiments

In this section, numerical experiments are conducted by using the GI/G/100 supercomputer model as the base of numerical analysis, with Weibull interarrival distribution (24) and Pareto service time distribution (10). In the first experiment, we consider and illustrate the PASTA inequality, whereas in the second experiment we set $a = 1$ to obtain M/G/100-type system and check the efficiency of direct/indirect waiting time estimation.

4.1 PASTA Inequality

In the first experiment, we used the following system configuration: $c = 100$ for the number of servers, the arrival epochs having Weibull distribution (24) where the shape parameter α was iterated over the range $[0.5, 2]$ with step 0.1 and the scale parameter calculated by formula

$$b = \frac{1}{C\Gamma(1 + \frac{1}{\alpha})},$$

where Γ is the gamma function and C is some fixed constant taken in such a way to guarantee system stability and relatively low system load. The service time had Pareto distribution (10) where the scale parameter x_0 and shape parameter α were taken as $x_0 = 1$ and $\alpha = 2.5$ respectively, for all customer classes. Finally, the customer class distribution was uniform, $p_i = 1/100$.

To estimate the workload for given Weibull shape parameter on arrivals, using the Kiefer-Wolfowitz recursion, we built a trajectory of 10^8 arrivals. Indirect estimate was obtained by GSMP model and Little's law. The results are depicted on Fig. 1, and the PASTA inequality is clearly visible, with inequality becoming equality at $a = 1$ as expected.

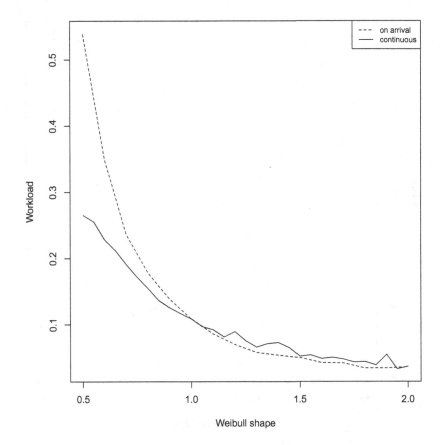

Fig. 1. The estimates of the mean stationary summary workload in continuous time, $W(\infty)$, and at arrival epochs, W_∞, in Weibull/Pareto/100 cluster model.

4.2   Estimator Efficiency

In this experiment, we take $a = 1$ to obtain PASTA equality in order to compare the efficiency of direct/indirect time-based performance estimation. For a fixed average service time, we want to compare the behavior of the system for different values of the shape parameter for Pareto distribution. As such, we use the GSMP to obtain average queue length and, by Little's law, average waiting time in the queue, and compare the width of the confidence interval with the corresponding estimate obtained from the modified Kiefer–Wolfowitz recursion. The point estimates are visualized on Fig. 2 and demonstrate nice coincidence. However, from the confidence intervals depicted on Fig. 3 it can be seen that direct estimate by stochastic recursion slightly outperforms the indirect one (the narrow interval is better) for the case of small values of the Pareto shape α (which correspond to higher variance in service time distribution).

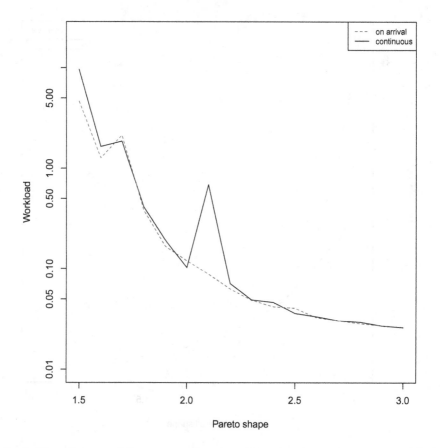

Fig. 2. The estimates of the mean stationary waiting time in continuous time, $W(\infty)$, and at arrival epochs, W_∞, vs. Pareto shape α in M/G/100-type supercomputer model.

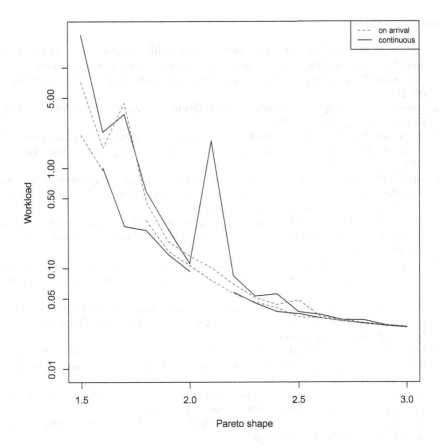

Fig. 3. The confidence intervals for the mean stationary waiting time in continuous time, $W(\infty)$, and at arrival epochs, W_∞, vs. Pareto shape α in M/G/100-type supercomputer model.

5   Conclusion

In this paper we demonstrated some important aspects of a novel supercomputer model by using simulation and heavy-tailed distributions. By numerical experiments we illustrated the PASTA inequality and compared direct/indirect waiting time estimator efficiency. These results are to help the researchers plan the experiment accordingly, by taking into account the important effects of heavy tails on system performance. It might also be interesting to deeply investigate these effects for a system of increasing size and/or under increasing load, however, we leave this for future research.

Acknowledgements. The publication has been prepared with the support of Russian Science Foundation according to the research project No.21-71-10135, https://rscf.ru/en/project/21-71-10135/.

References

1. Afanaseva, L., Bashtova, E., Grishunina, S.: Stability analysis of a multi-server model with simultaneous service and a regenerative input flow. Methodol. Comput. Appl. Probab. **22**(4), 1439–1455 (2019). https://doi.org/10.1007/s11009-019-09721-9
2. Asmussen, S.: Applied Probability and Queues. Springer, New York (2003). https://doi.org/10.1007/b97236
3. Asmussen, S., Glynn, P.W.: Stochastic Simulation: Algorithms and Analysis, vol. 57 in Stochastic modelling and applied probability. Springer, New York (2007). OCLC: ocn123113652
4. Brill, P.H., Green, L.: Queues in which customers receive simultaneous service from a random number of servers: a system point approach. Manag. Sci. **30**(1), 51–68 (1984). https://doi.org/10.1287/mnsc.30.1.51
5. Crane, M.A., Iglehart, D.L.: Simulating stable stochastic systems, i: general multiserver queues. J. ACM (JACM) **21**(1), 103–113 (1974). https://doi.org/10.1145/321796.321805
6. Evans, R.V.: Queuing when jobs require several services which need not be sequenced. Manag. Sci. **10**(2), 298–315 (1964). https://doi.org/10.1287/mnsc.10.2.298
7. Feitelson, D.G.: Random number generators and heavy-tail distributions, published: Technical report 2001–2, School of Computer Science and Engineering, The Hebrew University of Jerusalem
8. Feitelson, D.G.: Workload Modeling for Computer Systems Performance Evaluation. Cambridge University Press, Cambridge (2015). http://ebooks.cambridge.org/ref/id/CBO9781139939690
9. Fourneau, J.M., Quessette, F.: Tradeoff between accuracy and efficiency in the time-parallel simulation of monotone systems. In: Tribastone, M., Gilmore, S. (eds.) EPEW 2012. LNCS, vol. 7587, pp. 80–95. Springer, Heidelberg (2013). https://doi.org/10.1007/978-3-642-36781-6_6
10. Glynn, P.W.: A GSMP formalism for discrete event systems. Proc. IEEE **77**(1), 14–23 (1989)
11. Glynn, P.W.: Some topics in regenerative steady-state simulation. Acta Applicandae Math. **34**(1–2), 225–236 (1994). https://doi.org/10.1007/BF00994267
12. Glynn, P.W., Haas, P.J.: On Transience and recurrence in irreducible finite-state stochastic systems. ACM Trans. Model. Comput. Simul. **25**(4), 1–19 (2015). http://dl.acm.org/citation.cfm?doid=2774955.2699721
13. Grosof, I., Harchol-Balter, M., Scheller-Wolf, A.: Stability for two-class multiserver-job systems. arXiv:2010.00631. http://arxiv.org/abs/2010.00631 (2020)
14. Harchol-Balter, M.: The effect of heavy-tailed job size distributions on computer system design. In: Proceedings of ASA-IMS Conference on Applications of Heavy Tailed Distributions in Economics, Engineering and Statistics (1999). http://www.cs.cmu.edu/afs/cs.cmu.edu/user/harchol/www/Papers/h-t.pdf
15. Harchol-Balter, M.: Open problems in queueing theory inspired by datacenter computing. Queueing Syst. **97**(1), 3–37 (2021). https://doi.org/10.1007/s11134-020-09684-6
16. Harchol-Balter, M.: The multiserver job queueing model. Queueing Syst. **100**, 201–203 (2022). https://doi.org/10.1007/s11134-022-09762-x
17. Henderson, S.G., Glynn, P.W.: Regenerative steady-state simulation of discrete-event systems. ACM Trans. Model. Comput. Simul. **11**(4), 313–345 (2001). http://portal.acm.org/citation.cfm?doid=508366.508367

18. Kim, S.: M/M/s queueing system where customers demand multiple server use. PhD Thesis, Southern Methodist University (1979)

19. Rinne, H.: The Weibull Distribution: A Handbook. CRC Press, Boca Raton (2009). http://www.crcnetbase.com/isbn/9781420087437. OCLC: 399755324

20. Rumyantsev, A., Morozov, E.: Stability criterion of a multiserver model with simultaneous service. Ann. Oper. Res. **252**(1), 29–39 (2015). https://doi.org/10.1007/s10479-015-1917-2

Ensuring Data Integrity Using Merkle Trees in Desktop Grid Systems

Ilya Kurochkin[1]([✉]) [iD] and Svyatoslav Krasnov[2] [iD]

[1] Institute for Information Transmission Problems of Russian Academy of Sciences, Moscow, Russia
qurochkin@gmail.com
[2] National Research University Higher School of Economics, Moscow, Russia

Abstract. The use of distributed systems is one of the ways to solve computationally complex problems along with the use of clusters and other multiprocessor computing systems. Distributed systems have many features that must be taken into account when organizing calculations. The presence of errors in calculations, as well as possible malicious changes to data and results, can distort the results or make them incorrect. For example, in problems of finding a single solution, the presence of even one error can lead to a recalculation of the entire experiment. One way to overcome these features is to use job replication. But in this case, the computing power of a distributed system is greatly reduced. Another approach to identifying untrusted nodes and verifying the results are data integrity techniques. In this case, data integrity must be ensured from the start moment the input data transmission to the computing node until the results are stored on the control node of the distributed system. Currently, methods for solving various problems in distributed systems based on blockchain are popular. This paper proposes a method for ensuring data integrity based on the use of Merkle trees for a voluntary distributed computing project on the BOINC platform. The implementation of the proposed method for ensuring data integrity for two types of computing applications is discussed.

Keywords: Desktop grid · BOINC · Voluntary distributed computing project · Voluntary computing · Volunteer computing · Data integrity · Merkle tree · Blockchain · Orthogonal diagonal Latin squares

1 Introduction

Distributed systems began to gain popularity with the ubiquity of broadband Internet access. As soon as it became possible to link two separate computers based on the global Internet, ideas began to appear about organizing such devices into distributed systems. The first distributed systems using the Internet as a data transmission channel appeared in the 1990s. For example, the projects of the DEC Scientific Center [1] and the project distributed.net [2] served as distributed computing systems, and Napster [3] and Direct Connect [4] were the most famous file-sharing peer-to-peer net-works. At that time, the number of such systems was small, and they solved a limited range of tasks. Today, there are dozens of different distributed systems used for a variety of purposes.

V. Voevodin et al. (Eds.): RuSCDays 2022, LNCS 13708, pp. 670–685, 2022.
https://doi.org/10.1007/978-3-031-22941-1_49

Distributed computing systems have become more considered since the volume of data has grown rapidly over the past two decades. Tens of thousands of machines participate in such systems, which are often characterized by weak connectivity relative to each other when processing data. About 25 years ago, only desktop grid systems could be called distributed computing systems, but over the past twenty years, technologies in this area have made a sharp leap. In 2004, Google introduced the distributed computing paradigm on consumer devices MapReduce [5], for which the most famous open implementation today is Hadoop MapReduce [6] - a framework for processing multi-terabyte datasets on large computing clusters. Another popular distributed computing system used by Netflix, Yahoo and eBay is Apache Spark [7]. It is capable of processing unstructured or loosely structured data in RAM on top of the HDFS file system, supporting both batch and streaming data processing. Apache Hive [8], which is closely related to Spark, provides distributed data storage management capabilities using SQL-declarative language. Another popular big data frame-work used by Twitter, Yahoo! and Spotify companies is Apache Storm [9], which specializes in streaming data processing.

Large technology companies that can afford to build large data centers or rent a large amount of resources in them, organize their data processing processes at these facilities. However, complex tasks solved with the help of resource-intensive applications are found not only in a multibillion-dollar technological business environment. Various scientific institutes and centers solve extremely complex computational problems of molecular docking, identification of previously unknown parameters of asteroids, search for polymers and nanoclusters, problems in the field of combinatorics and orthogonal Latin squares, and many others. At the same time, the budgets of such organizations for computing resources are extremely limited and small, and scientific supercomputers can often be unavailable. In this regard, such a system as HTCondor (formerly known as Condor) appeared [10] in 1988. It served as a system for parallelizing computationally complex applications on devices that are not busy computing at a certain point in time. Such a system made it possible to perform calculations not only on dedicated university high-performance clusters, but also on ordinary user PCs in laboratories and computer classes. The actual use of these resources ranged from 5% to 20%, due to which it was possible to load the computer with background tasks by several tens of percent more. However, there is no doubt that such capacities were insufficient, and over time the heterogeneity of resources has grown greatly, so about 20 years ago the idea of Volunteer Computing as a type of distributed computing appeared. It involves the use of computing resources on a wide variety of platforms by volunteers who want to support a scientific project in their free time from the work of their devices. The most successful and well-known framework with potentially unlimited computing power was the BOINC (Berkeley Open Infrastructure for Network Computing) framework [11], which appeared in 2002 as a result of the development of one of the scientific projects SETI@home [12]. Today, it is the most advanced volunteer computing platform with millions of participants around the world.

A critical part of any distributed system is fault tolerance. It determines the ability of the system to function in the event of an unavoidable failure of one or more of its components. Data integrity can be considered as part of fault tolerance, since it is responsible for the correctness and consistency of the data processed by the system.

672   I. Kurochkin and S. Krasnov

And voluntary computing or volunteer computing is the most complex subdomain of distributed computing in the context of ensuring fault tolerance and data integrity of such a system. This is due to the fact that the volunteers and their intentions are completely unknown to the author of the project, which creates a wide space for various attacks. Moreover, in popular scientific projects, the number of computational tasks processed can be millions per day. Thus, the fault tolerance of the server architecture of the voluntary computing software is critically important.

Initially, the entire field of voluntary computing was limited to a small number of scientific projects such as GIMPS [13] or SETI@Home. The server part software of such projects was private, and details about the fault tolerance methods were not disclosed. In addition, at that time, there was neither a huge number of computing volunteers, nor a significant motivation to behave in bad faith. However, the success of the SETI@Home project inspired its creator to generalize the software into an open-source voluntary computing platform - BOINC. The fundamental success of this platform was that, like its close relative HTCondor, the full utilization of volunteer resources was not intended for use. The user could independently configure the quotas of resources allocated for calculations that he wanted. For example, he could set limits on processor time (no more than X%) or the number of cores involved, limit the download speed, sending, network traffic volume, set the maximum size of the disk used, etc. With the advent and increased number of BOINC users, issues of fault tolerance and data integrity became more and more relevant.

2   Review

If we consider Condor (HTCondor in the current view) as a close ancestor of BOINC in distributed computing, we can say that the framework has incorporated a checkpoint mechanism to provide some form of fault tolerance. In the original article about Condor [10], it is noted that a checkpoint is an intermediate state of a program executed on a remote machine, which is saved during its operation in order to resume work with a certain progress in the future. However, the difference between Condor and BOINC is the definition of this state. If Condor natively supported the preservation of the working state of the program, that is, the preservation of such sections of the program as text, data, stack segments, register values, statuses of open file descriptors, sent network messages, then from the BOINC side, the checkpoint means the state that the computing application itself will save. That is, the BOINC client, unlike Condor, is not responsible for saving the checkpoint, but only sends a message to the main application with a request to do it. Thus, application developers for BOINC independently determine which application states they wish to preserve. However, it is worth mentioning that BOINC later added support for running applications in VirtualBox virtual machines, for which it is possible to save states independently of applications using snapshots of virtual machines.

When analyzing the mechanisms of fault tolerance and data integrity directly in BOINC, this work is based on the paper [14] of BOINC developer. The replication-based approach is used as the main way to determine the correctness of the calculation results in BOINC. Its essence lies in the replication of a computational task to a quorum (min_quorum parameter) of independent client replicas. If the quorum results agree with each other, then the result is accepted as correct, otherwise an additional instance of the task is created and sent to another replica. This happens until a quorum is reached or the limits are exhausted (max_error_instances, max_succeess_instances). BOINC allows you to configure replication with great flexibility, taking into account the same equivalence classes by device, operating system, processor architecture (homogeneous redundancy), as well as on fixed versions of applications (homogeneous apps). BOINC also introduces mechanisms of trusted or reliable hosts that are highly likely (based on retrospective data) to correctly calculate the result and reduce the replication factor of tasks.

To ensure data integrity, the following are additionally applied:

1. Validation of the contents of input and output files using MD5 hashes;
2. Adding random substrings to output file names to prevent file name matching at-tacks (spoofing attacks);
3. Storing data based on immutable files after creation.

For fault tolerance of the BOINC server, the multi-daemon architecture was used [11]. The daemon implies an independent component of the server responsible for a specific function. For example, the transitioner is responsible for the transition of a computational task from one state to another, and the validator is responsible for validating the results of calculations sent by the client.

Each daemon does not interact directly with another, and functions on the basis of information from the database, that is, the output data of one daemon, recorded by it in the database, can be the input data of another daemon. This architecture provides high fault tolerance within the framework of inter-component interaction. After all, if one of the daemons dies, the other components will continue to work. The work for the fallen component accumulates in the database and will eventually be completed when the component returns to service. Also, in such an architecture, the responsibility for processing competitive requests and transactions is shifted to the database.

To ensure the fault tolerance of the server, the following are additionally used:

• Cryptographic tokens to limit the total size of downloaded files in order to prevent DDoS attacks;
• Exponential timeouts between the client and the server to reduce network load;
• Checkpoints of intermediate calculation results on the client.

3   Mechanisms for Ensuring Fault Tolerance and Data Integrity

In addition to certain mechanisms in the BOINC itself, in the context of fault tolerance and ensuring data integrity, there are methods that are not specifically related to any framework. Thus, in the Kan Watabe work [15] an approach is proposed to counteract a group of volunteers in collusion, behaving in bad faith and trying to sabotage the performance of the project. The idea of the authors is a mechanism for random verification of the client for the correctness of calculations on his part. A special task is sent to him, for which the server already knows the correct answer, and depending on the client's response, it is determined whether he is a participant in the sabotage or not. If the percentage of erroneous results is detected above the threshold, all the client's results are disabled. This mechanism is not bad at detecting intruders in calculations, but in comparison with the methods proposed in this paper, it does not reduce the replication factor, but even increases it, recognizing the calculations of some clients as untenable and re-creating new replicas of tasks.

The paper by Michele Ianni, Elio Masciari [16] emphasizes that there are a number of computational tasks that process data that cannot be disclosed. They may contain users' personal or any other sensitive data, such as patient diagnoses or financial information. If such calculations need to be performed within the framework of voluntary computing, then the volunteer should not see sensitive input or output data in any form. To do this, the authors' study suggests using trusted computing, a security technology that allows using the capabilities of additional hardware, often a special chip or cryptoprocessor, to provide OS integrity checks at the hardware level, generate and securely store cryptographic keys, securely and privately process input and output data, execute applications in isolation from users and OS administrators with the highest privileges and much more. Trusted computing is directly related to the hardware of a computing device and, depending on the platform, has a variety of implementations. In particular, the authors' article uses the Intel processor architecture, which implements Intel Software Guard Extensions for trusted computing, and integration with trusted computing on other platforms. For example, ARM TrustZone for processors with ARM architecture, is noted as not yet completed work. And indeed, AMD processors have a similar Secure Encrypted Virtualization (SEV) technology, Apple has an Apple T2 security chip with its API, Samsung has Samsung KNOX technology, etc. Undoubtedly, in the context of voluntary computing, this approach is guaranteed to secure any calculations on the user's device and ensure data integrity "out of the box" without additional effort. But in its current form, BOINC isn't adapted to the implementation of trusted computing in any way. The implementation of even one trusted computing platform for BOINC is a huge independent project that does not fit into the scope of this work, not to mention the huge variety of platforms that are currently supported by BOINC.

In paper [17] the framework for big data processing – ICE is presented. The authors consider fault tolerance of computing in the context of the state of clients processing computational tasks. In BOINC, for each task assigned to the client, a certain deadline for completing the task is calculated, and the client's status is determined by its compliance, that is, whether the client is active or not. The authors claim that this approach does not work well in conditions of complex graphs of streaming computing, since the task execution time, other things being equal, can vary greatly depending on dynamically changing input data, respectively, predictions on deadlines cannot be made. Instead, they implement a heartbeat mechanism to determine the status of the client and the maximum time of its unavailability (silence timeout). This approach really allows you to identify inactive clients in a timely manner and reassign computing tasks to other devices, but the current work focuses on server fault tolerance rather than client, since modification of the client program is not possible within the framework of a dedicated BOINC project.

Another interesting work on the topic of ensuring fault tolerance of voluntary computing is the work of Boxuan Shan [18]. It criticizes the client-server architecture approach of all modern voluntary computing frameworks, including BOINC. The author claims that a single point of failure in the form of a project server will always limit scaling and fault tolerance. The study presents a design in which there are volunteers and organizers of computing, exchanging information stored in the blockchain. They simultaneously serve as nodes that form one blockchain network and maintain consensus for conducting operations in this network. Accordingly, the organizer for sending tasks to the volunteer sends a task block to the blockchain (job block), the volunteer can find a block of this type in the blockchain. And send a processing block to it to signal to the rest of the volunteers that he has taken up this task and then send a result block as the results of calculations (result block). Due to the decentralized nature of the blockchain, asynchronous interaction between volunteers and organizers can be observed in such an architecture, and a single point of failure is no longer a bottleneck, so there are no restrictions on scalability and fault tolerance. However, this approach is not without a number of drawbacks. The total calculation time of one task is higher, since the time for adding and distributing blocks is added to the overall calculation process, which generates additional delays that are absent when the organizer interacts with the volunteer directly. The author's article also notes that volunteers can compete for the same task, which can lead to a fork of the block-chain. This effect can artificially increase the replication factor, reducing the overall computing performance. In the current work, one of the goals is to reduce the replication factor of the task and increase the throughput of calculations.

Despite the fact that the replication-based approach solves the problem of correctness of the calculations well enough, it still has a number of disadvantages. The approach is still vulnerable to the fact that the client can substitute the input and output files of a computational task without performing calculations at all. The approach is also susceptible to 51% type attacks, although in practice their implementation is quite rare due to inexpediency. It is difficult not to agree that replication greatly reduces the throughput of calculations in the context of many application tasks. Within the framework of this work, an approach is proposed based on validation of crypto-graphic hashes of input and output data calculated using Merkle trees, into which a secret encrypted using RSA asymmetric encryption and accessible only to the runtime of the computing application is mixed from the server side. The proposed approach will to some extent reduce the task replication factor by reducing the likelihood of data integrity violations. This will increase productivity within the project by directing the freed resources to the calculation of new tasks.

From the point of view of server fault tolerance, the obvious bottleneck in the en-tire architecture is the database. If, for some reason, it is unavailable, then the work of all server components is blocked since they can neither read the input data nor record the results of their work. The method of increasing the fault tolerance of the BOINC server investigated in this work is database replication. When researching the application of this method for the current architecture, there are many pitfalls that should be taken into account, which will be discussed later.

4 Methods

4.1 Data Integrity Threat Model

Before improving the protection of any system, it is important to understand the purpose, motivation, and the intentions of the attacker who will carry out the attacks. The main motivation to participate in voluntary calculations may be earning a rating. Of course, this is not the root cause of their help for all participants, many act only based on altruistic motives and aspirations for the development of science through joint efforts. However, for many, the rating may contain some value, because it is publicly visible, it can be included in a resume, and a significant contributor to scientific projects can gain popularity. The rating is also the basis for competitions between individual users and entire teams. With the help of the rating, individual projects measure computational performance. Moreover, there are cryptocurrencies, such as GridCoin [19], that reward participation in voluntary calculations, for which the rating serves as proof of the calculations performed (proof-of-work). All the above-mentioned characteristics of the rating of a participant in BOINC calculations are the main motivation of the attacker, whose goal will be to cheat the rating in one form or another.

In BOINC, credits are awarded for completed tasks that have successfully passed validation. However, there is a number of tasks with a small variety of answers, for example, prime number check, for which the answer to the question "is a prime number?" maybe "yes" or "no". Accordingly, the main goal of the attacker is to send a correct response in some way, without performing any real calculations or making a minimum of calculations. Let's denote the various attack vectors in this context:

1) Modification of network traffic. This attack can be carried out not only by the participant of the calculations, but by an attacker from the outside. In this scenario, a man-in-the-middle attack is considered. An attacker can substitute any data that is sent from the server to the client and back.
2) Modification of input files. On the user's side, the application's input files are substituted for the computational task. This attack can be carried out under the conditions that the application has a small set of correct application responses, and the user has calculated in advance some task that is fast in computing time and saved its input results. Thus, for new tasks, it replaces the input files in order to quickly calculate some result and send it.
3) Modification of the application checkpoints. The client, as part of the calculation of the task, can substitute the checkpoint to speed up its execution. With this approach, part of the iterations may be skipped for the application, and the result will still be correct.
4) Modification of output files. The most popular attack scenario is when the client, without doing any calculations (skipping them or killing the application process), creates or modifies the output files that have already been produced once. This attack is also relevant in conditions of a small set of correct application responses.

The features of the BOINC device make this system sufficiently open and accessible to attacks, since the source code of the server and client is freely available, and the input and output files are not encrypted before sending, so they are available to the user in their original form. Accordingly, the threat model under consideration is that the user can use one or combine several of the above attack vectors to achieve his goal in an optimal way. Additionally, the user can make their own changes to the BOINC client to facilitate some attack scenarios. Thus, it is necessary to develop a method that ensures data integrity throughout the life of a computational task, starting with sending input files to the client and ending with validating the results of calculations on the server.

4.2 Description of the Data Integrity Approach

The only computing component that is hidden from the user in some way is the application runtime. Compiled into executable files, the application represents some isolated environment to which an unprepared user does not have access. The original article notes that the target audience of BOINC is computer owners with a poor technical background, who may have never installed applications on their device. In this paper, a stricter premise is made, and an unprepared user means a person who does not have advanced skills at disassembling, reverse engineering and debugging executable files and their address space. Based on this idea, the premise is made that some secrets can be used to validate the correctness of all data in the executable application space. The proposed approach is based on the fact that, from the server side, a secret is mixed into the hash of all input data, encrypted using RSA asymmetric encryption and accessible only to the execution environment of the computing application. This secret is used to validate cryptographic hashes of input and output data calculated using Merkle trees. A detailed scheme of the proposed approach is presented in Fig. 1.

At the first stage, the client must generate a pair of RSA keys - public and private. To do this, the client accesses the server for tasks. The server observes that there is no public key in the database for the client and sends the corresponding key generation BOINC task to the client. After a generation, the client stores them and sends its public key to the server. The server stores the client's public key in its database. The keys are generated for each user's host, since one user can have multiple devices. However, such generation is required only once.

At the second stage, the client again contacts the server for the task. The server counts the Merkle tree root (hash_root) from all input files using the cryptographical-ly strong SHA-256 hash function. As a secret, the server uses the WUID - workunit id, which is the unique identifier of the computational task. It encrypts the WUID using the client's public key, receiving the WUID_enc ciphertext, and hashes it with the Merkle tree root, receiving the hash_input_server output hash. Then, the server sends all the input files, hash_input_server and WUID_enc to the client. All network interactions between the server and the client occur using secure TLS connections.

At the third stage, an application begins to be executed on the client side, the work of which consists of three stages - processing input files, launching a useful applica-tion, processing output files. At the stage of processing input files, hash_root is calcu-lated, WUID_enc is decrypted using the client's private key, hash_input_client is cal-culated. After that, hash_input_client is compared with hash_input_server, and if they match, then it can be argued that the input files were not substituted by the client. Otherwise, the task on the client is terminated, and a response is sent to the server about the violated integrity

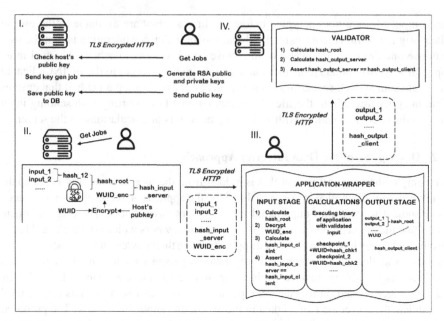

Fig. 1. A scheme for ensuring data integrity throughout the life of a computational task

of the input data. After validating the input files, the application starts performing useful calculations. During calculations, it can generate checkpoints, for which hashes with a mixed WUID will also be generated. If the application stops, then in order to resume from the checkpoint, it will similarly check that the checkpoint has not been replaced. After generating the results, the root hash of all output files (hash_root) is calculated in the same way, which is hashed with WUID, receiving the output hash hash_output_client, and then all this data is sent to the server.

At the last stage, the validator component on the server calculates hash_output_server in the same way as the input data processing stage on the client and compares it with hash_output_client. If they are equal, then we can assume that the computational task has passed validation and the integrity throughout the lifetime of the computational task is not violated.

The protection mechanism in the proposed approach is based on the client's ignorance of the secret (WUID), which is mixed into the resulting hashes, since its decryp-tion takes place in the application execution environment. Therefore, with any data change, be it input files, checkpoints or output files on his side, he also needs to change the corresponding hashes, but due to ignorance of the secret, he will not be able to do this, only by brute force. This method of protection allows you to guarantee with some degree of confidence not only the integrity of the data, but also the fact of actually performed calculations. The client can no longer prematurely terminate the process of executing a useful application and replace the output files for sending, because in this case the component responsible for generating output hashes (hash_root and hash_output_client) will find out about it and will not generate hashes.

Two objects can act as an application consisting of three components of the client. At best, all the components are embedded in the scientific application itself. That is, if the project owner has the opportunity to recompile a scientific application with data integrity components, then this provides all integrity guarantees. But sometimes scientific applications are not the property of the project owners, as well as the source codes are not freely available. Then the only possible scenario would be to use a wrapper application that will consistently perform all the steps shown in the diagram on the client. This approach has a significant drawback: the inability to implement the integrity of checkpoints. The fact is that the wrapper application will not be able to distinguish the real author of the checkpoint from the attacker in any way, in order to cache the contents of the checkpoint with a WUID. Therefore, the presented mechanism has the maximum protection efficiency when explicitly embedded in the executable file of a scientific application.

It is worth giving a justification for the choice of tools for the above algorithm. BOINC already has validation of separate input and output files based on MD5 hashes, but this hash function has long been considered cryptographically unstable to collision attacks [20]. In this algorithm, SHA-256 was chosen, which is currently considered cryptographically stable and has many uses in sensitive data applications, for example, in the Bitcoin mining algorithm, password hashing, SSH and TLS [21]. The concept of hashing using Merkle trees was used for two reasons:

1. To associate a complete set of input and output files with a single hash, and its binding with a secret – WUID.
2. To be able to store sticky input files on the client, which are not deleted after the task is completed and do not require reloading, but require validation each time the task is performed.

5   Results

The proposed approach to ensuring data integrity solves two problems: increasing the reliability of the results of calculations performed by the user, and accelerating the calculations themselves by reducing the replication factor. All components and utili-ties responsible for data integrity validation were written in Python, and their source code is available in the GitHub repository [22]. Moreover, changes were made to the BOINC server itself, written in C++: for this, a fork of the main BOINC repository was made [23]. In the experimental study of the data integrity mechanism, a real computing application KLPMD [24] – searching for canonical marriage DLSs was used, which searches for sets of combinatorial structures based on diagonal Latin squares.

5.1   Testing the Data Integrity Method

The model of data integrity threats was presented, in which the main attack scenarios by an intruder were listed. During testing, a wrapper application was used as an object executed on the client, since access to the source files of the scientific application was not possible.

Modification of Network Traffic

Obviously, this problem is solved not at the application level, but at the network transport level. In the proposed approach, all data is moved over a network with TLS/SSL protocols, which allows you to protect yourself from a man-in-the-middle attacks. To do this, a special option was enabled in the BOINC project in the html/project/project.inc.

Additionally, edits were made to the Apache configuration file to configure the HTTPS protocol. During testing, a server without SSL certificates was used. Accordingly, all data was transmitted over an unsecured channel, and its packets could be easily seen using a sniffer program. However, when SSL/TLS was included in the project, the traffic was encrypted, and the problem was resolved.

Modification of Input Files

Data integrity is monitored at the first stage of the wrapper program. There is a job configuration file for this program.xml that setup a set of tasks for it. The integrity of the input data is checked by the component input_validator.exe. For it, the input files of the computing application that need to be validated are set, including the job it-self.xml, which can also be substituted. Since the work of the validator is fast enough and manual substitution is difficult without the use of special tools, the testing of substitution of input files was carried out as follows: in job.xml the component was enabled sleep.exe, which provided some delay to manually have time to replace the data.

Then, during a 10-s pause, one input file in was edited (an extra line feed was added at the end of the file). After a pause input_validator.exe calculated the root hash of the Merkle tree from all input files, decrypted the WUID, and hashed it together with the root hash to get input_hash_client. Then the component compared the calculated hash with the one sent by the server and revealed their inequality, after which it terminated with a non-zero return code to stop the wrapper application.

It is worth emphasizing once again that the client can substitute everything except the contents of input_hash_server, since he does not know the encrypted WUID in order to calculate this hash from all the modified input files. Accordingly, to the server in the logs of the components input_validator.exe and the logs of the wrapper application reflected the fact of violation of data integrity verification at the stage of input files.

When modeling a scenario where the integrity check at the validation stage of input files is not violated, you can see the output in the validator logs.

Modification of Application Checkpoints

During operation, the computing application can save the state of its progress to the checkpoint files. As noted above, using a wrapper application, it is impossible to implement a mechanism to ensure the integrity of checkpoints. In this regard, a test application was written that does not produce a payload, but retains some checkpoints. The imitation of the attack was carried out as follows:

1. The application starts processing the computational task;

2. The user waits for the first checkpoint and hash to be saved from the concatenation of the checkpoint content and WUID by the application;
3. The user stops the program and replaces the checkpoint, but not the hash (due to ignorance of the WUID);
4. The user resumes the application;
5. The application violates the integrity check of the checkpoint, because the hash from the modified checkpoint with WUID does not match the original hash.

As a result, the application terminates with a non-zero return code and saves the information to the logs available on the server.

Modification of Output Files
After the computing application has worked and generated the output files, the component starts working output_submitter.exe, to which the names of the output files of the computing application are supplied as input. It similarly calculates the output hash for all output files, mixing the WUID into it and sends it to the server. To simulate file substitution in the same way as when modeling the substitution of input files, a component was added sleep.exe, during the operation of which one of the output files stdout was substituted. After replacing the output file, all files and the resulting hash (which was not changed by the client due to ignorance of the WUID) were sent to the server. On the server, a component such as output_validator calculated the root hash of the Merkle tree from all output files, took the WUID that was given to it for input from the outside, and hashed it together with the root hash to get output_hash_server. Then the component compared the calculated hash with the one sent by the client and revealed their inequality, after which it ended with a non-zero return code to signal to the BOINC server that the validation of the calculation result was violated, and the problem arose at the stage of creating output files.

This means that the entire processing pipeline of the computational task turned out to be correct, and validation of data integrity at all stages was successful.

5.2 Testing the Computing Performance Using the Proposed Method

The proposed approach to ensuring data integrity involves the transmission of additional data over the network that was previously missing. In this regard, it is relevant to estimate the overhead costs for the amount of data in comparison with what it was before the implementation of the described mechanism. Measurements of data volumes were performed on a test task with one input file in, which is used by a computing application and several dummy ones (in_dummy_1/2/3/4) for the exponential calculation of the Merkle tree hash. Based on the results of the comparison, it can be observed that the overhead costs for the volume of data amounted to only $\approx 2.13\%$. Moreover, these overhead costs are constant and do not depend on the volume of input and output data.

Thus, the proposed approach to ensuring data integrity, mainly due to the idea of hashing using the Merkle tree, makes it possible to achieve acceptable overhead in terms of traffic volume. Calculations of data volumes within the framework of the key generation task can be neglected, since it is performed only once for one user host.

The main purpose of the implemented data integrity mechanism is to increase the guarantees of the correctness of the calculations performed. Due to increased guarantees, it becomes possible to reduce the replication factor. Each project should empirically identify the level of the number of data integrity violations, determine the permissible threshold of violations, accuracy and error in the calculation results and calculate an acceptable replication factor depending on these parameters. In performance testing, the following hypothesis is tested: the replication level is inversely proportional to the computing performance. Based on the already mentioned KLPMD scientific application, performance was measured on 36 computational tasks (36 workunits), with a different set of application input parameters. Calculations were performed on a desktop computer with a 6-core (12 threads) Intel Core i5 10600K 4100 GHz processor and 32 GB of RAM on Windows 11. As an example, for a set of tasks that were calculated without a data integrity mechanism, the replication factor was set to 2 (min_quorum), which is equivalent to 2 computational results for the 1st task (workunit). Accordingly, for a set of tasks with data integrity, the replication factor was reduced by half and was 1 (for 1 workunit 1 result). The results of measurements of calculations can be seen in Figs. 2 and 3.

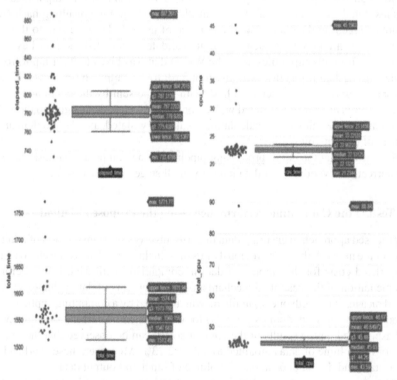

Fig. 2. The results of measuring the calculation times and processor time on 36 computing tasks without a data integrity mechanism

The duration of calculations in seconds (elapsed_time) and the percentage of CPU time (cpu_time) in %. The proposed hypothesis was confirmed by this example: the total calculation time of 36 tasks without a data integrity mechanism was 56,679 s, which is twice as long as the calculation time of the same tasks without a data integrity mechanism, which was 28,182 s due to a doubly reduced replication factor. For one workunit, its execution in a system without an integrity mechanism took an average of 1574 s (due to two computational results), and with a mechanism – 782 s. In the context of one result, the average time has not changed: for tasks without an integrity mechanism, it averages 787 s, and with a mechanism even slightly less – 782 s.

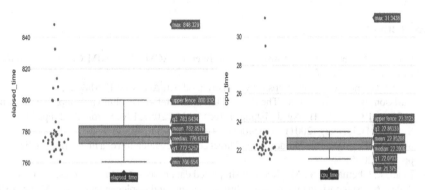

Fig. 3. Results of measurement of calculation times and processor time on 36 computational tasks with a data integrity mechanism

Thus, the implemented data integrity mechanism did not introduce significant overhead costs, not only in terms of input and output data, but also in terms of processor computing time. And in reality, the acceleration of throughput is twice as close to the upper estimate in the assumed hypothesis.

6 Conclusion

The mechanisms of fault tolerance and data integrity already existing in BOINC were studied in detail. The BOINC platform itself was compared with popular distributed computing systems. The existing mechanisms for ensuring fault tolerance and data integrity in voluntary computing without binding to a specific framework were also considered. In the main part of the study, a model of data integrity threats was presented in detail, as well as an approach based on Merkle tree hashes, designed to increase security against these threats. In an experimental study of the proposed method of ensuring data integrity, the simulation of the presented threats and the system's response to their implementation were described. It was also shown that when implementing the described mechanism into the executable file of a computing application, it is possible to protect yourself from the mentioned attack scenarios with a high degree of confidence and ensure the correctness of calculations of computational tasks. Testing of the proposed approach showed that the performance within a single computational result, as well as the amount of data, practically did not change, and for example, with the reduction of the replication factor by half, it was possible to increase the performance by the expected two times, which is close to the upper estimate. It is worth mentioning that this approach does not imply the complete neutralization of unfair behavior, the user can still try to replace the data from his side. The proposed approach can identify malicious nodes with greater speed and accuracy. And then it becomes possible to exclude them from trusted nodes as soon as possible, thereby increasing the proportion of reliable nodes for computing.

Acknowledgements. This work was funded by Russian Science Foundation (№ 22–11-00317).

References

1. Leiner, B.M., et al.: A brief history of the Internet. ACM SIGCOMM Comput. Commun. Rev. **39**(5), 22–31 (2009)
2. Distributed.net homepage. https://www.distributed.net. Accessed 17 May 2022
3. Carlsson, B., Gustavsson, R.: The rise and fall of napster - an evolutionary approach. In: Liu, J., Yuen, P.C., Li, C.-H., Ng, J., Ishida, T. (eds.) AMT 2001. LNCS, vol. 2252, pp. 347–354. Springer, Heidelberg (2001). https://doi.org/10.1007/3-540-45336-9_40
4. Schou, J., Engström, G., Nordqvist, T.: Direct connect : evaluation of a filesharing application, pp. 1–4 (2005)
5. Dean, J., Ghemawat, S.: MapReduce: simplified data processing on large clusters. In: OSDI 2004 – 6th Symposium on Operating Systems Design and Implementation, vol. 51, pp. 137–149 (2004)
6. Apache Hadoop MapReduce documentation. https://hadoop.apache.org/docs/r1.2.1/index.html. Accessed 17 May 2022
7. Apache Spark documentation. https://spark.apache.org/docs/2.4.7. Accessed 17 May 2022
8. Apache Hive documentation. https://cwiki.apache.org/confluence/display/Hive/Home. Accessed 17 May 2022
9. Apache Storm documentation. https://storm.apache.org/releases/2.3.0/index.html. Accessed 17 May 2022
10. Litzkow, M.J., Livny, M., Mutka, M.W.: Condor - a hunter of idle workstations. In: Proceedings of the International Conference on Distributed Computing Systems, vol. 8, pp. 104–111 (1988)
11. Anderson, D.P.: BOINC: A system for public-resource computing and storage. In: Proceedings of the IEEE/ACM International Workshop on Grid Computing, pp. 4–10 (2004)
12. Anderson, D.P., Cobb, J., Korpela, E., Lebofsky, M., Werthimer, D.: SETI@home: an experiment in public-resource computing. Commun. ACM **45**, 56–61 (2002)
13. Woltman, G., Kurowski, S., et al.: The great internet mersenne prime search. https://www.mersenne.org. Accessed 17 May 2022
14. Anderson, D.P.: BOINC: a platform for volunteer computing. J. Grid Comput. **18**(1), 99–122 (2019). https://doi.org/10.1007/s10723-019-09497-9
15. Watanabe, K., Fukushi, M., Horiguchi, S.: Collusion-resistant sabotage-tolerance mechanisms for volunteer computing systems. In: Proceedings of the IEEE International Conference on e-Business Engineering, ICEBE 2009, IEEE International Workshop - AiR 2009; SOAIC 2009; SOKMBI 2009; ASOC 2009, pp. 213–218 (2009)
16. Ianni, M., Masciari, E.: Trusted environments for volunteer computing. In: Proceedings of the 2018 IEEE 19th International Conference on Information Reuse and Integration for Data Science, IRI 2018, pp. 526–529 (2018)

17. Lv, Z., Chen, D., Singh, A.K.: Big data processing on volunteer computing. ACM Trans. Internet Technol. **21**, 1–20 (2021)
18. Shan, B.: A design of volunteer computing system based on blockchain. In: 2021 IEEE 13th International Conference on Computer Research and Development, ICCRD 2021, pp. 125–129 (2021)
19. Gridcoin Whitepaper: The computation power of a blockchain driving science & data analysis (2017). https://gridcoin.us/assets/docs/whitepaper.pdf. Accessed 17 May 2022
20. Wang, X., Feng, D., Lai, X., Yu, H.: Collisions for hash functions MD4, MD5, HAVAL-128 and RIPEMD. IACR Cryptol. ePrint Arch. **5**, 5–8 (2004)
21. SHA-256 algorithm overview. https://www.n-able.com/blog/sha-256-encryption. Accessed 17 May 2022
22. Github-repository. https://github.com/jellythefish/boinc_helpers. Accessed 17 May 2022
23. Github-repository with BOINC-server fork. https://github.com/jellythefish/boinc_improved_fault_tolerance_and_integrity/pull/1. Accessed 17 May 2022
24. Vatutin, E., Titov, V., Zaikin, O., Kochemazov, S., Manzuk, M., Nikitina, N.: Orthogonality-based classification of diagonal Latin squares of order 10. In: CEUR Workshop Proceedings, vol. 2267, pp. 282–287 (2018)

Optimization of the Workflow in a BOINC-Based Desktop Grid for Virtual Drug Screening

Natalia Nikitina[1]([✉]) [ID] and Evgeny Ivashko[1,2] [ID]

[1] Institute of Applied Mathematical Research, Karelian Research Center
of the Russian Academy of Sciences, 185910 Petrozavodsk, Russia
{nikitina,ivashko}@krc.karelia.ru
[2] Petrozavodsk State University, 185035 Petrozavodsk, Russia

Abstract. This paper presents an analysis of a BOINC-based volunteer computing project SiDock@home. The project implements virtual drug screening. We analyse the employed workflow describing the processes of task generation, results creation, validation and assimilation. Basing on this analysis, we propose an optimized workflow aimed at minimization of computing intensity and scaling up the granularity of the results.

Keywords: Distributed computing · Volunteer computing · Desktop grid · Task scheduling · BOINC · Virtual screening · Molecular docking

1 Introduction

Desktop Grid is a high-throughput computing paradigm based on using the idle time of non-dedicated geographically distributed general-purpose computing nodes (usually, personal computers) connected to the central server by the Internet or a local access network. The concept of Desktop Grid was introduced in 1987 [21] and used in many projects since then. Today, such a computing paradigm allows to efficiently solve computationally intensive scientific problems in mathematics (Gerasim@home [9], Amicable Numbers [2]), biology (Rosetta@home [30], Folding@home [34]), physics (LHC@home [17]), astronomy (Einstein@Home [7], Universe@Home [35]) and other areas of science.

Among the variety of high-performance and high-throughput computing systems, Desktop Grids hold a special place due to their enormous potential and, at the same time, high availability. For instance, in 2020, a volunteer computing project Folding@home gathered resources exceeding one exaflops and became the first world's exascale system, more powerful than the top 100 supercomputers combined [36]. The overall potential of Desktop Grids is estimated as hundreds of exaflops [3], exceeding the total power of all existing supercomputers. It makes Desktop Grid a credible alternative to other high-performance and high-throughput computing systems when solving urgent scientific problems [1].

V. Voevodin et al. (Eds.): RuSCDays 2022, LNCS 13708, pp. 686–698, 2022.
https://doi.org/10.1007/978-3-031-22941-1_50

In more than 30 years of the existence of Desktop Grids, multiple software platforms have been implemented and used for their operation. The high availability and ease-of-use of Desktop Grids complicate the enumeration and analysis of the variety of Desktop Grid-based projects. However, recent reviews of the public volunteer computing projects [6,20] show that up to 80% of them are based on BOINC (Berkeley Open Infrastructure for Network Computing) [3].

BOINC is an Open Source software platform for Desktop Grid deployment with a client-server architecture (Fig. 1). The server consists of a number of parallel services sharing a database (see [3] for detailed architecture). The client connects to the server to request tasks, performs computations and sends the results back to the server. The server validates and assimilates the results, aggregating them to obtain the solution of the initial scientific problem.

Fig. 1. Client-server architecture of BOINC.

In high-performance and high-throughput computing, the term scientific workflow generally stands for a data-intensive and computationally intensive scenario with interdependencies between parallel tasks [18]. Such a scenario is typically modeled in the form of a directed acyclic graph representing the tasks and dependencies between them. Optimization of scientific workflows is a broad subject that has been rigorously studied in the literature [5,10,15,18]. In BOINC-based Desktop Grids, however, the tasks are usually mutually independent and follow the model of "bag-of-tasks". In the present work, we restrict ourselves to such a model of a workflow. Concrete scientific problems and computational platforms impose specific requirements on the workflow optimisation. This is the case, in particular, for BOINC-based biomedical research [11,16,29].

Desktop Grid are aimed at gathering large amount of resources for a long period of time, so as to repeatedly process huge numbers of homogeneous tasks. With that, even small improvements could save years of CPU time. In this paper, we discuss the problem of performance optimization of a Desktop Grid-based computing project performing large-scale molecular docking. We perform analysis of the computational process, show that the issues of redundant computations and correctness are of high importance for such a project, and propose a design of the workflow which will address these issues.

The paper is organized as follows. In Sect. 2, we describe the scope of volunteer computing project SiDock@home aimed at drug discovery via high-throughput virtual screening. In Sect. 3, we summarise and analyse the computational efficiency of the project and propose a solution to the identified problems. In Sect. 4, we comment on the immediate implementation of the proposed solution. Finally, in Sect. 5, we conclude the paper.

2 Volunteer Computing Project SiDock@home

2.1 Project Setup

In March 2020, a citizen science project *"Citizen science and the fight against the coronavirus"* (COVID.SI) [12] was initiated in the field of drug design and medicinal chemistry. The project is aimed at drug discovery, first of all, against coronavirus infection, using high-throughput virtual screening (HTVS) [19, 33] on a small molecules library developed by the team. The problem of HTVS has the bag-of-tasks type and can be efficiently implemented in a Desktop Grid environment. At the same time, the scale of the problem requires a significant amount of computational resources that increases proportionally to the size of the small molecules library. These factors made volunteer computing an efficient tool for COVID.SI. The project received a good response from the community and showed the applicability of the volunteer computing to the ongoing research.

In the following months, SiDock@home, a BOINC-based extension of CO-VID.SI, was created and grew into a sizable, independent and competent research project for general drug design. We describe the project setup in detail in [25, 27] and estimate its performance in [26]. As of the end of March, 2022, there are 7540 registered users in SiDock@home providing about 8000 active computers with the total processing power 56 Teraflops as measured by means of BOINC.

2.2 High-Throughput Virtual Screening

Drug development is a time-consuming and expensive process which takes up to 12–17 years. In general case, it starts from the identification and validation of a biological *target*, a molecule which is associated with the disease and whose activity is expected to be modulated by a drug for a desired therapeutic effect.

The second stage is identification of *hits*, chemical compounds with high predicted binding activity against the target. The set of hits is subject to analysis and optimization to obtain *leads*, compounds that have several desired attributes in addition to high binding activity. Next stages of drug development are the additional optimization of leads, preclinical and clinical studies, registration of the new drug and postmarketing studies.

Identification of hits is a specific resource-consuming problem which may be seen as a funnel where a large library of chemical compounds is reduced to a set of $10 - 10^3$ hits to be tested in a laboratory [33]. HTVS allows to identify hits *in silico* so as to reduce time and cost of the first stages of drug development. For this purpose, hits are selected basing on molecular docking of the library of chemical compounds against the target.

In addition, identification of hits is a complex problem. There are many possible criteria for the selection of hits, and hardly any of them are absolute. The computational process should allow a flexible management of HTVS with the possibly minimal time to obtain a set of hits with desired characteristics.

3 Analysis and Optimization of the Computational Process

Performance is a permanent concern of a high-performance computing project. We believe that every developer should try to get the maximum out of available resources. At the same time, the workflow must be flexible enough to support the scalability of the computational project, which is especially important in case of volunteer computing resources known for their irregular nature (Fig. 2, 3).

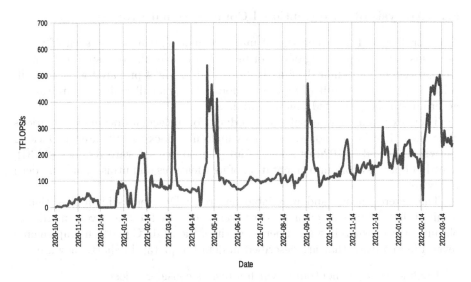

Fig. 2. Performance of SiDock@home, FLOPS/s, measured by means of BOINC.

Having in background a 1.5-year experience of running SiDock@home project, we analyze its computational process, aiming to obtain the set of hits faster and by spending less resources. The analysis is presented below.

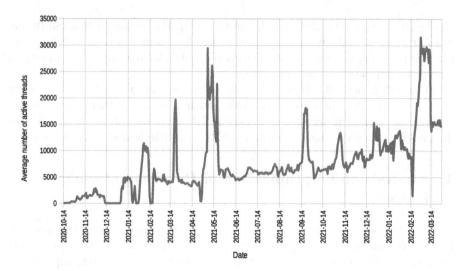

Fig. 3. Performance of SiDock@home, threads, measured by means of BOINC.

3.1 Analysis of a Conventional Computational Process

The workflow of HTVS consists of mutually independent tasks, each of which performs molecular docking of one or more small molecules to a specified target. The process of molecular docking is illustrated in Fig. 4 prepared with PyMOL software [32]. As a result of molecular docking, the small molecules are ranked according to the predicted binding affinity.

There exist a number of software products for molecular docking with various algorithms. In SiDock@home, we employ molecular docking software CmDock [4, 14] which started in 2020 as a fork of an open-source software RxDock [23,31], aimed at optimisation, implementation of new features and utilisation of modern hardware.

The heterogeneous and unreliable nature of Desktop Grid implies that a result of the task may be erroneous or never be returned to the server. In order to obtain correct results in a fixed period of time, the BOINC platform implements several mechanisms that are described in detail in [3,13]. In short, they are:

- deadline: time moment after which a task is considered lost;
- replication: issuing of several instances of the same task;
- quorum: the number of matching answers to consider a result valid.

In this section, we focus our attention on the tasks that have been executed at the client side correctly and within deadline. The results of such tasks provide the progress on the scientific problem being solved in the Desktop Grid.

In SiDock@home, the life cycle of such a task is, for the most part, the same as in other BOINC-based projects performing HTVS (for instance, the OpenZika project within World Community Grid [8]).

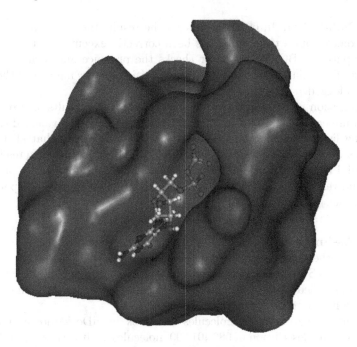

Fig. 4. Molecular docking of a small molecule to a target (in purple). (Color figure online)

Task Generation. The task is generated at the server side and includes an input file with a description of the target, docking parameters and a list of small molecules. If there is need for replication, the same task is created in two or more instances, and the value of quorum Q is specified. The generated task is put into the queue. When a client requests work from the server, it receives a portion of tasks from the queue.

Task Execution. At the client side, the following steps are taken for each molecule in a task:

1. A special software program performs molecular docking against the target in a limited number of runs. At each run, the program finds a docking pose and calculates the score based on the predicted binding energy.
2. If the best found score exceeds the given threshold, it is written into the output file together with the corresponding pose.

The result is a list of docking poses of the compounds with the score exceeding the threshold. Such a pre-filtration allows to omit the results with low predicted binding affinity so as to reduce the amount of transferred data which is important for Desktop Grid systems. In addition, a log file keeps the key information about all docked molecules in order to verify the result integrity.

The client sends ready results to the server upon the next communication.

Result Validation. In order to process the result, the server needs to verify that it comes from a task which has been correctly executed at the client side. For this purpose, BOINC validator checks the presence and format of output files. A result is considered valid if it has a positive integer number of the docked molecules logged.

If replication is used, the next step is to check if the results of two instances of a task are equivalent. Two valid results are considered equivalent if they have coinciding lists of the docked molecules logged. This means that all the input molecules were processed during the docking. If quorum Q has been reached, one of the valid results is considered canonical and is stored for further processing. Each valid result is awarded an equal amount of BOINC credits depending on task runtime.

Result Assimilation. Output files of canonical results are placed to a special directory at the server for further processing.

When HTVS has been performed over the whole library of small molecules against a specified target and the results have been assimilated, they undergo partially automated processing and expert analysis.

Currently, there are 500 molecules in a task in SiDock@home. The whole library contains description of 982 401 500 molecules, so it is covered by 1 964 803 tasks. Such a division of the library allows us to have an average task runtime of about 1–2 hours on a typical desktop computer, following the common practice of volunteer computing. Quorum $Q = 2$ is used. With such settings, the library of small molecules has been screened against 11 potential therapeutic targets during the first 17 months of the project operation. The quorum allowed to recognize a number of technical errors and problematic entries of small molecules in a semi-automated way and to update the docking application, the library of small molecules and server-side programs accordingly.

3.2   Known Drawbacks of the Conventional Computational Process

Due to replication and unreliability of the Desktop Grid nodes, there is an overhead in terms of tasks needed to obtain valid results. In Table 1, we present this overhead for five targets. At the time of the experiments, the screening of the whole library comprised 1 966 935 tasks for each target. On top of that, a number of tasks were added:

– *Excessive tasks.* These tasks ended with a computational error, validation error or were discarded because another result was accepted as canonical.
– *Lost tasks.* Results of these tasks were never received from a client, most likely because it left the project.

Such tasks have consumed computational resources but did not directly contribute to the hit identification.

Table 1. Overhead in terms of tasks. The basic number is 1 966 935 tasks (100%).

Target	Excessive tasks	Lost tasks
PLpro_v2	116.29%	0.35%
RdRp_v1	104.55%	0.71%
3CLpro_v4	100.87%	0.22%
3CLpro_v5	101.22%	0.32%
3CLpro_v6	100.87%	0.52%

Due to the randomized character of computations, the results of two replicas of the same task may not coincide regardless of technical errors or cheating. This is often the case in molecular simulations [16].

Recall that a task contains 500 molecules to dock. For a variety of reasons, the docking of some molecules in a task can fail. The result of such a task will be considered invalid, which leads to a wasting of time and computing power. Earlier, we considered a related problem in [22]. When small molecules are packed into "parcels" to form a task, too small a size of the parcel means a very high number of communications between the client and the server and, consequently, a high load on the server. Too large a size of the parcel, on the other hand, means that a high amount of computational time will be wasted in case of a single error. To calculate the optimal size of the parcel, we proposed a game-theoretical mathematical model. For an enterprise-level Desktop Grid, the derived solutions were shown to decrease server load by a factor of 3.

In the present work, we consider several factors in addition to the server load, and elaborate on a more reliable approach which is described in Subsect. 3.3 and will allow to save the intermediate docking results of separate molecules.

In the new approach, the task size remains an important issue. The size of 500 has been selected empirically to obtain a moderate average runtime. But the performance of individual Desktop Grid clients may vary a lot, and different targets may have different runtimes. Additionally, there are periods of an increased server load, such as the competitions in the BOINC community. A dynamically adjusted task size would allow to balance the load through generation of longer-running tasks when needed.

Another important question is the communication between the client and the server. Each client generates a number of requests to the server to obtain new tasks and send back the results. The output file may have a significantly larger size than the input data. The server load caused by these communications may be decreased, firstly, by an increase in the task size (as mentioned above), and secondly, by the transfer of output files to a dedicated file server.

Finally, the organization of the workflow influences the scope of results subject to expert evaluation, namely the set of identified hits. A docking configuration of a hit is important, but it is not reasonable to store all the docking results because it would require the storage and transfer of large amounts of data (about 0.7 terabytes per target), most of which will not pass a primary threshold.

For this reason, there is a preliminary filtration of results at the client's side. It allows to reduce the necessary amount of data, but comes at the price of losing information about molecules with low scores. If the threshold has been set too high, there may be a need to rescreen the whole library, leading to redundant use of computational resources and delaying testing of the results in a laboratory.

Let us summarize the problems described above:

– overhead due to the quorum $Q = 2$;
– wasting of time and computing power in case of a single fail in docking;
– a fixed size of a task;
– amount of client-server communications,
– scope of results.

In the next subsection we propose the solutions to the listed problems.

3.3   Optimization of the Computational Process

The current approach used in SiDock@home allows to automate, for the most part, the validation of results and identification of technical errors. At the same time, it has disadvantages that lead to a large amount of duplicated computations and, overall, slow down the hit discovery rate and limit the scope of hits selection. In this section, we describe a new organization of the computational process.

In the new approach, the workflow will base on a summary table describing the HTVS process and consisting of entries

<target_id, ligand_id, score, task_id>.

Here, `target_id` identifies the target of the virtual screening, `ligand_id` identifies a small molecule docked against the target, `score` contains the calculated docking score, and `task_id` identifies the computational task within which the docking score was calculated. The workflow will change as follows.

Task Generation. New tasks will be generated dynamically so as to include the molecules that have not been docked yet and form tasks of a desired length. Initially, only one instance of each task will be generated, and the quorum will be set to $Q = 1$. A list of molecules belonging to the task will be recorded at the server side.

Task Execution. At the client side, the resulting score will be logged for every small molecule. For the molecules with the score exceeding the threshold, the best pose will be written into the output file.

Result Validation. Instead of comparing the replicas, a result will be considered valid if it contains a positive number of successfully docked ligands from the recorded list of molecules associated with this task.

Result Assimilation. Target ID, ligand IDs and the calculated scores will be written into the summary table. Output files of validated results will be placed to a special directory at the server for further processing.

Upon completion of the virtual screening for a specified target, the summary table will contain consolidated information on the docking results for each target. It will support the expert selection of the set of hits with desired characteristics such as the number, chemical diversity, lead-likeness etc. Different hit cutoff metrics can be used for the selection, and some of them may be calculated basing on the present data without the need to repeat molecular docking. An example is ligand efficiency: the predicted binding energy normalized by the number of heavy atoms in the molecule.

Correct results will be accepted at the quorum of one, which will eliminate the need for duplication of computations and speed up the HTVS process. The size of new tasks can be adjusted for computational experiments of different runtimes. New tasks can be easily generated to dock selected molecules with complementary methods. For example, computationally expensive simulations may be performed for the top selected molecules.

In this way, the summary table will allow to better design new HTVS experiments. For example, one can create a representative sample of the library to run an initial screening and adjust the next HTVS process accordingly. With dynamic task generation, HTVS may be easily designed so as to prioritize a set of the most prospective molecules [28], balance between the number and diversity of hits [24], etc.

4   Implementation and Results

With the new approach, the architecture of the project database will be modified so as to include the summary table and auxiliary tables. The program code of BOINC validator and assimilator will be altered so as to implement the proposed approach. Other processes on the server side will remain unchanged.

As an intermediate step, the proposed design of the workflow can be implemented together with the existing mechanism of adaptive replication in BOINC. With adaptive replication, the results obtained by reliable hosts are accepted at the quorum $Q = 1$. If a result comes from an unreliable host, another replica of the task is issued and the quorum is set to $Q = 2$. Reliability is based on the number of consecutive valid results returned by the host and is constantly updated. The concept of validity depends on the considered scientific problem and the implementation of the computational process. The implementation described in Subsect. 3.3 allows to set any quorum without loss of reliability.

At the moment, the proposed design of the workflow has been implemented in an accompanying BOINC project operating for testing purposes. The clients in this project are heterogeneous computers belonging to the team of authors. The new approach is being tested and adjusted.

5   Conclusion

Virtual screening assists drug discovery and allows to reduce time and cost of its earliest stages. At the same time, it is a resource-demanding problem which usually requires a high-throughput computational infrastructure. An appropriate design of the workflow should allow efficient use of such an infrastructure.

Peculiar features of Desktop Grids make it necessary to control the reliability of results while ensuring their fastest discovery and rational use of the participating computers. Design and implementation of the workflow depends on the specific scientific problem being solved in the Desktop Grid.

In this paper, we analyze the workflow in a volunteer computing project SiDock@home and propose its optimization. We hope that the proposed design of the workflow will be of interest to other researchers at their computational experiments on virtual screening. In future work, we plan to investigate the performance of SiDock@home with the new workflow and derive new mathematical models and algorithms of task scheduling that will contribute to the further development of Desktop Grids.

References

1. Alnasir, J.J.: Distributed computing in a pandemic: a review of technologies available for tackling COVID-19. arXiv preprint arXiv:2010.04700 (2020)
2. Amicable numbers. https://sech.me/boinc/Amicable/. Accessed 12 Apr 2022
3. Anderson, D.P.: BOINC: a platform for volunteer computing. J. Grid Comput. **18**(1), 99–122 (2019). https://doi.org/10.1007/s10723-019-09497-9
4. Bahun, M., et al.: Inhibition of the SARS-CoV-2 3CLpro main protease by plant polyphenols. Food Chem. **373**, 131594 (2022). https://doi.org/10.1016/j.foodchem.2021.131594, https://www.sciencedirect.com/science/article/pii/S0308814621026005
5. Deelman, E., et al.: The future of scientific workflows. Int. J. High Perform. Comput. Appl. **32**(1), 159–175 (2018)
6. Distributed Computing - Computing Platforms. http://distributedcomputing.info/platforms.html. Accessed 12 Apr 2022
7. Einstein@Home. https://einsteinathome.org. Accessed 12 Apr 2022
8. Ekins, S., Perryman, A.L., Horta Andrade, C.: OpenZika: an IBM world community grid project to accelerate zika virus drug discovery. PLoS Negl. Trop. Dis. **10**(10), 1–5 (2016). https://doi.org/10.1371/journal.pntd.0005023
9. Gerasim@home main page. https://gerasim.boinc.ru/. Accessed 12 Apr 2022
10. Ghafarian, T., Javadi, B., Buyya, R.: Decentralised workflow scheduling in volunteer computing systems. Int. J. Parallel Emergent Distrib. Syst. **30**(5), 343–365 (2015)
11. Ghorbani, M., Swift, S., Taylor, S.J., Payne, A.M.: Design of a flexible, user friendly feature matrix generation system and its application on biomedical datasets. J. Grid Comput. **18**(3), 507–527 (2020). https://doi.org/10.1007/s10723-020-09518-y
12. Home - COVID.SI. https://covid.si/en. Accessed 12 Apr 2022
13. Ivashko, E., Chernov, I., Nikitina, N.: A survey of desktop grid scheduling. IEEE Trans. Parallel Distrib. Syst. **29**(12), 2882–2895 (2018)

14. Jukič, M., Škrlj, B., Tomšič, G., Pleško, S., Podlipnik, Č., Bren, U.: Prioritisation of compounds for 3CL pro inhibitor development on SARS-CoV-2 variants. Molecules **26**(10), 3003 (2021). https://www.mdpi.com/1420-3049/26/10/3003
15. Juve, G., Chervenak, A., Deelman, E., Bharathi, S., Mehta, G., Vahi, K.: Characterizing and profiling scientific workflows. Futur. Gener. Comput. Syst. **29**(3), 682–692 (2013)
16. Leguy, J., Glavatskikh, M., Cauchy, T., Da Mota, B.: Scalable estimator of the diversity for de novo molecular generation resulting in a more robust QM dataset (OD9) and a more efficient molecular optimization. J. Cheminform. **13**(1), 1–17 (2021). https://doi.org/10.1186/s13321-021-00554-8
17. LHC@home. https://lhcathome.web.cern.ch. Accessed 12 Apr 2022
18. Liew, C.S., Atkinson, M.P., Galea, M., Ang, T.F., Martin, P., Hemert, J.I.V.: Scientific workflows: moving across paradigms. ACM Comput. Surv. (CSUR) **49**(4), 1–39 (2016)
19. Lionta, E., Spyrou, G., Vassilatis, K.D., Cournia, Z.: Structure-based virtual screening for drug discovery: principles, applications and recent advances. Curr. Top. Med. Chem. **14**(16), 1923–1938 (2014). https://doi.org/10.2174/15680266146666140929124445, http://www.eurekaselect.com/article/62572
20. List of distributed computing projects. https://en.wikipedia.org/wiki/List_of_distributed_computing_projects. Accessed 12 Apr 2022
21. Litzkow, M.J.: Remote Unix: turning idle workstations into cycle servers. In: Proceedings of the Summer USENIX Conference, pp. 381–384 (1987)
22. Mazalov, V.V., Nikitina, N.N., Ivashko, E.E.: Hierarchical two-level game model for tasks scheduling in a desktop grid. In: 2014 6th International Congress on Ultra Modern Telecommunications and Control Systems and Workshops (ICUMT), pp. 541–545 (2014). https://doi.org/10.1109/ICUMT.2014.7002159
23. Morley, S.D., Afshar, M.: Validation of an empirical RNA-ligand scoring function for fast flexible docking using RiboDock®. J. Comput. Aided Mol. Des. **18**(3), 189–208 (2004). https://doi.org/10.1023/B:JCAM.0000035199.48747.1e
24. Nikitina, N., Ivashko, E., Tchernykh, A.: Congestion game scheduling for virtual drug screening optimization. J. Comput. Aided Mol. Des. **32**(2), 363–374 (2018). https://doi.org/10.1007/s10822-017-0093-7
25. Nikitina, N., Manzyuk, M., Jukić, M., Podlipnik, Č, Kurochkin, I., Albertian, A.: Toward crowdsourced drug discovery: start-up of the volunteer computing project SiDock@home. In: Voevodin, V., Sobolev, S. (eds.) RuSCDays 2021. CCIS, vol. 1510, pp. 513–524. Springer, Cham (2021). https://doi.org/10.1007/978-3-030-92864-3_39
26. Nikitina, N., Manzyuk, M., Podlipnik, Č, Jukić, M.: Performance estimation of a BOINC-based desktop grid for large-scale molecular docking. In: Malyshkin, V. (ed.) PaCT 2021. LNCS, vol. 12942, pp. 348–356. Springer, Cham (2021). https://doi.org/10.1007/978-3-030-86359-3_26
27. Nikitina, N., Manzyuk, M., Podlipnik, Č, Jukić, M.: Volunteer computing project SiDock@home for virtual drug screening against SARS-CoV-2. In: Byrski, A., Czachórski, T., Gelenbe, E., Grochla, K., Murayama, Y. (eds.) ANTICOVID 2021. IAICT, vol. 616, pp. 23–34. Springer, Cham (2021). https://doi.org/10.1007/978-3-030-86582-5_3
28. Pradeep, P., Struble, C., Neumann, T., Sem, D.S., Merrill, S.J.: A novel scoring based distributed protein docking application to improve enrichment. IEEE/ACM Trans. Comput. Biol. Bioinf. **12**(6), 1464–1469 (2015)

29. Quang, B.T., et al.: A comparative analysis of scheduling mechanisms for virtual screening workflow in a shared resource environment. In: 2015 15th IEEE/ACM International Symposium on Cluster, Cloud and Grid Computing, pp. 853–862. IEEE (2015)
30. Rosetta@home. https://boinc.bakerlab.org. Accessed 12 Apr 2022
31. Ruiz-Carmona, S., et al.: rDock: a fast, versatile and open source program for docking ligands to proteins and nucleic acids. PLoS Comput. Biol. **10**(4), e1003571 (2014)
32. Schrödinger, LLC and Warren DeLano: PyMOL. http://www.pymol.org/pymol, version 2.4.0. Accessed 20 May 2020
33. Tanrikulu, Y., Krüger, B., Proschak, E.: The holistic integration of virtual screening in drug discovery. Drug Discov. Today **18**(7–8), 358–364 (2013)
34. Together We Are Powerful - Folding@home. https://foldingathome.org. Accessed 12 Apr 2022
35. Universe@Home. https://universeathome.pl/universe. Accessed 12 Apr 2022
36. Zimmerman, M.I., et al.: SARS-CoV-2 simulations go exascale to predict dramatic spike opening and cryptic pockets across the proteome. Nat. Chem. **13**(7), 651–659 (2021)

Correction to: Fast Parallel Bellman-Ford-Moore Algorithm Implementation for Small Graphs

Alexei Vezolainen⬤, Alexey Salnikov⬤, Artem Klyuchikov⬤, and Sergey Komech⬤

Correction to:
Chapter "Fast Parallel Bellman-Ford-Moore Algorithm
Implementation for Small Graphs" in:
V. Voevodin et al. (Eds.): *Supercomputing*, **LNCS 13708,**
https://doi.org/10.1007/978-3-031-22941-1_32

In an older version of this paper, the presentation of Sergey Komech's affiliation was misleading. This has been corrected.

The updated original version of this chapter can be found at
https://doi.org/10.1007/978-3-031-22941-1_32

Author Index

Printed in the United States
by Baker & Taylor Publisher Services

Printed in the United States
by Baker & Taylor Publisher Services